101 961 241 X

ONE WEEK LOAN

27.4.16

RE'

Mental I
and trea
ism' is
individu
the Uni
it timel
liberty a
self or c

This
rights-b
The (

— Inti

— His

— The
    ven

— Gaj

— Rev

— Ac

Many
away fi
toward
always
ments,
The aim of this collection is to encourage
governing treatment, detention and care that are workable and conform to
international human rights documents.

D1342389

Rethinking Rights-Based Mental Health Laws

Edited by

Bernadette McSherry

and

Penelope Weller

·HART·
PUBLISHING

OXFORD AND PORTLAND, OREGON
2010

Published in the United Kingdom by Hart Publishing Ltd
16C Worcester Place, Oxford, OX1 2JW
Telephone: +44 (0)1865 517530
Fax: +44 (0)1865 510710
E-mail: mail@hartpub.co.uk
Website: http://www.hartpub.co.uk

Published in North America (US and Canada) by
Hart Publishing
c/o International Specialized Book Services
920 NE 58th Avenue, Suite 300
Portland, OR 97213–3786
USA
Tel: +1 503 287 3093 or toll-free: (1) 800 944 6190
Fax: +1 503 280 8832
E-mail: orders@isbs.com
Website: http://www.isbs.com

© The editors and contributors severally 2010

The editors and contributors have asserted their right under the Copyright, Designs and Patents Act
1988, to be identified as the authors of this work.

All rights reserved. No part of this publication may be reproduced, stored in a retrieval system,
or transmitted, in any form or by any means, without the prior permission of Hart Publishing,
or as expressly permitted by law or under the terms agreed with the appropriate reprographic
rights organisation. Enquiries concerning reproduction which may not be covered by the
above should be addressed to Hart Publishing Ltd at the address above.

British Library Cataloguing in Publication Data

Data Available

ISBN: 978-1-84946-083-5

Typeset by Columns Design Ltd, Reading
Printed and bound in Great Britain by
Antony Rowe Ltd, Chippenham, Wiltshire

SHEFFIELD HALLAM UNIVERSITY
WL
344.044
RE
COLLEGIATE LEARNING CENTRE

Acknowledgements

This book is based on research funded by an Australian Research Council Federation Fellowship. The authors would like to thank Sandra Pyke, Mel Hamill, Tali Budlender and Kathleen Patterson for their invaluable assistance in editing and formatting this book.

Cover Image

Donna Lawrence (1973–)
Triple Ouch, 2006
oil and encaustic on canvas
91.2 x 65 cm
Cunningham Dax Collection
www.daxcollection.org.au

Artist's statement about this painting:

'The title here says volumes about the suggested reading of the artwork. It speaks of the emotional pain of mental illness, sometimes physical pain and the social pain placed upon us by society at odds with understanding.

I have heavily cropped the figure to give a sense of anonymity and depicted the vehicle to demonstrate a more formal side of mental illness.'

Artist Profile

Donna is an award winning practising artist who has exhibited regularly over the past 15 years and has been involved in a wide variety of community arts festivals and projects.

Artist's Statement

'I believe visual artwork can be aesthetically pleasing as well as politically motivated or intellectual. I aim for both of these elements in my work.

I believe artwork can be empowering in its shared meaning as opposed to simply its aesthetic qualities. It can allow some people to feel a significant adherence to a group of similar minded/experienced people, and lead others to experience empathy and gain knowledge, concerning the occurrences of others. Similarly, I hope that my work will reach people who have experienced mental illness, and people who have not. It is ultimately an issue that affects us all.'

About the Cunningham Dax Collection

The Cunningham Dax Collection, amassed over a 60 year period, consists of over 15,000 works on paper, paintings, ceramics & textiles created by people with an experience of mental illness and/or psychological trauma. The Collection's mission is:

To promote widely a greater understanding of people who experience mental illness and/or psychological trauma, and to foster an appreciation of their creativity through the preservation and ethical presentation of their original works.

Table of Contents

List of Contributors

Peter Bartlett, Professor of Mental Health Law, University of Nottingham, England.

Terry Carney, Professor of Law and Director of Research, Sydney Law School, Australia.

John Dawson, Professor of Law, University of Otago, New Zealand.

Mary Donnelly, Senior Lecturer, Law Faculty, University College Cork, Ireland.

Philip Fennell, Professor of Law, Cardiff University, Wales.

Ian Freckelton, Senior Counsel and Professor, Law Faculty, Department of Psychological Medicine and Department of Forensic Medicine, Monash University, Australia.

Annegret Kämpf, PhD Candidate, Monash University, Australia.

Oliver Lewis, Director, Mental Disability Advocacy Centre, Hungary.

Bernadette McSherry, Australian Research Council Federation Fellow and Professor of Law, Monash University, Australia.

Tina Minkowitz, Founder of the Center for the Human Rights of Users and Survivors of Psychiatry, USA.

Jill Peay, Professor of Law, London School of Economics and Political Science, England.

John Petrila, Professor of Law, University of South Florida, USA.

Neil Rees, Chairperson, Victorian Law Reform Commission, Australia.

Genevra Richardson, Professor of Law, King's College London, England.

Penelope Weller, Postdoctoral Research Fellow, Monash University, Australia.

Joaquin Zuckerberg, Professor of Law, University of Toronto, Canada.

Table of Cases

European Union

New Zealand

Russia

South Africa

United Kingdom

United States of America

Table of Legislation

Canada

Secondary legislation

United States of America

Table of International Instruments

Part 1

Introduction

1

Rethinking Rights-Based Mental Health Laws

BERNADETTE MCSHERRY AND PENELOPE WELLER

I. Introduction

This book arises out of a Federation Fellowship project funded by the Australian Research Council entitled 'Rethinking Mental Health Laws'. In 2008, we invited a number of mental health law experts to write a paper in answer to one or more of the following questions:

- What do you think are the advantages and disadvantages of rights-based legalism governing the mental health system?
- Do you think there are any alternatives to rights-based legalism and the advantages/disadvantages of these alternatives?
- In the rights-based legalism model, what should be the scope of mental health laws?
- In what manner should an international human rights framework guide mental health laws?

The resulting papers were intensively workshopped in May 2009 at Monash University's Centre in Prato, Italy and subsequently revised prior to publication. What emerged were very different views of the meaning of rights-based mental health laws. Some authors took an historical approach, others a contemporary approach to problems in their own countries. Many focused on the Convention on the Rights of Persons with Disabilities (the CRPD)[1] and what this might mean for individuals with mental illnesses. Others were concerned with the link between civil and criminal laws via 'sexually violent predator' legislation and unfitness to plead statutes.

---

[1] Convention on the Rights of Persons with Disabilities, adopted 13 December 2006, GA Res 61/106, UN Doc A/Res/61/106 (entered into force 3 May 2008).

While the approaches may have differed, it was clear that there was a certain amount of overlap between the papers and certain themes began to emerge. The ensuing chapters have been grouped in five parts as follows:

- Historical Foundations
- The International Human Rights Framework and the United Nations Convention on the Rights of Persons with Disabilities
- Gaps Between Law and Practice
- Review Processes and the Role of Tribunals
- Access to Mental Health Services.

While this structure provides a suitable framework for the chapters, the five parts should not be seen as entirely separate, but interrelated. This introductory chapter outlines some of the common issues raised irrespective of where each chapter is placed in this volume.

II. The Meaning of Rights-Based Legalism

Patricia Allderidge has suggested that there are cycles in the care of those with mental illness, with phases of treatment in hospitals and phases of detention in private psychiatric institutions.[2] At the same time, Allderidge points out that there are cycles giving precedence to medical discretion and cycles giving precedence to mental health laws, which shift between protecting those with mental illnesses from society to protecting society from those considered dangerous. The current cycle can be viewed as being based 'upon an over-riding concept of legalism'[3] with mental health laws shaping the way in which certain individuals with mental illnesses can be detained and treated.

Like Patricia Allderidge, Kathleen Jones sees the history of detention and treatment of those with serious mental illnesses as shifting between the two extremes of legalism and clinical discretion.[4] In chapters two and three, both Phil Fennell and Penelope Weller point out that Kathleen Jones used the term 'legalism' in a pejorative manner, viewing it as leading to cumbersome and complex procedural processes.

---

[2] P Allderidge, 'Hospitals, Madhouses and Asylums: Cycles in the Care of the Insane' (1979) 134 *British Journal of Psychiatry* 321.
[3] H Prins, 'Whither Mental Health Legislation? Locking Up the Disturbed and the Deviant' (2001) 41(3) *Medicine, Science and Law* 241, 242.
[4] K Jones, 'The Limitations of the Legal Approach to Mental Health' (1980) 3 *International Journal of Law and Psychiatry* 1.

During the 1980s, Larry Gostin urged reform based on what he termed a 'new legalism'.[5] Phil Fennell comprehensively traces the way in which this approach drew on the European Convention on Human Rights. Penelope Weller in chapter three also explores the evolution of the rights-based movement in mental health law reform.

'Rights-based legalism' is thus a term that can be used to describe a cycle that gives precedence to mental health laws that refer to the rights of individuals with mental illnesses somewhere in their provisions. For example, section 4(1)(ac) of the Mental Health Act 1986 (Vic) states that one of the objects of the Act is to

protect the rights of people with a mental disorder.

Section 4(2)(b) then goes on to require that the Act must be interpreted so that

any restriction upon the liberty of patients and other people with a mental disorder and any interference with their rights, privacy, dignity and self-respect are kept to the minimum necessary in the circumstances.

Similar provisions can be found in other mental health legislation.

What the concept of rights-based legalism means in practice is the subject of many of the chapters in this collection.

III. Criticisms of Rights-Based Legalism

The conceptual framework of legalism based on human rights is not universally accepted. Nikolas Rose, for example, has criticised 'rights-strategists' on the basis that mental health laws based on rights simply switch the control of individuals with mental illnesses from doctors to lawyers.[6]

A similar scepticism can be found in some of the ensuing chapters. Phil Fennell in chapter two argues that modern mental health laws, despite using rights rhetoric, have created a codification of clinical authority to detain and treat without consent. Penelope Weller also argues in chapter three that rights have been 'lost in translation' because of the continued acceptance of medical authority.

An important point, however, is made by Peter Bartlett in chapter seventeen that criticisms of 'rights-based legalism' are usually voiced by those in countries where moves towards such legalism have been on the political agenda for some decades. The approach is of little relevance to countries such as those in Southern Africa where there has been no tradition of engagement of individuals with

---

[5] LO Gostin, 'Perspectives on Mental Health Reforms' (1983) 10 *Journal of Law and Society* 47; LO Gostin, 'The Ideology of Entitlement: The Application of Contemporary Legal Approaches to Psychiatry' in P Bean (ed), *Mental Illness: Changes and Trends* (Chichester, Wiley, 1983).
[6] N Rose, 'Unreasonable Rights: Mental Illness and the Limits of the Law' (1985) 12 *Journal of Law and Society* 199.

mental illnesses with the legal system. Bartlett also writes that in Central Europe, there are laws relating to civil confinement, but any rights lack real meaning.

This points to one of the limitations of this edited collection—it is largely centred on Western notions of human rights and how they influence legislation in common law countries. Considerations of time and space prevented a broader analysis of the topics in relation to other political cultures, and that remains a matter to be explored in the future.

John Dawson takes a different approach to general criticisms of rights-based legalism in chapter four by arguing that mental health law should not be based on balancing the rights of the individual against the state, but because individuals 'live our lives in the moral company of others',[7] a more pluralistic approach is needed. He is concerned in particular with mental health tribunal decision-making in relation to community treatment orders and how tribunal members might best take into account the interests of a range of persons who provide significant support to individuals with mental illnesses in the community.

There is also a question raised here as to the gap between what the law requires and the realities of clinical practice. Genevra Richardson in chapter eight explores how the notion of 'insight' and the conceptual difficulties raised by delusions and 'pathological' values can influence clinical decision-making. Similarly, Ian Freck-elton in chapter nine outlines some of the 'emotive and judgemental considerations' that may influence the decision-making of both clinicians and mental health review bodies.

IV. Which rights matter?

Many of the chapters in this collection highlight the question as to which rights should be central to mental health laws. The human rights debates concerning mental health laws have traditionally focused on the rights to liberty and autonomy in relation to the involuntary commitment of individuals with very serious mental illnesses. This reflects the traditional approach that civil and political rights (sometimes referred to as negative rights, in the sense of freedom *from* interference) have been seen as taking precedence over social, cultural and economic rights (sometimes referred to as positive rights, in the sense of rights to an entitlement).

The CRPD is significant in merging civil and political rights with economic, cultural and social rights. Oliver Lewis in chapter five outlines how the CRPD serves an 'expressive' function in altering social perceptions by taking a principled approach to disability equality.

---

[7] A McCall Smith, 'Beyond Autonomy' (1997–98) 14 *Journal of Contemporary Health Law and Policy* 26, 37.

Phil Fennell argues in chapter two that re-conceptualising mental health rights as disability rights is vital because it 'lays greater emphasis on positive rights and upholds the social inclusion, anti-stigma and equality agenda, without losing sight of the key imperatives of legality, due process and proportionality'.

In chapter thirteen, Joaquin Zuckerberg surveys the operations of the Canadian statutory standards of dangerousness, the need to provide treatment, capacity, civil commitment and the role of the Canadian Mental Health Tribunal. His analysis illustrates the failure of Canadian lawmakers to recognise that mental health laws operate within particular social, cultural and legal environments and that these must be taken into account if positive, social rights are to be recognised.

Similarly, in chapter twelve, Mary Donnelly's comparative analysis of the different mechanisms that have been developed to give effect to the right to the review of treatment decisions in England and Wales, Ireland and Victoria, respectively, describes the limited engagement of these processes with a human rights approach.

Brenda Hale has pointed out that mental health laws perpetually struggle 'to reconcile three overlapping but often competing goals: protecting the public, obtaining access to the services people need, and safeguarding users' civil rights' and 'the law finds it hardest to aim at obtaining access to services'.[8] John Petrila in chapter fifteen explores the lack of access to high-quality mental health care in the United States.

In chapter sixteen, Bernadette McSherry focuses on the right to health set out in Article 25 of the CRPD, which requires that States Parties

> shall take all appropriate measures to ensure access for persons with disabilities to health services that are gender-sensitive, including health-related rehabilitation.

She argues that there should be a shift away from focusing on laws dealing with the involuntary treatment of those with serious mental illnesses and protecting the right to liberty, to developing laws that support a right to mental health for *all* individuals with mental illnesses.[9]

In chapter eleven, Terry Carney suggests a practical solution to the disengagement of the law with positive rights. He argues that the recognition of positive rights can be achieved by expanding the role of mental health tribunals. In addition to their current role in the protection of negative rights, he suggests that tribunals could oversee the allocation and co-ordination of a full range of health and social services.

---

[8]   B Hale, 'Justice and Equality in Mental Health Law: The European Experience' (2007) 30(1) *International Journal of Law and Psychiatry* 18, 19.

[9]   See also S Bell, 'What Does the 'Right to Health' Have to Offer Mental Health Patients?' (2004) 28(2) *International Journal of Law and Psychiatry* 141.

V. The Convention on the Rights of Persons with Disabilities and Mental Health Laws

The CRPD makes no mention of involuntary detention and treatment for individuals with mental illnesses. This raises the question as to the significance of the rights listed in the CRPD to the reality of involuntary treatment.

Tina Minkowitz argues in chapter seven that the CRPD clearly requires that health care must be provided on the basis of free and informed consent. She emphasises the importance of understanding the CRPD as a reflection of the 'social model' of disability. The social model of disability locates the 'problem' in social organisation and the discriminatory attitudes of society. It follows that the CRPD requires the adjustment of social processes external to persons with disabilities. In relation to health care, it requires the provision of supported decision-making to enable persons with disabilities to make decisions about the matters that affect them.

Annegret Kämpf also argues in chapter six that domestic laws that are compliant with Convention principles must start with the presumption that individuals with mental illnesses possess legal capacity and the right to make self-determining health care decisions. She supports the call for supported decision-making, but argues that the law must also recognise diversity among those with mental illnesses and ensure that appropriate safeguards are in place to monitor the decisions that are made.

From another angle, Oliver Lewis points out in chapter five that the CRPD also requires States Parties to undertake comprehensive monitoring of all CRPD-based initiatives. In particular, the CRPD requires the establishment of an independent monitoring body, the collection of appropriate data and, above all, the participation of persons with disabilities in the evaluation of programmes designed to respect and support their human rights.

VI. Quasi-Criminal Laws

Two chapters are concerned with rights-based legalism in the context of those who have been brought before the criminal justice system, but have been civilly detained. In chapter ten, Jill Peay examines the procedural rules relating to those found 'unfit to plead' in England and Wales. She poses the question as to whether civil commitment following a finding of unfitness is an example of rights-based legalism working or simply the result of a 'health-based system inappropriately governed by paternalism'. Her exploration of the notion of capacity in relation to a finding of unfitness overlaps with some of Ian Freckelton's concerns with capacity in relation to involuntary detention and treatment in chapter nine.

In his comprehensive overview of rights-based legalism in the United States of America, John Petrila, in chapter fifteen, touches on the problems raised by the civil commitment of 'sexually violent predators' after the expiry of their sentences. He points out that due process rights are often skimmed over and that decisions can rely on scientifically questionable testimony. He argues that a rights-based approach is essential for individuals who face indefinite and/or preventive detention, but that it must go beyond the superficial.

VII.   Why have mental health laws at all?

While most authors engaged with the notion of rights underpinning mental health laws, Neil Rees raises the issue in chapter four as to whether there should be stand alone mental health legislation at all.

While clinicians such as Stephen Rosenman have strongly critiqued mental health laws, there is a general concession that '[l]aws are needed to ensure treatment, care and (in some cases) preventive custody for mentally ill patients'.[10] The question raised by Rees is whether such laws can take the form of a substituted decision-making scheme along the lines of guardianship laws rather than stand-alone mental health laws. He canvasses the advantages and disadvantages of such an approach and calls for a trial that allows for the concurrent operation of mental health and guardianship laws in order to gauge whether a fusion is realistic.

What is clear, following Genevra Richardson's analysis of the law in England and Wales in chapter eight, is that the current system of having two schemes, one governing those who lack capacity and one governing those with 'mental disorder', is excessively cumbersome and complicated.

Tina Minkowitz takes one step further in calling for the abolition of mental health laws in order to comply with the CRPD. She argues in chapter seven that the right to respect for physical and mental integrity set out in Article 17, together with the prohibition against torture or cruel, inhuman and degrading treatment or punishment in Article 15, provides the basis for understanding forced psychiatric interventions as a violation of human rights. It is unlikely that this view will resonate with Governments that, as Phil Fennell points out in chapter two, tend to take a narrow approach to what human rights laws require.

---

[10]   S Rosenman, 'Mental Health Law: An Idea Whose Time Has Passed?' (1994) 28 *Australian and New Zealand Journal of Psychiatry* 560, 564.

VIII. Conclusion

The current cycle of 'rights-based legalism' entrenches the law as the starting-point for the provision of services and access to them for those with serious mental illnesses. Many of the chapters in this collection emphasise the importance of moving away from the limitations of a negative rights approach to mental health laws towards more positive rights of social participation.

   The law may not always be the best way through which to alleviate social and personal ills,[11] but given that legislation is paramount for the functioning of the mental health system, it is important to ensure that legal provisions governing treatment, detention and care are workable and conform to international human rights documents.

---

[11] H Prins, 'Can the Law Serve as the Solution to Social Ills? The Case of the Mental Health (Patients in the Community) Act 1995' (1996) 36 *Medicine, Science and Law* 217.

Part 2

Historical Foundations

2

Institutionalising the Community: The Codification of Clinical Authority and the Limits of Rights-Based Approaches

PHILIP FENNELL

I. Introduction: Rights-Based Approaches

Contemporary discussion of disability law (which includes mental health and community care law) is based around the social model of disability and the need for a rights-based approach, particularly in the light of the adoption of the United Nations Convention on the Rights of Persons with Disabilities (the CRPD).[1] The social model of disability holds that disabled people are disabled by society's failure to provide the means to promote their social inclusion, and emphasises disabled people's human rights including the right to equality. Gerard Quinn defines the importance of the rights-based approach as the 'profound message in the Disability Rights Convention'.[2]

Bioethics examines the extent to which human rights instruments foster human dignity,[3] respect for autonomy (given that autonomy may be compromised by mental disorder), beneficence (given that psychiatric treatment may be required for the protection of others as well as for the benefit of the sufferer), non-maleficence (the medical precept '*primum non nocere*'—'above all do no harm'), and justice (the right to independent review of detention and compulsory treatment as well as fair access to treatment and support in the community).

---

[1] Convention on the Rights of Persons with Disabilities, opened for signature 13 December 2006, GA Res 61/106, UN Doc A/Res/61/106 (entered into force 3 May 2008).

[2] G Quinn, 'Resisting the Temptation of Elegance: Can the Convention Socialise States to Right Behaviour?' in OM Arnardóttir and G Quinn (eds), *The UN Convention on the Rights of Persons with Disabilities: European and Scandinavian Perspectives* (Leiden, Brill, 2009).

[3] D Beyleveld and R Brownsword, *Human Dignity in Bioethics and Biolaw* (Oxford, Oxford University Press 2001).

Bioethics Conventions emphasise the aspirational right to the highest attainable standard of health care, which should extend to mental as well as physical health care. Generic bioethics principles recognise that mentally disordered people may have their autonomy limited and that the principle of informed consent may be departed from, subject to safeguards for the right to personal integrity, and protection against stigmatisation and discrimination.

Legislation permitting detention on grounds of mental disorder recognises that there may be occasions when mentally disordered people need to be admitted to hospital or given treatment without consent where necessary in their own best interests or to protect others. 'Mental disorder' and 'unsoundness of mind', as the European Convention on Human Rights (the European Convention)[4] puts it, are generic concepts embracing all disabilities or disorders of mind, including mental illness, learning disability, and personality disorders. States have increasingly moved away from reliance on detention in hospital as the principal locus of care, and towards the provision of care in the community. Where compulsory treatment in the community is concerned, Article 5 of the European Convention, which deals with the deprivation of liberty, has only limited relevance, and Article 8 potentially allows treatment without consent in the community to be given where it is in accordance with law and necessary in a democratic society to protect health, prevent crime or disorder, or uphold the rights and freedoms of others. Community care brings a new emphasis on rights to social inclusion and protection against stigma. These rights are not set out in 'hard law' documents such as the European Convention. Rights to equitable access to health care, protection against discrimination on grounds of disability, and to protection against stigma are contained in such 'soft law' documents as UNESCO'S Universal Declaration on Bioethics and Human Rights and the Council of Europe Convention on Human Rights and Biomedicine (the Oviedo Convention 1997), as well as in the Charter of Fundamental Rights of the European Union[5] and the World Health Organization *WHO Resource Book on Mental Health, Human Rights and Legislation.*[6]

The effectiveness of rights-based approaches in achieving social inclusion and in protecting human rights depends on the social context. The prime driver of social policy and the raison d'être of mental health legislation is the management of risk—risk to the health and safety of mentally disordered people themselves,

---

[4] Convention for the Protection of Human Rights and Fundamental Freedoms (European Convention on Human Rights), opened for signature 4 November 1950, CETS No 005 (entered into force 3 September 1953).

[5] Official Journal of the European Communities (OJ) 2000/C 364/01.

[6] M Freeman, *WHO Resource Book on Mental Health, Human Rights and Legislation* (Geneva, World Health Organization, 2005), available at: www.who.int/mental_health/policy/resource_book _MHLeg.pdf.

but also risk to public safety. Risk management may be defined as the identification, assessment, elimination or reduction of the possibility of incurring misfortune.[7] Risk management justifies legislative mechanisms in overriding a person's
refusal to accept admission to hospital or treatment for mental disorder, and
since the 1990s philosophies of risk management now permeate decision-making
in both the psychiatric system and the penal system. As Nikolas Rose has put it,
risk management 'operates through transforming professional subjectivity':

> It is the individual professional who has to make the assessment and management of
> risk their central professional obligation … It appears that it is no longer good enough
> to say that behaviour is difficult to predict and 'accidents will happen'. Every unwel-
> come incident may be seen as a failure of professional expertise: someone must be held
> accountable.[8]

Ulrich Beck has written of the transition from industrial society to what he
describes as the risk society, speaking of a 'calculus of risks', where

> protection by insurance liability, laws and the like promise the impossible: events that
> have not yet occurred become the object of current action—prevention, compensation
> or precautionary after-care. The 'invention' of the calculus of risk lies in making the
> incalculable calculable. In this way a norm system of rules for social accountability
> compensation and precautions, always very controversial in its details, creates present
> security in the face of an open uncertain future.[9]

Beck writes of the 'technocratic authoritarianism' which results where the
presence of the technology to manage risk creates a political expectation that it
will be used, whatever the consequences in terms of expense or interference with
other fundamental values, such as the protection of individual rights.

Rights discourse has a lengthy pedigree in the history of mental health
legislation, and has appeared in different manifestations. Kathleen Jones, whose
work has greatly influenced thinking about English law and psychiatry, sees the
history of mental health legislation in terms of the movement of a pendulum
between the two extremes of legalism and medical discretion.[10] Jones uses the
term 'legalism' pejoratively to mean procedural formalism and a 'mechanistic

---

[7] R Castel, 'From Dangerousness to Risk' in G Bruchell, C Gordon and P Miller (eds), *The Foucault Effect: Studies in Governmentality* (London, Harvest Wheatsheaf, 1991).

[8] N Rose, 'At Risk of Madness: Law, Politics and Forensic Psychiatry'. Paper Delivered at the Cropwood Conference on 'The Future of Forensic Psychiatry', St John's College, Cambridge, 19-21 March 1997.

[9] U Beck, 'From Industrial Society to Risk Society: Questions of Survival, Social Structure and Ecological Enlightenment' (1992) 9(1) *Theory, Culture and Society* 97, 120.

[10] K Jones, *Lunacy, Law and Conscience 1744–1845* (London, Routledge and Paul, 1955); *A History of the Mental Health Services* (London, Routledge and Kegan Paul, 1972); 'The Limitations of the Legal Approach to Mental Health' (1980) 3 *International Journal of Law and Psychiatry* 1; 'Law and Mental Health: Sticks or Carrots' in GE Berrios and H Freeman (eds), *150 Years of British Psychiatry 1841–1991* (London, Royal College of Psychiatrists, 1991); and *Asylums and After: A Revised History of the Mental Health Services: From the Early 18th Century to the 1990s* (London, Athlone Press, 1993).

approach'.[11] 'Open-textured law' was preferable—'enabling rather than regulatory, permitting the maximum of discretion within a loose framework of
regulation'.[12] Underlying this critique is the assumption that a rights-based
approach leads to increasingly complex and detailed legal regulation, and
impedes effective pursuit of the interests of the welfare of the patient and reflects
little more than 'resuscitated Diceyism'.[13]

During the public debate prior to the passage of the Mental Health Act 1983
(England and Wales), Larry Gostin, the legal officer of MIND (the National
Association for Mental Health) urged the introduction of more effective procedural safeguards and regulation of psychiatry, describing reform proposals which
he had drafted for MIND as based on a 'new legalism'.[14] Gostin argued that
Jones's attacks were aimed at a cumbersome and technical legal formalism which
few would support. His critique of the 1959 Mental Health Act, which conferred
wide discretionary power on doctors and state authorities, was put forward
against a background of revelations of serious institutional malpractice in a series
of inquiries into abuses in psychiatric hospitals.

The 'new legalism' was based on the European Convention. In the 1970s and
1980s Gostin and MIND had brought a series of test cases under the Convention
before the European Commission and Court of Human Rights, highlighting the
absence of possibilities for legal review of detention for many patients. The
European Court of Human Rights upheld the legalist view of psychiatric detention as a form of arrest, holding that Article 5 of the Convention requires any
decision to detain a person on grounds of unsoundness of mind to be free from
arbitrariness.[15] In *Winterwerp v The Netherlands*,[16] the European Court of
Human Rights held three conditions to be necessary for there to be a 'lawful
detention of a person of unsound mind'. First, except in emergency cases, the
individual must be reliably shown to be of unsound mind, entailing 'the
establishment of a true mental disorder before a competent authority on the
basis of objective expertise'.[17] Secondly, the mental disorder must be of a kind or

---

[11] K Jones, 'The Limitations of the Legal Approach to Mental Health' (1980) 3 *International Journal of Law and Psychiatry* 1, 10–11.
[12] K Jones, 'The Limitations of the Legal Approach to Mental Health' (1980) 3 *International Journal of Law and Psychiatry* 1, 11.
[13] *ibid.*
[14] LO Gostin, 'Perspectives on Mental Health Reforms' (1983) 10 *Journal of Law and Society* 47; and 'The Ideology of Entitlement: The Application of Contemporary Legal Approaches to Psychiatry' in P Bean (ed), *Mental Illness: Changes and Trends* (New York, Wiley, 1983). Gostin estimated that approximately two-thirds of the provisions of the 1982 Mental Health (Amendment) Act derived from proposals of MIND (the National Association for Mental Health) contained in his book *A Human Condition Vols I and II* (London, National Association for Mental Health, 1977), see Gostin, 'Perspectives on Mental Health Reforms' (1983) 10 *Journal of Law and Society* 47, 67.
[15] *Van der Leer v The Netherlands* (1990) 12 EHRR 567; *Winterwerp v The Netherlands* (1979) 2 EHRR 387; *X v United Kingdom* (1981) 4 EHRR 181.
[16] *Winterwerp v The Netherlands* (1979) 2 EHRR 387.
[17] *Winterwerp v The Netherlands* Commission Report, Publications of the European Court of Human Rights, Series B, Pleadings, Oral arguments and documents (1979) Vol 31 at [76].

degree warranting compulsory confinement.[18] Thirdly, the validity of continued confinement depends on the persistence of such a mental disorder.[19] If detention is to be prolonged, the authorities must satisfy themselves at reasonable intervals that the criteria for detention continue to be met. In *X v United Kingdom*[20] the Court stated:

> [A] person of unsound mind compulsorily confined in a psychiatric institution for an indefinite or lengthy period is in principle entitled, at any rate where there is no automatic review of a judicial character, to take proceedings before a court at reasonable intervals to put in issue the lawfulness ... of his [or her] detention, whether that detention was ordered by a civil or criminal court, or by some other authority.[21]

In addition to traditional notions of due process, two principles underpinned Gostin's new legalism: 'the ideology of entitlement', that patients should have enforceable rights to the care which they need; and 'the least restrictive alternative', that they have a right to expect to be cared for in the least restrictive alternative setting.[22] The least restrictive alternative is based on *Winterwerp's* case and, as Gostin points out, if taken seriously, 'would require the government to create a full range of community services including housing, crisis intervention, medical and nursing support, training and employment'.[23] The ideology of entitlement and the least restrictive alternative also entail the protection of mentally disordered people against discrimination and the creation of legal rights to appropriate care and treatment.[24] The novelty of the 'new' legalism was its legal recognition of an 'ideology of entitlement'[25] to treatment in the least restrictive setting and support services in the community so as to avoid the need for detention. The new legalism was reflected in the English Mental Health Act 1983 with its increased rights to challenge detention and to seek review of compulsory treatment, as well as the entitlement (under section 117 of the Act) of detained patients to after-care services on discharge from longer term detention. The European Court of Human Rights has provided an important underpinning for the due process component of the 'new legalism' as far as psychiatric detention is concerned, but the scope for using the Convention to challenge coercive treatment or to uphold rights to adequate services has been more limited.

---

[18] *Winterwerp v The Netherlands* (1979) 2 EHRR 387 at [37].

[19] *X v United Kingdom* (1981) 4 EHRR 181 at [40]; *Winterwerp v The Netherlands* (1979) 2 EHRR 387 at [39]; *Luberti v Italy* (1984) 6 EHRR 440.

[20] *X v United Kingdom* (1981) 4 EHRR 181.

[21] *ibid*, at [52].

[22] LO Gostin, 'The Ideology of Entitlement' in P Bean (ed), *Mental Illness: Changes and Trends* (New York, Wiley, 1983) 49–50.

[23] *ibid*, 30.

[24] LO Gostin, 'Perspectives on Mental Health Reforms' (1983) 10 *Journal of Law and Society* 47, 61.

[25] LO Gostin, 'The Ideology of Entitlement' in P Bean (ed), *Mental Illness: Changes and Trends* (New York, Wiley, 1983) 27.

Exploring the limits of a rights-based approach entails identifying the nature of the rights involved—the right to protection against torture or inhuman or degrading treatment (Article 3 of the European Convention on Human Rights), the right to liberty (Article 5 of the Convention), the right to physical integrity (Article 8 of the Convention), and the right to community care support to ensure that detention is only used where it is a proportionate response to the patient's situation (the beginnings of a positive obligation under Article 5). It is important to explore the nature and effectiveness of the mechanisms through which these rights are enforced. It is vital to identify both the negative aspects of the obligation on states to desist from infringements of these rights, and the positive obligations to uphold them that may arise under these articles.[26] Negative obligations under the European Convention require states and their agents to desist from arbitrary detention, from disproportionately severe treatment, and from infringements of human dignity. Positive obligations require states to take positive steps to uphold individual human dignity, to protect against inhuman or degrading treatment, arbitrary detention or unwarranted treatment by third parties, to impose duties to place people detained on grounds of mental disorder in a hospital, clinic, or similar institution, and not in a prison, and to ensure that a patient's release is not unreasonably delayed by failure to provide support in the community.

The Richardson Committee's proposals for reform of English mental health legislation recommended a principle of reciprocity, meaning that society's assumption of the power to detain or treat without consent entails reciprocal obligations to provide appropriate treatment and community support.[27] The Committee proposed a further condition of compulsion that there must be positive clinical measures that are likely to prevent deterioration or secure an improvement in the patient's condition. Without this, healthcare professionals might be forced 'to engage in activities they would regard as inappropriate and possibly unethical'.[28]

A key issue is whether law can be used effectively to pursue the ideology of entitlement. Article 5 creates positive rights to treatment in the least restrictive setting. *Stanley Johnson v United Kingdom*[29] established that where a court reviewing the lawfulness of detention finds that a person is no longer suffering from mental disorder, it is not under an obligation to discharge immediately, but may order discharge subject to the provision of after-care support. If this

---

[26] P Fennell, 'The Third Way in Mental Health Policy: Negative Rights, Positive Rights and the Convention' (1999) 26 *Journal of Law and Society* 103 and P Fennell, 'Convention Compliance, Public Safety, and the Social Inclusion of Mentally Disordered People' (2005) 32 *Journal of Law and Society* 90.

[27] Great Britain. Department of Health. Expert Committee, *Review of the Mental Health Act 1983: Report of the Expert Committee* (London, Department of Health, 1999) at [2.21].

[28] *ibid*, at [5.99].

[29] *Stanley Johnson v United Kingdom* (1997) 27 EHRR 296.

happens, the court must have the power to ensure that discharge is not unreasonably delayed. The scope of the duties of the court and the after-care authorities under *Johnson* was the key issue in *R v Secretary of State for the Home Department ex p IH*.[30] Resolving it, the House of Lords reaffirmed the fundamental principle of English law that, regardless of whether psychiatrists are public authorities for the purposes of the Human Rights Act 1998, a doctor cannot be ordered to do anything against his or her clinical judgement of the patient's best interests.[31] Neither a tribunal nor a health authority could order a doctor to take on the care of a patient if the doctor, in his or her clinical judgement, considered that care could not safely be provided.

In *IH's* case, Lord Bingham maintained a narrow approach to the ruling in *Johnson v United Kingdom*[32] limiting the scope of the duty to ensure that discharge is not unreasonably delayed to cases where the patient is no longer suffering from mental disorder—the '*Johnson* type of case'. In *IH's* case, the second *Winterwerp* criterion was no longer met, because there was still mental disorder but no longer of a kind or degree justifying detention, as long as adequate placement and supervision in the community could be arranged. The Court of Appeal and the House of Lords agreed that where the basis of discharge is the nature or degree of the illness rather than its absence,

> [i]f a health authority was unable, despite the exercise of all reasonable endeavours, to procure for a patient the level of care and treatment in the community that a tribunal considered to be a prerequisite to the discharge of the patient from hospital, the continued detention of the patient in hospital would not violate the right to liberty under Article 5.

Patients will rarely be pronounced free of mental disorder by psychiatrists or tribunals, so the ruling limits significantly the impact of *Johnson's* case, and the extent to which Article 5 is capable of imposing positive duties on state authorities to provide after-care to facilitate discharge.

In the United States of America, the Supreme Court dealt with a similar issue in *Olmstead, Commissioner, Georgia Department Of Human Resources v LC*.[33] The Court held that under the Americans with Disabilities Act, States are required to provide persons with mental disabilities with community-based treatment rather than placement in institutions. This duty applies where (1) the State's treatment professionals have determined that community placement is appropriate; (2) the transfer from institutional care to a less restrictive setting is not opposed by the

---

[30] *R v Secretary of State for the Home Department ex parte H* [2003] UKHL 59.

[31] A principle which has since been modified by Munby J in *R (Burke) v General Medical Council* [2004] EWHC 1879.

[32] An approach first adopted by Lord Phillips of Worth Matravers MR, at [32]–[36] of his judgment in *R (on the application of K) v Camden and Islington Health Authority* [2001] EWCA Civ 240.

[33] *Olmstead, Commissioner, Georgia Department Of Human Resources v LC* 527 US 581 (1999).

affected individual; and (3) the community placement can be reasonably accommodated, taking into account the resources available to the State and the needs of others with mental disabilities.

This overview of the case law indicates that the courts are showing commitment to the idea of a right to treatment in the least restrictive setting, a potential positive obligation in relation to psychiatric detentions. However, this is subject to the significant limitation that it must accord with the clinical judgement of the health professionals, and will no doubt be subject to the availability of resources, as *Olmstead's* case makes clear in the United States. *IH's* case, like *Olmstead*, shows how the powers of competent courts under Article 5(4) are subject to the important limitation of the clinical judgement of the doctor who will be treating the patient in the community, and his or her view of whether the risk posed by the patient to self or to others can safely be managed in the community. *IH's* case subjects the rule in *Johnson's* case to strict limits in the interests of risk management.

II. Disability Rights and the Future of Mental Health Legislation

I have argued elsewhere that the rights of mentally disordered people are disability rights.[34] Although people with mental health problems may be viewed as 'a special case' justifying exceptions to the principle of autonomy and informed consent, as disabled people they are entitled to the protection of international instruments on the human rights of people with disabilities. The relevant rights under the CRPD are explored in other chapters of this volume.[35] Although the enforcement mechanisms for the CRPD are weak, instruments such as these have been used to demonstrate in national and international courts, so far with only limited success, a developing international consensus on the rights of people with mental health problems.[36]

Traditional responses to mental ill health have been based on social segregation and separate treatment, and rights to safeguards to protect against wrongful confinement. Contemporary approaches draw on the philosophies of social

---

[34] P Fennell, 'Human Rights, Bioethics and Mental Disorder' (2008) 27 *Medicine and Law* 95.

[35] See Part Three of this volume: The International Human Rights Framework and the CRPD.

[36] Cases where the English courts have proved resistant to the developing international consensus approach include *R (on the application of B) v Dr SS (1) Dr AC (2) and the Secretary of State for Health* [2005] EWHC 86 (Admin); *R (on the application of B) v Dr Haddock* [2005] EWHC 921 (Admin), on appeal *R (on the application of B) v Dr Haddock and Others* [2006] EWCA Civ 961; and *R (on the application of B) v SS, Responsible Medical Officer, Broadmoor Hospital and Others* [2005] EWHC 1936 (Admin), on appeal [2006] EWCA Civ 28. However, the European Court of Human Rights has proved receptive to the idea in cases such as *Glass v United Kingdom* (2004) 39 EHRR 15, and *Dybeku v Albania* (App No 41153/06) Judgment of 18 December 2007.

inclusion and non-stigmatisation developed by the disability rights movement. Mental ill health is a disability as defined in Article 1 of the CRPD, which states that

[p]ersons with disabilities include those who have long-term physical, mental, intellectual or sensory impairments which in interaction with various barriers may hinder their full and effective participation in society on an equal basis with others.

Psychiatric patients who have long-term mental impairments hindering their full and effective participation have the same 'positive' rights to human dignity, non-discrimination, social inclusion, independent living, education and employment as other disabled people. Re-conceptualising mental health rights as disability rights is vital to the protection of the individual human dignity of mentally disordered people in that it lays greater emphasis on positive rights and upholds the social inclusion, anti-stigma and equality agenda, without losing sight of the key imperatives of legality, due process and proportionality. It is also clear that there is a positive duty on states to exercise effective supervision and review of decisions to detain and treat without consent,[37] and to protect vulnerable or incapacitated people against abuse.[38]

It is important to remember that government agencies may adopt a different kind of rights-based approach to law reform, adopting a narrow approach to human rights legislation. Just as legislation and policy have been 'judicial review proofed', Government now seeks to put forward legislation which is 'Convention proof', in the sense that the minimum necessary to achieve Convention compliance has been done. Moreover, human rights discourse may be used by government to promote a particular reform agenda, attaching varying weight to competing rights that may be at play. I have written elsewhere about a 'new human rights agenda', based on the idea that the community should have strong rights to protection against the risk of harm at the hands of mentally disordered people.[39] The rights of the community should be weighed in the balance against those of individual psychiatric patients, and in certain cases should trump those individual rights.

The new human rights agenda involves 'reading up' the state's positive duty to uphold the public's right to life under Article 2 of the European Convention. In *Osman v United Kingdom*,[40] the European Court of Human Rights held that Article 2 is breached if the authorities

knew or ought to have known at the time of the existence of a real and immediate risk to the life of identified individual or individuals from the criminal acts of a third party,

---

[37] *Storck v Germany* (2005) 43 EHRR 96.

[38] *Z v United Kingdom* (2002) 34 EHRR 3.

[39] P Fennell, 'Convention, Compliance, Public Safety, and the Social Inclusion of Mentally Disordered People' (2005) 32 *Journal of Law and Society* 90, 110.

[40] *Osman v United Kingdom* (1998) 29 EHRR 245.

and failed to take action within the scope of their powers which, judged reasonably, might have been expected to avoid that risk.[41]

Reading up the positive duty under Article 2 provides the justification for widening the scope of powers, and in the new human rights agenda is accompanied by a 'reading down' of the Article 5 and Article 8 rights of psychiatric patients to protection against arbitrary detention and against arbitrary compulsory treatment (by widening the definition of mental disorder and loosening the criteria for compulsion). Throughout the reform process leading to the Mental Health Act 2007 (England and Wales), the Government aimed for the minimum level of restraint on compulsory powers consonant with Convention compliance.[42]

Any assessment of the limits of rights-based approaches must adopt an historical perspective to chart, in the context of the risk management agenda, the development of new modes of exercise of psychiatric power, new sites where it may be exercised, and the extent to which mechanisms of supervision and review are capable of providing effective protection for the right to physical and psychological integrity under Article 8. Rather than adopt Kathleen Jones's concept of legalism, Clive Unsworth uses the term 'juridicism' to denote 'adherence to an ideology embodying a preference for rule-bound relationships entailing rights, duties and other law-centred concepts'.[43]

The history of mental health legislation is the history of the codification of clinical authority for mental health professionals to deprive mentally disordered people of their liberty and to treat without consent. That codification has become increasingly elaborate and has been, in Unsworth's term, 'juridicised' in that new areas of clinical power and authority have been redefined in terms of express rights, powers, and duties. It has also developed new sites for the exercise of clinical power, extending beyond the hospital walls into the community.

III. The Tutelary Relationship

As Clive Unsworth and I have suggested, Robert Castel's concept of tutelary relationships ('relations de tutelle') offers a useful perspective on the historical

---

[41] *ibid*, 305.

[42] House of Lords, House of Commons, Joint Committee on Human Rights, *Legislative Scrutiny: Mental Health Bill Fourth Report of Session 2006–07*, HL 40 HC/288, 4 February 2007; House of Lords, House of Commons, Joint Committee on Human Rights *Legislative Scrutiny: Seventh Progress Report: Fifteenth Report of Session 2006–07*, HL 112/HC555.

[43] C Unsworth, 'Law and Lunacy in Psychiatry's Golden Age' (1993) 13 *Oxford Journal of Legal Studies* 479, 501. See also C Unsworth, *The Politics of Mental Health Legislation* (Oxford, Oxford University Press, 1987).

development of mental health law and policy.[44] A tutelary relationship arises where decision-making power over the affairs of an adult is conferred on others. Law confers clinical authority to detain and treat without consent and legitimises a wide range of interventions by providing a broad definition of the parameters of medical treatment. It also subjects clinical power to supervision and review. In England and Wales, mental health law has undergone radical reform via the Mental Capacity Act 2005 and the Mental Health Act 2007. Read together, mental health and mental capacity legislation codify clinical authority, broaden the professional groups who may exercise it, and provide statutory authority for non-consensual treatment in the community.

The first key question is the scope of clinical authority. What powers over mentally disordered people are granted to professionals? These include the power to detain, to treat without consent, to place in seclusion, and to restrain. The second question is which professional groups are qualified to exercise tutelary power? Is decision-making power limited to doctors or can other disciplines exercise powers to detain and treat without consent? The third issue is the 'open textured' nature of the statutory criteria which must be met before rights can be interfered with, and the breadth of discretionary power conferred on professionals. The fourth issue concerns the sites where clinical or tutelary power, in the sense of forcible treatment, may be exercised. Is use of force confined to institutional settings or may it be used in the community? The fifth question concerns the mechanisms of clinical authority be they through the conferment of express powers subject to procedural safeguards, or through the granting of legal immunity from suit in respect of actions complying with certain criteria, or through other methods. Finally, there is the vital issue of how the supervision and review of exercises of clinical authority are carried out, and the extent to which it is possible to seek review of the need for, or the terms of, a tutelary relationship.

This section explores the mechanics of tutelary authority, focusing on the power to treat without consent and the power to seclude and restrain. Michel Foucault has written evocatively of the development and refinement of a 'carceral network', where deviancy and delinquency can be controlled through the development not just of penal institutions but other institutions such as asylums and poor-houses aimed at cure and reformation, and the development of surveillance mechanisms in the community. The hallmark of these developments is that risky individuals posing a threat to the social fabric can be detained and monitored,

---

[44] R Castel, *L'Ordre Psychiatrique: L'age d'or de l'alienisme* (Paris, Editions de Minuit, 1976); R Castel, F Castel and A Lovell, *The Psychiatric Society* (New York, Columbia University Press, 1982); R Castel, *The Regulation of Madness: The Origins of Incarceration in France* (trans WD Halls) (Berkeley CA, University of California Press, 1988). See CR Unsworth, 'Mental Disorder and the Tutelary Relationship: From Pre- to Post-carceral Legal Order' (1991) 18 *Journal of Law and Society* 2; CR Unsworth, 'Law and Lunacy in Psychiatry's Golden Age' (1993) *Oxford Journal of Legal Studies* 479; P Fennell, 'Law and Psychiatry' in PA Thomas (ed), *Legal Frontiers* (Aldershot, Dartmouth, 1996).

and that legal mechanisms exist to move them from one set of institutions to another with relative ease if risk management dictates.[45]

Of equal importance in the twenty-first century is what can be called 'the tutelary archipelago': a network of interconnected tutelary relationships, where those clothed with clinical or disciplinary authority have the power to impose compulsory residence, treatment, access on the part of professionals, and restrictions on conduct to the extent that the community is institutionalised in that it becomes a site where compulsory power may be exercised. However, the prison and the psychiatric hospital remain pivotal to the whole system, since the ultimate sanction against non-compliance with these tutelary obligations is detention in an institution. The institutionalisation of the community entails the creation of a network of tutelary relations extending from the criminal justice and penal system from prison through to community sentences, through the various psychiatric hospital sectors—high-secure, medium-secure, and low-security—to compulsory care in the community, and deprivation or restriction of liberty of elderly people in residential care homes. Detention, forcible treatment without consent, seclusion and restraint are the ultimate mechanisms of clinical power. A person may consent to treatment or to remain in hospital if they know that they will be compelled in the event of refusal. Compliance in the shadow of compulsion is an important feature of the psychiatric system.

The reforms introduced by the Mental Health Act 2007 mark the culmination of a lengthy period of debate which began in July 1998 when the then Secretary of State for Health, Frank Dobson, declared that community care had failed, and that 'a third way' in mental health was necessary.[46] The third way would steer a path between reliance on putting all mentally ill people in institutions—'out of sight, out of mind'—and community care where people with mental health problems could be 'left off the books', thereby putting themselves and other people at risk. The third way involved developing a range of services, from the high-security special hospitals which provide care for patients with dangerous or violent propensities through specialist regional secure units in every National Health Service Region; accommodation in every locality to provide short-term, round the clock nursing care and supervision; assertive outreach teams to keep tabs on people who have been discharged and make contact with people who shy away from getting help; and changes to enable carers and professionals to respond promptly and effectively to the needs of mentally ill patients in the community. The 'third way' included a promise of 'root and branch review' of mental health law 'to reflect the opportunities and limits of modern therapies and drugs'. Frank Dobson stated that the third way 'will cover such possible measures as compliance orders and community treatment orders to provide a

---

[45] M Foucault, *Discipline and Punish: The Birth of the Prison* (trans Alan Sheridan) (New York, Pantheon Books, 1977).

[46] During the last years of the Conservative Government, policy was packaged in 'point-plans' (usually 10-point plans); for the Blair Government the mantra was 'the Third Way'.

prompt and effective legal basis to ensure that patients get supervised care if they do not take their medication and their condition deteriorates'.[47]

The rest of this chapter focuses on two aspects of tutelary power and examines the extent to which they can be subject to effective supervision and review. One which is subject to direct legal regulation is the power to require acceptance of medication. The other, which is regulated by Codes of Guidance, is the power to place individuals in seclusion (solitary confinement). In *Storck v Germany*[48] the Strasbourg Court held that there was a positive obligation for the state to take measures under the European Convention of Human Rights to protect the right to liberty under Article 5 and the right to personal integrity under Article 8 against infringements by private persons, and that both Article 5 and Article 8 had been infringed. The Court stated that

> [i]nsofar as the applicant argued that she had been medically treated against her will while detained, the court reiterates that even a minor interference with the physical integrity of an individual must be regarded as an interference with the right of respect for private life *if it is carried out against the individual's will* (emphasis added).[49]

This statement suggests that the crucial factor in identifying a breach of Article 8 is the fact that the intervention is carried out against the individual's will, in other words that there is some resistance. However, in *HL v United Kingdom*[50] the European Court of Human Rights refused to treat compliant incapacitated patients as being on a par with capable patients who were consenting.[51] Reaffirming the importance of the right to liberty, the Court stated:

> [T]he right to liberty in a democratic society is too important for a person to lose the benefit of Convention protection simply because they have given themselves up to detention, especially when they are not capable of consenting to, or disagreeing with, the proposed action.[52]

The Court emphatically rejected the argument that a compliant incapacitated patient should be treated on the same basis as a capable consenting patient in relation to deprivations of liberty under Article 5 of the European Convention. The same principle must apply to interferences with physical integrity. It is too important to be lost simply because a person has given themselves up to the intervention, especially if he or she lacks the capacity to consent to treatment.

It is important also to bear in mind the statement of the scope of the positive obligation under Article 8, as outlined in *Storck's* case: 'The Court … considers that on account of its obligation to secure to its citizens the right to physical and

---

[47] Department of Health, *Frank Dobson Outlines Third Way for Mental Health*, Press Release 98/311, 29 July 1998.

[48] *Storck v Germany* (2005) 43 EHRR 96.

[49] *ibid*, at [143].

[50] *HL v United Kingdom* (2004) 40 EHRR 32.

[51] See D Bruckard and B McSherry, 'Mental Health Laws for Those "Compliant" with Treatment' (2009) 17(1) *Journal of Law and Medicine* 16; and Bernadette McSherry, this volume, ch 16.

[52] *HL v United Kingdom* (2004) 40 EHRR 32 at [90].

moral integrity, *the state remained under a duty to exercise supervision and control over private psychiatric institutions*' (emphasis added).[53] The possibility of retrospectively establishing criminal or tortious liability was not enough to provide appropriate protection of vulnerable people detained in institutions. Effective supervision and review were required.

IV. Two Mental Health Statutes in England and Wales

Currently there are two statutes which are relevant to the treatment of mental disorder in England and Wales: the Mental Health Act 1983 and the Mental Capacity Act 2005.[54] Detention under the Mental Health Act 1983 is likely to be used if a person diagnosed with mental disorder needs hospitalisation and treatment in his or her own interests but also for the protection of others, and/or if he or she is resisting admission. Once detained, a person who is incapable of consenting or refusing may be given medication for mental disorder without consent subject to approval by a second opinion doctor acting under Part IV of the Mental Health Act 1983.[55] A detained patient does not become entitled to a second opinion until three months have elapsed from the first time when medicine was given during that period of detention. The question arises whether the second opinion system provides effective supervision and review as required by *Storck's* case, given this time lag in relation to entitlement to a second opinion for medicine. If a patient has been detained for treatment, the Responsible Clinician may, with the agreement of an Approved Mental Health Professional make that person subject to a Community Treatment Order. If the person is to receive medication in the community, this can only be given after one month if it is authorised by a second opinion doctor acting under Part IVA of the 1983 Act.

If persons with mental disorder lack capacity and need treatment for mental disorder in their own best interests, and they are not resisting treatment, their care is likely to be managed under the Mental Capacity Act 2005. Unlike the Mental Health Act, which operates by a procedure requiring applications and supporting medical evidence on statutory forms, the Mental Capacity Act operates by providing (in sections 5 and 6) a defence in respect of acts of care and treatment done for a person where reasonable steps have been taken to assess capacity, where the person is reasonably believed to lack capacity and where the intervention is reasonably believed to be in the person's best interests.

If the incapacitated person needs to be deprived of his or her liberty to be given treatment that may be done under the Deprivation of Liberty (DoL)

---

[53] *Storck v Germany* (2005) 43 EHRR 96 at [150].
[54] See also Genevra Richardson, this volume, ch 8.
[55] Mental Health Act 1983 (England and Wales) s 58. On this point, see Mary Donnelly, this volume, ch 12.

procedures introduced into the Mental Capacity Act 2005 by the Mental Health Act 2007. The Mental Health Act 1983 allows long-term deprivation of liberty in a hospital, but not in a care home. The DoL procedures in Schedules A1 and 1A to the Mental Capacity Act 2005 authorise deprivation of liberty in a hospital or a care home. They allow deprivation of liberty of a mentally disordered person who lacks capacity where the deprivation is necessary in the patient's best interests. Unlike the Mental Health Act 1983, the DoL procedures allow deprivation of liberty of people with learning disabilities who do not exhibit abnormally aggressive or seriously irresponsible conduct.

The treatment of incapacitated people detained under the DoL procedures is governed by sections 5 and 6 of the 2005 Act. The defences to a battery action are available to anyone who can demonstrate that they took reasonable steps to assess capacity, reasonably believed that the person lacked capacity and reasonably believed that they were acting in the person's best interests. If the patient is resisting treatment, section 6 provides a defence in respect of the use or threat of physical force if it is necessary to prevent harm to a patient who lacks capacity, and the intervention is a proportionate response both to the likelihood of harm and the seriousness of harm. There is no second opinion procedure to authorise treatment without consent, such as exists under Part IV of the Mental Health Act 1983.

V. Medicine for Mental Disorder Under Part IV And Part IVA of The Mental Health Act 1983

Although powers may exist to authorise treatment without consent, the Council of Europe's European Committee for the Prevention of Torture and Inhuman or Degrading Treatment or Punishment (CPT), has developed 'CPT Standards' that emphasise the need to seek consent:

> Patients should, as a matter of principle, be placed in a position to give their free and informed consent to treatment … every competent patient, whether voluntary or involuntary, should be given the opportunity to refuse treatment or any other medical intervention. Any derogation from this fundamental principle should be based upon law and only relate to clearly and strictly defined exceptional circumstances.[56]

Under section 58 of the Mental Health Act 1983, if the patient is capable of consenting and has consented to treatment, the Approved Clinician in charge of treatment certifies that (1) the patient is capable, and (2) consenting to the

---

[56] Available at: www.cpt.coe.int/en/documents/eng-standards.pdf, Part V section C at [41].

treatment.[57] If the patient is incapable of consenting or refusing, the Approved Clinician asks the Care Quality Commission to send a second opinion appointed doctor (SOAD) independent of the hospital to come and give a second opinion. No appeal lies to the Care Quality Commission against a SOAD's decision to refuse or grant authority to treat.

The emergency power in section 62 provides that any treatment for mental disorder may be given without consent or a second opinion if immediately necessary to save the patient's life. Any treatment which is not irreversible may be given if immediately necessary to prevent serious deterioration in the patient's condition. Any treatment which is not irreversible or hazardous may be given if immediately necessary to alleviate serious suffering on the part of the patient. Finally, any treatment which is not irreversible or hazardous may be given if immediately necessary and the minimum interference necessary to prevent the patient from behaving violently or being a danger to himself or others.

The figures for second opinions under section 58 showed an increase, from 4,032 for the two years from 1983–85, to 8,839 for the period 1991–93.[58] Second opinions for electro-convulsive therapy continued to run at around 4,000 per two-year period, although the figure for 2007–09 showed a drop to 3,781.[59] However, second opinions for medication increased dramatically since the 1990s, reaching 18,831 for the period 2005–07 and 19,919 for the period 2007–09. As for the reasons for the increase in medicine second opinions, the Commission said this in 2008:

> We suspect a combination of increasingly unwell patients and increasing awareness of consent issues by clinicians, the latter including a growing appreciation by clinicians of the Second Opinion service (whether as a protection for their patient or as a protection for themselves).[60]

In deciding whether treatment ought to be given under the 1983 Act, the SOAD had to have regard to 'the likelihood that it would alleviate or prevent deterioration in the patient's condition?'[61] A Circular letter to SOADs made it clear that the role of SOADs is not to substitute their own decision as to what the treatment

---

[57]   Mental Health (Hospital, Guardianship and Consent to Treatment) Regulations 1983 (SI 1983 No 893) reg 16(2)(b) and Sch 1, Form 38.

[58]   The sources for these figures are Mental Health Act Commission *First–Fifth Biennial Reports of the Mental Health Act Commission*, 1985, 1987, 1989, 1991, 1993 (London, HMSO) and *11th Biennial Report 2003–2005: In Place of Fear* (London, TSO, 2006) para [4.67], and *12th Biennial Report 2005–2007: Risks, Rights and Recovery* (London, TSO, 2008) para [6.20], *13th Biennial Report 2005–2007: Coercion and Consent* (London, TSO 2009) para [3.30]. For a general discussion of these issues see P Fennell, *Treatment Without Consent: Law, Psychiatry and the Treatment of Mentally Disordered People since 1845* (London, Routledge, 1995).

[59]   Mental Health Act Commission, *13th Biennial Report 2005–2007: Coercion and Consent* (London, TSO, 2009) para [3.44].

[60]   Mental Health Act Commission, *12th Biennial Report 2005–2007: Risks Rights and Recovery* (London, TSO, 2008) para [6.8].

[61]   Mental Health Act 1983 s 58(3)(b).

should be for that of the clinician making the treatment proposal.[62] Where there is no consent, the question for the SOAD is 'whether or not the treatment plan is one which should be followed even if it is not necessarily the one which the appointed doctor would make himself'. The Circular went on to say that 'doctors vary in their therapeutic approach and appointed doctors should feel able to support a consultant proposing a programme which others would regard as one which should be followed'.[63] This approach is based on similar principles to those by which a doctor would be adjudged not to have been negligent under the test in *Bolam v Friern Barnet Hospital Managers*,[64] whereby any doctor has a defence to a negligence action if he or she behaves in accordance with practice accepted at the time by a responsible body of medical opinion (however small) skilled in the specialty concerned. Here, too, the question is would the treatment be supported by a responsible body of opinion skilled in the specialty?

In *R (Wilkinson) v Responsible Medical Officer, Broadmoor Hospital*,[65] the *Bolam* test was rejected. Simon Brown LJ held that the requirement on the SOAD in deciding whether the treatment should be given was to have regard to the likelihood that the treatment will alleviate or prevent deterioration in the patient's condition, essentially mirrored the 'best interest' test. His Lordship went on to criticise the Circular letter and its 'deferential' approach, and emphasised that the test required the SOAD to

> reach his [or her] own independent view of the desirability and propriety of the treatment ... Whilst, of course, it is proper for the SOAD to pay regard to the views of the RMO who has, after all, the most intimate knowledge of the patient's case, that does not relieve him [or her] of the responsibility of forming his [or her] own independent judgment as to whether or not 'the treatment should be given.' And certainly, if the SOAD's certificate and evidence is to carry any real weight in cases where, as here, the treatment plan is challenged, it will be necessary to demonstrate a less deferential approach than appears to be the norm.[66]

Wilkinson was an important case for another reason. It reset the parameters of review of decisions of Responsible Medical Officers (RMOs) and SOADs.

Prior to the coming into force of the Human Rights Act 1998 (England and Wales), in *R v Collins and Ashworth Hospital Authority, ex p Brady*,[67] Maurice Kay J had held that the appropriate standard of review of decisions to treat without consent (in this case forcible feeding under section 63) was so-called 'super

---

[62] DHSS Circular Letter DDL(84)4.

[63] *ibid*, at [17].

[64] *Bolam v Friern Barnet Hospital Managers* [1957] 1 WLR 582.

[65] *R (on the application of Wilkinson) v Responsible Medical Officer, Broadmoor Hospital* [2001] EWCA Civ 1545.

[66] *ibid*, at [33]–[34].

[67] *R v Dr Collins and Ashworth Hospital Authority, ex parte Brady* [2000] Lloyds Medical Reports 355.

Wednesbury.[68] This meant that the court should subject the decision to heightened scrutiny to ensure that the decision is not so unreasonable that no reasonable doctor could have made it, and that the more substantial the interference with human rights, the more the court would require by way of justification. 'Super *Wednesbury*' was held by the European Court of Human Rights to be an inadequate standard of review.[69] The correct standard was the test of 'proportionality', which in the words of Lords Steyn in *R v Home Secretary ex p Daly*,[70] required assessment of 'the balance which the decision maker has struck, not merely whether it is within the range of rational or reasonable decisions, [and] may require attention to be directed to the relative weight accorded to interests and considerations'.

In *Wilkinson's* case, the argument was that where the right of physical integrity and the right to be protected from inhuman or degrading treatment were engaged, it was insufficient to deal with the matter by evaluating written witness statements; there should also be an opportunity for oral examination of witnesses. Here there was a conflict of evidence between the RMO and the SOAD on the one hand, and on the other the expert witness for the applicant, first as to whether the applicant (a 69-year-old man) was competent to decide for himself, secondly as to whether the treatment would put his life at risk, and thirdly as to whether the treatment was medically necessary in his case. The Court of Appeal (Simon Brown LJ, quoting the ECtHR) held that the Court would need to be satisfied 'that medical necessity has been convincingly shown to exist ... according to the psychiatric principles generally accepted at the time'.[71] Therefore, in the event of a fresh decision to subject the appellant to forcible treatment, the court ordered the attendance of all three specialists for cross-examination at the review hearing. No further treatment was subsequently imposed on Mr Wilkinson.

In *R(N) v M*,[72] Dyson LJ held that before permission could be given for treatment of a patient without consent the court had to be satisfied that the treatment was both medically necessary and in the patient's best interests, otherwise there might be a potential breach of Article 3. As to the need for an oral hearing, his Lordship seemed to row back from the test in *Wilkinson* slightly, suggesting

> that it should not often be necessary to adduce oral evidence with cross-examination where there are disputed issues of fact and opinion in cases where the need for forcible medical treatment of a patient is being challenged on human rights grounds. Nor do we

---

[68]   ibid, 359. *Associated Provincial Picture Houses v Wednesbury Corporation* [1948] 1 KB 223 set down the standard of unreasonableness of administrative decisions which render them liable to be quashed on judicial review.

[69]   *Smith and Grady v United Kingdom* (1999) 29 EHRR 493.

[70]   *R v Home Secretary, ex parte Daly* [2001] 2 WLR 1622 (HL) 1634–5.

[71]   *Herczegfalvy v Austria* (1992) 15 EHRR 437.

[72]   *R (on the application of N) v M* [2003] 1 WLR 562 (CA).

consider that the decision in ... *Wilkinson* ... should be regarded as a charter for routine applications to the court for oral evidence in human rights cases generally.[73]

In *R (JB) v Haddock*,[74] Auld LJ reasserted the entitlement to cross-examine witnesses, in the following terms:

> The effect of the ruling of this Court in *R (Wilkinson) v Broadmoor* is that a court must conduct a 'full merits review' as to whether the proposed treatment infringed the patient's human rights, and that, to that end, a patient is entitled to require the attendance of witnesses to give evidence and to be cross-examined.

In *Haddock's* case, Collins J at first instance had carried out a full merits review evaluating the evidence and had asked himself whether he was satisfied that the treatment was medically necessary. The judge had dealt with the application on the written evidence and had not acceded to the appellant's request to call the latter as a witness. In the Court of Appeal, Auld LJ held that the judge had been right to take the appellant's witness statement at face value and was right to conclude that oral evidence from him could not conceivably have assisted him in reaching his decision. Auld LJ took the view that that 'the Court, in *Wilkinson*, could not have intended or contemplated that every case would require the hearing and testing of oral medical evidence, especially where, as here, none of the parties requested it'.[75]

As to the standard of proof, Auld LJ rejected the argument that it should be higher than the civil standard, doubting whether the requirement to be convinced of medical necessity was capable of being expressed in terms of a standard of evidential proof.

> If it was to be expressed in forensic terms at all, [his Lordship doubted whether] it amounts to more than satisfaction of medical necessity on a balance of probabilities, or as a 'likelihood' of therapeutic benefit—the test in section 58(3)(b) for triggering a decision on medical necessity for the treatment in question.[76]

Since the enactment of the Human Rights Act 1998, there have been various attempts to test the compatibility of Part IV with the European Convention. The courts have not accepted that it is a breach of the prohibition on inhuman or degrading treatment to give treatment in the face of refusal by a capable patient.[77] In *Wilkinson*, counsel for the applicant had floated the idea that there was a developing international consensus to the effect that treatment of a capable patient without consent could only be justified if necessary for the patient's safety or for the protection of others, and that necessity for health or welfare should not be sufficient grounds. Hale LJ observed that 'we have not yet reached the point

---

[73] *ibid*, 575.
[74] *R (on the application of B) v Responsible Medical Officer, Dr Haddock* [2006] EWCA Civ 961 at [64].
[75] *ibid*, at [65].
[76] *ibid*, at [42].
[77] *R v Collins & Ashworth Hospital Authority, ex parte Brady* [2000] Lloyds Medical Reports 355.

where it is an accepted norm that detained patients who fulfil the ... criteria for capacity can only be treated against their will for the protection of others or for their own safety'.[78]

Further efforts to argue the 'developing international consensus' point have not met with success. The Court of Appeal has rejected the argument that section 58 is incompatible with Articles 3 and 8 of the European Convention in that it does not specify in sufficiently precise terms the circumstances in which a competent refusal may be overridden, which should only be where (i) such treatment is necessary to protect other persons from serious harm, or (ii) without such treatment, serious harm is likely to result to the patient's health. The most the courts have conceded is that refusal by a patient with capacity is a factor to be taken into account by a SOAD and the RMO, but it cannot operate as a bar to treatment.[79]

In *R (Wooder) v Fegetter and MHAC*,[80] the court held that fairness demanded that the SOAD give reasons why medication should be given against the patient's will and those reasons should be disclosed to the patient unless the SOAD or the RMO considers that such disclosure would be likely to cause serious harm to the physical or mental health of the patient or any other person. However this duty did not require the SOAD to 'dot every "i" and cross every "t"' so long as he gives his reasons clearly on what he reasonably regards as the substantive points on which he formed his clinical judgment. The court stated that

> [u]nless a patient can show a real prospect of establishing that a SOAD has not addressed any substantive point which he [or she] should have addressed, or that there is some material error underlying the reasons that he [or she] gave, the court will not grant permission for judicial review.[81]

In 2006 the Court of Appeal in *R(B) v SS (Responsible Medical Officer) & Others*[82] stated that 'issues requiring cross-examination of medical witnesses should not often arise if the SOAD complies with section 58(3)(b) by giving clear reasons why, in his [or her] opinion, treatment is a therapeutic necessity and should, therefore, be given'.

Following a flurry of case law on section 58, the position is as laid down by the Court of Appeal in *R (on the application of N) v Dr M*[83] that a court (and by implication a SOAD) deciding whether to authorise treatment without consent

---

[78] *R (Wilkinson) v Responsible Medical Officer, Broadmoor Hospital* [2001] EWCA Civ 1545 at [80].

[79] *R (on the application of PS) v Dr G and Dr W* [2003] EWHC 2335 (Admin); *R (on the application of B) v Dr SS, Dr AC and the Secretary of State for Department of Health* [2005] EWHC 86 (Admin); *R (or the application of B) v Dr SS, Responsible Medical Officer, Broadmoor Hospital and Others* [2006] EWCA Civ 28.

[80] *R (on the application of Wooder) v Fegetter and Mental Health Act Commission* [2003] QB 219.

[81] *ibid*, at 227.

[82] *R (on the application of B) v SS, Responsible Medical Officer, Broadmoor Hospital and Others* [2006] EWCA Civ 28 at [64].

[83] *R (on the application N) v Dr M* [2002] EWCA Civ 1789.

must satisfy itself not only that the treatment is medically necessary but also that it is in the patient's best interests. Dyson LJ, emphasised that 'best interests' is wider than medical necessity, in the sense that it can produce a greater list of justifications for treatment without consent. Two years previously, in *Re S (Sterilisation: Patient's Best Interests)*[84] Thorpe LJ had held that interests could embrace a wide range of interests beyond medical ones, such as social interests.

This expansive approach to best interests is exemplified in cases like *JS v an NHS Trust*,[85] where the court held there was a duty to consider and assess the best interests of patients in the widest possible way to include the medical and non-medical benefits and disadvantages, the broader welfare interests of patients, their abilities, their future with or without treatment, the impact on their families, and the impact of denial of the treatment. The patient's best interests are to be decided by first determining whether the treatment is in 'the *Bolam* range' of treatments that would be supported by a responsible body of medical opinion, and then deciding which of them best serves the patient's social and medical interests.

'Best interests' has thus become relevant to decision-making under Part IV of the Mental Health Act 1983, but it serves to extend clinical discretion which is already wide as a result of the broad definition of treatment for mental disorder, by extending beyond the medical the range of interests which may be served by treatment without consent.

The Mental Health Act 2007 has introduced a new test to be applied in deciding whether treatment ought to be given with consent under section 57 or without consent under section 58. The test is that it is 'appropriate for the treatment to be given'. The word appropriate gives great scope for subjective judgement on the part of the second opinion doctor. Under section 58, it is appropriate for treatment to be given to a patient

> if the treatment is appropriate in his [or her] case, taking into account the nature and degree of the mental disorder from which he [or she] is suffering and all other circumstances of his [or her] case.

In order to comply with the European Convention, the tests of medical necessity and best interests will have to be applied, but as outlined, these do not represent a particularly strict limitation on clinical discretion, even though the concurrence rate between first and second opinion doctors is now nearer to 80 per cent than 90 per cent. During the first 10 years following the 1983 Act the agreement rate between the treating doctor and second opinion doctor was between 94 and 96 per cent. In a study of 1009 second opinions in 1991–92, less than one per cent (7) of visits resulted in significant changes to the treatment plan, and six per cent (60) resulted in slight changes. Of the 60 'slight changes' only 11 (eight drug-related and three for electro-convulsive therapy) had limited the original proposal by the patient's doctor; in 13 cases the second opinion visit resulted in a

---

[84] *Re S (Sterilisation: Patient's Best Interests)* [2000] 2 FLR 389 (CA).
[85] *JS v an NHS Trust* [2002] EWHC 2734 (Fam).

more permissive authority to treat than had been sought; and in 35 cases the 'slight change' made no substantive difference to the parameters of the treatment authorised.[86]

By 1997, the MHAC was able to report that 15 per cent of all second opinion visits over the previous two years had led to some change to the proposed treatment plan.[87] Until recently this proportion of changes resulting from second opinions remained roughly the same. For the Eleventh and Twelfth Biennial Reports (2003–05 and 2005–07) the agreement rate was calculated at 80 per cent, with around nine per cent of cases recording slight changes in the treatment plan, leaving only two per cent where significant changes were made (in the remaining eight per cent of cases there is no record of whether the plan was changed).[88] In its Thirteenth (and final) Biennial Report, the Mental Health Act Commission refers to the question of the effect of second opinion visits, and reports that '2008 saw a significant rise in the number of changes made as a result of SOAD visits. In the nine months from April to the end of December 2008, the percentage of changes increased to an average of 27%'.[89] The MHAC acknowledged the importance and continued relevance of the finding that 'slight change' does not necessarily equate with a restriction of the parameters of treatment. They pointed out that 'this would be a useful area for further monitoring and analysis by the Care Quality Commission and Healthcare Inspectorate Wales when they take over the administration of the second opinion service'.[90]

The issue of the level of disagreement between first and second opinion doctors can only be a crude measure of the effectiveness of the second opinion system. However, the fact that second opinions have been called a 'safeguard' and a 'service' prompts the question: Safeguard for whom, and service to whom? Is the second opinion system more geared to providing a safeguard for the patient's right to physical integrity, or is the safeguard/service more oriented towards clinicians' desire to acquire a 'flak jacket' against potential legal liability?

---

[86]   P Fennell, *Treatment without Consent: Law, Psychiatry and the Treatment of Mentally Disordered People Since 1845* (London, Routledge, 1996) 208–11.

[87]   Mental Health Act Commission, *Seventh Biennial Report 1995–1997* (London, HMSO, 1997) 106.

[88]   Mental Health Act Commission, *First Biennial Report 1983–1985* (London, HMSO, 1985) at [11.4]; *Second Biennial Report 1985–1987* (London, HMSO, 1987) 22; *Third Biennial Report 1987–1989* (London, HMSO, 1989) 5; *Fourth Biennial Report 1989–1991* (London, HMSO, 1991) 31; *Fifth Biennial Report 1991–1993* (London, HMSO, 1993) 37.

[89]   Mental Health Act Commission, *13th Biennial Report 2005–2007: Coercion and Consent* (London, TSO, 2009) at [3.36].

[90]   *ibid*, at [3.35]–[3.36].

VI. Other Treatment of Detained Patients without Consent Under MHA 1983 Section 63

An important concern behind Part IV was to clarify the powers of staff to treat for mental disorder without consent. 'Medical treatment for mental disorder' is defined broadly and extends beyond those treatments which require a second opinion. Section 63 provides that any medical treatment for mental disorder not specifically identified under sections 57, 58 or 58A as requiring a second opinion may be given to a detained patient without consent by or under the direction of the clinician in charge of treatment. In *R (on the application of B) v Ashworth Hospital Authority*[91] Baroness Hale stated that the Mental Health Act 1983: 'enacted the general power in s 63, defined in s 56 the patients to whom it applied, and provided safeguards for the most controversial treatments specified in or under ss 57 and 58'. Hence, section 63 provides the general power to treat without consent, section 58 provides the procedures and safeguards attending its exercise in relation to medicine, and section 62 provides for emergency treatment without a prior second opinion.

In Lord Elton's words, spoken in the Lords debate in 1982, section 63 was included 'to put the legal position beyond doubt ... for the sake of the psychiatrists, nurses and other staff who care for these very troubled patients'.[92] When faced with the criticism that this provision might authorise a disturbingly wide range of interventions, Lord Elton emphasised that this provision was not intended to apply to 'borderline' or 'experimental' treatments but: 'things which a person in hospital for treatment ought to undergo for his [or her] own good and for the good of the running of the hospital and for the good of other patients ... perfectly routine, sensible treatment'.[93] Leaving aside sensibleness, subsequent case law has made it clear that section 63 extends far beyond the routine. Force-feeding patients suffering from anorexia nervosa[94] or from any personality disorder as a result of which the sufferer ceases eating[95] can be 'treatment for mental disorder' covered by section 63. Case law has also made it clear that treatment for mental disorder includes treatment of the symptoms and sequelae of mental disorder as well as treatment of the core disorder itself.[96]

In *Tameside and Glossop Acute Services NHS Trust v CH (A Patient)*,[97] section 63 was held to authorise the use of reasonable force to secure the delivery of a

---

[91]   *R (on the application of B) v Ashworth Hospital Authority* [2005] UKHL 20 at [26].

[92]   *Hansard*, HL Deb, vol 426, ser 5, cols 1064–5 (1 February 1982).

[93]   *ibid*, col 1071 (1 February 1982).

[94]   *Re KB (Adult) (Mental Patient: Medical Treatment)* (1994) 19 BMLR 144, 146.

[95]   *B v Croydon Health Authority* [1995] 1 All ER 683; *R v Collins and Ashworth Hospital Authority, ex parte Brady* [2000] Lloyd's Med Rep 355.

[96]   *B v Croydon Health Authority* [1995] 1 All ER 683.

[97]   *Tameside and Glossop Acute Services NHS Trust v CH (A Patient)* [1996] 1 FLR 762. See also *Norfolk and Norwich Healthcare NHS Trust v W* [1996] 2 FLR 613; and *Rochdale Healthcare NHS Trust*

baby by Caesarean section, where the mother was detained under section 3. The doctors feared placental failure. Administering a Caesarean was held to be a treatment for mental disorder because CH's schizophrenia could otherwise only be treated by tranquillisers rather than the antipsychotic drugs she needed, since the latter would cross the placental barrier and might damage the foetus. It was therefore in the interests of her mental health that her pregnancy be brought to a swift conclusion to enable the new drug regime to start. It was also in CH's interests that the baby be born alive, since if it were not she would blame herself and the doctors and this would exacerbate her schizophrenic illness. This case stretched the concept of treatment for mental disorder to the very limit. It also revealed the permeability of the boundary between the best interests of the patient and the interests of others.

The case of *St George's Healthcare NHS Trust v S*[98] represented a step back from the *CH* position. Here the Court of Appeal held that a person who is detained under the Act cannot be forced to undergo medical procedures unconnected with the patient's mental condition unless he or she is deprived of capacity to decide for him or herself. In that case the treatment could be authorised under common law (now the Mental Capacity Act 2005) as being necessary in the patient's best interests.

If treatment is needed to cope with a physical cause or behavioural symptom or consequence of a person's mental disorder, it can be a 'treatment for mental disorder'. The broad definition of medical treatment, which can include treatment of behaviours consequent on the disorder which might pose a risk to others, is reinforced by section 145(4) of the Mental Health Act 1983. This states that

> [a]ny reference in this Act to medical treatment, in relation to mental disorder, shall be construed as a reference to medical treatment the purpose of which is to alleviate, or prevent a worsening of, the disorder or one or more of its symptoms or manifestations.

The case law on section 63 shows how 'open textured' clinical discretion is under Part IV, and how expansively the courts are prepared to interpret it. Although it might be said to reflect legalism by subjecting clinical decision-making to outside audit by second opinion, it is a medical second opinion, operating according to criteria whereby the treating doctor's judgement will be questioned only in the most exceptional circumstances. It is concerning that invasive treatments such as forcible feeding are authorised under section 63 and not subject to a second opinion procedure.

---

v C [1997] 1 FCR 274, where force was authorised at common law to administer a caesarean. These cases are discussed in E Fegan and P Fennell, 'Feminist Perspectives on Mental Health Law' in S Sheldon and M Thomson (eds), *Feminist Perspectives on Health Care Law* (London, Cavendish, 1998).

[98] *St George's Healthcare NHS Trust v S* [1998] 3 All ER 673 (CA).

VII. Medicines for Community Treatment Order Patients Under MHA 1983 Part IVA

Within one month of a Community Treatment Order (CTO) being made, a Second Opinion Appointed Doctor (SOAD) must visit the patient. If any medicine for mental disorder is to be given to the patient in the community it must be authorised by a SOAD certificate under Part IVA. The basic principle is that a patient with capacity may only be given medicine for mental disorder if he or she consents (or a deputy or someone with lasting power of attorney, with power to consent on the patient's behalf consents) and there is a SOAD certificate authorising the treatment. Treatment may be given in an emergency if the patient lacks capacity. If the patient is capable and refusing, treatment may only be given without consent by recalling the patient and treating under section 62A. But of course if a patient is capable and knows that refusal will probably lead to recall, he or she is likely to consent.

Section 62A applies where a community patient is recalled, or where the CTO is revoked. For the purposes of section 58, the patient is to be treated as if he or she had remained liable to be detained since the making of the CTO. This means that if there was a Part IV certificate covering section 58 treatment before the CTO was made which covers the patient's current treatment, there is no need for a new section 58 certificate on recall. If the period from the time the patient first received medication during that period of detention is less than three months, then a new section 58 certificate will not be required until that three-month period has elapsed.

On recall to hospital, a patient may be given medicine which would otherwise require a certificate under section 58, on the basis of a certificate given by a SOAD under the new Part IVA of the 1983 Act. However, that certificate must specify the treatment as being appropriate to be given on recall, and giving the treatment must not be contrary to any condition in the certificate. If a patient's CTO is revoked, so that the patient is once again detained in hospital for treatment, treatment can be given on the basis of a Part IVA certificate only until a section 58 certificate can be arranged. If the Part IVA certificate does not specify any such treatment, then medicines cannot be given on recall unless or until their administration is permitted under Part IV.

The aim of the rather abstruse provisions of section 62A is to provide authority to give treatment, using force if necessary, to patients who are recalled or have their CTO revoked, either under Part IV or Part IVA. If patients are recalled and advised to take their medication, they are likely to comply if they know that refusal will lead to revocation, which will mean that they are detained for treatment for up to six months running from the date of revocation. This in turn means that they may be given medication without consent or a second opinion for up to three months.

The effective operation of the CTO depends to a great extent on the psychiatric equivalent of the principle of less eligibility. A person is likely to consent to treatment if the alternative is recall or revocation and detention in hospital—there is compliance, but it is compliance in the shadow of compulsion. Although much is made of entitlement to treatment in the least restrictive alternative setting, compliance in such settings is often achieved by the shadow of a more restrictive environment and regime. In mental health law a principle applies which may be expressed in the words of the moral of Hillaire Belloc's wonderful cautionary poem, 'Jim who ran away from his nurse and was eaten by a lion': 'Always keep a-hold of nurse for fear of finding something worse'.[99]

The key question is what are the limits of rights in this arena? The patient is entitled to a second opinion, which is likely to support the proposed treatment plan. Indeed, the patient will probably be willing to agree to the plan even if not actively supporting all its elements, as a price worth paying for life in the community rather than hospital.

The main means of redress will be via the Mental Health Tribunal, which must direct discharge if it is not satisfied that the patient is then suffering from mental disorder or mental disorder of a nature or degree which makes it appropriate for him or her to receive medical treatment. The Tribunal is likely to be satisfied that the patient is then suffering from mental disorder even though the symptoms are controlled by medication. This is because of the use of the term 'nature or degree'. The symptoms of the patient's disorder may not be of a degree making it appropriate for him or her to receive treatment, but its underlying nature may be such that continued treatment is appropriate.[100]

The Tribunal must direct discharge if it is not satisfied that it is necessary for the patient's health or safety or for the protection of other persons that he or she should receive such treatment. A Tribunal is likely to reason that it is necessary for the patient's health that he or she receives the treatment, because otherwise there is a strong likelihood of relapse. The Tribunal must direct discharge if not satisfied that it is necessary for the responsible clinician to be able to exercise the power to recall the patient to hospital. In deciding whether it is satisfied that the power of recall is necessary, the Tribunal must *in particular* consider, having regard to the patient's history of mental disorder and any other relevant factors, what risk there would be of a deterioration of the patient's condition if he were to continue not to be detained in a hospital (as a result, for example, of his refusing or neglecting to receive the medical treatment he requires for his mental disorder).

Finally the Tribunal must discharge the patient if not satisfied that appropriate treatment is available. The main issue here will relate to medication, and if the treatment is within the range of appropriate treatments: a patient will only

---

[99]   H Belloc, *Cautionary Tales* (London, Duckworth, 1940) 12.
[100]   See *R v Mental Health Review Tribunal for the South Thames Region, ex parte Smith* (1998) 47 BMLR 104.

succeed on this ground if the treatment is established as inappropriate. In the face of the broad discretionary power of clinicians, and in the face of clear instructions to the Tribunal to take account of the risk ensuing from non-compliance with medication, it is unlikely that many patients will succeed in obtaining discharge from CTOs.

VIII. Treatment Under the Mental Capacity Act 2005

Part IV applies only to treatment for mental disorder, and allows treatment without consent only if the patient is detained under the longer term powers of detention in the 1983 Act. The common law doctrine of necessity was developed by the House of Lords in 1989 in *Re F (Mental Patient: Sterilisation)*,[101] where the patient had a learning disability and was not detained and the treatment (sterilisation for contraceptive purposes) could not be described as treatment for mental disorder. Common-law necessity provided that mentally incapacitated adults might be restrained using reasonable force and given treatment without consent which was necessary in their best interests, without those carrying out the treatment incurring liability in battery. Necessity is now codified in sections 5 and 6 of the Mental Capacity Act 2005 (England and Wales), which allow a range of steps to be taken on behalf of a mentally incapacitated person by carers, health and care professionals; indeed, anyone where it is reasonable for that person to take action and the action is in the patient's best interests. Treatment given under this Act may be for physical or mental disorder, and medicines for mental disorder may be given if reasonably believed to be in the best interests of a person reasonably believed to lack capacity.

The Mental Capacity Act 2005 and its accompanying rules, regulations and Code of Practice are intended to provide a complete legislative framework of decision-making for mentally incapacitated adults. The jurisdiction to grant declarations and to appoint deputies has been taken over by the Court of Protection.[102] The Act recognises the binding nature of 'valid and effective' advance decisions made by individuals, while they are still capable, to refuse specified treatments should they lose capacity in the future. It provides for individuals who are still capable to grant a lasting power of attorney to a person of their choice to take decisions about their property and affairs or health and personal welfare, in the event that they become incapable in the future. It confers jurisdiction on the Court of Protection to appoint a deputy, a proxy decision-maker on matters concerning property and affairs, or health and personal welfare.

---

[101] *Re F (Mental Patient: Sterilisation)* [1990] 2 AC 1.
[102] Mental Capacity Act 2005 ss 15–19.

One of the principles of the Mental Capacity Act 2005 is that any act or decision for or on behalf of a person who lacks capacity must be done, or made, in his or her best interests. Under common law, a person's best interests were initially to be determined according to the test set out in *Bolam v Friern Barnet Hospital Managers*.[103] The House of Lords decided in *Re F (Mental Patient: Sterilisation)*[104] that a doctor's decision that a treatment was in the patient's best interests was to be tested against the *Bolam* formula, that is, it had to be supported by a responsible body of medical opinion skilled in the specialty (not necessarily the majority). This was widely criticised, as meaning that a doctor's duty in deciding what was in an incapacitated patient's best interests amounted to little more than a duty to act non-negligently. Subsequent case law has responded to this criticism.

In *Re A (Male Sterilisation)*,[105] a two-stage 'balance sheet' was introduced as the new test. The first question is whether the treatment is within the *Bolam* range? The second is which treatment provides the most 'significant credit' in the balance sheet of probable advantages over disadvantages? In *JS v an NHS Trust*,[106] the High Court insisted on a broader concept of best interests, including all the medical and non-medical benefits and disadvantages, the broader welfare interests of patients, their abilities, their future with or without treatment, the impact on their families, and the impact of denial of the treatment. These remain the matters which are to be considered.

Section 4 of the 2005 Act sets out the approach to be adopted in assessing a patient's best interests. It does not redefine best interests, but sets out how they are to be determined. The person making the determination must not make it merely on the basis of the person's age or appearance or condition, or an aspect of his or her behaviour which might lead others to make unjustified assumptions about what might be in his or her best interests. The assessor must take into account all the circumstances of which he or she is aware and which might reasonably be regarded as relevant. He or she must consider whether it is likely that the person will at some time have capacity in relation to the matter in question, and, if it appears likely that he or she will, when that is likely to be.

The person making the 'best interests' determination must, as far as reasonably practicable, permit and encourage the person to participate, or to improve his or her ability to participate, as fully as possible in any act done for him or her and any decision affecting him or her. The decision-maker must take into account the person's past and present wishes and feelings, his or her beliefs and values which might be likely to influence the decision, and any other factors which he or she would be likely to consider if able to do so. If practicable and appropriate, the decision-maker must consider the views of anyone named by the person to be

[103]   *Bolam v Friern Barnet Hospital Managers* [1957] 1 WLR 582.
[104]   *Re F (Mental Patient: Sterilisation)* [1990] 2 AC 1 (HL).
[105]   *Re A (Male Sterilisation* [2000] 1 FLR 549 (CA) 560 (Thorpe LJ).
[106]   *JS v an NHS Trust* [2002] EWHC 2734 (Fam).

consulted, any carer or person interested in his or her welfare, any donee of a lasting power of attorney granted by the person, and any deputy appointed by the Court of Protection.

The Deprivation of Liberty (DoL) procedures in Schedules A1 and 1A to the Mental Capacity Act 2005 enable the deprivation of liberty of a mentally disordered person by detention in a residential care home where the person lacks capacity and deprivation is necessary in the patient's best interests. For patients deprived of their liberty there are no second opinion procedures provided under the Mental Capacity Act. If the treatment is defined as serious and there is no one other than a paid carer to consult, the responsible body must appoint an Independent Mental Capacity Advocate, but this does not amount to supervision and review. In 2008 the All Party Parliamentary Group on Dementia published *Always a Last Resort: Inquiry into the Prescription of Antipsychotic Drugs to People Living in Care Homes.*[107] This Report raised serious concerns that there was widespread inappropriate prescribing of antipsychotic medication in care homes. For example, antipsychotics were being used for patients with mild behavioural symptoms as a first rather than a last resort, and prescribing drugs was often continued for long periods of time. These drugs have a serious side-effect profile, including excessive sedation leading to dizziness, falls and potential injury, doubling the risk of mortality and trebling the risk of stroke. There is a 2007 National Institute for Clinical Excellence guideline, which says that those with mild to moderate non-cognitive symptoms should not be prescribed antipsychotic drugs.[108]

If a patient detained under the Mental Health Act were to be given these drugs without consent beyond three months from the time of first administration, a statutory second opinion would be needed. A second opinion safeguard is available even if it only arises after three months from the time the drug is first given. The three-month stabilising period during which treatment may be given without consent remains a human rights concern, but the position under the Mental Capacity Act is that there is no procedural safeguard against prolonged inappropriate prescribing of the nature described in *Always a Last Resort.*

Patients in care homes may not be given treatment without consent under the Mental Health Act unless they are on leave from Mental Health Act detention somewhere else. These strong psychotropic drugs are given to elderly people in care homes without procedural safeguards and quite often covertly. This may be done under the Mental Capacity Act 2005, and the person giving the treatment will have a defence if he or she has taken reasonable steps to assess the person's

---

[107] All-Party Parliamentary Group on Dementia, *Always a Last Resort: Inquiry into the Prescription of Antipsychotic Drugs to People with Dementia Living in Care Homes* (April 2008), available at: www.alzheimers.org.uk/downloads/ALZ_Society_APPG.pdf.

[108] National Institute for Health and Clinical Excellence and the Social Care Institute for Excellence, *Dementia: The NICE-SCIE Guideline on Supporting People with Dementia and their Carers in Health and Social Care* (London, British Psychological Society, 2007).

capacity, reasonably believed at the time that the patient lacked capacity to consent, and reasonably believed that the treatment was in the person's best interests.

In the case of covert medication it must be believed that it is in the person's best interests to give the medicine covertly. The *Always a Last Resort* Report found that the processes of consultation of the patient and carers and relatives required by the Mental Capacity Act 2005 to determine best interests were not widely understood and followed in care homes.[109] The Report recommended that education about the use of antipsychotics be included as a compulsory element in Mental Capacity Act training for care home staff, that sufferers and their carers should be consulted so that they are fully involved in decision-making, and that for people with dementia who lack capacity and have no one else to support them an Independent Mental Capacity Advocate must be consulted because of the serious nature of the treatment.[110] The Report also recommended the introduction of prescribing protocols for antipsychotic medication, which would provide for involvement of service users, carers and, where appropriate, Independent Mental Capacity Advocates in initial prescribing and in review, which must take place frequently.[111] The Report does not recommend new legislation but the introduction of decision-making and review procedures in guidance and protocols.

The Mental Capacity Act 2005 applies to patients who are incapable of consenting. Hence a care home patient who is deemed capable of consenting may not be given antipsychotic medication without consent under the Mental Capacity Act 2005. Such treatment might be given under common law necessity, regardless of capacity, only if it was the minimum interference and was reasonably necessary to prevent immediate harm to others.[112]

The Mental Health Act 1983, the Mental Capacity Act 2005, and the common law provide a complete legal framework authorising detention and treatment without consent, a consolidation of clinical power and authority, subject always to the proviso that the correct procedural steps must be taken. The 2007 Act reforms have extended considerably the scope of clinical tutelary power and the range of sites where it may be exercised, so that detention may now take place in a residential care home, and the obligation to accept treatment can be imposed in

---

[109]   All-Party Parliamentary Group on Dementia, *Always a Last Resort: Inquiry into the Prescription of Antipsychotic Drugs to People with Dementia Living in Care Homes* (April 2008), available at: www.alzheimers.org.uk/downloads/ALZ_Society_APPG.pdf, p 27.

[110]   *ibid*, p 35.

[111]   *ibid*, p 36.

[112]   In *Munjaz v Mersey Care National Health Service Trust and S v Airedale National Health Service Trust* [2003] EWCA Civ 1036, Hale LJ as she then was, stated at para [46] 'the common law doctrine of necessity ... has two aspects. There is a general power to take such steps as are reasonably necessary and proportionate to protect others from the immediate risk of significant harm. This applies whether or not the patient lacks the capacity to make decisions for himself [or herself]. But where the patient does lack capacity, there is also the power to provide him [or her] with whatever treatment or care is necessary in his [or her] own best interests'.

the community. Patients with learning disabilities who do not meet the conduct requirement may be detained under the DoL procedures. Any mentally disordered patient who lacks capacity to decide where to live may be detained in a residential care home if it is necessary in his or her best interests.

The 2007 Act also has resulted in the dismantling of the medical monopoly of the role of the clinician in charge of a patient's case. Under the 1983 Act the only person who could be the responsible medical officer (RMO) in charge of the patient's medical treatment was a doctor. Under the Mental Health Act 1983 as amended, the RMO role is replaced by the Responsible Clinician who has 'overall responsibility for the patient's case'. A Responsible Clinician could be a nurse, a clinical psychologist, an occupational therapist or a social worker, provided he or she has passed the appropriate accreditation as an Approved Clinician. The power of the Responsible Clinician includes the power to renew detention and the power to discharge. In relation to medicines for mental disorder, if the Responsible Clinician is not a doctor, then a doctor Approved Clinician who has prescribing rights for medicine will be the Approved Clinician in charge of the patient's treatment. Although it may be some time before other professionals take up the statutory possibilities, the 2007 Act has created the possibility of a diffusion of clinical power to other occupational groups.

IX. Seclusion

Under nineteenth-century lunacy legislation, it was simply assumed that because all psychiatric inpatients had been certified, they could be treated for mental disorder without consent. The only areas of 'treatment' subject to regulation were seclusion and mechanical restraint, which until 1959 were defined in regulations and were required to be recorded in a register, which would be inspected by members of the Board of Control on their visits to the hospital.[113] Under the Mental Health Act 1959, seclusion and restraint ceased to be subject to any legal regulation. Under the 1959 Act, the power to treat without consent, to seclude and to restrain were all treated as implicit in the legislation. When the Mental Health Act 1983 came into force, seclusion was dealt with in the Code of Practice, which required all hospitals to have a seclusion policy.

In *R (on the application of Munjaz) v Mersey Care NHS Trust; R (on the application of S) v Airedale NHS Trust*[114] the applicants challenged their seclusion as being in breach of the Mental Health Act Code of Practice. The decisions of the Court of Appeal and the House of Lords establish that legal powers to seclude exist under the 1983 Act (as part of the general power to control detained

---

[113] Mental Deficiency Regulations 1948 (SI 1948 No 1000).
[114] *R (on the application of Munjaz) v Mersey Care NHS Trust; R (on the application of S) v Airedale NHS Trust* [2003] EWCA Civ 1036.

patients), and outline the impact of Articles 3 and 8 of the European Convention on Human Rights on those powers. The effects had not reached the level of severity necessary to engage Article 3. However, the Court of Appeal held that there was a potential breach of Article 8, under the test in *Raininen v Finland*,[115] where it was held that respect for privacy under Article 8(1) includes the physical and moral integrity of the individual. The European Court of Human Rights held in *Raininen's* case that conditions during detention may produce effects on physical or moral integrity which might not reach a level of severity sufficient to breach Article 3, but might nevertheless infringe Article 8.[116]

The Court of Appeal in *Munjaz's* case upheld both challenges to seclusion, holding that European Convention rights obliged the Court to afford a status and weight to the seclusion provisions in the Code of Practice consistent with the state's obligation to avoid ill-treatment of patients detained by or on the authority of the state. Seclusion would infringe Article 8 unless justified under Article 8(2) as strictly necessary for the prevention of disorder or crime, for the protection of health or morals, or for the protection of the rights and freedoms of others. Since the justifications under the 1983 Act were very broad, the Code of Practice had an important role to play in securing that they had the necessary degree of predictability and transparency to comply with Article 8(2). Moreover, frequent review of the continued need for seclusion was necessary in order to comply with the requirements of Article 13 as specified in *Keenan v United Kingdom*.[117] The Court of Appeal ruling in *Munjaz's* case established a lawful basis for seclusion, as part of the implied power to control, and also sought to meet the requirements of Article 13 by affording judicial remedies and requiring the review of seclusion by nursing and medical staff and its immediate termination if no longer necessary.

In its 2004 report on *Deaths in Custody*,[118] the Joint Committee on Human Rights supported the recommendation of the Mental Health Act Commission and called for the regulation of seclusion and other forms of restraint. The Mental Health Act Commission renewed its call for legal regulation in its *11th Biennial Report* 'not least because of the widespread failure of services to meet the Code's requirements'.[119] The Commission remained of the view that legal regulation is necessary,

---

[115] *Raininen v Finland* (1997) 26 EHRR 563.

[116] *ibid*, at [63]–[64].

[117] *Keenan v United Kingdom* (2001) 33 EHRR 38.

[118] House of Lords, House of Commons, Joint Committee on Human Rights, *Third Report of Session 2004–05:Deaths in Custody*, HL 15–1/HC 137–1 at [245].

[119] Mental Health Act Commission, *11th Biennial Report 2003–2005: In Place of Fear?* (London, TSO, 2006) at [4.237].

[g]iven that seclusion has potential to infringe Articles 3 and 8 of the ECHR it is essential to meet obligations of Government and Service providers that its implementation is premised upon consistent and predictable standards and that all hospitals employ the same approach.[120]

At that time it appears that the Government may have been prepared to consider legal regulation, as the Commission stated that '[t]he Government has informed us that it intends to pursue the statutory regulation of seclusion through the mechanism of the new Mental Health Bill concerned with medical treatment'.[121] The Commission considered that seclusion should not be considered a form of treatment, but should be legally regulated as a management technique.

The Government's willingness to contemplate legal regulation of seclusion seemed to evaporate after the House of Lords granted the hospital's appeal in the *Munjaz* case.[122] The House of Lords held that, assuming Article 8 to be engaged, it was not necessary for seclusion to be regulated by legal rules rather than the 'soft law' Code in order to comply with the requirement in Article 8(2) that 'interferences be in accordance with law'.[123] Lord Bingham confirmed the status of the Code as 'soft law':

> It is plain that the Code does not have the binding effect of statute or a statutory instrument Guidance not instruction. It is guidance which any hospital should consider with great care and from which it should depart only if it has cogent reason for doing so.[124]

The court held that the hospital had demonstrated a cogent reason (the fact that the hospital was a special hospital with many difficult patients) for having less frequent observations for patients detained for more than seven days. Therefore their policy did not breach Articles 3, 5, or 8 of the European Convention. It is interesting that the Secretary of State intervened on the side of the hospital and against making it difficult to justify departures from her own Code.

Lord Bingham considered that whilst it was obvious that seclusion, improperly implemented, could infringe Article 8, seclusion properly implemented and for the shortest period necessary would not. Even if Article 8 were engaged, properly implemented seclusion for the shortest periods necessary would find justification in Article 8(2). Lord Bingham went on to say that the requirement in Article 8(2) that interferences with the right to respect for privacy be in accordance with law was 'intended to ensure that any interference is not random and arbitrary but governed by clear pre-existing rules, and that the circumstances and procedures

---

[120] *ibid*, at [4.238].
[121] *ibid*, at [4.240].
[122] *R (on the application of Munjaz) v Mersey Care NHS Trust* [2004] 1 WLR 441.
[123] *R (on the application of Munjaz) v Mersey Care NHS Trust* [2005] 3 WLR 793, 799
[124] *ibid*, 805.

adopted are predictable and foreseeable by those to whom they are applied'.[125] Although compliance with Article 8 could have been achieved by statutory provisions or regulations,

> that was not the model Parliament adopted. It preferred to require the Secretary of State to give guidance and (in relation to seclusion) to call on hospitals to have clear written guidelines. Given the broad range of institutions in which patients may be treated for mental disorder … it is readily understandable why a single set of rules, binding on all, was thought to be undesirable and perhaps impracticable.[126]

This judicial endorsement of the need for flexibility in relation to seclusion clearly had an impact on Government thinking. Although the Joint Committee on Human Rights's Report on the Mental Health Bill 2006[127] recommended that seclusion be regulated by law rather than the Codes, the Government has chosen the status quo and has avoided subjecting seclusion to direct legal regulation. Instead it remains regulated by the Mental Health Act Code of Practice and by the National Institute of Clinical Excellence Guidance on the short-term management of violence.[128] Generally speaking, health professionals are expected to take the Guidance fully into account when exercising their clinical judgement, but it is emphasised that the Guidance does not override the individual responsibility of health professionals to make decisions appropriate to the circumstances of the individual patient, in consultation with the patient and/or guardian or carer. However, the Guidance warns in its preface that

> [f]ailure to act in accordance with the guideline may not only be a failure to act in accordance with best practice, but in some circumstances may have legal consequences. For example, any intervention required to manage disturbed behaviour must be a reasonable and proportionate response to the risk it seeks to address. The service should ensure access to competent legal advice when required in relation to the management of disturbed/violent behaviour.[129]

---

[125] *ibid*, 809.

[126] *ibid*, 809.

[127] House of Lords, House of Commons Joint Committee on Human Rights, *Fourth Report of Session 2006–7: Legislative Scrutiny: Mental Health Bill* HL 40/HC 288 (London, TSO, 2007) paras [102]–[106].

[128] National Institute of Clinical Excellence, *Violence: The Short-term Management of Disturbed/Violent Behaviour in In-patient Psychiatric Settings and Emergency Departments* CG 25 (London, Royal College of Nursing, 2005).

[129] *ibid*, 10.

X. Conclusion: The Codification of Clinical Authority and the Limits of Rights

The development of twenty-first century mental health legislation in England and Wales shows the emergence of a comprehensive and multi-layered codification of clinical tutelary authority. Clinical authority under legislation has been extended to new professional groups, it has been extended into the community and into residential care homes. Power may be conferred expressly by statute, as in the power to detain and treat without consent, or impliedly and regulated by Codes of Practice, as in the case of seclusion. Conferring clinical authority to detain and treat without consent is the primary aim of mental health legislation, and this is usually done by open textured rules granting extensive discretion to clinicians. Rights are generally rights to seek review of the need to impose restrictions on liberty or interfere with physical integrity, and rights to challenge arbitrary exercise of clinical power.

There has been a steady process of juridification of mental health law, whereby tutelary power is expressed in legislation, regulations and Codes of Practice/ Guidance—a colonisation of legal forms and concepts, with the creation of a special regulatory apparatus for mental health rights via the procedural safeguards in the Mental Health Act and the Mental Capacity Act, the specialist Mental Health Tribunals to review compulsory powers under the Mental Health Act, and the specialist Court of Protection exercising jurisdiction over care and welfare decisions for mentally incapacitated adults.

There are apparent illogical elements in the system. Some of the most invasive interventions—seclusion, restraint and forcible feeding—are not subject to direct legal regulation but are dealt with in the Code of Practice. Treatment without consent under the Mental Health Act is subject to second opinion regulation, while treatment without consent under the Mental Capacity Act does not have a second opinion system. The Care Quality Commission will inspect institutions where patients are detained under the Mental Health Act or the Mental Capacity Act. A requirement to document interferences with the right to liberty or physical integrity, with scrutiny of the sufficiency of those documentary justifications, remains a key feature of regulating psychiatry.

There is a system of institutions where patients may be detained, ranging from the special hospitals for patients who require treatment in conditions of high security on account of their dangerous or violent propensities, through medium-secure units to local hospitals, and now also residential care homes. A voluntary patient who becomes disturbed and requires to be restrained from leaving hospital may be detained under holding powers. A detained patient who becomes too challenging to be cared for in conditions of lesser security may be transferred to a more secure setting. All these interventions take place under express legal powers. Those who become disturbed and threaten others may be given rapid tranquillisation under section 62 of the Mental Health Act. They may be physically restrained or secluded under control powers implied into the Mental Health Act by the courts and regulated by the Mental Health Act Code of Practice and the National Institute of Clinical Excellence Guidance. These are the mechanisms by which compliance may be enforced in hospital. Compliance in the community under a CTO may be enforced by the threat of recall to hospital.

There is great emphasis on recovery programmes where patients manage their own illness and recovery, and these lay great stress on compliance with medication. Compliance will undoubtedly be greatly motivated by the service user's desire to recover, but it will also be significantly influenced by the fact that it takes place in the shadow of compulsion. The psychiatric system is a system of institutions, but also a system of legal relations, where tutelary clinical power is conferred on mental health professionals, and where powers and duties are used to institutionalise the community, to make it into a site where clinical power may be exercised. The example of the CTO shows how the extension of power comes first and limited rights to seek review of that power follow behind. This chapter has outlined how the criteria for the CTO are extremely open textured, and the likelihood will be that few patients will succeed in obtaining discharge from the CTO or in challenging their drug regime. They will only be able to challenge the conditions of a CTO by judicial review, not via the tribunal.

The 2009 Annual Report of the United Nations High Commissioner for Human Rights contains a 'thematic study' on enhancing awareness and understanding of the CRPD.[130] The Report suggests that the maintenance by states of specific mental health legislation authorising the deprivation of liberty on grounds of mental disability contravenes the Convention. Giving as an example the 1991 UN Principles for the Protection of Persons with Mental Illness and the Improvement of Mental Health Care,[131] the Report notes that 'prior to the entrance into force of the Disability Rights Convention, the existence of a mental disability represented a lawful ground for deprivation of liberty and detention under international human rights law'. However, according to the High Commissioner, the CRPD

> radically departs from this approach by forbidding deprivation of liberty based on the existence of any disability, including mental or intellectual, as discriminatory. Article 14, paragraph 1(b), of the Convention unambiguously states that 'the existence of a disability shall in no case justify a deprivation of liberty'... As a result, unlawful detention encompasses situations where the deprivation of liberty is grounded in the combination between a mental or intellectual disability and other elements such as

---

[130] Office of the United Nations High Commissioner for Human Rights, *Annual Report of the United Nations High Commissioner for Human Rights and Reports of the Office of the High Commissioner and the Secretary-General: Thematic Study by the Office of the United Nations High Commissioner for Human Rights on Enhancing Awareness and Understanding of the Convention on the Rights of Persons with Disabilities* (2009), available at: www.un.org/disabilities/documents/reports/ohchr/A.HRC.10.48AEV.pdf

[131] Adopted by UN GA Res 46/119 of 17 December 1991.

dangerousness, or care and treatment. Since such measures are partly justified by the person's disability, they are to be considered discriminatory and in violation of the prohibition of deprivation of liberty on the grounds of disability, and the right to liberty on an equal basis with others prescribed by article 14.[132]

The Report emphasises that this does not mean that 'persons with disabilities cannot be lawfully subject to detention for care and treatment or to preventive detention', but that 'the legal grounds upon which restriction of liberty is determined must be de-linked from the disability and neutrally defined so as to apply to all persons on an equal basis'.[133]

To bring the rights of mentally disordered individuals under the umbrella of disability rights will not be an easy task, either in technical legal terms, or in political terms, since governments seem strongly committed to specific mental health legislation authorising detention on grounds of mental disorder plus the presence of risk to own health or safety or the safety of others. The Joint Parliamentary Scrutiny Committee on the English Mental Health Bill 2004 expressed the view that '[t]he primary purpose of mental health legislation must be to improve mental health services and safeguards for patients and to reduce the stigma of mental disorder'.[134] The Government's Response was dismissive and blunt: 'The Bill is not about service provision, it is about bringing people under compulsion'.[135]

England and Wales have recently introduced two statutes authorising detention: the Mental Capacity Act 2005, where the person has a mental disorder and lacks capacity to decide where to reside, and deprivation of liberty is necessary in the person's own best interests; and the Mental Health Act 2007, which amends the 1983 Act and allows detention where the person has mental disorder of a nature or degree warranting detention in the interests of own health or safety or for the protection of others. However worthy the aim, there would seem to be little immediate prospect of new legislation authorising therapeutic detention on the basis of risk to own health or safety or the safety of others which is 'de-linked from the disability and neutrally defined so as to apply to all persons on an equal basis'.[136]

---

[132] Office of the UNHCHR, *Enhancing Awareness and Understanding of the CRPD* (1990), above n 130, at [48].

[133] Office of the UNHCHR, *Enhancing Awareness and Understanding of the CRPD* (1990), above n 130, at [49]. The scope of the CRPD is explored further in this volume, Part Three: The International Human Rights Framework and the CRPD.

[134] House of Lords, House of Commons, Joint Committee Report on the Draft Mental Health Bill, *First Report:* Session 2004–2005 HL 79–1/HC 95–1, 5.

[135] House of Lords, Sessional Papers, *Government Response to the Report of the Joint Committee on the Draft Mental Health Bill* (Cm 6624, 2005) HLP 79 04/05 at [10].

[136] Office of the UNHCHR, *Enhancing Awareness and Understanding of the CRPD* (1990), above n 130, at [49].

3

Lost in Translation: Human Rights and Mental Health Law

PENELOPE WELLER

I. Introduction

The development of rights-based legalism as the dominant model for contemporary mental health law illustrates the complex relationship between human rights and mental health law reform. The conceptual tool that is popularly used to explain rights-based legalism refers to a pendulum swinging between the two fixed poles of patient rights and medical welfare paternalism.[1] In the pendulum analogy, rights and welfare are posed as mutually exclusive opposites. In contrast, contemporary human rights discourse incorporates traditional welfare principles into the rights framework through the conceptualisation of rights as universal, interconnected, interdependent and indivisible. This chapter analyses the limitations of rights-based legalism, and explores the emerging strength of the human rights approach to mental health law reform.

II. Characterising Consumer Rights

The rights-based movement in mental health law reform grew from a wave of public concern over unacceptable psychiatric practices in the 1960s and 1970s, coupled with the influential exposition of medicine as an institution of social

---

[1] K Jones, 'The Limitations of the Legal Approach to Mental Health' (1980) 3 *International Journal of Law and Psychiatry* 1; K Jones, *A History of the Mental Health Services* (London, Routledge and Kegan Paul, 1972); GL Lipton, 'Politics of Mental Health: Circles or Spirals' (1983) 17 *Australian and New Zealand Journal of Psychiatry* 5.

control.[2] The ground-swell of response was critical of mental health laws that allocated a broad statutory discretion to the medical profession.[3] Discretionary powers of this type were typical of mental health laws in the inter- and post-war periods in developed western jurisdictions. The discretionary model sought to bring mental illness under the umbrella of 'health'. The objective was to provide accessible, modern services that were untarnished by the stigmatising label of insanity.[4] The rights movement saw the privileging of medical discretion as the legal foundation of the (discredited) asylum system, and a dangerous entrench-ment of medical power.[5] This set the twin objectives of rights-based law reform as the limitation of medical power and the dismantling of the asylum system.[6] This characterisation of rights has persisted over time. It belies the more comprehensive analyses that were developed in the 1980s in response to the articulation of international human rights.

III.   The Ideology of Entitlement

Larry Gostin's influential work provides an example of the aspiration for broad social change envisaged by the human rights movement.[7] According to Gostin, law could be used as a strategic tool to legitimately uphold the integrity of people who were de-humanised in institutions, who were subject to the opprobrium of society and whom the discriminatory character of legislation marginalised.[8] By

---

[2]   T Szasz, *Coercion as Cure: A Critical History of Psychiatry* (New Brunswick, Transaction, 2007); P Fennell, *Treatment without Consent: Law, Psychiatry and the Treatment of Mentally Disordered People since 1845* (London, Routledge, 1996); IK Zola, 'Medicine as an Institution of Social Control' (1972) 20 *Sociological Review* 487.

[3]   See T Szasz, *The Myth of Mental Illness: Foundations of a Theory of Personal Conduct* (New York, Hoeber-Harper, 1961).

[4]   C Unsworth, *The Politics of Mental Health Legislation* (Oxford, Clarendon Press, 1987); see also Great Britain, *Report of the Royal Commission on the Law Relating to Mental Illness and Mental Deficiency 1954–1957* (Cmnd 169), (Percy Commission) (London, HMSO, 1957).

[5]   See E Goffman, *Asylums: Essays on the Social Situation of Mental Patients and Other Inmates* (Harmondsworth, Penguin, 1961).

[6]   LO Gostin, 'Contemporary Social Historical Perspectives on Mental Health Reform' (1983) 10 *Journal of Law and Society* 47, 49.

[7]   Larry Gostin was the Welfare Rights Officer and later Legal Director of MIND, the National Association of Mental Health in the United Kingdom. Available at: www.mind.org.uk. He published an extensive critique of mental health law in the UK in 1975: *A Human Condition (Volume 1): The Mental Health Act from 1959 to 1975: Observation, Analysis and Proposals for Reform* (London, MIND, 1975). A second volume related to mentally disordered offenders appeared in 1977. Gostin referred to his 'new rights approach' as the 'ideology of entitlement'. See LO Gostin, 'Contemporary Social Historical Perspectives on Mental Health Reform' (1983) 10 *Journal of Law and Society* 47; LO Gostin, 'The Ideology of Entitlement: The Application of Contemporary Legal Approaches to Psychiatry' in P Bean (ed), *Mental Illness: Changes and Trends* (Chichester, Wiley, 1983). See also Philip Fennell, this volume, ch 2.

[8]   LO Gostin, 'Contemporary Social Historical Perspectives on Mental Health Reform' (1983) 10 *Journal of Law and Society* 47, 50.

imposing specific statutory duties, law could secure mental health services through the pursuit of identified individual rights: statutory rights to services, statutory rights to refuse medical treatment, and statutory rights to review of detention and imposed treatment decisions.[9] Gostin argued that the right to treatment derived from the broad traditions of the common law that obliged governments to provide social and welfare services to all members of the community. As the principle of non-discrimination required that the benefits of the general law be extended to people with mental illness, governments were obliged to provide a full range of community services to people with mental illness including crisis intervention, medical and nursing support, housing, training and employment.[10]

Gostin's 'right to treatment' theory emphasised the importance of voluntary treatment and 'the least restrictive alternative' as a foundation principle of mental health law. He accepted the need to limit recourse to treatment without consent and the need to recognise a 'right to refuse treatment', particularly in relation to psychiatric practices that are shown to be hazardous and/or unsupported by an acceptable evidentiary base. Compulsory admission and treatment on health grounds were acceptable, provided the intervention was limited and aimed at restoring the person to a position of health and social stability. In Gostin's view, compulsory powers in legislation should be tempered by the parallel duty to provide appropriate and legitimate treatment for inpatients.[11] It followed that confinement in the absence of treatment, either because it is unavailable or non-existent, is unacceptable; that treatment that fails to accord with established medical standards is unacceptable; and that the imposition of treatment according to what people may objectively surmise is in the 'best interests' of the person is also inappropriate.[12]

Included in Gostin's 'right to treatment' theory was the obligation to provide publicly financed legal representation for people whose detention or treatment is being considered by Mental Health Review Tribunals or their equivalent. Gostin saw legal representation as an essential component of effective mechanisms of review. He recognised that tribunal systems should aim to provide a fair hearing without unnecessary recourse to formality. But he regarded legal representation in mental health matters as necessary to enable the person with mental illness to critically engage with the difficult task of examining the reasons for detention, the clinical assessment of the need for ongoing intervention, and the plausibility of alternatives to care. Gostin also articulated a role for legislation in ensuring that psychiatric practice remains within the law.[13] He argued that mental health law could set outer limits on practice without intruding unjustifiably on the

---

[9]   *ibid*, 50.
[10] *ibid*, 52.
[11] *ibid*, 53.
[12] *ibid*, 67.
[13] *ibid*, 55.

medical domain. The strategies he suggested included careful restriction of the statutory definition of mental disorder, strict statutory criteria for compulsory admission, recognition of the right to refuse treatment and extension of review mechanisms.

Gostin's approach can be viewed as an 'ideology of entitlement' in that it provided an integrated framework for law that emphasised access to appropriate mental health services (entitlement), freedom from unwarranted detention (liberty), freedom from inappropriate medical intervention (dignity), and the amelioration of stigma and discrimination (equality).[14] In sum, such an integrated framework anticipated the principles that are now recognised in international articulation of the 'right to health'.[15] These principles also point to persistent tensions at the interface between law and psychiatry. In terms of law reform, they reflect an overall transition from a civil rights focus, to a human rights sensibility.[16]

IV. Lost in Translation—The Model of Rights-Based Legalism

The strong human rights ethos that informed the ideology of entitlement was substantially lost in its translation into domestic law. Larry Gostin's work as Legal Officer and later Legal Director of MIND was highly influential. His critique of the Mental Health Act 1959 (England and Wales) appeared in 1975.[17] At that time, MIND was also instrumental in the development of relevant human rights jurisprudence in the European Court of Human Rights.[18] The case of *Winterwerp v The Netherlands*[19] set the fundamental framework for the civil commitment of individuals with mental illnesses. That decision held that civil detention cannot be arbitrary and must follow a 'procedure prescribed by law'. The person concerned must have 'a recognized mental illness', the nature of which must be

---

[14] LO Gostin, '"Old" and "New" Institutions for Persons with Mental Illness: Treatment, Punishment or Preventive Confinement?' (2008) 122 *Public Health* 906.

[15] P Hunt, 'The UN Special Rapporteur on the Right to Health: Key Objectives, Themes, and Interventions' (2003) 7(1) *Health and Human Rights* 26; P Hunt, 'The Health and Human Rights Movement: Progress and Obstacles' (2008) 15 *Journal of Law and Medicine* 714; P Hunt, *Reclaiming Social Rights: International and Comparative Perspectives* (Aldershot, Dartmouth, 1996).

[16] A third limb of the ideology of entitlement concerned the retention of the civil status of the person who was admitted to a psychiatric institution.

[17] LO Gostin, *A Human Condition (Volume 1): The Mental Health Act from 1959 to 1975: Observation, Analysis and Proposals for Reform* (London, MIND, 1975).

[18] G Niveau and J Mater, 'Psychiatric Commitment: Over 50 years of Case Law from the European Court of Human Rights' (2006) 21 *European Psychiatry* 427.

[19] *Winterwerp v The Netherlands* (1979) 2 EHRR 387.

established before the competent national authority on the basis of objective medical expertise, and confinement must be required for the purposes of treatment.[20]

The rights-oriented model of law that emerged from the amalgam of human rights and rights-based critique, and international jurisprudence, is known as 'rights-based legalism'. It is essentially a hybrid model that framed the existing discretionary model with 'rights' armature. Aspects of the rights-based legalism model differ across jurisdictions depending upon the social, political and cultural context in which legislation is adopted. Nevertheless, the characteristic features of the model can be summarised as:

- a diagnostic threshold for the operation of mental health powers;
- restrictive criteria for civil commitment;
- statutory consent requirements for special medical treatments; and
- tribunal review for decisions made pursuant to the legislation.

On their face, these elements accord with the principles expressed in *Winterwerp's* case. They do not, however, engage with the comprehensive framework of statutory powers suggested by Gostin. Discussion about the appropriate content and orientation of these core features has occupied much of the subsequent law reform debate. In focusing on these characteristic elements, rights-based law reform debate misses the opportunity to engage with emerging human rights themes. More recently, frameworks that address decision-making capacity have begun to reshape the rights-based law reform debate. These debates highlight the deficits of the original rights-based model.

V. Diagnostic Thresholds

Rights-based legalism seeks to define the group of people to whom mental health legislation applies with reference to internationally recognised medical criteria. Setting a diagnostic threshold is intended to prevent the misuse of psychiatry as a means of political or social control. In some legislatures there is an additional list of specifically excluded categories. For example, the Mental Health Act 1986 in Victoria, Australia, excludes people who merely

- express a particular political opinion or belief;[21]
- express a particular religious opinion or belief;
- express a particular philosophy;
- express a particular sexual preference or sexual orientation;
- engage in a particular political activity;

---

[20] *ibid.*
[21] The full wording includes the phrase 'express or refuses or fails to express' or 'engage'.

- engage in a particular religious activity;
- engage in sexual promiscuity;
- engage in immoral conduct;
- engage in illegal conduct;
- have an intellectual disability;
- take drugs or alcohol;
- have an antisocial personality.[22]

Exclusion provisions recognise the social construction of diagnostic categories and their close association with prevailing social norms. This approach to the law understands that the adoption of strictly medical categories may compromise the coherence of law by importing controversial, unworkable or unstable diagnostic categories.

At a practical level, threshold definitions dictate access to services and set the interface between the mental health and forensic systems. For example, categorical exclusions may have the effect of excluding people with dual diagnoses, or people in whom mental illness is regarded as a secondary aspect of the primary problem of drug use, from sorely needed services. More fundamentally, exclusion criteria directly invoke the debate about treatability and the proper clinical categorisation of conditions such as antisocial personality disorder and psychopathy. The treatability issue raises questions about whether detention in psychiatric facilities can be justified if no formal treatment is available. In turn, this questions the definition of 'treatment'. Adopting a broad definition of treatment may facilitate access to services, but it may also inappropriately extend the reach of the law. It has been noted by Elizabeth Fistein and colleagues that current trends in mental health law reform seek to achieve flexibility by adopting broad definitions of mental illness that are tempered by both exclusion and treatability requirements.[23] It is not clear whether these new formulations assist in solving issues of access to treatment that arise from the diagnostic threshold.

The ongoing debate about definition points to an underlying tension in rights-based legalism. Rights-based legalism accepts that populations of people with mental illness, regardless of their capacity to make decisions, are legitimately subject to medical authority. In defining the limits of medical authority on perennially uncertain diagnostic grounds, rights-based legalism glosses over its underlying distinction between the (capable) subjects of law and the (incapable) objects of medical welfare. This tension is reiterated in the civil commitment criteria adopted in rights-based legalism.

---

[22] This reflects s 8(2) of the current Mental Health Act 1986 (Vic), save for the addition in 1995 'that the person has a particular economic or social status or is a member of a particular cultural or racial group'.

[23] EC Fistein, AJ Holland, IC Clare and MJ Gunn, 'A Comparison of Mental Health Legislation from Diverse Commonwealth Jurisdictions' (2009) 32 *International Journal of Law and Psychiatry* 147, 153.

VI. The Dangerousness Ground for Civil Commitment

Rights-based legalism adopts restrictive criteria for lawful civil commitment. In earlier formulations of the law, people could be treated involuntarily on the basis of a need for 'care or treatment'.[24] Rights-based legalism restricts meaning of the need for care to immediate or urgent care, and necessitates in addition that the person's safety or the safety of others requires protection. Rights-based legalism therefore seeks to limit compulsory intervention to people who are a danger to themselves or others and who have an immediate need for treatment. The restrictive aspect of these dual criteria has been criticised for setting the intervention criteria too narrowly, and unduly limiting access to preventive intervention or early treatment.[25] Many legislatures have expanded the dangerousness grounds to include the likelihood of a deterioration of physical or mental health. Nevertheless, although empirical evidence shows that there is a weak relationship between violence and mental illness (except in some instances of some psychotic illnesses), the position of risk and danger as the pivotal criteria in rights-based mental health law is linked to the increased prevalence of stigma and discrimination directed toward people with mental illness.[26] On this view, the rights-based approach has contributed to substantive infringements of human rights.

The exposure of people with mental illness to harassment in the community underscores the implicit emphasis in rights-based legalism on community-based treatment. This reflects the requirement that treatment should be provided in the least restrictive manner. From a human rights perspective, the notion of the least restrictive indicates that compulsory intervention is a practice of last resort. In rights-based legalism, the concept of the least restrictive alternative has been predominantly linked with the principle of liberty and the global trend toward de-institutionalisation.[27] The dismantling of stand-alone institutions in the 1980s and 1990s shifted service provision from institutional to community care. De-institutionalisation in many jurisdictions was accompanied by a failure to invest resources in community-based services.[28] The effect of under-resourcing is an inevitable reliance on emergency services and the creation of crisis-driven mental health systems. Clinical interaction with patients who present in crisis is often fraught, and may increase resistance to treatment. In a stressed system,

[24] For example, s 42(3) and s 7(a) and (b) Mental Health Act 1959 (Vic).
[25] R Hayes, O Nielssen, D Sullivan, M Large and K Bayliff, 'Evidence-Based Mental Health Law: The Case for Legislative Change to allow Earlier Intervention in Psychotic Illness' (2007) 14 *Psychiatry, Psychology and Law* 35, 36.
[26] G Thornicroft, *Shunned: Discrimination Against People with Mental Illness* (Oxford, Oxford University Press, 2006); M Brown and J Pratt (eds), *Dangerous Offenders: Punishment and Social Order* (London, Routlege, 2000).
[27] P Appelbaum, 'Law and Psychiatry: Least Restrictive Alternative Revisited: Olmstead's Uncertain Mandate for Community-Based Care' (1999) 50 *Psychiatric Services* 1271, 1278.
[28] LO Gostin, '"Old" and "New" Institutions for Persons with Mental Illness: Treatment, Punishment or Confinement?' (2008) 122 *Public Health* 906, 910.

refusal of treatment is more likely to operate as an indicator of the potential risk of violence or dangerousness and to be interpreted as a proxy indicator of the two other elements that are usually required to justify civil commitment—the need for treatment and a lack of capacity. The observation that stressed systems produce cyclical escalations of crisis, refusal and aggressive intervention has been made in New Zealand, Canada and the United States.[29]

Civil commitment laws that rely on the notion of dangerousness in under-resourced systems therefore work to impose involuntary psychiatric detention in an arbitrary way. Fear of the prospect of imposed treatment may deter people from approaching mental health services. Conversely, scarce treatment resources may be imposed on people who are legitimately non-compliant. While non-compliance as a result of lack of insight is a recognised element of mental illness, non-compliance may also represent a reasoned response to inappropriate intervention. In failing to distinguish between legitimate refusal and non-compliance, rights-based legalism misses its mark. As Matthew Large and colleagues have argued, criteria based on dangerousness in mental health laws are fundamentally problematic.[30] As both Genevra Richardson and Ian Freckelton contend in chapters eight and nine of this volume, close attention must be paid to the significance of the concept of 'insight' in the formulation of mental health laws.

VII.　Limiting Consent

The third and most controversial characteristic of rights-based legalism is its removal of the requirement of consent to medical treatment for all but the most invasive treatments. For example, the Mental Health Act 1983 (England and Wales) included comprehensive arrangements for treatment of patients without their consent. In the case of psychosurgery, the consent of the patient and a second medical opinion were required before the surgery could be performed. A second category of invasive treatments, which included electro-convulsive therapy, required the consent of the person *or* a second medical opinion.[31] Treating clinicians are authorised to provide substituted consent for all other

---

[29] S Bell, 'What Does the "Right to Health" have to offer Mental Health Patients?' (2005) 28 *International Journal of Law and Psychiatry* 141; S Wildeman, 'The Supreme Court of Canada at the Limits of Decisional Capacity' in J Downie and E Gibson (eds), *Health Law at the Supreme Court of Canada* (Toronto, Irwin Law, 2007); BJ Winick, 'A Therapeutic Jurisprudence Approach to Dealing with Coercion in the Mental Health System' (2008) 15 *Psychiatry, Psychology and Law* 25.

[30] M Large, C Ryan, O Nielssen and R Hayes, 'The Danger of Dangerousness: Why we must Remove the Dangerousness Criterion from our Mental Health Acts' (2008) 34 *Journal of Medical Ethics* 877, 879.

[31] LO Gostin, 'Contemporary Social Historical Perspectives on Mental Health Reform' (1983) 10 *Journal of Law and Society* 47, 58.

treatments.[32] Gostin was highly critical of the 1983 amendments, arguing that except in the case of psychosurgery, the provisions failed to provide effective safeguards for the non-consenting patient because they merely required consultation with another member of the clinical team who is unlikely to be in a position to question the treatment programme.[33] A similar criticism can be made of the example found in the Mental Health Act 1986 in Victoria, Australia. In Victoria, psychosurgery may only be performed with the informed consent of the person and the authorisation of the Psychosurgery Review Board.[34] An authorised psychiatrist may give substituted consent to electro-convulsive therapy provided the treatment has clinical merit and will prevent deterioration of the person's condition, or is urgently necessary.[35] All other treatment can be authorised by the treating clinician. The consent provisions indicate that rights-based legalism explicitly sanctions compulsory intervention for people who fall within the scope of the Act. Rights-based legalism therefore excludes the common law principles that apply to the consent and refusal of medical treatment in general health, including the principle of informed consent. By defining people who are subject to mental health legislation as incapable of consenting to medical treatment, the legislation encourages a culture of exclusion and non-participation.

In fixing the ability to consent as the fulcrum for the exercise of medical power, rights-based legalism creates and defines the contemporary tensions in mental health law. Challenging the exclusion of people with mental illness from participation in medical decision-making has emerged as a central theme in the current human rights debate. Contemporary human rights approaches emphasise the right of all people to participate in decision-making processes that affect their human rights. Rights-based legalism assumes that people with mental illness not only lack the capacity to make decisions, but lack the capacity to contribute to the decision-making process. In excluding the principles of participation and informed consent from the matrix of decision-making, rights-based legalism limits the extent to which clinical decisions may be informed by the expressed preferences of the person, or the subjective experience of mental illness. These factors are recognised as principles of best practice in contemporary medical care. They are not supported by the rights-based model.

---

[32] *ibid*, 59.
[33] *ibid*, 60.
[34] Mental Health Act 1986 (Vic) ss 53–71.
[35] Mental Health Act 1986 (Vic) ss 72–82.

VIII. The Review of Medical Decisions

The final feature of rights-based legalism is the introduction of systems of review. The mechanism of review is generally a specialist tribunal. The importance of independent systems of review to oversee the exercise of power granted in mental health legislation as a matter of human rights principle was affirmed in the landmark case of *Winterwerp v The Netherlands*,[36] which is mentioned above. *Winterwerp's* case requires that decisions about detention and medical treatment should be established before a 'competent national authority' vested with the authority to approve ongoing treatment and confinement.[37] The necessity of authoritative review was further entrenched in the case of *X v United Kingdom*.[38] In that decision, the European Court of Human Rights established that the availability of speedy periodic judicial review was necessary in all cases of civil confinement on the basis of mental illness, pursuant to Article 5 of the European Convention on Human Rights. In light of these decisions, debates about the human rights compliance of the rights-based model have focused on the timeliness of tribunal review. For example, in Australia, the shortened average length of the admission period means that, contrary to established human rights principles, most admissions to psychiatric facilities are rarely reviewed.[39] An additional review issue is raised by the question of compliant, voluntary patients whose real consent to medical treatment is questionable. In *HL v United Kingdom*[40] the European Court of Human Rights found that non-protesting patients were entitled to the benefits of review.[41] Finding a breach of Article 5(1)(e) of European Convention on Human Rights, the Court stated that

> the right to liberty in democratic society is too important for a person to lose the benefit of ... [Review] ... simply because they have given themselves up to detention, especially when they are not capable of consent to or disagreeing with, the proposed action.[42]

From a human rights perspective, review processes must have real substance.

Debate about the quality of tribunal review in mental health matters coalesces around the issue of formality and its relationship to the requirements of procedural fairness.[43] Consideration of the substantive content of the requirement of procedural fairness generally requires a consideration of whether people

---

[36] *Winterwerp v The Netherlands* (1979) 2 EHRR 387.
[37] *Luberti v Italy* (1984) 6 EHRR 440.
[38] *X v United Kingdom* (1981) 4 EHRR 181.
[39] N Rees, 'International Human Rights Obligations and Mental Health Review Tribunals' (2003) 10 *Psychiatry, Psychology and Law* 33, 37.
[40] *HL v United Kingdom* (2004) 40 EHRR 32.
[41] *R v Bournewood Community and Mental Health NHS Trust, ex parte L* [1998] 3 All ER 289.
[42] *HL v United Kingdom* (2004) 40 EHRR 32 at [90].
[43] N Rees, 'International Human Rights Obligations and Mental Health Review Tribunals' (2003) 10 *Psychiatry, Psychology and Law* 33, 38, 39.

who appear before mental health tribunals are adequately informed of the matters to be heard, and are provided with the opportunity to put evidence before the tribunal and to respond to any adverse information that is relevant to the decision being made.[44] It is often assumed that procedural fairness requirements, and by implication human rights requirements, will be satisfied if legal representation is available for people who appear before mental health tribunals or their equivalent. Human rights jurisprudence establishes that rights must not be rendered 'theoretical or illusory' by the operation of the law, and must be 'practical and effective'.[45] Moreover, the European Court of Human Rights has affirmed the obligation to provide public finance for legal representation before mental health tribunals.[46] Given the complex nature of the matters before such tribunals and the vulnerability of persons who appear before them, it is unlikely that legal representation alone will adequately attend to the question of whether human rights are rendered practical and effective within tribunal systems of review.

The substantive requirements that attach to the principle of procedural fairness draw attention to the underlying question of how tribunals should approach their task of review. Bruce Winick has described proceedings before mental health tribunals in the United States as dominated by lawyers who either fail to understand the therapeutic needs of patients, or alternatively, lack sufficient legal expertise to understand the requirements of the law. He argues that this results in processes that merely 'rubber stamp' medical decisions.[47] Similarly, a recent report from the Mental Health Legal Centre in Victoria, entitled '*Lacking Insight*', questions the capacity of the Victorian Mental Health Review Tribunal to effectively challenge medical decisions.[48] These critical accounts of tribunal systems invoke the enduring association of rights-based legalism with the protection of rights. However, in rights-based legalism, tribunals are charged with the task of ensuring that medical decisions are made according to law. The resounding entrenchment of medical discretion at the core of the rights-based model effectively operates to preclude tribunals from determinations that substantially challenge medical opinion.[49]

In summary, the contradiction at the heart of rights-based legalism is its explicit limitation of rights within a rights framework. First, the model is principally concerned to protect people who are wrongly subject to medical expertise. Secondly, when people are deemed to have a mental illness, the model

---

[44] *ibid*, 39.

[45] *Airey v Ireland* (1979–80) 2 EHRR 305 at [24].

[46] *Collins v United Kingdom* (2003) 36 EHRR CD6.

[47] BJ Winick, 'Therapeutic Jurisprudence Approach to Dealing with Coercion in the Mental Health System' (2008) 15 *Psychiatry, Psychology and Law* 25, 29.

[48] V Topp, M Thomas and M Ingvarson, *Lacking Insight: Involuntary Patient Experience of the Victorian Mental Health Review Board* (Melbourne, Mental Health Legal Centre, 2008).

[49] N Rees, 'International Human Rights Obligations and Mental Health Review Tribunals' (2003) 10 *Psychiatry, Psychology and Law* 33, 39.

hinges on the unwieldy and contradictory assessment of dangerousness and the need for treatment. Thirdly, the model requires only limited procedural review of treatment decisions. Because the model assumes a dichotomous division between people without mental illness who can exercise rights, and those with mental illness who cannot, it founders on the slippery ground of the clinical categorisation of mental illness. Challenging the strict distinction between capacity and incapacity, and the consequences of that determination, is the principal contribution of contemporary human rights thinking to the mental health field.

IX. Re-Asserting Rights With Psychiatric Advance Directives

Understanding the ethos of rights-based legalism as the ability to impose medical treatment on people with mental illness provides an explanation for the parallel amplification of a global law reform campaign that has sought to secure the right to refuse treatment.[50] The early focus of this campaign was the legal recognition of psychiatric 'advance directives'.[51] Psychiatric advance directives claim their legitimacy from the deeply-embedded common law recognition of the right to bodily integrity, which encompasses the right to consent and refuse medical treatment.[52] As the common law developed prior to the distillation of human rights principles represented by the Universal Declaration of Human Rights, the notion of bodily inviolability pre-empts and informs the emphasis in international human rights law on protection of bodily integrity.

Like its counterpart in general health concerning end-of-life decisions, the psychiatric advance directive movement claimed the right to make binding future decisions about psychiatric treatment. Although they remain the subject of controversy, several jurisdictions introduced legislative provision for psychiatric advance directives during the 1990s.[53] Where psychiatric advance directives have been introduced as an adjunct to a rights-based model, their impact has been disappointing. The difficulties encountered in implementing advance directives across jurisdictions vary according to the legislative mechanisms that have been

---

[50] BJ Winick, *The Right To Refuse Mental Health Treatment* (Washington DC, American Psychological Association, 1997).

[51] T Szasz, 'The Psychiatric Will: A New Mechanism for Protecting Persons against "Psychosis" and Psychiatry' (1982) 37 *American Psychology* 762.

[52] AR Maclean, 'Advance Directives and the Rocky Waters of Anticipatory Decision-making' (2008) 16 *Medical Law Review* 1; JM Atkinson, HC Garner and WH Gilmour, 'Models of Advance Directives in Mental Health Care: Stakeholder Views' (2004) 39 *Social Psychiatry and Psychiatric Epidemiology* 673.

[53] J Atkinson, *Advance Directives in Mental Health: Theory, Practice and Ethics* (London, Jessica Kingsley Publishers, 2007).

adopted. Nevertheless, these difficulties further illuminate the tensions in rights-based legalism that arise from the underlying assumption that people with mental illness lack the capacity to make valid medical decisions.

From a rights perspective, psychiatric advance directives are supposed to give substance to the autonomy rights of a person with mental illness by enabling them to retain control over their medical treatment during periods of anticipated incapacity. However, they intrude uncomfortably upon a legal framework that allocates the authority for medical decision-making to the clinician. As the discussion of the detail of rights-based legalism has indicated, rights-based legalism does not seek to challenge the authority of medicine. Instead, rights-based legalism entrenches the medical obligation to provide the treatment that the clinician considers to be in the best interests of the person. In the legal framework of rights-based legalism, where the obligation falls on clinicians to act in the person's 'best interests', the legal ramifications of following a psychiatric advance directive are far from clear.

The operation of the best interests principle in psychiatric decision-making has not been the subject of extended analysis. In the absence of guidelines to direct the decision-making process, the best interests model invites imposition of the subjectively determined judgement of the decision-maker, whether that be the tribunal or a clinician. As illustrated above, rights-based legalism gives precedence to the medical view. One approach to ensuring that best interests determinations include holistic, socially-based assessments is to ensure that decision-makers take into account different stakeholder perspectives. Another is to consider the wishes or preferences of the person as part of the best interests determination. Exhortations to clinicians to take into account the expressed preferences of the person when determining the treatment in the person's best interests, however, are unlikely to alter the legal conundrum clinicians face when making decisions in a framework that imposes an ethical and legal obligation upon them to provide treatment that is in the best interests of the person. New conceptions of the capacity of psychiatric advance directives to assist people in negotiating effective systems of care are transforming the advance directive debate. As the above discussion indicates, however, psychiatric advance directives have a limited scope when they are merely a reaction to the coercive power of rights-based legalism.

X. Rights-Based Legalism and the International Community

The international community has also struggled to articulate a human rights-based standard for mental health law. The first statement of international principle specifically addressing the rights of people living with mental illness appeared in 1991.[54] At the time of their adoption, the *Principles for the Protection of Persons with Mental Illness and the Improvement of Mental Health Care* (MI Principles) were highly persuasive. On their face, the MI Principles construct a coherent human rights framework for mental health care. They require that medical treatment is provided in the least restrictive manner, according to an individual plan. Treatment must also reflect accepted medical standards and be delivered in a manner that is supportive of autonomy (Principle 9). Medication must be given for therapeutic purposes only (Principle 10), and all treatment is to be provided with free and informed consent (Principle 11). The principle of informed consent, however, is modified by lengthy qualifications that strongly endorse involuntary medical treatment when a person is considered to lack capacity. Like rights-based legalism, the MI Principles enshrine a broad discretion to impose medical treatment upon persons who are subject to involuntary detention procedures, which is limited only by the standards of medical practice and the principle of best interests.

The MI Principles were strongly criticised by consumers and academics because of their uncritical acceptance of the medical model of disease and treatment, and their related endorsement of involuntary detention and treatment. For example, Eric Rosenthal and Leonard Rubenstein described the consent provisions in the MI Principles as an unacceptably loose standard that permits the imposition of medical treatment according to a vague and unlimited 'best interests' standard.[55] Caroline Gendreau has argued that the MI Principles actually limited the scope of the human rights that were thought to apply to persons living with mental illnesses at the time they were adopted.[56]

A valuable aspect of the MI Principles is the clarification they provide to the role of tribunals. Tribunal review must be independent and impartial, and assisted by one or more qualified and independent mental health practitioners. Initial review of a treatment decision must take place as soon as possible, be periodically reviewed, and be subject to a right of judicial appeal. As is discussed above, elaborating upon the detail of tribunal procedure begs a question about the role and focus of the review itself. In this regard the MI Principles are significant because they require review of the determination of incapacity itself.[57]

---

[54] *Principles for the Protection of Persons with Mental Illness and the Improvement of Mental Health Care* (1991) GA Res 46/119. UN Doc A/Res/46/.

[55] E Rosenthal and L Rubenstein, 'International Human Rights Advocacy under the Principles for the Protection of Persons with Mental Illness' (1993) 16 *International Journal of Law and Psychiatry* 257.

[56] C Gendreau, 'The Rights of Psychiatric Patients in the Light of the Principles Announced by the United Nations: A Recognition of the Right to Consent to Treatment?' (1997) 20 *International Journal of Law and Psychiatry* 259.

[57] Ontario, Canada has adopted tribunal review of capacity. See J Zuckerberg, 'International Human Rights for Mentally Ill Persons: The Ontario Experience' (2007) 30 *International Journal of Law and Psychiatry* 512, and Wildeman, S, 'The Supreme Court of Canada at the Limits of Decisional Capacity' in J Downie and E Gibson (eds), *Health Law at the Supreme Court of Canada* (Toronto, Irwin Law, 2007).

The human rights-based requirement to determine the question of capacity contrasts with the assumption in rights-based legalism that the clinical determination of incapacity is non-reviewable. MI Principle 1(3) also provides that the person 'shall be entitled to be represented by a counsel' who is independent of the mental health facility and of the family of the person. The MI Principles therefore recognise that a determination of mental illness does not automatically foreclose the question of capacity. This echoes the recent move toward capacity-based legislation, and statutory requirements that capacity be determined with reference to the ability of the individual to understand the nature of treatment or admission, weigh up the benefits of such, make a choice and communicate that choice.[58] In England and Wales, where the capacity-based legislation sits alongside mental health laws, a finding of capacity determines whether or not the person will be the subject of voluntary or involuntary admission.[59] Capacity-based laws have the potential to ameliorate some of the difficulties posed by the rights-based model.

Subsequent international statements concerning people living with mental illness have been incorporated within statements concerning disability. In 1993, the United Nations adopted the *Standard Rules on the Equalization of Opportunities for Persons with Disabilities* (Standard Rules).[60] The Standard Rules are regarded as the major outcome of the Decade of Disabled Persons; they represent a summary of the World Programme of Action Concerning Disabled Persons. At the time, they represented the principal international instrument guiding state action on human rights and disabilities. The Standard Rules emphasised the importance of human dignity and personal self-determination in the provision of health care. They required the implementation of programmes addressing impairment, the non-discriminatory provision of regular health care and the appropriate training of medical and paramedical personnel. They also informed the Economic and Social Council's 'General Comment 5' on Persons with Disability.[61] Paragraph 34 of General Comment 5 reaffirms that people with disabilities have a right to have access to, and to benefit from, medical and social services that enable persons with disabilities to become independent, that prevent further disabilities and that support their social integration. General Comment 5 also recognises that services should enable people with disabilities to reach and sustain an optimum level of independence and functioning, and should be provided in a way that the persons concerned are able to maintain full respect for their rights and dignity.

---

[58] As in the Mental Capacity Act 2005 (England and Wales). This approach is also adopted by the Steering Committee on Bioethics (CDBI) of the Council of Europe, 10.1, 2000.

[59] G Richardson, 'Balancing Autonomy and Risk: A Failure of Nerve in England and Wales?' (2007) 30 *International Journal of Law and Psychiatry* 71.

[60] Adopted by the United Nations General Assembly, 48th session, resolution 48/96, annex, 20 December 1993.

[61] United Nations Office of the High Commissioner for Human Rights, *Persons with Disabilities* CESR General Comment 5, 9 December 1994.

In conjunction with the ongoing concern with disability, international recognition of mental health as a public health issue is reflected in the contributions of the World Health Organization to the development of international legal standards. In 1996, WHO developed 10 basic principles, with accompanying guidelines, that were intended to assist in the interpretation of the MI Principles.[62] The 10 basic principles were:

- promotion of mental health and prevention of mental disorders;
- access to basic mental health care;
- mental health assessments in accordance with internationally accepted principles;
- provision of least restrictive type of mental health care;
- self-determination;
- right to be assisted in the exercise of self-determination;
- availability of review procedure;
- automatic periodic review mechanism;
- qualified decision-makers; and
- respect of the rule of law.

WHO continued its work on human rights and mental health legislation resulting in the publication in 2001 of *The World Health Report 2001: Mental Health Law: New Understanding, New Hope*.[63] The report sought to encourage a community care paradigm and respect for the rights and dignity of patients.[64] In 2004, a paper discussing the role of international human rights in national mental health legislation was followed by the publication of a resource book to guide the formulation of mental health laws according to human rights principles.[65]

The *WHO Resource Book* lists the fundamental aims of mental health legislation as the

- protection, promotion and improvement of the lives and mental well-being of citizens;
- protection of vulnerable citizens (including people with mental disorders);
- promotion of access to mental health care;
- promotion and protection of the rights of persons with mental disorders;
- reduction of stigma and discrimination; and
- promotion of the mental health of populations.[66]

---

[62] M Freeman, *WHO Resource Book on Mental Health, Human Rights and Legislation* (Geneva, World Health Organization, 2005) 15, available at: www.who.int/mental_health/policy/resource_book_MHLeg.pdf.

[63] *The World Health Report 2001: Mental Health Law: New Understanding, New Hope* (Geneva, World Health Organization, 2001).

[64] ibid, 54.

[65] E Rosenthal and C Sundram, *The Role of International Human Rights in National Mental Health Legislation* (Geneva, World Health Organization, 2004).

[66] ibid, 1.

Legislation can also support the recommended policy goals of:

- establishing high-quality mental health facilities and services;
- ensuring access to quality mental health care;
- protecting human rights;
- protecting the patient's right to treatment;
- developing procedural protections;
- integrating people with mental disorders into the community; and
- promoting mental health throughout society.[67]

To achieve these goals, legislation should support the rights of equality and non-discrimination, the right to privacy and individual autonomy, freedom from inhuman and degrading treatment, the principle of the least restrictive environment, and the rights to information and participation.[68] The 2004 WHO report is also supportive of a legislative obligation to provide a full range of services for people with mental disorders.[69] This broader potential is stated more restrictively in the WHO Policy Framework on Mental Health, Human Rights and Legislation.[70] The framework recommends that:

- mental health care be available at the community level for anyone who may need it;
- procedural safeguards be put in place to protect against the overuse and abuse of involuntary admission and treatment;
- monitoring bodies be established to ensure that human rights are being respected in all mental health facilities;
- people with mental illnesses be protected from discrimination; and
- people with mental illnesses be diverted away from the criminal justice system and towards mental health services.

Specific rights issues discussed in the *Resource Book* include respect for confidentiality, access to information, and the rights and conditions in mental health facilities. In relation to the question of competence, capacity and guardianship, the *Resource Book* recognises that 'most persons with mental disorders retain the ability to make informed choices and decisions regarding important matters affecting their lives'.[71] In relation to consent to medical treatment, the *Resource Book* specifically adopts the MI Principles, thereby importing into the model the most controversial aspect of the MI Principles.

Acceptance of the provision of involuntary treatment is reinforced by the *Resource Book*'s reference to the Siracusa Principles on the Limitation and

---

[67] *ibid*, 2.
[68] *ibid*, 3.
[69] *ibid*, 6.
[70] M Freeman, *WHO Resource Book on Mental Health, Human Rights and Legislation* (Geneva, World Health Organization, 2005) 63.
[71] *ibid*, 39.

Derogation of Provisions in the International Covenant on Civil and Political Rights (Siracusa Principles) as an authoritative framework for the limitation of human rights.[72] The Siracusa Principles permit restrictions of rights, provided that the restriction is

- provided for and carried out in accordance with the law;
- in the interest of the legitimate objective of general interest;
- necessary in a democratic society to achieve the objective;
- necessary to respond to a public health need;
- proportional to the social aim, there being no less intrusive and restrictive means available to reach this social aim; and
- not drafted or imposed arbitrarily.

As a cursory examination of this list confirms, any limitation of the principle of free and informed consent on medical grounds is easily justified in law. The WHO model therefore replicates the contradictions and limitations of rights-based legalism. From a contemporary human rights perspective, its most salient feature is the continued preoccupation of the framework with the imposition of the provision of medical treatment as the primary response to mental illness. This focus is fundamentally challenged by the Convention on the Rights of Persons with Disabilities.[73]

XI.   Re-Inventing a Human Rights Response

The Convention on the Rights of Persons with Disabilities (the CRPD) came into force internationally on 3 May 2008. People with disabilities, including people with mental illness, were closely involved in its design.[74] Drafting of the CRPD followed publication of a discussion paper by Gerard Quinn and Theresia Degener that emphasised the fundamental, but overlooked, entitlement of people with disabilities to benefit from the human rights already contained in binding international documents.[75] The report identified two barriers to the realisation of human rights for people with disability. These were the dominance of a medical, rather than social model of disability, and the unwarranted conceptual separation of civil, political, and economic, social and cultural rights. The social model encompasses the dual recognition that disability is a social construct and that health and illness are socially determined. Unlike earlier Convention models that

---

[72]   *ibid*, 16.

[73]   Convention on the Rights of Persons with Disabilities, adopted 13 December 2006, GA Res 61/106. UN Doc A/Res/61/106 (entered into force 3 May 2008).

[74]   For an overview of the CRPD, see Oliver Lewis, this volume, ch 5.

[75]   G Quinn and T Degener, with A Bruce, *Human Rights and Disability: The Current Use and Future Potential of United Nations Human Rights Instruments in the Context of Disability* (New York, United Nations, 2002).

have sought to achieve human rights through the assertion of rights, the CRPD addresses the foundation human rights of non-discrimination, equality and social participation as entitlements that must be constructed in the social fabric.

Gerard Quinn summarises the potential impact of the Convention as one that establishes disability politics as a matter of equity, the rule of law, justice and human rights.[76] He argues that people with disabilities, as subjects of law, are entitled to protection from violence, to live independently and to be provided with the social supports that make life choices and freedoms a reality for everybody. If people with disabilities have different needs, that recognition should engender the provision of additional supports—not their limitation. To achieve this, States Parties to the CRPD are obliged to embed reflective process within government, to consult with people with disabilities, to set measurable goals, and to establish independent monitoring authorities.

These goals fundamentally challenge the limited focus of rights-based legalism, which is solely concerned with the compulsory medical treatment of people living with mental illnesses. They invite a re-evaluation of the broader role for the law in providing the social infrastructure that enables people living with mental illnesses to participate fully in social life as the subject of law. In the 1970s, Larry Gostin alluded to the obligation of governments to provide a full range of community services to people with mental illnesses, including crisis intervention, medical and nursing support, housing, training and employment. The Richardson report, in evaluating new directions in mental health law in England and Wales, referred to this concept as 'the principle of reciprocity'.[77] The CRPD returns the human rights approach to this emphasis.

XII. Human Rights and Domestic Law

The challenge for a human rights approach to mental health law is the translation of Convention principles into domestic law. As Sylvia Bell has noted, attempts to secure service entitlement through the courts have met with a persistent refusal by the judiciary to intercede in what it regards as the proper sphere of executive power.[78] Important decisions in the South African and Indian Supreme Courts

---

[76] G Quinn, Seminar for the European Coalition for Community Living, Drammen, Norway, 12-13 September 2008.

[77] Great Britain, Department of Health Expert Committee, *Review of the Mental Health Act 1983: Report of the Expert Committee* (London, Department of Health, 1999).

[78] S Bell, 'What Does the "Right to Health" Have to Offer Mental Health Patients?' (2005) 28 *International Journal of Law and Psychiatry* 141.

that recognise the justiciability of economic, social and cultural rights, at least where human rights are constitutionally entrenched, indicate that a shift is afoot.[79]

The changing approach to the justiciability of economic, social and cultural rights is underpinned by the burgeoning recognition of the false dichotomy between the two sets of rights that has structured the development of the law. Amita Dhanda has analysed the entrenched distinction between civil and political and economic, social and cultural rights.[80] In her view, civil and political rights were traditionally seen as negative rights. They were easily expressed in laws that prohibited action by the state, and, it was thought, could be promptly and effectively guaranteed without requiring significant resource allocation. Civil and political rights were principally a creature of law, and could thus be adjudicated and defended in the courts. Social, economic and cultural rights, on the other hand, were assumed to be positive, resource-dependent rights that were policy-driven and essentially non-justiciable. The dichotomy between the two sets of rights accepted that judicial intervention is integral to the protection of civil-political rights, and relegated social-economic rights to the discretion of the mechanisms of state governance. The marginal role allocated to courts in the realisation of social, economic and cultural rights therefore reflects acceptance of the doctrine of judicial essentialism, which requires courts to only execute legislative intention and not make law.

The false dichotomy between civil and political and economic, social and cultural rights has been clearly illustrated in the work of Armatya Sen and others.[81] This recognition underpins the adoption by the United Nations of the Vienna Declaration and Programme of Action that recognises human rights as universal, indivisible, interdependent and interrelated.[82] The CRPD similarly acknowledges the deep interconnection of all rights. In addition, it indicates that the discriminatory provision of resources and services may not be subject to the principle of progressive realisation. For people with mental illnesses, an important implication of this expression of the human rights framework is the recognition that the provision of medical services is one aspect of a broad social infrastructure to which they are entitled. The challenge is to ensure the translation of CRPD principles into domestic law.

---

[79] S Bell, *ibid*, cites *Soobramoney v Minister of Health (Kwazulu-Natal)* 1998 (1) SA 756 (CC); *Grootboom v Oosteenberg Municipality* 2001 (1) SA 46 (CC); and *Minister of Health v Treatment Action Campaign* 2002 (5) SA 721 (CC). The Constitution of the Republic of South Africa Act No 108 (1996) incorporates the International Convention on Economic, Social and Cultural Rights.

[80] A Dhanda, 'The Right to Treatment of Persons with Psychosocial Disabilities and the Role of the Courts' (2005) 28 *International Journal of Law and Psychiatry* 155, 168.

[81] A Sen, *Poverty and Famines: An Essay on Entitlement and Deprivation* (Oxford, Oxford University Press, 1981); A Sen and M Nausbaum (eds), *The Quality of Life* (Oxford, Oxford University Press, 1993); A Sen, *Development as Freedom* (Oxford, Oxford University Press, 1999).

[82] World Conference on Human Rights, Vienna Declaration and Programme of Action (1993). UN Doc A/CONF.157/23.

In Larry Gostin's most recent work, he continues to articulate a comprehensive role for the law in terms of rights, duties and justice.[83] Gostin observes that the law has a broad remit. It grants power to governments, sets limits, prescribes government process, specifies measures of accountability and adjudicates disputes. In health, the law affords individuals a broad set of rights in the health system that includes the protection of autonomy, bodily integrity, privacy and liberty.[84] Inspiration that can be drawn from Gostin's contemporary work is the appreciation to harness the law in the light of a full recognition of the social construction of disability and social determinants of health and illness.

XIII. Conclusion

The metaphor of a pendulum swinging in mental health law invokes a sense of a historical prevarication between legalism and medical paternalism, and between rights and welfare. It also denotes a deep frustration with the structures and institutions of the law. Rights-based legalism contributes to this frustration by its apparent acceptance of the prevailing critique of medical power, and simultaneous affirmation of the deeply felt humanism of psychiatric medicine. Contemporary human rights-thinking welds the two perspectives. It emphasises the indivisible nature of rights and the problematic exclusion of economic, social and cultural rights. In recognising people with mental illness as bearers of human rights, the human rights approach inverts the point of departure of rights-based legalism. It requires the assumption of capacity, questions the welfare principle, and asserts an entitlement to services. This means that people with mental illnesses must be included in the decisions that affect them, and must be provided with services that are appropriate to their needs on an equal basis with others.

The principles of equality, participation and non-discrimination that provide the core of the ethos of the CRPD require the adoption of a human rights approach in mental health care that asserts the human capabilities of people with mental illness. This notion fundamentally challenges the foundation principles of the western political order, which is derived from the enlightenment principles of constitutionalism and the rule of law.[85] The enlightenment rule of law takes the autonomous, fully rational self-determining person as its subject. The subjects of rational law are characterised as independent individuals, who are the bearers of civil and political rights. In this framework, the rights of people who lack rationality are limited because they cannot participate in the structures of formal freedom and equality. The problem created by the exclusion of people who lack

---

[83] LO Gostin, *Public Health Law: Power, Duty, Restraint*, 4th edn (Berkeley CA, University of California Press, 2008).

[84] LO Gostin, 'National and Global Health Law' (2008) 96 *Georgetown Law Journal* 17.

[85] C Unsworth, *The Politics of Mental Health Legislation* (Oxford, Clarendon Press, 1987) 36.

rationality is resolved by welfare principles and best interests determinations. Welfare and best interests principles characterise people who lack rationality as wholly dependent. Those principles renders their views, wishes and preferences irrelevant to the decision-making process.

Contemporary human rights law recognises all people as equal subjects of law. This requires the revision of the black-and-white distinction between capacity and incapacity, and determinations on the basis of a diagnosis of mental illness, which lie at the heart of rights-based legalism. Instead, mental health laws must seek to conceptualise capacity and competence along a continuum of capability. Recognition of the decision-making capacity of people with mental illnesses will be a first step in challenging the deeply discriminatory legacy of the law.[86]

---

[86]   *ibid*, 40.

4

The Fusion Proposal: A Next Step?[*]

NEIL REES

I. Introduction

While Australia is highly likely to have rights-based laws governing the involuntary treatment of people with a mental illness into the foreseeable future, debate about the precise nature of that legal regime will continue.

Support for the fusion of Australian mental health and guardianship laws appears to be gaining ground as expert commentators in many countries question the need for two separate bodies of law that deal with what seem to be the same, or similar, legal issues.[1] Those issues may be broadly characterised as authorising the medical treatment and, in some instances, the containment of people who are unable, or unwilling, to consent to these actions because of impaired capacity resulting from disability.

At present mental health legislation deals with the detention and involuntary treatment of people with a mental illness, while Australian guardianship laws provide a generic substitute decision-making regime for people with impaired capacity because of any disability, including mental illness. Despite the breadth of guardianship laws, they are generally unavailable for use in the circumstances covered by the civil commitment provisions in mental health statutes.

The case for continuing to treat people with a mental illness differently to the way in which others who have impaired decision-making capacity are treated

[*] Any opinions expressed in this paper are the personal views of the author. I wish to acknowledge the research assistance of Aviva Berzon and Claire Gallagher.

[1] See, eg G Richardson, 'Autonomy, Guardianship and Mental Disorder: One Problem, Two Solutions' (2002) 65 *Modern Law Review* 702; P Bartlett, 'The Test of Compulsion in Mental Health Law: Capacity, Therapeutic Benefit and Dangerousness as Possible Criteria' (2003) 11 *Medical Law Review* 326; J Dawson and G Szmukler, 'The Fusion of Mental Health and Incapacity Legislation' (2006) 188 *British Journal of Psychiatry* 504; J Dawson and G Szmukler, 'Why Distinguish "Mental" and "Physical" Illness in the Law of Involuntary Treatment?' in M Freeman and O Goodeneough (eds), *Law, Mind and Brain* (Farnham, Ashgate, 2009) 173.

must be able to withstand scrutiny at a time when human rights, such as the equal protection of the law, are at the forefront of our thinking.[2]

Like the separate rules of common law and equity prior to the advent of legislation[3] which brought about their fusion,[4] modern Australian mental health and guardianship laws have generally operated as parallel bodies of law, providing quite different substitute decision-making regimes for people unable to make their own decisions because of disability. In some Australian jurisdictions attempts have been made to integrate the two bodies of law,[5] while in others one body of law expressly defers to the other.[6] In Victoria the two sets of laws have co-existed in silence until quite recently, the general assumption having been that mental health laws govern most substitute decision-making for people with a mental illness, and that guardianship laws have a limited role to play.[7]

The purpose of this chapter is, first, to examine the Australian history of mental health and guardianship laws in order to explain why these two separate bodies of law exist. Secondly, the chapter will describe the current operation of mental health and guardianship laws in Victoria and New South Wales, the two most populous Australian jurisdictions. Thirdly, it will identify some of the arguments for and against the fusion of mental health and guardianship laws and, fourthly, it will consider the feasibility of a 'legal trial' which would not bring about fusion but would permit these two bodies of substitute decision-making law to operate concurrently for people with a mental illness over a reasonable period of time. The 'legal trial' would permit consumers, clinicians

---

[2] See, eg Convention on the Rights of Persons with Disabilities, adopted 13 December 2006, GA Res 61/106, UN Doc A/Res/61/106 (entered into force 3 May 2008) Art 5.1; Charter of Human Rights and Responsibilities Act 2006 (Vic) s 8(3).

[3] In England this step came about in the 1870s (the Judicature Acts 1873–75). Victoria followed in the 1880s (Supreme Court (Judicature) Act 1883 (Vic)). In New South Wales, this step was not taken until the 1970s (Supreme Court Act 1970 (NSW) ss 57–63; Law Reform (Law and Equity) Act 1972 (NSW)).

[4] There are still some prominent Australian lawyers who dispute the assertion that the common law and equity have been fused (RP Meagher, JD Heydon and MJ Leeming, *Meagher, Gummow and Lehane's Equity, Doctrines and Remedies*, 4th edn (Sydney, Butterworths, 2002) xi). For a more modern view, see M Kirby, 'Equity's Australian Isolationism' (WA Lee Equity Lecture, 19 November 2008, Queensland University of Technology, Brisbane) available at: www.michaelkirby.com.au/images/stories/speeches/2000s/vol65+/2008/2323-W_A_Lee_Equity_Lecture_2008_(final).doc.

[5] In Tasmania, for example, decisions about detention in hospital are made by the Mental Health Tribunal (see s 52 Mental Health Act 1996 (Tas)), while decisions about involuntary treatment for mental illness are made by the Guardianship and Administration Board (see s 32 Mental Health Act 1996 (Tas)).

[6] Section 3C of the Guardianship Act 1987 (NSW) provides that while guardianship may continue to operate when a person is either a voluntary or involuntary patient in a mental health facility, all of the powers in the Mental Health Act 2007 (NSW) prevail over those in the Guardianship Act whenever there is inconsistency. Section 7 of the Mental Health Act permits a guardian to admit a person under guardianship to a mental health facility as a voluntary patient.

[7] In Victoria a guardian may be a substitute decision-maker in relation to non-psychiatric treatment for a voluntary patient (Mental Health Act 1986 (Vic) s 85). While Victorian law does not specifically prevent the use of guardianship laws to provide involuntary psychiatric treatment for a person with impaired capacity, there are strong indications in the legislation that this step should not be taken (see, eg Mental Health Act 1986 (Vic) s 3A).

and carers to evaluate which system better caters for the legal needs of people with a mental illness when they lack capacity to make decisions for themselves. The ultimate outcome may be evidence-based law reform.

II. The History of Australian Mental Health and Guardianship Laws

A. The History of Mental Health Law

Australia has traditionally looked to England for guidance when preparing mental health laws. Until the 1980s our Mental Health Acts were little more than local versions of English statutes. Since that time some important differences, such as the Australian emphasis upon involuntary treatment in the community, have emerged.

Early English mental health laws were concerned with the protection of private property. While those statutes—which date from the reign of Edward I during the late thirteenth century—had a protective purpose, they also contributed to the royal income. As feudal lords had abused people of unsound mind, the sovereign intervened, as *parens patriae*, to protect their lands. The monarch had the prerogative power to manage the lands of these people and to share in the profits for doing so. People of unsound mind became wards of the sovereign, and the sovereign could determine where they were to live and what could be done to them.[8]

Medieval law made no specific provision for mentally ill people without interests in land. It was not until the eighteenth century that legislation dealt with the detention of mentally ill persons who had no property. The Vagrancy Act 1744 permitted justices to order that 'pauper lunatics' be locked up and chained in a secure place. This move reflected concerns of the day that insane people would interfere with the property of others unless they were placed in institutions.[9]

Legislative interest in the actual care and treatment of people with a mental illness commenced three decades later, in 1774, with the passage of the Madhouses Act. This Act sought to regulate private asylums in response to complaints

---

[8] J Lithiby, *The Law Relating to Lunacy and Mental Deficiency*, 4th edn (London, Knight & Co, 1914) 52; J McClemens and J Bennett, 'Historical Notes on the Law of Mental Illness in New South Wales' (1962) 4 *Sydney Law Review* 49, 49–53.

[9] N Glover-Thomas, *Reconstructing Mental Health Law and Policy* (London, Butterworths LexisNexis, 2002) 4.

about appalling conditions.[10] For the first time legislation introduced a system for licensing and inspecting madhouses—which, historians suggest, was ineffectual.[11]

During the nineteenth century, various legal procedures and bureaucracies were established in England with the aims of protecting people in private asylums and safeguarding people who were at risk of being committed to these institutions. Certification procedures involving medical practitioners were introduced, provision was made for public mental health hospitals and a Lunacy Commission was established.[12] There were strongly competing views then, as now, about the processes to be followed when determining who could be admitted to an institution as an involuntary patient:

> [M]edical men… desired early and easy treatment of persons afflicted with mental disease, and at the same time demanded protection against the risks they ran in certifying persons as lunatics; lawyers … attached more weight to the liberty of the person than to the possibility of a cure by facility for compulsory confinement.[13]

The English Lunacy Act of 1890 was a legislative response to the unsatisfactory care provided to people in mental health facilities. At the time, the asylum was essentially custodial rather than curative, often acting as a dumping ground for the socially undesirable as well as the mentally ill.[14] According to Nicola Glover-Thomas, these conditions led to the emergence of 'a pessimistic attitude towards medical judgement and a fear that the sane might also be subjected to wrongful confinement'.[15] The Act established a formalised legal structure, with involuntary detention and treatment procedures being heavily regulated.

The Act remained in force for 40 years, strongly influencing the shape of both English[16] and Australian mental health laws ever since. As the well-known Australian psychiatrist John Ellard has observed, most subsequent Australian mental health acts have been little more than local revisions of the Lunacy Act of 1890.[17]

While there have been pendulum swings in the precise content of Australian mental health laws, their legal purpose has remained the same. Mental health Acts authorise conduct that would otherwise be unlawful: loss of liberty and loss of the right to choose whether to accept medical treatment. They also establish

---

[10]   J Lithiby, *The Law Relating to Lunacy and Mental Deficiency*, 4th edn (London, Knight & Co, 1914) 54.

[11]   See, eg N Glover-Thomas, *Reconstructing Mental Health Law and Policy* (London, Butterworths LexisNexis, 2002) 7.

[12]   *ibid.*

[13]   H Theobold, *The Law Relating to Lunacy* (London, Oxford University Press, 1987) 78.

[14]   N Glover-Thomas, *Reconstructing Mental Health Law and Policy* (London, Butterworths LexisNexis, 2002) 16.

[15]   *ibid*, 3.

[16]   P Bartlett and R Sandland, *Mental Health Law, Policy and Practice*, 3rd edn (Oxford, Oxford University Press, 2007) 18–19.

[17]   J Ellard, 'The Madness of Mental Health Acts' (1990) 24 *Australian and New Zealand Journal of Psychiatry* 167, 174.

administrative machinery to facilitate and review these authorisations. Examples include the powers given to police officers to take people to psychiatric hospitals for assessment, and the requirement that magistrates or tribunals review the cases of involuntarily detained people.

B.   The History of Guardianship Laws

The history of Australian guardianship laws is very different to that of mental health laws. Since the 1980s, Australia, together with some Canadian provinces and New Zealand, has been a world leader in the development of laws which permit the appointment of a substitute decision-maker when people with a disability are incapable of making their own decisions about important personal or financial matters.[18]

While Australian statutory guardianship laws are a relatively recent phenomenon, guardianship laws date back to the time of the Roman Empire. The law of the Roman XII Tables prescribed that

> if a person is a fool, let this person and his goods be under the protection of his family or paternal relatives, if he is not under the care of anyone.[19]

These ancient principles of caring for the vulnerable underpinned the concept of guardianship that developed in medieval English law.[20] However, English (and subsequently Australian) law 'evidenced a preoccupation with estate administration at the expense of guardianship'.[21] Until the early sixteenth century, royal officials acted as agents of the Crown in handling petitions and appointing tutors or guardians.[22]

In the seventeenth century this jurisdiction passed to the Courts of Chancery.[23] These courts could appoint a guardian, known as a 'committee', to look after the property and the person of the ward.[24] The courts also relied on juries to determine whether the wards would be deemed 'idiots' or 'lunatics', and the

---

[18]   See generally, T Carney and D Tait, *The Adult Guardianship Experiment: Tribunals and Popular Justice* (Sydney, Federation Press, 1997).

[19]   AF Johns, 'Guardianship Folly: The Misgovernment of *Parens Patriae* and the Forecast of its Crumbling Linkage to Unprotected Older Americans in the Twenty-first Century—A March of Folly? Or just a Mask of Virtual Reality?' (1997) 27(1) *Stetson Law Review* 10.

[20]   T Carney, 'Civil and Social Guardianship for Intellectually Handicapped People' (1981–1982) 8 *Monash University Law Review* 205.

[21]   Victoria. Minister's Committee on Rights and Protective Legislation for Intellectually Handicapped Persons (Cocks Committee), *Report of the Minister's Committee on Rights and Protective Legislation for Intellectually Handicapped Persons* (Melbourne, Victorian Government Printer, 1982) 18.

[22]   T Carney and D Tait, *The Adult Guardianship Experiment: Tribunals and Popular Justice* (Sydney, Federation Press, 1997) 10.

[23]   T Carney, 'Civil and Social Guardianship for Intellectually Handicapped People' (1981–82) 8 *Monash University Law Review* 205, 206.

[24]   T Carney and D Tait, *The Adult Guardianship Experiment: Tribunals and Popular Justice* (Sydney, Federation Press, 1997) 10.

juries sometimes used their discretion to avoid financially ruinous findings of idiocy. Lunacy was preferred to idiocy because if the latter were found, the ward's assets were forfeited to the Crown.[25]

The jury system was abolished in the nineteenth century when responsibility for decision-making reverted to judges and court officials. The English Lunacy Act of 1890 consolidated this shift and provided a framework for regulating the personal and property affairs of people with a mental illness and those who were intellectually disabled.[26] As previously noted, many of the Australian colonies copied this legislation. Lunacy powers were plenary. They fell within the jurisdiction of the State Supreme Courts and were exercised by Masters in Lunacy.[27]

In England, the Mental Deficiency Act 1913 and later the Mental Health Act 1959 allowed mentally ill and intellectually disabled people to be taken into guardianship. The legislation gave the guardian the power to make decisions as though the subject of the order were under the age of 14 and the guardian were his/her father.[28] Because reliance on confinement in hospitals was strong, however, guardianship laws were rarely used.[29]

The Mental Health Act 1983 (England and Wales) defined and confined the powers of a guardian. This legislation gave the guardian three specific powers: first, to require the person to reside at a specified place; secondly, to require the person to attend at places and times for the purpose of medical treatment, education, occupation or training; and thirdly, to require that a doctor or some other specified individual have access to the person under guardianship.[30]

The guardianship powers in the 1983 Act were seldom used for a number of reasons, including the fact that guardians were not actually empowered to authorise compulsory treatment or detention at specified places in the community.[31] A report of the English Law Commission in 1995[32] led to the enactment of the Mental Capacity Act 2005 (England and Wales), which provides a substitute decision-making regime that promotes autonomy and is based on a 'best interests' approach.[33] This legislation is broadly similar to contemporary Australian guardianship statutes.

In Australia, personal guardianship was little used until the 1960s because of the focus on institutionalisation. The legal powers of a guardian were seldom needed because the institution itself made decisions about matters such as

---

[25]   *ibid*, 11.

[26]   *ibid*, 11.

[27]   *ibid*, 11.

[28]   P Bartlett and R Sandland, *Mental Health Law, Policy and Practice*, 3rd edn (Oxford, Oxford University Press, 2007) 488.

[29]   N Glover-Thomas, *Reconstructing Mental Health Law and Policy* (London, Butterworths LexisNexis, 2002) 75.

[30]   Mental Health Act 1983 s 8(1); P Bartlett and R Sandland, *Reconstructing Mental Health Law and Policy* (London, Butterworths LexisNexis, 2002) 488.

[31]   *ibid*, 489.

[32]   Law Commission, *Mental Incapacity*, Report No 231 (London, HMSO, 1995).

[33]   See Philip Fennell, this volume ch 2.

treatment, lifestyle and education.[34] Even when de-institutionalisation began, Australian courts were rarely asked to exercise their powers to appoint guardians because of the expense involved.[35] As Terry Carney and David Tait observed, 'superior courts were almost inaccessible due to their financial cost, the lack of public familiarity, and the absence of psychological comfort'.[36] Moreover, the use of 'trial leave', which later became formalised as 'community treatment orders', allowed psychiatrists to direct the treatment of people with a mental illness outside of an institution without the use of guardianship powers.[37]

Once guardianship law was substantially reformed in the late twentieth century, it became popular as a means of providing a substitute decision-making regime for people with an intellectual disability who were moving from institutions to the community.[38] South Australia was the first jurisdiction to enact new laws,[39] while Victoria[40] and New South Wales[41] followed within a decade.

In 1982 a Victorian ministerial committee (the Cocks Committee) examined the traditional guardianship system and identified deficiencies in the law.[42] The Committee found the law to be uncertain and inflexible, referring to the absence of guidelines for selecting and discharging guardians, and to the fact that the plenary nature of guardianship led to an extraordinary loss of autonomy. The Cocks Committee also took issue with the cumbersome process for appointing a guardian, and with the absence of a process for reviewing the continuing need for a substitute decision-maker.[43] It supported steps taken in South Australia to establish a Guardianship Board with the power to make various decisions for people with intellectual disability.[44]

The committee recommended setting up a 'one-stop shop' where both personal and property matters could be handled.[45] The aim was for guardianship to operate as a 'last resort' option under legislation which promoted autonomy and self-sufficiency, encouraged the appointment of family members rather than representatives of the state as substitute decision-makers, and resulted in limited

---

[34] The statutory powers of appointment, vested in state Supreme Courts, were very similar to those in the 1913 and 1959 English Mental Health Acts. See, eg Public Trustee Act 1958 (Vic) ss 32 and 39.

[35] T Carney, 'The Limits and the Social Legacy of Guardianship in Australia' (1988–89) 18 *Federal Law Review* 235.

[36] T Carney and D Tait, *The Adult Guardianship Experiment: Tribunals and Popular Justice* (Sydney, Federation Press, 1997) 13.

[37] *ibid.*

[38] *ibid*, 15.

[39] Mental Health Act 1977 (SA).

[40] Guardianship and Administration Board Act 1986 (Vic).

[41] Guardianship Act 1987 (NSW).

[42] Victoria. Minister's Committee on Rights and Protective Legislation for Intellectually Handicapped Persons, *Report of the Minister's Committee on Rights and Protective Legislation for Intellectually Handicapped Persons*, Cocks Committee (Melbourne, Victorian Government Printer, 1982).

[43] *ibid*, 24–5.

[44] *ibid*, 12.

[45] *ibid.*

and reviewable orders.[46] Other Australian States soon enacted similar laws, which have been constantly developed and refined ever since.[47]

III.   Current Australian Mental Health and Guardianship Laws

A.   Mental Health Laws

(i)   The Legal Purpose of Mental Health Laws

As has been noted, the primary legal purpose of all contemporary mental health laws is to authorise activities which would otherwise be unlawful: the detention and involuntary treatment of some people who have a mental illness. These actions would constitute false imprisonment and assault if not expressly permitted by law.

These laws exist on the basis that some people with a mental illness should be required to accept treatment for their own good, or for the protection of others. The law permits them to be involuntarily detained in a hospital, or required to interact with community mental health services, while the compulsory treatment regime is implemented.

Current Australian mental health laws are influenced by notions of beneficence, by a concern to protect the community from harm, and by the desire to ensure that liberty is not lightly lost. The legislation seeks to strike a balance between reducing the risk of harm and protecting the core value of liberty. The concern with liberty transcends the interests of people with a mental illness. This is not a modern phenomenon. Mental health laws have always sought to ensure that people are not lightly deprived of their freedom, or their property, because of mistaken judgements about mental illness.

(ii)   The Process Provisions

Mental health laws include many provisions that are designed to facilitate actions which may ultimately result in a person's compulsory treatment and loss of liberty once various clinical assessments have been made. They permit emergency intervention by the police and first instance clinical decision-making. They proceed on the assumption that some people will actively resist clinical intervention. The statutes create processes for use when apprehending people in the

---

[46]   T Carney and D Tait, *The Adult Guardianship Experiment: Tribunals and Popular Justice* (Sydney, Federation Press, 1997) 19.

[47]   R Creyke, 'Privatising Guardianship—The EPA Alternative' (1993) 15 *Adelaide Law Review* 79.

community, transporting them to hospital, undertaking medical examinations, and deciding whether to authorise involuntary treatment and detention.

The usual trigger for the operation of mental health laws is a 'street-level' judgement[48] that clinical intervention is required because a person is at *risk of harm* to themselves or others because of mental illness.[49] A person's *capacity*, or lack of it, to consent to any interference with their liberty or freedom to choose medical treatment is not a primary consideration.[50]

Modern mental health laws contain comprehensive 'process provisions' which permit emergency intervention when there is a risk of harm. These powers parallel, and in some respects surpass,[51] those possessed by police officers to apprehend and detain people suspected of engaging in serious criminal activities.

The following powers are found in most modern Australian mental health laws:

- Police officers may apprehend a person in the community suspected of being at serious risk of harm because of mental illness and cause them to be examined by a medical practitioner.[52]
- Police officers may forcibly enter the premises of a person suspected of being at serious risk of harm because of mental illness, apprehend that person and cause them to be examined by a medical practitioner.[53]
- Police officers may transport a person to a hospital for examination.[54]
- A medical practitioner at a psychiatric hospital may conduct a psychiatric

---

[48] Police officers (and others) are given the power to cause a person who appears to be mentally ill and at risk of harm to be medically examined (Mental Health Act 1986 (Vic) ss 10, 12; Mental Health Act 2007 (NSW) ss 20–22.

[49] The terms 'mental illness' and 'mentally ill person' are similarly defined in the New South Wales and Victorian statutes (Mental Health Act 2007 (NSW) s 4; Mental Health Act 1986 (Vic) s 8(1A)). The Victorian Act provides that 'a person is mentally ill if he or she has a mental illness, being a medical condition that is characterised by a significant disturbance of thought, mood, perception or memory'. Both Acts also contain lists of disqualifying factors, such as political opinion and sexual preference, which cannot of themselves be used to indicate that a person has a 'mental illness' (Mental Health Act 2007 (NSW) s 16; Mental Health Act 1986 (Vic) s 8(2)).

[50] The New South Wales legislation does not even require the medical practitioners involved in causing a person to become an involuntary patient, or the external reviewing authorities (Magistrates and the Mental Health Review Tribunal), to consider the person's capacity to consent to treatment. The criteria are mental illness (or mental disorder) and risk of serious harm (Mental Health Act 2007 (NSW) ss 14 –15). In Victoria the medical practitioners involved in causing a person to become an involuntary patient and the external reviewing authority (the Mental Health Review Board) must be satisfied that 'the person has refused or is unable to consent to the necessary treatment for the mental illness' (Mental Health Act 1986 (Vic) s 8(1)(d)).

[51] For instance, s 10(2) of the Mental Health Act 1986 (Vic) permits a police officer to forcibly enter premises, without a warrant, when the police officer has reasonable grounds for believing, amongst other things, that a person who appears to be mentally ill is likely to cause serious harm to themselves or some other person. Compare the general police power to enter premises and arrest a person suspected of crime: Crimes Act 1958 (Vic) s 459A.

[52] See, eg Mental Health Act 1986 (Vic) s 10(1), (4); Mental Health Act 2007 (NSW) s 22.

[53] See, eg Mental Health Act 1986 (Vic) s 10(2); Mental Health Act 2007 (NSW) s 21.

[54] See, eg Mental Health Act 1986 (Vic) ss 9A, 9B; Mental Health Act 2007 (NSW) s 22.

assessment of a person brought to that hospital and cause the person to be detained at the hospital until a second opinion may be sought from a psychiatrist.[55]

- A psychiatrist at a psychiatric hospital may subject a person to a psychiatric assessment and cause a person to be detained at the hospital and given psychiatric treatment without the consent of that person.[56]

Once 'full' involuntary patient status[57] has been confirmed by the use of these processes, a person experiences absolute loss of liberty and total loss of power to refuse psychiatric treatment. Mental health laws impose a form of clinical guardianship, with the senior psychiatrist at a hospital having the power to authorise involuntary treatment.[58]

(iii)   Accountability and Review Mechanisms

Modern mental health laws contain a range of accountability and review mechanisms, which seek to ensure that the powers granted to emergency workers and clinicians are used properly and with good cause. Various authorisation or licensing mechanisms deal with recording information, the places where people may be involuntarily detained, and the qualifications and responsibilities of the person in charge of that facility. Provisions of this nature deal with the following matters:

- prescribed forms to be used when exercising the various powers granted by the legislation;[59]
- the licensing of premises that are permitted to receive involuntary patients;[60]
- the appointment of a senior psychiatrist at each licensed facility;[61]
- the responsibilities of that senior psychiatrist.[62]

Modern mental health laws also contain an array of checks and balances designed to ensure that there is review of the merits of a decision to deprive a person of their liberty and to require them to accept treatment without consent. Those review mechanisms include the following matters:

---

[55] See, eg Mental Health Act 1986 (Vic) ss 12, 12AA; Mental Health Act 2007 (NSW) s 27.

[56] See, eg Mental Health Act 1986 (Vic) ss 12AC, 12AD; Mental Health Act 2007 (NSW) ss 27, 29 and 84.

[57] It is also possible in both Victoria and New South Wales to use these processes to cause a person to be placed on a community treatment order, which does not result in the loss of liberty experienced by involuntary inpatients (Mental Health Act 1986 (Vic) s 12; Mental Health Act 2007 (NSW) s 51).

[58] See, eg Mental Health Act 1986 (Vic) s 12AD; Mental Health Act 2007 (NSW) s 84.

[59] See, eg Mental Health Act 1986 (Vic) s 9; Mental Health Act 2007 (NSW) s 19.

[60] See, eg Mental Health Act 1986 (Vic) s 94; Mental Health Act 2007 (NSW) s 109.

[61] See, eg Mental Health Act 1986 (Vic) s 96; Mental Health Act 2007 (NSW) s 111. In New South Wales the 'medical superintendent' does not have to be, but is usually, a psychiatrist.

[62] See, eg Mental Health Act 1986 (Vic) s 96(2); Mental Health Act 2007 (NSW) s 124.

- The senior psychiatrist, or delegate, must review any decision made by an admitting medical officer to detain a person as an involuntary patient.[63]
- A tribunal must review any decision to detain a person as an involuntary patient.[64]
- A person detained as an involuntary patient has the right to appeal to a tribunal at any time for review of their detention.[65]
- Some forms of psychiatric treatment must be approved by a tribunal before they may be used.[66]
- Independent community visitors have the right to enter a psychiatric hospital, to talk to patients and to examine records concerning treatment.[67]

B. Guardianship Laws

(i) The Legal Purpose of Guardianship Laws

Modern Australian guardianship laws provide for the appointment of substitute decision-makers for people who do not have the capacity to make their own decisions about important matters such as where they will live, whether they should have a particular form of medical treatment, and how their financial affairs should be managed.[68] These laws permit a tribunal to appoint a suitable person, such as a relative or friend, as guardian to make personal or 'lifestyle decisions' for a person incapable of making their own decisions as a result of disability, and, similarly, to appoint such a person as an administrator (or financial manager) to make financial decisions. A public official is available for appointment as a guardian or administrator of last resort.[69]

Australian guardianship laws also encourage forward planning and, in some circumstances, informal decision-making.[70] These laws aim to promote the autonomy of people with impaired decision-making capacity and they seek to

---

[63] See, eg Mental Health Act 1986 (Vic) s 12AC; Mental Health Act 2007 (NSW) s 27.

[64] See, eg Mental Health Act 1986 (Vic) s 30; Mental Health Act 2007 (NSW) s 34. In New South Wales, a magistrate conducts the initial 'tribunal' review.

[65] See, eg Mental Health Act 1986 (Vic) s 29; Mental Health Act 2007 (NSW) s 44.

[66] See, eg Mental Health Act 1986 (Vic) s 57; Mental Health Act 2007 (NSW) s 94.

[67] See, eg Mental Health Act 1986 (Vic) s 112; Mental Health Act 2007 (NSW) s 131.

[68] There is a separate branch of most guardianship legislation which deals with the management of financial affairs. For example, in Victoria, Part 5 of the Guardianship and Administration Act 1986 (Vic) deals with 'Administration Orders'. In New South Wales, Part 3A of the Guardianship Act 1987 (NSW) deals with 'Financial Management Orders'. These parts of the legislation are not discussed in this chapter as they are beyond the scope of the matters under consideration.

[69] In Victoria the Public Advocate and in New South Wales, the Public Guardian.

[70] See, eg Guardianship and Administration Act 1986 (Vic) Part 4; Guardianship Act 1987 (NSW) s 4.

discourage default decision-making by professionals such as medical practition-ers, except in relation to life-threatening medical emergencies or relatively minor matters.[71]

As outlined above, the primary purpose of modern Australian guardianship laws was originally to establish a substitute decision-making regime for people with an intellectual disability who no longer fell within mental health legislation and were no longer required or able to live in psychiatric hospitals. These laws established a 'light touch' substitute decision-making regime with strong empha-sis upon promoting the autonomy of people to make their own decisions whenever possible. This was achieved by granting the guardian only those substitute decision-making powers which were clearly necessary, and through encouraging the use of informal decision-making processes whenever possible.[72]

Much has changed since these statutes were first enacted in the 1980s. Appointment of a guardian by a tribunal is no longer the preferred way of providing a substitute decision-maker for people who are incapable of making their own decisions and who are in need of another person to make decisions on their behalf. The legislation now establishes a tiered approach to substitute decision-making. It encourages forward planning, with a guardian appointed by tribunal being the final option when a substitute decision-maker is required. The preferred approach is for people to appoint their own substitute decision-maker. The legislation permits a person who is over the age of 18 and has capacity, to appoint an enduring guardian to make decisions on their behalf when they are incapable of doing so.[73] In Victoria, there is also an overlapping power to appoint a person as an agent for the specific purpose of making future medical treatment decisions.[74]

The legislation also creates a default substitute decision-making regime in the area of medical treatment. It declares that a range of people automatically become substitute decision-makers when a person becomes incapable of con-senting to most types of medical treatment.[75] These statutorily appointed default decision-makers, such as a person's spouse or primary carer, are permitted to make most treatment decisions for a person who lacks the capacity to do so.[76]

---

[71] Medical practitioners have statutory default decision-making power in relation to these matters: see, eg Guardianship and Administration Act 1986 (Vic) s 42L; Guardianship Act 1987 (NSW) s 37.

[72] See the 'objects' or 'general principles' sections in the Acts: Guardianship and Administration Act 1986 (Vic) s 4; Guardianship Act 1987 (NSW) s 4.

[73] See, eg Guardianship and Administration Act 1986 (Vic) Part 4 Division 5A; Guardianship Act 1987 (NSW) Part 2.

[74] Medical Treatment Act 1988 (Vic) s 5A.

[75] The nature of the incapacity is set out in the legislation. The person must be incapable of understanding the general nature and effect of the proposed treatment, or incapable of indicating whether he or she consents to that treatment (see, eg Guardianship and Administration Act 1986 (Vic) s 36(2); Guardianship Act 1987 (NSW) s 33(2)).

[76] See, eg Guardianship and Administration Act 1986 (Vic) Part 4A; Guardianship Act 1987 (NSW) Part 5.

The outer limits of the powers that may be given to and exercised by a guardian are not particularly clear. While a guardian may be given the power to consent to medical treatment on behalf of a represented person,[77] the power of a guardian to authorise the detention of a person in a hospital or a community residence is uncertain.

The extent of a guardian's powers is best determined by considering the legislative description of the powers of a plenary guardian. Both the New South Wales and Victorian statutes use the drafting device of referring to powers set out in other bodies of law to describe the powers of a plenary guardian. In the Victorian Act the powers are those

> which the plenary guardian would have if he or she were a parent and the represented person his or her child.[78]

In New South Wales, as well as having 'custody of the person', the plenary guardian

> has all of the functions …that a guardian has at law or in equity.[79]

It is highly unlikely that the drafters of these provisions considered whether guardianship powers could be used to authorise the detention in either a hospital or a community setting of a person who was actively resisting deprivation of their liberty.

The use of guardianship has changed quite markedly over the past two decades and it is now the primary substitute decision-making regime for people with all forms of disability other than mental illness.[80] People who are unable to make their own decisions because of disabilities generally associated with the ageing process have become the major users of guardianship laws.[81]

(ii)   Process Provisions

The trigger for the operation of guardianship laws is a determination by any interested person that somebody is in need of a substitute decision-maker because they appear to lack *capacity* to make an important decision.[82] While that lack of capacity must be the result of a disability, the term 'disability' is so broadly defined that it is difficult to imagine circumstances in which it does not cover a

---

[77]   Guardianship and Administration Act 1986 (Vic) s 24(2)(d).

[78]   Guardianship and Administration Act 1986 (Vic) s 24(1); Guardianship Act 1987 (NSW) s 40.

[79]   Guardianship Act 1987 (NSW) s 21(1).

[80]   Section 1 of the Guardianship and Administration Act 1986 (Vic) provides as follows: 'The purpose of this Act is to enable persons with a disability to have a guardian or administrator appointed when they need a guardian or administrator'.

[81]   See, eg New South Wales Guardianship Tribunal, *Annual Report 2007–2008* (Balmain, Guardianship Tribunal, 2008) 23.

[82]   See, eg Guardianship and Administration Act 1986 (Vic) s 22; Guardianship Act 1987 (NSW) s 14.

person who lacks capacity to make an important decision.[83] In practice, a friend or relative, health worker or other person involved in the care of a person with a disability will usually make an application to a tribunal for the appointment of a guardian when there is a perceived need for a substitute decision-maker.

Guardianship statutes do not contain any of the process provisions for emergency intervention found within mental health laws. Guardianship legislation does not permit the police (or any other public officials) to enter the premises of people who are suspected of being at risk of harm because of lack of capacity. Nor does it allow them to apprehend people and cause them to be medically assessed in order to determine whether a guardianship order should be made, and to convey them to hospital for further examination or treatment. In practice, informal steps are usually taken when emergency action is required because few people who lack capacity actively resist that intervention.

(iii)   Accountability and Review Mechanisms

Guardianship laws contain relatively few mechanisms which permit review of any decisions made by a guardian or the decision by a tribunal to make a guardianship order. In New South Wales, it is possible to appeal from a tribunal decision to appoint a guardian on a question of law alone and, with leave, on the merits of the decision.[84] It is also possible to request the tribunal to review a guardianship order.[85] In Victoria, there is a right to appeal on a question of law alone,[86] and it is possible to apply to the tribunal for a re-hearing of a decision to make a guardianship order.[87]

In both jurisdictions there is no capacity to review individual decisions made by a private guardian acting pursuant to a guardianship order. In New South Wales, it is possible to review individual decisions made by the statutory guardian of last resort, the Public Guardian[88] but, other than in this circumstance, the broad powers of a guardian may be exercised without any opportunity for external review of individual decisions. While this issue is a matter of ongoing debate, any new mechanism for external review of individual decisions by a guardian is likely to be labour- and resource-intensive.

---

[83]   See, eg Guardianship and Administration Act 1986 (Vic) s 3; Guardianship Act 1987 (NSW) s 3(2).

[84]   Guardianship Act 1987 (NSW) s 67A; Administrative Decisions Tribunal Act 1997 (NSW) s 118B.

[85]   Guardianship Act 1987 (NSW) s 25.

[86]   Victorian Civil and Administrative Tribunal Act 1998 (Vic) s 148(2).

[87]   Guardianship and Administration Act 1986 (Vic) s 60A.

[88]   Administrative Decisions Tribunal Act 1997 (NSW) s 80A.

IV. Fusion of Mental Health and Guardianship Laws

A. Arguments in Favour of Fusion

The fusion of mental health and guardianship laws would cause guardianship to become the only legal means of providing substitute decision-making for people who lack the capacity to make their own decisions because of any disability, including mental illness. John Dawson and George Szmukler, two of the most prominent advocates of the fusion proposal, describe how the law would operate:

> This scheme would not rely on any specific reference to 'mental disorder'. Instead, it would rely squarely on the criterion of incapacity to make necessary treatment decisions, *but* it would still authorise both a person's detention and their involuntary treatment ... Under it [the fusion proposal], the incapacity of a person to consent would be *the* fundamental criterion governing *all* involuntary health interventions, and that criterion would be applied to *both* detention *and* involuntary treatment, of *both* 'physical' *and* 'mental' conditions.

> ... [W]e are not advocating the intermediate (or hybrid) legal position now followed in many parts of North America and continental Europe that involves the application of different legal criteria to the detention and involuntary treatment decisions. Under that approach, mental disorder and threat of harm criteria may be applied to a person's detention, while incapacity criteria may be applied to their treatment. That approach has the significant disadvantage that it can lead to a position wherein a person may be lawfully detained in a psychiatric facility on the basis of their mental disorder, but they cannot be treated if they retain or regain their capacity to consent to psychiatric treatment.[89]

In practical terms, fusion would mean that when a person loses capacity because of mental illness, decision-making responsibility about matters such as treatment and detention would shift from a public official (as is now the case under mental health laws) to the family member or friend who had been appointed as the guardian, or to the statutory guardian of last resort (as occurs under guardianship legislation). This change may promote the dignity and autonomy of a person who loses capacity because of mental illness, as in many instances the substitute decision-maker would be a close and trusted person rather than an unfamiliar doctor at a psychiatric hospital.

The principal theme that runs through the arguments in favour of fusion is that it is discriminatory to have a separate body of law that deals with the

---

[89] J Dawson and G Szmukler, 'Why Distinguish "Mental" and "Physical" Illness in Involuntary Treatment?' in M Freeman and O Goodenough (eds), *Law, Mind and Brain* (Farnham, Ashgate, 2009) 174–5.

involuntary treatment and detention of people with a mental illness, when statutory guardianship laws exist as a generic substitute decision-making regime for people with all forms of disability.[90]

Tom Campbell argues that the existence of such separate legislation allows for the manifestation of 'institutional discrimination',[91] since the coercive measures permitted under the legislation are confined to people with a mental illness.[92] He also suggests that 'mental illness prejudice'[93] is confirmed and perpetuated through the existence of separate mental health legislation. According to Campbell,

> [b]y having separate mental health legislation empowering the detention and treatment of persons with mental illness, these prejudices are legitimated and channelled so that compulsion is used disproportionately and unreasonably against this section of the population.[94]

Campbell argues that a serious consequence of having separate legislation is that it 'institutionalises the idea that there is something about "mental illness" itself which invites a system of control and coercion'.[95] He suggests that although issues of medical treatment and social control are conceptually and practically different, they become dangerously entangled in the context of mental illness, thereby allowing stereotyped prejudice to flourish.[96] The stereotyping stems from ignorance, he contends, because public opinion wrongly attributes 'the anti-social characteristics of psychopaths to people with a mental illness.[97]

This ignorance, according to Campbell, has led to the widespread assumption that all people with a mental illness are dangerous, which is reinforced by legislation that permits preventative detention of mentally ill people in anticipation of dangerous conduct. Campbell does not take issue with the notion of preventative detention, but argues that the rules should apply equally to everyone regardless of whether or not they have a mental illness.[98]

Stephen Rosenman argues that it is both discriminatory and therapeutically undesirable to have separate mental health laws:

> Once they have qualified for compulsory hospitalisation, patients lose their autonomy and personal standing. Not only treatment but all facets of the patient's personal life fall completely under the power of the hospital staff. However benevolent the staff may be,

---

[90]   See, eg T Campbell and C Heginbotham, *Mental Illness: Prejudice, Discrimination and the Law* (Aldershot, Dartmouth, 1991).

[91]   T Campbell, 'Mental Health Law: Institutionalised Discrimination' (1994) 28 *Australian and New Zealand Journal of Psychiatry* 554.

[92]   *ibid.*

[93]   *ibid.*

[94]   *ibid*, 556.

[95]   *ibid*, 556.

[96]   *ibid*, 555.

[97]   *ibid*, 556.

[98]   *ibid*, 556.

patients resent staff who are at once their custodians and carers. Such resentment discourages the development of collaboration in treatment.[99]

Rosenman suggests that guardianship laws be used to provide substitute decision-making for people with a mental illness in need of involuntary treatment. He believes that this shift would allow guardians to remain involved throughout the process and thus play a role 'which separates medical advice from consent'.[100]

Dawson and Szmukler advocate the fusion of mental health and guardianship legislation because it is both unnecessary and discriminatory to have separate laws that govern psychiatric treatment.[101] They suggest that the law should always respond to a person's incapacity to make their own decisions about medical treatment in the same way, regardless of the cause of that incapacity.

Dawson and Szmukler argue that reliance on incapacity as the trigger for legal intervention would 'shift the focus away from potential "risk of harm" as the central ground upon which psychiatric treatment may be imposed'.[102] They suggest that this shift is likely to have two main benefits: earlier clinical intervention for both physical and mental illnesses, and uniform application of the criminal law.[103] These authors suggest that if clinical involvement may be authorised as soon as a person lacks capacity, even though there is no imminent threat of harm, early intervention would become a real possibility at critical moments. George Szmukler has written elsewhere that this would also help reduce discrimination[104] because the current law permits the non-consensual treatment of people for a mental disorder regardless of whether or not they have the capacity to make treatment decisions. On the other hand, a person with a physical disorder cannot be treated non-consensually if they have capacity, even if the rejection of treatment may result in death.[105]

Dawson and Szmukler also argue that a legal shift to an incapacity focus would permit all people (whether mentally ill or not) who harmed or attempted to harm somebody while retaining capacity to be controlled through the criminal justice system, while those who lacked capacity (whether mentally ill or not) could be managed under involuntary treatment legislation. The shift would allow for 'consistent ethical principles [to be applied] across medical law'.[106]

---

[99] S Rosenman, 'Mental Health Law: An Idea Whose Time has Passed' (1994) 28 *Australian and New Zealand Journal of Psychiatry* 562.

[100] *ibid*, 565.

[101] J Dawson and G Szmukler, 'Fusion of Mental Health and Incapacity Legislation' (2006) 188 *British Journal of Psychiatry* 504.

[102] *ibid*.

[103] *ibid*.

[104] G Szmukler and F Holloway, 'Mental Health Legislation is Now a Harmful Anachronism' (1998) 22 *Psychiatric Bulletin* 662.

[105] *ibid*.

[106] J Dawson and G Szmukler, 'Fusion of Mental Health and Incapacity Legislation' (2006) 188 *British Journal of Psychiatry* 504, 504.

Genevra Richardson suggests that discrimination against people with a mental disorder would be avoided if 'mental health care could be provided according to the same principles, including respect for patient autonomy, as those which cover all other forms of health care'.[107]

Richardson also suggests that the existence of guardianship laws in Australia further entrenches prejudice against mental illness so long as this system co-exists with separate mental health legislation.[108] Richardson argues that the existence of the two systems 'encourages the perception of mental disorder as a condition apart':[109] 'Where two parallel decision making structures exist, based on two distinct sets of principles, mental disorder will be regarded as the more threatening and its pariah-status will thus be reinforced'.[110]

B. Arguments Against Fusion

There are many arguments which may be raised in opposition to the suggestion that mental health and guardianship laws should merge. First, it may be argued that mental health laws are 'special measures' which promote the interests of people with a mental illness rather than unfairly discriminate against them. 'Special measures' do not infringe the equal protection and non-discrimination provisions in domestic and international human rights charters.[111]

It may be argued that separate mental health laws are 'special measures' that implement a policy of beneficence towards people with a mental illness. Mental illness is different to most other forms of disability because it is sometimes accompanied by a lack of awareness of impaired functioning. A person with a mental illness, unlike someone with most physical disorders, may be unaware of any disturbance of functioning which may be alleviated by treatment. This difference may be used to justify separate, interventionist mental health laws that are designed to promote the well-being of people with mental illness who are unable to perceive their own need for treatment.[112] It has been argued that 'in the

---

[107] G Richardson, 'Autonomy, Guardianship and Mental Disorder: One Problem, Two Solutions' (2002) 65 *Modern Law Review* 450.

[108] *ibid*, 459.

[109] *ibid*, 459.

[110] *ibid*, 459.

[111] Section 7(4) of the Victorian Charter of Human Rights and Responsibilities provides that: 'Measures taken for the purposes of assisting or advancing persons or groups of persons disadvantaged because of discrimination do not constitute discrimination'. Art 5.4 of the Convention on the Rights of Persons with Disabilities, adopted 13 December 2006, GA Res 61/106, UN Doc A/Res/61/106 (entered into force 3 May 2008) contains similar language.

[112] For example, s 3(d) of the Mental Health Act 2007 (NSW) provides that one of the objects of the legislation is to give people an opportunity to have access to appropriate care.

tussle between autonomy and coercion, a short period of coercion may be a precursor to a long period of autonomy'.[113]

Secondly, it may be argued that the safeguards which have slowly developed over time about the use of coercive powers may be jeopardised if guardianship rather than mental health laws were used to authorise the detention and involuntary treatment of a person with a mental illness. The use of guardianship laws for these purposes would result in the delegation of what have been seen as significant state powers—detention and coercive treatment—to a single person, the guardian. In many instances the use of these powers would be privatised because the guardian may be a friend or relative of the person who is the subject of the guardianship order.

It is arguable that because of the fundamental importance of the issues of liberty and bodily integrity, there is a great need for independent and transparent decision-making processes when these rights are lost. These processes are a central feature of mental health laws. Guardianship laws contain far fewer mechanisms for supervising the use of coercive powers. With few exceptions, there is no external review of individual decisions made by guardians concerning deprivation of liberty and coercive treatment.

Thirdly, it may be argued that guardianship laws lack the necessary process provisions to respond effectively to the circumstances in which some people with a mental illness come to the attention of police and ambulance services. As outlined, mental health laws contain detailed provisions concerning the emergency intervention that may take place when a person poses a risk of harm because they are in the acute stage of a mental illness. Guardianship laws do not contain any of the emergency intervention processes found in mental health laws.

Fourthly, the trigger for the operation of guardianship laws—lack of capacity—may not be an effective means of providing assistance in some cases involving people with a mental illness. If a person's capacity to make decisions for themselves is a contestable issue, as is the case for people with some mental illnesses, the processes which exist under guardianship laws to resolve disputes about capacity may be too slow and awkward to permit timely clinical intervention in many cases.

Fifthly, a guardian is required to act in the best interests of the represented person and, whenever possible, to consider that person's wishes before making any decisions.[114] In some instances this task may be very difficult if guardianship were used to authorise involuntary detention and treatment for people with a mental illness. It is inevitable that there would be instances in which the guardian was encouraged by clinical staff to make decisions contrary to the expressed wishes of the represented person. In some instances, the guardian may conclude

---

[113] J Peay (ed), *Seminal Issues in Mental Health Law* (Aldershot, Ashgate, 2005) at xxii, summarising an argument first made in N Rose, 'Unreasonable Rights: Mental Illness and the Limits of the Law' (1985) 12 *Journal of Law and Society* 199.

[114] Guardianship and Administration Act 1986 (Vic) s 28.

that it is in the best interests of the represented person to accept clinical advice rather than follow the wishes of the represented person. This is a recipe for conflict. The ongoing relationship between a friend or relative who accepts appointment as a guardian and the represented person may be irrevocably damaged in these circumstances.

V. Conclusion

Recent experience in England and Wales suggests that the path to fusion of mental health and guardianship laws is probably a long one. The introduction of generic substitute decision-making legislation based on lack of capacity rather than risk of harm was pressed strongly during the community debates which ultimately led to the passage of the Mental Health Act 2007 (England and Wales).[115] The fusion argument was not successful, resulting in mental health and incapacity (or guardianship) laws operating side by side in England and Wales, as they do in Australia.[116]

The recent events in England and Wales suggest that the fusion proposal will succeed only if consensus can be reached among a coalition of consumers, clinicians, carers and human rights lawyers who are able to persuade the broader community that the suggestion is fair and workable. That consensus may not be easily achieved given the struggles that invariably accompany attempts to rewrite mental health laws.

While the arguments in favour of fusion are strong, so too are many of the counter arguments. At present, there is only some limited interaction between Australian mental health and guardianship laws—a guardian may cause a person to be admitted to a psychiatric hospital as a voluntary or informal patient.[117]

A way forward may be to permit the concurrent operation of mental health and guardianship laws, so that either statutory regime may be used to authorise involuntary treatment and detention (in hospital or in the community) of a person with a mental illness who is unable to consent to their own treatment. Under this system, mental health laws would continue to operate in those circumstances where the issue of capacity is not easily resolved and there is a clear risk of harm resulting from a person's untreated mental illness.

If both bodies of law are able to operate concurrently, however, a guardian (including an enduring guardian appointed by the person concerned) could

---

[115] R Daw, 'The Mental Health Act 2007—The Defeat of an Ideal' (2007) *Journal of Mental Health Law* 131.

[116] *ibid*, 131.

[117] Mental Health Act 2007 (NSW) s 7; Guardianship Act 1987 (NSW) s 3C. In Victoria the power of a guardian to admit a person to a psychiatric hospital as a voluntary patient is not specifically dealt with in legislation but arises by implication from the broad powers granted under guardianship legislation.

authorise detention and involuntary treatment in some circumstances now covered by the civil commitment provisions of mental health laws. The choice of legal regime in a particular case would be a matter for all people with a direct interest in the decision, including carers, clinicians and, whenever possible, consumers.

During a trial period of the proposed system it is highly likely that mental health laws would continue to be the regime of choice in those circumstances where emergency intervention is needed to promptly deal with the risk of harm to the person concerned, or to other members of the community. Guardianship laws may be preferred, however, in instances where a person with a strong support network has acknowledged the cyclical nature of their illness and has appointed a trusted relative or friend to be their enduring guardian. The guardian would have the capacity to intervene in a more personal and less dramatic way than is generally available under mental health laws when the need for compulsory treatment arises. Guardianship laws may also be preferred when there is little or no dispute about lack of capacity and the person concerned is not actively resisting clinical intervention.

Concurrent operation of mental health and guardianship laws during a trial period merits discussion as one means of advancing the fusion proposal.

Part 3

The International Human Rights Framework and the United Nations Convention on the Rights of Persons with Disabilities

5

The Expressive, Educational and Proactive Roles of Human Rights: An Analysis of the United Nations Convention on the Rights of Persons with Disabilities*

OLIVER LEWIS

I. Introduction

Addressing dignitaries on the day the United Nations Convention on the Rights of Persons with Disabilities (CRPD)[1] opened for signature, Louise Arbour the then United Nations High Commissioner for Human Rights, said:

> At the time of the adoption of the Universal Declaration of Human Rights, Eleanor Roosevelt famously asked: 'Where do human rights begin?' and answered 'In small places, close to home'. This is as true in the area of human rights and disability as with any other area of human rights.[2]

People with psychosocial (mental health) disabilities[3] are among those who suffer most from the compliance gap between lofty declaration and rights reality. This

---

* The views expressed in this paper are the author's own. Thanks to Aart Hendriks, Anna Lawson and Kathryn Vandever for feedback on earlier drafts. All remaining mistakes are mine.
[1] Convention on the Rights of Persons with Disabilities, adopted 13 December 2006, GA Res 61/106, UN Doc A/Res/61/106 (entered into force 3 May 2008).
[2] L Arbour, Opening address of the High Level Dialogue on the day of the signing of the Convention on the Rights of Persons with Disabilities and its Optional Protocol: From Vision to Action: The Road to Implementation of the Convention, 30 March 2007.
[3] I use the term 'psychosocial disabilities' to mean people labelled or living with mental health problems. The Convention says that '[p]ersons with disabilities include those who have long-term physical, mental, intellectual or sensory impairments which in interaction with various barriers may hinder their full and effective participation in society on an equal basis with others'. The global disability communities fought to have the phrase 'psychosocial' instead of 'mental' used, but the latter

chapter attempts to suggest how the CRPD, an international human rights treaty agreed unanimously by the global community, may serve as an innovator of change, in small places, close to home.

The chapter examines the CRPD by applying Sandra Fredman's framework of the expressive, educational and proactive roles of human rights.[4] In doing so, it seeks to analyse the values which the CRPD expresses, the forms of communication it encourages, and the range of actions it demands. 'Groundbreaking' and 'landmark' are among the adjectives which have been used to describe the CRPD. It is both of these and more. This is the first human rights treaty to be adopted in the twenty-first century, and it was negotiated more quickly than any other human rights treaty in history, taking four years from start to finish. It involved the greatest level of participation from civil society of any human rights treaty throughout its negotiation process, and benefited from being the first human rights treaty to be the subject of an extensive and co-ordinated internet lobbying campaign.[5] It is the first to oblige States Parties to take measures to eliminate discrimination 'by any person, organization or private enterprise',[6] thus taking international human rights law into the private sphere for the first time. It is by far the longest and most detailed 'status'-based treaty, perhaps making it more likely that it will be implemented.[7]

This chapter suggests that the CRPD has the potential to become a transformative international legal instrument which innovates domestic politics as much as policies.[8] The first part of the chapter argues that the CRPD embodies the expressive role of human rights by encouraging actors to rethink assumptions, evaluate positions and shift existing concepts or paradigms. The global community has agreed on the values to which it aspires, elevating the CRPD into a 'focus

---

prevailed. There is a significant difference in the terminology used by the Convention and that used by the disability communities and other human rights instruments. Prior to the Convention, 'mental disability' had clumsily been the umbrella term including both people with psychosocial (mental health) disabilities and people with intellectual disabilities.

[4] S Fredman, *Human Rights Transformed: Positive Rights and Positive Duties* (Oxford, Oxford University Press, 2008) 32.

[5] See, eg comments made by K Annan, UN Secretary General, 'Secretary General Hails Adoption of Landmark Convention on Rights of People with Disabilities', UN Press Release, 13 December 2006, Ref SG/SM/10797, HR/4911, L/T/4400, available at www.un.org/News/Press/docs/2006/sgsm10797.doc.htm.

[6] Convention on the Rights of Persons with Disabilities, adopted 13 December 2006, GA Res 61/106, UN Doc A/Res/61/106 (entered into force 3 May 2008) Art 4(1)(e).

[7] The CRPD comes in at 9,954 words excluding its title, compared with the other UN treaties protecting the rights of other people due to their 'status': the Convention on the Rights of the Child (Adopted by General Assembly resolution 44/25 of 20 November 1989) contains 7,559 words, the International Convention on the Elimination of All Forms of Racial Discrimination (adopted by General Assembly resolution 2106 (XX) of 21 December 1965) contains 4,739 words, and the Convention on the Elimination of All Forms of Discrimination against Women (adopted by General Assembly resolution 34/180 of 18 December 1979) contains 4,427 words.

[8] For an insightful analysis on how the Convention influences and challenges international human rights law, see F Mégret, 'The Disabilities Convention: Towards a Holistic Concept of Rights' (2008) 12 *International Journal of Human Rights* 261.

for political and grass-roots campaigning, giving a specific and authoritative legitimacy to demands for their fulfilment'.[9]

The second part of the chapter addresses the ways in which the CRPD embodies the educational value of human rights. If the expressive value of human rights is about thinking, the educational value is about talking. The CRPD sets up and encourages communication horizontally: between organisations in the same country, between government departments, between non-governmental organisations (NGOs) across borders and between various states. It encourages information flow vertically: between people with disabilities and their NGOs and the authorities within a state; and internationally between the treaty monitoring body and domestic actors in each state.

The third section of the chapter looks at how the CRPD can be seen as embodying a proactive role of human rights, moving from talking to doing. It does this by outlining how the CRPD creatively sets up domestic policy processes to increase the chances of effective implementation. The CRPD itself obliges States Parties to establish national independent mechanisms to promote and protect the rights of people with disabilities and monitor the implementation of the CRPD. It provides for participation of people with disabilities in the monitoring process at both international and domestic levels, and it obliges States Parties to designate a disability rights focal point at the heart of government to co-ordinate policy. In setting out the expressive, educational and proactive values of the CRPD, the chapter acknowledges the artificiality of separating these values. Permeation between them is both inevitable and encouraged.

Whilst this chapter does not seek to build upon the scholarship of an expressive theory of international law, it is influenced by the literature. Expressive law theory may help explain a government's willingness to ratify and implement treaties.[10] Alex Geisinger and Michael Stein, for example, suggest that states operate a 'need-reinforcement principle' by which states ratify international treaties to signal attraction to a group of states, and over time the group collectively develops shared values.[11] This version of expressive international law works on the assumption that the desire to be seen as a member of an international club is the key reason why states ratify treaties. There is little empirical evidence to back up this assertion, and it would be interesting to conduct research to gather data from civil servants and diplomats who were members of the Ad Hoc Committee which negotiated the CRPD. Expressive law theory takes us only so far, as it accords insufficient weight to the dynamics of domestic politics during treaty negotiation, the decision to sign and ratify which

---

[9] S Fredman, *Human Rights Transformed: Positive Rights and Positive Duties* (Oxford, Oxford University Press, 2008) 33.

[10] For an expressive law analysis of a specific disability law provision, see MA Stein, 'Under the Empirical Radar: An Initial Expressive Law Analysis of the ADA' (2004) 90 *Virginia Law Review* 1151.

[11] A Geisinger and MA Stein, 'A Theory of Expressive International Law' (2007) 60 *Vanderbilt Law Review* 75, 111.

is negotiated across ministries, and any governmental department's genuine willingness to implement the provisions. In terms of international disability politics, the supposition put forward in this chapter is that it is not a state's desire to be a member of a club which drives CRPD ratification, but rather the pressure from people with disabilities – including within government by politicians and civil servants with disabilities, NGOs of and for people with disabilities, academics and the media. People with disabilities constitute a sizeable voting minority: all incumbent governments want to be re-elected and the sensible ones will have figured out that ratifying this treaty may earn them votes.[12]

An expressive theory of law is a holistic one in which, although not explicitly stated, the three elements—of thinking, talking and doing—are inextricably linked. Alex Geisinger and Michael Stein nearly go as far when they suggest that the '[l]egal process provides not just focal points for co-operation, but also an iterative process of norm development and entrenchment that carries with it strong influence on the behaviour of States'.[13] Thus the development of law, including international law, can itself be a 'paradigm shift'. Additionally it can set up processes through which ideas are developed and action is taken. As an example of how these three elements are cyclically linked, the CRPD arose from an interaction of new ideas, discussions among and between NGOs and state officials, and action through negotiations and drafting, being continually influenced by communication with others, adjusting ideas to reach compromise positions, and so on. Having said that, it is possible that ideas alone instigate conversations. As one public policy theorist has suggested, 'discursive power can determine the very field of action, including the tracks on which political action travels'.[14] The CRPD is inspiring not because it codifies a pre-existing reality, but because it articulates a shared reality which has yet to be explained. It is this new reality of disability rights to which the chapter now turns.

II. Expressive Value of Human Rights: Thinking

The CRPD succinctly explains the reason for its existence. It is that all existing human rights treaties apply equally to persons with disabilities,[15] yet 'despite these various instruments and undertakings, persons with disabilities continue to

---

[12] The caveat is that people under guardianship in many countries are prohibited, through the denial or restriction of their legal capacity, from voting. Art 12 (legal capacity) and Art 29 of the Convention compel legislative reform.

[13] A Geisinger and MA Stein, 'A Theory of Expressive International Law' (2007) 60 *Vanderbilt Law Review* 75, 118.

[14] F Fischer, *Reframing Public Policy: Discursive Politics and Deliberative Practices* (Oxford, Oxford University Press, 2003) viii.

[15] Convention on the Rights of Persons with Disabilities, adopted 13 December 2006, GA Res 61/106, UN Doc A/Res/61/106 (entered into force 3 May 2008) preambulatory para (d).

face barriers in their participation as equal members of society and violations of their human rights in all parts of the world'.[16] It is worth pointing out that every single member state of the United Nations agreed with this proposition when they voted unanimously in the General Assembly to adopt the CRPD, signalling a globally-agreed consensus on a new understanding of disability.[17] The 'paradigm shift' championed by the CRPD seeks to move societies away from viewing people with disabilities as passive objects of treatment, management, charity and pity (and sometimes fear, abuse and neglect), towards a world view of people with disabilities as active subjects of human rights and dignity.

The then United Nations Secretary General, Kofi Annan, described the adoption of the CRPD as, 'the dawn of a new era—an era in which disabled people will no longer have to endure the discriminatory practices and attitudes that have been permitted to prevail for all too long'.[18] In promoting a shift of attitudes, the CRPD embodies the expressive value of human rights, 'signalling the values a society stands for'.[19] Human rights activists celebrating the adoption of the CRPD soon turned their attention to ratification and implementation, encouraging states to do the same. In her speech on the day of the CRPD's entry into force, to which this chapter has referred above, Louise Arbour set out the urgent need for domestic law reform. In a direct message to her audience of ambassadors she injected a sense of urgency by saying that '[w]e need to get moving on the implementation now, which means transposing the provisions of the CRPD into national laws. Changes to the law help speed up changes of attitude'.[20] In her speech, Arbour hinted at the transformative potential of the CRPD. By doing so she addressed a goal of the expressive value of law, which scholars have claimed seeks to 'affect preferences and behaviour by altering social perceptions and conventions'.[21] In seeking to adjust social perceptions, the CRPD contains a list of principles, which the next section analyses.

---

[16] *ibid*, preambulatory para (k).

[17] The Convention on the Rights of Persons with Disabilities and its Optional Protocol was adopted unanimously by the United Nations General Assembly on 13 December 2006.

[18] UN Press Release: *Secretary General Hails Adoption of Landmark Convention on Rights of People with Disabilities*, 13 December 2006, Ref SG/SM/10797, HR/4911, L/T/4400, available at: www.un.org/News/Press/docs/2006/sgsm10797.doc.htm.

[19] S Fredman, *Human Rights Transformed: Positive Rights and Positive Duties* (Oxford, Oxford University Press, 2008) 32.

[20] UN Press Release, 'Arbour Welcomes Entry into Force of "Ground-breaking" Convention on Disabilities', 4 April 2008, available at: www.unhchr.ch/huricane/huricane.nsf/view01/1AD533A6AB95F873C1257421003A8DA8?opendocument.

[21] M Stein, and J Lord, 'Future Prospects for the United Nations Convention on the Rights of Persons with Disabilities' in OM Arnardóttir and G Quinn (eds), *The UN Convention on the Rights of Persons with Disabilities: European and Scandinavian Perspectives* (Leiden, Martinus Nijhof, 2009).

A.   Articulated Principles

The CRPD lists several principles which flesh out the specificities of the paradigm shift. This itself is innovative, the CRPD being the first international human rights treaty to explicitly list a set of guiding principles. Article 3 of the CRPD sets these out:

(a)   Respect for inherent dignity, individual autonomy including the freedom to make one's own choices, and independence of persons;
(b)   Non-discrimination;
(c)   Full and effective participation and inclusion in society;
(d)   Respect for difference and acceptance of persons with disabilities as part of human diversity and humanity;
(e)   Equality of opportunity;
(f)   Accessibility;
(g)   Equality between men and women;
(h)   Respect for the evolving capacities of children with disabilities and respect for the right of children with disabilities to preserve their identities.

Principles (b) on non-discrimination, (c) on participation and inclusion in society, (e) on equality of opportunity and (g) on gender equality are what Gerard Quinn calls the 'legacy values of human rights theory and law'.[22] They are not disability-specific and could apply to disability as they could to, for example, women, persons of ethnic minorities or any other discriminated against 'group'. However, when applied to people with disabilities these regular human rights principles become quite revolutionary. One only has to do a quick internet search to find out about how women and girls with disabilities fare much worse than those without disabilities, or men and boys with disabilities. Similarly, the ways in which persons with disabilities are prevented solely because of their disability from participation and inclusion on an equal basis with others has been well documented. It is of interest to note that the principles firmly reject a 'best interests' or protection approach, a principle contained in the United Nations Convention on the Rights of the Child,[23] and one which is applied in domestic laws throughout the world to provide a legal basis in substitute decision-making for those assessed as lacking functional capacity to make particular decisions. More dubiously 'best interests' is a feel-good vehicle for those making decisions which ignore or override the choices of children and adults with disabilities who have functional capacity to make such decisions.

---

[22]   G Quinn, 'Resisting the 'Temptation of Elegance': Can the Convention on the Rights of Persons with Disabilities Socialise States to Right Behaviour?' in MO Arnardóttir and G Quinn (eds), *The UN Convention on the Rights of Persons with Disabilities: European and Scandinavian Perspectives* (Leiden, Martinus Nijhof, 2009).
[23]   Convention on the Rights of the Child, adopted by UN GA Res 44/25 of 20 November 1989, Art 3(1).

The CRPD is silent on how the principles laid out in Article 3 are to be used, but the accompanying United Nations website asserts that the principles 'underlie the CRPD and each one of its specific articles'.[24] This can be understood to mean that the principles represent the moral basis of the CRPD, explaining the reasons for the CRPD's existence, and providing guidance for national authorities, courts and the treaty monitoring body on how to interpret the CRPD. The principles cut across all substantive CRPD rights so that, for example, the right to education for children with disabilities in Article 24, read in conjunction with the principle of non-discrimination as set out in Article 3, may well be interpreted to mean that education shall not be denied to Roma children with disabilities, or to girls with disabilities. Article 24 may also be interpreted to mean that discrimination against children with a particular disability is also prohibited—thus the right to education applies equally to all children with disabilities, which 'include those who have long-term physical, mental, intellectual or sensory impairments which in interaction with various barriers may hinder their full and effective participation in society on an equal basis with others'.[25] The two disability-specific principles are Principle (a), which restates autonomy and the right to make one's own choices, and Principle (d), which celebrates persons with disabilities as part of humanity. These principles may be useful when interpreting controversial or ambiguous topics which were subject to heated debate by the Ad Hoc Committee negotiating the CRPD.

B.   Silence as Expression

An example of a controversial topic on which the CRPD has no explicit provision for or against, is forced psychiatric treatment of persons diagnosed/labelled with a mental illness. Such treatment is lawful in domestic legislation in most countries. The global disability movement fought hard for the CRPD to include an explicit prohibition against forced psychiatric interventions, and the text is quite clear on the prohibition of detention, with Article 14 stating that 'the existence of a disability shall in no case justify a deprivation of liberty.' Some negotiating states sought a specific exception to the general right to consent to treatment so as to explicitly allow forced psychiatric treatment. Instead, the CRPD is silent on psychiatric treatment.[26] Instead, Article 25 on the right to health places an obligation on States Parties to

---

[24] United Nations Enable, *Guiding Principles of the Convention*, available at: www.un.org/disabilities/default.asp?navid=14&pid=156.

[25] Convention on the Rights of Persons with Disabilities, adopted 13 December 2006, GA Res 61/106, UN Doc A/Res/61/106 (entered into force 3 May 2008) Art 1—Purpose.

[26] I am grateful to Professor Amita Dhanda for enlightening me about the potential implications of the Convention's silence on forced psychiatric treatment: see A Dhanda, 'Legal Capacity in the Disability Rights Convention: Stranglehold of the Past or Lodestar for the Future?' (2007) 34(2) *Syracuse Journal of International Law and Commerce* 429 and Annegret Kämpf, this volume, ch 6.

[r]equire health professionals to provide care of the same quality to persons with disabilities as to others, including on the basis of free and informed consent.

The principle of consent to treatment is phrased as a state obligation rather than an individual right and the word 'consent' remains undefined, leaving open the proposition that consent includes a person's current functional capacity, or previous functional capacity during which a future wish was expressed (including in the form of an advance directive).

In analysing the range of possible interpretations of the CRPD, their politically palatability and operational viability, those interpreting the CRPD may want to utilise the expressive value of human rights. This would mean, for example, interpreting the substantive articles by giving meaning to the principles of respect for autonomy, freedom to make one's own choices, inclusion in society and acceptance of persons with disabilities as part of human diversity. The gap between the CRPD's values and the current reality of many mental health laws all over the world may be an example of an area where the CRPD is trying to set out a future reality which has yet to be explained. Ambiguity is awkward for policy-makers and for black-letter lawyers, but it represents a triumph of shared norms over policy detail, whereby those negotiating the treaty agreed on the fundamental principles, but were not able—at that moment in time, on this particular issue—to find consensus on how these principles should play out in the psychiatric emergency room.

Some English-speaking jurisdictions have introduced mental health laws which contain principles such as measures to minimise the restrictions. These include, among others, the principle of 'least restrictive environment and with the least restrictive or intrusive treatment', 'minimum restriction on the freedom of the patient that is necessary in the circumstances',[27] 'least restrictive environment',[28] and 'minimising restrictions on liberty'.[29] That the CRPD is silent on forced treatment may be viewed as simply naïve, offering domestic policy-makers little guidance on the content of domestic mental health legislation, or indeed offering them plenty of room to be creative and progressive, or it may have been simply a political compromise to finalise the treaty. Whichever of these truths emerges, the CRPD is less open to be criticised for hypocrisy, unlike the United Nations Mental Illness Principles which contain a lofty principle on non-discrimination of persons

---

[27] Principles for the Protection of Persons with Mental Illness and the Improvement of Mental Health Care, Adopted by UN GA res 46/119 of 17 December 1991, Principle 9(1).

[28] See, eg Mental Health Act 2007 (NSW) s 68(a).

[29] Mental Health Act 2007 (England and Wales), s 8, which inserts into the Mental Health Act 1983 (England and Wales), s 118(2B)(c) compelling the Secretary of State to ensure this principle is addressed when preparing a statement of principles for the Code of Practice.

with mental illness,[30] and then goes on to list five exceptions to the right to consent to treatment without offering any legal or moral justifications for the exceptions.[31]

The law's communication process has been described as creating 'a normative framework, a vocabulary and a set of open concepts to structure normative discussion'.[32] The CRPD's silence on forced psychiatric treatment provides space and time for reflection and communication, perhaps demonstrating the inter-connectivity between the expressive and the educational roles of human rights.

The CRPD's existence is predicated upon the supposition that, 'the typical welfare response ... of maintaining rather than empowering persons with disabilities has been relatively immune from pressure to change'.[33] However strong the vision and rhetoric of the CRPD, governments and other actors may find themselves stuck in repeating the behaviours of the past, thwarting change. A filtration of ideas from the grassroots disabilities movement is a good start, but ideas alone will be insufficient to ensure an internalisation of a new disability politics. States' inability or unwillingness to accord persons with disabilities sufficient power to set, implement, monitor and adjust policies was one of the reasons the CRPD was needed. It also represents the greatest risk that it will remain unimplemented. Empowering individuals with disabilities can be achieved by the inclusion of CRPD beneficiaries into the domestic policy cycle. This means moving beyond the rhetoric of paradigms and principles, and engaging vigorously and respectfully with those who hold opposing views to unleash the CRPD's potential.

III. Educational Value of Human Rights: Talking

The playwright and political activist Harold Pinter was once asked a question on the actions which individuals who feel compelled to do something about injustices should take. He answered, '[t]o speak. The appropriate response is simply to look for the truth and tell it'.[34] If the expressive value of human rights aims at seismic shifts in societal thinking, then the educational role of human rights gets us talking, speaking truth to power. The adoption of the CRPD

---

[30] Principles for the Protection of Persons with Mental Illness and the Improvement of Mental Health Care, Adopted by UN GA Res 46/119 of 17 December 1991, Principle 1(4).

[31] *ibid*, Principle 11(1).

[32] W van der Burg, 'The Expressive and Communicative Functions of Law, Especially with Regard to Moral Issues' (2001) 20 *Law and Philosophy* 31.

[33] G Quinn, 'Resisting the "Temptation of Elegance": Can the Convention on the Rights of Persons with Disabilities Socialise States to Right Behaviour?' in MO Arnardóttir and G Quinn (eds), *The UN Convention on the Rights of Persons with Disabilities: European and Scandinavian Perspectives* (Leiden, Martinus Nijhof, 2009).

[34] Harold Pinter interviewed by Harry Burton, British Library, 8 September 2008.

provides closure on an intensive global conversation about the notion of disability, the rights of people with disabilities, and the duties on states and others towards them. It is a dusk as well as a dawn.

A substantial amount of time and resources will need to be spent in structuring normative discussion on how the CRPD is to be interpreted, on finding new 'institutional champions' at domestic levels,[35] and educating key stakeholders about what the paradigm shift actually means. Stakeholders will hold a variety of views about CRPD interpretation, and those putting forward views may well assume that their own view is correct, and other interpretations are wrong. Appropriate forums to allow communication to take place in a open dialogue will be crucial to exploring the various interpretations out there and persuading each other of the pros and cons of different viewpoints.[36] The public policy theorist Jan Kooiman suggests that communication between stakeholders is crucial because, '[n]o single actor, public or private, has all the knowledge and information required to solve complex dynamic and diversified problems; no actor has sufficient overview to make the applications or needed instruments effective'.[37] This is as true for disability as it is for any other area of public policy. In this section of this chapter, it is suggested that the CRPD encourages a culture of continuous communication by creating bodies at both the United Nations level and state level, and by placing obligations upon those bodies to specifically seek out the views of persons who have experienced disabilities.

A.   Transposing International Norms

Given the stark gap between the text of the CRPD and the reality on the ground, education at various levels clearly needs to take place. The United Nations High Commissioner for Human Rights has called for states to 'transpose international

---

[35]   G Quinn, 'Resisting the 'Temptation of Elegance': Can the Convention on the Rights of Persons with Disabilities Socialise States to Right Behaviour?' in MO Arnardóttir and G Quinn (eds), *The UN Convention on the Rights of Persons with Disabilities: European and Scandinavian Perspectives* (Leiden, Martinus Nijhof, 2009).

[36]   These discussions will need to start at a basic level and those holding discussions should be prepared for unexpected re-opening of the paradigm shift. For example, in December 2008 the author was a co-trainer at a three-day Council of Europe sponsored training seminar on disability rights for staff of various national human rights institutions across Europe. The training schedule had to be adjusted to allow for an unexpected and lengthy debate on why people with disabilities should have the right to vote. Although Art 29(a) of the CRPD unambiguously provides the right of persons with disabilities to vote and stand for election, several participants—who are all charged with monitoring the rights of persons with disabilities—initially laughed at the proposition that persons with mental health problems should have the right to stand for parliament, and after much explanation they remained less than convinced of the merits of the provision.

[37]   J Kooiman, 'Social-political Governance' in J Kooiman (ed), *Modern Governance: New Government-Society Interactions* (London, Sage, 1993).

obligations into meaningful programmes for change at the national level'.[38] It is suggested that there are three elements to such a transposition. First, stakeholders need to understand the CRPD's vision and ask themselves 'What are the elements of this aspiration?' In doing so they will reach back to the expressive role of human rights, be aware of the paradigm shift, and conduct an appreciative inquiry into the sort of changes the CRPD envisions. Secondly, the participants in the conversation will need to assess the current human rights situation of people with various disabilities and analyse the reasons for any gap in compliance, asking the questions 'Where are we now?' and 'What has caused this situation?'. They will have to reach out and hold conversations with a range of groups and individuals, actively listening to their needs and wishes. Thirdly, there will need to be some sort of majority (of whom?!) opinion about the steps which stakeholders need to take in order to make CRPD provisions a reality; in other words they will need to answer questions such as, 'What needs to change?' How are these changes going to be made, by whom, and by when?' In pursuing these discussions, participants may not reach a consensus (although an open discussion certainly makes this more likely), but they may well be able to better understand each others' positions, explore the reasons underlying deeply-held views, critically appraise their own and others' viewpoints, and find ways of accommodating competing claims.[39]

Taking one of the CRPD's provisions as an example, Article 12 on legal capacity contains two provisions which will require quite significant shifts in thinking, a series of conversations, and steps to bring norms and behaviours into compliance. The Article sets out first, that everyone with disabilities has the right to legal capacity, and secondly that those who need support in exercising their legal capacity to make decisions get such support. Recognising that '[r]especting the legal capacity of persons with disabilities is fundamental not only as a right in itself, but also as a basis to protect other human rights', Louise Arbour went on to set out the challenge of implementation:

> What do these provisions mean for lawyers, for notaries, for institutions, for support-oriented organizations, for justice departments, for courts? To make this right a reality, it will be important to identify good practices in legislative and policy approaches and to examine how these rights and obligations can be incorporated into different legal and developmental contexts.

Let me give some examples about the educative value of the CRPD in this regard. During 2008 and 2009 my colleagues at the Mental Disability Advocacy Center (MDAC) have been working in Hungary and the Czech Republic with other civil

---

[38] L Arbour, Opening address of the High Level Dialogue on the day of the signing of the Convention on the Rights of Persons with Disabilities and its Optional Protocol: From Vision to Action: the Road to Implementation of the Convention, 30 March 2007.

[39] On the naivity of consensus, see W van der Burg, 'The Expressive and Communicative Functions of Law, Especially with Regard to Moral Issues' (2001) 20 *Law and Philosophy* 31, 56.

society organisations on Article 12 implementation, and advocating at governmental level for the requisite changes. Exchanges of opinions and ideas have taken place horizontally, in coalitions of non-governmental organisations (NGOs). MDAC, a legal advocacy organisation which is not a disabled people's organisation, carried out research on the extent to which these two countries' guardianship arrangements complied with international law. Following the publication of those reports, MDAC worked with a range of NGOs, including disabled people's organisations, national umbrella organisations, local service providers and small self-help groups. Coalition members reached out to mainstream human rights NGOs. People with disabilities in the coalitions shared their experiences, ideas and concerns. MDAC lawyers listened to these personal testimonies and framed them as legislative issues. In parallel, colleagues were in contact with NGOs and other experts internationally to gain an understanding of the CRPD's provisions. They also identified best practice in other countries such as Canada, evaluated these programmes and adapted them to the different contexts. In parallel, horizontal exchanges also happened across ministries in these countries, and the governments engaged in discussions, for example, through the European Union's Disability High Level Group, which was established partly to act as a forum for countries to share promising practices.

The advocacy coalitions reached out to central government, taking their research on legislative compliance together with their proposals on how to bring law and services into compliance with Article 12. In this vertical exchange of views, government officials in both countries were initially hesitant to work so closely with civil society, but were soon receptive to ideas when it became clear that the NGOs brought CRPD knowledge together with the testimony of people with disabilities, whose rights could be better protected by domestic implementation. Officials also noticed that NGOs have technical assistance which went above and beyond the competencies of civil servants. The NGOs set out in detail how the government could bring laws into compliance with the CRPD. At the time of writing (November 2009), the Hungarian parliament became the first in the world to enact CRPD-inspired root and branch legal capacity reforms (which abolishes plenary guardianship, and introduces supported decision-making), and the Czech government had agreed with the majority of the submissions made by the NGO coalition. These examples are provided to demonstrate how NGOs can take a proactive role in encouraging states to transpose international law into the domestic arena. There are examples from other parts of the world too.

B.   Bringing New Actors into Disability Rights Discourse

As noted, the educational value of human rights encourages communication between actors, bringing together people holding diverse views who may share common ground at a deeper value-based level. Most people agree on the concept of equality but may differ on how the concept should manifest itself across policy areas. The CRPD encourages such communication, giving primacy to persons with disabilities and their respective organisations.[40] Through its inclusive approach, the CRPD may encourage groups who have not previously done so to work with each other. A small example is lawyers (attorneys as well as academic ones) in English-speaking jurisdictions. Disability lawyers tend to focus on discrimination-in-employment law, whereas mental health lawyers usually do not cover employment at all, but focus on detention and forced treatment. Perhaps the CRPD will bring these groups together? Another example is of 'mainstream' human rights organisations which have traditionally been slow to recognise that human rights of persons with disabilities is actually a legitimate topic of human rights. Human Rights Watch is among the most respected human rights organisations in the world but until summer 2009, when it came out with a report looking at corporal punishment of students with disabilities in the United States,[41] it paid little attention to the rights of persons with disabilities. Its Executive Director acknowledged this in 2002, writing that

> [t]here is little doubt that a disability is a 'status' entitling one to protection under, for example, the anti-discrimination provision of Article 26 of the International Covenant on Civil and Political Rights. In some cases involving children, the human rights movement has begun to take on the cause of people with disabilities. But an embrace of this broad sector of humanity has barely begun. Remedying this failure is a major challenge facing the movement.[42]

In 2009 Human Rights Watch announced that it had obtained funding to start some specific programming on the rights of persons with disabilities, and it is hoped that Human Rights Watch will contribute to raising the visibility and credibility of the rights of persons with disabilities within the 'mainstream' human rights community and its donors.

Seeking out and bringing on board partners was evident when the CRPD was being negotiated by states and NGOs at the United Nations. Louise Arbour has reflected that the process was a 'significant learning process' and one which has 'helped us forge partnerships with new actors beyond our typical human rights

---

[40] Convention on the Rights of Persons with Disabilities, adopted 13 December 2006, GA Res 61/106, UN Doc A/Res/61/106 (entered into force 3 May 2008) Art 4(3).

[41] Human Rights Watch, *Impairing Education: Corporate Punishment of Students with Disabilities in US Schools* (New York, Human Rights Watch, 2009) available at www.hrw.org/sites/default/files/reports/us0809webwcover_0.pdf

[42] K Roth, 'Foreword' in Mental Disability Rights International, *Not on the Agenda: Human Rights of People with Mental Disabilities in Kosovo* (Washington DC, Mental Disability Rights International, 2002). Art 26 of the International Covenant on Civil and Political Rights states: 'All persons are equal before the law and are entitled without any discrimination to the equal protection of the law. In this respect, the law shall prohibit any discrimination and guarantee to all persons equal and effective protection against discrimination on any ground such as race, colour, sex, language, religion, political or other opinion, national or social origin, property, birth or other status'.

partners—in particular persons with disabilities and their representative organizations'.[43] She has pointed out that the involvement of her office in the negotiation process instigated a process of changing the way the United Nations works—from office layout to the choice of technology.

The CRPD has secured the attention of United Nations officials who had previously not addressed the rights of persons with disabilities. For example, in December 2007, the Office of the United Nations High Commissioner for Human Rights organised a seminar on disability and torture, which was attended by two members of the United Nations Committee against Torture, and Manfred Nowak who holds the mandate of United Nations Special Rapporteur on Torture.[44] Within a year Nowak had produced a report in which he stated that the CRPD 'provides a timely opportunity to review the anti-torture framework in relation to persons with disabilities'.[45] The report cited examples of how persons with disabilities are subjected to neglect, severe forms of restraint and seclusion, as well as physical, mental and sexual violence. A reframing of the anti-torture framework is necessary, Nowak claims, so that ill-treatment which is perpetrated in public institutions as well as in the private sphere, begins to be recognised as torture or other cruel, inhuman or degrading treatment or punishment.

In many states across the world, NGOs are using the CRPD as a catalyst to reach out to others, discuss the benefits for their constituents of adopting a human rights based approach, and build constituencies for advocacy. The need to develop one's own and other people's understanding of disability and to bring new actors into the disability rights field should go hand in hand with the attempt to do something over and above CRPD's aims, namely to reduce world poverty.

C. Poverty and Disability

The educational value of the CRPD has the potential to encourage communication to highlight the intimate link between disability and poverty and to implement inclusive poverty reduction strategies. The key actors in these conversations are host governments, donor governments, other donors and civil society organisations, including disabled people's organisations. The statistics are astonishing. The United Nations estimates that approximately 80 per cent of the 650 million people with disabilities worldwide live in developing countries, and of these some 426 million live below the poverty line, often representing the 15 to 20

---

[43] L Arbour, Statement to the General Assembly Ad Hoc Committee, 8th session, New York, 5 December 2006.

[44] For more information, see: www2.ohchr.org/english/issues/disability/torture.htm.

[45] M Nowak, *Interim Report of the Special Rapporteur of the Human Rights Council on Torture and other Cruel, Inhuman or Degrading Treatment or Punishment*, 28 July 2008, A/63/175 at [41].

per cent most vulnerable and marginalised poor in such countries.[46] The drafters of the CRPD wanted funding to flow between States Parties by inserting a provision which recognises 'the importance of international cooperation for improving the living conditions of persons with disabilities in every country, particularly in developing countries.'[47] The CRPD encourages communication between and among states in co-operation with regional and intergovernmental organisations and civil society, in order to, amongst other things, ensure international development programmes are inclusive of and accessible to people with disabilities, facilitate capacity-building and sharing of best practices, co-operate in research, share information, and provide economic and technical assistance.[48] That the CRPD is a human rights treaty as well as a development tool may be one of the reasons why so many low- and middle-income countries have swiftly ratified the CRPD.

A recent report of the United Nations Economic and Social Council has found that

> [t]here is a strong bidirectional link between poverty and disability. Poverty may cause disability through malnutrition, poor health care, and dangerous living conditions. Case studies in developing countries show that higher disability rates are associated with higher rates of illiteracy, poor nutritional status, lower immunization coverage, lower birth weight, higher rates of unemployment and underemployment, and lower occupational mobility.[49]

More explicitly, disability needs to become a focus for the United Nations' Millennium Development Goals[50] for these goals to stand any chance of being achieved. The United Nations Commission for Social Development 2008 report puts it bluntly:

> The high numbers of persons with disabilities who are disproportionately represented among the world's most marginalized groups have a profound significance with respect to the achievement of the Millennium Development Goals, which thus far seems to have gone largely unnoticed in the international discourse on the Goals. The Millennium Development Goals, in fact, cannot be achieved if persons with disabilities are not included in these efforts. We are now at the halfway point to the target date of 2015, yet in The Millennium Development Goals Report 2007,[51] persons with disabilities as a

---

[46] A O'Reilly, *The Right to Decent Work of Persons with Disabilities*, revised edn (Geneva, International Labour Office, 2007).

[47] Convention on the Rights of Persons with Disabilities, adopted 13 December 2006, GA Res 61/106, UN Doc A/Res/61/106 (entered into force 3 May 2008) preambulatory para (l).

[48] *ibid*, Art 32.

[49] United Nations, Economic and Social Council, *Mainstreaming Disability in the Development Agenda* Report for the Commission for Social Development, 46th Session 6–15 February 2008, ref E/CN.5/2008/6, 23 November 2007, available at: www.un.org/disabilities/default.asp?id=358, at [3].

[50] The Millennium Development Goals are eight goals aimed to be achieved by 2015 that respond to the world's main development challenges, available at: www.undp.org/mdg/basics.shtml.

[51] United Nations, Department of Economic and Social Affairs, *The Millennium Development Goals Report 2007* (New York, United Nations, 2007).

group are not mentioned, and the issue of disability is briefly mentioned twice. The Human Development Report 2006[52] discusses persons with disabilities within the development context of sanitation. It is hoped that current efforts to integrate disability within the United Nations system will increase the importance of persons with disabilities in such reports in the future.[53]

Article 32 of the CRPD is dedicated to international co-operation and highlights action-oriented measures which states can undertake to support inclusive development. The Article ensures that development programmes become inclusive and accessible to persons with disabilities, putting to bed the idea that the only way to increase the wealth of disabled people is by focusing on disability-specific programming. A consequence of the CRPD's insistence that disability be mainstreamed into all development programmes,[54] is that

> once a country ratifies the CRPD, it will need to be reflected in its national development framework such as the Common Country Assessment, United Nations Development Assistance Framework, and Poverty Reduction Strategy Papers. It is through these broad-reaching approaches to development that the CRPD will become a reality on the ground and in the daily lives of individuals.[55]

Thus, the CRPD sets up a communication process among people leading on different policies. The treaty's focus on poverty reduction may well have a direct impact on domestic implementation, as well as on the methods with which international and domestic actors communicate with each other. Boosted communications in the mainstream will result in persons without disabilities being exposed to those with disabilities. Such exposure may help reduce stigma and discrimination against persons with disabilities.

Prerequisites to rebalancing global inequalities by redistributing financial and informational resources include elements of the educational value of human rights: willingness by states to share information with other states; an appreciation by development agencies of the damage caused by inappropriate grant-making (such as renovating children's institutions instead of investing into community-based services); an increased effort by United Nations and regional bodies to facilitate exchange; and more transparent processes to allow civil society organisations to participate and hold states to account. Exchanging information, of course, only goes so far. People's lives will change only if action is

---

[52] United Nations, Department of Economic and Social Affairs, *The Human Development Report 2006* (New York, United Nations, 2006).

[53] United Nations Commission for Social Development, *Mainstreaming Disability in the Development Agenda* Report for the Commission for Social Development, Forty-sixth Session 6–15 February 2008 ref E/CN.5/2008/6, 23 November 2007 available at: www.un.org/disabilities/default.asp?id=358.

[54] Convention on the Rights of Persons with Disabilities, adopted 13 December 2006, GA Res 61/106, UN Doc A/Res/61/106, preambulatory para (g) also emphasises 'the importance of mainstreaming disability issues as an integral part of relevant strategies of sustainable development'.

[55] United Nations Enable, *Relationship between Disability and Development*, available at: www.un.org/disabilities/default.asp?id=33.

taken as a result of the information exchange, and it is the proactive value of human rights which this chapter now considers.

IV. Proactive Value of Human Rights: Doing

Having laid out the expressive value of human rights which presents a new paradigm for the conceptualisation of disability, and the educational value of human rights which opens up conversations inside and between organisations and states, it is the proactive value of human rights which turns thinking and talking into action. The pre-existing international human rights landscape applies to people with disabilities, but as the CRPD points out,

> despite these various instruments and undertakings, persons with disabilities continue to face barriers in their participation as equal members of society and violations of their human rights in all parts of the world.[56]

The drafters of the CRPD made it their aim to plug the compliance gap between rights and implementation, and they inserted into the text several structural features which make it likely that the CRPD will be implemented to a greater extent than other human rights treaties.

A. Specificity of Action

The drafters were acutely aware that the need for the CRPD was that international human rights treaties and their mechanisms had failed people with disabilities. The CRPD contains a wealth of action points which states will find difficult to ignore. Whereas the United Nations Convention on the Rights of the Child obliges States Parties to take 'all appropriate legislative, administrative, and other measures' to ensure that children are protected against all forms of discrimination,[57] it does not actually specify what these appropriate measures should be.

The CRPD does not hold back on specificity, making it easier for States Parties to understand their obligations, and for the United Nations Committee on the Rights of Persons with Disabilities, as well as domestic bodies, to hold States Parties to account. The CRPD goes much further than the Convention on the Rights of the Child, obliging States Parties to 'modify or abolish existing laws,

---

[56] Convention on the Rights of Persons with Disabilities, adopted 13 December 2006, GA Res 61/106, UN Doc A/Res/61/106 (entered into force 3 May 2008) preambulatory para (k).
[57] Convention on the Rights of the Child, adopted by UN GA Res 44/25 of 20 November 1989 Art 2(2).

regulations, customs and practices that constitute discrimination against persons with disabilities,'[58] to refrain from acting in any way which is inconsistent with the CRPD,[59] to take 'all appropriate measures to eliminate discrimination on the basis of disability by any person, organization or private enterprise,'[60] to promote training of professionals and staff working with persons with disabilities about the CRPD,[61] and (quite remarkably) to 'take into account the protection and promotion of the human rights of persons with disabilities in *all* policies and programmes.'[62] States Parties are therefore under a duty to take broad action across government to ensure that rights are protected, respected and fulfilled in public and private spheres and considered in all policies and services.

B. Independent Mechanisms

It is commonly acknowledged in human rights that it is easy for states to ratify treaties, because they need not do anything about implementation, placing at risk the potential of international law to bring positive changes to people's lives. The CRPD guards against backsliding by establishing an independent body at United Nations level, and by obliging States Parties to establish/designate an independent monitoring body at domestic level. These two mechanisms will be examined in turn.

Despite numerous innovative proposals put forward by a variety of organisations, the CRPD has quite a mundane arrangement at the United Nations level to monitor state compliance. The CRPD establishes a Committee on the Rights of Persons with Disabilities,[63] which consists of 12 experts (increasing to 18 after 80 ratifications of the CRPD)[64] who 'shall serve in their personal capacity and shall be of high moral standing and recognized competence and experience in the field covered by the Convention.'[65] When nominating prospective members, States Parties are encouraged to 'closely consult with and actively involve persons with disabilities, including children with disabilities, through their representative organizations.'[66] The CRPD calls for States Parties to 'consider' the prospect of achieving 'equitable geographical distribution, representation of the different

---

[58] Convention on the Rights of Persons with Disabilities, adopted 13 December 2006, GA Res 61/106, UN Doc A/Res/61/106 (entered into force 3 May 2008) Art 4(1)(b).
[59] *ibid*, Art 4(1)(d).
[60] *ibid*, Art 4(1)(e). Note how the CRPD views State intervention into the private spheres as unproblematic.
[61] *ibid*, Art 4(1)(i).
[62] *ibid*, Art 4(1)(c), emphasis added.
[63] *ibid*, Art 34(1).
[64] *ibid*, Art 34(2).
[65] *ibid*, Art 34(3).
[66] *ibid*, Art 4(3), to which Art 34(3) invites States Parties to give due consideration when nominating their candidates.

forms of civilization and of the principal legal systems, balanced gender representation and participation of experts with disabilities.'[67] The members serve for
four years, except for six members from the first batch who serve for two years
only, ensuring a staggered turnover.[68]

The role of the Committee is two-fold. First, the Committee receives reports by
States Parties on measures taken to implement the CRPD. The reports 'may
indicate factors and difficulties affecting the degree of fulfilment of [CRPD]
obligations.'[69] These reports must be submitted within two years of the entry into
force of the CRPD in each particular State Party,[70] and thereafter every four
years.[71] The CRPD uses rather tentative language when it invites States Parties 'to
consider [preparing their reports] in an open and transparent process and to give
due consideration to ... closely consult[ing] with and actively involv[ing] persons
with disabilities, including children with disabilities, through their representative
organizations.'[72] The Committee will consider these reports, and 'shall make such
suggestions and general recommendations on the report as it may consider
appropriate.'[73] Interestingly enough, the CRPD places an obligation on States
Parties to 'make their reports widely available to the public in their own countries
and facilitate access to the suggestions and general recommendations relating to
these reports.'[74] This is worth dwelling on a little. The CRPD is the first United
Nations human rights treaty to contain an obligation on States Parties to make
widely available to the public either their own report on compliance or the treaty
monitoring body's suggestions and recommendations relating to that report.
This is another example of how the CRPD pioneers a new participatory politics
and promotes a dynamic of domestic discussion and participation. Presumably
the obligation to make reports widely available means producing the reports in
various formats—for the public without disabilities, and various accessible
formats for people with disabilities who require different formats. So the reports
would at a minimum have to include: easy-to-read format for children with
disabilities, easy-to-read format for adults with intellectual disabilities, large
print, Braille, and electronic versions. The public also consists of people without
disabilities. One can read into the CRPD an implicit obligation that the government takes the responsibility to translate its report and the Committee's suggestions and recommendations into indigenous languages accurately and promptly,
and to issue all of the above-mentioned formats in each of these languages.

The second role of the Committee applies only in relation to those states which
have ratified the Optional Protocol to the CRPD. The Committee can receive and

---

[67] *ibid*, Art 34(4).
[68] *ibid*, Art 34(7).
[69] *ibid*, Art 35(6).
[70] *ibid*, Art 35(1).
[71] *ibid*, Art 35(2).
[72] *ibid*, Art 35(5), citing Art 4(3) on participation.
[73] *ibid*, Art 36(1).
[74] *ibid*, Art 36(4).

consider communications from or on behalf of individuals or groups of individuals subject to its jurisdiction of that state who claim to be victims of a violation by that State Party of any CRPD provision.[75] The Optional Protocol sets out various procedural rules, including the requirement that the victim(s) must exhaust domestic legal remedies before submitting the communication to the Committee. After considering the Applicant's and the respondent state's positions in a given communication the Committee may make recommendations and suggestions to the respondent state.[76] In addition to dealing with individual communications the Committee can also instigate an 'inquiry' where it receives information 'indicating grave or systematic violations' of the CRPD.[77] The Committee can ask a state to include in its periodic reports under Article 35 of the CRPD any measures which it has taken in response to such an inquiry.[78]

The rather mundane international arrangement for monitoring compliance is compensated for by innovative domestic monitoring mechanisms. The CRPD follows a recently-established trend in international human rights treaties to oblige States Parties to establish domestic mechanisms for monitoring implementation. The obvious parallel is the Optional Protocol to the United Nations Convention against Torture (OPCAT) which obliges States Parties to 'maintain, designate or establish … one or several independent national preventive mechanisms for the prevention of torture at the domestic level.'[79] These national preventive mechanisms may be ombudsman offices, national human rights institutions or fresh bodies. States must give them the power to enter places of detention in order to examine the rights of persons deprived of liberty, make recommendations to the authorities on each place of detention and make recommendations on draft legislation.[80]

The CRPD takes this idea and runs with it, obliging States Parties to 'maintain, strengthen, designate or establish … a framework, including one or more independent mechanisms, as appropriate, to promote, protect and monitor implementation of the present [CRPD].'[81] In carrying out this obligation states must take into account the Paris Principles,[82] which set out minimum standards for the functioning, composition, financing, guarantees of independence and pluralism, and methods of operation of national human rights institutions. Although the national monitoring mechanisms are seen as quite innovative, during the negotiations of the CRPD, states rejected even more creative proposals

---

[75] Optional Protocol to the Convention on the Rights of Persons with Disabilities, Art 1.
[76] *ibid*, Art 5.
[77] *ibid*, Art 6.
[78] *ibid*, Art 7(1).
[79] *ibid*, Art 17.
[80] *ibid*, Art 19.
[81] Convention on the Rights of Persons with Disabilities, adopted 13 December 2006, GA Res 61/106, UN Doc A/Res/61/106 (entered into force 3 May 2008) Art 33(2).
[82] National Institutions for the Promotion and Protection of Human Rights, UN GA res 48/134, 20 December 1993.

put forward by both the International Disability Caucus (comprising all sorts of disability NGOs) and the grouping of National Human Rights Institutions.[83]

The national independent mechanisms foreseen by the CRPD will in many countries likely be crucial in conjoining the government to focus on effective implementation. The CRPD inventively mandates States Parties to ensure that these independent mechanisms do three quite different things: 'to promote, protect and monitor implementation of the [CRPD].' To get round the linguistic ambiguity, my reading of this sentence is that the duties to promote and protect refer to the rights of people with disabilities and not to promoting or protecting implementation.

What sorts of activities would fall under these three headings? Promoting human rights of persons with disabilities means anything which 'valourises' the paradigm shift.[84] This would include activities in the public arena and in the corridors of power to promote the ratification of the CRPD (if the state has not already done so), and encouraging ratification without reservations or interpretative declarations which unravel the CRPD. Promoting rights means getting out of the office and meeting key officials to encourage them to take action to ensure the full and effective implementation of the CRPD. Other activities would include awareness-raising campaigns for the general public including delivering messages to the public through the media.[85] It would also include organising training for people working with and caring for people with disabilities,[86] and capacity-building of organisations of and for persons with disabilities so that they can better participate in public policy-making on issues which affect them, as envisioned by the CRPD.[87] Promoting human rights means working with

---

[83] For an analysis of these proposals, see G Quinn, 'Resisting the 'Temptation of Elegance': Can the Convention on the Rights of Persons with Disabilities Socialise States to Right Behaviour?' in MO Arnardóttir and G Quinn (eds), *The UN Convention on the Rights of Persons with Disabilities: European and Scandinavian Perspectives* (Leiden, Martinus Nijhof, 2009). These included a direct obligation on the national monitoring mechanism not just to hold the government to account with regard to the CRPD, but also domestic disability policies, and that the national body should make legislative recommendations. The proposal for an international monitoring body included a set of facilitative, solution-oriented activities rather than a passive role which receives reports from States Parties. It also contained an elaborate mechanism to ensure that the Committee contained experts with disabilities proposed not by states, but by the Office of the UN High Commissioner for Human Rights.

[84] Thanks to Gerard Quinn for this phrase and for encouraging me to delve into domestic monitoring mechanisms.

[85] In the CRPD, 'States undertake to adopt immediate, effective and appropriate measures' (Art 8(1)) on awareness-raising, with measures including 'encouraging all organs of the media to portray persons with disabilities in a manner consistent with the purpose of the present Convention' (Art 8(2)(c)).

[86] Convention on the Rights of Persons with Disabilities, adopted 13 December 2006, GA Res 61/106, UN Doc A/Res/61/106 (entered into force 3 May 2008) Art 4(1)(i) requires states 'to promote the training of professionals and staff working with persons with disabilities in the rights recognized in the present Convention so as to better provide the assistance and services guaranteed by those rights'.

[87] ibid, Art 33(3)—this is addressed below.

education systems to integrate disability into human rights education in primary and secondary schools. It also means encouraging law faculties and human rights institutes to include the rights of persons with disabilities as part of their regular human rights teaching and research.

As already noted, the CRPD places a general obligation on states '[t]o take into account the protection and promotion of the human rights of persons with disabilities in all policies and programmes.'[88] So too should an Ombudsman office or national human rights institution ensure that in addition to carrying out specific programming to promote and protect the rights of persons with disabilities, they integrate and mainstream disability into all areas of existing work. For example, they need to promote disability rights within thematic areas such as the prevention of torture, promotion of sexual and reproductive rights, freedom of expression, election monitoring, domestic violence and hate crime. Mainstreaming also means dealing authentically with double (and triple, and more) discrimination by ensuring that people with disabilities feature as part of work regarding all discriminated-against groups: women, refugees, people of ethnic or religious minorities, lesbian, gay, bisexual and transgender people, children and young people, elderly people, poor people, detained people and so on. The national monitoring mechanisms need not do this alone; they can call for assistance from sister organisations abroad, working in concert to share practices and to develop ideas.

So much for promoting rights. Protecting rights has more of a hard-edged feel. This may include providing legal advice and assistance to individuals and— depending on the mandate of the independent mechanism—representing them in domestic courts or before the United Nations Committee on the Rights of Persons with Disabilities in individual complaints under the Optional Protocol. The independent mechanism could seek to advance jurisprudence by piggy-backing on litigation by intervening as a friend-of-the-court by submitting an *amicus curiae* brief. Protecting rights means reacting in a speedy and appropriate manner to cases revealed by the media. It means vigorously holding governments to account and ensuring that independent bodies are seen and heard to be doing so. It also means travelling the breadth and width of the country to monitor the rights of people with disabilities where they live, including in places of detention such as psychiatric facilities and social care institutions, as well as in smaller group homes. There is an inevitable crossover here between the role of the CRPD independent mechanisms, and the national preventive mechanism of places of detention under the Optional Protocol to the United Nations Convention against Torture (OPCAT), noted above. Coordination between the two bodies will be necessary, as will cross-fertilisation of skills and experience. In some countries

---

[88]   *ibid*, Art 4(1)(c).

they will be different departments of the same Ombudsman's office or national human rights institution, in which case cross-departmental cooperation is called for.

If the independent body is doing its job properly, it will come head-to-head with governmental authorities. Part of being an independent human rights structure means speaking truth to power. In the area of human rights, truths can be uncomfortable, and some governments go to great lengths to crush criticism. It is vital that legislation protects the independence of national human rights structures to prevent their budgets being slashed by government, to prevent summary dismissal of staff, or raiding of premises.

The third function of the national independent body as set out in the CRPD is to monitor the implementation of the CRPD. This is an unusual task, unparalleled in international human rights law. It is quite remarkable that states negotiating the CRPD agreed that they would each establish and finance a body at arms-length to government with the mandate to monitor how well the government is implementing the CRPD. Such a task will be challenging even for well-established independent mechanisms. The CRPD is detailed and complex and most existing national human rights institutions are already overloaded even without this significant additional mandate.

Monitoring the implementation of the CRPD will mean carrying out an array of concrete activities distinct from those falling under the headings of promoting and protecting the rights of persons with disabilities. The first activity when monitoring anything is likely to be to establish the 'current reality'. Each national independent mechanism will have to analyse how national laws and policies compare with the CRPD and publish a base-line report which highlights areas on which the independent body needs to focus, and, flowing from this, a work-plan with measurable objectives. Monitoring CRPD implementation also means tracking draft legislation which has or ought to have an impact on people with disabilities, analysing it through the lens of the CRPD, and coming out with a view as to its CRPD compliance. A legislative scrutiny role such as this will feed into or from a parliamentary human rights committee (where such a body exists).

Conducting analyses of actual and draft laws and policies for Convention compliance requires staff working for the independent mechanism to have a high level of understanding of the CRPD, the skills to conduct such analyses, and the resources to ensure that analyses are available in a variety of formats. In building its own capacity such a mechanism might want to draw on the expertise of disabled people's organisations, other NGOs and academics. The independent mechanism will need to develop and adopt indicators or precise standards against which laws or practice can be measured. A useful early task for the United Nations Committee on the Rights of Persons with Disabilities is to develop— with the participation of persons with disabilities and their NGOs—a reporting template with basic indicators of compliance, and make it clear that they expect States Parties to use this template when compiling their reports under Article 35 of the CRPD. This will help the national independent mechanisms to carry out their base-line analyses, and to repeat these periodically so that information is tracked through time. Assessing compliance at various points in time is a vital tool to be able to comment on whether a particular state is, to the maximum of its available resources, progressively realising the economic, social and cultural rights set out in the CRPD.[89]

A compliance analysis requires data. The lack of meaningful data and statistics is a major problem in some countries where governments fail to collect and collate national data on disability rights issues, such as (if we are analysing compliance with Article 12 of the CRPD) how many people in a particular country have been deprived of legal capacity. States Parties are obliged by the CRPD to 'collect appropriate information including statistical and research data to enable them to formulate and implement policies to give effect to the present CRPD.'[90] The data should be disaggregated, so as to monitor potentially discriminatory practices, and the independent monitoring body would be wise to ensure that it makes its expectations clear at the outset, so that the government can start collecting the appropriate data.

Evaluating policy implementation is no easy task, and the national monitoring body—as well as the United Nations Committee on the Rights of Persons with Disabilities itself—will need to be well-resourced. Difficulties which these bodies may face include evaluating several initiatives in parallel; dealing with governmental 'initiativitis', whereby policies change quickly without proper evaluation or sometimes explanation; evaluating policies serving multiple policy objectives which rely on the input of various departments, services and organisations; and dealing with the incredible breadth of legislation and policies which implement the CRPD: from inclusive education of children with visual disabilities to the disability inclusivity of international aid, from accessibility of police stations to the sexual and reproductive rights of adults with intellectual disabilities in group homes. The scope of the topics covered by the CRPD could easily become overwhelming for those responsible for monitoring and evaluating its implementation.

The United Nations Committee on the Rights of Persons with Disabilities will need to be the watchdog of watchdogs, monitoring the performance of the national monitoring bodies, as well as compiling and sharing information about 'best practices' among them. To give meaning to the proactive role of human rights, the national monitoring bodies should ensure the participation of people with disabilities, as well as draw on the expertise of people within their own

---

[89] *ibid*, Art 4(2). It is not clear which of the CRPD rights fit into the seemingly neat box of 'economic, social and cultural rights'. For a discussion of this point, see F Mégret, 'The Disabilities Convention: Towards a Holistic Concept of Rights' (2008) 12 *International Journal of Human Rights* 261, 265–6.

[90] Convention on the Rights of Persons with Disabilities, adopted 13 December 2006, GA Res 61/106, UN Doc A/Res/61/106 (entered into force 3 May 2008) Art 31.

country and gather information from abroad. In combining information-sharing with carrying out concrete activities, such bodies will demonstrate the connectivity between the educational role and the proactive role of human rights.

C.   Participation by People with Disabilities

One of the CRPD's principles is ' [f]ull and effective participation and inclusion in society.'[91] Specifically the CRPD guarantees participation in political and public life by reaffirming the right to vote and stand for office.[92] Participation in public life, however, means more than voting every few years. The CRPD sets out the right to participation in strong terms, and locates this obligation in Article 4(3) on general obligations:

> In the development and implementation of legislation and policies to implement the present Convention, and in other decision-making processes concerning issues relating to persons with disabilities, States Parties shall closely consult with and actively involve persons with disabilities, including children with disabilities, through their representative organizations.

As noted above, the duty on the state to ensure participation of persons with disabilities in legislative and policy reforms is extended to the process for states to nominate candidates for the United Nations Committee on the Rights of Persons with Disabilities. When nominating their candidates, 'States Parties are invited to give due consideration' to consulting with and actively involving persons with disabilities through NGOs.[93] When States Parties elect the members of the Committee they are asked that consideration be given to the 'participation of experts with disabilities'.[94]

The CRPD guarantees that persons with disabilities and their organisations are involved in monitoring its implementation.[95] This means that the domestic independent monitoring bodies (discussed in sub-section B above) must find ways of reaching out to people with disabilities and including them in their work. Participation of persons with disabilities in the monitoring of the CRPD will likely result in the monitoring being more relevant, accurate and sensitive to the needs of those whose rights the CRPD aims to advance.

Across the world, people with disabilities have been denied access to information and therefore denied power. Those in positions of influence and wealth (for example, disability service providers, psychiatrists, lawyers, family members and carers, not to mention pharmaceutical companies) have traditionally been the

---

[91]   *ibid*, Art 3(c).
[92]   *ibid*, Art 29.
[93]   *ibid*, Art 34(3).
[94]   *ibid*, Art 34(4).
[95]   *ibid*, Art 33(3) says that, '[c]ivil society, in particular persons with disabilities and their representative organizations, shall be involved and participate fully in the monitoring process.'

policy-making power players, lobbying governments to adopt policies which are professionally and financially beneficial. The CRPD is premised on the belief that

> persons with disabilities should have the opportunity to be actively involved in decision-making processes about policies and programmes, including those directly concerning them,[96]

and in doing so the treaty seeks to repatriate power towards those who have most to gain from Convention implementation. The CRPD organises this power redistribution by creating a general obligation to ensure participation, an obligation which should be read into each CRPD provision. The general obligations need also to be read into the various bodies which the CRPD establishes and which are referred to in this chapter, namely the Conference of States Parties to the Convention,[97] the Committee on the Rights of Persons with Disabilities,[98] the focal point(s) in the domestic executive structure,[99] and the national independent monitoring bodies,[100] in all of which '[c]ivil society, in particular persons with disabilities and their representative organizations, shall be involved and participate fully.'[101] An insistence that people with disabilities and their NGOs participate in monitoring the CRPD's implementation makes it more likely that implementation will actually happen. It is also more likely that the United Nations Committee on the Rights of Persons with Disabilities and the domestic independent monitoring bodies receive relevant, informed and accurate information from civil society so that they in turn can provide specific, measurable and time-bound objectives for States Parties to bring their laws, policies and practices in line with CRPD requirements. The CRPD's insistence on ensuring the participation of persons with disabilities suggests a post-hierarchical politics, one in which there is greater transparency, ownership of results, and likelihood of implementation.

Research has suggested that participation allows for a greater and more varied set of voices to be brought into decision-making processes in order to counteract the dominance of previously more powerful voices. It has also indicated that participation increases the effectiveness of service delivery. A group of British researchers puts it succinctly in observing that, '[e]ffective governance requires an informed, engaged citizenry which votes in elections, participates in decision making and works with service providers in designing, delivering and monitoring

---

[96] *ibid*, preambulatory para (o).
[97] *ibid*, Art 40.
[98] *ibid*, Art 34.
[99] *ibid*, Art 33(1).
[100] *ibid*, Art 33(2).
[101] *ibid*, Art 33(3).

services'.[102] In other words, participation in CRPD processes goes beyond superficial attempts at political correctness: it is beneficial for persons with disabilities, and for politicians and civil servants too.[103]

D. Co-ordinating Implementation

As well as establishing independent mechanisms at the domestic and international levels and insisting on the participation of people with disabilities at both those levels, the CRPD demands executive co-ordination of implementation at both intergovernmental and governmental levels.

The CRPD is the first United Nations human rights treaty to require the States Parties to 'meet regularly in a Conference of States Parties in order to consider any matter with regard to the implementation of the present CRPD.'[104] The Conference can be convened however regularly the States Parties decide, but no less regularly than every two years.[105] Although most other treaties have a provision for calling a Conference of States Parties, the CRPD is the only one to mandate its Conference to consider implementation.[106] Early indications are that the Conference of States Parties to the CRPD will be held more or less annually, and will be inclusive of civil society organisations.[107] The Conference of States Parties is serviced not by the Geneva-based Office of the High Commissioner for

---

[102]   SR Andrews, R Cowell, J Downe, S Martin and T Turner, *Promoting Effective Citizenship and Community Empowerment: A Guide for Local Authorities on Enhancing Capacity for Public Participation* (London, Office of the Deputy Prime Minister, 2006).

[103]   For a discussion on participation in the mental health arena, see O Lewis and N Munro, 'Civil Society Involvement in Mental Health Law and Policy Reform' in M Dudley, D Silove and F Galeeds (eds), *Mental Health and Human Rights* (Oxford, Oxford University Press, forthcoming 2010).

[104]   Convention on the Rights of Persons with Disabilities, adopted 13 December 2006, GA Res 61/106, UN Doc A/Res/61/106 (entered into force 3 May 2008) Art 41(1).

[105]   *ibid*, Art 41(2).

[106]   Although a Conference of States Parties is envisioned in Art 51 of the International Covenant on Civil and Political Rights (adopted by GA Res 2200A (XXI) of 16 December 1966), Art 29 of the International Covenant on Economic, Social and Cultural Rights (adopted by GA Res 2200A (XXI) of 16 December 1966), Art 29 of the Convention against Torture and Other Cruel, Inhuman or Degrading Treatment or Punishment (adopted by General Assembly resolution 39/46 of 10 December 1984), Art 50 of the Convention on the Rights of the Child (adopted by GA Res 44/25 of 20 November 1989), Art 90 of the International Convention on the Protection of the Rights of All Migrant Workers and Members of Their Families (adopted by GA Res 45/158 of 18 December 1990), Art 34 of the Optional Protocol to the Convention against Torture and other Cruel, Inhuman or Degrading Treatment or Punishment (adopted by GA Res 57/199 of 18 December 2002), all of these treaties limit the formal mandate of such a conference to a consideration of proposed amendments to the treaty by States Parties. Curiously neither the International Convention on the Elimination of All Forms of Racial Discrimination (adopted by GA Res 2106 (XX) of 21 December 1965) nor the Convention on the Elimination of All Forms of Discrimination against Women (adopted by GA Res 34/180 of 18 December 1979) contain provision for a Conference of States Parties.

[107]   The second Conference of States Parties was held over three days in September 2009. The agenda included panels, dialogues and side events, all discussing the subject 'Legislative measures to implement the Convention on the Rights of Persons with Disabilities'. There was significant participation of NGOs.

Human Rights (which services the Committee on the Rights of Persons with Disabilities), but by the Department for Economic and Social Affairs based in New York. This reflects, perhaps, the fact that the Conference is governmental, whereas the Committee is supposed to be independent.

The CRPD encourages states to talk to each other and (possibly) make decisions on implementation, through the Conference of States Parties. At the domestic level, it requires that States Parties, ' designate one or more focal points within government for matters relating to the implementation of the present CRPD.'[108] The purpose of the focal points is to co-ordinate action across ministries, departments and agencies to deliver a coherent disability policy. Central government has a duty under the CRPD to ensure that its provisions are implemented everywhere within the state's jurisdiction (even in federal states). It has a further duty to co-ordinate action across local and regional authorities. The drafters of the CRPD (which were, after all, state representatives themselves) were aware that many of the rights violations suffered by people with disabilities are caused by failures in communication and co-ordination of policy. This proposition is supported by empirical evidence which suggests that a key element in policy implementation failure is that many actors do not talk to each other and do not co-ordinate policy delivery.[109]

That the CRPD sets out *how* States Parties should organise the executive branch of government in order to implement the treaty is an audacious constitutional masterstroke. The CRPD insists on 'joined-up' government, a new concept for many countries which govern by departmental machine. Governments may like to consider adopting the following objectives for their disability rights focal point(s):[110]

- To create an integrated, holistic approach to the development and delivery of disability policy;
- To overcome departmental barriers and the problems of 'silo' management;
- To reduce transition costs from overlapping policies and initiatives;
- To deliver better policy outcomes by ensuring the participation of and contributions from people with disabilities;[111]
- To encourage greater coordination and integration of service delivery among providers at the local level;

---

[108] Convention on the Rights of Persons with Disabilities, adopted 13 December 2006, GA Res 61/106, UN Doc A/Res/61/106 (entered into force 3 May 2008) Art 33(1).

[109] S Barrett, 'Implementation Studies: Time for a Revival? Personal Reflections on 20 Years of Implementation Studies' (2004) 82 *Public Administration* 249. Barrett suggests that the three other factors deemed to contribute to implementation failure are lack of clear policy objectives; inter- and intra-organisational value and interest differences; and relative autonomies of implementing agencies coupled with limits of administrative control.

[110] Adapted from J Newman, 'Joined-up Government: The Politics of Partnership' in *Modernising Governance: New Labour, Policy and Society* (London, Sage, 2001).

[111] This is a requirement under CRPD Arts 4(3) and 33(3).

- To develop innovative approaches to policies and services by eliciting the contributions of various partners;[112] and
- To increase the financial resources flowing into the disabilities sectors.[113]

A pre-requisite to pursuing joined-up government will be for politicians overseeing these focal points to provide leadership towards Convention implementation. Despite strong political backing, an enabling approach to delivering disability policy may be undermined by the strong traditions of rational planning and the continued centralisation of power associated with mechanical models of the 'policy-action dynamic'. It is crucial therefore that the effectiveness of CRPD focal points is closely monitored by civil society, by the relevant state's independent monitoring body, and by the United Nations Committee on the Rights of Persons with Disabilities.

In many countries the focal points are being set up within traditionally low-power ministries, such as ministries of social affairs, or ministries of employment. In placing the focal points in these ministries, states perpetuate the myth that disability policy is a soft social issue, or that its only aim is to reduce discrimination in employment. The CRPD is a cross-disciplinary treaty which, of course, does cover public policy areas of employment and social affairs, but goes much broader into policy areas of education, criminal justice, civil justice, family, foreign affairs,[114] international development, home/interior affairs, data protection, data and statistics. Given that the CRPD's main goal is to achieve equality and non-discrimination, it may be more prudent for activists to suggest that the relevant government's focal point is housed by the ministry of justice which, in many countries, has power and authority across a variety of other ministries. It will be interesting to see what the United Nations Committee on the Rights of Persons with Disabilities says about the ideal mother ministry for the focal points.

A further pre-requisite to pursuing a 'holistic' approach of policy co-ordination will be for all actors to be clear about the role of government. Such clarity is needed when coordinating policy, ensuring the participation of persons with disabilities, and delivering policy and services. In hierarchical models of governance, the government sets the agenda, develops the policy and implements

---

[112] This could mean facilitating the sharing of promising practices within the country, and importing practices from outside the country—perhaps by working with sister focal points in other countries or via organisations such as the UN or international NGOs.

[113] This could be achieved, for example, by quantifying the needs of persons with disabilities, ensuring that ministries contribute to providing the funding, developing partnerships which can deliver on providing appropriate services. Such partnerships these could, depending on the local circumstances, involve State bodies, quasi-State agencies, private companies, and non-profit organisations.

[114] For example, people entering the United States risk not being allowed in the country if they fail to tick the box certifying that they do not have a major mental illness. Another example is that it could be argued that the Convention requires embassies to be accessible for persons with disabilities, and another example is that embassies act as polling stations, and Art 29 of the Convention requires voting procedures to be accessible.

it or orders others to do so. In encouraging an alternative politics, the CRPD sets up potential conflicts which will have to be managed. The policy theorists Erik-Hans Klijn and Joop Koppenjan suggest that in a network-like situation, the government may choose not to join in discussions at all.[115] Alternatively the government could communicate with other public agencies and NGOs, or they may choose to play the role of process manager facilitating iterative discussions, or they may choose to be a network builder using their resources and their credibility as legitimately elected representatives of the majority. Klijn and Koppenjan warn that if government is inexperienced (which will inevitably be the case for the majority of CRPD focal points around the world) there is a risk that behaviours will revert to established and safer routines in which 'misunderstandings and conflict among actors can prove to be costly in terms of effectiveness and efficiency, but especially with regard to the reliability and legitimacy of governments'.[116] This may be especially the case in countries with active focal points, with civil servants who want to combine the roles of a body which has a political 'opinion' with a more neutral process manager role or a network builder role. In time we will be able to assess how well the focal points manage their new and complex role. It is hoped that the Conference on States Parties will take the lead in sharing promising practices in executive coordination.

The politics of power has inevitably surfaced in this section on the proactive value of human rights. Power exists also in formulating ideas and discussions between stakeholders, so it is a consideration which runs through the expressive, educational and proactive roles of human rights. This section has looked at the structures established at the international and domestic levels to ensure policy coordination and those set up to monitor the implementation of the CRPD. The strong participation of people with disabilities in these mechanisms will re-balance power and ensure that policies and monitoring methodologies are relevant and owned by disability communities. Ownership will happen if governments acknowledge the disenfranchisement of persons with disabilities and their respective organisations, and ensure that these citizens are empowered to participate in and have the capacity to intervene on an equal basis with others in the policy cycle. The combination in the CRPD of substantive rights coupled with process requirements is unusual in human rights treaties. Its innovative implementation mechanisms may well contribute to closing the gap between rights rhetoric and reality.

---

[115] EH Klijn and FM Koppenjan, 'Public Management and Policy Networks: Foundations of a Network Approach to Governance' (2000) 2(2) *Public Management* 135.
[116] *ibid*, 154.

V. Conclusion

This chapter has suggested that a way of conceptualising the potential of the United Nations Convention on the Rights of Persons with Disabilities to effectuate social change is through the framework of the expressive, educational and proactive roles of human rights. The interdependence of these roles mirrors the rights enshrined in the CRPD as well as the institutions established by the CRPD at United Nations and domestic levels to ensure implementation. Interdependence itself is a core feature of human rights law and practice. The CRPD is now one of the nine core United Nations human rights treaties, but as Gerard Quinn has suggested, we should think of it

> less as a means for coercing States and more as a powerful tool for enabling its revolutionary insights to percolate into the political process (by 'persuasion' and 'socialisation') and hence transform the political process to the point that justice and rights for persons with disabilities is seen as the primary departure point and not as an annoying distraction.[117]

Political processes are likely to be transformed if persons with disabilities, their family members and carers, providers of services, governmental authorities, and a range of civil society actors are open to thinking about ideas which may initially be uncomfortable. Political processes are likely to be transformed if people talk to those whose views may have been marginalised and with whom they have previously not talked or with whom they have vehemently disagreed. Political processes are likely to be transformed if programmes outside their drafters' comfort zones are implemented. In other words, the expressive, educational and proactive roles of human rights may be relevant to this Convention's implicit goal of changing the politics which have marginalised people with disabilities worldwide.

Creative problem solving will mean that policy-makers will have to take risks, and try out programmes, for example to put in place supported decision-making to comply with Article 12 of the CRPD. On such issues the 'correct' thing to do may be to take risks and put in place services for which there are no best practices, but rather promising practices which will have to be evaluated over time. Some of these programmes will work; others will flop. The United Nations Commission for Social Development has lent its weight to the notion of programme experimentation and knowledge-transfer, suggesting that, '[n]ew and innovative thinking and collaboration are required to utilize the CRPD so as

---

[117] G Quinn, 'Resisting the "Temptation of Elegance": Can the Convention on the Rights of Persons with Disabilities Socialise States to Right Behaviour?' in MO Arnardóttir and G Quinn (eds), *The UN Convention on the Rights of Persons with Disabilities: European and Scandinavian Perspectives* (Leiden, Martinus Nijhof, 2009).

to bring the maximum benefit to persons with disabilities and society'.[118] The negotiation process was an example of innovative collaboration, and the resultant text of creative thinking.

The CRPD attempts to redistribute power and creates new forums for stakeholder communication, policy co-ordination and implementation monitoring. These are all reasons to be optimistic that this Convention, more than others, will be implemented in small places, close to home. Implementation will depend on the genuine willingness of policy-makers to embrace a new kind of politics, an embrace which no treaty can guarantee.

[118] UN Commission for Social Development, *Mainstreaming Disability in the Development Agenda*, E/CN.5/2008/6, prepared for the Commission's 46th Session, 6–15 February 2008 (23 November 2007), available at: www.un.org/disabilities/default.asp?id=358, at [30(b)].

6

Involuntary Treatment Decisions: Using Negotiated Silence to Facilitate Change?

ANNEGRET KÄMPF

I. Introduction

In many jurisdictions, mental health legislation is based on the idea that a mentally ill person can be involuntarily treated if treatment is necessary for that person's own health or safety or for the protection of others. While the person's legal capacity to make a decision is often a consideration, it is not always crucial. Rather, the treatment decision can be a clinical one that may be based on public interest considerations. However, international human rights have increasingly influenced mental health laws and facilitated a stronger focus on rights-based mental health schemes. In particular, the recent United Nations Convention on the Rights of Persons with Disabilities (CRPD)[1] has the potential to influence reforms in law and politics because it clarifies and amplifies in unprecedented detail what human rights mean in the context of disability.

The CRPD marks an important shift in the understanding of legal capacity.[2] It recognises that legal capacity is central to a person's equal recognition before the law, and clarifies that all persons with disabilities not only possess but may also exercise legal capacity on an equal basis with others. It further clarifies that decision-making must be safeguarded by measures such as respecting a person's rights, will and preferences. Decision-making must also be proportional, tailored to individual circumstances and subject to regular review by a competent, independent and impartial authority.

---

[1] Convention on the Rights of Persons with Disabilities, adopted 13 December 2006, GA Res 61/106, UN Doc A/Res/61/106 (entered into force 3 May 2008). For an overview of the CRPD, see Oliver Lewis, this volume, ch 5.

[2] *ibid*, Art 12.

In contrast to Article 12 of the CRPD, which sets out the requirements for legal capacity, Article 17, which concerns the right to physical and mental integrity, does not give further clarification. Article 17 does not explicitly permit involuntary treatment, nor does it prohibit it. This is a negotiated silence. Australia, for example, ratified the CRPD with the declaration that it understands that the CRPD allows for fully substituted decision-making and compulsory treatment for mental disability, if it is necessary, as a last resort and subject to safeguards.

This chapter addresses the ways in which international human rights can guide mental health laws. Using Australia as an example, it will examine some of the features of its mental health laws before outlining the framework which the CRPD establishes for treatment decisions. It will assess the practicability and limitations of having such a framework and of using its terminology for rights-based arguments. It will then examine the CRPD's silence on involuntary treatment. Finally, the chapter will assess the effect of Australia breaking that silence, and why silence was feared by some and preferred by others.

II. Features of Australian Mental Health Laws

Mental health laws in Australia exist in all six States and two Territories but vary in content. All have been subject to international human rights scrutiny, in particular after a national inquiry into human rights and mental health revealed in 1993 that individuals with mental illnesses were amongst the most vulnerable and disadvantaged persons in Australia.[3] The human rights point of reference at that time was the United Nations international human rights treaties, as interpreted in the United Nations Principles for the Protection of Persons with Mental Illness and for the Improvement of Mental Health Care.[4] These Principles have been criticised for falling short in clarifying an appropriate standard.[5]

Subsequent reform processes initiated a move to bestow rights on persons with mental illnesses in mental health policy and strategy.[6] However, the genuine empowerment of persons with mental illnesses was not achieved.[7] Rather, mental health legislation and policies were criticised for insufficiently focusing on

---

[3] Human Rights and Equal Opportunity Commission, Human Rights and Mental Illness: Report of the National Inquiry into the Human Rights of People with Mental Illness (vol 2) (Canberra, Australian Government Publishing Service, 1993) 908.

[4] Principles for the Protection of Persons with Mental Illness and for the Improvement of Mental Health Care (GA Res 119, UN GAOR, 46th session, Supp no 49, Annex, at 188–92, UN Doc A/46/49), 1991.

[5] See, eg: N Rees, 'International Human Rights Obligations and Mental Health Review Tribunals' (2003) 10(1) *Psychiatry, Psychology and Law* 33, 34*ff*.

[6] Mental Health Council of Australia and the Brain and Mind Research Institute, *Not For Service: Experiences of Injustice and Despair in Mental Health Care in Australia: Summary* (Canberra, Mental Health Council of Australia, 2005) 35.

[7] *ibid*, 36.

monitoring processes to ensure implementation and adherence to human rights-based principles.[8] Other points of criticism were that the shift to facilitating treatment outside of institutional settings was not delivered effectively[9] and that failures in accessing services resulted in 'serious and systematic neglect'[10] of persons with mental illnesses.

Reform processes aimed to reduce the regulation of mental health care for involuntary measures in the least restrictive environment. The aim was to prevent liberties being unnecessarily restricted by regulating voluntary-based mental health services. However, such reform processes were not accompanied by sufficient resources or clarity as to how voluntary-based care should be delivered.[11] Rather, the legislation's focus on involuntary measures meant that involuntary treatment became the primary form of care,[12] leaving systematic gaps in the care of many people who need mental health services, but are not at the point of crisis. Thus, after approximately 10 years, legislative reforms have been criticised as having failed to achieve high-quality care,[13] leaving 'any person seeking mental health care run[ning] the serious risk that his or her basic needs will be ignored, trivialised or neglected'.[14]

Australian mental health legislation still has a strong focus on involuntary care, including community-based involuntary care. Although the various Mental Health Acts include differences in safeguards and specific criteria for involuntary detention and treatment, the main similarities are that involuntary treatment can be administered if it is necessary to prevent harm to the person's own health and safety or if he or she poses a threat to others, and if no less restrictive alternative is available.[15] Some of the Mental Health Acts allow for the involvement of carers in treatment decisions, but the decision as to whether a person requires involuntary treatment, as well as the decision as to what that treatment should be, are

---

[8] T Carney, 'Mental Health Law in Postmodern Society: Time for New Paradigms?' (2003) 10(1) *Psychiatry, Psychology and Law* 12, 12.

[9] Mental Health Council of Australia and the Brain and Mind Research Institute, *Not For Service: Experiences of Injustice and Despair in Mental Health Care in Australia: Summary* (Canberra, Mental Health Council of Australia, 2005) 35.

[10] *ibid*, 36.

[11] V Topp, M Thomas and M Ingvarson, *Lacking Insight: Involuntary Patient Experience of the Mental Health Review Board* (Melbourne, Mental Health Legal Centre, 2008) 28.

[12] Senate Select Committee on Mental Health, *A National Approach to Mental Health: From Crisis to Community, First Report* (Canberra, Select Committee on Mental Health, 2006) 55 stated that involuntary admissions and treatment are common, referring to one facility in which 83% of patients are under involuntary orders and suggesting that the number of people treated against their will is higher.

[13] G Groom, I Hickie and T Davenport, *Out of Hospital, Out of Mind! A Report Detailing Mental Health Services in Australia in 2002 and Community Priorities for National Mental Health Policy for 2003–2008* (Canberra, Mental Health Council of Australia, 2003) ii.

[14] *ibid*, 12.

[15] Senate Select Committee on Mental Health, *A National Approach to Mental Health: From Crisis to Community, First Report* (Canberra, Select Committee on Mental Health, 2006) 55; F Beaupert, 'Mental Health Tribunals: From Crisis to Quality Care?' (2007) 32(4) *Alternative Law Journal* 219, 219.

basically clinical decisions. The decision-making is, by law, guided by what is necessary for the person concerned or necessary in the public interest. Over the years, the terminology of mental health legislation has shifted away from 'best interest' considerations to decision-making guided by what is 'necessary' for the mentally ill person (or the safety of others). This concept of necessity does not provide a substantially different standard, as it ties in with clinical considerations and does not facilitate consideration of what the person would have wanted and for what reasons. The degree of reliance on clinical assessment is in conflict with developments in general health care settings, where self-determination is a central consideration and subject to certain elements of control outside of clinical settings. While self-determination should be approached carefully in all kinds of decision-making, the degree to which the current mental health legislation relies on clinical assessment is concerning.

In general health care settings, decision-making is predominantly guided by what that person wants or would have wanted, rather than what would be in that person's best interest. Exceptions apply, but they are subject to a high level of scrutiny. In contrast, the decision-making process concerning involuntary treatment is based on broad criteria with limited safeguards. It becomes justifiable to make a presumption of incapacity or to disregard a person's refusal of treatment primarily on the basis that the person has been diagnosed with a mental illness. However, legal capacity is crucial to being recognised as a person before the law, and if limitations are not subject to thorough safeguards they run the risk of cutting people off from the position of being able to claim their rights.

In current mental health legislation, only certain intensive kinds of treatment come with special safeguards which pay respect to autonomous decision-making in such a way that the will of the treated person is at least a consideration. For example, psychosurgery cannot be executed against the will of the individual who is recommended for such surgery. Overall, however, decision-making in relation to involuntary treatment is focused on deciding *for* the person concerned, rather than *with* that person, and it seems to rest on the idea that in cases of doubt, coercion is the preferred option. The following sections will address in what ways the CRPD challenges such substituted decision-making.

III. The Human Rights Framework of the CRPD

A. Background to the CRPD

The CRPD significantly affects key issues of domestic mental health legislation—up to the point of questioning whether the existence of specific mental health law itself is a discriminatory state practice.[16]

---

[16] See Neil Rees, this volume ch 4.

The CRPD emerged under strong influence from Non-Governmental Organisations (NGOs) and people with disabilities, who lobbied for increased international human rights protection with appropriate implementation.[17] These groups successfully called for systematic change to international recognition and realisation of their human rights in one comprehensive international treaty.

Central to their claims was the idea that people with disabilities have inherent human dignity worthy of protection equal to that of other human beings.[18] While this may have previously existed on paper, the meaning of equality despite differences did not come to mainstream society's attention. Many people with disabilities referred to this as an issue of invisibility: people with disabilities experienced systematic marginalisation, institutionalisation and exclusion from society, and their physical or mental differences were perceived as a basis for subjecting them to welfare, rather than seeing them as subjects of rights.[19] The CRPD embraces the aim of making persons with disabilities visible as different, but equal, members of society. In order to facilitate change it clarifies and amplifies in unprecedented detail what human rights mean in the context of disability.

The CRPD applies to all persons

> who have long-term physical, mental, intellectual and sensory impairments which in interaction with various barriers may hinder their full and effective participation in society on an equal basis with others.[20]

It considers disability as an

> evolving concept [that] … results from the interaction between persons with impairments and attitudinal and environmental barriers that hinders their full and effective participation in society on an equal basis with others.[21]

Thus, the application of the CRPD is very broad and emphasises that disability can be a social construct whereby impairments can arise from social factors, such as social interaction or social standing.

---

[17] See Oliver Lewis, this volume ch 5.

[18] T Degener, 'Menschenwürde und Behinderung' (Paper presented at the 'Menschenwürde' Conference on the 60th anniversary of the Universal Declaration of Human Rights, Berlin, 1 December 2008) (author's translation).

[19] G Quinn and T Degener, *Human Rights and Disability: The Current Use and Future Potential of United Nations Human Rights Instruments in the Context of Disability* (New York, United Nations, 2002) 23 *ff.*

[20] Convention on the Rights of Persons with Disabilities, adopted 13 December 2006, GA Res 61/106, UN Doc A/Res/61/106 (entered into force 3 May 2008) Art 1.

[21] *ibid*, Preamble(e).

B. The Dignity and Equality of Human Beings as Guiding Principles

The CRPD places the inherent dignity and worth of human beings at the heart of human rights protection for persons with disabilities, and interlinks it with the equality of all human beings. The following sections will address in what ways this is consistent with the foundational human rights documents of the United Nations. It will then assess the correlation between the concept of human dignity and the equality of human beings and their autonomy. Subsequently, it will discuss the use of human dignity and equality for rights-based arguments and for guiding the interpretation and application of the CRPD.

(i) Human Dignity within the United Nations Human Rights Framework

The protection of human dignity is fundamental to the human rights framework of the United Nations. It has been incorporated into the Charter of the United Nations (UN Charter),[22] the Universal Declaration of Human Rights (UDHR)[23] and many other documents of the United Nations, including all the United Nations' core treaties on human rights.[24] The preamble of the UN Charter starts by recalling the experiences of the World Wars and reaffirming faith in fundamental human rights, in the dignity and worth of the human person, and in the equal rights of men and women and of nations large and small. The preamble to the UDHR begins by recognising the inherent dignity of all human beings and the idea that the equal and inalienable rights of all members of the human family are the foundation of freedom, justice and peace in the world. In its proclamation of human rights, it first guarantees in Article 1 that

> [a]ll human beings are born free and equal in dignity and rights.[25]

Thus, both documents place the protection of human dignity and equality at the top of their actual formulation.

---

[22] United Nations, Charter of the United Nations, 24 October 1945, 1 UNTS XVI.

[23] Universal Declaration of Human Rights, GA Res 217A (III), UN Doc A/810 (1948).

[24] International Covenant on Civil and Political Rights, opened for signature 19 December 1966, 999 UNTS 171 (entered into force 23 March 1976) Preamble, Art 10; International Covenant on Economic, Social and Cultural Rights, opened for signature 19 December 1966, 993 UNTS 3 (entered into force 3 January 1976) Preamble, Art 13; International Convention on the Elimination of All Forms of Racial Discrimination, opened for signature 7 March 1966, 660 UNTS 195 (entered into force 4 January 1969) Preamble; Convention on the Elimination of All Forms of Discrimination against Women, opened for signature 1 March 1980, 1249 UNTS 13 (entered into force 3 September 1981) Preamble; Convention against Torture and Other Cruel, Inhuman or Degrading Treatment or Punishment, opened for signature 10 December 1984, 1465 UNTS 85 (entered into force 26 June 1987) Preamble; Convention on the Rights of the Child, opened for signature 26 January 1990, 1577 UNTS 3 (entered into force 2 September 1990) Preamble, Arts 23, 28, 37, 39, 40; International Convention on the Protection of the Rights of All Migrant Workers and Members of Their Families, opened for signature 18 December 1990, 2220 UNTS 3 (entered into force 1 July 2003) Arts 17, 70.

[25] Universal Declaration of Human Rights, GA Res 217A (III), UN Doc A/810 (1948) Art 1.

The UDHR has a central standing in the actual human rights protection of the United Nations. Despite its originally non-binding character and some initial scepticism as to its use in enforcing human rights, it is still the most recognised and most accepted human rights standard throughout the world. The UDHR can be viewed as a milestone in establishing the basic rights of the individual comprehensively, internationally and inclusively, not only for civil and political rights but also for economic, social and cultural rights.[26] Philip Alston referred to it as 'the greatest ethical and normative achievement of the United Nations ... a beacon of light in a fog of inhumanity'.[27] He considered Article 1, which guarantees the freedom, dignity and equality of all human beings, as 'probably the single most important principle which underpins the Universal Declaration'.[28]

To understand the international human rights framework of the United Nations, it is important to keep in mind that it developed in reaction to the atrocities of the Nazi regime and the 'massacres and barbarities'[29] during the time of World War II.[30] The development of international human rights was a reaction against the objectification of human beings through totalitarian systems[31] and the experience that human beings are capable of subjecting fellow human beings to extermination, forced labour, medical experimentation, starvation and other forms of inhuman and degrading treatment. The United Nations aimed to introduce international standards that direct states to grant basic rights to individuals who are subjected to state powers. While it was hard to find universal agreement on many human rights standards, there was agreement that human beings are born with equal dignity and worth, understood as a pre-existing inherent value of all human beings which calls for unconditional respect[32] and which is not confined to a pre-set religious, philosophical or cultural belief. One core element of early human rights protection under the aegis of the United Nations was guaranteeing that this intrinsic value of human life must ultimately be protected from intrusions. The human rights framework

---

[26] T Buergenthal, 'Centerpiece of the Human Rights Revolution' in B van der Heijden and B Tahzib-Lie (eds), *Reflections on the Universal Declaration of Human Rights—A Fiftieth Anniversary Anthology* (The Hague, Martinus Nijhoff Publishers, 1998) 91.

[27] P Alston, 'The Universal Declaration in an Era of Globalisation' in B van der Heijden and B Tahzib-Lie (eds), *Reflections on the Universal Declaration of Human Rights—A Fiftieth Anniversary Anthology* (The Hague, Martinus Nijhoff Publishers, 1998) 28.

[28] *ibid*, 29.

[29] M Koskenniemi, 'The Preamble of the Universal Declaration of Human Rights' in G Alfredsson and A Eide (eds), *The Universal Declaration of Human Rights: A Common Standard of Achievement* (The Hague, Martinus Nijhoff Publishers, 1999) 27, 32 in reference to E/CN.4/21, 69.

[30] J Morsink, *The Universal Declaration of Human Rights: Origins, Drafting, and Intent* (Philadelphia PA, University of Pennsylvania Press, 2000) 36 *ff*.

[31] J Reiter, 'Menschenwürde als Maßstab' (2004) 23/24 Das Parliament—Aus Politik und Zeitgeschehen, available at: www.das-parlament.de/2004/23–24/Beilage/002.html (author's translation).

[32] K Dicke, 'The Founding Function of Human Dignity in the Universal Declaration of Human Rights' in D Kretzmer and E Klein (eds), *The Concept of Human Dignity in Human Rights Discourse* (The Hague, Kluwer Law International, 2002) 111, 116.

aimed to ensure that everyone is treated not as a pure object or means to an end, but rather is recognised as a bearer of basic human rights. This idea is encompassed in Article 1 of the UDHR, a provision which 'provides the crucially important and cross-culturally unobjectionable normative premise'[33] of universal human rights protection.

(ii)   The Interrelationship between Human Dignity and Equality

The UDHR and the UN Charter clearly link the inherent dignity and worth of all human beings with equality. The way both documents address human dignity and equality in their preambles conceptualises human dignity and equality as more than basic rights to freedom from interference that need to be granted by states. The preambles address dignity and worth as pre-existing conditions of all human beings, which serve as the underlying rationale as to why all human beings need to have their basic rights respected on an equal basis. The subsequently formulated human rights and fundamental freedoms elaborate what that means in terms of specific rights and freedoms.

In other words, protecting human dignity within the international human rights framework of the United Nations has two important elements. First, it reiterates that all individuals have human dignity as an inherent value simply because they are human beings. Secondly, respecting and protecting human dignity serves as the foundation for equality. The idea that all human beings have dignity as an inherent value is the inspiration for why they ought to have equal protection and not be subjected to discriminatory treatment. When discussing human dignity and its interrelationship with equality, Arthur Chaskalson defined discrimination as the 'differentiation based on attributes and characteristics that [has] the potential to impair the fundamental human dignity of persons as human beings or to affect them adversely in a comparable serious manner'.[34] He continued to explain the interrelationship by stating:

> Dignity and equality are interdependent. Inequality is established not simply through group-based differential treatment, but through differentiation, which perpetuates disadvantage and leads to the scarring of the sense of dignity and self-worth. Conversely, an invasion of dignity is more easily established when there is an inequality of power and status between violator and victim.[35]

René Cassin, a member of the Drafting Committee of the UDHR, emphasised the need to develop a human rights document to respond to the Holocaust. He insisted that equality must be fundamental to the human rights declaration and

---

[33]   T Lindholm, 'Article 1' in G Alfredsson and A Eide (eds), *The Universal Declaration of Human Rights: A Common Standard of Achievement* (The Hague, Martinus Nijhoff Publishers, 1999) 62.

[34]   A Chaskalson, 'Human Dignity as a Constitutional Value' in D Kretzmer and E Klein (eds), *The Concept of Human Dignity in Human Rights Discourse* (The Hague, Kluwer Law International, 2002) 140 with references therein.

[35]   *ibid*, 140.

he recalled that Hitler 'started by asserting the inequality of men before attacking their liberties'.[36] The notion that some people are intrinsically different can facilitate and perpetuate uncritical acceptance of unequal treatment—up to the point of questioning other human beings as bearers of rights and disrespecting their inherent dignity. Conor Gearty states that equality of esteem is

> the bridge that leads us to a fuller set of principles. The reason we are interested in human rights to start with, and why we are looking for foundations in the first place, is because of our commitment to this kind of equality ... [T]alk of esteem takes us inevitably to the notion of individual human dignity.[37]

(iii)   Human Dignity as the Underlying Principle in the CRPD

The CRPD includes the protection of human dignity and equality as the underlying foundation for the interpretation and application of rights and freedoms. Its preamble starts by recalling the UN Charter's foundation position in recognising the inherent dignity and worth of all human beings. The first provision re-states its commitment to protecting human dignity by providing that the purpose of the CRPD is to promote, protect and ensure the full and equal enjoyment of rights and freedoms and to promote respect for inherent human dignity. It links the protection of inherent dignity with equality and considers both to be the essence of the CRPD and the underlying rationale for non-discrimination. Apart from the position of human dignity and equality mentioned in the CRPD's preamble and its general principles, the central standing of human dignity and equality can be further seen by the treaty's consistent reference to human dignity in many of its provisions—more so than in any other international human rights treaty.[38]

The CRPD's extensive emphasis on human dignity can be explained as a reaction to disabled persons' experiences of injustice and systematic discrimination. Previous international human rights treaties granted persons with disabilities rights on an equal basis by prohibiting discrimination based on disability, but they failed to bring about equality when it came to placing persons with disabilities in a position where they could exercise their rights and freedoms.[39] In other words, while formal equality of persons with disabilities had long been established in theory, simply granting rights on an equal basis did not achieve substantive or material equality. Now, the CRPD utilises the concept of human dignity to underpin the realisation of human rights. It 'extrapolates the principle

---

[36]   J Morsink, *The Universal Declaration of Human Rights: Origins, Drafting, and Intent* (Philadelphia PA, University of Pennsylvania Press, 2000) 39 in reference to (SR13/p 4).

[37]   C Gearty, *Can Human Rights Survive?* (Cambridge, Cambridge University Press, 2006) 46.

[38]   Convention on the Rights of Persons with Disabilities, adopted 13 December 2006, GA Res 61/106, UN Doc A/Res/61/106 (entered into force 3 May 2008) Arts 2, 3(b), 4(b), 5, 12(2), 13(1), 14(1), 14(2), 15(2), 17, 18, 19, 23(1), 24(1), 25(1) and 27(1).

[39]   See, eg M Jones and LA Basser Marks (eds), *Disability, Divers-ability and Legal Change* (The Hague, Martinus Nijhoff Publishers, 1999).

of non-discrimination throughout its text, addressing the many facets and effects of discrimination'[40] and it clarifies what actions need to be taken to achieve that.

In order to promote equality and to eliminate discrimination, the CRPD provides that States Parties must take appropriate steps to ensure reasonable accommodation for people with disabilities (Article 5(3)) and sets out, in unparalleled detail, what measures are necessary to accelerate or achieve equality (Article 5(4)). By requiring reasonable accommodation, the CRPD clarifies that it aims to achieve substantive or material equality of persons with disabilities.[41] It now explicitly requires States Parties not only to refrain from discriminatory practices, but also to provide devices, services or facilities to allow persons with disabilities to achieve equal standing and recognition within society. In order to achieve substantial or material equality, the CRPD systematically addresses common obstacles to including persons with disabilities in society, includes details as to how to apply and enforce established human rights and fundamental freedoms in the context of disability, and clarifies what it requires to facilitate their realisation.[42] It interweaves civil and political rights as well as social, economic and cultural rights, refusing to distinguish between traditional negative freedoms from interference and positive rights to entitlement. Even though this distinction seems to have been diminishing to a point where it may have become obsolete within the international human rights framework of the United Nations, the CRPD has significantly marked the understanding and development of international human rights protection. A crucial element of the CRPD is that it adheres to the idea that it is necessary to overcome structural inequalities, rather than to simply treat people alike on a formal basis.

When elaborating on the content of its specific rights, the CRPD recognises the importance of individual autonomy,[43] but it focuses on dignity-based terminology, rather than autonomy-based terminology—an interesting aspect given that in the history of human rights development, respect for a person's autonomy and right to self-determination have been predominant.[44] However, in mental health care settings autonomous decision-making has been less determinate, as mental illnesses can impede the rationality of decision-making and inhibit autonomous decision-making. The concept of autonomy has limited use for protecting and

---

[40] P Weller, 'Supported Decision-Making and the Achievement of Non-Discrimination: The Promise and Paradox of the Disabilities Convention' (2009) 26(2) *Law in Context* 85, 95.

[41] R Kayess and P French, 'Out of Darkness into Light? Introducing the Convention on the Rights of Persons with Disabilities' (2008) 8(1) *Human Rights Law Review* 1, 10; A Hendriks, 'Disabled Persons and Their Right to Equal Treatment: Allowing Differentiation while Ending Discrimination' (1995) 1(2) *Health and Human Rights* 152, 157.

[42] L Gable, 'The Proliferation of Human Rights in Global Health Governance' (2007) 35(4) *Journal of Law, Medicine & Ethics* 534, 535.

[43] Convention on the Rights of Persons with Disabilities, adopted 13 December 2006, GA Res 61/106, UN Doc A/Res/61/106 (entered into force 3 May 2008) Preamble (n), Arts 3, 16 and 25.

[44] See also F Mégret, 'The Disabilities Convention: Human Rights of Persons with Disabilities or Disability Rights?' (2008) 30 *Human Rights Quarterly* 494, 513.

realising the human rights of persons with mental illnesses because autonomy can be over-ridden if they are deemed incapable of consenting to treatment. Mary Donnelly has pointed out that autonomy can be denied through broadly applicable legal schemes that do not even require assessment of individual capacity to make decisions, leading to claims that such schemes are discriminatory.[45] In contrast, the CRPD values decision-making based on individual capacities, social factors, a sliding scale of the degree to which decision-making may be compromised because of disability, and the wishes of the individual concerned.

People with disabilities have claimed that respect for human dignity requires respecting the diversity of disability. Thus, the kind and degree of disability must be considered on an individual level. Mental health schemes that readily base involuntary treatment on the existence, or even appearance, of a mental illness combined with some level of dangerousness conflict with that claim. In regard to general as well as mental health care, people with disabilities have voiced their experience of injustice in systematically not being involved in their own health decisions. The CRPD now serves as a tool of empowerment for people with disabilities by placing strong emphasis on the diversity of disability, and guarantees that people with disabilities have the opportunity to conduct their lives with support, but with a high level of self-determination, including access to services, advocacy and review.

C. Summary

Human dignity and equality are fundamental principles in the international human rights framework of the United Nations. Both are interdependent and interrelated principles. They protect the universal idea that all human beings have an inherent value that needs to be protected on a non-discriminatory basis. Central to developing the CRPD were claims that persons with disabilities were not treated equally and that it was not sufficiently recognised that they are fully entitled subjects of rights. Many of the specific rights and freedoms of the CRPD consistently refer back to human dignity and equality, thus guiding its interpretation and application. The fundamental objectives of the CRPD are to prohibit discrimination based on disability, and to establish the full recognition of persons with disabilities as subjects of rights. These central objectives can now be used as rights-based arguments to challenge state practices.

---

[45] M Donnelly, 'From Autonomy to Dignity: Treatment for Mental Disorders and the Focus for Patient Rights' (2008) 26(2) *Law in Context* 37, 38.

IV. The Impact of the CRPD

The question arises as to what effect the CRPD may have on mental health legislation. Treatment decisions are critical issues in the area of mental health law and human rights. This section assesses in what ways the CRPD addresses decision-making in relation to involuntary mental health treatment. It contrasts the detailed provisions of Article 12 with the silence of Article 17 in relation to requirements, safeguards and limitations.

A. Article 12: Treatment Decisions as a Matter of Equal Possession and Exercise of Legal Capacity

In Article 12, the CRPD guarantees equal recognition before the law and provides that legal capacity is crucial to respecting persons with disabilities. It clearly signals that legal capacity is vital to any realisation of rights. Article 12 further provides the right to possess and exercise legal capacity. By guaranteeing the possession of legal capacity, the CRPD clarifies that persons with disabilities have to be recognised as full bearers of rights regardless of their disabilities. Exercising legal capacity guarantees that persons with disabilities enjoy and realise their rights to the full degree of their capabilities. The CRPD further clarifies that exercising legal capacity may require support. In other words, if deficits in decision-making exist, they do not exclude persons with disabilities from having their rights respected and realised; rather, the individual concerned remains an integral driver of decision-making. Article 12 sets out specific safeguards to prevent abuse and includes respect for the wishes and preferences of the person as one of the safeguards. There are three important core messages in Article 12.

First, Article 12 represents a move away from legal presumptions of incapacity based on disabilities, including mental illness. Legislation such as the Disability Discrimination Act 1992 (Cth), and similar disabilities or equal opportunity legislation at federal and State and Territory level, clarify that the legal capacity of people with disabilities must be presumed. However, the specific provisions of mental health legislation do not fully respect the legal presumption of capacity, as clinical treatment decisions rest on the existence, or even appearance, of mental illness combined with some level of risk assessment. People with disabilities can often be judged to be incapable of controlling their own affairs simply because of their disabilities.[46] Article 12 provides that decision-making is a matter of individual capacities.

Secondly, Article 12 clarifies that while decision-making abilities are central to exercising legal capacity, the free will and preferences of the person concerned are

---

[46] M Jones and LA Basser Marks (eds), *Disability, Divers-ability and Legal Change* (The Hague, Martinus Nijhoff Publishers, 1999) 18.

also of fundamental importance. The underlying reason why Article 12 looks at more than decision-making abilities is that the CRPD has been designed to counteract the power imbalances and abuse of people with disabilities as expressed before and throughout the drafting process. Systematic violation of basic rights occurred despite the inherent good will of many laws. One element that made these violations *invisible* for so long was that people with disabilities were marginalised and systematically placed under guardianship, with their will and preferences being ignored, trivialised or readily trumped by ideas of protection. The CRPD reacted to claims that, while people with disabilities need to have their individual abilities respected, they are not defined by their abilities or disabilities, but by their inherent self-worth.[47] An expression of how people with disabilities want to define their lives must be an integral part of decision-making, as a driver and as a safeguard of decision-making. Placing value on individual preferences and respecting other forms of decision-making safeguards are central to respecting someone as a subject of rights.

Thirdly, Article 12 calls for a nuanced model of decision-making that is marked by self-direction, support and a set of important safeguards. The following section addresses the conceptualisation of this model in further detail.

(i)   Self-Direction as a Guiding Principle

The important starting premise of the CRPD is that it clearly recognises persons with disabilities as equal bearers of human rights and fundamental freedoms. Stemming from this premise, it guarantees that people with disabilities are presumed to be legally capable of making their own decisions and having their right to self-determination respected on an equal basis with people in general health care settings. Article 12 aims to facilitate a clear move away from clinician-based decision-making: a move that has taken place in general health care settings, but has not yet translated to the mental health disability sector. Respect for self-direction is central to the CRPD's paradigm shift in the perception of people with disabilities from objects of welfare to subjects of rights.

The CRPD clearly recognises the diversity and social context of disabilities, and it incorporates that kind of understanding of disabilities into its decision-making model. It recognises that decision-making is typically not a clear-cut matter where people have either full or no capacity to decide on treatment decisions. Rather, what is relevant is the decision at hand and the abilities of the individual. Mental illness can impede the rationality of decision-making on different levels, as decision-making is a process of understanding the facts involved, appreciating their nature and significance, processing information and reasoning, as well as

---

[47]   G Quinn and T Degener, *Human Rights and Disability: The Current Use and Future Potential of United Nations Human Rights Instruments in the Context of Disability* (New York, United Nations, 2002) 14.

deliberating and choosing one option.[48] Assessing whether an individual with mental illness has capacity to make a decision is complicated and often a matter of degree. However, the CRPD clearly provides that States Parties must take action in order to accommodate the realisation of the rights and freedoms of persons with disabilities, and must finance improved services.

Persons who are not mentally ill can refuse even potentially life-saving treatment based on beliefs that others might find incomprehensible, while those subject to a restrictive mental health scheme cannot take any risks when the mental health legislation is based on best interest considerations or considerations of what is necessary for that person. However, taking risks is an element of many health decisions and life in general that should be safeguarded, not excluded. Legal schemes that exclude people with mental illness from all significant levels of decision-making run counter to human rights principles and can result in counter-therapeutic resignation or hostility towards the providers of treatment. The CRPD emphasises respect for the preferences of persons with disabilities.

Rather than strictly defining to what point preferences need to be protected, the CRPD aims to guarantee the greatest possible collaboration between the person with disability and the clinician. It carefully refrains from using language that can be interpreted in absolute terms.[49] However, by respecting the preferences of the individual concerned, the CRPD readily allows for guiding decision-making based on previous decisions or psychiatric advance directives as an indicator as to what the person would have wanted.

(ii)   Self-Direction through Supported Decision-Making

Following from the position that capacity is a central consideration to decision-making and that capacity is a matter of a sliding scale, the CRPD endorses that deficits in capacity should lead to supported decision-making.[50] It aims to enhance equality by considering impairments only where necessary and only to the degree to which they make a difference to decision-making.

---

[48]   Loosely based on considerations of the MacArthur Competence Assessment Tool for Treatment considerations, as developed by T Grisso, PS Appelbaum and C Hill-Fotouhi, 'The MacCAT-T: A Clinical Tool to Assess Patient's Capacities to Make Treatment Decisions' (1997) 48 *Psychiatric Services* 1415.

[49]   Some scholars interpret the CRPD in more absolute terms, eg see Tina Minkowitz, this volume, ch 7.

[50]   See also A Lawson, 'The United Nations Convention on the Rights of Persons with Disabilities: New Era or False Dawn?' (2007) 34(2) *Syracuse Journal of International Law and Commerce* 563, 597.

The CRPD aims to facilitate a careful approach to identifying deficits and developing assistance to overcome these deficits, rather than automatically subjecting persons with impairments in decision-making to substituted decision-making.[51] Methods to achieve supported decision-making include establishing and improving existing support services, community engagement and networks, as well as personal assistance.[52] This approach ensures that persons with disabilities are properly assessed as to their capabilities and that impairments only make a difference to the extent that they actually affect decision-making. The CRPD aims to prevent people with disabilities being systematically cut off from decision-making purely based on their 'status' as being 'disabled'.

Article 12 calls for States Parties to develop models of supported decision-making that respect, protect and fulfill a person's legal capacity most effectively and accommodate deficits in decision-making capacities. The range of people who can act as a support person can vary quite significantly, and support schemes may need to be adjusted to the realities of countries with limited resources. It is possible to incorporate a system of nominated or appointed persons to assist in decision-making, ranging from lay persons and independent advocates to experts in the field. Lay support persons may range from family members, friends and partners to any other selected person. Independent advocates may be social workers, lawyers, carers or persons with other relevant qualifications and experience who are able to provide formal advice and legal assistance to the person. If the person is unable to nominate a support person, an appropriate authority can be granted power to appoint a support person for them. The details as to how such a system will meet the demands of practice have to be trialed and subjected to regular review.

Importantly, Article 12 suggests that treatment decisions for people with mental disabilities are guided by clinical criteria, as in general health settings, but not decided by a clinician alone.

(iii) Decision-Making Safeguards

Article 12 includes important decision-making safeguards. It clarifies that any measure relating to exercising legal capacity must respect the rights and preferences of the person concerned. It must also be free of any conflict of interest and undue influence, be proportional and tailored to the person's circumstances, apply for the shortest time possible and be subject to regular review by a competent, independent and impartial authority or judicial body.

---

[51] See G Quinn and T Degener, *Human Rights and Disability: The Current Use and Future Potential of United Nations Human Rights Instruments in the Context of Disability* (New York, United Nations, 2002) 16.

[52] T Minkowitz, 'The United Nations Convention on the Rights of Persons with Disabilities and the Right to Be Free from Nonconsensual Psychiatric Interventions' (2007) 34(2) *Syracuse Journal of International Law and Commerce* 405, 409.

These specifications ensure that capacity is assessed as a matter of degree and that any limitations in exercising legal capacity are subject to proper review procedures. They also aim to ensure an environment that clearly recognises and respects the rights of people with disabilities. The formulation of these safeguards is precise and careful, and it appears that Article 12 was drafted in the light of the great potential for abuse in placing limitations on exercising legal capacities.

The CRPD considers the preferences of persons with disabilities without scrutinising them as to whether those preferences are reasonable—an element that is unusual in domestic laws dealing with involuntary treatment. Mental Health legislation typically deals with the truly problematic cases or worst-case scenarios in order to clarify the application of the law. It would not have been surprising to find an exception outlined in Article 12, such as an exception for people with such severe disabilities that they may not be able to form or express a preference; for example, those who are unconscious or suffer from severe brain damage or severe dementia. However, Article 12 outlines no exceptions, but assumes that those who need support with their decision-making will make better decisions when they are thoroughly engaged with their support persons and that overriding their preferences will have counter-productive effects. Considering a person's preferences may also lead to their trust in treatment decisions.

One other specifically mentioned safeguard for exercising legal capacity is the respect of other rights. This opens the way to interpret and apply Article 12 in light of other human rights and fundamental freedoms of equal importance, as assessed and balanced in the individual circumstances.

(iv) *The Silence on Substituted Decision-making*

As Article 12 aims to facilitate decision-making *with* the person, rather than *for* the person, it moves away from the concept of substituted decision-making. In its extensive clarifications, Article 12 does not mention substituted decision-making as a legitimate limitation at all, even though substituted decision-making was extensively debated during the drafting process of the CRPD. There are arguments stressing that the reality of mental health services means that support is not always sufficient in all cases: thus substituted decision-making must exist as a measure of last resort, at least on a case-by-case basis.[53] There are people who have undergone involuntary treatment that was beneficial to them and improved their lives. However, the CRPD, by not mentioning substituted decision-making, indicates that there should be no disability-specific exceptions to decision-making models, and that limitations should be subject to the same high level of scrutiny that they are in general health care settings. If substituted decision-making must take place, it must be a matter of individual assessment and must be applied restrictively and consistently with other rights and freedoms of the

---

[53] R Kayess and B Fogarty, 'The Rights and Dignity of Persons with Disabilities: A United Nations Convention' (2007) 32(1) *Alternative Law Journal* 22, 23.

CRPD. In particular, substituted decision-making must be based on principles of equality and respect elements of self-direction, such as advance directives.

Current mental health legislation clearly conflicts with the tenor of Article 12. It rests on a scheme of substituted decision-making based on requirements that can be applied and interpreted very broadly. This scheme of substituted decision-making lasts for extended periods of time, allows for a broad range of treatment, including intensive and irreversible kinds of treatment, and is subject to limited review.

B.   Article 17: The Integrity of the Person

Article 17 ensures that every person with disabilities has the right to respect for his or her physical and mental integrity on an equal basis with others. It is remarkable that Article 17 is the only provision within the formulation of the CRPD that does not include any further clarification or amplification. During the drafting process matters of involuntary treatment and detention were discussed under Article 17, as involuntary interventions clearly affect the physical and mental integrity of the person.[54] However, Article 17 does not provide insight into whether involuntary interventions can be justified or, if they are justified, whether they should be subjected to limitations or safeguards. During the drafting process it was suggested that the following amendments to the text of Article 17 be incorporated:[55]

2.   States Parties shall protect persons with disabilities from forced interventions or forced institutionalization aimed at correcting, improving or alleviating any actual or perceived impairment.
3.   In cases of medical emergency or issues of risk to public health involving involuntary interventions, persons with disabilities shall be treated on an equal basis with others.
[4.   States Parties shall ensure that involuntary treatment of persons with disabilities is:

   (a)   minimized through the active promotion of alternatives;
   (b)   undertaken only in exceptional circumstances, in accordance with procedures established by law and with the application of appropriate legal safeguards;
   (c)   undertaken in the least restrictive setting possible, and that the best interests of the person concerned are fully taken into account;
   (d)   appropriate for the person and provided without financial cost to the individual receiving the treatment or to his or her family.]

---

[54] On the drafting process, see B McSherry, 'Protecting the Integrity of the Person: Developing Limitations on Involuntary Treatment' (2008) 26(2) *Law in Context* 111.

[55] United Nations, General Assembly's Ad Hoc Committee on a Comprehensive and Integral International Convention on the Protection and Promotion of the Rights and Dignity of Persons with Disabilities, 7th session, 16 January–3 February 2006, A/AC.265/2006/2, available at: www.un.org/esa/socdev/enable/rights/ahc7report-e.htm.

However, these amendments were dropped entirely. Some commentators criticised the mention of involuntary interventions as authorising their existence, inhibiting their substantial scrutiny and re-establishing differential treatment for people with disabilities; while others feared that not mentioning safeguards and limitations would leave people without any real protection.[56] As agreement was not reached, Article 17 remains a single statement, the development and interpretation of which is subject to continuous scrutiny.

V. The Use of Silence

The question arises in what ways the CRPD actually challenges involuntary treatment schemes through Article 17, given that it is silent as to what it means in practice. This will be discussed in comparison with Article 12 and its detailed specifications.

A. The Clear Guidance of Article 12 on Treatment Decision-Making Processes

(i) The Use of Terminology within the CRPD

The CRPD drafters incorporated a remarkably careful approach to using terminology. They aimed to elaborate on already established human rights terminology and yet endeavoured to clarify what certain terminology means in the context of disability. This careful approach resulted from experiences of abuse and exclusion that occurred systematically despite the fact that the international human rights framework already protected the human rights of people with disabilities. It reflected the experience that even well-intentioned legislation could be interpreted and applied restrictively, thus hindering the achievement of substantial equality. Even the crucial clarification of to whom the CRPD applies is significantly marked by this careful approach. During the drafting process of the CRPD a definition of disability was considered. However, it was feared that a definition could unintentionally exclude some individuals, as disability is so divergent and capable of changing. The CRPD thus incorporated a description of

---

[56] See A Lawson, 'The United Nations Convention on the Rights of Persons with Disabilities: New Era or False Dawn?' (2007) 34 *Syracuse Journal of International Law and Commerce* 563, 608*ff*; AA Dhir, 'Human Rights Treaty Drafting through the Lens of Mental Disability: The Proposed International Convention on Protection and Promotion of the Rights and Dignity of Persons with Disabilities' (2005) 41 *Stanford Journal of International Law* 181, 202*ff*; R Kayess and B Fogarty, 'The Rights and Dignity of Persons with Disabilities: A United Nations Convention' (2007) 32(1) *Alternative Law Journal* 22, 26; B McSherry, 'Protecting the Integrity of the Person: Developing Limitations on Involuntary Treatment' (2008) 26(2) *Law in Context* 111, 112*ff*.

disability, rather than a definition, in order not to exclude people who should be covered by the CRPD and to safeguard against such an interpretation.

The remarkable length of the CRPD in comparison with other human rights treaties also shows that it followed a very descriptive approach to clarifying human rights and fundamental freedoms in the context of disability. The extensive preamble and lengthy formulations of specific rights and freedoms illustrate the fine interaction between the formulation of underlying principles and values with the concrete expressions of rights and freedoms. The terminology used in Article 12 clarifies the meaning and understanding of legal capacity and its interconnection with the right to equal recognition before the law, and addresses clear safeguards and limitations. As such, Article 12 provides set terminology for rights-based arguments and links it back to underlying values and principles to assure their consistent interpretation and application.

(ii) Limitations of Set Terminology

While the choice of terminology can enhance the understanding and application of rights, it also runs the risk of abuse or narrow interpretation—a risk that seems to grow where interpretation is as politically motivated as it is in international human rights law.

For example, involuntary orders in domestic mental health laws have been based on loose criteria that can give rise to undefined concepts in practice, such as 'lack of insight'.[57] This concept has been subject to criticism, as it is open to broad interpretation with the potential for overuse. 'Lack of insight' is a term that has been criticised for being frequently used as a justification for not discharging people from involuntary orders.[58] It is also difficult to determine what level of insight is necessary in deciding whether a person can consent to treatment.[59] Beyond this, the term runs the risk of being interpreted interchangeably with non-compliance.[60] It has the potential to be loosely used, referring generally to a person who has not fully accepted a particular diagnostic label.[61] Also, as medication can affect the processing of information and communication with

---

[57] See Genevra Richardson and Ian Freckelton, this volume, chs 8 and 9.

[58] K Diesfeld, 'Insight: Unpacking the Concept in Mental Health Law' (2003) 10(1) *Psychiatry, Psychology and Law* 63, 63 and references therein.

[59] See K Diesfeld and B McKenna, *Insight and Other Puzzles: Undefined Terms in the New Zealand Mental Health Review Tribunal*, Summary Report (Wellington, Mental Health Commission, 2006) available at: www.mhc.govt.nz/users/Image/Resources/2006%20Publications/20061207DIESFELD_SUMMARY.PDF; I Freckelton, 'Distractors and Distressors in Involuntary Status Decision-Making' (2005) 12(1) *Psychiatry, Psychology and Law* 88, 91 and 93.

[60] See K Diesfeld and B McKenna, *Insight and Other Puzzles: Undefined Terms in the New Zealand Mental Health Review Tribunal*, Summary Report (Wellington, Mental Health Commission, 2006) available at: www.mhc.govt.nz/users/Image/Resources/2006%20Publications/20061207DIESFELD_SUMMARY.PDF; I Freckelton, 'Distractors and Distressors in Involuntary Status Decision-Making' (2005) 12(1) *Psychiatry, Psychology and Law* 88, 91.

[61] I Freckelton, 'Distractors and Distressors in Involuntary Status Decision-Making' (2005) 12(1) *Psychiatry, Psychology and Law* 88, 91.

the clinician, it can affect 'insight'. The criterion of 'lack of insight' has been identified as also running the risk of being applied with circularity, if lack of insight is seen as an indicator of mental illness.[62]

As explored by Penelope Weller in chapter three of this volume, the criterion of dangerousness, which is also commonly used in mental health legislation, has also been subject to criticism.

B.   The Vagueness of Article 17

The advantage of Article 17's silence as to its meaning is that it does not provide terminology that can be interpreted narrowly, possibly with the intent to avoid change. In particular, it does not re-instate established terminology. The silence of Article 17 suggests that States Parties must re-think their involuntary treatment schemes in the light of CRPD principles. Considerations of dangerousness will, in particular, have to be justified in departing from the general principle that treatment should be voluntary-based.

C.   Australia's Declaration Breaking the Silence

The idea of not including set terminology within the scope of Article 17 has been disregarded by Australia. When Australia ratified the CRPD, it declared its understanding that the CRPD allows for 'fully supported or substituted decision-making arrangements, which provide for decisions to be made on behalf of a person, only where such arrangements are necessary, as a last resort and subject to safeguards' and it allows for 'compulsory assistance or treatment of persons, including measures taken for the treatment of mental disability, where such treatment is necessary, as a last resort and subject to safeguards'. As a true measure of last resort, substituted decision-making and involuntary treatment do seem to reflect the reality of clinical practice, as it is hard to imagine that there will no longer be any instances where substituted decision-making and forced treatment may take place.

However, the actual formulation of this declaration is very broad and contravenes the spirit of the CRPD, in particular in regard to its careful use of terminology. Resting the declaration on what is 'necessary' may lead to scrutiny of State and Territory measures that impede human rights and fundamental freedoms. This may in particular be the case in a legal system that has a strong and well-established human rights culture with clear guidance as to how to interpret and apply human rights principles within the framework of domestic laws. However, the human rights culture in domestic Australian law is still in its infancy and lacks potency in terms of enforcing human rights. Thus, including

---

[62]   *ibid.*

set terminology such as what is 'necessary' has the potential to be interpreted broadly and runs the risk of re-instating the status quo.

In Australia, previous reforms of domestic mental health legislation were drafted under the premise of delivering involuntary measures in the least restrictive environment only. They have reportedly failed to realise the basic human rights and fundamental freedoms of people with mental illnesses— measured on a standard lower than that of the CRPD. The vague formulation of what is 'necessary', 'a last resort' and 'subject to safeguards' does not seem to deliver a new standard of treatment and care. The formulation Australia used in its declaration is susceptible to the risk of continuing differential treatment to people based on the existence of mental illness.

As a declaration, Australia's declaration serves to clarify the understanding and the interpretation of Articles 12 and 17. Unlike a reservation, it cannot exclude or alter the legal effect of the CRPD.[63] However, the political effect of such a declaration is nevertheless wide-ranging. On a formal basis, it can be easily quoted in policy-making, service delivery and law reform to confirm that the current mental health legislation complies with international human rights standards as interpreted in light of Australia's declaration. When people with disabilities voiced their experience of being systematically cut off from their human rights realisation, it was central to their claims that this kind of formal equality was not sufficiently translated into concrete terms that could have established their substantial equality.

D. Concluding Comments

The silence of Article 17 can be interpreted in light of its historical development, its underlying principles and values and other rights and freedoms of the CRPD. The fact that Article 17's silence aimed to deliberately expose involuntary measures to ongoing scrutiny is an important starting-point for its interpretation and application. It has the potential to challenge the substance, and even existence, of established mental health schemes that readily expose people with mental illness to involuntary treatment. It can facilitate a thorough re-assessment of mental health care and how best outcomes can be achieved. This incentive towards re-assessment is underpinned by the approach of Article 12, which considers mental illness and impaired decision-making capacities as matters to be resolved through support rather than substitution. Australia's declaration seems to prevent such a discussion and rather seems to reiterate that the status quo of mental health care is satisfactory, despite many reports to the contrary.

---

[63] Vienna Convention on the Law of Treaties, opened for signature 23 May 1969, 1155 UNTS 331 (entered into force 27 January 1980) Art 2.

Considerations supporting involuntary treatment may still be based on respecting and realising other human rights and fundamental freedoms. However, weighing conflicting rights requires a high level of scrutiny and individual assessment. What the CRPD aims to portray is that disability itself cannot justify differential treatment, as it contradicts respecting the dignity, worth and equality of human beings. Respecting the dignity, worth and equality of human beings is central to the interpretation and application of all the human rights and fundamental freedoms of the CRPD.[64] The dignity of a person is a concept that may enhance the human rights protection of people with disabilities further than the principle of autonomy; at the very least it will supplement respecting the principle of autonomy in instances where the autonomy of people with mental disabilities has been readily questioned. The CRPD thus provides people with disabilities with a standard to articulate their human rights claims and to call for equality beyond differences.

---

[64] P Carozza, 'Human Dignity and Judicial Interpretation of Human Rights: A Reply' (2008) 19(5) *European Journal of International Law* 931, 932.

7

Abolishing Mental Health Laws to Comply with the Convention on the Rights of Persons with Disabilities

TINA MINKOWITZ

I. Introduction

The Convention on the Rights of Persons with Disabilities (CRPD)[1] requires not only a rethinking of mental health laws (laws that simultaneously legitimise and limit coercive state power in relation to confinement and psychiatric 'treatment' of people labelled with a mental illness), but a rethinking of the concept of 'mental health law'. 'Mental health law' suggests the regulation of a profession or service industry, in which case the natural constituency for consultation is the clinicians and service providers. The CRPD starts from a broader and more fundamental premise, non-discrimination based on disability, and takes as its natural constituency the people whose rights are affected, that is, people with disabilities.

The CRPD, in contrast to earlier standards such as the non-binding Principles for the Protection of Persons with Mental Illness and for the Improvement of Mental Health Care (the MI Principles),[2] does not permit the imposition of coercive measures in the supposed 'best interest' of an adult person with a disability (such as guardianship, psychiatric detention and compulsory treatment).[3] Instead, the CRPD takes a holistic approach to human rights and

---

[1] Convention on the Rights of Persons with Disabilities (CRPD), adopted 13 December 2006, GA Res 61/106, UN Doc A/Res/61/106 (entered into force 3 May 2008).

[2] Principles for the Protection of Persons with Mental Illness and for the Improvement of Mental Health Care, UN Doc A/RES/48/119, 17 December 1991.

[3] Interim Report of the Special Rapporteur on Torture and other Cruel, Inhuman and Degrading Treatment or Punishment (SR Torture Interim Report), 28 July 2008, UN Doc A/63/175, at [44].

provides for supportive measures to facilitate individual development and autonomy, with equal rights and responsibilities as fundamental to human dignity.

II. Status of the CRPD

The CRPD is the eighth core human rights treaty of the United Nations, having entered into force on 3 May 2008.[4] As such, it is binding international law on all States Parties.

As a thematic treaty dealing with the rights of persons with disabilities, the CRPD also affects the interpretation of other treaty obligations both directly and indirectly. The United Nations human rights system, particularly with reference to the core treaties, is moving towards harmonisation, with increased co-ordination of reporting and unification of standards.[5] Treaty bodies dealing with civil and political rights, torture, children's rights and other areas will look to the CRPD for guidance in developing their own jurisprudence and normative guidelines affecting the rights of persons with disabilities.

The CRPD also governs the United Nations agencies in their work on the rights of persons with disabilities. Thus, the Office of the High Commissioner for Human Rights has issued documents going to the Human Rights Council and to their own field offices, applying the CRPD in areas such as legal capacity and detention based on disability.[6]

Holders of mandates under the Special Procedures of the Human Rights Council, such as the Special Rapporteur on Torture, also draw on the CRPD as part of the international legal framework. Manfred Nowak, the current Special Rapporteur on Torture (the Special Rapporteur), has articulated standards relating to torture and persons with disabilities in a report,[7] drawing on provisions of the CRPD 'complementary to the international legal framework against torture'.[8] These standards are likely to be used by treaty bodies considering country reports and individual complaints, as well as by the Special Rapporteur

---

[4] For further background to the CRPD, see T Minkowitz, 'Disability Convention Advocacy by the World Network of Users and Survivors of Psychiatry: The Emergence of a User/Survivor Perspective in Human Rights', in M Sabatello and M Schultze (eds) *Voices from Within – Civil Society's Involvement in the Drafting of the CRPD* (Forthcoming).

[5] See, *Strengthening of the United Nations: An Agenda for Further Change* Report of the Secretary-General, 9 September 2002, UN Doc A/57/387 at [54].

[6] Thematic Study by the Office of the United Nations High Commissioner for Human Rights on Enhancing Awareness and Understanding of the Convention on the Rights of Persons with Disabilities (OHCHR Legal Measures Study) UN Doc A/HRC/10/48, 26 January 2009, see especially paras 48–49; Dignity and Justice for Detainees Week, Information Note No 4: Persons with Disabilities available at: psychrights.org/Countries/UN/detentioninfonote1.pdf.

[7] Interim Report of the Special Rapporteur on Torture and other Cruel, Inhuman and Degrading Treatment or Punishment (SR Torture Interim Report), 28 July 2008, UN Doc A/63/175.

[8] *ibid*, at [44].

himself in his exercise of the mandate to transmit urgent appeals and letters of allegation regarding cases of torture and ill-treatment.

The CRPD supersedes the MI Principles, which should no longer be considered valid even as a non-binding standard. While there is no established mechanism by which declarations of the United Nations can be disavowed, adoption by the UN General Assembly of the CRPD constitutes a subsequent declaration on the same subject-matter, so that the MI Principles must be considered as superseded to the extent of any conflict.[9] Direct conflict exists with respect to guardianship, detention, and forced or non-consensual treatment (permitted by the MI Principles, excluded by the CRPD)[10]. In addition, the MI Principles contain a general limitation clause on the exercise of all rights,[11] beyond what is permissible under the International Covenant on Civil and Political Rights[12] and the Convention against Torture and Other Cruel, Inhuman or Degrading Treatment or Punishment,[13] and extending even to non-derogable rights such as the right to be free from torture. For this reason, the MI Principles as a whole cannot be considered compatible with current human rights standards and should be abandoned. Since the CRPD comprehensively guarantees all human rights and fundamental freedoms to all persons with disabilities, anything of value remaining in the MI Principles can be derived from the CRPD, and in many cases is set forth in the CRPD in stronger terms. For example, the right of persons with

---

[9] See (2008) 3 *Enable Newsletter* 3, in which the UN Secretariat for the CRPD acknowledges: 'It is important to note that some provisions of the Principles for the Protection of Persons with Mental Illness and the Improvement of Mental Health Care have been criticised and the Convention on the Rights of Persons with Disabilities now supersedes these standards to the extent that there is any conflict between the two instruments'. See also, International Disability Alliance, *Position Paper on the Convention on the Rights of Persons with Disabilities (CRPD) and Other Instruments*, available at: www.internationaldisabilityalliance.org/documents_working_group/IDA_CRPD_paper_final.doc.

[10] Interim Report of the Special Rapporteur on Torture and other Cruel, Inhuman and Degrading Treatment or Punishment (SR Torture Interim Report), 28 July 2008, UN Doc A/63/175, at [44].

[11] The general limitations clause of the Principles for the Protection of Persons with Mental Illness and the Improvement of Mental Health states: 'The exercise of the rights set forth in the present Principles may be subject only to such limitations as are prescribed by law and are necessary to protect the health or safety of the person concerned or of others, or otherwise to protect public safety, order, health or morals or the fundamental rights and freedoms of others'. In the International Covenant on Civil and Political Rights, there are some rights that are non-derogable, others that are derogable in situations of 'public emergency which threatens the life of the nation and which is officially proclaimed' (ICCPR Art 4.1), and still others that are limited in terms such as: 'The above-mentioned rights shall not be subject to any restrictions except those which are provided by law, are necessary to protect national security, public order (*ordre public*), public health or morals or the rights and freedoms of others, and are consistent with the other rights recognized in the present Covenant' (ICCPR Art 12). The limitations clause in the Principles for the Protection of Persons with Mental Illness and the Improvement of Mental Health encompasses all these rights insofar as they are 'set forth' in that document, and thus goes farther then any of the ICCPR limitations.

[12] International Covenant on Civil and Political Rights, opened for signature 16 December 1966, 999 UNTS 171 (entered into force 23 March 1976).

[13] Convention against Torture and Other Cruel, Inhuman or Degrading Treatment or Punishment, adopted by UN GA Res 39/46 of 10 December 1984 (entered into force 26 June 1987).

disabilities to live in the community in the CRPD is unequivocally recognised on an equal basis with others,[14] rather than 'to the extent possible'[15] as in the MI Principles.

All states should be encouraged to ratify and fully implement the CRPD and its optional protocol, without any reservations or declarations. States that have not yet done so should not apply the MI Principles but instead should accept the CRPD as non-binding guidance and work towards ratification; in addition they are bound by CRPD standards to the extent they are used in the authoritative interpretation of treaties to which the state is a party, and to the extent they may become part of customary international law.

One other aspect of the CRPD must be noted in relation to its status in international law. This is the high level of participation of civil society as well as states in its creation, particularly the participation of the persons whose human rights are affected.[16] Christiana Ochoa and other scholars argue that civil society and individuals, as well as states, have a role in the creation of customary international law.[17] The rejection of the MI Principles by international organisations of users and survivors of psychiatry—particularly by the World Network of Users and Survivors of Psychiatry (WNUSP), which is governed by a democratically elected board and is open to all users and survivors without ideological limitation—is evidence that this document is unacceptable to those whose human rights are directly affected.[18] In contrast, WNUSP played a central role in the drafting and negotiation of the CRPD, which is strongly informed by a user/survivor perspective.

III. Users and Survivors of Psychiatry Covered By the CRPD

CRPD Article 1 on 'purpose' includes the language:

---

[14] Convention on the Rights of Persons with Disabilities (CRPD), adopted 13 December 2006, GA Res 61/106, UN Doc A/Res/61/106 (entered into force 3 May 2008) Art 19.

[15] Principles for the Protection of Persons with Mental Illness and the Improvement of Mental Health Care, Principle 3.

[16] See T Minkowitz, 'Disability Convention Advocacy by the World Network of Users and Survivors of Psychiatry: The Emergence of a User/Survivor Perspective in Human Rights', in M Sabatello and M Schultze (eds) *Voices from Within – Civil Society's Involvement in the Drafting of the CRPD* (Forthcoming).

[17] C Ochoa, 'The Individual and Customary International Law Formation' (2007–08) 48 *Virginia Journal of International Law* 119.

[18] Statement of WNUSP – the World Network of Users and Survivors of Psychiatry, for the Meeting of Experts on the International Convention to Promote and Protect the Rights and Dignity of Persons with Disabilities in Mexico City, 11–14 June 2002, Produced by T Minkowitz in cooperation with K Bach Jensen; World Network of Users and Survivors of Psychiatry, Position Paper on the Principles for the Protection of Persons with Mental Illness (2001).

Persons with disabilities include those who have long-term physical, mental, intellectual or sensory impairments which in interaction with various barriers may hinder their full and effective participation in society on an equal basis with others.

In this context, 'persons with mental impairments which in interaction with various barriers may hinder their full and effective participation in society on an equal basis with others' refers to users and survivors of psychiatry or persons with psychosocial disabilities (two alternative terms referring to the same group of people, which WNUSP has promoted in preference to 'mental illness' or other language).[19] Negotiating states preferred the term 'mental' to 'psychosocial' for the CRPD text, but it is clear that it means psychosocial rather than intellectual disability, as 'intellectual impairment' is mentioned separately.

The reference to 'long-term' impairment should not be taken to exclude those whose disability is intermittent or of shorter duration. Elsewhere in the CRPD, there are obligations that must be complied with at an early stage of disability before it may become clear whether an impairment is of long or short duration (such as early provision of services),[20] and obligations of non-discrimination that do not even depend on the actual existence of a disability but would also apply in the case of imputed or perceived disability.[21] The experience of disability depends on the degree to which disability (including discrimination based on imputed disability) has affected and continues to affect one's life, and can vary depending on accommodations and social context.

Post-adoption application of the CRPD by the Special Rapporteur on Torture[22] and the Office of the High Commissioner for Human Rights[23] affirms that people with psychosocial disabilities as a group of persons with disabilities, and forms of discrimination arising in the mental health context as such, are indeed covered by the CRPD. However, the relationship of psychosocial disability to 'mental illness' and health status needs to be clarified. Diagnosis of a mental illness or subjective experience of oneself as having a mental illness comes within the concept of 'mental disability' under the CRPD, and discrimination based on

[19] See WNUSP Statutes, available at: wnusp.rafus.dk/wnusp-statutes.html, and the International Disability Alliance CRPD Forum submission to the Office of the High Commissioner for Human Rights (OHCHR) Thematic Study on Psychosocial disability, available at: www.internationaldisabilityalliance. org/advocacy-work/office-of-the-high-commissioner-on-human-rights/.

[20] Art 25(b) of the CRPD refers to health services, including early identification and intervention as appropriate, and Art 26(a) requires states to ensure that habilitation and rehabilitation programmes begin at the earliest possible stage.

[21] See particularly Art 2 of the CRPD (definition of discrimination based on disability) and Arts 4 and 5 (general obligations and obligations relating to non-discrimination).

[22] Interim Report of the Special Rapporteur on Torture and other Cruel, Inhuman and Degrading Treatment or Punishment (SR Torture Interim Report), 28 July 2008, UN Doc A/63/175.

[23] Thematic Study by the Office of the United Nations High Commissioner for Human Rights on Enhancing Awareness and Understanding of the Convention on the Rights of Persons with Disabilities (OHCHR Legal Measures Study) UN Doc A/HRC/10/48, 26 January 2009, see especially paras 48–49; Dignity and Justice for Detainees Week, Information Note No 4: Persons with Disabilities available at: www.psychrights.org/Countries/UN/detentioninfonote1.pdf.

'mental illness' or 'mental health status' is governed by the CRPD as the most recent set of standards, with enhanced legitimacy due to the high degree of participation by this group in the creation of the CRPD. In general, discrimination based on 'health status'[24] is likely to be covered under the CRPD, as the concept of disability includes the allegation or experience of health problems insofar as they have a social dimension and human rights implications.

IV. Analysis of Specific Provisions of the CRPD

A. Legal Capacity

Article 12 of the CRPD requires States Parties to

> recognize that persons with disabilities enjoy legal capacity on an equal basis with others in all aspects of life.[25]

This is complemented by an obligation to

> provide access to support that persons with disabilities may require in exercising their legal capacity[26]

and to ensure that

> all measures related to the exercise of legal capacity establish safeguards to prevent abuse in accordance with international law.[27]

Safeguards must ensure that measures

> respect the rights, will and preferences of the person, are free from conflict of interest and undue influence, are proportional and tailored to the person's circumstances, apply for the shortest time possible and are subject to regular review by a competent, independent and impartial authority or judicial body. The safeguards shall be proportional to the degree to which the measures affect the person's rights and interests.[28]

Article 12 does not provide for substituted decision-making, unlike another version that was considered by the negotiating parties.[29]

---

[24] See Committee on Economic, Social and Cultural Rights (CESCR), *General Comment No 14*, para 18; also CESCR *General Comment No 20*, compare paras 28 and 33. Persons living with HIV/AIDS are considered persons with disabilities under the US Americans with Disabilities Act, *Bragdon v Abbott*, 524 US 624 (1998).

[25] Convention on the Rights of Persons with Disabilities (CRPD), adopted 13 December 2006, GA Res 61/106, UN Doc A/Res/61/106 (entered into force 3 May 2008) Art 12, para 2.

[26] *ibid*, Art 12, para 3.

[27] *ibid*, Art 12, para 4.

[28] *ibid*, Art 12, para 4.

[29] Substituted decision-making is not explicitly prohibited in Art 12 of the CRPD, and the phrase 'measures related to the exercise of legal capacity' in para 4 could, standing alone, be read as including

(i) Implications of the Support Model

Simply put, Article 12 means that a person who experiences difficulties with decision-making must be supported to make his or her own decisions, rather than having the right to make decisions taken away and given to another person (substitute decision-maker) to exercise in his or her place. If a person does not want support, he or she has the right to make decisions without using support. Safeguards to prevent abuse of support are aimed at making sure that support is adequate to meet the person's needs and that such support does not represent a limitation on autonomy.[30]

Article 12 does not answer all questions that may arise in relation to legal capacity, but provides guidance in resolving such questions so as to respect the equal rights and dignity of persons with disabilities. Even in quite extreme situations such as the conditions known as persistent vegetative state and coma, or loss of consciousness, the principles of support can be applied so as to give full respect to any present communications by the person (which can sometimes be discerned by close associates though missed by others), and if such communications are indeterminate, following the person's previously expressed wishes, abiding values and experience with similar situations. Such principles have already begun to inform decision-making in extreme medical situations, and Article 12 can help to complete the transformation to an autonomy-based approach consistent with the CRPD and the social model of disability. While there is still a need for some residual protocol for immediate life-saving measures when an individual is unconscious, and for ongoing care when there is no

substituted as well as supported decision-making among the measures that must be safeguarded against abuse. However, that phrase must be read in the context of the mandate to respect the will and preferences of the person, which is a key element of the safeguards and expressed in obligatory language, as well as the recognition of equal legal capacity in Art 12, para 2 and the inclusion of 'respect for … individual autonomy including the freedom to make one's own choices' among the guiding principles of the CRPD. The spectrum of safeguards developed under para 4, including the availability of regular review by an independent body, do not presume the existence of substituted decision-making, but on the contrary, will be applied differentially depending on the type of support as well as the nature of the legal act(s) for which support is provided.

[30] See Thematic Study by the Office of the United Nations High Commissioner for Human Rights on enhancing awareness and understanding of the Convention on the Rights of Persons with Disabilities (OHCHR Legal Measures Study), UN Doc A/HRC/10/48, 26 January 2009 para 43 et seq; and *From Exclusion to Equality: Realizing the Rights of Persons with Disabilities: Handbook for Parliamentarians on the Convention on the Rights of Persons with Disabilities and its Optional Protocol* (Parliamentarians Manual) No 14–2007 (Geneva, UNHCR, 2007) 68–70, 89–91, available at: www.ohchr.org/Documents/Publications/training14en.pdf. See also International Disability Alliance CRPD Forum, *Principles on the Implementation of Article 12* (IDA Article 12 Principles), available at: www.internationaldisabilityalliance.org/documents_working_group/Article_12_Principles_Final. doc; World Network of Users and Survivors of Psychiatry, *Implementation Manual for the United Nations Convention on the Rights of Persons with Disabilities* (Odense, WNUSP, 2008), available at: www.wnusp.rafus.dk/documents/WNUSP_CRPD_Manual.doc; Inclusion Europe, *Key Elements of a System of Supported Decision-Making: Position Paper of Inclusion Europe* (Brussels, Inclusion Europe, 2008).

evidence of the person's will and preferences to use as a guide, the use of support to exercise legal capacity and accessible communication[31] should make the latter situation increasingly rare.[32]

The use of support to exercise legal capacity represents a substantial departure from earlier thinking about legal capacity, in which people were socially shamed and legally annihilated (by interdiction or guardianship) if they admitted to having a disability that had an impact upon their decision-making. Even partial guardianship perpetuates this shame and annihilation by removing individual autonomy in particular areas of life. The notion of legal incapacity permeates much law and policy-making about people with disabilities, such as coercive mental health laws, creating a legal limbo in which virtually anything can be justified. Making support available without the loss of autonomy can make it easier for people to acknowledge a need for support and accept such support if desired. Support can only merit the name when it is truly voluntary and when those providing support understand their role as facilitative rather than directive, that is, as an adjunct to the person's own decision-making process rather than as central participants in that process. While the degree and nature of support must be worked out by the parties to a support relationship, the person receiving support always has the right to a final say in his or her own decisions.

The reasoning behind Article 12 is that differences in decision-making ability do not justify the limitation of the right to make decisions, which is an aspect of personhood.[33] People with disabilities, equally as others, have the right to make bad decisions, face the consequences, and to go on with their lives. To mitigate the harsh effects of holding people responsible for bad decisions, protective measures need to be available to all persons, and made relevant to persons with

---

[31] See Convention on the Rights of Persons with Disabilities (CRPD), adopted 13 December 2006, GA Res 61/106, UN Doc A/Res/61/106 (entered into force May 3, 2008) Arts 2, 9, 21.

[32] Inclusion Europe, *Key Elements of a System of Supported Decision-Making: Position Paper of Inclusion Europe* (Brussels, Inclusion Europe, 2008) In their recent position paper, Inclusion Europe reminds us of 'the importance of one of the basic statements of communication theory for people with severe and profound disabilities: "You cannot not communicate!"'. See also *Principles on the Implementation of Article 12* (IDA Article 12 Principles), available at: www.international disabilityalliance.org/documents_working_group/Article_12_Principles_Final.doc; *From Exclusion to Equality: Realizing the Rights of Persons with Disabilities: Handbook for Parliamentarians on the Convention on the Rights of Persons with Disabilities and its Optional Protocol* (Parliamentarians Manual) No 14–2007 (Geneva, UNHCR, 2007) 88–91.

[33] Legal Opinion on Art 12 of the CRPD, signed by, in Argentina: Santos Cifuentes, Christian Courtis, Agustina Palacios; in Australia: Duncan Chappell, Bernadette McSherry; in Brazil, Ana Paula Crosara de Resende, Patricia Garcia Coelho Catani; in Chile: Maria Soledad Cisternas Reyes; in Costa Rica: Rodrigo Jiménez; in Denmark: Holger Kallehauge; in India: Amita Dhanda; in Ireland: Gerard Quinn; in Japan: Yoshikazu Ikehara, Makoto Iwai, Hirobumi Uchida, Mitsuhide Yahiro; in Mexico: Santiago Corcuera Cabezut, Carlos Rios Espinosa; in The Netherlands: Lisa Waddington; in New Zealand: Susan Jane (aka Huhana) Hickey; in Nicaragua: Carlos Emilio Lopez; in Peru: Juan Vicente Ugarte del Pino; in the United Kingdom: Peter Bartlett; in the United States of America: Robert Dinerstein, Arlene S Kanter, Tina Minkowitz, Michael L Perlin, Stephen A Rosenbaum, Susan Stefan, Michael Stein, Michael Waterstone, available at: www.leeds.ac.uk/disability-studies/archiveuk/legal%20opinion/LegalOpinion_Art12_Final.pdf.

disabilities. For example, Argentina's Civil Code includes a provision that can be used by persons with disabilities whose difficulty in decision-making is exploited by other parties in a transaction:

> Acts vitiated by error, fraud, violence, intimidation or subterfuge may be annulled. The nullity or modification of legal acts may also be demanded when one of the parties exploiting the need, recklessness or inexperience of the other obtained thereby an evidently disproportionate and unjustified financial benefit.[34]

(ii)   Capacity to Act

In a background paper prepared for the Ad Hoc Committee during its negotiation of the CRPD, the Office of the High Commissioner for Human Rights concluded that legal capacity is

> a wider concept [that is, wider than legal personality] that logically presupposes the capability to be a potential holder of rights and obligations (static element), but also entails the capacity to exercise these rights and to undertake these duties by way of one's own conduct, i.e. without assistance of representation by a third party (dynamic element).[35]

The static element is sometimes referred to as 'capacity for rights' and the dynamic element as 'capacity to act'. The dynamic element also comprises 'functional' or 'contractual' capacity, and the exercise of legal capacity.

Legal capacity as referred to in Article 12 does not distinguish between the static and the dynamic elements but accords legal capacity as a whole to persons with disabilities on an equal basis with others. There can be no legal consequences to an assessment of a person's decision-making abilities or request for support in making decisions. The doctrine that competence (in the sense of ability) is a prerequisite for valid decision-making needs to be reviewed in all subject-matter areas of the law and changed in appropriate ways to reflect Article 12, so that persons with disabilities are not legally disadvantaged in exercising autonomy and participating in the legal system.

The term 'capacity' has two meanings that have been conflated in the traditional understanding of 'legal capacity', to the detriment of persons with disabilities. Capacity can mean ability, or internal resources, as in 'capacity-building' enabling an individual or organisation to take on new tasks. However, it can also mean legal standing of a sort, as in the capacity of a court to hear a particular type of case. Legal standing rather than ability is implied by 'capacity for rights', which is applied to all human beings from birth, and similarly the capacity to act

---

[34] Argentina Civil Code Art 954.

[35] *Background Conference Document Prepared by the Office of the United Nations High Commissioner for Human Rights: Legal Capacity,* available at: www.un.org/esa/socdev/enable/rights/documents/ahc6ohchrlegalcap.doc. This paper, written during the negotiations, concluded that legal capacity could be limited based on disability, based on the law as it stood then. However, the adoption and entry into force of the CRPD adds to the relevant body of law and modifies it from a disability perspective.

is the standing to take action within a legal system, without any necessary connotation of ability. Thus, it can also be said that functional capacity (in the sense of ability) can be assessed for the purpose of providing support, but such an assessment does not limit the person's functional capacity (in the sense of standing to take action).

(iii)   Implementation

Practical questions arise with regard to the implementation of support to exercise legal capacity, and the role to be played by legal safeguards and formalities in relation to this support.

The first step in making sure that persons with disabilities are enabled to exercise legal capacity on an equal basis with others is accessible communication. CRPD Article 21 requires States Parties to

> take all appropriate measures to ensure that persons with disabilities can exercise the right to freedom of expression and opinion, including the freedom to seek, receive and impart information and ideas on an equal basis with others and through all forms of communication of their choice, as defined by Article 2 of the present Convention.[36]

That definition is as follows:

> 'Communication' includes languages, display of text, Braille, tactile communication, large print, accessible multimedia as well as written, audio, plain-language, human-reader and augmentative and alternative modes, means and formats of communication, including accessible information and communication technology.[37]

Thus, accessible communication includes methods usable for people with different kinds of disabilities. People with psychosocial disabilities may benefit from plain language, as well as a communication style that is free of hidden agendas and allows for digressions and creative self-expression, and for the person to take his or her own time to feel comfortable enough to speak. Accessible communication in this sense can be practised by lawyers, health professionals, bankers, judges and court personnel in situations where legal capacity is being exercised, and training should be provided for this purpose.[38] Peer advocates may play a supplementary role and should also be trained and certified for particular settings. Informal support by close associates should always be permitted when the individual so chooses.

Accessible communication is an essential part of compliance with the support obligation in Article 12, as the need for support may arise unexpectedly, either because the disability itself is sudden, or because the transaction for which support is needed was not anticipated. Thus, accessible communication provides

---

[36] Convention on the Rights of Persons with Disabilities (CRPD), adopted 13 December 2006, GA Res 61/106, UN Doc A/Res/61/106 (entered into force 3 May 2008) Art 21.

[37] *ibid*, Art 2.

[38] See *ibid*, Art 4.1(i) and Art 13.2.

support at the point when a need arises, which can be tailored to a particular context (eg, health care, access to justice and so on).

The second step is needed when a person has longer-term needs for support or a more intensive need for support in multiple areas of life.

Support to exercise legal capacity is often provided informally by family members and close friends. People rely on such networks to give them advice and feedback about decisions they need to make, to explain confusing information, and for emotional support in dealing with stressful aspects of transactions (bureaucracy, jargon, the high stakes of such decisions as marriage, buying a house, having an operation, whether to settle a lawsuit and so on). Such support can be tailored to the person's needs in the context of an ongoing relationship, in which both parties can negotiate how the relationship should work, with the understanding that each person is responsible for his or her own choices.

Support networks (or one-to-one support relationships) can be formalised so as to make them accountable. Such a system is envisioned in the seminal Report of the Canadian Association for Community Living Task Force on Alternatives to Guardianship,[39] but attempts to introduce this model of supported decision-making into domestic legislation have fallen short of realising key principles.[40] Formal registration of supporters and laws setting out their obligations, along with an oversight mechanism of some sort, can provide the safeguards required by CRPD Article 12, para 4. Such formalities should be focused on protecting the individual autonomy of the person receiving support, and should not revert to a guardianship-like institution, questioning the choices of people with disabilities.

Formal registration and review mechanisms can also be criticised for bringing too much scrutiny to bear on a relationship that itself is the result of choices made in the exercise of individual autonomy. The CACL model is designed to replace guardianship without fundamentally changing the law of informed consent and its requirement of 'mental capacity' as an element of valid decisions.[41] If support is characterised as a way for people with disabilities to make valid decisions that they are not entitled to make independently, supported decision-making is premised on inferior, rather than equal, legal capacity. The safeguards arising in such a model may be designed more to appease the formal process (which remains discriminatory) rather than to protect the autonomy of people with disabilities.

---

[39] Canadian Association for Community Living, *Report of the C.A.C.L. Task Force on Alternatives to Guardianship* (CACL Report) (Toronto, Canadian Association for Community Living, 1992).

[40] See Representation Agreement Act [RSBC 1996] c 405, British Columbia, Canada. See also overview in S Herr, 'Self-Determination, Autonomy, and Alternatives for Guardianship' in S Herr, LO Gostin and H Koh, *The Human Rights of Persons with Intellectual Disabilities* (Oxford, Oxford University Press, 2003). The British Columbia Act and other legislation discussed by Herr provide only for limited autonomy while retaining the option of appointing a substitute decision-maker, not limited to situations such as coma or loss of consciousness. The British Columbia Act furthermore excludes mental health decisions from its coverage, Art 11.

[41] See for example, Canadian Association for Community Living, *Report of the C.A.C.L. Task Force on Alternatives to Guardianship* (CACL Report) (Toronto, CACL, 1992) 29–32.

There may still be some value to legal formalities in supported decision-making; almost by definition an exercise of legal capacity is a decision that carries legal consequences depending in part on the formality of execution. The participation of supporters in a person's decision-making might be noted, so as to hold him or her accountable for the support provided (such as explanation of a contract) in case of any dispute. Such formalities could be optional depending on the wishes of the parties, the nature of the support (for example, interpretation of a person's non-verbal communication may require greater oversight in general), and the degree of formality required for a particular legal act.

Safeguards can also be implemented in a way that does not depend on legal formalities. For example, a law reform project that has been submitted to the Costa Rican parliament provides for assessment and referral for supported decision-making services together with other types of support for personal autonomy (such as personal assistance with daily living needs).[42] This reform would eliminate interdiction and guardianship, and does not appear to have any mechanism by which a person's decisional autonomy can be legally violated. Safeguards consist of an opportunity for the level of support to be reviewed,[43] and sanctions imposed on supporters for acts of abuse and neglect.[44] Although cognitive and volitional incapacity has been retained as a ground to nullify a legal act,[45] this concept appears to be less disability-specific than 'mental capacity' in common law jurisdictions; for example consent may be vitiated by fear, lack of knowledge or understanding, or error.[46] The Costa Rican project draws on the independent living movement and personal assistance services as its model, rather than the blend of informal support and legal formality that characterises the CACL approach. This project deserves serious consideration and analysis, and further study of its success in implementation.

(iv) Implications for Mental Health

Legal capacity has both direct and indirect implications for the mental health system. If persons with disabilities are deemed to have the capacity to make decisions in all aspects of life, this applies to decisions about mental health treatment and hospitalisation. Such decisions may only be made by the person concerned, after being provided with all available information from non-biased sources regarding the nature of the treatment, likelihood of particular benefits,

---

[42] Asamblea Legislativa de la República de Costa Rica, *Proyecto de Ley: Autonomía de las Personas Con Discapacidad (Ley de Autonomía)*, Ana Helena Chacón Echeverría, Ofelia Taitelbaum Yoselewich, Lesvia Villalobos Salas, Diputadas.

[43] *ibid*, Artículo 35: Revisión del grado y del nivel de las necesidades de apoyo y de la prestación reconocida.

[44] *ibid*, Capítulo IX: Infracciones y Sanciones; also Capítulo XII: Modificaciones de Otras Leyes, Seccion IV: Incumplimiento de derechos y deberes familiares.

[45] *ibid*, Capítulo XII: Modificaciones de Otras Leyes, Seccion VII: Reforma del Código Civil, y sus reformas, Ley No 63, de 19 de abril de 1885, Art. 91.

[46] Personal communication with Rodrigo Jiménez, Professor, University of Costa Rica.

likelihood of particular adverse effects, and less intrusive alternatives. If it is unclear whether a person understands this information, or whether he or she accepts or rejects the proposed treatment, the principles of supported decision-making must be applied, for example: making sure that information is presented in an accessible way and that the person's chosen mode of self-expression is respected and if necessary facilitated; involving close associates of the person's choice; and following the guidance of a pre-crisis plan so long as the person is still comfortable with his or her earlier choices.

The support model also frames a new way of looking at mental health issues, one that is in keeping with values that are already informing a wide range of good practices in mental health, and alternatives to the mental health system. The main aim of such a model is to support a person in a mental health crisis to come to his or her own way out, rather than breaking the chain of events and suppressing inner potential. The key is support: this is not abandonment in a cruel world, but caring engagement that has to be mutual at some level, in the sense that no individual exists solely for another, so a carer's needs and limitations can be acknowledged even while focusing attention on the person who needs support.

The following are examples of programmes and methodologies that can be among the building blocks for a system of services for people in altered states of consciousness or psychic distress who may need support and accommodation, from a perspective that puts the person first and sees the social context as enabling or disabling.[47] Such a system could incorporate psychiatry to serve those individuals who prefer a medical approach, but non-medical services would not be subordinated to psychiatry as they are at present.

Shery Mead's work on intentional peer support has brought a coherent theoretical approach to practical questions of how to support people in crisis.[48] Key to her method is the concept of shared power and shared responsibility, so that a supporter is not expected to ensure a predetermined outcome (such as preventing the individual from committing suicide) but instead a conversation is allowed to take place to explore both individuals thoughts and feelings on the subject. Mead has conducted training for users and survivors of psychiatry as well as mental health providers in the United States and other countries.

Maths Jesperson describes the 'Personaligt Ombud' programme,[49] as implemented by himself and others through the Skåne branch of RSMH, a user/survivor organisation in Sweden. As there is no elegant and gender-neutral way to

---

[47] I do not fully endorse all the approaches presented here, but have tried to bring out the elements of each one that I find useful components of a support framework.

[48] S Mead, 'Trauma-informed Peer Run Crisis Alternatives' in Peter Stastny and Peter Lehmann (eds), *Alternatives Beyond Psychiatry* (Berlin, Peter Lehmann, 2007). Also see S Mead, *Intentional Peer Support: An Alternative Approach* (Plainfield, The Author, 2008).

[49] M Jesperson, 'Personal Ombudsman in Skåne: A User-controlled Service with Personal Agents' in P Stastny and P Lehmann (eds), *Alternatives Beyond Psychiatry* (Berlin, Peter Lehmann, 2007). See also Socialstyrelsen, *A New Profession is Born—Personligt ombud, PO* (Vastra Aros, Socialstyrelsen, 2008).

write the term in English, I will use 'PO'. The PO programme is designed to reach out to people living in isolated circumstances, often self-chosen, who may be experiencing longer-term mental health problems. The PO works to establish communication, and then gets to know the person, before asking if the individual wants him or her to be the person's PO. If not, then nothing further is attempted. If the person agrees, the PO will take the individual's requests and help with advocacy or support as needed, but can do nothing that the person does not authorise. The PO programme has been successful in large part because it avoids bureaucracy and is accountable only to the person being served; this allows people to access services even when they do not want to be found by the authorities.

Bhargavi Davar and Madhura Lohokare have researched the value of traditional healing centres in India, motivated in part by a 'witch-hunt' against these centres after a tragic fire exposed human rights violations in some of them (such as people being chained to their beds). Similar violations in mental institutions were ignored, and the authorities campaigned to close down the 'unlicensed' healing centres and promote western-style mental health services as a replacement, without considering how well the respective systems were meeting people's needs. Davar and Lohokare found:

> Users are inclined to access places where they can express their problem as they experience it, where they sense a match between their causal models of illness and the models prevalent in the healing space; places which will address cosmological and personal, existential issues; where they will not be forced to directly confront their problems at the individualistic level, as a 'disorder', but can depend on divine [serendipitous] or collective mediation.[50]

The authors characterise the healing centres as social institutions integrated in the community, not as part of the medical system. They might be key building blocks for an alternative service system based on a social model of disability, and should be allowed to develop and evolve with the new human rights standards,[51] rather than fall into disuse or be absorbed into the medical system.

It is especially important not to censor spiritual explanations of experiences that are now being labelled as madness or mental illness. Traditional faith healing methods are still a vital institution in many developing countries,[52] and serve as examples of good practice in this regard. In countries where such healing is no longer integrated with community institutions and cultural beliefs, individual spiritual journeys of a difficult nature may need support from the mental health

---

[50] BV Davar and M Lohokare, 'Recovering from Psychosocial Traumas: The Place of Dargahs in Maharashtra' (2009) 44(16) *Economic and Political Weekly* 60–67. See also: www.camhindia.org/hhwm_review_report.html.

[51] See Convention on the Rights of Persons with Disabilities (CRPD), adopted 13 December 2006, GA Res 61/106, UN Doc A/Res/61/106 (entered into force 3 May 2008) Arts 4.1(b), 16.3.

[52] Members of the World Network of Users and Survivors of Psychiatry have also informally reported benefiting from traditional healing in Kenya and Uganda.

system, religious institutions, peer support groups, and/or friends and family. While supporters don't have to share the person's understanding, they should be willing to accept it as equally valid for the individual as psychological or biological explanations might be for someone else.

Involvement of social networks in finding solutions to problems existing at multiple levels is also a feature of the Open Dialogues programme currently being used on a large scale in Finland.[53] A team of mental health professionals organises an initial discussion with all those who are concerned, including the person who is identified as having a problem. Everyone can talk and share their views, and the aim is for the multiple perspectives to be heard and commented on, to arrive at a better understanding. I have reservations about this approach as it leaves room for overt and subtle coercion if the person's own voice is not privileged in deciding what he or she needs. The voices of others in the network can lend a valuable perspective and are needed to resolve social and interpersonal aspects of a crisis, and the programme has a good reputation among promoters of mental health alternatives. But not everyone will welcome this exposure of sensitive matters, or feel that it is fair to focus on one person as needing help, and so this practice needs to be subject to free and informed consent, and not used if an individual finds it uncomfortable.

The Soteria Project was developed as an alternative to psychiatric hospitalisation for young people newly diagnosed with schizophrenia. Loren Mosher, its founder, described it as follows:

> Basically, the Soteria method can be characterized as the 24 hour a day application of interpersonal phenomenologic interventions by a nonprofessional staff, usually without neuroleptic drug treatment, in the context of a small, homelike, quiet, supportive, protective, and tolerant social environment. The core practice of interpersonal phenomenology focuses on the development of a nonintrusive, non-controlling but actively empathetic relationship with the psychotic person without having to *do* anything explicitly therapeutic or controlling. In shorthand, it can be characterized as 'being with,' 'standing by attentively,' 'trying to put your feet into the other person's shoes,' or 'being an LSD trip guide' [remember, this was the early 1970s in California].[54]

While the original project ended for lack of funding, despite consistently positive results, versions of Soteria have been established in other states in the United States and in Europe.

At the Icarus Project[55] and associated local support groups, individuals diagnosed with bipolar disorder create a conversation about their experiences,

---

[53] J Seikkula and B Alakare, 'Open Dialogues' in P Stastny and P Lehmann (eds), *Alternatives Beyond Psychiatry* (Berlin, Peter Lehmann, 2007).

[54] LR Mosher, 'Soteria and Other Alternatives to Acute Psychiatric Hospitalization: A Personal and Professional Review' (1999) 187 *Journal of Nervous and Mental Disease* 142.

[55] The Icarus Project, *Navigating the Space Between Brilliance and Madness*, available at: www.theicarusproject.net/.

including struggles over whether or not to use medication, the spiritual dimension of high or manic states, and their sensitivity to large-scale social forces seemingly bent on destruction of human beings and the earth. Taking a 'harm reduction' approach to psychiatric drugs, the Icarus project provides a good example of peer support as a way to develop collective knowledge as well as a sense of not being alone.[56]

The Hearing Voices movement brings together voice hearers, mental health professionals and other interested people to explore different ways of understanding what it means to hear voices and how people can cope with voices that cause them distress. These ways may be psychological (for example, seeking meaning from events in the person's life), spiritual (for example, dealing with spirit intrusion, a calling to become a shaman, and other events beyond ordinary understanding), or practical methods to limit the power of the voices or change their character from harmful to helpful.[57]

Initiatives to reduce and eliminate the use of seclusion and restraint, often motivated by an awareness that such practices are extremely traumatising, are examples of good practice at the level of policy-making and implementation in the public mental health system. These initiatives have been collaborative at many levels, involving users and survivors as experts and working with individuals to make pre-crisis plans and debrief all concerned after any incident where seclusion and restraint have been used. In some cases, the use of any coercion is also addressed in a similar way. This approach, while not yet fully human rights compliant, can be useful as a practical and non-adversarial way of engaging the mental health system in reform.[58]

Finally, mutual accommodation and finding ways to resolve interpersonal crises, including but not limited to those that could result in violence, needs to be a part of an alternative service system. This relates to the dimension of responsibility as an aspect of legal capacity. While people with disabilities cannot be excused for all bad behaviour, some level of tolerance is needed as a reasonable accommodation, understood in a philosophical sense as applicable to our informal interactions and to standards of behaviour generally, as well as situations involving law enforcement and other authorities. Users and survivors of psychiatry have helped to train police departments in the de-escalation of hostility and avoiding violence; however, coercing someone to go to a psychiatric hospital needs to be equally avoided, as is not yet the case.

---

[56] ibid.
[57] Intervoice, *The International Community for Hearing Voices*, available at: www.intervoiceonline.org/.
[58] See eg, United States of America Department of Health and Human Services, Substance Abuse and Mental Health Administration, Center for Mental Health Services, *Roadmap to Seclusion and Restraint Free Mental Health Services*, DHHS Publication No (SMA) 05–4055 (2005), available at: www.mentalhealth.samhsa.gov/publications/allpubs/sma06–4055/.

B.   Liberty

Article 14 of the CRPD requires States Parties to

> ensure that persons with disabilities, on an equal basis with others, enjoy the right to
> liberty and security of person … and that the existence of a disability shall in no case
> justify a deprivation of liberty.[59]

The Office of the High Commissioner for Human Rights has recognised that this
provision requires

> the repeal of provisions authorizing institutionalization of persons with disabilities for
> their care and treatment without their free and informed consent, as well as provisions
> authorizing the preventive detention of persons with disabilities on grounds such as the
> likelihood of them posing a danger to themselves or others, in all cases in which such
> grounds of care, treatment and public security are linked in legislation to an apparent
> or diagnosed mental illness.[60]

Thus, mental health legislation as we know it must be abolished and detention in
psychiatric institutions treated as unlawful imprisonment.

Article 14 also obliges States Parties to

> ensure that if persons with disabilities are deprived of their liberty through any process,
> they are, on an equal basis with others, entitled to guarantees in accordance with
> international human rights law and shall be treated in compliance with the objectives
> and principles of the present Convention, including by provision of reasonable accom-
> modation.[61]

The significance of this paragraph for users and survivors of psychiatry is
two-fold. First, it underscores that the article as a whole is framed in terms of
non-discrimination and is not dealing with separate or special standards that
uniquely apply to persons with disabilities. Persons with disabilities are subject to
lawful arrest and detention exercised by states on disability-neutral grounds, such
as law enforcement or immigration status violations. When such detention
occurs, persons with disabilities have equal rights as others to guarantees of due
process and humane treatment, which is complemented by reasonable accommodation and compliance with the objectives and principles of the CRPD.

Since the prison system is designed for punishment, some users and survivors
question the relevance of reasonable accommodation. However, there may be
instances where people with psychosocial disabilities can argue for supports or
rule modifications to mitigate conditions that would otherwise have the effect of

[59] Convention on the Rights of Persons with Disabilities (CRPD), adopted 13 December 2006,
GA Res 61/106, UN Doc A/Res/61/106 (entered into force 3 May 2008) Art 14.1.

[60] Thematic Study by the Office of the United Nations High Commissioner for Human Rights on
enhancing awareness and understanding of the Convention on the Rights of Persons with Disabilities
(OHCHR Thematic Study) UN Doc. A/HRC/10/48, 26 January 2009 at [49].

[61] Convention on the Rights of Persons with Disabilities (CRPD), adopted 13 December 2006,
GA Res 61/106, UN Doc A/Res/61/106 (entered into force 3 May 2008) Art 14.2.

punishing them to a greater extent than others. In addition to providing reasonable accommodation, mental health and other support services should be made available to people who want them, on the basis of free and informed consent. The prison or detention setting does not legitimise coercive medical treatments, and people with disabilities who are detained for lawful, disability-neutral reasons should not be placed under medical authority. Neuroleptic drugs and other psychiatric interventions should not be used to subdue any person or control behaviour.

Article 19 of the CRPD reinforces and complements Article 14, requiring States Parties to ensure that

> persons with disabilities have the opportunity to choose their place of residence and where and with whom they live on an equal basis with others and are not obliged to live in a particular living arrangement.[62]

Article 19, like Article 12, also provides for support in the service of autonomy. States Parties must ensure that

> persons with disabilities have access to a range of in-home, residential and other community support services, including personal assistance necessary to support living and inclusion in the community, and to prevent isolation or segregation from the community.

In addition, they must ensure that

> community services and facilities for the general population are available on an equal basis to persons with disabilities and are responsive to their needs,

reflecting a mainstreaming principle that is also relevant to supported decision-making.

C.   Free and Informed Consent

Article 25(d) of the CRPD sets out that States Parties must

> require health professionals to provide care of the same quality to persons with disabilities as to others, including on the basis of free and informed consent by, inter alia, raising awareness of the human rights, dignity, autonomy and needs of persons with disabilities through training and the promulgation of ethical standards for public and private health care.[63]

The key obligation for purposes of this discussion is that States Parties must require health professionals to provide care to persons with disabilities, equally as to others, on the basis of free and informed consent. Mental health services might be provided to people with and without disabilities, for example, mental health

---

[62]   *ibid*, Art 19.
[63]   *ibid*, Art 25(d).

promotion activities might be made available to the entire community, and some forms of counselling and therapy might not necessarily be limited to people who are in great distress. However, it is precisely when people are in great distress, significantly impacting upon their lives in combination with various barriers, that coercive treatment has been applied. This constitutes discrimination against persons with psychosocial or 'mental' disabilities, contrary to Article 25 of the CRPD.

V. Forced or Non-Consensual Psychiatric Interventions as Torture

For the disability community, medical torture and ill-treatment have been an ongoing sources of pain, anger and frustration. Medical doctors have a social status and power that comes from their knowledge and skill in dealing with injury and sickness, areas in which most people feel vulnerable and welcome expert help. People with disabilities have had a mixed relationship with medical professionals. For many people with disabilities, medical help is needed to sustain life, health and well-being. However, this also means that when doctors misuse their power, such as by performing a treatment without disclosing serious known risks, or promoting treatments that are risky and of dubious benefit, people with disabilities can be disproportionately affected.

The medical profession also has a dark side in relation to people with disabilities, which had its peak expression in the eugenics movement that called for sterilisation and culminated in systematic murder during the Nazi era. Psychiatrists were active participants in the selection of patients for killing, and euphemised the killing as 'treatment'. Doctors in the United States of America called for eugenic policies before the Nazi era; doctors in Germany requested and received the power to kill their patients, and the murders continued after Hitler issued an order to stop.[64]

There is a continuum between deliberate killing, sterilisation and other atrocities committed in the name of treatment. The field of psychiatry in particular has been marked by a search for 'great and desperate cures' unchecked by the subjective suffering of their patients.[65] Psychiatry is also compromised by its use of legally protected force to compel compliance with treatment and to detain

---

[64] See L Lapon, *Mass Murderers in White Coats: Psychiatric Genocide in Nazi Germany and the United States* (Springfield IL, Psychiatric Genocide Research Institute, 1986); L Andre, *Doctors of Deception: What They Don't Want You to Know About Shock Treatment* (Piscataway, Rutgers University Press, 2009) 13–43; RD Strous, 'Psychiatry During the Nazi Era: Ethical Lessons for the Modern Professional' (2007) 6:8 *Annals of General Psychiatry*; E Klee, 'Killing by Starvation in the Institutions and Other Previous Crimes of Psychiatry', available at: www.irren-offensive.de/kleespeech.htm.

[65] ES Valenstein, *Great and Desperate Cures: The Rise and Decline of Psychosurgery and other Radical Treatments for Mental Illness* (New York, Basic Books, 1986) 23–44.

people against their will. This puts people in need of help in a dangerous situation, where seeking support can easily result in betrayal and harm. Institutionalised and systemic discrimination creates an untenable situation where doctors can become perpetrators of ill-treatment and torture.

In July 2008, the Special Rapporteur on Torture, Manfred Nowak, (the Special Rapporteur) included a section on torture and persons with disabilities in his Interim Report to the General Assembly. The Special Rapporteur addressed several issues of concern to the disability community, and one of the highlights was his attention to abuses in the medical context, including forced or non-consensual psychiatric interventions.

A.   Non-discrimination and the Medical Context

The Special Rapporteur contextualises his discussion of torture and persons with disabilities, including the medical context, with reference to non-discrimination as defined in Article 2 of the CRPD,[66] and the phrase in the Convention against Torture 'any reasons based on discrimination of any kind' among the proscribed purposes of torture.[67]

The Special Rapporteur goes on to clarify the connection between discrimination and intent or purpose:

> Furthermore, the requirement of intent of article 1 of the Convention against Torture can be effectively implied when a person has been discriminated against on the basis of disability. This is particularly relevant in the context of medical treatment of persons with disabilities, where serious violations and discrimination against persons with disabilities may be masked as 'good intentions' on the part of health professionals. Purely negligent conduct lacks the intent required under article 1, and may constitute ill-treatment if it leads to severe pain and suffering.[68]

---

[66]   That definition reads: '"Discrimination on the basis of disability" means any distinction, exclusion or restriction on the basis of disability which has the purpose or effect of impairing or nullifying the recognition, enjoyment or exercise, on an equal basis with others, of all human rights and fundamental freedoms in the political, economic, social, cultural, civil or any other field. It includes all forms of discrimination, including denial of reasonable accommodation'.

[67]   Convention against Torture and Other Cruel, Inhuman or Degrading Treatment or Punishment, adopted by UN GA Res 39/46 of 10 December 1984 (entered into force 26 June 1987). Art 1 states in full: '1. For the purposes of this Convention, the term "torture" means any act by which severe pain or suffering, whether physical or mental, is intentionally inflicted on a person for such purposes as obtaining from him or a third person information or a confession, punishing him for an act he or a third person has committed or is suspected of having committed, or intimidating or coercing him or a third person, or for any reason based on discrimination of any kind, when such pain or suffering is inflicted by or at the instigation of or with the consent or acquiescence of a public official or other person acting in an official capacity. It does not include pain or suffering arising only from, inherent in or incidental to lawful sanctions. 2. This article is without prejudice to any international instrument or national legislation which does or may contain provisions of wider application'.

[68]   Interim Report of the Special Rapporteur on Torture and other Cruel, Inhuman and Degrading Treatment or Punishment (SR Torture Interim Report), 28 July 2008, UN Doc A/63/175, at [49].

Significantly, this analysis rejects the doctrine of 'therapeutic necessity'[69] as the decisive factor in determining whether medical treatment is torture or cruel, inhuman or degrading treatment.

B. Legal Capacity, Free and Informed Consent and Powerlessness

As outlined above,[70] the CRPD sets out a new paradigm for respecting the autonomous decision-making of people with disabilities rather than vesting decision-making power in another person. Mental health coercion relies on a judgement that the person is 'incapable' of making decisions—that is, that the person's choices need not be respected due to limitations in their decision-making ability. The Special Rapporteur points out how deprivation of legal capacity facilitates torture and ill-treatment:

> Torture, as the most serious violation of the human right to personal integrity and dignity, presupposes a situation of powerlessness, whereby the victim is under the total control of another person. Persons with disabilities often find themselves in such situations, for instance when they are deprived of their liberty in prisons or other places, or when they are under the control of their caregivers or legal guardians. In a given context, the particular disability of an individual may render him or her more likely to be in a dependent situation and make him or her an easier target of abuse. However, it is often circumstances external to the individual that render them 'powerless', such as when one's exercise of decision-making and legal capacity is taken away by discriminatory laws or practices and given to others.[71]

The Special Rapporteur says that the CRPD provisions on legal capacity and free and informed consent, and the principle of respect for individual autonomy, complement the prohibition of torture and ill-treatment by 'providing further authoritative guidance'.[72] As noted above,[73] he affirms that 'the acceptance of involuntary treatment and involuntary confinement runs counter to' these provisions.[74] In his conclusions and recommendations, the Special Rapporteur calls on states to ratify the CRPD and its Optional Protocol, and makes specific recommendations about legal capacity and free and informed consent:

> In keeping with the Convention, States must adopt legislation that recognizes the legal capacity of persons with disabilities and must ensure that, where required, they are provided with the support needed to make informed decisions.[75]

---

[69] *Herczegfalvy v Austria* (1992) 15 EHRR 437 at [82].

[70] See Section IV(A) of this chapter.

[71] Interim Report of the Special Rapporteur on Torture and other Cruel, Inhuman and Degrading Treatment or Punishment (SR Torture Interim Report), 28 July 2008, UN Doc A/63/175, at [50].

[72] *ibid*, at [44]. In addition, he refers to Art 14 on liberty, in the section on involuntary commitment to psychiatric institutions, paras 64–65.

[73] *ibid*, s I.

[74] *ibid*, at [44].

[75] *ibid*, at [73].

States should issue clear and unambiguous guidelines in line with the Convention on what is meant by 'free and informed consent', and make available accessible complaints procedures.[76]

C.   Treatments 'Aimed at Correcting or Alleviating a Disability'

The Special Rapporteur sets out a three-pronged analysis for treatments that may constitute torture or ill-treatment: (1) medical treatments of an intrusive and irreversible nature; (2) lacking a therapeutic purpose OR aimed at correcting or alleviating a disability; (3) enforced or administered without free and informed consent of the person concerned.[77]

The strength of the obligation to ensure free and informed consent increases to the degree to which a treatment is intrusive and irreversible, with lobotomy and psychosurgery falling at the highest point on this spectrum.[78]

The Rapporteur cites 'electroshock and mind-altering drugs including neuro-leptics' as paradigmatic examples of 'intrusive and irreversible treatments aimed at correcting or alleviating a disability'.[79] He notes that such practices performed on persons with disabilities without their consent have not been properly recognized as torture or ill-treatment.[80]

Intrusive treatments for a non-therapeutic purpose include psychiatric drugs used for coercion and punishment[81] (as well as compulsory abortion and sterilisation).[82] Behaviour control cannot be transformed into a medical issue by the existence of a disability. The standard ensures that neither behaviour control (a non-therapeutic purpose) nor the aim of correcting a disability will suffice to justify forced psychiatric interventions.

More detailed guidance is provided for several issues in the medical context, which is a site of serious abuse, 'notably in relation to experimentation or treatments directed to correct and alleviate particular impairments'.[83] He addresses medical and scientific experimentation; medical interventions gener-ally and in relation to children; abortion and sterilisation; electro-convulsive therapy (ECT); forced psychiatric interventions; and involuntary commitment to psychiatric institutions. In other sections of the report he deals with conditions of detention as well as seclusion and restraint.

---

[76]   *ibid*, at [74].
[77]   *ibid*, at [47].
[78]   *ibid*, at [59].
[79]   *ibid*, at [40].
[80]   *ibid*, at [41].
[81]   *ibid*, at [62]–[63].
[82]   *ibid*, at [60].
[83]   *ibid*, at [57].

(i)   Forced and Non-consensual Administration of Drugs

The Special Rapporteur discusses human rights precedents recognising non-consensual administration of neuroleptics and other psychiatric drugs as a form of torture or ill-treatment, and the fact that such measures have been used not only against political dissidents but also routinely on people with disabilities. He concludes:

> The Special Rapporteur notes that forced and non-consensual administration of psychiatric drugs, and in particular of neuroleptics, for the treatment of a mental condition needs to be closely scrutinized. Depending on the circumstances of the case, the suffering inflicted and the effects upon the individual's health may constitute a form of torture or ill-treatment.[84]

The 'suffering inflicted' should be assessed with reference to subjective experience, for example, fear and terror, grief, disturbing sensations of body and mind produced by the drugs,[85] and long-term consequences such as traumatic reactions and the loss of significant relationships and opportunities. 'Effects on the individual's health' can take into account diagnoses of medical problems commonly caused by neuroleptic drugs, including neurological disorders like tardive dyskinesia,[86] and the likelihood of a shortened life span.[87] This standard should not be applied in such a way as to negate the subjective experience of suffering by professional assessments of the person's mental health. For a person recently subjected to forced or non-consensual psychiatric interventions, to require such an assessment would be tantamount to repeating abuse.

In addition, to ensure that consent is both free and informed, protocols for informed consent need to be developed to ensure that accurate and unbiased information is provided to individuals who are considering treatment with psychiatric drugs, including information about less intrusive alternatives.

(ii)   Electro-Convulsive Therapy

The Special Rapporteur emphasises the need for accurate information about electro-convulsive therapy (ECT), as long advocated by survivors:

---

[84]   *ibid*, at [63].

[85]   See PR Breggin, *Psychiatric Drugs: Hazards to the Brain* (New York, Springer, 1983); D Cohen, 'A Critique of the Use of Neuroleptic Drugs' in S Fisher and RP Greenberg (eds), *From Placebo to Panacea: Putting Psychiatric Drugs to the Test* (New York, John Wiley, 1997); GE Jackson, *Rethinking Psychiatric Drugs: A Guide for Informed Consent* (Bloomington, AuthorHouse, 2005).

[86]   PR Breggin, *Psychiatric Drugs: Hazards to the Brain* (New York, Springer, 1983); D Cohen, 'A Critique of the Use of Neuroleptic Drugs' in S Fisher and RP Greenberg (eds), *From Placebo to Panacea: Putting Psychiatric Drugs to the Test* (New York, John Wiley, 1997).

[87]   M Joukamaa, M Heliövaara, P Knekt, A Aromaa, R Raitasalo and V Lehtinen, 'Schizophrenia, Neuroleptic Medication and Mortality' (2006) 188 *British Journal of Psychiatry* 122. The PsychRights website at: www.psychrights.org/index.htm has collected many more studies documenting adverse health effects of neuroleptics and other psychiatric drugs.

In its modified form, it is of vital importance that ECT be administered only with the free and informed consent of the person concerned, including on the basis of information on the secondary effects and related risks such as heart complications, confusion, loss of memory and even death.[88]

In addition, he follows established jurisprudence in considering unmodified ECT (without anaesthesia, muscle relaxant or oxygenation) to be an unacceptable medical practice that may constitute torture or ill-treatment. It should be noted that some of the adverse effects the Special Rapporteur cites as a reason for the unacceptability of unmodified ECT, in particular cognitive deficits and loss of memory, are equally applicable to the modified version, and survivors of the modified form of ECT find severe and permanent memory loss devastating to personal identity.[89] Texas in the United States requires disclosure of both 'the possible degree and duration of memory loss and 'the possibility of permanent irrevocable memory loss'.[90] The Rapporteur says that even in its modified form, ECT may only be administered with free and informed consent of the person concerned, implying as suggested elsewhere in his report that ECT without consent may constitute torture or ill-treatment.

(iii) Medical and Scientific Experimentation

The Special Rapporteur re-affirms the prohibition of medical and scientific experimentation without the free and informed consent of the person concerned, and underlines that the 'very nature of the experiment' in some instances might be deemed torture or cruel, inhuman or degrading treatment.[91] Advocates have called for polypharmacy (prescribing two or more drugs at one time, with untested interactions), off-label and excessive dosages of psychiatric drugs to be considered experimental and subject to more stringent informed consent protocols. The same is true for ECT, which, in the United States, remains classified as a medical 'device' whose safety and efficacy has not been proven.[92]

---

[88] Interim Report of the Special Rapporteur on Torture and other Cruel, Inhuman and Degrading Treatment or Punishment (SR Torture Interim Report), 28 July 2008, UN Doc A/63/175, at [61].
[89] L Andre, *Doctors of Deception: What They Don't Want You to Know About Shock Treatment* (Piscataway, Rutgers University Press, 2009) 1–12. See also, PR Breggin, 'Electroshock: Scientific, Ethical and Political Issues' (1998) 11 *International Journal of Risk and Safety in Medicine* 5, and HA Sackeim, J Prudic, R Fuller, J Keilp, PW Lavori and M Olfson, 'The Cognitive Effects of Electroconvulsive Therapy in Community Settings' (2007) 32 *Neuropsychopharmacology* 244.
[90] Texas Health and Safety Code, section 578.003(b).
[91] Interim Report of the Special Rapporteur on Torture and other Cruel, Inhuman and Degrading Treatment or Punishment (SR Torture Interim Report), 28 July 2008, UN Doc A/63/175, at [58].
[92] The United States of America regulatory body overseeing electroshock devices, the Food and Drug Administration, classifies the machines as Class III devices, pre-market approval, 21 CFR 882.5940. See also L Andre, *Doctors of Deception: What They Don't Want You to Know About Shock Treatment* (Piscataway, Rutgers University Press, 2009) 156–88.

(iv)   Restraint and Seclusion

The Special Rapporteur addresses cage-beds and other physical restraints used on adults and children with disabilities, as well as psychiatric drugs used as chemical restraint. He concludes:

> It is important to note that 'prolonged use of restraint can lead to muscle atrophy, life-threatening deformities and even organ failure', and exacerbates psychological damage. The Special Rapporteur notes that there can be no therapeutic justification for the prolonged use of restraints, which may amount to torture or ill-treatment.[93]

With regard to seclusion, he emphasises that this practice cannot be justified either 'for therapeutic reasons, or as a form of punishment'. He concludes: 'The Special Rapporteur notes that prolonged solitary confinement and seclusion of persons may constitute torture or ill-treatment'.[94]

Given the traumatising nature of both restraint and solitary confinement or seclusion, it would be better to say that these practices should not be used for any duration in treatment or service settings.[95] Standards applicable in law enforcement and public safety situations should also aim at avoiding these measures and ensure that they are not applied disproportionately or with disproportionate effect on people with disabilities.[96]

(v)   Involuntary Commitment to Psychiatric Institutions

The Special Rapporteur notes that Article 14 of the CRPD prohibits

> the existence of a disability as a justification for the deprivation of liberty,[97]

and states:

> In certain cases, arbitrary or unlawful deprivation of liberty based on the existence of a disability might also inflict severe pain or suffering on the individual, thus falling under the scope of the Convention against Torture. When assessing the pain inflicted by deprivation of liberty, the length of institutionalization, the conditions of detention and the treatment inflicted must be taken into account.[98]

These factors are broad enough to encompass lengthy institutionalisation as well as shorter periods of detention that include forced drugging or ECT, restraint or solitary confinement that inflicts lasting harm.

---

[93]   Interim Report of the Special Rapporteur on Torture and other Cruel, Inhuman and Degrading Treatment or Punishment (SR Torture Interim Report), 28 July 2008, UN Doc A/63/175, at [55].
[94]   *ibid*, at [56].
[95]   See Section IV(A) of this chapter.
[96]   See Section IV(B) of this chapter.
[97]   Interim Report of the Special Rapporteur on Torture and other Cruel, Inhuman and Degrading Treatment or Punishment (SR Torture Interim Report), 28 July 2008, UN Doc A/63/175, at [64].
[98]   *ibid*, at [65].

D. Application of the Standards

The Special Rapporteur has refrained from declaring that a particular practice per se constitutes torture or ill-treatment, except where this is well established in international law, such as custodial rape being a form of torture.[99] With regard to emerging issues such as forced psychiatric interventions and other as uses in the medical context, he provides guidelines and factors for evaluating allegations of torture and ill-treatment against persons with disabilities, and strongly suggests that these practices will be considered torture or ill-treatment when the elements of the definition are met. His analysis, based on the international framework of torture together with the CRPD, is a meaningful and well-considered application of the disability perspective to issues long mired in prejudice and ignorance. The use of these standards by advocates, and their adoption by United Nations bodies, national human rights institutions and torture prevention mechanisms, and others, should result in 'victims and advocates [being] afforded stronger legal protection and redress for violations of human rights'.[100]

The obligation to take effective measures to prevent torture and ill-treatment[101] has broader implications than prohibition of practices that are known to constitute torture and ill-treatment in all circumstances. If a practice violates other human rights and may also constitute torture and ill-treatment, this should be enough to invoke the obligation to prevent torture and ill-treatment by banning the offending practice. Mental health laws on the contrary violate the CRPD and other international human rights norms,[102] and facilitate torture and ill-treatment. These laws must be abolished and the practices of compulsory treatment and confinement on mental health grounds must be prohibited.

VI. Conclusion

The CRPD sets out both legal obligations and a framework for social development in which people with disabilities can participate with equal opportunity. Support to facilitate the exercise of legal capacity is paradigmatic of the inclusion of people with disabilities in all aspects of life on an equal basis with others. While people with disabilities may need specific kinds of support, support does not negate autonomy. Everyone needs support at times, and everyone also cherishes personal freedom.

---

[99] *ibid*, at [67].

[100] *ibid*, at [45].

[101] Convention against Torture Articles 2 and 16; Committee against Torture General Comment No. 2, paragraphs 1–4.

[102] See Dignity and Justice for Detainees Week, Information Note No. 4: Persons with Disabilities (see footnote 21 above).

The CRPD complements other core human rights treaties and requires changes in jurisprudence in some cases. The Special Rapporteur on Torture, Manfred Nowak, has demonstrated the value of the CRPD as complementary to the Convention against Torture, with particular relevance to users and survivors of psychiatry, who can now begin to assert claims for traumatising forced interventions as a form of torture or ill-treatment.

This chapter has argued that mental health laws violate the CRPD and may facilitate torture and ill-treatment. They cannot be reformed and should be abolished, to be replaced by non-coercive practices, services based on a social model with room for medical support, and legal reforms ensuring that users and survivors of psychiatry have the right to exercise legal capacity on an equal basis with others in all aspects of life.

These reforms need to be developed in each country and local jurisdiction, with the active involvement and participation of people with psychosocial disabilities, as well as other sectors of the community. This may take time, as the old model still holds sway and everyone will need to consider what the new one has to offer. At the same time, legal remedies should be pursued for human rights violations, both to give satisfaction to individual victims and to help motivate change.

Part 4

Gaps between Law and Practice

8

Rights-Based Legalism: Some Thoughts from the Research*

GENEVRA RICHARDSON

I. Introduction

Underlying the early literature on rival approaches to the provision of mental health care was a clear assumption that over-reliance on rights would lead to the negative consequences of legalism. This debate, which is fully described by Phil Fennell in chapter two of this volume, must now be set in the context of the more energetic international framework of rights that has emerged over the last decades. From at least the early 1980s people with mental disorders have sought to protect their traditional, largely negative, rights through the guarantees provided by the European Convention on Human Rights (the ECHR).[1] While the ECHR was not drafted with the position of the mentally disordered especially in mind, save in relation to Article 5(1)(e), people with mental disorder, together with other vulnerable groups, have been able to call on the Convention to limit the interventions permitted by national laws. Certainly the shape of much mental health law in the United Kingdom has been directly influenced by the requirements of the ECHR.[2] The ECHR is concerned mainly with the protection of individuals from unjustified interference. In the years since its initial drafting, recognition of the particular vulnerability of disabled people and their consequent need for protection from interference has grown significantly. International recognition of the vulnerability of disabled people does not now stop at protection from interference. There is a growing recognition of the need to facilitate access to essential services. That is a case for positive rights. Both these developments have recently found expression in the CRPD. Far from withering

---

* Some of the material contained within this chapter has appeared in G Richardson, 'Mental Capacity at the Margin: The Interface Between Two Acts' (2010) 18 *Medical Law Review* 56.
[1] Convention for the Protection of Human Rights and Fundamental Freedoms (European Convention on Human Rights), opened for signature 4 November 1950, CETS No 005 (entered into force 3 September 1953).
[2] See, for example *X v United Kingdom* (1982) 4 EHRR 118 and *HL v United Kingdom* (2005) 40 EHRR 32.

on the vine, rights-based approaches to mental health law have flourished, but the question remains: What good do they do?

At the national level mental health law is still primarily concerned with the authorisation of intervention. Typically this intervention will take the form of involuntary hospitalisation and treatment. The law thus specifies the point at which coercion becomes lawful. The precise identification of that point is likely to be influenced by the cultural and political contexts, and to be the subject of much negotiation and debate. Once identified, the respect the point is afforded in practice will depend on the attitude of the relevant professionals. In a rights-based system patients can in theory use rights to police the border between lawful and unlawful coercion. In practice, dilemmas arise from the attempt to select mental disorder for special legal attention. This chapter will review the findings of recent empirical research that has been designed to throw light on the operation of mental health law. It will focus on the law's traditional role of policing the border between lawful and unlawful coercion. It will not consider the possibly more difficult question of the law's role in relation to the provision of services, an issue explored by Bernadette McSherry in chapter sixteen and Peter Bartlett in chapter seventeen of this volume.

The application and impact of mental health law has been the subject of empirical research in a number of, mainly developed, jurisdictions. This research has focused on the admission into compulsory hospitalisation and treatment, the administration of compulsory treatment both in hospital and in the community, and the discharge from compulsory powers. More than anything this research has served to place in stark relief the context in which mental health law has to operate: 'a heady mixture of questionable science, individual prejudice and overpowering beneficent intentions'.[3] In particular it has revealed a picture of pragmatic interpretation, a desire to minimise risk, the importance of context and of organisational demands, and the seductive quality of the non-decision. It has also, most significantly, emphasised the importance of the patient's perceptions of the experience. It would not be possible to do justice to all this work here. Elegant and valuable accounts exist elsewhere.[4] Instead this chapter will focus on research recently conducted in the United Kingdom which has attempted to investigate some of the concepts central to the relationship between law and psychiatry, including capacity, insight and compliance. In the light of the emerging data it will consider how these concepts are interpreted in practice and what this might reveal about the nature and location of the boundary between lawful and unlawful coercion.

---

[3] J Peay (ed), *Seminal Issues in Mental Health Law* (Aldershot, Ashgate, 2005) xxiv.
[4] *ibid*; K Diesfeld and I Freckelton (eds), *Involuntary Detention and Therapeutic Jurisprudence* (Aldershot, Ashgate, 2003); P Bartlett and R Sandland, *Mental Health Law: Policy and Practice*, 3rd edn (Oxford, Oxford University Press, 2007).

II. Law at the Interface

By making an exception of mental disorder and providing special powers of intervention in relation to it, the law not only specifies the nature and limits of those powers but also identifies the population to whom they apply—people with mental disorder. The question of demarcation can cause difficulties and uncertainties: at the interface between mental disorder and physical disorder, for example, or between mental disorder and criminality, or between mental disorder and mental incapacity. The interface between mental disorder and deviance or anti-social behaviour has proved notoriously problematic over the years and will no doubt continue to do so.[5] In England and Wales it is the interface between mental disorder and mental incapacity that is causing the most practical concern at present.

England and Wales, like many other jurisdictions, has two schemes, one governing those who lack capacity and one governing people with mental disorder. To be lawful, involuntary intervention that interferes with the rights of an individual must meet the requirements of one or other scheme. Thus, for a significant section of the inpatient population, clinical teams in England and Wales are now required to decide which scheme to employ: the Mental Health Act 1983 (England and Wales) (the MHA) or the Mental Capacity Act 2005 (the MCA).

The MHA establishes a framework for the provision of medical treatment for those people who suffer from mental disorder to the necessary degree, on an involuntary, or even compulsory basis. The main criteria for the application of the MHA are the presence of mental disorder and risk to the patient or to others. The MCA provides a more general framework through which decisions may be made on behalf of adults who lack the relevant decision-making capacity. These decisions may include those relating to medical treatment. The absence of decision-making capacity is the main criterion for the application of the MCA. To some extent, the populations covered by these two statutory schemes overlap. Many of those with a mental disorder of sufficient gravity to trigger the MHA will lack decision-making capacity,[6] while some adults who lack capacity and fall under the MCA will require treatment for mental disorder.[7] Individuals who require treatment for mental disorder but who lack the necessary capacity to make decisions about that treatment could be covered by either framework.

---

[5] D Bolton, *What is Mental Disorder?: An Essay in Philosophy, Science and Values* (Oxford, Oxford University Press, 2008).

[6] G Owen, G Richardson, A David, G Szmukler, P Hayward and M Hotopf, 'Mental Capacity to Make Decisions on Treatment in People Admitted to Psychiatric Hospitals: Cross Sectional Study' (2008) 337 *British Medical Journal* 448.

[7] V Raymont, W Bingley, A Buchanan, A David, P Hayward, S Wessely and M Hotopf, 'Prevalence of Mental Incapacity in Medical In-patients and Associated Risk Factors: Cross Sectional Study' (2004) 364 *Lancet* 1421.

Despite this significant overlap in coverage, the two statutes are designed for very different jobs. The MHA is primarily concerned with the reduction of the risks flowing from mental disorder both to the patient and to others.[8] The MCA is designed to 'empower people to make decisions for themselves wherever possible, and to protect people who lack capacity'.[9] The MCA is governed by principles which ensure that decisions reflect the individual's best interests and that the least restrictive intervention is used. This bifurcation of principle and the discrimination which flows from it have been the subject of much heated debate in both the academic literature and the political process preceding the recent legislative reforms.[10] This chapter will not rehearse further this sorry tale. Instead it will concentrate on the practical implications which flow from the interface between the two Acts in an attempt to understand the performance of the law. Because of the particular issues raised by the need to comply with Article 5 of the ECHR, it will focus on the provision of treatment in hospital, not in the community. As suggested above, this legislative separation between mental capacity and mental disorder is by no means special to England and Wales. It is common throughout developed legal systems.[11] Thus, although the precise legal and service context will differ across jurisdictions, the essential dilemmas will remain: Can we distinguish between mental disorder and mental capacity? Why do we do so? And what are the consequences?

A.   The Statutory Structure in England and Wales

The MHA provides for the legal detention of patients in hospital for assessment and treatment for mental disorder. Prior to the enactment of the MCA patients who lacked the capacity to consent to stay in hospital but who did not openly object were typically accommodated in hospital informally under the common law without resort to the MHA.[12] In *HL v United Kingdom*[13] this practice was held to be in breach of Article 5 of the ECHR in cases where the restrictions imposed on the individual amounted to a deprivation of liberty under the terms

---

[8]   Great Britain. Department of Health, *Reforming the Mental Health Act* Parts I and II (London, TSO, 2000).

[9]   *Mental Capacity Act 2005 Code of Practice* (London, TSO, 2007) Foreword.

[10]   See, eg, J Peay, 'Reform of the Mental Health Act 1983: Squandering an Opportunity' (2000) 3 *Journal of Mental Health Law* 5; A Eldergill, 'Is Anyone Safe? Civil Compulsion under the Draft Mental Health Bill' (2002) 8 *Journal of Mental Health Law* 331; G Richardson, 'Balancing Autonomy and Risk: A Failure of Nerve in England and Wales?' (2007) 30 *International Journal of Law and Psychiatry* 71; A Boyle, 'The Law and Incapacity Determinations: A Conflict of Governance?' (2008) 71 *Modern Law Review* 433; Joint Committee on the Draft Mental Health Bill, *Report*, vol I [2005] HL 79–I, HC 95–I (London, TSO, 2005).

[11]   See E Fistein, A Holland, I Clare and M Gunn, 'A Comparison of Mental Health Legislation from Diverse Commonwealth Jurisdictions' (2009) *International Journal of Law and Psychiatry* 147.

[12]   *R v Bournewood Community Mental Health Trust NHS, ex parte L* [1999] 1 AC 481 (HL).

[13]   *HL v United Kingdom* (2005) 40 EHRR 32.

of that article. As it was originally drafted, the MCA did nothing to remedy this non-compliance. Since April 2009 safeguards introduced via the Mental Health Act 2007 have been in place to enable patients who lack capacity lawfully to be deprived of their liberty in their own best interests.

Finding exactly the right mechanism to safeguard properly the interests of a highly vulnerable group of patients without imposing a disproportionate burden on limited resources was always going to be extremely difficult.[14] It would be in no one's interests to burden the system with complex legal processes at the expense of improvements in care, that is, to elevate legalism over quality of care. It is still far too early to judge whether the 2007 amendments to the MCA have found the right balance, or anything approaching it, but a preliminary glance at MCA Schedules A1 and 1A, and at the MCA Code of Practice supplement *Deprivation of Liberty Safeguards*[15] is very far from reassuring. Mercifully it is not the intention here to describe the nature of these safeguards; that has been done elsewhere.[16] Instead this chapter will identify some of the crucial factors that clinical teams will now have to confront when deciding which statutory framework to adopt. It will consider those factors in the light of existing research.

According to current guidance in relation to all inpatients who lack capacity, clinical teams must decide which framework to employ.[17] The MCA as amended specifies some of the factors governing the choice. In particular Schedule 1A, paragraph 5, indicates that if *P* meets the criteria for MHA detention and objects either to being in hospital or to any element of the treatment proposed, then the MHA should be preferred.[18] Of course clinical teams will not be puzzled by the choice of framework in relation to every patient who is admitted to a psychiatric ward. There will be those patients for whom detention under the MHA is the only realistic option and still others for whom neither scheme is required because they clearly retain mental capacity and are content to remain in hospital as voluntary patients. The group in relation to whom the choice is relevant and must consciously be made is of those who require treatment for mental disorder in hospital and lack the relevant capacity. Patients in this group have effectively been given new rights in the form of safeguards which must now be applied to their involuntary treatment and hospitalisation. How will these rights be implemented and to what effect?

---

[14] For early recognition of the problems see, Great Britain, Department of Health. Expert Committee. *Review of the Mental Health Act 1983: Report of the Expert Committee* (London, Department of Health, 1999) ch 14.

[15] *Mental Capacity Act 2005: Deprivation of Liberty Safeguards Code of Practice* (London, TSO, 2008).

[16] A Weereratne, S Hadfield, U Burnham and A Gerry, *Butterworths New Law Guide: Mental Capacity Act 2005* (London, LexisNexis, 2008).

[17] *Mental Health Act 1983 Code of Practice* (London, TSO, 2008) at [4.13]–[4.17].

[18] See for further guidance, *Mental Capacity Act 2005: Deprivation of Liberty Safeguards Code of Practice* (London, TSO, 2008).

A recent study involving patients admitted to three psychiatric wards in inner London between February 2006 and June 2007 gives some idea of the likely size of this relevant population.[19] Two hundred patients were interviewed and both their capacity and their legal status were recorded.[20] The results are set out in Table 1.

Table 1: Capacity and Legal Status of 200 Patients in Three London Wards

	Capacity	Incapacity
Informal	73	47
Formal	12	68
Total	**85**	**115**

A large minority of patients, around 40 per cent, retained capacity and would not therefore attract the choice under consideration. Indeed the largest single group was that of the informal patients with capacity. The clear majority of all the patients, just under 60 per cent, lacked capacity and 47 of those, or 24 per cent of the whole sample, fell clearly into the target group, that is, informal patients who lack capacity. If this sample is at all representative of the inpatient population in England and Wales then it suggests that clinical teams will be confronted with the choice between the MHA and the MCA in over half of all admissions to acute wards. Of course in many cases the decision to use the MHA might be clearly indicated: after all, 68 of the incapable patients in the sample were detained under the MHA and we may assume that the MHA would still have been used in the majority of those cases even if detention via the MCA had been available. This leaves at least 24 per cent of all admissions where incapacity was found and the MHA was not used. Here the choice will be very real.

So the recent legal reforms present the clinical team with a series of questions:

- Does the patient lack the relevant decision-making capacity?
- If so which framework should apply? MHA or MCA?
- In particular, does the patient object to either admission or treatment?
- Is deprivation of liberty required?

Strictly speaking, the first question applies to all admissions. If capacity is absent then the next two questions will apply whether or not deprivation of liberty is at issue, but the focus here is on deprivation of liberty. When that is in issue clinical

---

[19] G Owen, G Richardson, A David, G Szmukler, P Hayward and M Hotopf, 'Mental Capacity to Make Decisions on Treatment in People Admitted to Psychiatric Hospitals: Cross Sectional Study' (2008) 337 *British Medical Journal* 448.

[20] G Owen, G Szmukler, G Richardson, A David, P Hayward, J Rucker, D Harding and M Hotopf, 'Mental Capacity and Psychiatric Inpatients: Some Implications for the New Mental Health Law' (2010) *British Journal of Psychiatry* (forthcoming). The capacity assessment was achieved using both the MacCAT-T assessment tool and a clinical interview.

teams will have to become familiar with the application of three concepts: mental capacity/incapacity, objection and deprivation of liberty. While the relevance of these concepts has increased enormously in England and Wales, thanks to the recent reforms, they, or concepts like them, are likely to be familiar in most jurisdictions where parallel statutes apply to mental disorder and mental capacity. Some understanding of how they might be interpreted in practice is therefore essential if we are to understand the role of the law in policing the boundaries of coercion at the interface between mental disorder and mental capacity.

B. Capacity/Incapacity

(i) The Legal Criteria

In law the concept of decision-making capacity is commonly used to distinguish decisions or choices which attract the law's respect from those which do not.[21] Only decisions made with capacity are regarded as autonomous and thus worthy of respect. In the medical context capacity is central to the law of consent. The law will not recognise a consent to medical treatment, nor a refusal of medical treatment unless it is made with capacity. Capacity thus performs a crucial role in setting the threshold for the legal protection of a patient's decision. In England and Wales the concept of capacity emerged originally through the common law and to a large extent the statutory definition builds on the position at common law.[22]

At the heart of the MCA lies the principle that 'a person must be assumed to have capacity unless it is established that he lacks capacity'.[23] Once there is reason to doubt a person's capacity, his or her decision-making ability must be assessed according to the statutory criteria. Accordingly, a person lacks capacity in relation to a particular matter if he is unable to make a decision for himself because of 'an impairment of, or a disturbance in the functioning of, the mind or brain'.[24] A person

> is unable to make a decision for himself if he is unable a) to understand the information relevant to the decision, b) to retain that information, c) to use or weigh that information as part of the process of making the decision, or d) to communicate his decision.[25]

---

[21] The emphasis on individual autonomy and the importance consequently placed on capacity can be seen as a very Western notion: C Foster, *Choosing Life, Choosing Death: The Tyranny of Autonomy in Medical Ethics and Law* (Oxford, Hart Publishing, 2009) and M Kara, 'Applicability of the Principle of Respect for Autonomy: The Perspective of Turkey' (2007) 33 *Journal of Medical Ethics* 627.

[22] Law Commission, *Mental Incapacity* Report No 231 (1995).

[23] Mental Capacity Act 2005 s 1(2).

[24] *ibid*, s 2(1).

[25] *ibid*, s 3(1).

In the context of inpatient psychiatric care it may be reasonable to assume the presence of the first requirement: 'an impairment of, or a disturbance in the functioning of, the mind or brain'. The criteria set out in section 3 are more open to interpretation. Here clinical teams will have to use their judgement, guided by the MCA Code of Practice. While mental health professionals may well differ in their application of the criteria to individual cases, research has indicated that the use of established assessment tools can achieve high levels of inter-rater consistency.[26] Ultimately, of course it will be for the courts to resolve any disputes, but it is necessary to consider the dilemmas raised in applying these criteria to psychiatric patients.

Although this statutory definition applies only to England and Wales, it closely resembles the tests for capacity refined from US case law.[27] In relation to treatment decisions these tests or criteria have been expressed by Thomas Grisso and Paul Applebaum as the ability to express a choice about treatment, to understand information relevant to the treatment decision, to appreciate the significance of that treatment information for one's own situation, and to reason with relevant information so as to engage in a logical process of weighing treatment options.[28]

While Grisso and Appelbaum's analysis is designed as a descriptive definition written to inform clinical practice rather than as an authoritative statement of the law in the United States of America, it has provided the basis for a clinical tool now used widely to assess mental capacity, the MacArthur Competence Assessment Tool for Treatment (MacCAT-T).[29] This tool provides a semi-structured interview, which enables the assessor to evaluate capacity in terms of four abilities closely resembling, although not precisely replicating, the criteria listed in MCA, section 3(1): understanding, appreciation, reasoning and expressing a choice. It has been used in the United States to assess decision-making capacity in relation to treatment decisions in many different clinical contexts.[30] The high inter-rater agreement that has been reported by a number of research groups indicates that it can achieve high levels of consistency between evaluators.[31] In the United Kingdom, it has also been used to determine the incidence of incapacity on

---

[26] R Cairns, C Maddock, A Buchanan, A David, P Hayward, G Richardson, G Szmukler and M Hotopf, 'Reliability of Mental Capacity Assessments in Psychiatric In-patients' (2005) 187 *British Journal of Psychiatry* 372.

[27] W Berg, P Appelbaum and T Grisso, 'Constructing Competence: Formulating Standards of Legal Competence to make Medical Decisions' (1995–1996) 48 *Rutgers Law Review* 345.

[28] T Grisso and P Applebaum, *Assessing Competence to Consent to Treatment: A Guide for Physicians and Other Health Professionals* (New York, Oxford University Press, 1998).

[29] T Grisso and P Appelbaum, *MacArthur Competence Assessment Tool for Treatment (MacCAT-T)* (Sarasota, Professional Resources Press, 1998).

[30] P Appelbaum, 'Assessment of Patients' Competence to Consent to Treatment' (2007) 357 *New England Journal of Medicine* 1834.

[31] *ibid*; L Dunn, M Nowrangi, B Palmer, D Jeste and E Saks, 'Assessing Decisional Capacity for Clinical Research or Treatment: A Review of Instruments' (2006) 163 *American Journal of Psychiatry* 1323.

general medical wards[32] and on acute psychiatric wards.[33] Again, high levels of inter-rater agreement have been reported.[34] The MacCAT-T can therefore be used with some confidence to measure decision-making capacity against criteria that satisfy the requirements of the MCA.

(ii) The Application to Psychiatric Disorders

Reliable though the MacCAT-T may be in assessing capacity against its own criteria and, by analogy, against those provided by the MCA, those criteria have themselves been the object of some debate.[35] To a significant extent both the MacCAT-T and the MCA criteria have been developed in the context of physical or cognitive disorders and are not specifically designed to capture the complexities of decision-making within the psychiatric sphere. It has been suggested that, as a consequence, they are ill-suited to use in relation to psychiatric disorders where they might run the risk of either under- or over-identifying incapacity. In particular it has been suggested that the MacCAT-T places too much emphasis on cognition and rationality, leading to an inadequate treatment of insight and a lack of understanding of delusions,[36] and that it gives insufficient weight to the role of values and emotion.[37] In the context of eating disorders, in particular, the work of Tan *et al* has illustrated the difficulties which may arise from the development of 'pathological' or 'inauthentic' values—difficulties which cannot adequately be described in terms of deficiencies in understanding or retaining information, or as gross disturbances in thinking.[38]

Certainly the requirements of understanding, retaining and communicating contained in section 3 of the MCA, can be seen as predominantly cognitive. They cannot on their own capture the core clinical concept of insight, nor can they fully reflect the role of emotions and values. The requirement to 'use or weigh' may be more flexible and is often seen as a close equivalent of the notion of

---

[32] *X v United Kingdom* (1982) 4 EHRR 118 and *HL v United Kingdom* (2005) 40 EHRR 32.

[33] R Cairns, C Maddock, A Buchanan, A David, P Hayward, G Richardson, G Szmukler and M Hotopf, 'Prevalence and Predictors of Mental Incapacity in Psychiatric In-patients' (2005) 187 *British Journal of Psychiatry* 379.

[34] *ibid*, 372.

[35] G Owen, F Freyenhagen, G Richardson and M Hotopf, 'Mental Capacity and Decisional Autonomy: An Interdisciplinary Challenge' (2009) 52 *Inquiry: An Interdisciplinary Journal of Philosophy* 79.

[36] M Jackson and K Fulford, 'Spiritual Experience and Psychopatholgy' (1997) 4 *Philosophy, Psychiatry and Psychology* 41.

[37] L Charland, 'Appreciation and Emotion: Theoretical Reflections on the MacArthur Treatment Competence Study' (1998) 8 *Kennedy Institute Ethics Journal* 359; T Breden and J Vollmann, 'The Cognitive Based Approach of Capacity Assessment in Psychiatry: A Philosophical Critique of the MacCAT-T' (2004) 12 *Health Care Analysis* 273.

[38] J Tan, T Hope and A Stewart, 'Competence to Refuse Treatment in Anorexia Nervosa' (2003) 23 *International Journal of Law and Psychiatry* 697; and J Tan, T Hope, A Stewart and R Fitzpatrick, 'Competence to Make Treatment Decisions in Anorexia Nervosa: Thinking Processes and Values' (2006) 13 *Philosophy, Psychiatry and Psychology* 267.

appreciation included in case law in the United States and the MacCAT-T.[39] On the other hand, in relation to rationality and logical reasoning, which is said to be over-emphasised in the MacCAT-T, the MCA is less vulnerable to criticism. Section 3 makes no express reference to either rationality or the need to reason logically, although it is possible that the need to reason is incorporated in the requirement to 'use or weigh'.[40] In order to examine these issues further it is useful to look at both the research data and the relevant case law. The law cannot provide effective guidance at the boundaries if the concepts it employs are deficient or irrelevant.

(iii) Insight

As Ian Freckelton explores in chapter nine of this volume, insight has long been recognised as core to the clinical understanding of schizophrenia;[41] it has acquired an acknowledged place in psychiatric assessments[42] and it has proved capable of measurement.[43] Despite its widespread use, however, insight remains controversial even within psychiatry[44] and notoriously hard to define. Like the concept of time, insight is easier to use than to define.[45] For present purposes lack of insight can be understood as a lack of awareness of illness, but even this reduced definition harbours tensions within it. At its core lies a judgement about the patient's ability to accept certain experience or behaviour as pathological, thus giving it an inherently subjective character. It is this subjective, or as some would say normative or value-laden,[46] character of insight that perhaps lies at the heart of some of our instinctive suspicion of the concept.

Whatever its value in clinical practice, it is clear that insight is a concept utilised, even if not defined, by law. It is evident in the context of both detention decisions and capacity judgements. In relation to detention it is widely employed across jurisdictions by those responsible for decisions regarding the discharge from hospital of involuntary patients. According to Kate Diesfeld, both research and case law indicate that insight is of considerable significance in discharge

---

[39]   G Owen, F Freyenhagen, G Richardson and M Hotopf, 'Mental Capacity and Decisional Autonomy: An Interdisciplinary Challenge' (2009) 52 *Inquiry: An Interdisciplinary Journal of Philosophy* 79.

[40]   *ibid.*

[41]   J McEvoy, P Applebaum, L Apperson, J Geller and S Freter, 'Why must some Schizophrenic Patients be Involuntarily Committed? The Role of Insight' (1989) 30 *Comprehensive Psychiatry* 13.

[42]   A David, 'Insight and Psychosis' (1990) 161 *British Journal of Psychiatry* 599.

[43]   *ibid*; G Owen, A David, G Richardson, G Szmukler, P Hayward and M Hotopf, 'Mental Capacity, Diagnosis, and Insight in Psychiatric Inpatients: A Cross Sectional Study' (2008) 39 *Psychological Medicine* 1389.

[44]   R Perkins and P Moodley, 'The Arrogance of Insight?' (1993) 17 *Psychiatric Bulletin* 233.

[45]   K Fulford, 'Insight and Delusion: From Jaspers to Kraeplin and Back Again via Austin' in X Amador and A David (eds), *Insight and Psychosis* (Oxford, Oxford University Press, 2004). See also Ian Freckelton, this volume, ch 9.

[46]   G Owen, F Freyenhagen, G Richardson and M Hotopf, 'Mental Capacity and Decisional Autonomy: An Interdisciplinary Challenge' (2009) 52 *Inquiry: An Interdisciplinary Journal of Philosophy* 79.

decision-making in the United Kingdom, Australia and New Zealand. She observes that '[r]eview bodies and clinicians are disinclined to discharge until patients demonstrate insight'.[47] It is effectively a de facto discharge criterion but remains without formal definition.

In the context of treatment decisions, the relationship between insight and capacity has also been subjected to scrutiny. Writing in 2004, Ken Kress argued that in light of advances in the understanding and measurement of insight, it should now play a more significant role in mental health law as a determinant of involuntary treatment.[48] He is not suggesting that it should replace the consideration of decision-making capacity but that it should be employed alongside it. To some extent this argument is supported by the results of recent research conducted at the Maudsley Hospital, London.[49] This study assessed both the incapacity status and the insight of 200 patients admitted to three acute general psychiatric wards. The research concluded that low insight is associated with incapacity. Indeed of all the clinical constructs applied in the research, insight was the strongest discriminator of capacity status and it discriminated across all diagnostic groups. It was most discriminatory in patients with psychotic disorders and in those in the manic episodes of bipolar affective disorder. For patients with non-psychotic disorders it was less successful. Thus, insight and incapacity, as defined by MacCAT-T,[50] appear to coincide in common psychiatric disorders—very closely in some, less so in others. This suggests that even though the MacCAT-T makes no direct reference to insight it appears, through the notion of appreciation, to capture the same population of patients, particularly in the context of psychotic disorders. In relation to the non-psychotic disorders incapacity may mean something other than or in addition to lack of insight as understood by clinicians.

The research conducted at the Maudsley used the MacCAT-T criteria for incapacity rather than those from the MCA or the common law, neither of which contains appreciation. This immediately raises the question whether the requirement 'to use or to weigh' employed by English law would display the same close relationship to insight. There can be no definitive answer to this, particularly in the absence of any case law on the interpretation of section 3 itself. Nevertheless there is some indication in the common law case law that the courts see lack of insight as intimately linked with lack of capacity. Two judgments from 2006 give

---

[47] K Diesfeld, 'Insights on 'Insight': The Impact of Extra-legislative Factors on Decisions to Discharge Patients' in K Diesfeld and I Freckelton (eds), *Involuntary Detention and Therapeutic Jurisprudence* (Aldershot, Ashgate, 2003).

[48] K Kress, 'Why Lack of Insight Should have a Central Place in Mental Health Law' in X Amador and A David (eds), *Insight and Psychosis* (Oxford, Oxford University Press, 2004).

[49] G Owen, G Richardson, A David, G Szmukler, P Hayward and M Hotopf, 'Mental Capacity to Make Decisions on Treatment in People Admitted to Psychiatric Hospitals: Cross Sectional Study' (2008) 337 *British Medical Journal* 448.

[50] T Grisso and P Appelbaum, *MacArthur Competence Assessment Tool for Treatment (MacCAT-T)* (Sarasota, Professional Resources Press, 1998).

a flavour of the judicial approach. In *Trust A, Trust B v H*,[51] having described the patient's delusional state, the Family Division concluded:

> [I]t is clear from a number of observations that she does not appreciate the seriousness of her condition and the sense of threat to life which it presents if unalleviated by such surgery. I am thus satisfied that H lacks capacity to make decisions about her medical treatment for her ovarian cyst and gynaecological condition.[52]

In the same year the Court of Appeal considered the case of a patient detained in Broadmoor who refused the antipsychotic medication prescribed by his responsible doctor:

> [W]e think that it is plain that a patient will lack that capacity if he is not able to appreciate the likely effects of having or not having the treatment. The judge found that this was the position so far as Mr B was concerned in that he did not accept even the possibility that he might be mentally ill and thus in need of treatment.[53]

If this case law can be taken as a guide to the way in which section 3 will be interpreted, then it seems likely that the coincidence established between insight and capacity as defined by the MacCAT-T will be equally strong when capacity is assessed according to section 3. The conclusions to be drawn from this for the choice between capacity and insight as possible determinants of involuntary treatment will not be pursued here. The above discussion does suggest that whatever the reservations attaching to insight and its definition, its essence can be captured through the assessment of capacity whether by way of the MacCAT-T or the MCA. To this extent the law's understanding of capacity coincides with that of psychiatric practice, which would indicate that the legal notion of capacity does have a relevant clinical meaning.

(iv)   Delusions

Within psychiatry the complex relationship between insight and delusions is well recognised. Indeed early approaches to insight drew the two very closely together. Suzanne Jolley and Philippa Garety write: 'delusions and conventional psychiatric insight are inextricably linked—one cannot hold a delusional belief with conviction and have insight into its nature as a symptom'.[54] In the case law, however, although evidence of delusional belief and lack of insight may both be present, the connection between the two is seldom made explicit.[55] Delusions have proved very hard to define but for present purposes they can be taken to involve a 'false, fixed belief based on incorrect inference about external reality

---

[51]   *Trust A and Trust B v H (an adult patient) (Represented by her Litigation Friend, the Official Solicitor)* [2006] EWHC 1230 Fam.

[52]   *ibid*, at [23] (Sir Mark Potter, P).

[53]   *R(B) v Dr SS* [2006] EWCA Civ 28 at [34] (Lord Philips CJ).

[54]   S Jolley and P Garety, 'Insight and Delusions: A Cognitive Psychological Approach' in X Amador and A David (eds), *Insight and Psychosis* (Oxford, Oxford University Press, 2004).

[55]   See, eg *Trust A v H (an adult patient)* [2006] EWHC 1230 Fam.

and out of keeping with that person's culture'.[56] At first sight delusions, so understood, present a dilemma for legal definitions of capacity. The law typically operates a presumption in favour of capacity. An individual will be presumed to have the capacity to consent to or to refuse treatment unless there is evidence to the contrary.[57] Further, at the level of rhetoric, the English common law is prepared to recognise capacity despite the presence of irrationality in either the decision-making process or the outcome. In relation to the process, the Court of Appeal has stated:

> A mentally competent patient has an absolute right to refuse to consent to medical treatment for any reason, rational or irrational, or for no reason at all, even where that decision may lead to his or her own death.[58]

And with regard to the decision itself: 'that [the patient's] choice is contrary to what is to be expected by the vast majority of adults is only relevant if there are other reasons for doubting his [or her] capacity to decide'.[59] Thus, a person may be able to understand and retain the information relevant to his or her treatment but his or her final decision may be based on a delusional belief. The delusional belief may constitute an 'irrational reason', but according to the Court of Appeal, that cannot on its own amount to incapacity. In practice the courts have avoided this conclusion by employing a generous interpretation of the requirements relating to understanding and to using or weighing. In *Re T*[60] the court was clear that a refusal of a blood transfusion based on the patient's belief that her blood was evil should not be respected. The patient's misperception of reality had rendered her incapable of using and weighing the relevant information. Similarly, in *Trust A and Trust B v H*[61] the court recognised that the patient's belief that she had no children and her desire to bear children in the future were delusional and this contributed to the eventual finding of incapacity.

So whatever the formal legal position, in individual cases the courts seem willing to adopt an interpretation of the criteria that will enable them to find incapacity when a decision is based on a delusional belief. Such a pragmatic approach enables the courts to avoid the need to respect decisions which they regard as not truly autonomous. It also leaves them latitude in the definition of delusion or false belief, thus providing ample scope for the reflection of judicial values in determining when a belief becomes delusional. In this respect, incapacity may be as open to manipulation as mental disorder itself.

---

[56] *The Diagnostic and Statistical Manual of Mental Disorders*, 4th edn text revision (Washington DC, American Psychiatric Association, 2000).

[57] Mental Capacity Act 2005 s 1(2).

[58] *Re MB (an adult: medical treatment)* [1997] 2 FCR 541, 549.

[59] *Re T (adult: refusal of treatment)* [1992] 4 All ER 649, 662. See also Mental Capacity Act 2005 s 1(4).

[60] *NHS Trust v T* [2004] EWHC 1279 (Fam).

[61] *Trust A and Trust B v H (An Adult Patient) (Represented by her Litigation Friend, the Official Solicitor)* [2006] EWHC 1230 (Fam).

(v)   Values

The conceptual difficulties raised by delusions are further illustrated by the presence of 'pathological' values. People suffering from certain forms of mental disorder may experience quite extreme changes in values. In anorexia nervosa, for example, being thin may be of paramount importance, more important than being healthy or possibly even than staying alive. A similar distortion of values may also occur in acute depression. Following a study of 10 patients with anorexia nervosa, Jacinta Tan and colleagues have argued that the MacCAT-T is ill-equipped to capture the distorted reasoning that can lead to the refusal of life-saving treatment.[62] They argue that the patients in the study were able to score well on the MacCAT-T test of competence—'exhibiting excellent under-standing, reasoning, and ability to express a choice'[63]—and yet their decisions in relation to treatment were compromised by their difficulties in relation to factual beliefs and changed values, in ways which threw doubt on their true capacity to consent to or to refuse treatment. Tan and colleagues consider whether the development of a notion of pathological values, values springing from the disorder, might assist in the application of standard tests of capacity to disorders such as anorexia nervosa.[64] In answer, the authors of the MacCAT-T argue that the distortions of reality resulting from the changes in value experienced by those with anorexia nervosa are precisely those that are captured by the existing 'lack of appreciation' criterion.[65]

Two English cases in the 1990s addressed the question of anorexia nervosa and capacity to consent. Both involved young women under the age of 18 but the courts' attitude to the impact of anorexia on mental capacity specifically does not appear to have been significantly affected by age considerations. In *Re W*[66] the court of appeal accepted the trial court's finding that a 16 year old with anorexia was competent to decide her medical treatment. However, in his judgment Lord Donaldson expressed doubts about this conclusion arguing: 'that it is a feature of anorexia nervosa that it is capable of destroying the ability to make an informed choice. It creates a compulsion to refuse treatment or only to accept treatment which is likely to be ineffective'.[67] In *Re C*[68] there was medical evidence to the effect that a 16 year old was not capable of consent due to the distorting effects of anorexia:

---

[62]   J Tan, T Hope, A Stewart and R Fitzpatrick, 'Competence to Make Treatment Decisions in Anorexia Nervosa: Thinking Processes and Values' (2006) 13 *Philosophy, Psychiatry and Psychology* 267.

[63]   *ibid*, 270.

[64]   *ibid.*

[65]   T Grisso and P Appelbaum, 'Appreciating Anorexia: Decisional Capacity and the Role of Values' (2006) 13 *Philosophy, Psychiatry and Psychology*, 293.

[66]   *Re W (a minor) (medical treatment)* [1992] 4 All ER 627 (CA).

[67]   *ibid*, 637.

[68]   *Re C (a minor)* [1997] 2 FLR 180.

It is a feature of anorexia and related eating disorders that information is distorted in this way. The immediate gratification involved in being able to override the pangs of hunger, and to feel in control, is such that worries about the effects on the body, and eventually threats to life itself, are ignored.[69]

On the basis of such evidence, Wall J concluded that *C* was unable to weigh the information relevant to her treatment and was thus incapable of giving a valid consent.[70] Thus, as with delusions, in cases of distorted values the English courts are willing to interpret the incapacity criteria flexibly in order to avoid the need to respect decisions which they clearly regard as 'disordered'.

So, despite the cognitive origins of the criteria and the reservations that have been expressed about their ability to capture the complexity of mental disorder, the case law itself suggests that the courts' pragmatic attitude, coupled with a disinclination to condone withholding treatment where it is medically indicated, will tend to avoid under-inclusion. Lack of insight, the presence of delusions and a distortion in values have all been regarded as included within the flexible requirements of understanding, using and weighing. While this might answer the specific fears of under-inclusion, it does so by providing generous scope for the exercise of judicial values, thus raising concerns about possible over-inclusion.

What can we conclude from this about the validity of the law's distinction between capacity and incapacity when it is applied to psychiatric disorders? It is a distinction which, from both the research on insight and the case law itself, appears able to reflect a psychiatric understanding of the severity of disorder. While this would suggest that the capacity/incapacity distinction is compatible with the therapeutic endeavour, it may at the same time throw doubt on its ability to provide sufficient clarity on which effectively to build rights protection.

(vi) Objecting

As already described, the amended MCA specifies some of the factors which are to govern the choice between the use of the MHA and the MCA in cases where a patient lacks capacity and deprivation of their liberty is considered. In particular where a patient meets the criteria for admission under the MHA and objects to either the admission to hospital or some element of their proposed treatment, then the MHA should be used. Thus the presence or otherwise of an objection can become a crucial factor. There are certainly questions to be asked about why objecting should be regarded as so significant and whether some other determining factor might be more appropriate. Any jurisdiction which maintains parallel statutes will have to include some factors to govern the choice. In England and Wales it happens to be objection.

[69] Quoted in I Kennedy and A Grubb, *Medical Law*, 3rd edn (London, Butterworths, 2000) 640.
[70] For further discussion of the courts' attitude to the treatment of anorexia nervosa see P Lewis, 'Feeding Anorexic Patients who Refuse Food (1999) 7 *Medical Law Review* 21, and S Giodano, *Understanding Eating Disorders: Conceptual and Ethical Issues in the Treatment of Anorexia and Bulimia Nervosa* (Oxford, Clarendon Press, 2005).

Whatever those factors might be, it can be assumed that clarity in their interpretation would be valued both by those who have to apply them and by those directly subjected to them. Unfortunately in the case of 'objects' in England and Wales no definition is provided by the relevant statutes, although the MCA does specify the issues that have to be taken into account when determining whether an incapable patient is objecting.[71] Thus, provided these statutory factors are *taken into account*, clinicians will in practice be able to use their own judgement in determining the presence or absence of objection.

However, given the plasticity of the notion of objection it is difficult to predict exactly where the cut-off point will be. In the study of psychiatric inpatients described above the patients' level of compliance with treatment was assessed using a scale contained within the Expanded Schedule for the Assessment of Insight (SAI-E).[72] This is a seven-point scale, ranging from complete rejection to active participation. If anything from occasional reluctance downwards is equated with objection, then 38 per cent of the informal patients who lacked capacity must be regarded as objecting. On the other hand, if P must reject treatment either partially or completely before objection is present then only six per cent of the patients were objecting. In England and Wales the immediate consequence of adopting the broader understanding of objection would be a significant increase in the use of the MHA as a result of the recent reforms. More widely, the data illustrates the difficulty of establishing a workable criterion on which to choose between the two statutory frameworks. A jurisdiction which has parallel statutes has to have some way of knowing which patients fall into which framework. The presence of objection without further definition, it seems, is not a sensible basis on which to police the boundary.

(vii)   Deprivation of Liberty

In England and Wales patients who lack capacity can still be accommodated and treated in hospital or residential care informally provided their treatment complies with the principles of the MCA and the conditions do not amount to a deprivation of liberty. However, since the case of *HL v UK* it is clear that the conditions under which an individual is accommodated in a hospital or nursing home may amount to a deprivation of liberty under Article 5 of the ECHR, in which case that deprivation must comply with the requirements of that article if it is to be lawful.[73] According to the ECtHR the common law which had been widely used to detain in cases of incapacity was not so compliant. Consequently, in jurisdictions covered by the ECHR, it has become essential for clinical teams and other health and social care decision-makers to be able to recognise a

---

[71]   Mental Capacity Act 2005 Sch 1A, para 5.6.
[72]   G Owen, G Szmukler, G Richardson, A David, P Hayward, J Rucker, D Harding and M Hotopf, 'Mental Capacity and Psychiatric Inpatients: Some Implications for the New Mental Health Law' (2010) *British Journal of Psychiatry* (forthcoming).
[73]   *HL v United Kingdom* (2005) 40 EHRR 32.

deprivation of liberty (DoL) and to know when the restrictions imposed on a patient are sufficient to amount to a DoL. In England and Wales if DoL is required a choice must now be made between the two statutory schemes,[74] and if the MCA route is preferred then the new DoL safeguards will have to be used.[75] Whatever the precise mechanism that a jurisdiction chooses to employ in order to comply with the requirements of Article 5 and the *HL* judgment, it will be necessary to develop a clear understanding of what constitutes a deprivation of liberty for the purposes of Article 5.

(a)   Defining a DoL

The European Court of Human Rights in *HL* itself provided general guidance on the identification of a DoL, but admitted that: 'the distinction between a deprivation of, and restriction upon, liberty is merely one of degree or intensity and not one of nature or substance'.[76] Several European and domestic cases both before and since *HL* have considered various aspects of the distinction.[77] In a helpful attempt to distill these judgments, the DoL Code of Practice lists seven relevant factors emerging from them.[78] The Code explains that there

> is unlikely to be any simple definition that can be applied in every case, and it is probable that no single factor will, in itself, determine whether the overall set of steps being taken in relation to the relevant person amount to a deprivation of liberty.

It then offers six issues/questions which 'the decision-maker should always consider' when determining whether a deprivation of liberty is likely to occur.[79] Unfortunately some of these are more circular than explanatory, for example:

> How are any restraints or restrictions implemented? Do any of the constraints on the individual's personal freedom go beyond 'restraint' or 'restriction' to the extent that they constitute a deprivation of liberty?
> Does the cumulative effect of all the restrictions imposed on the person amount to a deprivation of liberty, even if individually they would not?

So decision-makers in England and Wales guided by our domestic Code are effectively confronted with a range of factors which they need to consider, but no clear indication of the priority to be accorded to each. It has been suggested that the relevant decision-makers would be better advised to be guided by the formulation in *JE v DE*.[80] In that case Munby J took the opportunity to review all

---

[74]   For current advice on this choice see *Mental Health Act 1983: Code of Practice* (London, TSO, 2008) [4.13]–[4.24].

[75]   See *Mental Capacity Act 2005: Deprivation of Liberty Safeguards Code of Practice* (London, TSO, 2008).

[76]   *HL v United Kingdom* (2005) 40 EHRR 32 at [89].

[77]   For an excellent analysis of the case law, see A Weereratne, S Hadfield, U Burnham and A Gerry, *Butterworths New Law Guide: Mental Capacity Act 2005* (London, LexisNexis, 2008) ch 9.

[78]   *Mental Capacity Act 2005: Deprivation of Liberty Safeguards* (London, TSO, 2008) at [2.5].

[79]   *ibid*, at [2.6].

[80]   *JE v DE* [2007] MHLR 39.

the relevant European and domestic case law and broke the question down into three constitutive elements,[81] which may be paraphrased as follows:

1. The objective element, the fact of confinement in a restricted space for a non-negligible period of time. The key factor is whether the person is free to leave. This may be tested by determining whether those treating and managing the person exercise complete and effective control over the person's care and movements. Whether the person is in a ward which is 'locked' or 'lockable' is relevant but not determinative.

2. The subject element, the person has not given valid consent to the confinement. A person may give valid consent only if they have the capacity to do so.

3. The deprivation must be imputable to the state.

Aswini Weereratne and colleagues conclude that all three elements ought to be satisfied before there is a deprivation of liberty, but that paramountcy must be given to the question of whether or not the person is free to leave.[82] While this judicial formulation may offer more precision than that provided by the Code, the law remains obstinately uncertain, an uncertainty only exacerbated by the House of Lords' renewed reliance on motive in *Austin v Commissioner of Police of the Metropolis*.[83] To date we have no research evidence available on how the constituents of DoLs will be interpreted in practice.[84] If international human rights law is effectively to protect individuals from unauthorised deprivations of liberty, then we need to know with some certainty what a deprivation of liberty is.

(viii)   The Retrospective Views of Patients

The discussion so far has concerned the dilemmas presented by the law's attempts to maintain a distinction between mental health and mental capacity and to police the choice between the two. In England and Wales both the MCA and the MHA provide for *involuntary* treatment and hospitalisation, in the sense of treatment and hospitalisation in the absence of consent. The MHA has always provided for not just involuntary, but *compulsory* treatment and hospitalisation, in the sense of treatment and hospitalisation against the express wishes of the patient, whether capable or incapable. With the introduction of objection as a criterion for selecting the MHA over the MCA in cases where both are available, the relevance of that compulsory element of the MHA was further expanded. It may therefore be relevant to ask how patients view the use of compulsion and the role of the law in regulating its use.

---

[81]   *ibid*, at [77].

[82]   A Weereratne, S Hadfield, U Burnham and A Gerry, *Butterworths New Law Guide: Mental Capacity Act 2005* (London, LexisNexis, 2008) at [9.12].

[83]   *Austin v Commissioner of Police of the Metropolis* [2009] UKHL 5.

[84]   A small pilot is underway at the Maudsley Hospital, London.

Jurisdictions which provide for the compulsory treatment of mental disorder are authorising the formal use of coercion. There is an extensive literature concerned with the clinical implications of the use of coercion in psychiatry. This literature is not limited to the formal use of coercion. It tends to concentrate rather on coercion as perceived by the patient and this perception can be present in relation to compulsory, involuntary or even informal admissions.[85] While recent research has indicated that patients do resent coercion, some studies have suggested that this resentment may be reduced if the procedures of admission are seen to be fair.[86]

In a recent study involving 1570 compulsorily admitted patients in eight English NHS trusts 50 per cent were interviewed within the first week of admission and of these, 51 per cent were re-interviewed after a year.[87] Forty per cent of those interviewed after a year considered that their original admission had been justified. In the Maudsley study, described above, 115 patients who lacked capacity were interviewed after one month of treatment and asked for their views on the treatment they had received.[88] Eighty-five per cent of those who had regained capacity indicated approval and there was no discernable difference between those who had been compulsorily admitted and those who had been informal. Of those who did not regain capacity and were able to give a

[85]   J Monahan, S Hoge, C Lidz, L Roth, N Bennett, W Gardner and E Mulvey, 'Coercion and Commitment: Understanding Involuntary Hospital Admission' (1995) 18 *International Journal of Law and Psychiatry* 249; H Poulsen, 'Perceived Coercion among Committed, Detained and Voluntary Patients' (1999) 22 *International Journal of Law and Psychiatry* 167; H Poulsen, 'The Prevalence of Extralegal Deprivation of Liberty in a Psychiatric Hospital Population' (2002) 25 *International Journal of Law and Psychiatry* 29; G Hoyer, L Kjellin, M Engberg, R Kaltiala-Heino, T Nilstun, M Sigurjonsdottir and A Syse, 'Paternalism and Autonomy: A Presentation of a Nordic Study on the use of Coercion in the Mental Health Care System' (2002) 25 *International Journal of Law and Psychiatry* 93; B McKenna, A Simpson, and J Coverdale, 'Patients' Perceptions of Coercion on Admission to Forensic Psychiatric Hospital: A Comparison Study' (2003) 26 *International Journal of Law and Psychiatry* 355.

[86]   J Monahan, S Hoge, C Lidz, L Roth, N Bennett, W Gardner and E Mulvey, 'Coercion and Commitment: Understanding Involuntary Hospital Admission' (1995) 18 *International Journal of Law and Psychiatry* 249; V Hiday, M Swartz, J Swanson and H Wagner, 'Patient Perception of Coercion in Mental Hospital Admission' (1997) 20 *International Journal of Law and Psychiatry* 227; B McKenna, A Simpson, J Coverdale and T Laidlaw, 'An Analysis of Procedural Justice during Psychiatric Hospital Admission' (2001) 24 *International Journal of Law and Psychiatry* 573. This research relies on psychological studies of procedural justice which have emphasized the importance of 'voice', E Lind and T Tyler, *The Social Psychology of Procedural Justice* (New York, Plenum, 1988) and E Lind, R Kanfer and P Early, 'Voice, Control and Procedural Justice: Instrumental and Non-instrumental Concerns in Fairness Judgements' (1990) 59 *Journal of Personality and Social Psychology* 952, and to that extent reflects a familiar debate in law about the underlying purpose of fair procedures and due process, M Bayles, *Procedural Justice: Allocating to Individuals* (Dordrecht, Kluwer, 1990), G Richardson, *Law, Process and Custody: Prisoners and Patients* (London, Weidenfeld & Nicolson, 1994) and D Galligan, *Due Process and Fair Procedures: A Study of Administrative Procedures* (Oxford, Clarendon Press, 1996).

[87]   S Priebe, C Katsakou, T Amos, M Leese, R Morriss, D Rose, T Wykes and K Yeeles 'Patients' Views and Readmissions 1 Year after Involuntary Hospitalisation' (2009) 194 *British Journal of Psychiatry* 49.

[88]   G Owen, A David, P Hayward, G Richardson, G Szmukler and M Hotopf, 'Retrospective Views of Psychiatric Inpatients Regaining Mental Capacity' (2010) *British Journal of Psychiatry* (forthcoming).

view only 41 per cent expressed approval. Thus, the Maudsley study reports a much higher approval rate in relation to the patients who regained capacity than the overall rate reported by Priebe et al. The higher rate in the case of regained capacity may imply that patients who 'recover' are more inclined to judge their incapable states of mind as having required surrogate decision-making, whether they were detained compulsorily under the MHA or were informal (under the common law as was). Priebe et al did not consider the patients' capacity status and all their patients were compulsory, but they did record the patients' satisfaction with treatment in the first week. Lower initial satisfaction with treatment was associated with higher involuntary re-admission rates, while higher initial satisfaction with treatment was linked with more positive retrospective views of the admission. This leads Priebe et al to conclude that better procedures and communication from admission onwards could improve patients' initial satisfaction and thus their long-term outcomes.

Can any conclusions be drawn from these data with regard to the role of the law? The Maudsley study may suggest that what matters most is recovery. The process of admission and treatment is not determinative and, however coercive the intervention may be, patients will give retrospective approval provided it promotes recovery. Is the law's role then simply to facilitate beneficent intervention? To adopt such a permissive view of the law's role would be to ignore the patients who do not recover capacity and perhaps to abandon the 'benefits' of legalism entirely? The lower rates of approval reported by Priebe et al are not related to the recovery of capacity and in this sample initial satisfaction with the process is identified as an important variable. The authors do not claim to know what aspects of the admission process give rise to a more positive view of initial treatment but they do suggest that it is important to explore the processes behind patients' initial views. Here the law as a regulator of process in the protection of individual rights might have a crucial role to perform. However, to adopt such a conclusion might be to assume a positive role for process irrespective of outcome, an assumption that has attracted considerable debate in other contexts.[89]

III. Conclusions

In England and Wales, as in so many other jurisdictions, the law has created a distinction between mental disorder and mental incapacity. Two distinct legal frameworks exist which differ significantly in substance, purpose and underlying principle. For those potentially subject to either framework, the boundary between the two matters because their rights will be affected by the choice of framework. Can the law adequately police the boundary it has created? Both the

---

[89] A Weereratne, S Hadfield, U Burnham and A Gerry, *Butterworths New Law Guide: Mental Capacity Act 2005* (London, LexisNexis, 2008).

research data and the case law considered in this chapter suggest that the distinguishing factors applied by the law are insufficiently clear to provide an adequate basis for the determination of rights.

The capacity/incapacity distinction in the case of certain disorders does appear to match the psychiatric assessment of illness, and the flexibility contained within the legal criteria for incapacity has been used by the courts to avoid the under-inclusion of decisions affected by delusions and distorted values. However, the very flexibility contained within the legal criteria may make capacity/incapacity an inadequate distinction on which to rest significant legal consequences until we gain a better understanding of its implications in practice. By virtue of the recent reforms in England and Wales the concepts of objection and deprivation of liberty have also gained considerable legal significance. Unfortunately both remain ill-defined. The presence of an objection may be an appropriate factor to be taken into account in choosing between the two frameworks but, in the absence of a definition, it provides little guidance and considerable scope for inconsistency. Finally the confusion surrounding the core concept of deprivation of liberty is in urgent need of resolution. A right to be protected from unauthorised deprivations of liberty is of little value if there is no agreement on what constitutes such a deprivation.

9

Extra-Legislative Factors in Involuntary Status Decision-Making

IAN FRECKELTON

I. Introduction

This chapter reflects upon a number of emotive and judgemental considerations that have the potential to have an impact, covertly or explicitly, on the imposition of involuntary status by clinicians and mental health review tribunals. It identifies a series of extra-legislative descriptors that commonly figure in clinical assessments of those who are the subject of involuntary inpatient and outpatient status and which are common in decisions of mental health review tribunals. Decisions of the Victorian Mental Health Review Board are used to illustrate the phenomenon.

The descriptors examined are 'insightlessness', 'non-compliance'/'non-adherence', 'promiscuity', 'absconding', 'violence', 'substance dependence', 'disorganisation', 'poor hygiene', 'impairment of judgement' and 'personality disorders'. It is argued that in light of the clinical significance of insight and compliance considerations, there would be merit in incorporating the essence of them explicitly into mental health legislation. In respect of the other descriptors, it is important for clinicians and review tribunals alike to be precise in the meanings attributed to them, to use them with great care, always to assess whether their employment is justified by reliable, contemporary evidence, to probe their contexts, and to determine whether they are the product of subjective judgements which may have alternative explanations. These have no place in legislation and only a limited role in decision-making about involuntary status.

A. The Risk Posed by the 'No Formality' Mandate

Many mental health review tribunals are mandated to proceed without undue formality and regard to technicalities.[1] However, procedural and evidentiary latitude should not constitute a licence for unstructured and paternalistic decision-making in what from time to time is regarded as the best interests of a patient. As Michael Perlin argues, the practice of mental disability law contains significant and persisting elements that are 'sanist'.[2]

> [Sanism] is based predominantly upon stereotype, myth, superstition, and deindividualisation, and is sustained and perpetuated by our use of alleged 'ordinary common sense' and heuristic reasoning in an unconscious response to the events of everyday life and in the legal process.[3]

Michael Kirby has also warned, in another context, that the resort to 'common-sense', is 'at best an uncertain guide involving subjective, unexpressed and undefined extra-legal values' that vary from one decision-maker to another.[4] The sanist or common sense usage of epithets, short-hand descriptors and judgemental labels has been facilitated by loose patterns of language that are routinely employed by clinicians in reports for review tribunals, and by the relaxedness of review tribunals regarding the information coming before them and the procedures they follow. The risk is that such 'relaxedness' can become a licence for lack of clinical and decision-making rigour, over-ready judgementalism and paternalism. It can lead to a variety of forms of unfairness and unwarranted prejudice toward those with psychiatric disorders.

B. Therapeutic Jurisprudence and Decision-making

Therapeutic jurisprudence has made many contributions to reflection about decision-making processes concerning the involuntary status of inpatients and outpatients in the context of psychiatric illness.[5] Initially it exposed patterns of inappropriate detention of persons under cover of their having mental illnesses.[6]

---

[1] See, eg Mental Health Act 2007 (NSW) s 151; Mental Health Act 2000 (Qld) s 438; Mental Health Act 2009 (SA), s 79(3); Mental Health Act 1986 (Vic) s 24(1).

[2] M Perlin, *The Hidden Prejudice: Mental Disability on Trial* (Washington DC, American Psychological Association, 2000).

[3] M Perlin, 'Preface' in K Diesfeld and I Freckelton (eds), *Involuntary Detention and Therapeutic Jurisprudence: International Perspectives on Civil Commitment* (Aldershot, Ashgate, 2003).

[4] *Chappel v Hart* (1998) 195 CLR 232, 269; See I Freckelton, 'Health Law and Bioethics' in I Freckelton and H Selby (eds), *Appealing to the Future: The Legacy of Michael Kirby* (Pyrmont, Lawbook Co, 2009).

[5] For an overview of therapeutic jurisprudence see the Therapeutic Jurisprudence Network, available at: www.law.arizona.edu/depts/upr-intj/.

[6] See, eg BJ Winick, *The Right to Refuse Mental Health Treatment* (Washington DC, American Psychological Association, 1997); I Freckelton, 'Ideological Divarication in Civil Commitment Decision-making' (2003) 10(2) *Psychiatry, Psychology and Law* 390.

Then it highlighted the potential for legislation to provide inadequately for rights of review for clinicians' decision-making.[7] It has identified inadequacies in criteria for deprivation of liberty by mandated inpatient and outpatient treatment.[8] It has shown that decision-making processes that are coercive and non-participatory for patients tend to engender alienation, distress and resentful passivity in persons with mental illnesses.[9] This is especially problematic. One of the greatest challenges for psychiatric patients is to come to terms with a long-term illness that needs to be managed so that they can function at the best possible level, and assume control of their life as part of a 'wellness' or recovery strategy.

Therapeutic jurisprudence has also identified the need for patients to have a voice that is expressed and heard in civil commitment hearings. Disempowerment is demoralising and counter-therapeutic, especially for individuals with disabilities such as psychiatric illnesses.[10] Therapeutic jurisprudence scholarship has emphasised the need for decision-making to be fair and evidence-based, and not contaminated by assumptions and value judgements loaded in favour of a deprivation of liberty. It has identified that hearings by bodies such as mental health review tribunals can be therapeutic, but can also be harmful if they leave a patient feeling stigmatised, hopeless and demoralised.[11] Therapeutic jurisprudence suggests that it is important that hearings are conducted (and determined) in accordance with proper legal principles but with sensitivity to the unhelpfulness of dwelling upon embarrassing and distressing matters from the past. These matters can range from symptoms displayed shortly after admission and behaviour just before admission, to conduct which gave rise to concerns on the part of family and friends, and in due course clinicians' recommendations.[12]

---

[7]   See, eg BJ Winick, *The Right to Refuse Mental Health Treatment* (Washington DC, American Psychological Association, 1997).

[8]   *ibid.*

[9]   See BJ Winick, *Civil Commitment: A Therapeutic Jurisprudence Model* (Durham NC, Carolina Academic Press, 2005); BJ Winick, 'Coercion and Mental Health Treatment' (1997) 74 *Denver Law Review* 1145; TT Tyler, 'The Psychological Consequences of Judicial Procedures: Implications for Civil Commitment Hearings' in DB Wexler and BJ Winick (eds), *Law in a Therapeutic Key: Developments in Therapeutic Jurisprudence* (Durham NC, Carolina Academic Press, 1996). See also V Topp, M Thomas and M Ingvarson, *Lacking Insight: Involuntary Patient Experience of the Victorian Mental Health Review Board* (Melbourne, Mental Health Legal Centre, 2008).

[10]   See, eg S Du Fresne, 'Preparation and Presentation of Medical Evidence for Civil Commitment Hearings' (1996) 3 *Journal of Law and Medicine* 256; S Du Fresne, 'Therapeutic Potential in Review of Involuntary Detention' in K Diesfeld and I Freckelton (eds), *Involuntary Detention and Therapeutic Jurisprudence: International Perspectives on Civil Commitment* (Aldershot, Ashgate, 2003).

[11]   See, eg BJ Winick, 'The Side Effects of Incompetency Labeling and the Implications for Mental Health Law' in DB Wexler and BJ Winick (eds), *Law in a Therapeutic Key* (Durham NC, Carolina Academic Press, 1996).

[12]   V Topp, M Thomas and M Ingvarson, *Lacking Insight: Involuntary Patient Experience of the Victorian Mental Health Review Board* (Melbourne, Mental Health Legal Centre, 2008); see further I Freckelton, 'Involuntary Detention Decision-making, Criteria in Hearing Procedures: An Opportunity for Therapeutic Jurisprudence in Action' in K Diesfeld and I Freckelton (eds), *Involuntary Detention and Therapeutic Jurisprudence: International Perspectives on Civil Commitment* (Aldershot, Ashgate, 2003).

In particular, therapeutic jurisprudence serves to highlight the potential for considerations that are not particularly helpful to clinician decision-making and review tribunal reasoning to become dominant, or even an end in themselves. Often such factors are extra-legislative.[13] First, they are likely to be unauthorised by statute and to be problematic in this respect alone. Secondly, they may distract from the core tasks imposed upon clinicians and review tribunals by the legislative scheme.[14] Thirdly, they may impoverish decision-making because they are prone to looseness of analysis by virtue of their connotations and resonances. Finally, they may be counter-therapeutic because they not only detract from patients' confidence in the fairness and objectivity of decision-making processes but also because they employ terminology and suggest values that are value-laden and condemnatory.[15]

Insofar as descriptors and reasoning have such characteristics and do not usefully advance fair and evidence-based decision-making, they risk compounding the stigma attaching to persons with mental illness, contaminating reasoning processes and reducing the confidence that can reasonably be vested in involuntary commitment processes.[16] The remainder of this chapter scrutinises the problems attaching to 'dangerous descriptors'. It endeavours to distinguish those descriptors that have a potential for utility from those that do not and advances suggestions for statutory reform.

II. Extra-Legislative Factors

A. 'Insightless'

In involuntary status hearings it is common for patients to be described by clinicians and by mental health tribunals as 'insightless', 'lacking in insight' or 'with only partial insight'.[17] The concept of 'insight', or its absence, is clinically orthodox but can carry with it highly pejorative connotations as to a patient's capacity to make informed decisions and as to the likelihood of the patient

---

[13] See, eg I Freckelton, 'Ideological Divarication in Civil Commitment Decision-making' (2003) 10(2) *Psychiatry, Psychology and Law* 390.

[14] See, eg I Freckelton, 'Distractors and Distressors in Involuntary Status Decision-making' (2005) 12(1) *Psychiatry, Psychology and Law* 88.

[15] See, eg K Diesfeld and B McKenna, 'The Therapeutic Intent of the New Zealand Mental Health Review Tribunal' (2006) 13 *Psychiatry, Psychology and Law* 100; S Stevens, 'Where is the Asylum?' in K Diesfeld and I Freckelton (eds), *Involuntary Detention and Therapeutic Jurisprudence: International Perspectives on Civil Commitment* (Aldershot, Ashgate, 2003).

[16] See, eg BJ Winick, *Civil Commitment: A Therapeutic Jurisprudence Model* (Durham NC, Carolina Academic Press, 2005) 145 *ff*.

[17] See, eg J Peay, *Tribunals on Trial: A Study of Decision-making under the Mental Health Act 1983* (Oxford, Clarendon Press, 1989); E Perkins, S Arthur and J Nazroo, *Decision-making in Mental Health Review Tribunals* (Liverpool, University of Liverpool Health and Community Care Research Unit, 2000).

co-operating with needed treatment. This latter issue has ramifications for the patient's risk to self or others if there is relapse as a result of non-compliance with treatment.

The concept of insight is difficult because on the one hand it is said to be highly characteristic of schizophrenia across cultures, and even the most reliably present feature of the disorder,[18] but on the other has been identified as unclear in its features and boundaries.[19] In reviewing the literature on insight in respect of schizophrenia in 2008, Stéphane Raffard and colleagues identified that between 50 and 80 per cent of patients with schizophrenia do not believe they have a disorder.[20] They noted that studies published on the subject over the previous two decades stressed the specificity of this phenomenon in patients with schizophrenia, taking into account both its prevalence and its clinical consequences by comparison with other mental disorders. They argued that although in bipolar disorders a lack of insight amongst patients is linked with the intensity and acuteness of symptomatology, there is only a limited relationship between these factors in schizophrenia, thus making lack of insight a trait rather than a mental state-related symptom. However, Marc Adida and colleagues have contended that manic patients clearly show defects in decision-making, which are strongly related to their lack of insight.[21]

Stéphane Raffard and colleagues[22] have identified four current explanatory models of lack of insight:

- resulting either from adaptation or defence mechanisms to environmental stressors;
- resulting from cognitive bias of data processing;
- resulting from neuropsychological functional deficits; and
- resulting from meta-cognitive deficits.

They have argued that research in neuropsychology and cognitive psychology has provided consistent results concerning the link between deficit in executive functions, frontal lobe dysfunction and poor insight, with recent studies on bias

---

[18] WH Tan, TA Ban and W Guy, 'Flexible Systems Criteria in Chronic Schizophrenia' (1986) 27(6) *Comprehensive Psychiatry* 259; S Raffard, S Bayard, M-C Gely-Nargeot, D Capdeveille, M Maggi, E Barbotte, D Morris and J-P Boulenger, 'Insight and Executive Functioning in Schizophrenia: A Multidimensional Approach' (2009) 167(3) *Psychiatry Research* 239.

[19] See, eg X Amador, D Strauss, S Yale, M Flaum, J Endicott and J Gorman, 'Assessment of Insight in Psychosis' (1993) 150 *American Journal of Psychiatry* 873.

[20] S Raffard, S Bayard, D Capdevielle, F Garcia, JP Boulenger and MC Gely-Nargeot, 'Lack of Insight in Schizophrenia: a Review. Part I: Theoretical Concept, Clinical Aspects and Amador's Model' (2008) 34(6) *Encephale* 597. See too TM Lincoln, E Lullmann and W Rief, 'Correlates and Long-term Consequences of Poor Insight in Patients with Schizophrenia. A Systematic Review' (2007) 33(6) *Schizophrenia Bull* 1324.

[21] M Adida, L Clark, P Pomietto, A Kaladjian, N Besnier, J-M Azorin, R Jeanningros and GM Goodwin 'Lack of Insight May Predict Impaired Decision Making in Manic Patients' (2008) 10 *Bipolar Disorders* 829.

[22] S Raffard, S Bayard, D Capdevielle, F Garcia, JP Boulenger and MC Gely-Nargeot, 'Lack of Insight in Schizophrenia: A Review' (2008) 34 *Encephale* 511.

in cognitive information treatment and social cognition theories opening new avenues for understanding of the phenomenon.

Anthony David has argued that 'insight' has three elements: recognition by a person that they have a mental illness; acknowledging that certain mental events are pathological; and complying with treatment.[23] However, additional components can be identified:

- Acceptance of having a mental illness;
- Acceptance of having a particular mental illness, howsoever termed;
- Recognition of the signs and symptoms of the mental illness for the particular person, for example, delusions about persecuting neighbours or about a family member poisoning their food;
- Acceptance of requiring medical treatment for a mental illness;
- Acceptance of requiring a particular form of treatment for a mental illness, for example antipsychotic medication, not just vitamin C;
- Recognition of the efficacy of pharmacotherapy or other interventions for maintenance of their mental health;
- Acceptance of the need for lifestyle limitations as a result of having a mental illness, eg not drinking alcohol, not using marijuana, and avoiding certain stressors;
- Recognition of the person's relapse signature, ie the pattern of the return of symptoms;
- Ability to identify suitable remedial steps when symptoms are returning; and
- Capacity to formulate and implement a plan for responding when symptoms are recurring.

This has led to the suggestion of a 'Mental Health Insight Scale' which would enable the evaluation on an objective basis of the degree of insight in a relevant sense possessed by a patient.[23a]

Insight, in respect of each of these factors, lies on a continuum, with few patients having total insight and most patients shifting up and down the continuum at different times in relation to the extent of their appreciation of factors relevant to their experience of mental illness.[24] In other words, insight is temporally and contextually influenced, as well as affected by a number of other variables. Insight is often affected by the seriousness of symptomatology and

---

[23] A David, 'Insight and Psychosis' (1990) 156 *British Journal of Psychiatry* 798; see also A David, A Buchanan, A Reed and O Almeida, 'The Assessment of Insight in Psychosis' (1992) 161 *British Journal of Psychiatry* 798.

[23a] Freckelton, 'The Mental Health Insight Scale: In Quest of Objectivity', (2010) 17 *Psychiatry, Psychology and Law* (in press).

[24] See further: K Diesfeld, 'Insights on Insight: The Impact of Extra-legislative Factors on Decisions to Discharge Detained Patients' in K Diesfeld and I Freckelton (eds), *Involuntary Detention and Therapeutic Jurisprudence: International Perspectives on Civil Commitment* (Aldershot, Ashgate, 2003); K Diesfeld, 'Insight: Unpacking the Concept in Mental Health Law' (2003) 10(1) *Psychiatry, Psychology and Law* 63; K Diesfeld and S Sjostrom, 'Interpretive Flexibility: Why Doesn't Insight Incite Controversy in Mental Health Law?, (2007) 25 *Behavioral Sciences and the Law* 1.

factors such as intelligence and educational levels.[25] Some aspects of insight are affected by medication, by psychotherapy and by psycho-education; others are not. A variety of studies have identified a correlation between poor insight and low levels of medication adherence amongst those with mental illnesses.[26] Some studies have suggested a positive correlation between good insight and treatment outcome.[27] As John Dawson and Richard Mullen have put it: 'Clearly no automatic association can be assumed between impaired insight and non-compliance with treatment'.[28] However, in an empirical study, Dawson and Mullen found that improved insight in the course of a treatment is an important factor in predicting future compliance with treatment. Insofar as insight is a predictor of compliance with clinically indicated treatment, it is useful but is not determinative.

For clinicians, insight is relevant to the likelihood of a patient's deterioration if he or she is not involuntary, to the patient's ability to consent to treatment,[29] and to the potential for him or her to be treated less restrictively than as an involuntary patient—namely on a voluntary basis.

Some patients are deferential and co-operative by disposition, meaning they are likely to be compliant with what is recommended for them by clinicians, even though they may have little understanding of the reasons why it may be necessary or advantageous. Alternatively, their insight may extend no further than that without being compliant they are liable to be (again) involuntarily detained as a hospital inpatient; this may be quite enough to secure their co-operation. This was the situation encountered by McDonald J in *Re An Application by DC*,[30] where the patient did not consider he had a mental illness but was very keen to

---

[25] See, eg MA De Hert, V Simon, D Vidovic, T Franic, M Wampers, J Peuskens and R van Winkel, 'Evaluation of the Association Between Insight and Symptoms in a Large Sample of Patients with Schizophrenia' (2009) *European Psychiatry* (forthcoming). See also H Yoshizumi, K Hirao, K Ueda and T Murai, 'Insight in Social Behavioral Dysfunction in Schizophrenia. A Preliminary Study' (2008) 62(6) *Psychiatry and Clinical Neurosciences* 669.

[26] See, eg T Trauer and T Sacks, 'The Relationship between Insight and Medication Adherence in Severely Mentally Ill Clients Treated in the Community' (2000) 102 *Acta Psychiatrica Scandinavica* 211.

[27] See, eg J McEvoy, S Freter, G Everett, J Geller, P Appelbaum, L Apperson and L Roth, 'Insight and the Clinical Outcome of Schizophrenic Patients' (1989) 177 *Journal of Nervous and Mental Disease* 48; X Amador, D Strauss, S Yale, M Flaum, J Endicott and J Gorman, 'Assessment of Insight in Psychosis' (1993) 150 *American Journal of Psychiatry* 873. Paul Lysaker and colleagues argue that awareness of the nature of an illness such as schizophrenia can be accompanied by depression, low self-esteem and possibly an increased risk of suicide; PH Lysaker, KD Buck, G Salvatore, R Popolo and G Dimaggio, 'Lack of Awareness of Illness in Schizophrenia: Conceptualizations, Correlates and Treatment Approaches' (2009) 9 *Expert Review of Neurotherapeutics* 1035; see also I Hasson-Ohayon, S Kravetz, T Meir and S Rosencwaig, 'Insight into Severe Mental Illness, Hope and Quality of Life for Persons with Schizophrenia and Schizoaffective Disorders' (2009) 167(3) *Psychiatry Research* 231.

[28] J Dawson and R Mullen, 'Insight and the Use of Community Treatment Orders' (2008) 17 *Journal of Mental Health* 269, 271.

[29] See D Capdevielle, S Raffard, S Bayard, F Garcia, O Baciu, I Bouzigues and J-P Boulenger, 'Competence to Consent and Insight in Schizophrenia. Is There an Association? A Pilot Study' (2009) 108 *Schizophrenia Research* 272.

[30] *Re An Application by DC*, unreported, Victorian Supreme Court, 9 December 1998, p 24–5.

retain his liberty. The result was that the patient took the antipsychotic medication which he needed, thereby making relapse (and dangerousness) relatively unlikely. Justice McDonald summed it up in this way, responding to a contention on behalf of the Attorney-General that DC lacked insight and therefore should not be released from custody:

> The fact is however, in the circumstances of this case, that which motivates the applicant to be compliant with medical treatment prescribed [for] him is that it is necessary for him to do so if he wishes to enjoy the freedom of movement that he presently enjoys. It is in consequence of this that he accepts the prescribed treatment and by accepting the same the treatment has the effect as sought by his treating psychiatrist. This demonstrates that the applicant has in this respect insight. He appreciates that it is necessary to be compliant with treatment to be able to live in the circumstances that he currently enjoys.

This meant that his Honour was prepared to find that

> [a]lthough the applicant does not have insight into his condition or is not prepared to accept that he suffers from schizophrenia, nevertheless I am satisfied on the evidence that he appreciates that it is necessary for him to comply with conditions of a like nature that have been imposed as a condition for him being granted leave including his compliance with a medical regime prescribed for him, if he is to continue to live in the community.[31]

Since 2000, the Victorian Mental Health Review Board has tended to look behind the bare assertion that a patient 'lacks insight', is 'insightless' or 'has only partial insight'. This has been part of an effort to distill what is significant in terms of predictive factors relevant to a patient's attitude toward their mental illness. The new approach began with the case of *Re NI*,[32] which involved a woman with what were said by her clinicians to be bulimia nervosa, paranoid schizophrenia, dysmorphophobia and depression. It was said by NI's treaters that her insight was so low that she could only be treated on an involuntary basis.

The Board analysed NI's limitations of insight in order to determine whether she was able to provide consent for treatment. NI acknowledged, although with a number of qualifications and rationalisations, that she had an eating disorder but did not accept that she had schizophrenia. She expressed reservations at a philosophical level about the legitimacy of the concept of mental illness. The Board found that this impacted upon her attitude toward whether she had a mental illness and required medication. NI stated that she agreed that she needed treatment (although she denied that she had an illness for which she required treatment) but in practice was inclined to reject treatments when she perceived that they had unwanted side-effects upon her weight status, regardless of the impact that they had in ameliorating the symptoms of her mental illness. The

---

[31] *ibid*, p 28.
[32] *Re NI*, 01–039 [2000] VMHRB 1, 27 September 2000.

Board found that she was unable to draw a clear nexus between the lessening of her experience of hallucinations or delusions and the impact of the injection of intra-muscular Modecate.

It also found that NI had very limited appreciation of the symptoms of the illness that she experienced, when they were recurring and what she could constructively do to address any relapse symptomatology. In light of this combination of matters, although the Board accepted NI's honesty and good intentions, when she said that she would submit to Modecate injections if released from hospital, it concluded that she was unable to consent to treatment in any real sense, given how many limits there were to her understanding of her illness, its characteristics, its sequelae and her need for treatment. The Board acknowledged the unhelpfulness of uncritical and generalised reference to insight but conducted a contextualised and focused inquiry into certain deficits in insight when undertaking its statutory inquiries.

The concept of insight was further examined by the Victorian Board in *Re LW*.[33] The patient again suffered from an eating disorder. It was submitted on her behalf that she was prepared to stay in hospital until discharged, after which she would return to her supportive family. She argued that she had shown a steady improvement in weight gain, and was complying with the eating programme recommended by the hospital. However, her doctor contended that LW could not be treated less restrictively because of the physical risk of further weight loss, and reduction in ability to function physically. He argued that LW's lack of understanding about how she became so thin, and her actions in continuing to lose weight for two weeks after her diagnosis, demonstrated her inability to give informed consent to treatment. The Board was split in its decision with the majority concluding that LW's insight into her illness was of such a low order as to preclude her capacity to give informed consent. Although LW indicated that she understood how serious her mental illness was, and the necessity of treatment in the hospital programme, this 'insight' was classified by the majority as recent, and had not been reflected in sustained weight gain. In other words her understanding of her condition and its need for remediation was shallow and of recent origin. The majority of the Board formed the view in the context of these limited aspects of LW's insight that, without the involuntary status, LW would not comply with the necessary treatment, and would risk further weight loss, accompanied by serious medical problems.

The existence or otherwise of insight in each of the senses previously identified clearly enough can be affected by a range of factors other than mental illness. These can include the perceived and actual stigmatisation of mental illness, family pressures, embarrassment, stress, intelligence levels, and disabilities, cultural and

[33]   *Re LW*, unreported, VMHRB, 1 July 2003.

even religious factors.[34] In addition, insight lies on a spectrum, with few patients having total insight and most patients shifting up and down in their appreciation of issues relevant to their illness at different times. It is unrealistic for clinicians and review tribunals to expect that patients have complete insight and for them to dichotomise in a raw way between patients with and without insight. Sometimes aspects of insight are affected by medication, by psychotherapy and by psycho-education; sometimes they are not.

Another form of insight which figures in decision-making about whether a patient should be treated involuntarily is insight on the part of families. Often enough it is very difficult for family members and carers to come to terms with the fact that their loved one has an illness such as schizophrenia or a bipolar disorder. It is far from unknown for a patient to be resigned to their diagnosis of illness and to be co-operative with taking their medication but for their family to be antagonistic and unaccepting of their relative's diagnosis and need for pharmacotherapy. This can result in an attitudinal osmosis by which the patient becomes mistrustful of, non-consensual to, and/or non-compliant with treatment by reason of an antagonistic attitude on the part of their family.

On occasions the antagonism of relatives of a patient toward his or her clinicians, and their absence of insight into the patient's mental illness and need for treatment, can lead to a need to move the patient to a location where the relatives will exercise less of an adverse influence over the patient's recovery. Thus, in *Re MS*[35] the Victorian Board authorised the transfer of a patient away from easy contact with a family who were very caring of him and even taking it upon themselves to feed him every day, because their lack of insight into his illness was causing counter-therapeutic conflict between them and his treaters—resulting in distress and entrenchment of his symptomatology. Similarly, in *Re GD*[36] the Board was presented with a scenario in which the conduct of family members of a person on a community treatment order featured thoroughgoing denial of the patient's mental illness and need for pharmacotherapy, and consequently ongoing antagonism toward the clinical team. It accepted a proposal for transfer of the unwell person to a facility where significant constraints would be placed upon the father of the patient in order to reduce his obstruction of the patient's treatment.

A risk with the tag of 'insightlessness' is that there will be an invitation to circularity of reasoning. This was apparent in a 2005 case before the Victorian Mental Health Review Board, *Re AW*.[37] In relation to a patient who had relatively recently converted to Islam, the Board was invited to conclude that the patient

---

[34] See, eg X Amador and A David (eds), *Insight and Psychosis* (New York, Oxford University Press, 1998); KM Fung, H Tsang and F Chan, 'Self-stigma, Stages of Change and Psychosocial Treatment Adherence among Chinese People with Schizophrenia: A Path Analysis' (2009) *Social Psychiatry and Psychiatric Epidemiology* 561.
[35] *Re MS* [1] [1997] VMHRB 3, 5 February 2007.
[36] *Re GD*, unreported, VMHRB, 24 June 2008.
[37] *Re AW* 05–088 [2005] VMHRB 3, 22 February 2005.

appeared to be mentally ill in substantial part because he was 'insightless' and had 'impaired judgement'. It declined to do so, observing that

> [w]e accept that it can be an indicator of mental illness that a person is unable to come to terms with having a mental illness. However, there is a risk of unfair circularity in such an argument—a person is mentally ill because they deny that they are mentally ill.

In essence, then, the concept of 'insight' is fundamental to many psychiatric illnesses, especially schizophrenia. However, whenever it is invoked, it needs to be examined carefully. In its cryptic form it can convey different things to different people. It has the potential to be a portmanteau for many different components and it is important for clinicians, advocates and review tribunals to be clear about those to which they are referring. This maximises the prospect of drawing sound inferences relevant to likelihood of compliance with medication and therapy, and thus the likelihood of a person staying well or deteriorating, their being able to consent to treatment; and their being treated in the least restrictive way possible in accordance with the 1991 United Nations Principles for the Protection of Persons with Mental Illness and for the Improvement of Mental Health Care. Thus, while the notion of insight carries risks in both the clinical and review tribunal decision-making contexts, inevitably it is part of reasoning processes, meaning that it has the potential to be constructively harnessed by suitably carefully worded legislative recognition.

B.   'Non-compliant'/'Non-adherent'

Commonly it can be seen in the files of patients diagnosed with mental illnesses that they have been classified as 'non-compliant/non-adherent' or 'unlikely to be compliant/adherent'. What is being described or predicted is generally a patient who does not take medication as prescribed or (less commonly) who fails to be monitored or to receive psychotherapy at some time in the future. It can also be a patient who is unco-operative, who does not exhibit expected deference to clinicians (that is, a patient who is 'challenging') and who might be a management problem on the ward or at the clinic.[38]

Generally, the non-compliance or non-adherence is said to arise, amongst other things, from 'insightlessness' (see above). The assessment is made on the basis of:

- previous failure to 'comply';
- antagonism by the patient toward treaters;
- known or reputed hostility toward a particular form of intervention;
- campaigning by the patient against medication;
- patterns of sowing dissent amongst other patients;

---

[38]   See, eg I Freckelton, 'Madness, Migration and Misfortune: The Challenge of the Bleak Tale of Cornelia Rau' (2005) 12(1) *Psychiatry, Psychology and Law* 1.

- challenging or threatening behaviour toward clinicians;
- refusal on the part of the patient to co-operate with the prescription of medication or with ward or clinic rules; or
- low insight on the part of the patient.

The clinical literature discloses a number of factors responsible for the significant rates of non-adherence to pharmacotherapy amongst those with psychiatric disorders. Jonathan Lacro and colleagues[39] reviewed a series of studies on levels of non-adherence to psychotropic medications amongst those with schizophrenia, and found them to vary between 41.2 and 49.5 per cent, with the factors most consistently associated with non-adherence including poor insight, negative attitude or subjective response toward medication, previous non-adherence, substance abuse, shorter illness duration, inadequate discharge planning or aftercare environment, and poor therapeutic alliance. Recent research on non-adherence amongst patients diagnosed with bipolar disorder has identified co-morbid substance abuse, negative attitudes toward mood-stabilising medication, and difficulty managing to take medication in the context of one's daily schedule as primary determinants of medication adherence.[40]

An example of the resort to 'non-compliance' as a reason to retain a person as an involuntary patient occurred in the context of SL, a Samoan man living on the banks of the Murray River outside Mildura.[41] He became involved in a fracas with council employees, which in turn led to criminal charges and a stay at Melbourne's inpatient forensic psychiatric hospital, Thomas Embling. On release he was disinclined to take his medication, as he did not accept that he had a mental illness.

The psychiatric evidence before Victoria's Mental Health Review Board was that SL was 'insightless' about his illness and highly likely to be 'non-compliant'. Thus the recommendation was that he be retained on mandated outpatient treatment. Ultimately, the Board disagreed and was not satisfied that SL's illness was serious enough or that the medications he was being prescribed were effective enough to coerce his compliance. On balance, it would have been counter-therapeutic.

A risk with 'non-compliance' tags is that persons can be unreasonably judged for past conduct. This is a particular issue with mental illness because for most patients, especially those with early onset schizophrenia, it takes time for them to come to terms with having their illness and with the need to adapt their life to its consequences. Psycho-education plays a role. So also does the passage of time and

---

[39] JP Lacro, LB Dunn, CR Dolder, SG Leckband and DV Jeste, 'Prevalence of and Risk Factors for Medication Nonadherence in Patients with Schizophrenia: A Comprehensive Review of Recent Literature' (2002) 63 *Journal of Clinical Psychiatry* 892.

[40] M Sajatovic, RV Ignacio, JA West, KA Cassidy, R Safavi, AM Kilbourne and FC Blow, 'Predictors of Nonadherence Amongst Individuals with Bipolar Disorder Receiving Treatment in a Community Mental Health Clinic' (2009) 50(2) *Comprehensive Psychiatry* 100.

[41] *Re SL* 04–057 [2004] VMHRB 2, 27 October 2003.

the acquisition of maturity. In other words, the fact that a patient at an early presentation was slow to accept that they had a mental illness or that they needed a particular kind of medication, or was querulous on the ward, demanding their rights or challenging, for instance, their stay in a high dependency unit, does not mean that it is useful or accurate for them to be designated 'non-compliant'.

An example of such a problematic categorisation occurred in the case of *Re AC*.[42] Evidence from a clinician referred to AC having a 'history of assaulting his mother' and a 'history of paracetamol overdose in 1998'. AC's doctor also stated that AC had an 'established history' of non-compliance with oral medication. However, when scrutinised, it emerged that there was no pattern of failure to co-operate with recommended treatment. The issue was that a number of problematic events had occurred, but, when analysed, they tended to be one-off issues; they were not repeated.

This phenomenon is not particularly unusual. But there was probably a particular reason for AC attracting a series of pejorative descriptors. He had effectively alienated his treaters by being repeatedly antagonistic toward them and by making abusive phone-calls to his outpatient clinic when disinhibited by intoxication with marijuana. Part of the consequences of his behaviour was his being given the descriptor of non-compliant, principally because of his hostile attitude toward being diagnosed as having schizophrenia. He was difficult to manage and was regarded as having 'nil insight' into his condition and as a result highly likely to cease taking needed medication if given the opportunity. There appeared to be concern that his verbal abuse could at some stage transmute into physical violence, especially in light of his 'history of assaulting his mother.'

Many mental health patients at first rail against their clinicians, reject the diagnoses they feel to be 'imposed' upon them, are deeply affronted by the stigma of mental illness, fail to get on with their clinicians and are distressed by the side-effects of the medication prescribed for them. Patients with bipolar disorders often miss their highs and feel as though they are losing a significant part of themselves when those highs, and aspects of what they feel to be their creativity, are taken away.[43]

However, just as it is unfair to judge patients later on the basis of their presentation when acutely unwell, it is wrong to place a patient in a time-warp and classify them as forever non-compliant on the basis of their having been hesitant about or resistant to treatment or a particular form of treatment at a time in the past. Attribution of what is almost asserted to be the character defect of 'non-compliance' risks de-contextualising previous episodes and unfairly extrapolating, from an incident or incidents, to a trait or propensity.

Like 'insight', alleged 'non-compliance' is a concept that always needs to be scrutinised before it is embraced as an accurate descriptor by a clinician or a

---

[42] *Re AC*, unreported, VMHRB, 22 July 2004.
[43] See K Jamison, *Touched with Fire: Manic Depressive Illness and the Artistic Temperament* (New York, Free Press, 1994); K Jamison, *An Unquiet Mind* (New York, AA Knopf, 1996).

mental health tribunal. For instance, non-compliance can be the product of a personality conflict between a clinician and a patient. It can also be created by a patient's fear (reasoned or otherwise) about the effects of medication. It can have resulted from a life context that was fraught and which militated against the patient's co-operation with a treating team. It may have come about from a patient's difficulties in integrating into the unwonted world of the clinical ward with its many unwell people, its rules and strictures and its authority structures. It can be exacerbated by an inability on the part of a patient's family to come to terms with an unwelcome diagnosis of their relative.

There are people who, by disposition, are oppositional and unco-operative. However, they are relatively few in number. More common is that people from fear, confusion or misunderstanding act contrary to their own best interests on some occasions. There are few amongst us who, in circumstances of stress, could not be said to have behaved in this manner at times. This is also the case with people with psychiatric illnesses. It can be a precipitate and unfair step to classify a patient as 'non-compliant' because in the past they have failed to take advice or to take recommended medication. When such behaviours have occurred, a number of questions need to be asked:

- Is it right that the person was non-compliant?
- When was the person non-compliant?
- What can be said with accuracy about the factual context of the non-compliance?
- Has it been repeated?
- Was the non-compliance attributable to a level of symptomatology of mental illness that has now been addressed?
- Does it appear to be part of a pattern likely to recur?

In evaluating the significance of prior incidents, the dissenting decision in the Victorian Mental Health Review Board of *Re AC*[44] suggested as follows:

> The value of prior matters as predictive factors stems, amongst other things, from their nature, their context, their frequency and their recency. It is important for patients' dignity that they not be assailed with restatements (that may have little contemporary relevance) of matters that occurred in the historical past and which there is no good reason to conclude are likely to be repeated. Such revisiting of embarrassing or distressing incidents, such as behaviour when floridly ill, when forcibly taken into custody, or when initially received as an inpatient in a psychiatric ward can be counter-therapeutic by stigmatising, demeaning and demoralising patients—to no particularly useful end from a decision-making perspective. There is the counter-therapeutic risk that a patient can form the view that there is no potential to live down past actions documented in their medical records. This can detract from motivation to start afresh and take control of life and the symptoms of illness.

---

[44] *Re AC*, unreported, VMHRB, 22 July 2004.

However, none of this is to deny the fact that previous episodes of failure to take medication as prescribed or certain actions or statements may not connote that a patient is unlikely in the short or medium term to comply with medication that they require to stay well.

In addition, it is useful to have regard to the phenomenon of treatment non-compliance by patients in contexts other than mental illness. Patients' non-compliance with treatment has been described for some time as one of the major challenges faced by contemporary health service providers.[45] For instance:

1. Marshall Becker and Lois Maiman found that fewer than 50 per cent of patients take medication as prescribed;[46]

2. Henry Milgrom and colleagues found 37 per cent non-compliance with corticosteroids by children with asthma;[47]

3. Paul Beardon and colleagues found 14.2 per cent of patients in a general practice sample did not redeem prescriptions;[48]

4. Carl Salzman and colleagues documented between 40 and 75 per cent drug non-compliance in the elderly;[49]

5. Véronique Rabenda and colleagues documented the problems caused for women with osteoporosis by low rates of compliance with oral biophos-phenate treatment;[50]

6. Holger Schmid and colleagues documented that more than 50 per cent of dialysis patients were non-compliant in some way with treatment;[51] and

7. Dorothy Faulkner and colleagues found that after one year 54 per cent of patients were non-compliant with HRT.[52]

---

[45] See, eg MH Becker, 'Patient Adherence to Prescribed Therapies' (1985) 23 *Medical Care* 539; C Cameron, 'Patient Compliance: Recognition of Factors Involved and Suggestions for Promoting Compliance with Therapeutic Regimens' (1996) 24(2) *Journal of Advanced Nursing* 244.

[46] MH Becker and LA Maiman, 'Sociobehavioral Determinants of Compliance with Health and Medical Care Recommendations' (1975) 13(1) *Medical Care* 10.

[47] H Milgrom, B Bender, L Ackerson, P Bowry, B Smith and C Rand, 'Noncompliance and Treatment Failure in Children with Asthma' (1996) 98 *The Journal of Allergy and Clinical Immunology* 1051. See also JA Coutts, NA Gibson and JY Paton, 'Measuring Compliance with Inhaled Medication in Asthma' (1992) *67 Archives of Disease in Childhood* 332.

[48] PHG Beardon, MM McGilchrist, AD McKendrick, DG McDevitt and TM MacDonald, 'Primary Non-compliance with Prescribed Medication in Primary Care' (1993) 307 *British Medical Journal* 846.

[49] C Salzman, DJ Kupfer and E Frank, 'Medication Compliance in the Elderly' (1995) 56 (supp 1) *Journal of Clinical Psychiatry* 18.

[50] V Rabenda, M Hiligsmann and JY Reginster, 'Poor Adherence to Oral Bisphosphonate Treatment and its Consequences: a Review of the Evidence' (2009) *Expert Opinion on Pharmaco-therapy* 2303.

[51] H Schmid, B Hartmann and H Schiffl, 'Adherence to Prescribed Oral Medication in Adult Patients Undergoing Chronic Hemodialysis: A Critical Review of the Literature' (2009) 14(5) *European Journal of Medical Research* 185.

[52] DL Faulkner, C Young, D Hutchins and JS McCollam, 'Patient Noncompliance with Hormone Replacement Therapy: A Nationwide Estimate using a Large Prescription Claims Database' (1998) 5(4) *Menopause* 226.

This selection of studies indicates that the phenomenon of treatment non-adherence is commonplace within medicine and a significant impediment to pharmacotherapeutic efficacy. Its extent in the mental health context needs to be acknowledged and worked with, just as it is in all other medical contexts. However, what distinguishes the mental health context is the combination of a high incidence of non-adherence to pharmacotherapy and the fact that it is mental illness itself which can be responsible for the inability to be treatment adherent. It is in these circumstances that the phenomenon retains an inevitable relevance when predicting the likelihood of future mental health.

C. 'Promiscuous'

Generally, promiscuity as a behavioural concern said to be consistent with or the product of mental illness is raised in the context of individuals diagnosed with bipolar disorders, but occasionally too with schizophrenia spectrum disorders. The concern, often not fully articulated, is that a female patient may become pregnant, be raped or exploited when her capacity to consent to sexual activity is impaired by her symptomatology. Another public health issue is that a patient may be infected by a sexually transmissible disease, or if already infected, may spread it to others. Thus it is relevant in terms of vulnerability and dangerousness.

A common clinical scenario giving rise to the use of the descriptor 'promiscuous' occurs where a patient becomes sexually or romantically involved with another patient or patients, or shows sexual interest 'inappropriately' in another patient. An associated concern may be that the patient is 'sexually disinhibited'. As with many matters involving a sexual component, there can be a tendency toward pathologisation of behaviour and toward over-reaction, judgementalism and prurience. The labels of 'sexually disinhibited' or 'promiscuous' when unwell tend to be particularly adherent especially when applied to women.[53]

The risk in the utilisation of such epithets is that a person's expression of sexual needs, practices or wishes may be misinterpreted. What to one person is promiscuity may be healthy sexual expression to someone else. A patient who exhibits sexual interest in one or more fellow patients in a psychiatric ward runs the risk of being labelled sexually disinhibited or promiscuous when, if their behaviour took place in a night-club or other social venue, it would be conventional and would not attract the stigma of any adverse epithet.

It can be useful in the context of what is categorised as 'promiscuity' in relation to an inpatient in a psychiatric ward—especially a female inpatient—to recall that an integral part of involuntary hospitalisation is deprivation of most aspects of autonomy. Sexual expression can be a form of rebellion and a search for self-esteem, comfort and validation in such a context. It may or may not be indicative of mental illness. No doubt it is for this reason that there is a preclusion

---

[53] See, eg *Re MH*, unreported, VMHRB, 5 February 2003.

in mental health legislation in a number of jurisdictions against a person being accounted as mentally ill by reason alone of their engaging in promiscuity.[54]

D. 'Violent'

Generally the risk of commission of violence to oneself or others is a legislatively articulated indicator in favour of involuntary detention. My focus in this context though is upon the recording in clinical files of a patient as being 'violent', 'having a history of violence', 'having exhibited aggressive tendencies' or being 'prone to violent behaviours'.

Three categories of violence tend to be referred to in clinical reports in respect of involuntary patients:

- Persons regarded as potentially violent toward others, such as family members;
- Persons regarded as potentially violent toward their clinicians; and
- Persons regarded as potentially self-harming.

In the real world of the ward, where clinician records are generated, concern is generally especially significant in respect of patients said to have previously injured or threatened injury to others—staff, patients, family members, or neighbours.

The recycling of accounts of patients' acts of violence (especially in hospital records) and the drawing of an inference because of one instance of aggressive conduct or instances of such conduct in a particular context that a person is 'violent' can be unfairly prejudicial and counter-therapeutic to patients. A risk, too, is the assumption that psychiatric patients' violence is the product of their mental illness and therefore that it is prone to repetition unless adequately treated, including with sedating medication. There can of course be many reasons for anti-social conduct—the incidence of domestic violence bears eloquent testimony to its frequency. Commonly, violent behaviour occurs in the context of anti-social personality, low impulse control, intoxication, distress, familial conflict and relationship stressors, to name but some scenarios that can be independent of mental illness. A difficulty in the context of clinical and review tribunal decision-making is that a causal nexus can be imputed to mental illness because of the assumption of correlation between violence and mental illness. Secondly, the fact of aggressive acting-out years previously can often linger in assessments for longer than is reasonable and can be de-contextualised from factors which may have given rise to it originally. Thirdly, violent behaviour can make its way onto hospital files in an exaggerated or inaccurate form from information

---

[54] See, eg Mental Health Act 1986 (Vic) s 8(2)(g); Mental Health Act 2000 (Qld) s 12(2)(e); Mental Health Act 1996 (WA) s 4(2)(b); Mental Health Act 2007 (NSW) s 16(g); Mental Health and Related Services Act (NT) s 6(3)(c); Mental Health (Treatment and Care) Act 1994 (ACT) s 5(g).

provided by persons who cannot easily be consulted a considerable time after-wards, when such assessment would be preferable in order to gauge the likeli-hood of the connection between mental illness and some form of violent conduct which may have become mythologised or the subject of 'Chinese whispers'.

Two cases that came before the Victorian Mental Health Review Board are illustrative of these issues for decision-making.

In *Re AC*[55] the patient was described by his treating doctor as having 'an established history of violence'. However, examination of the files and question-ing of the doctor and the patient by the Board revealed that AC had hit his mother once when 15 years old, eight years previously and had attempted suicide three years later in the aftermath of a teenage relationship breakdown. There was no evidence that either incident had been repeated. Yet, in spite of the incidents now being historical, they consistently re-appeared in clinical files, reports for the Board and in evidence as a potential ground for maintaining a patient's involun-tary status because of the risk that he might pose to others.

In *Re AW*[56] a similar scenario was presented. AW was described as having a 'history of aggressive and assaultive behaviour'. It was only when this was scrutinised by the Board that it emerged that AW's mother maintained no more than that on one occasion, when aged 17 and in the midst of very heavy marijuana usage, he had grabbed her by the throat. In the five subsequent years he had not repeated his conduct but he continued to be afflicted by an uncritical descriptor of having a history of violent conduct. Again, this was advanced as a reason for maintaining his involuntary status.

A sub-category that prompts a form of prejudicial recording in notes that is often repeated for many years is where a patient has threatened a staff member or clinician, or lashed out at them when distressed, angry or delusional. To a lesser degree the same can be said in relation to violence or threatened violence against members of mobile support teams, crisis assessment teams, ambulance officers or apprehending police officers.

The patient who attracts the reputation of being a risk to others or themselves when symptomatic is particularly likely to be detained involuntarily as an inpatient longer than others. However, the descriptor is often generated by behaviour some years previous and can have come about in circumstances that are ambiguous to say the least. Family conflict can be complex in its dynamics; intervention by police can be heavy-handed; and distress can be precipitated by those who intervene insensitively during crises. Harm or threatened harm to clinical staff can occur in the context of sub-optimal handling of distressed or psychotic patients. The actual context of the violence or threatened violence is often lost in the mists of time. It is helpful for clinicians and review tribunals to be conscious that accounts in records, which are often the product of second-hand or confused

---

[55] *Re AC*, unreported, VMHRB, 22 July 2004.
[56] *Re AW* 05–088 [2005] VMHRB 3, 22 February 2005.

narratives, can be unreliable but difficult for patients to contest because of the context. Yet they can be extremely damaging and stigmatising in an enduring way. Again, more is required to ensure that the circumstances of previous acts are properly understood so that reasonable inferences for the contemporary context can be drawn from them.

E. 'Absconder'

If a patient is designated an 'absconder' or a 'runner', their release from mandated inpatient status (including from a high dependency ward) becomes significantly more difficult. A history of one or more actual or attempted escapes from confinement can lead to the adoption of much more stringent measures to ensure their continuing presence on a locked ward. Trust is difficult to regain when it is perceived as having been breached. There can be a link between the descriptors of 'absconder', 'non-compliant' and 'insightless'; in *Re DS*[57] the Victorian Board made an explicit connection between absconding behaviour and likely lack of compliance with medication as a result of absence of insight.

However, there can be many reasons why a person has been absent without permission from a ward and there are a number of forms of such behaviour. The 'absconding' may, for instance, be attributable to:

- a physical craving for illicit drugs;
- a personal matter that needs to be attended to (eg care of children, parents or pets);
- a tryst;
- fears that are contextually reasonable (eg because of having been assaulted on the ward) or unreasonable;
- confusion;
- a conflict with a staff member; or
- the experience of paranoid hallucinations or delusions.

It is important for clinicians, advocates and review tribunal members to endeavour to ascertain what caused the 'absconding behaviour' in order to be able to gauge its relevance for matters such as the existence of insight and potential for ongoing compliance with medication by a patient and thus informed prediction of likely prognosis of a patient without the coercion of involuntary status.

Moreover, unauthorised absences can take many forms, including the merely 'technical', such as returning a few minutes late from authorised off-site leave during the day or from weekend leave. These can still be recorded in the files and return later as a suggestion that a patient has 'absconded'. By contrast, there are serious and dangerous 'break-out' attempts by some patients. The principal relevance of 'genuine' absconding for clinicians and review tribunals is its

---

[57] *Re DS*, unreported, VMHRB, 10 May 2001.

potential to indicate disinclination to co-operate with treatment. It is this aspect of absconding which needs to be the subject of investigation and assessment.

F. 'Substance Dependent'

The reality of dual and multiple disabilities, especially of substance dependence and mental illness, is increasingly a paradigm of mental health work. The correlation of schizophrenia and marijuana usage has received a good deal of critical analysis over recent years.[58] However, what is pertinent in this context is the recording on some patients' files that they are 'substance dependent', that they have engaged in 'poly-substance abuse' or that they are a 'known drug addict'. The reality is that a high percentage of persons with serious mental illnesses have used illicit substances or have drunk to excess at some stage. What clinicians and review tribunal members need to know is whether current or previous symptomatology may have been affected by either co-morbid substance use or dependence or by substance use or dependence alone.

The appeal of *Re AC*[59] is an example of the difficulties that can exist when mental illness intersects with high levels of cannabis usage. AC was a 24-year-old man on a community treatment order from whose strictures he desired to be released. He lived with his parents, worked up to 28 hours per week and had his income administered by his mother and father. His treating doctor explained to the Board that AC had dual diagnoses of paranoid schizophrenia and cannabis abuse. She stated that he used as much marijuana as he could obtain and that he had been threatening toward clinicians on occasions. His symptoms of illness were described as persecutory and grandiose delusions about the writing of famous music, which he believed had been stolen from him and illicitly broadcast. His doctor told the Board that AC became irritable and disorganised around the time preceding a previous admission. She also said that his most prominent symptomatology as of the time of the hearing was negative symptoms of schizophrenia, which had not been addressed by his antipsychotic medication. She expressed the view that the fact he had not had an admission for three years

---

[58] See, eg X Lauqueille, 'Is Cannabis a Vulnerability Factor in Schizophrenic Disorders?' (2009) 16(9) *Archives of Pediatrics and Adolescent Medicine* 1302; E Fernandez-Espejo, MP Viveros, L Núñez, BA Ellenbroek, F Rodriguez de Fonseca, 'Role of Cannabis and Endocannabinoids in the Genesis of Schizophrenia' (2009) 206 *Psychopharmacology* 531; C Hjorthøj, A Fohlmann, and M Nordentoft, 'Treatment of Cannabis Use Disorders in People with Schizophrenia Spectrum Disorders—A Systematic Review' (2009) 34 *Addictive Behaviours* 520; M Frisher, I Crome, O Martino and P Croft, 'Assessing the Impact of Cannabis Use on Trends in Diagnosed Schizophrenia in the United Kingdom from 1996 to 2005' (2009) 113 *Schizophrenia Research* 123; R Miller, G Ream, J McCormack, H Gunduz-Bruce, S Sevy and D Robinson, 'A Prospective Study of Cannabis Use as a Risk Factor for Non-adherence and Treatment Dropout in First-episode Schizophrenia' (2009) 113 *Schizophrenia Research* 138; J Koskinen, J Löhönen, H Koponen, M Isohanni and J Miettunen, 'Rate of Cannabis Use Disorders in Clinical Samples of Patients With Schizophrenia: A Meta-analysis' (2010) *Schizophrenia Bulletin* (forthcoming). Advance access online: doi:10.1093/schbul/S6p031.
[59] *Re AC*, unreported, VMHRB, 22 July 2004.

was attributable to the antipsychotic medication which he had been prescribed. However, AC continued to smoke cannabis regularly. The difficulty for the Board in the absence of clear, primary symptomatology of mental illness, other than some slightly odd ideas about music, which did not seem to preoccupy him, was whether he still appeared to be mentally ill or whether such symptoms as he was then displaying, such as amotivation and lassitude, were attributable to a drug-affected lifestyle. Ultimately, the Board was split, with two members concluding he appeared to be mentally ill and the other member dissenting.

Descriptions of patients as having drug or alcohol dependencies can impact diversely upon clinicians' and decision-makers' expectations and reasoning processes. An important question for clinicians, advocates and review tribunal members is whether such substance use is continuing, rather than being simply a phenomenon that was recorded in mental health files years before and which lingers as a potential distraction. Associated questions include:

- What is the substance dependency or usage?
- How serious is its nature and extent?
- What interaction does it have with the patient's mental illness—eg is it separate and distinct or potentiating? and
- Whether it could it be responsible for the patient's psychiatric symptomatology—for example, a drug-induced psychosis.

G. 'Disorganised' and 'Poor Hygiene'

An effect of mental illness can be disorganisation and poor self-care. Indeed, these can be both symptoms and effects of mental illness, leading to real risks. However, the descriptors can also be highly judgemental and reflective of a mindset that suspects that persons who are not well organised and well-presented are unwell. This is not always the case. There can be many explanations other than mental illness for some level of disorganisation and for indifferent hygiene. These can include domestic ineptitude, disinclination to focus upon the quality of surroundings, eccentricity and poverty. Such phenomena can also have a significant subjective and pejorative component.

'Disorganisation' and 'poor hygiene', while having emotive connotations, are sensitive to but not specific for mental illness. It is always advisable for mental health professionals, patient advocates and mental health review tribunals to obtain details of such matters so as to enable evaluation of whether they are simply value judgements or whether they are actually indicative of pathology.

H. 'Impaired Judgement'

An effect of mental illness can be impoverishment of judgement. However, there can be many other aetiologies for such a characteristic. These can include sheer eccentricity.[60] Judgement is a highly relative concept, laden with values and assumptions that are not shared in all contexts and which vary amongst cultures and timeframes. Put another way, the exercise of poor judgement is not co-terminous with impaired judgement. Moreover, the exercise of poor judgement may be a subjective evaluation of another's lifestyle or may be reflective of attitudinal unorthodoxy in the patient and not relate to impairment caused by mental illness.

In *Re AW*,[61] for example, a psychiatrist contended that one of the reasons for regarding a patient as appearing to be mentally ill was that the patient's judgement was 'impaired'. This had the potential to relate to an impairment of thought and thus to be indicative of the current presence of mental illness. When scrutinised, however, this assertion related simply to the patient not accepting the diagnosis of schizophrenia. Similarly, the Board was asked to consider whether a patient's religious practices and ascetic lifestyle, living long-term on a riverbank beside the Murray River in a tent, justified the inference that he was mentally ill, rather than eccentric. The Board ultimately concluded that the evidence did not establish a significant disturbance of thought or perception as a result of a medical condition, simply a decision to live an unorthodox lifestyle.[62]

The notion of 'impairment of judgement', which should be interpreted by way of its indicating the active, current presence of mental illness, can readily evolve into a critique of the quality of a person's decisions—rather than an assessment of the person's capacity to exercise reasoned judgement, regardless of whether they choose to make decisions which, objectively or conventionally speaking, are in their best interests. As such, the making of apparently odd or heterodox decisions can unfairly be characterised as indicative of impairment of thinking (or of impoverished ideation) and thus evidence of the presence of mental illness. A responsibility of clinicians, advocates and mental health review tribunals is to identify whether a person has been deprived of the ability to make reasoned decisions on their own behalf in relation to matters of health and safety, and then whether it is mental illness (as against, for instance, substance dependence or intellectual disability) which has caused this.

I.   Personality Disordered

One of the most prejudicial epithets that can be applied to a person with mental illness is that they also have a personality disorder, particularly an antisocial personality disorder or a borderline personality disorder. At the extreme end of the spectrum is the term 'psychopath', generally used outside Europe in recent

---

[60] D Weeks and J James, *Eccentrics: A Study of Sanity and Strangeness* (New York, Kodansha International, 1995).

[61] *Re AW*, 05–088 [2005] VMHRB 3, 22 February 2005.

[62] *Re SL*, 04–057 [2004] VMHRB, 27 October 2003.

years as a result of the administration of Robert Hare's PCL-R (Psychopathy Checklist Revised).[63] The most significant connotations attaching to the use of personality disorder descriptors are that the person has characteristics which can involve mendacity,[64] anti-social behaviour (especially violence) and manipulativeness, none of which are likely to be particularly amenable to pharmacotherapy or orthodox therapeutic techniques. This can induce a level of mistrust and despair in treaters in relation to the success likely to be accomplished by pharmacotherapy and even psychotherapy. What can make such a diagnosis prejudicial is its propensity to lead to a confirmation of involuntary status by reason of the concern that the person will commit acts of harm toward themselves or others.

In *Re GW*,[65] the Victorian Mental Health Review Board, in relation to an earlier legislative regime, concluded, after hearing very extensive evidence from psychiatrists, that an earlier decision in *Re KMC*[66] that a woman with a Borderline Personality Disorder could be classified as mentally ill was insupportable. The essence of the decision was that a Borderline Personality Disorder could not properly be described as a mental illness. The Board concluded that, giving the term 'mental illness' its non-technical meaning, it was not satisfied that GW appeared to be suffering from a mental illness, as he had not recently demonstrated any symptoms of disturbance of mental functioning which formed an identifiable syndrome. Nor had he demonstrated symptoms of disturbance of mental functioning which were pathological in nature.

In the context of another patient diagnosed with Borderline Personality Disorder, the Board applied this definition, concluded in *Re ASB*[67] that the patient did not appear to be mentally ill. In particular, it commented that

> however naive or ill advised her actions may have been, we cannot accept that ASB's purported attempt to hang herself in custody or her suggestion that she was pregnant provide evidence to support a conclusion that she is mentally ill. In response to our questions it appeared probable that both the play-acted hanging and her supposed pregnancy were devices she used to attract attention to facilitate her release.[68]

In 1995, amendments to the Mental Health Act 1986 (Vic) introduced a phenomenological definition of 'mental illness', focusing not on its classification but upon the manifestation of symptomatology. Section 8(2) of the Act was also amended to provide that a person could not be considered mentally ill by reason

---

[63] See generally RD Hare, *Without Conscience: The Disturbing World of the Psychopaths Among Us* (New York, Pocket Books, 1993).

[64] *Farrell v The Queen* (1998) 194 CLR 286.

[65] *Re GW* [1990] VMHRB 4, 27 March 1990.

[66] *Re KMC* [1989] VMHRB 13, 7 November 1989.

[67] *Re ASB* [1994] 2 VMHRB 188, 2 November 1994.

[68] *Re ASB* [1994] 2 VMHRB 188, 3 November 1994, at 192.

only of their having 'an antisocial personality'.[69] The definition was the subject of interpretation in 1996 in the context of a woman with Borderline Personality Disorder in *Re CG*.[70] CG also had the dual diagnosis of a severe depressive episode, including hallucinations, requiring Electro-Convulsive Therapy. The Board concluded that she suffered from symptoms of a condition characterised by a significant disturbance of mood and perception.

Similarly, in *Re AM*,[71] the Board heard a case involving a woman with the diagnosis of Borderline Personality Disorder. She had a history of psychotic episodes and suicide attempts. On occasions she claimed that she was possessed by demons, was communicating with Satan and believed she was 'special'. The Board noted that she had experienced severe episodes of psychosis which had been characterised by a significant disturbance of thought, mood and perception and concluded that she appeared to be mentally ill.

In the 2003 case of *Re SK*,[72] the Board was called upon to review its previous decisions in the context of a woman whose only condition was Borderline Personality Disorder, at times characterised by apparent psychotic symptomatology. The clinical view was that for the most part such apparently psychotic symptoms were pseudo-symptoms, rather being utterances and behaviour designed to attract clinical attention, rather than being indicative of genuinely underlying false beliefs or experiences. The Board found that SK experienced dramatic oscillations in mood at regular intervals. While she was said to cope at work and enjoy it, her persistent episodes of self-harm occurred at night when she was alone and became anxious and unhappy. At that stage her affect became extremely labile and she tended to descend into self-loathing, harming herself in a variety of ways. The Board found her behaviour to be characterised by a significant disturbance of mood. It also found SK's thinking to be significantly distorted with some regularity:

> She becomes obsessed by views about her worthlessness. She has also given vent consistently, according to her clinical record, to views about being a sacrifice to God. Her self-image becomes substantially disordered, in a way comparable with the somatic distortions of perception which characterise the experiences of those with eating disorders. She then acts out her feelings and has repeatedly put her life at risk. She told the Board on a number of occasions that she believed herself to be in control when she self-harms by attacking her neck or other part of her body with a weapon or by taking overdoses of medication. This is plainly wrong and a cognitive distortion. She has been admitted to the Intensive Care Unit on a number of occasions and only days ago was found hanging in her hospital room. Her acts are lethal. It is only a matter of time until they will be fatal, if she continues with them. We accept that generally she draws herself

---

[69] See also Mental Health Act 2000 (Qld) s 12(2)(i); Mental Health (Treatment and Care) Act 1994 (ACT) s 5(i); Mental Health Act 2007 (NSW) s 16(1)(l); Mental Health and Related Services Act (NT) s 6(3)(c); Mental Health Act 1996 (WA) s 4(2)(f); Mental Health Act 1996 (Tas) s 4(2)(a).

[70] *Re CG* [1996] 2 VMHRB 353, 28 November 1996.

[71] *Re AM* [1996] 2 VMHRB 358, 5 December 1996.

[72] *Re SK*, unreported, VMHRB, 28 May 2003.

to the attention of clinical staff before and/or after self-harming. However, given the frequency of her behaviour and the escalation in its seriousness, we have no doubt that she will successfully commit suicide unless the cycle of her self-harm is interrupted. SK does not accept the level of risk that she is posing to herself.

Thus, it found her to have a condition characterised by a significant disturbance of thought.

A challenge for clinicians, advocates and review tribunal members is to attempt the complex exercise of disentangling a personality disorder from mental illness, at the same time refraining from using the coercive powers of mental health legislation to render a person an involuntary patient when what is causing the concern about public safety is the person's personality disorder alone.

III. The Clinical and Review Tribunal Imperatives

It is tempting and easy for clinicians to have ready resort to the short-form expressions described above and for review tribunal members to rely upon them without being sufficiently cautious about the risks of misevaluation or error. On occasions it is entirely appropriate for such descriptors to be employed. The clinical literature makes it clear that they relate to real attributes and conse-quences of mental illness commonly encountered by treaters and experienced by patients. It is in good part upon proven instances of unwell behaviour or sub-optimal coming to terms with illness that informed decisions about likely future behaviour and relapse-risk can be predicted. The relevant past remains the best predictor of the future. The sting often lies in discerning what constitutes the 'relevant past'.

The essence of the descriptors outlined above, though, is that they can typecast and stereotype inaccurately and in a way prejudicial to the therapeutic and liberty interests of persons who are involuntarily treated. In short, they can communi-cate what they should not by being inappropriately cross-sectional, one-dimensional and de-contextualised. Much of the problem lies not within the relevance or potential relevance of such descriptors. It comes with over-ready and uncritical usage of them and too ready extrapolation from one episode or too limited a set of data, especially if de-contexualised. One instance of unco-operativeness does not make a patient 'non-compliant'; one sexual dalliance on a ward does not make them 'promiscuous'; one attempted escape does not make them an 'absconder'; one episode of self-harm does not make them 'suicidal'; one episode of violence does not render them 'violent'; one poor exercise of judge-ment does not mean they have 'impaired judgement'; usage of illicit drugs in the past does not make them for all time a 'drug user' or 'substance dependent'.

There is no easy answer to the question of how often a person has to behave in a certain way to be the appropriate recipient of what can be a prejudicial descriptor. What is clear is that if such descriptors are to be properly employed, there should be evidence to justify the contemporary relevance of them—to suggest that it is likely on the basis of the comparability of events from the past to the currently presenting circumstances that the descriptors can fairly be applied to the patient now and be useful for assessing ongoing risks. Further, matters which are likely to be distressing, embarrassing and demeaning should only be the subject of ongoing justifications for involuntary status to the extent that they need to be.

To the extent that past behaviour is indicative of an ongoing propensity, a number of questions need to be asked:

- To what extent is the descriptor relevant?
- Might the descriptor be culturally determined or influenced?
- To what extent is the evidence for previous behaviour accurately recorded?
- To what extent was the past behaviour a product of a particular factual context that no longer exists?
- To what extent was the behaviour generated by mental illness symptomatology which is no longer present?
- To what extent has the person been shamed by their behaviour to a point where they are unlikely to repeat it?

In the mental illness context, there are additional considerations about the extent to which it is reasonable or therapeutically legitimate for a clinician or decision-maker to investigate past incidents of the kind that give rise to the short-hand descriptors described in this chapter. Dwelling on past incidents, be they episodes of violence, sexual disinhibition, attempts to leave a ward without permission, resort to violence, previous levels of self-care, or usage of illicit substances, can be counter-therapeutic—it can persuade a patient that they are forever tarred with the brush of symptoms experienced acutely in the past. Repeated canvassing of such matters, especially those that resonate with periods of florid mental illness, is embarrassing and distressing for a patient. Having to relive certain kinds of incidents is degrading and demoralising. It does little to instill hope and promote preparedness to assume responsibility for self-care and to come to terms with mental illness and its symptoms. In short, such investigations should only be undertaken to the minimum extent necessary to enable accurate decision-making.

IV. Conclusion

The argument that the descriptors relating to insight and compliance/adherence should be incorporated within mental health legislation dealing with imposition of involuntary status has previously been flagged in this chapter.

Both descriptors have the potential for misapplication. However, problems can be substantially addressed by insight and treatment compliance being framed in terms of clinical knowledge for instance by reference to a mechanism for falsifiable measurement[73], carefully moulded by legislative draftspersons, and regulated by the words of statutory provisions.

At present legislation does not include explicit reference to issues arising from insight or treatment adherence/compliance. The considerations in the real world of provision of treatment and decision-making about involuntariness function as free-floating, de facto yardsticks. This is less than transparent and is imprecise and confusing. There is a risk both that they will function, in the sense described by Michael Perlin,[74] as sanist conduits for unarticulated paternalism and that they will overtake (or at least interact unclearly with, or even contaminate) the criteria that are legislatively prescribed.

Thus, there is a problematic gap between considerations actually taken into account in making important decisions about involuntary status, and the criteria formally stipulated for the exercise by legislatures. Disjunctions between law and practice of this kind do not conduce either to transparency or confidence in decision-making processes.

One of the distinctive attributes of both concepts is that they lie at the heart of decision-making by clinicians and review tribunals alike. Inevitably they have an impact upon assessment of risk to self or others and upon the capacity for psychiatric patients to make decisions about their treatment without coercion, that is, to be voluntary. The degree of understanding of relevant matters exhibited by patients, and their history of co-operation with clinicians' treatment on every occasion, are part of decision-making by clinicians and then on review by mental health tribunals. It would be unrealistic and ill-conceived to propose that they be jettisoned from the clinical and review tribunal lexicon or decision-making process. Such a step would be unrealistic and would deprive decision-makers of important reference points they need to make decisions about involuntariness.

John Dawson and Richard Mullen are not in favour of taking the bold step of incorporating insight as a yardstick in itself.[75] They favour accepting that insight is a relevant factor in the decision-making process but fear rigidity if 'improved insight' is formally recognised as a criterion for discharge from involuntary status. A compromise may be to incorporate the following provisions that make clear the relevance of insight and treatment compliance/adherence for decision-making in relation to risk and inability to consent:

---

[73] See Freckelton 'The Mental Health Insight Scale: In Quest of Objectivity' (2010) 17 *Psychiatry, Psychaology and Law* (in press).

[74] M Perlin, *The Hidden Prejudice: Mental Disability on Trial* (Washington DC, American Psychological Association, 2000).

[75] J Dawson and R Mullen, 'Insight and the Use of Community Treatment Orders' (2008) 17 *Journal of Mental Health* 269, 279.

- In evaluating the existence of risk to the health and safety of the patient and risk to the safety of members of the community, and the capacity of the patient to make informed decisions about treatment for their mental illness, regard may be had, amongst other things, to:
- The history of the patient's mental illness;
- The severity and nature of the patient's symptoms of mental illness;
- The circumstances in which its symptoms have been manifested and become more or less serious, if this has happened;
- The attitude of and understanding by the patient at relevant times toward his or her illness, its symptoms and his or her need for treatment;
- The previous response of the patient to clinicians' recommendations for treatment for his or her illness;
- Any recurrence of symptoms of the patient's mental illness and the circumstances of such recurrence;
- The nature, circumstances and recency of any acts of harm or attempted harm engaged in by the patient toward himself or herself or others.

In evaluating the capacity of a patient to be able to provide consent to treatment required for the patient's mental illness, consideration may be given, amongst other things, to any symptoms of the mental illness which are significantly adversely affecting the patient's ability to understand in general terms the nature and symptoms of his or her illness and to evaluate rationally/reasonably his or her need for treatment and his or her treatment options.

The advantage of such formulations is that they capture the essence of patients' understanding of relevant issues and of failures to adhere to treatment on previous occasions, without resorting to catch-all descriptors. However, such formulations still enable evaluation of the significance of such factors in a way which is sensitively contextual. They are fair to patients in the sense of being transparent and advantageous to decision-makers—clinicians and review tribunals alike.

10

Civil Admission Following a Finding of Unfitness to Plead

JILL PEAY

I. Introduction

The problems posed to legal systems by persons accused of criminal offences who, at the point of their trial, are in no fit mental state to participate in that trial, manifest themselves in a number of ways across a number of jurisdictions.[1] Similarly, the statutory provisions vary in their relative friendliness to the accused, the nature of the disorders they embrace and the aspects of the trial process they cover.[2] In England and Wales, the focus of this chapter, such persons may be subject to a finding of 'unfitness to plead', which is still governed by the

---

[1] See, eg N Poythress, R Bonnie, J Monahan, R Otto and S Hoge, *Adjudicative Competence: The MacArthur Studies* (New York, Kluwer Academic/Plenum Publishers, 2002); J Dawson, 'Capacity to Stand Trial: Old and New Law in New Zealand' (2008) 15 *Psychiatry, Psychology and Law* 251; T Exworthy, 'Commentary: UK Perspective on Competency to Stand Trial' (2006) 34 *Journal of the American Academy of Psychiatry and the Law* 446; T Rogers, N Blackwood, F Farnham, G Pickup and M Watts, 'Fitness to Plead and Competence to Stand Trial: A Systematic Review of the Construct and its Application' (2008) 19 *Journal of Forensic Psychiatry and Psychology* 576.

[2] For example, in s 2 of the Criminal Code for Canada, 'unfit to stand trial' means unable on account of mental disorder to conduct a defence at any stage of the proceedings before a verdict is rendered or to instruct counsel to do so, and, in particular, unable on account of mental disorder to (a) understand the nature or object of the proceedings, (b) understand the possible consequences of the proceedings, or (c) communicate with counsel. Similarly, in s 4 of the New Zealand Criminal Procedure (Mentally Impaired Persons) Act 2003, unfit to stand trial (a) means a defendant who is unable, due to mental impairment, to conduct a defence or to instruct counsel to do so; and (b) includes a defendant who, due to mental impairment, is unable (i) to plead (ii) to adequately understand the nature or purpose or possible consequences of the proceedings or (iii) to communicate adequately with counsel for the purposes of conducting a defence. Neither provision makes explicit reference to the person's ability to give evidence in their own defence. Jersey's approach of requiring the defendant to have 'the capacity to participate effectively in the proceedings' arguably separates the ability to make rational decisions which reflect true and informed choices about plea and those about participation in the trial: see R Mackay, 'On Being Insane in Jersey Part Three—The Case of *Attorney- General v O'Driscoll*' [2004] *Criminal Law Review* 291.

Pritchard test dating back to 1836.[3] At that time the science of psychiatry was, as the Law Commission recognises, 'in its infancy', and the criteria are now widely regarded as outmoded and outdated.[4] They are, in essence, a test of whether an accused can comprehend the course of proceedings so as to make a proper defence. But the test benefits from none of the advances in modern psychiatric thinking which might better discriminate between accused persons who can and should be exposed to a criminal trial and those vulnerable, mentally disordered persons who manifestly should not.

This chapter considers questions of rights-based legalism in the context of those who straddle the range between wholly civil commitment, a health-based disposal following a criminal conviction, and a punitive sentence. Depending on what test is applied, what procedures are followed and what objectives are sought, these disordered individuals facing criminal proceedings might find themselves either within a health-based system or a penal system or neither. Would a broader test of 'unfitness to plead' result in a fairer disposal of those who have committed the actus reus of an offence, but who do not have the necessary mental capacity at the point of trial to determine whether they met the necessary mens rea criteria, and accordingly be in a position to be held culpable of a criminal offence? Is subsequent civil commitment in this context an example of rights-based legalism working, or of a health-based system governed by paternalism? Indeed, are some offenders convicted, following a guilty plea, of offences for which they could not be held liable in a full trial process if a test more in keeping with current understandings of the nature of mental responsibility were devised?

Since the various outcomes of a determination of fitness include full trial followed by acquittal or conviction and conventional punishment, or by a determination that the accused performed the actus reus of the offence (followed by health-based disposal), or did not (followed by acquittal), the nature of the test used to determine unfitness will be critical. Should its scope be primarily legalistic, or capacity-based, or based on a 'best interests' determination? Consideration of unfitness to plead thus permits an examination of the range of potential bases for mental health law—whether primarily legalistic, paternalistic or dominated by a human rights framework—in the context of what are difficult cases with complex and overlapping objectives for all the participants concerned.

---

[3]   *R v Pritchard* (1836) 7 C & P 303.

[4]   Available at: www.lawcom.gov.uk/insanity.htm. The *Pritchard* test is also in conflict with the test of capacity in the Mental Capacity Act 2005 (England and Wales) and with the new definition of mental disorder in the Mental Health Act 1983 (England and Wales), as amended by the Mental Health Act 2007 (England and Wales). The scope of the law on unfitness is currently being reviewed by the Law Commission.

II. Fitness to Plead: The Problem of Numbers

In all jurisdictions significant numbers of mentally ill and cognitively impaired individuals pass through the criminal justice system. In a proportion of these cases, psychiatrists and psychologists will be asked to advise upon whether the defendants are capable of standing trial. Without a proper clinical test or evidence base for the legal test these judgements are likely to be inconsistent and arbitrary. A number of such clinical tests do exist,[5] but within England and Wales the approach is currently ad hoc. While clinicians may agree on their findings, they may disagree on how they relate to the legal test; or they may just disagree on their findings per se.[6]

What is evident is that many unfit defendants end up in the penal system following conviction. The numbers revealed by Nicola Singleton, Howard Meltzer and Rebecca Gatward on learning disability alone in the prison population are worrying.[7] In July 1997 the prison population in England and Wales was 61,944: five per cent of the male sentenced population (then at 46,872), would, according to the authors, have fallen into the lowest category on the Quick Test of intellectual functioning (ie 25 and below, which is the approximate equivalent of 65 on the IQ scale.)[8] Thus, there would have been some 2,340 men in the sentenced population with the most serious of learning disabilities. How many of these men pleaded guilty in either the Crown Court or the Magistrates' Court is hard to determine, but their mere presence in the prison population should raise concerns. In particular, it should raise concerns about the viability of the test for unfitness to plead. In 1997 there were only 50 findings of unfitness to plead nationwide.[9]

Nor has the situation changed. A systematic review involving some 12,000 prisoners has estimated that up to 1.5 per cent of prisoners would be diagnosed with intellectual disabilities.[10] Even given the preponderance of sentencing by

---

[5] For example, the AAPL guideline which also incorporates decisional incompetence, see R Mackay, 'AAPL Practice Guideline for the Forensic Evaluation of Competence to Stand Trial: An English Legal Perspective' (2007) 35 *Journal of the American Academy of Psychiatry and the Law* 501 and the MacCAT-FP instrument, see A Akintunde, 'The MacArthur Competence Assessment Tool—Fitness to Plead: A Preliminary Evaluation of a Research Instrument for Assessing Fitness to Plead in England and Wales' (2002) 30 *Journal of the American Academy of Psychiatry and the Law* 476.

[6] D James, G Duffield, R Blizard and L Hamilton, 'Fitness to Plead: A Prospective Study of the Inter-relationships Between Expert Opinion, Legal Criteria and Specific Symptomatology' (2001) 31 *Psychological Medicine* 139.

[7] N Singleton, H Meltzer and R Gatward, *Psychiatric Morbidity among Prisoners in England and Wales* (London, The Stationery Office, 1998).

[8] R Ammons and C Ammons, 'The Quick Test (QT): Provisional Manual' (1962) 11 *Psychological Reports* 111.

[9] R Mackay, B Mitchell and L Howe, 'A Continued Upturn in Unfitness to Plead—More Disability in Relation to the Trial under the 1991 Act' [2007] *Criminal Law Review* 530.

[10] S Fazel, K Xenitidis and B Powell, 'The Prevalence of Intellectual Disabilities among 12000 Prisoners—A Systematic Review' (2008) 31 *International Journal of Law and Psychiatry* 369.

magistrates in short-term sentences of imprisonment, and their evident failure to utilise fully their powers under the Mental Health Act 1983 (England and Wales), it is clear that the test of unfitness to plead is failing to filter some of the most intellectually impaired away from the criminal justice process. Moreover, arguments that the disability might have developed after sentence (as can happen with some mental illnesses) are less persuasive with respect to mental impairment. Two other recent reports have also confirmed worryingly high levels of mental disorder in the prison population.[11] Lord Bradley's review has only served to emphasise the seriousness of the situation with his assertion that '[c]ustody can exacerbate mental ill health, heighten vulnerability and increase the risk of self-harm and suicide'.[12]

Indeed, the Bradley Report[13] estimates that there are some 9,143 people appearing at Magistrates' Courts annually with a serious mental illness, having been bailed, and a further 8,081 with serious mental illness having been held in custody before their court appearance (out of a total of approximately 821,000 defendants making their first appearance). Amongst Lord Bradley's recommendations is the proposal that '[i]mmediate consideration should be given to extending to vulnerable defendants the provisions currently available to vulnerable witnesses'.[14] In short, he suggests special measures to reduce the stresses associated with the court environment and facilitate effective communication.

Documenting the extent of mental ill health and mental incapacity within those caught up in the criminal justice process should come as no surprise. Research on incapacity amongst those admitted to acute medical inpatient wards,[15] and to those admitted to psychiatric wards from the community,[16] reveals significant levels of incapacity at the point of critical decision-making in people's lives. What is also interesting is the evidence of clinical professionals failing to pick-up on the incapacity documented by researchers.[17] This may be

---

[11] K Edgar and D Rickford, *Too Little, Too Late: An Independent Review of Unmet Mental Health Need in Prison* (London, Prison Reform Trust, 2009); Great Britain. Her Majesty's Chief Inspector of Prisons for England and Wales, *The Mental Health of Prisoners: A Thematic Review of the Care and Support of Prisoners with Mental Health Needs* (London, HM Inspectorate of Prisons, 2007).

[12] KJC Bradley, *The Bradley Report: Lord Bradley's Review of People with Mental Health Problems or Learning Disabilities in the Criminal Justice System* (London, COI for the Department of Health, 2009) Executive Summary at [1].

[13] *ibid,* 59, citing the work of J Shaw, F Creed, J Price, P Huxley and B Tomenson, 'Prevalence and Detection of Serious Psychiatric Disorder in Defendants Attending Court' (1999) 353 *The Lancet* 1053.

[14] KJC Bradley, *The Bradley Report: Lord Bradley's Review of People with Mental Health Problems or Learning Disabilities in the Criminal Justice System* (London, COI for the Department of Health, 2009) 61.

[15] V Raymont, W Bingley, A Buchanan, A David, P Hayward, S Wessely and M Hotopf, 'Prevalence of Mental Incapacity in Medical In-patients and Associated Risk Factors: A Cross-sectional Study' (2004) 364 *Lancet* 1421.

[16] G Owen, G Richardson, A David, G Szmukler, P Hayward and M Hotopf, 'Mental Capacity to Make Decisions on Treatment in People Admitted to Psychiatric Hospitals: Cross-Sectional Study' (2008) 337 *British Medical Journal* 448.

[17] See also Genevra Richardson, this volume, ch 8.

because clinical professionals are focusing on other things at the time of admission; and in this sense, lawyers at pre-trial hearings may be similarly distracted.

Given the general incidence of incapacity in the population and the levels of mental disability within the prison population, all of the figures would suggest that there is either a failure to detect problems of fitness to plead amongst defendants or, if they are detected, a failure by the legal system to be able to respond appropriately. Either way, there is a clear problem to be resolved. Getting the balance right is critical, since too low a threshold for establishing unfitness will result in many accused persons being diverted into the health system inappropriately, when they could properly be tried. Setting it too high produces the alternative problem of too many unfit accused being tried and, potentially, inappropriately punished.

III. Fitness to Plead: Background, Procedure, Theory and Practice

A. Statutory Background

The law governing fitness to plead is to be found in the Criminal Procedure (Insanity) Act 1964. This Act has been subject to considerable procedural reform. First, the Criminal Procedure (Insanity and Unfitness to Plead) Act 1991 provided more flexible disposal options. Prior to these amendments indefinite confinement in a mental hospital followed a finding of unfitness, and counsel would occasionally advise clients to avoid such mandatory outcomes by pleading guilty to minor offences even where there may have been doubt about the prosecution's ability to prove the accused's guilt. Not surprisingly, findings of unfitness were uncommon.[18] Although the Mental Health Act 1983 (England and Wales) had also introduced the entitlement to be discharged by a Mental Health Review Tribunal (MHRT) where the presence of a continuing disorder could not be established, use of the provisions remained minimal. Given the underlying ethos of unfitness findings, under-usage of these orders was an indictment of the law's fairness, a frustration of the purposes of punishment and led to the possibility of unnecessary but costly appeals. The second procedural reform came via the Domestic Violence, Crime and Victims Act 2004, which abolished the remaining mandatory disposal to hospital where the charge was murder.[19] This

---

[18] R Mackay, 'The Decline of Disability in Relation to the Trial' [1991] *Criminal Law Review* 7; R Mackay, *Mental Condition Defences in the Criminal Law* (Oxford, Clarendon Press, 1995).

[19] For a detailed analysis of the effects of the Domestic Violence, Crimes and Victims Act 2004 see *The Domestic Violence, Crime And Victims Act 2004: Provisions For Unfitness To Plead And Insanity*, Home Office Circular 24/2005 available at: www.homeoffice.gov.uk/about-us/publications/home-office-circulars/circulars-2005/024–2005/.

had, of course, been in conflict with the need to satisfy the criteria for the deprivation of liberty of those of unsound mind under Article 5 of the European Convention on Human Rights. Undoubtedly, these statutory reforms have increased the use
of the unfitness procedures, but even so, they remain palpably low.[20]

B. Procedure

The legislation now requires unfitness to be determined by a judge, on the
evidence of two or more doctors, according to the *Pritchard* criteria. If an accused
is found unfit, the trial will not proceed, but a jury will then consider whether the
accused did the act or made the omission required for the offence charged.[21] The
provisions accordingly do not allow for the legal issues to remain in limbo.
Accused persons found to be unfit will either be acquitted if the actus reus is not
made out, or be found to have done the act or made the omission charged and be
liable to therapeutic intervention.[22]

During the 'trial of the facts' there is no examination of the accused's intention
per se, although the House of Lords has asserted (obiter) that if there is objective
evidence of 'mistake or accident or self-defence, then the jury should not find the
defendant did the "act" unless it is satisfied beyond all reasonable doubt on all the
evidence that the prosecution has negatived that defence'.[23] Ronnie Mackay, Barry
Mitchell and Leonie Howe note that having raised the issue of unfitness successfully, some defendants are acquitted following the trial of the facts or, curiously,
such a trial does not take place at all.[24] If the actus reus is made out then the court
has access to the range of disposals for unfit accused, namely:

- a hospital order under section 37, with or without an indefinite restriction
  order under section 41 (Mental Health Act 1983 (England and Wales) as
  amended by the Mental Health Act 2007 (England and Wales))
- a supervision order (under which treatment can be given for both physical
  and mental disorders, although it is a non-punitive order and there are no
  sanctions for non-compliance)
- an order for absolute discharge.

---

[20] R Mackay, B Mitchell and L Howe, 'A Continued Upturn in Unfitness to Plead—More
Disability in Relation to the Trial under the 1991 Act' [2007] *Criminal Law Review* 530: they report
329 unfitness findings for the period 1997–2001, an average of less than 66 accused persons per year.
Notably, findings relating to serious mental illness marginally outweighed those relating to learning
disability.

[21] See *Attorney General's Reference (No 3 of 1998)* [1999] 3 All ER 40 (CA).

[22] Notably, Szymon Serafinowicz, the first person (not) to be tried under the War Crimes Act
1991, was found unfit to plead by a jury who heard conflicting evidence as to his dementia. Rather
than moving to a 'trial of the facts', the Attorney General entered a plea of *nolle prosequi*, permanently
staying the proceedings.

[23] Lord Hutton in *R v Antoine* [2001] 1 AC 340 (HL) 376.

[24] R Mackay, BJ Mitchell and L Howe, 'A Continued Upturn in Unfitness to Plead—More
Disability in Relation to the Trial under the 1991 Act' [2007] *Criminal Law Review* 530: namely, in 31
cases of their sample of 329.

Hospital orders may only be made, regardless of the charge, where the accused meets the criteria for admission. Medical evidence is required. Notably, the court has the power to *require* a hospital to admit the accused: it does not have this power generally with respect to admission under section 37, and this reflects the unusual position of the court in not having the option of a criminal disposal where the accused is found unfit. The anomalous position of the courts having the power to, in effect, order clinicians to provide a treatment environment, is in conflict with the otherwise prevailing situation that the decision as to whether treatment is appropriate for any patient is a clinical one.[25] The situation contrasts with other cases where the court is considering making a section 37 order, as the offender will have been convicted and accordingly a penal option remains possible.

Lord Hutton has further noted in *R v Antoine*[26] that once an accused person has been found unfit to stand trial, the trial of the facts under section 4A of the 1964 Act strives to achieve the balance inherent in the European Convention on Human Rights:

> The purpose of section 4A … is to strike a fair balance between the need to protect a defendant who has, in fact, done nothing wrong and is unfit to plead at his trial and the need to protect the public from a defendant who has committed an injurious act which would constitute a crime if done with the requisite mens rea. The need to protect the public is particularly important where the act done has been one which caused death or physical injury to another person and there is a risk that the defendant may carry out a similar act in the future. I consider that the section strikes this balance by distinguishing between a person who has not carried out the actus reus of the crime charged against him and a person who has carried out an act (or made an omission) which would constitute a crime if done (or made) with the requisite mens rea.[27]

It is clear that this balance is found to be most difficult to draw if the issues relate to instances where serious harm has occurred, and there is a perceived risk of future harm. No mention is made here of the seriousness of the accused's disorder or of any perceived need for treatment. Here the legalistic, protective model is dominant in the procedural arrangements.

One other procedural matter is worthy of note. Under section 4(2) of the 1964 Act the court may postpone consideration of the question of fitness to be tried until, at the latest, the opening of the defence case. The court would need to be of the opinion that it would be expedient and in the interests of the accused so to do, but such a tactic on the part of the defence does allow the strength of the prosecution case to be tested on the issue of both actus reus and mens rea without formally assessing the accused's fitness. As Ronnie Mackay and Gerry

---

[25] *R (on the application of Burke) v General Medical Council* [2004] EWHC 1879 (Admin).
[26] *R v Antoine* [2001] 1 AC 340 (HL).
[27] *ibid*, 375–6.

Kearns note,[28] this could lead to some odd conclusions. For example, a special verdict of not guilty by reason of insanity where an individual suffering from epileptic automatism is fit to plead but then found legally insane, but a complete acquittal either where the individual has their fitness put into abeyance and the prosecution then fail sufficiently to negative any factual evidence of automatism, or where the prosecution fail to negative an arguable defence during a trial of the facts. The decision in *Antoine's* case similarly has the potential to lead to inconsistent conclusions: even though a plea of diminished responsibility could not be relied upon during a trial of the facts for murder,[29] the prosecution still have to negative any arguable defences of mistake, accident or self-defence. If the section 4(2) route is chosen the position with respect to diminished responsibility is even more complex.

Finally, it should be noted that in the Magistrates' Court, which will inevitably account for the greatest number of sentenced mentally disordered offenders, there are no provisions for determining fitness to plead per se. Proceedings can be discontinued by the Crown Prosecution Service in accordance with the terms of the Code for Crown Prosecutors; accused persons may thereafter be civilly admitted to hospital where they meet the necessary criteria under the Mental Health Act 1983 (England and Wales). And, in a procedure more akin to that in the Crown Court, magistrates can utilise section 37(3) of the Mental Health Act 1983 (England and Wales). Where they are satisfied both that the accused 'did the act or made the omission charged' and that the accused satisfies the criteria for a hospital order admission, magistrates may make the order without, obviously, convicting the individual.

C.   Theory

The justifications for having 'fitness to plead' safeguards have been set out by the House of Lords:

> Throughout history, seriously anti-social acts, particularly acts of violence, have been committed by people whose mental capacity was such that they were not responsible, or not fully responsible, for their acts, or could not fairly be required to stand trial. Such cases pose an inescapable public, moral and human rights dilemma: for while such people may present a continuing danger from which the public deserve to be protected, it would be offensive to visit the full rigour of the law on those who are not mentally

---

[28]   R Mackay and G Kearns, 'An Upturn in Unfitness to Plead? Disability in Relation to the Trial under the 1991 Act' [2000] *Criminal Law Review* 532, 544.

[29]   In *R v Antoine* [2001] 1 AC 340, the House of Lords expressly overruled *Egan v The Queen* [1998] 1 Cr App R 121 (CA), which had problematically held that it was necessary for the prosecution to establish during any trial of the facts both that the defendant did the act charged and had the necessary mens rea at the time.

responsible, or not able to defend themselves, as an ordinary person of sound mind would be taken to be, and who may (despite their mental incapacity) have done nothing wrong or dangerous.[30]

Thus, fitness to plead in part stems from a desire to protect the individual from what could be an unfair trial; and in part constitutes a forward-looking and necessarily quite broad approach with its desire to protect others from the potential for further injurious acts. Whether the phrase 'the full rigour of the law' implicitly acknowledges the problems of imposing punishment on those of questionable mental capacity is unclear. For the moment it is sufficient to note the complexity of the dilemmas individuals with reduced capacity pose for both criminal law and, for the purposes of this chapter, for the subsequent civil provisions that follow a finding of 'unfitness'.

The 1836 *Pritchard* criteria draw a distinction between those who have the ability to enter a plea (in the sense of being able to indicate what their plea is) and those who, despite being able to do so, are still considered unfit to plead.

> There are three points to be inquired into—first, whether the prisoner is mute of malice or not; secondly, whether he can plead to the indictment or not; thirdly, whether he is of sufficient intellect to comprehend the course of proceedings on the trial, so as to make a proper defence—to know that he might challenge any of you to whom he may object—and to comprehend the details of the evidence, which in a case of this nature must constitute a minute investigation. Upon this issue, therefore, if you think that there is no certain mode of communicating the details of the trial to the prisoner, so that he can clearly understand them, and be able properly to make his defence to the charge; you ought to find that he is not of sane mind. It is not enough, that he may have a general capacity of communicating on ordinary matters.[31]

The case law on what the criteria have come to include is somewhat contradictory. The recent summary in *R v Friend*[32] is helpful; and it also stresses the element of the defendant being able to give evidence in his own defence:[33]

> [T]he accused will be able to comprehend the course of the proceedings so as to make a proper defence. Whether he can understand and reply rationally to the indictment is obviously a relevant factor, but [the jury] must also consider whether he would be able to exercise his right to challenge jurors, understand the details of the evidence as it is given, instruct his legal advisers and give evidence himself if he so desires.

The *Pritchard* criteria have been repeatedly approved even though they do not necessarily include accused people with various handicaps that might impair the chances of a fair trial. For example, in *R v Podola* (1959) loss of memory about the events themselves would not qualify as unfitness; indeed the Court of Appeal

---

[30] Lord Bingham, *R v Antoine* [2001] 1 AC 340 (HL) 344.
[31] Baron Alderson in *R v Pritchard* (1836) 7 C & P 303, 304.
[32] Otton LJ, in *R v Friend* [1997] 2 All ER 1011 (CA) 1018.
[33] See also *R v John M* [2003] EWCA Crim 3452 and *R v Stewart Michael Diamond* [2008] EWCA Crim 923 at [44].

rejected the notion that comprehending the course of proceedings entailed an ability properly to 'appreciate the significance of the evidence', rather the test was narrow—could the defendant understand the case as it proceeded?[34] There is thus a problem for a defendant affected by delusional thinking where a disorder of mind may cause him or her to act unwisely. One consequence of the rejection of this approach is that a defendant may well have the capacity to enter a plea, in the sense of knowing what guilty or not guilty means, but be unable to appreciate the significance of failing to act on legal advice to pursue a defence of diminished responsibility because the defendant's disorder leads him or her wrongly to conclude that they will be acquitted.[35] In turn, this would militate in favour of treating the ability to enter a plea, and the ability to stand trial separately.

In short, fitness to plead means fitness to enter a plea and to be tried if that plea is not guilty. The conflation of the two under *Pritchard* is problematic: can the anticipatory nature of a decision about the likely elements of a trial and their complexity be properly evaluated? If not, legal and health-based approaches will come into conflict. Moreover, the *Pritchard* criteria do not equate with legal certifiability, which leads to problems with the Article 5 (deprivation of liberty) provisions under the Human Rights Act 1998,[36] nor do they 'fit neatly with any diagnostic criteria'.[37] Questions have also been raised about their potential conflict with the Article 6 (right to a fair trial) requirements, although the House of Lords in *R v H*[38] held that the procedural arrangements for dealing with unfitness do not require compliance with Article 6(2), as they do not constitute criminal proceedings.

D.   Practice

The empirical evidence suggests that the application of the test is malleable in the hands of those who apply it: psychiatrists, for example, will also take into account other criteria, such as whether the defendant can understand the consequences of the charge and whether they would be able to control themselves during a trial.[39]

---

[34]   *R v Podola* (1959) 43 Cr App R 220, 229, 238–9 (CA).

[35]   See *R v Stuart Michael Diamond* [2008] EWCA Crim 923.

[36]   Resolved under the Domestic Violence Crime and Victims Act 2004; see also L Scott-Moncrieff and G Vassall-Adams, 'Capacity and Fitness to Plead: Yawning Gap' (October 2006) *Counsel* 14 at [2]–[3].

[37]   D Chiswick, 'Fitness to Stand Trial and Plead Mutism and Deafness' in R Bluglass and P Bowden (eds), *Principles and Practice of Forensic Psychiatry* (Edinburgh, Churchill Livingston, 1990).

[38]   *R v H (Fitness to Plead)* [2003] UKHL 1.

[39]   R Mackay and G Kearns, 'An Upturn in Unfitness to Plead? Disability in Relation to the Trial under the 1991 Act' [2000] *Criminal Law Review* 532. See also T Ward, 'Hearsay, Psychiatric Evidence and the Interests of Justice' [2009] *Criminal Law Review* 415. Tony Ward notes two examples from *R v Friend (No 1)* [1997] 1 WLR 1433 (CA) 1442, where the Court of Appeal acknowledged that the sorts of condition that might satisfy s 35(1)(b) of the Criminal Justice and Public Order Act 1994 would be epilepsy and latent schizophrenia where the experience of giving evidence might trigger an attack or florid state. In *R v Friend (No 2)* [2004] EWCA Crim 2661 the CA added Attention Deficit

Similarly, in practice, those with psychotic illnesses do seem to be included in 'unfitness' findings,[40] which now are as frequently imposed in practice in cases of psychosis as in cases of intellectual impairment, implying an expansive application of the test in defiance of the more narrow legal approach.[41] Some criminal barristers regard the threshold for fitness as too low, meaning that unfit defendants do stand trial unfairly, and that defendants with mood disorders and delusions who don't satisfy a cognitively-based test may, in practice, be unable to appreciate and contribute to their own trial.[42] In short, whilst the courts[43] may have asserted that the test of fitness is not set at too low a level, practitioners' actions and beliefs, and the evidence from prison populations and studies of incapacity in those not involved with the criminal justice system, would suggest otherwise.

Very little, if anything, is known about the determination of unfitness by the judge; and the absence of reasoned decisions will only hinder such understanding. Whilst research[44] sheds light on the numbers and types of accused persons who are found to be unfit, little is known about the numbers and types of cases where, the issue of fitness having been raised, it is rejected by the judge (or in earlier times, the jury). Even less is known about cases where unfitness might properly be raised, but is not. What is known is that the 1991 Act has enhanced the use of the 'unfit' provisions: the indications are that these have begun to rise as lawyers and psychiatrists have become more familiar with the workings of the revised legislation.[45]

Hyperactivity Disorder where a defendant might blurt out something or give conflicting evidence. Thus, a defendant in such circumstances might be fit to plead but not to give evidence under s 35 and have adverse inferences drawn. Tony Ward also notes (at 419) the Court of Appeal's approval in *R v John M* [2003] EWCA Crim 3452, wherein the Court approved a direction adding an ability to give evidence, namely to understand questions and give intelligible replies, to the *Pritchard* criteria.

[40] See, eg, the case of *R v Davies* (1853) 3 C & K 328.

[41] R Mackay, B Mitchell and L Howe, 'A Continued Upturn in Unfitness to Plead—More Disability in Relation to the Trial under the 1991 Act' [2007] *Criminal Law Review* 530; see also D James, G Duffield, R Blizard and L Hamilton, 'Fitness to Plead: A Prospective Study of the Inter-relationships Between Expert Opinion, Legal Criteria and Specific Symptomatology' (2001) 31 *Psychological Medicine* 139.

[42] T Rogers, N Blackwood, F Farnham, G Pickup and M Watts, 'Fitness to Plead and Competence to Stand Trial: A Systematic Review of the Constructs and Their Application' (2008) 19 *Journal of Forensic Psychiatry and Psychology* 576.

[43] See, eg, *Robertson* (1968) 52 Cr App R 690, cited by R Mackay, B Mitchell and L Howe, 'A Continued Upturn in Unfitness to Plead—More Disability in Relation to the Trial under the 1991 Act' [2007] *Criminal Law Review* 530.

[44] R Mackay and G Kearns, 'An Upturn in Unfitness to Plead? Disability in Relation to the Trial under the 1991 Act' [2000] *Criminal Law Review* 532; and R Mackay, B Mitchell and L Howe, 'A Continued Upturn in Unfitness to Plead—More Disability in Relation to the Trial under the 1991 Act' [2007] *Criminal Law Review* 530.

[45] Mackay's work generally has noted significant increases in the use of 'unfit' provisions rising from 13 in 1990 to 76 in 2001: see R Mackay, B Mitchell and L Howe, 'A Continued Upturn in Unfitness to Plead—More Disability in Relation to the Trial under the 1991 Act' [2007] *Criminal Law Review* 530; and R Mackay and G Kearns, 'An Upturn in Unfitness to Plead? Disability in Relation to the Trial under the 1991 Act' [2000] *Criminal Law Review* 532.

In Ronnie Mackay and Gerry Kearns's study of 110 disposals under the 1991 Act, 77 per cent received hospital disposals, with or without restrictions.[46] Whilst this might suggest that judges are still not making as great a use of the new flexible (non-hospital-based) disposals as they might, the authors note that defendants found unfit to plead at trial are quite likely to be ill at the point of trial and accordingly in need of hospital treatment. This contrasts with those pleading not guilty by reason of insanity, where the disorder has to have been present at the time of the offence, but not necessarily at the time of trial. Here, over 50 per cent of disposals were non-hospital-based.[47] Therapeutic imperatives at the point of plea may thus be a current concern, rather than as an issue that touches merely on the question of responsibility for the crime.

IV. Options and Outcomes

To summarise, under the current arrangements for trial accused persons finding themselves in the Crown Court will be faced with a range of options. Where there are doubts about an individual's fitness to plead, or fitness to stand trial, that range becomes confusingly complex for both the accused and the legal advisor. And the issue is further complicated where an accused's mental state may fluctuate or deteriorate during a trial. But in short they can:

1. Plead not guilty—with capacity—trial with formal legal safeguards;
2. Plead guilty—with capacity—a calculated decision with advantages of sentence discount that stem from an early plea;
3. Plead not guilty—without capacity—trial, but may not benefit from safeguards—risk of inappropriate conviction and inappropriate disposal;
4. Plead guilty—without capacity—risk of inappropriate sentence (ie may not benefit from health-based disposal);
5. Raise the issue of potential disability and ask the court to postpone the consideration of fitness to be tried until the opening of the defence case; if the prosecution fails to make out the actus reus or present sufficient factual evidence to allow the jury safely to infer that the accused had the requisite mens rea then the defence can make a submission of no case to answer. The Judge can accede to this, leading to a complete acquittal, or move to the assessment of the defendant's fitness to stand trial;[48]

---

[46] R Mackay and G Kearns, 'An Upturn in Unfitness to Plead? Disability in Relation to the Trial under the 1991 Act' [2000] *Criminal Law Review* 532.

[47] R Mackay and G Kearns, 'More Facts about the Insanity Defence' [1999] *Criminal Law Review* 714.

[48] Criminal Procedure (Insanity) Act 1964 (England and Wales) s 4(2).

Or ... raise the issue of unfitness to plead at the start of proceedings and be found ...

6.   Currently unfit to plead—judge-based determination on 1836 criteria, leading to

7.   Trial of the facts before jury—finding of did or did not commit the act or make the omission charged

   (a)   Did commit act: leads to health-based disposal

   (b)   Did not commit act: acquittal but possible risk of civil admission.

Perceived difficulties or uncertainties with the fitness to plead criteria, or a desire to avoid any determination of unfitness, can lead to errors outlined in (3) and (4). Similarly, an outdated or outmoded test for fitness (6) can lead to both inappropriate guilty pleas and findings of guilt, and can fail to embrace defendants who are not fit to plead, but are treated as fit.

Limitations in the trial of the facts 'test' can result in not guilty offenders being inappropriately held to have committed the act and hence receive a (potentially) inappropriate health-based disposal. Accused persons who are found not to have committed the act or made the omission for the offence charged, will nonetheless have drawn their mental state to the attention of those who have the power thereafter to pursue civil admission if thought appropriate. Whether this ever happens is a moot point; but it is not wholly illusory.

What is evident from the case law is that accused persons whose fitness to plead is compromised, even though they may be deemed fit to plead under the current narrow legal test, find themselves, often many years later, caught up in complex appeals. Most frequently, these appeals concern cases where defendants have been convicted of murder and they subsequently seek to have a finding of manslaughter on grounds of diminished responsibility substituted for the murder conviction. Such cases may arise where a defendant refuses, for reasons attributable to their mental state at the time, to allow such a defence to be put forward: improvement in their mental state over a period of years can lead to a re-evaluation by them (if not by the courts) of the wisdom of this course of inaction.[49] Perhaps most poignant is the case of *Murray*, who killed her five-year-old daughter and pleaded guilty to murder seemingly because she wished to be punished for her crime.[50] Her paranoid schizophrenia was sufficient in the eyes of the clinicians to prevent her from understanding the impact of her disorder on her actions, but it was not sufficient to bring her within a legal test of unfitness; nor, accordingly, to prevent her rejecting advice to plead to manslaughter on grounds of diminished responsibility.[51]

---

[49]   See, eg, *R v Stewart Michael Diamond* [2008] EWCA Crim 923; *R v Moyle* [2008] EWCA Crim 3059; *R v Neaven* [2006] EWCA Crim 955.

[50]   *R v Murray* [2008] EWCA Crim 1792.

[51]   I am indebted to Ronnie Mackay for drawing attention to these cases in his presentation to the Law Commission seminar on unfitness on 19 March 2009.

A. Problems and Possibilities

It is evident that the current test of unfitness is insufficiently either defined or consistently applied to ensure that those with mental disorder are appropriately protected, where that mental disorder is likely to have an impact on the fairness of the plea or trial. Only a tiny proportion of the most worrying cases gain any benefit from the current provisions. The judicially-based, case-specific approach to this is deficient where there is no objective standard by which the judge can judge unfitness, and no guarantee that relevant cases will be brought before the judge for such a determination.

Aside from this fundamental difficulty, a series of mismatches can occur between rights-based and paternalistic objectives because decisions about fitness to plead do involve a clash of ideologies, perspectives and objectives between the criminal justice system and the health system. At trial, and somewhat crudely, the criminal justice system's general approach is that the interest in not convicting innocent people takes precedence over ensuring that everybody who is guilty is convicted (although this has shifted over the last 12 years with a 're-balancing' of the justice system in favour of victims and the protection of wider society). At sentence, the dominant philosophy to determine what is appropriate punishment involves a determination of the seriousness of the offence and the culpability of the offender, tempered by the secondary objectives of deterrence, compensating the victim and rehabilitating the individual. Incapacitative and protective objectives remain pertinent. Criminal trials, partly in anticipation of the consequences that can follow, are subject to the Article 6(2) and (3) protections, as evidenced in *R v H*,[52] but preventive detention, even for those found unfit, is a justified outcome.

In contrast, the health system's dominant philosophy is in the health interests/ needs of the individual. Arguably it is tempered by a growing interest in public protection, albeit that this interest may be imposed uncomfortably on clinicians. Indeed, 'the primary purpose of mental health units is to provide healthcare and to promote the physical and mental health of the patients'.[53] Article 6(1) should apply to proceedings prior to compulsory admission following an unfitness determination. So, when unfitness determinations intercede in a criminal trial the objective would appear to be avoiding manifestly unfair trials (and hence the exposure of unfit individuals to the potential rigours of punishment; either just or unjust punishment) and ensuring an appropriate disposal where justified. Having an inappropriate test, getting the determination wrong, or having an unfair 'trial of the facts' have potentially grave consequences for the individual. The risks for inadequate societal protection are partially ameliorated by the

---

[52] Lord Bingham, *R v H (Fitness to Plead)* [2003] UKHL1 at [2] (with additions).

[53] Pill LJ in *R (On the Application of G) v Nottinghamshire Healthcare NHS Trust* [2008] EWHC 1096 (Admin) at [33], summarising the view of the smoke free legislation team at the Department of Health.

potential for a secure health-based disposal, but then only if the individual meets the criteria for compulsory admission to hospital, and largely only if a finding that the individual 'did the act' is made.

Whether the 'unfitness test', and in particular whether the 'trial of the facts' under section 4A of the 1964 Act is essentially criminal or civil in nature, has been determined by the House of Lords in *R v H*.[54] The case concerned two charges of indecent assault by a 13-year-old boy on a 14-year-old. The boy was held unfit to plead, but was determined to have committed the acts alleged, and given an absolute discharge. However, this finding attracted the application of the Rehabilitation of Offenders Act 1974 and the notification requirements under the Sex Offenders Act 1997. The House of Lords concluded that both of these orders were non-punitive: the first was for the purposes of rehabilitation and for the benefit of the accused person; and the second was to protect the public and not to punish the accused. Thus, they asserted that these were orders analogous to civil anti-social behaviour orders (ASBOs).[55] In so doing the House of Lords relied on the tests laid down by the European Court of Human Rights in *Engel v The Netherlands (No 1)*,[56] and concluded that the preceding section 4A procedure was not criminal in nature. It could not result in conviction, only acquittal; and a positive finding could not be followed by punishment. Although there was a finding 'adverse' to the accused the procedure for so doing lacked the essential features of a criminal process, since the interventions that could follow were not essentially 'criminal'. Although the degree of severity of the penalty the person risked incurring was relevant to a determination of what was 'criminal', some deprivations of liberty were not relevant, since 'by their nature, duration or manner of execution' they could not be 'appreciably detrimental'.[57]

That criminal proceedings culminate in the potential to impose penalties is their purpose. And, as any first year criminal law student will know, it is the marking out of defendants through this act of censure that defines the scope of criminal law and deters that conduct deemed sufficiently damaging to merit penal sanctions. But it is essentially a circular argument. We know what is criminal because it is followed by punishment: we know what is punishment because it is preceded by criminal processes.

Arguably, the strength of the appellant's argument in *R v H* lay in the notification and rehabilitative requirements mentioned above. To the unfit accused person these may well be experienced as censuring and punishing. Similarly, other compulsory rehabilitative measures which can be imposed under the Criminal Justice Act 2003 would be deemed punitive; moreover, these follow conviction. Thus, whilst rehabilitation is said to be for the benefit of the offender,

---

[54] *R v H (Fitness to Plead)* [2003] UKHL 1.
[55] *R v H (Fitness to Plead)* [2003] UKHL 1 at [16].
[56] The third *Engel* test, *Engel v The Netherlands (No 1)* (1976) 1 EHRR 647.
[57] See *Engel v The Netherlands (No 1)* (1976) 1 EHRR 647, 678–9 at [82], cited in *R v H (Fitness to Plead)* [2003] UKHL 1 at [19].

such measures are clearly demanding and are intended to have a symbolic punitive value. For the House of Lords to cite authorities to say that notification and registration measures are not punitive is not determinative of their reality. Is it hair splitting to maintain that a rehabilitative measure cannot be punishing because the court says so when they are applied in a civil context, even if they can have a punitive element in a criminal context? Is it a failure to appreciate the fundamental qualities of these orders which leads the House of Lords inextricably to the conclusion that the decision that precedes them cannot be criminal in nature? Undoubtedly, it is not going to be to the individual's advantage in finding work, for example, if he or she is obliged to disclose an adverse finding under the Criminal Procedure (Insanity) Act 1964. Indeed, since a restriction order can otherwise only be made following conviction in the Crown Court, this would imply that the restriction order has a dual potential status, following both criminal convictions and findings adverse to the accused. In essence these are muddy and muddied waters with considerable overlap between civil and criminal provisions, and one might expect some greater cognitive dissonance here from the courts, particularly since the application of Article 6(2) and (3) would make a difference to the nature of 'trials of the facts'.

This raises the third problem, of whether this is essentially an exercise by the courts in civil admission based on the nature and degree of the individual's disorder, leavened by some appreciation of the likelihood of harm to others, or whether this is the criminal courts essentially disposing of an accused person to a secure environment, but recognising that the objective of security is being achieved through a health-based route, since the penal route is unavailable in the absence of a criminal conviction? Although not a sentencing function, requiring admission to a psychiatric hospital under a section 37/41 order (hospital order with restrictions) will necessarily entail deprivation of liberty (on grounds of mental disorder) and potentially entail the subsequent continuation of that deprivation of liberty on grounds of risk to the public, even where the disorder may ameliorate or be unresponsive to treatment.[58] It achieves an amalgam of penal and health objectives, where these could not be justified in a purely criminal context.

Fourthly, it is open to accused persons and their representatives to be treated as mentally competent up until the close of the prosecution case. Thus, it is possible for the defence to attack the merits of the prosecution case without jeopardising (if jeopardising it is) the accused's position with respect to their mental state.[59] Similarly, both findings of fitness and unfitness may be appealed under section 6(1)(b) and section 15(1) respectively, preserving the legalistic approach beyond the disposal stage. Moreover, the finding by a jury that the unfit accused did the act or made the omission charged is also subject to appeal under section 15 of the

[58] *Hutchison-Reid v UK* (2003) 37 EHRR 9.
[59] Section 4(3) of the Criminal Procedure (Insanity) Act 1964 (England and Wales).

Criminal Appeal Act 1968. Thus, legal certainty about final disposal may take some time to crystallise. Meanwhile, treatment in conditions of uncertainty about the permanence of the therapeutic disposal may undermine both the offender's motivation to engage and the therapist's ability to deliver treatment. Equally, the results of therapeutic endeavours, for example, in enabling an accused to recover sufficiently to acknowledge his or her own part in an offence, may be too delayed to ensure a legally just outcome. A greatly delayed appeals process may prevent the courts from being able, retrospectively, to accept that the accused was sufficiently disordered at the point of offending to merit, for example, a finding of diminished responsibility.[60] After disposal and treatment, and assuming a section 37 or 41 order was made, a full trial can subsequently be held to determine guilt or innocence. But for those given other disposals—for example, an unrestricted hospital order—there is no right to a subsequent trial and any such determination would lie with the Crown Prosecution Service. Given its public interest criteria, this is unlikely to be exercised. Decisions about disposal per se, since they do not follow a conviction and are not sentences, are not subject to appeal, only to subsequent review by the Mental Health Review Tribunal.

This raises the fifth problem of uncertainty from an accused's perspective. Whilst the introduction of indeterminate sentences for public protection under the Criminal Justice Act 2003 somewhat lessens the power of this point, it remains true that for an accused the choice between an indeterminate and uncertain therapeutic disposal and a certain, albeit unattractive, penal disposal may incline an accused towards the latter. Although counsel may be alive to the consequences of the differing legal provisions, it is expecting a great deal of them to expect them also to be alive to the realities of indefinite detention under either a penal or therapeutic regime, and the operating standards of the various safeguards and decision-makers, such as the Parole Board, the Mental Health Review Tribunal, and the Secretary of State, who will affect and effect the implementation of those detention periods. Thus, much decision-making is likely to take place on the basis of 'best guesstimates' as to what will transpire.

Sixth, the criminal justice system has an operating assumption that defendants will act strategically, sometimes with the benefit of legal advice, but nonetheless act in their own best interests. Where an accused person's fitness is in doubt, acting strategically cannot be relied upon as an operating assumption. Thus, an accused's (disordered) beliefs about a number of aspects relevant to the decisions to be made may well interfere with informed decision-making.[61] Similarly, an accused's prior experience of either health or penal disposals may influence decision-making, unbeknownst to a legal advisor. What role, for example, is the

---

[60]   See *R v Stewart Michael Diamond* [2008] EWCA Crim 923.

[61]   Instructions may be based on false premises (eg *R v Stewart Michael Diamond* [2008] EWCA Crim 923, where there was an unrealistic expectation of an acquittal and a desire, arising out of paranoid beliefs, to 'get one over on the police') or out of a deluded belief that they deserve punishment on the most serious charge (eg *R v Murray* [2008] EWCA Crim 1792).

ban on smoking in health institutions, but not in prison, likely to have on decision-making where an accused might go in either direction? Similarly, instability in an accused's condition might enable them to act strategically and make consistent decisions at one point in the process, only to revoke those decisions or refuse to engage or be unable to make any further decisions at another point in the process. These are not easy cases to deal with but they have a chronology of their own. In other jurisdictions, such decisions faced by the accused may be even more dramatic: the role of 'three strikes and you are out' provisions in the United States, and the continuing existence of the death penalty, have seemingly contributed to the inexorable rise in the population of detained incompetent persons, which now includes those with personality disorder who would not normally be considered lacking in capacity or unfit to plead. Evidently, standards are relaxed where the consequences of not so doing are manifestly harsh. Whether in England and Wales, where the broadened definition of mental disorder under the amended Mental Health Act (England and Wales) 1983 (now including those with personality disorder) will have similar unintended consequences has yet to be revealed; but the risk of a many-headed health hydra eating-up scarce resources in diverting accused persons from trial and punishment is ever present.

Finally, there is the issue of the extent to which an accused needs to be 'fit to be punished' as opposed to being sufficiently unfit to merit a therapeutic disposal. Meeting the criteria for admission under the Mental Health Act 1983 (England and Wales) does permit those who deteriorate in prison to be transferred away from circumstances where they no longer remain fit to be punished. But should there be some other determination of fitness for punishment before it is imposed on those of already suspect mental vulnerability? One interesting development is noteworthy. In the recent case of *R (On the Application of Cooke) v DPP*,[62] which concerned the imposition of an Anti-Social Behaviour Order, the court made plain that when imposing this civil order, where the consequences of breach led to punitive interventions, decision-makers should not make an order where the individual, by reason of mental ill-health, did not have the capacity to understand and comply with the terms of the order being imposed. Without such capacity the accused was being doomed to future failure. Developing this approach, one might question whether we ought to think more carefully about the need to meet some threshold for fitness to be punished, rather than adhering to the default position, namely that those who are not convicted, but sufficiently disordered, can only be held in a therapeutic environment, whilst those who deteriorate in prison will only be transferred once the criteria are met, a bed is available and clinicians are willing to accept the patient.

Further problems arise out of the disjunction between the law's binary, one-point-in-time, approach to decisions (fit/unfit; guilty/not guilty;

---

[62]   *R (On the Application of Cooke) v DPP* [2008] EWHC 2703.

punishment/health-based disposal) and the clinical approach, which is based more on degrees of disorder and uncertainty, with its sliding scales of capacity and the recognition that individuals can vary in their abilities, needs and treatability not only over time, but within relatively brief periods of time. Thus, someone may have the capacity to instruct counsel but not to give evidence on their own behalf; they may have the capacity to understand the basis of the prosecution case, but not to be able to give a coherent account of their own defence where that intersects with their mental disorder and the medical assessment of that disorder (where, for example, an accused refuses psychiatric assessment); and an individual may be well enough at the point of plea to plead with capacity, but then deteriorate due to the demands of a trial so as not to be in a position properly to comprehend the course of proceedings. Leaving an appeal system to sort out these unfairnesses, perhaps many years later, is not a solution when it becomes so much more difficult with hindsight to ascertain exactly what the accused's mental state was at the time determinations were made (or not made) about their fitness.

In summary, considering the role of unfitness to plead as a basis for civil admission raises a number of difficulties, arising out of the clash of multiple perspectives which are concentrated on this particularly complex junction for decision-making in mental health. Even the roles of the various parties do not conform to traditional expectations. Counsel, who act on instructions from their clients, may find themselves precluded from pursuing the best defence and yet bound to accept instructions from those clients who meet a narrow test for fitness, but who are manifestly not thereafter able to act in their own best interests vis-à-vis any subsequent trial. And judges sitting in the Crown Court, who are now asked to adjudicate on unfitness on the basis of expert medical evidence, may equally find themselves managing the process where the accused person appears only briefly in court, and then does not behave in the traditional self-interested mode of the bulk of defendants.

V. Reform

Whilst the Law Commission has launched an initiative to explore the possibilities of developing a better legal test and rules for determining fitness to plead, two other issues arise: the processes for determining whether an individual meets the criteria (namely, the clinical assessments that feed into the judicial determination); and the underpinning philosophy of the law, with which this book is primarily concerned. With respect to the former, it is worth noting that research is underway to develop a bespoke dynamic test of fitness that more accurately reflects the nature of the capacities people need to participate in the decision about plea and the process of trial.[63] If capable of consistent application such a test might better meet the needs of both justice and an individual's interest in treatment, by initially delineating those who can and those who can't fairly stand trial, on the minimum grounds of their inability to comprehend trial proceedings.

With respect to the latter, the legal approach that might best underpin decisions about unfitness and the disposal of those found unfit, three possible albeit crude bases present themselves: a formally legalistic approach which may trade-off health considerations for the individual against protective imperatives with respect to the public's risk of future harm (albeit not offending per se); an approach which attempts to treat the mentally incapacitated on the same basis as the physically incapacitated, and which draws on human rights principles of non-discrimination; and a 'best interests' approach which is most clearly paternalistic and is heavily influenced by an assessment of the individual's clinical needs.

A. Legalistic

Putting the prosecution to proof before having the issue of unfitness determined would be one route to injecting a more legalistic approach. Giving primacy to a legal determination by the judge that there was sufficient evidence that the act or omission had occurred as alleged (as would happen with any half-time submission of no case to answer) would put the accused on a more equal footing with ordered defendants. Following on from a determination of unfitness a health-based disposal would result; no conviction as such would arise for those found unfit, since the accused would not have been able fully to participate in the trial, so could not satisfy the requirements of Article 6(2) or 6(3). This approach should lead to more acquittals (since the prosecution would have to establish any mental element, insofar as it required rebutting any evidence of mistake, accident etc to a 'beyond reasonable doubt' standard). From the perspective of protecting an accused's legal rights, this has the advantage of potentially securing more acquittals without formally raising their mental health status and ensuring that, for those found unfit, conviction per se cannot ensue; but it has the marginal disadvantage of exposing an unfit accused to the unfairness of a hearing of the prosecution case without their being able properly to participate in that hearing. If they are found to be fit, the ensuing full trial still holds out the possibility of a complete acquittal. There would need to be consideration of whether the unfitness relates primarily to entering a plea, taking part in a trial, or being punished. Whether this is a formally legalistic approach, or one seeped in 'new

---

[63] N Blackwood, J Peay and M Watts, 'Fitness to Plead: The Impact of Cognitive Abilities and Psychopathology' (2008) Application to the Nuffield Foundation (funded from January 2009).

legalism', will depend on the extent to which it facilitates entitlements and ensures outcomes that are the least restrictive in their nature.

B. Capacity-based—Human Rights

With the passage of the Mental Capacity Act 2005 (England and Wales) (the MCA), some statutory assistance with the meaning of capacity has occurred. In an ideal world, which applied legal concepts consistently, only those who were sufficiently capacitous according to the MCA to make a decision about plea would be permitted to engage with the criminal justice process. Section 2(1) of the MCA presumes an individual to have capacity until they are unable to make a decision because of

an impairment of, or a disturbance in the functioning of, the mind or brain

with respect to a particular matter. The capacities entailed include understanding and retaining relevant information, being able to use it and to communicate any decision made. Critically, with respect to its potential application to unfitness, section 3(4) notes that 'relevant information' includes

information about the reasonably foreseeable consequences of—

(a)   deciding one way or another, or
(b)   failing to make the decision.

And although the capacity test might be thought of as being set at a low threshold, to facilitate autonomous decision-making, in the context of unfitness, where the decisions are both complex and have foreseeable consequences down the line, many accused may find the task more demanding than their capacities permit.

Were a substantive test for fitness to be updated in this way a number of issues would arise. Many more offenders might be drawn into a health-based disposal when they might otherwise have been appropriately eligible for a criminal justice based determination. If the capacity required to plead guilty and the capacity required to plead not guilty are not co-terminous, there could not be a perfect allocation between the two options—Is more capacity required to risk the higher penalty of conviction following a contested trial, or is more capacity required to acknowledge legal (as opposed to moral) guilt, without an independent determination of guilt? A more forward-looking approach would be required, since complex anticipatory questions entailing consideration of the consequences of different pleas would arise, particularly with respect to the differing disposal options, some with a more punitive element than others, some with greater indeterminacy. A capacity-based approach is also decision-specific, not person-specific, so a person may have the capacity to plead guilty to an offence that, for example, is unlikely to result in a custodial sentence, but not to a more serious charge that might result in imprisonment. This will complicate any negotiations over charge or plea.

A test of 'decisional incompetence', as advocated by Ronnie Mackay and adopted in Jersey, could form the basis of a capacity-based test of unfitness, by expanding it beyond its current narrow cognitive base.[64] This would better capture the defendant's ability to participate meaningfully in the trial process, and could embrace principles such as the need for everything to be done that can reasonably be done to assist people to have the capacity to make particular decisions, and that one is entitled to make foolish, risky and unwise decisions that are not in one's best interests without being found to lack capacity.

The complexity of the decisions faced along the way (entering a plea, instructing counsel, understanding proceedings, giving evidence etc) might also result in accused persons shifting above and below the threshold for unfitness as proceedings progressed. Disposal following unfitness and an adverse finding on the facts would be governed by the need for treatment and a continuing lack of capacity. Deprivation of liberty to facilitate treatment would need to be justified under the Mental Health Act 1983 (England and Wales) or the MCA. For an equitable approach this would need to apply both to compulsory treatment for physical and mental disorders (raising further problems). For those lacking capacity, where there may be no disorder to treat, some form of third way civil detention might, albeit controversially, be justified on grounds of proven and continuing dangerousness. Depending on the threshold for what constitutes a lack of capacity for the task(s), this is a potentially highly interventionist route. Whilst it avoids the stigma of conviction, it replaces punishment with a potentially open-ended form of detention. Given the very widespread nature of offending, and the demonstrated levels of task-specific incapacity in the population, this could draw in large numbers of people. Proper representation might permit people with minimal capacity to be tried, but then result in the problem of punishing those without the capacity to benefit from it, and potentially ineligible for a health-based disposal. Since capacity is task-specific, it would need to be constantly under review, both in respect of individual fluctuation, and in respect of the different decisions over time with which people are faced. Without careful review the possibility remains that punishment would be imposed on those who cannot benefit from it.

C. Best Interests/Paternalism

Without a good definition of what is meant by best interests in this context (what interests? from whose perspective?) this is tricky. If one assumes best health

---

[64] R Mackay 'On Being Insane in Jersey Part Three—The Case of *Attorney-General v O'Driscoll*' [2004] *Criminal Law Review* 291.

interests then that would entail having a very inclusive test for unfitness to plead, on the grounds that punishment, or the conditions in which it is imposed, are rarely good for one's health. The accused's choice at the point of trial would not be central. Rather, professionals' views about his or her mental state and health needs would determine the route followed and the alleged offending would just be another way of drawing attention to such needs. Intervention thereafter would be determined by a continuation of those needs. This approach is redolent of the (controversial) mental health courts in, for example, North America. The denial of a 'right to punishment' and its replacement with the medicalisation of offending is amongst those controversial elements.

A paternalistic approach would probably also suggest that after the period of health intervention there would be no return to court for trial, since this would not be in one's overall best interests. The risk of undoing the good interventions to date outweighs the stigma of unresolved allegations. This reflects the current arrangements, where magistrates can make an order for admission under section 37 without any formal determination of the facts, as is required in the Crown Court, or where the Crown Court makes a hospital order without restrictions, and there is no right for the accused to return to court to contest the allegations should their mental state recover. Unfitness would be determined on a case-by-case basis, perhaps invoking a sliding scale of seriousness of offending and degree of unfitness to inject some element of proportionality into the compulsory health intervention.[65] The task of determining individual unfitness could also be supplemented by some objective criteria to determine whether a given standard of unfitness was met. Under this process, it is not immediately evident how the interests of any victim might be met.

VI. Conclusions

None of these three models looks particularly attractive. Yet both the latter two look likely to divert a significantly greater number of accused persons away from the criminal justice system, and potentially into the health system if the necessary criteria for admission or supervision are satisfied. Given the numbers of individuals in prison with serious mental disorder and significant learning disability, that may be regarded as a good thing. And even the legalistic model has the potential to divert given a more inclusive test for unfitness. Of course, in the absence of a robust and agreed basis on which to determine unfitness there would be an enhanced risk of clinician-based inconsistent (and potentially

---

[65] See the discussion of Winnick's 'sliding scale of competence' in Loughnan, *Mental Incapacity Defences in Criminal Law*. Thesis submitted to the Law Department, London School of Economics and Political Science for the Degree of Doctor of Philosophy (2008, unpublished) 780.

discriminatory) practice. The lessons learnt on the use of compulsion under the Mental Health Act 1983 (England and Wales) do not suggest that this is likely to be the fairest of approaches between individuals.[66]

All three models also raise the potential for greater conflict between hospitals and the courts, since in unfitness cases the courts exceptionally have the power to order a hospital to admit a patient. Of course, the court has to hear medical evidence that the patient satisfies the criteria for admission, but not evidence that a bed is available and being offered. Moreover, if the pool of unfit but potentially untreatable accused persons is significantly increased, the courts' well-documented anxieties about future offending may come to play a more prominent role.

Would the ideal solution be a pluralistic merging of the best features of each approach, or perhaps, as Tim Exworthy notes, the injection of more rights-based thinking, for example of proportionality, into health care decisions?[67] Even so, the reality is that such rights are context-specific in their application. The moving feast of dilemmas that the unfit accused poses, will shift as the individual moves through the different systems and is differently perceived by individuals wearing different hats. Thus, procedural rights can trump in the criminal context, human rights trump potentially for the competent patient, and paternalism triumphs with incompetent individuals, tempered by protectionism for competent risk posers. Perhaps the real answer lies in ensuring that fewer people pass through the criminal justice process; that more are dealt with voluntarily in the community where their disorders can be dealt with on the same basis as those with physical disorders; and that we dramatically reduce the size of our prison population. Achieving the latter would in turn make prison a potentially less damaging and more therapeutic environment for all. And to end with an adynaton: pigs might fly.

---

[66] J Peay, *Decisions and Dilemmas: Working with Mental Health Law* (Oxford, Hart Publishing, 2003).

[67] T Exworthy, 'Commentary: UK Perspective on Competency to Stand Trial' (2006) 34(4) *Journal of the American Academy of Psychiatry and Law* 466.

Part 5

Review Processes and the Role of Tribunals

11

Involuntary Mental Health Treatment Laws: The 'Rights' and the Wrongs of Competing Models?

TERRY CARNEY

I. Introduction

In 2007, Samuel Jan Brakel wrote:

> To make a police operation out of the state's efforts to provide needed [mental health] care and treatment is misguided, as is the adversarial inclination to exploit the already excessive criminal-law style protections that surround the [admissions and review] process in an effort to keep as many people from obtaining treatment as possible.[1]

As a long-standing primary author of the American Bar Association's text *The Mentally Disabled and the Law*,[2] Brakel's critique of the excesses of 'rights-based' models of mental health laws of the kind championed and favourably audited in Australia[3] cannot be ignored.

Similarly, there is a serious case for total repeal of dedicated mental health legislation on the basis that principles of consent to health care (and competence as a basis for substitute decision-making) are already perfectly capable of balancing competing interests in mental health care as in somatic health care generally. While Brakel argues for a less 'legalistic' model, these commentators argue, among other things, that it is discriminatory and stigmatising (or even unnecessary) to retain

---

[1] SJ Brakel, 'Searching for the Therapy in Therapeutic Jurisprudence' (2007) 33 *New England Journal on Criminal and Civil Confinement* 455, 498–9.

[2] SJ Brakel, J Pery and BA Weiner, *The Mentally Disabled and the Law*, 3rd edn (Chicago IL, American Bar Foundation, 1985).

[3] H Watchirs, 'Human Rights Audit of Mental Health Legislation—Results of an Australian Pilot' (2005) 28(2) *International Journal of Law and Psychiatry* 99.

separate mental health laws at all.[4] From a different standpoint, writers such as Amita Dhanda,[5] and Tina Minkowitz in chapter seven of this volume, argue that, properly interpreted, the Convention on the Rights of Persons with Disabilities (the CRPD)[6] undermines current models of mental health legislation, since it is unclear whether either coercion into treatment[7] or a 'competence' assumption[8] is permitted.[9]

---

[4]   J Dawson and G Szmukler, 'Fusion of Mental Health and Incapacity Legislation' (2006) 188(6) *British Journal of Psychiatry* 504; G Richardson, 'Autonomy, Guardianship and Mental Disorder: One Problem, Two Solutions' (2002) 65 *Modern Law Review* 702; T Wand and M Chiarella, 'A Conversation: Challenging the Relevance and Wisdom of Separate Mental Health Legislation' (2006) 15(2) *International Journal of Mental Health Nursing* 119. See also Neil Rees, this volume, ch 4.

[5]   A Dhanda, 'Legal Capacity in the Disability Rights Convention: Stranglehold of the Past or Lodestar for the Future?' (2007) 34(2) *Syracuse Journal of International Law and Commerce* 429.

[6]   Convention on the Rights of Persons with Disabilities, adopted 13 December 2006, GA Res 61/106. UN Doc A/Res/61/106 (entered into force 3 May 2008). For a recent overview: A Kämpf, 'The Disabilities Convention and its Consequences for Mental Health Laws in Australia' (2008) 26(2) *Law in Context* 10.

[7]   One argument is that the Convention is *silent* about the use of coercion (neither authorising nor banning its use), while Art 12(4) walks both sides of the fence on the issue of 'competence' in using language consistent with competence-based substitute-decision-making (adult guardianship) as well as espousing a 'supported-decision-making' model which would be incompatible with retention of competence-based reasoning: See A Dhanda and T Narayan, 'Mental Health and Human Rights' (2007) 370 *Lancet* 1197, 1198; A Dhanda, 'Constructing a new Human Rights Lexicon: Convention on the Rights of Persons with Disabilities' (2008) 8 *SUR International Journal on Human Rights* 43 and Annegret Kämpf, this volume, ch 7. This argument may add *rhetorical* weight to the case for greater reliance on supported decision-making, or chart the *direction* for legal reform in mental health (such as greater encouragement of medical enduring powers of attorney or honouring of values and directions set out in advance directives), but it surely pitches its case too high. Neither silence nor 'doublespeak' language can support an argument to displace *prior explicit* language in previous international instruments expressly addressing mental health care, given accepted principles of treaty interpretation: see P Weller, 'Supported Decision-Making and the Achievement of Non-Discrimination: The Promise and Paradox of the Disabilities Convention' (2008) 26(2) *Law in Context* 85, 87–90. Moreover, Australia expressly reserved its right to retain, 'subject to safeguards' and as a 'last resort', coercion within mental health and retention of adult guardianship laws when ratifying the Convention on 17 July 2008, available at: www.un.org/disabilities/default.asp?id=475 at 19 (June 2009).

[8]   Autonomy/capacity-based legislation rather short-changes mental health patients in practice: M Donnelly, 'From Autonomy to Dignity: Treatment for Mental Disorders and the Focus for Patient Rights' (2008) 26(2) *Law in Context* 37, 49–51.

[9]   The argument which is made that Art 17 of the CRPD, endorsing the right to respect for physical *and* mental integrity, totally precludes involuntary treatment is not borne out either by the history of negotiation of the Convention, or regional human rights jurisprudence. Instead it may be read as limiting resort to unbeneficial and overly intrusive treatment, or other than rare resort to physical restraint or seclusion: B McSherry, 'Protecting the Integrity of the Person: Developing limitations on involuntary treatment' (2008) 26(2) *Law in Context* 111, 121–3.

A. 'Rights' (or not) Hinge on the Context?

Mental health laws of the kind found in the developed world, like all laws, are a product of many forces, including their history, cultural values,[10] constitutional settings, available resources, styles of delivery of mental health services, and institutional arrangements.

Thus, there is a strong degree of path dependence in social policy,[11] which leads to considerable continuity of practice, irrespective of shifts in mental health models.[12] A cultural endorsement of liberal values of personal autonomy accounts for the prominence of rights models in common law countries.[13] Confucian value systems privilege family decision-making,[14] as the Japanese mental health and adult guardianship law demonstrates.[15] Constitutional inter-pretations pushed mental health law in the United States into its current 'quasi-criminal' standard for admissions, based on imminent risk and strong procedural protections, while Britain and other common law countries mainly opted for 'health and safety' approaches[16] and (European derived) post-admission tribunal review rather than court-approved admissions.[17] In practice,

---

[10] A US study of attitudes towards community treatment laws suggests they tend to be supported by those who are '*hierarchical* and *communitarian* ... while those who are *egalitarian* and *individual-istic* tend to oppose them': DM Kahan, D Braman, J Monahan, L Callahan and E Peters, 'Cultural Cognition and Public Policy: The Case of Outpatient Commitment Laws' (2010) 34(2) *Law and Human Behavior* 118. Services too have a cultural dimension: see for instance the Bradford psychiatric services in the United Kingdom which seek to attune themselves to cultural diversity by avoiding 'Eurocentric notions of dysfunction and healing': P Bracken and P Thomas, 'Postpsychiatry: A New Direction for Mental Health' (2001) 322 *British Medical Journal* 724, 726.

[11] W Arts, 'Pathways to the Future of the Welfare State: Institutional Persistence, Hybridization, Reflexive Modernization, or What?' in J Berghman, A Nagelkerke, M Boos, R Doeschot and G Vonk (eds), *Social Security in Transition* (The Hague, Kluwer Law International, 2001) 21; P Pierson, 'Coping with Permanent Austerity' in P Pierson (ed), *The New Politics of the Welfare State* (New York, Oxford University Press, 2001) 410; P Pierson, 'Coping with Permanent Austerity: Welfare State Restructuring in Affluent Democracies' (2002) 43 *Revue Francaise de Sociologie* 369, 372–4.

[12] GN Grob, 'Mental Health Policy in the Liberal State: The Example of the United States' (2008) 31(2) *International Journal of Law and Psychiatry* 89.

[13] See further, T Carney, 'The Mental Health Service Crisis of Neoliberalism—An Antipodean Perspective' (2008) 31 *International Journal of Law and Psychiatry* 101.

[14] SC Lee (ed), *The Family, Medical Decision-making and Biotechnology: Critical Reflections on Asian Moral Perspectives* (London, Springer, 2007).

[15] I Doran, 'Elder Guardianship Kaleidoscope: A Comparative Perspective' (2002) 16 *International Journal Law, Policy and the Family* 368, 374–5. See also, M Arai, 'Guardianship for Adults: A New Safety Net in Japan' (Paper presented at the Society for Legal Guardianship 'Japan-Australia Adult Guardianship Workshop', Sydney, 29 September 2003); T Carney, 'Aged Capacity and Substitute Decision-making in Australia and Japan' (2003/4) *LawASIA Journal* 1; D Weisstub and T Carney, 'Forensic Mental Health Law Reform in Japan: From Criminal Warehousing to Broad-spectrum Specialist Services?' (2006) 29(2) *International Journal of Law and Psychiatry* 86.

[16] P Appelbaum, 'Almost a Revolution: An International Perspective on the Law of Involuntary Commitment' (1997) 25(2) *Journal of the American Academy of Psychiatry and the Law* 135.

[17] Y Thoret and S Kantin, 'Historical Development of Legal Protection for the Rights of Mentally Ill Persons in France' (1994) 45(12) *Hospital and Community Psychiatry* 211.

however, the system in the United States remained accessible[18] until, as John Petrila describes in chapter fifteen of this volume, mental health *services* contracted. This demonstrates that socio-legal or systems factors, not the law, are most decisive.[19] Indeed similar control/committal outcomes may be reached despite differences in legislative form.[20]

Rights models also presuppose the existence of residential- and community-based professional mental health care, whether delivered by government or the market. If some commentators in wealthy developed countries, such as Australia, query rights models for depleting already strained mental health budgets,[21] it is unsurprising that developing countries prioritise services ahead of rights protection. This issue is discussed by Peter Bartlett in chapter seventeen of this volume. Rights models face many challenges, even in developed countries with strong traditions of liberalism and protection of civil rights. These include the neo-liberal contraction of the regulatory, distributive and social protection roles of the state, the emergence of community-based care models more reliant on private/civil society responsibilities of families and non-government supports, and implications for the atomistic 'liberal model' of autonomy posed by philosophical positions such as an 'ethic of care' or the practical question of whether or how to involve carers.[22]

B. The Argument

This chapter argues that the strengths of Australia's 'rights protection' model outweigh its weaknesses, but agrees in part with Jan Brakel that the model should be seriously renovated.

The renovation of mental health laws outlined in this chapter comprises several strands. In terms of their core task of adjudicating on the use of coercion, it is argued that mental health tribunals (MHTs) should not only be enabled to more fully discharge their existing rights protection mandate (currently at risk of being something of a charade), but also be *broadened* in two ways. MHTs should be empowered to fully engage the domain of *treatment access* (and service appropriateness), and be enabled to better perform their important *social* (or

---

[18]   P Fennell and RL Goldstein, 'The Application of Civil Commitment Law and Practices to a Case of Delusional Disorder: A Cross-national Comparison of Legal Approaches in the United States and the United Kingdom' (2006) 24(3) *Behavioral Sciences and the Law* 385.

[19]   S Anfang and PS Appelbaum, 'Civil Commitment—The American Experience' (2006) 43(3) *Israel Journal of Psychiatry and Related Sciences* 209.

[20]   P Fennell and RL Goldstein, 'The Application of Civil Commitment Law and Practices to a Case of Delusional Disorder: A Cross-national Comparison of Legal Approaches in the United States and the United Kingdom' (2006) 24 *Behavioral Sciences and the Law* 385.

[21]   R Vine, 'Review Boards in a Mainstreamed Environment: A Toothless Tiger in a Bedless Desert?' (Paper presented at the 30th Congress of the International Academy of Law and Mental Health, Padua, Italy, June 2007).

[22]   T Carney, 'The Mental Health Service Crisis of Neoliberalism—An Antipodean Perspective' (2008) 31 *International Journal of Law and Psychiatry* 101.

'community') role. To achieve these core reforms it is envisaged that MHTs would not only broaden their role from a sole focus on civil rights to engage the treatment and social domains, but would also operate in more flexible, more subtle and 'fluid' (or responsive) ways characteristic of a 'case conference', as developed more fully elsewhere.[23] Other areas of the reform package, such as social advocacy arrangements and recognition of the roles of carers, remain for future consideration. There must be better harnessing of quality treatment, housing, employment and social support options to overcome much unnecessary suffering and deprivation among the mentally ill.[24] As argued here, the overall goal is to advance *social participation* and socio-economic (social citizenship) and civil rights of mentally ill people at various levels of interaction with governmental or civil society.[25]

Section II of this chapter reports on the findings of an Australian Research Council Linkage study. Section III outlines the elements of different models and canvasses their respective strengths and limitations as judged against broad basic principles. Section IV summarises the main conclusions.

II. Background Building Blocks for Reconsideration of Australian Mental Health Law

A. The Research Story So Far

Research on the operation of Australian mental health tribunals largely mimics equivalent work from Britain,[26] with important exceptions. As in overseas studies, procedural fairness for people appearing before tribunals is an issue in Australia.[27] Advocacy (or, conversely, the lack of representation, time and information) plays a part in the degree of patient participation,[28] but the *structural* features of tribunals are critical. Multi-member tribunal panels, and adequate

---

[23] See also T Carney, 'Mental Health Tribunals: A "Relational Case-conference" to Pursue Fairness, Freedom and Treatment?' (Paper presented at the 31st Congress of the International Academy of Law and Mental Health, New York, 29 June–3 July 2009).

[24] K Brown and E Murphy, 'Falling Through the Cracks: The Quebec Mental Health System' (2000) 45 *McGill Law Journal* 1037.

[25] A Dixon, D McDaid, M Knapp and C Curran, 'Financing Mental Health Services in Low- and Middle-income Countries' (2006) 21(3) *Health Policy and Planning* 171.

[26] J Peay, *Tribunals on Trial: A Study of Decision-making Under the Mental Health Act 1983* (Oxford, Clarendon Press, 1989); E Perkins, *Decision-Making in Mental Health Review Tribunals* (London, Policy Studies Institute, 2003).

[27] T Carney, D Tait, D Chappell and F Beaupert, 'Mental Health Tribunals: "TJ" Implications of Weighing Fairness, Freedom, Protection and Treatment' (2007) 17(1) *Journal of Judicial Administration* 46.

[28] T Carney, F Beaupert, J Perry and D Tait, 'Advocacy and Participation in Mental Health Cases: Realisable Rights or Pipe Dreams?' (2008) 26(2) *Law in Context* 125.

funding and staffing to sustain acceptable durations of hearings appear essential both on the merits,[29] and in order to meet procedural fairness standards (unless statutorily exempted)[30] or any requirements imposed by human rights legislation.[31]

Mental health tribunals already subtly exercise some limited leverage around treatment and service access for some mental health consumers[32] by 'pushing the boundaries' of their jurisdiction.[33] However, structural impediments of underfunding and pressures towards 'production line' justice—the median length of hearings in NSW is 15 minutes, and 9 in 10 are less than 30 minutes (likewise in Victoria)—currently preclude proper exploration of the health and social domains.[34] In some States, such as New South Wales, involuntary admissions or orders were (until very recent repeal) further complicated by separate property management laws, which presumed *incompetence* to manage (contrary to adult guardianship laws presuming 'competence', as laid down in international instruments) and favoured indefinite rather than finite periods of administration.[35]

Significantly for this chapter, studies suggest that current laws do little to connect the more acutely ill to required mental health and other services. Larissa Hallam's qualitative study of Queensland's mental health legislation found that families felt mental health services 'denied services' and took 'no action' unless they could 'recall the correct procedures' for accessing involuntary committal.[36] Mobilisation of involuntary treatment orders was said to be like gaining admission to a secret society, where entry depends on verbatim recital of a complicated password. In

---

[29] T Carney and F Beaupert, 'Mental Health Tribunals: Rights Drowning in Un-"chartered" Health Waters?' (2008) 13(2) *Australian Journal of Human Rights* 181.

[30] L Sossin and Z Yetnikoff, 'I Can See Clearly Now: Videoconference Hearings and the Legal Limit on How Tribunals Allocate Resources' (2007) 25(2) *Windsor Yearbook of Access to Justice* 247, 271–2.

[31] See, eg *Human Rights Acts 2004* (ACT); *Charter of Human Rights and Responsibilities Act 2006* (Vic). In *Kracke v Mental Health Review Board (General)* [2009] VCAT 646, Bell J issued a declaration that the MHRB had breached Mr Kracke's right to a fair hearing under s 24 of the Victorian Charter of Human Rights and Responsibilities by 'unreasonably' delaying the routine review of involuntary treatment (scheduled to take place every 12 months) and Community Treatment Orders (scheduled for review within 8 weeks of any extension). Although Mr Kracke contributed by requesting adjournments and a second opinion, the delay was found to be excessive, and the Board was held responsible for 'driving' compliance with the statutory timeframes: see [700]–[702], especially at [702].

[32] E Grundell, 'Burden to Benefit? Psychiatric Perspectives on the Impact of Administrative Review in Victoria, Australia' (Paper presented at the 30th Congress of the International Academy of Law and Mental Health, Padua, Italy, June 2007); E Grundell, 'Psychiatrists' Perceptions of Administrative Review: A Victorian Empirical Study' (2005) 12(1) *Psychiatry, Psychology and Law* 68.

[33] T Carney, D Tait and F Beaupert, 'Pushing the Boundaries: Realising Rights through Mental Health Tribunal Processes?' (2008) 30(2) *Sydney Law Review* 329.

[34] T Carney and F Beaupert, 'Mental Health Tribunals: Rights Drowning in Un-"chartered" Health Waters?' (2008) 13(2) *Australian Journal of Human Rights* 181–208.

[35] F Beaupert, T Carney, D Tait and V Topp, 'Property Management Orders in the Mental Health Context: Protection or Empowerment?' (2008) 31(3) *University of New South Wales Law Journal* 795.

[36] L Hallam, 'How Involuntary Commitment Impacts on the Burden of Care of the Family' (2007) 16(4) *International Journal of Mental Health Nursing* 247.

consequence, early intervention was rare, and families reported that their opinions and views about emerging illness patterns were ignored or devalued on bases such as 'patient confidentiality' or lack of urgency of the need for services.

Once involuntary status had been obtained, families reportedly feared losing legal backing for treatment compliance due to the difficulty in re-instating orders (resorting to subterfuges and de facto coercion/paternalism instead), and were concerned that the termination of orders would be perceived as license for patients not to comply with medication regimes. Orders reportedly provided respite for carers and leverage for better *clinical* care, compared to the haphazard care levels without an order 'validating' a mental illness, though orders did little to access allied resources like accommodation or professional case planning.

Carers and families are another key resource for people with mental illness in Australia[37] (as elsewhere),[38] but as will be argued later, too little attention has been given to devising relational and inclusive forms of engagement.

B. Searching for the 'Access' Key

The studies such as those in the previous sub-section demonstrate that the lexicon of mental health has shifted dramatically away from excessive institutionalisation in recent decades. The focus now is on 'barriers' to accessing needed treatment, and mainly involves community-based management of people with a mental illness.[39]

Community treatment orders, as variously described around the world,[40] are now the setting for exercise of state power over individuals, though in more subtle ways than for institutional care.[41] Power mainly now cultivates compliance with clinical and social management plans (including accommodation or other lifestyle features), stopping just short of *enforced* medication in the community;[42]

---

[37] J Shankar and S Muthuswamy, 'Support Needs of Family Caregivers of People Who Experience Mental Illness and the Role of Mental Health Services' (2007) 88(2) *Families in Society* 302.

[38] I Crombie, L Irvine, L Elliott and H Wallace, 'Carers of People with Mental Health Problems: Proposals Embodied in Current Policies in Nine Countries' (2007) 28(4) *Journal of Public Health Policy* 465.

[39] T Carney and F Beaupert, 'Mental Health Tribunals: Rights Drowning in Un-"chartered" Health Waters?' (2008) 13(2) *Australian Journal of Human Rights* 181. T Carney, 'The Mental Health Service Crisis of Neoliberalism—An Antipodean Perspective' (2008) 31(2) *International Journal of Law and Psychiatry* 101–15.

[40] N Wagle, F Levy and A Allbright, 'Outpatient Civil Commitment Laws: An Overview' (2002) 26 *Mental and Physical Disability Reporter* 179.

[41] V Pinfold and J Bindman, 'Is Compulsory Community Treatment Ever Justified?' (2001) 25(7) *Psychiatric Bulletin* 268; M Swartz and J Monahan, 'Special Section on Involuntary Outpatient Commitment: Introduction' (2001) 52(3) *Psychiatric Services* 323.

[42] J Dawson, *Community Treatment Orders: International Comparisons* (Dunedin, University of Otago, 2005); P Power, 'Community Treatment Orders: The Australian Experience' (1999) 10 *Journal of Forensic Psychiatry* 9; N Preston, S Kisely and J Xiao, 'Assessing the Outcome of Compulsory Psychiatric Treatment in the Community: Epidemiological Study in Western Australia' (2002) 324 *British Medical Journal* 1244.

sometimes as low-volume alternatives to institutionalisation (eg in North America and Britain) and sometimes as larger scale 'preventive' interventions (as mainly in Australasia).[43] While often criticised for *in practice* allowing social control (or 'risk management') to displace therapeutic aims,[44] a small-scale Victorian study by Lisa Brophy et al found that risk was concentrated on a sub-group with serious, complex and more chronic needs. In other instances CTOs were made for other defined groups, including a sub-group with chaotic lives presaging clinical deterioration or burden on carers, and a third group of mainly isolated young males with paranoid schizophrenia.[45] This diversity of sub-populations, and the relevance of *social context* for the majority of patients, it was argued, reinforced the importance of good case planning processes, combining clinical and social perspectives. Since CTOs account for at least two thirds of MHT caseloads, it seems that they should engage both the clinical and the social domains in the course of their reviews.

Any contemporary model of mental health law (including rights protections) must surely be judged mainly by how well it engages with these new patterns of service, and the degradation of service quality and resourcing often associated with contemporary delivery of community mental health services. It is here that current models of mental health adjudication, and any wider human rights laws, are most found wanting. The recently enacted human rights 'Charters' in Victoria and the Australian Capital Territory only protect civil, or so-called 'negative' rights,[46] such as rights to freedom, respect, equality and dignity.[47] As Mary Donnelly explains, such protections have generally been interpreted around the world as not extending to the subtler forms of social control associated with CTOs (such as restrictions on travel, housing or socialising).[48] Overseas experience in Canada[49] or the United

---

[43] J Dawson, *Community Treatment Orders: International Comparisons* (Dunedin, University of Otago, 2005); T Rolfe, *Community Treatment Orders: A Review* (Perth, Office of the Chief Psychiatrist, Department of Health, 2001); H Wales and V Hiday, 'PLC or TLC: Is Outpatient Commitment the/an Answer?' (2006) 29(6) *International Journal of Law and Psychiatry* 451.

[44] L Brophy, J Reece and F McDermott, 'A Cluster Analysis of People on Community Treatment Orders in Victoria, Australia' (2006) 29(6) *International Journal of Law and Psychiatry* 469, 472; see also, D Ring, L Brophy and A Gimlinger, 'Examining Community Treatment Orders in Victoria: A Preliminary Inquiry into their Efficacy' (2001) 66 *Health Issues* 13.

[45] L Brophy, J Reece and F McDermott, 'A Cluster Analysis of People on Community Treatment Orders in Victoria, Australia' (2006) 29(6) *International Journal of Law and Psychiatry* 469, 478–9.

[46] Charter of Human Rights and Responsibilities Act 2006 (Vic); Human Rights Act 2004 (ACT).

[47] *The Victorian Charter of Human Rights and Responsibilities: Civil and Political Rights Explained* (Melbourne, Victorian Equal Opportunity and Human Rights Commission, 2007) available at: www.humanrightscommission.vic.gov.au/pdf/CPRsexplainedLR.pdf.

[48] M Donnelly, 'Community-based Care and Compulsion: What Role for Human Rights?' (2008) 15(5) *Journal of Law and Medicine* 782.

[49] J Arboleda-Florez and D Weisstub, 'Mental Health Rights: The Relation Between Constitution and Bioethics' in D Weisstub and G Pintos (eds), *Autonomy and Human Rights in Health Care: An International Perspective* (Dordrecht, Springer, 2008) 309; J Zuckerberg, 'International Human Rights for Mentally Ill Persons: The Ontario Experience' (2007) 30(6) *International Journal of Law and Psychiatry* 512.

Kingdom[50] demonstrates that the omission of *positive* ('economic and social') rights, such as 'the right of everyone to the enjoyment of the highest attainable standard of physical and mental health',[51] renders human rights laws of little assistance in leveraging access to treatment services or resources. Tasmania's tentative proposal for inclusion of economic, social and cultural rights holds some possibilities perhaps.[52]

If human rights instruments influence, but are unlikely to dictate, the shape of the crucial social and economic aspects of contemporary mental health law, we must ask whether guidance is offered either by consideration of competing 'models' for reform, or the 'autonomy-harm-beneficence' rationales on which these models are commonly predicated. Since the answer appears to be 'no', and the debates are becoming well rehearsed, our attention will mainly focus on those features which appear to lend themselves to contemporary circumstances, such as how or on what basis to engage carers and social networks associated with a person experiencing mental illness.

III. Models of Mental Health Law and Administration

A 'rights' model is privileged by entrenchment of 'Charters of Rights' at both the international and, in most developed countries, also at the domestic level (so far only in Victoria and the ACT in Australia). That is a powerful normative reason for retaining the *basic* architecture of mental health laws, at least in reviewing the exercise of State powers of coercion,[53] but it is rather unsatisfying so far as implementation of economic and social rights are concerned.

---

[50] G Davidson, M McCallion and M Potter, 'Connecting Mental Health and Human Rights' (Belfast, Northern Ireland Human Rights Commission, 2003); K Gledhill, 'Human Rights Instruments and Mental Health Law: The English Experience of the Incorporation of the European Convention on Human Rights' (2007) 34 *Syracuse Journal of International Law and Commerce* 359.

[51] International Covenant on Civil and Political Rights, opened for signature 16 December 1966, 999 UNTS 171 (entered into force 23 March 1976) Art 12.

[52] Tasmania, Law Reform Institute, *A Charter of Rights for Tasmania* (Hobart, Tasmania Law Reform Institute, 2007) Rec 15, 118–22. The South African constitutional experience demonstrates the potential to realise social and economic rights, such as the Constitutional Court ruling in *Khosa v Minister of Social Development; Mahlaule and Another v Minister of Social Development* (2004) (6) SA 505 (CC) that it was a breach of the Bill of Rights to deny social benefits available to citizens to otherwise eligible *resident* children and the elderly (here Mozambican citizens holding permanent residence status as refugees): E Christiansen, 'Adjudicating Non-Justiciable Rights: Socio-economic Rights and the South African Constitutional Court' (2007) 38(2) *Columbia Human Rights Law Review* 321. For a sober view of institutional and other impediments to realisation of health rights, see: M Pieterse, 'Health, Social Movements, and Rights-based Litigation in South Africa' (2008) 35(3) *Journal of Law and Society* 364, 378–88.

[53] T Carney and F Beaupert, 'Mental Health Tribunals: Rights Drowning in Un-"chartered" Health Waters?' (2008) 13(2) *Australian Journal of Human Rights* 181.

A. Philosophical Base-lines

The question of what (if anything) is required beyond respect for a civil rights
core in 'rights'-based legislation necessarily raises fundamental philosophical
issues, such as the validity of positions derived from classical liberalism (with its
strong enunciation of 'autonomy' values), utilitarian liberalism (where harm to
others is a limitation on autonomy), or more communitarian models, where,
among other things, an 'ethic of care'[54] and 'relational' ethics are valued.[55]
Certainly these various philosophical positions undergird particular 'aspects' of
the mosaic comprising current mental health and adult guardianship laws in
different jurisdictions.[56]

Emmanuel Kant's endorsement of individual autonomy as the highest obligation and expression of human dignity, for instance, finds expression in 'capacity-
based' models of mental health law that privilege 'consent' as the arbiter of
treatment when illness sets in,[57] or informal community treatment models such
as found in Trieste, Italy.[58] Traditional mental health laws presently found in most
countries instead adopt the utilitarian liberal rationale expressed by writers such
as JS Mill, envisaging a balance between respect for individual autonomy of
action and harms to others, often expressed in so-called 'legalistic' models of
mental health.[59] These are characterised by restrictive definitions of mental
illness, independent verification of involuntary admissions, and strong procedural guarantees.[60]

---

[54] See W Brookbanks, 'Therapeutic Jurisprudence: Conceiving an Ethical Framework' (2001) 8
Journal of Law and Medicine 328.

[55] S Loue, *Textbook of Research Ethics: Theory and Practice* (New York, Kluwer Academic, 2000),
51-8.

[56] For a through taxonomy and 'rating' of laws in Commonwealth of nations countries, see: E
Fistein, A Holland, I Clare and M Gunn, 'A Comparison of Mental Health Legislation from Diverse
Commonwealth Jurisdictions' (2009) 32(3) *International Journal of Law and Psychiatry* 147.

[57] Capacity-based models of mental health are promoted as a radical alternative to present
legislative models on the basis that focusing on 'competence' avoids the need to distinguish between
physical and mental conditions, enables treatment to be provided more promptly, removes the stigma
and discrimination of separate identification of psychiatric patients, and largely avoid the task of
assessing future 'risk': T Wand and M Chiarella, 'A Conversation: Challenging the Relevance and
Wisdom of Separate Mental Health Legislation' (2006) 15 *International Journal of Mental Health
Nursing* 119. JJ Dawson and G Szmulker, 'Fusion of Mental Health and Incapacity Legislation' (2006)
118 *British Journal of Psychiatry* 504.

[58] For a description of this 'minimalist' usage of formal coercion (but higher reliance on extra
legal persuasion to win acquiescence), see J Lesser, *Lessons from Abroad: Australian Mental Health Law
and Practice in an International Context* (Melbourne, Mental Health Review Board, 2008) 52–7
available at: www.mhrb.vic.gov.au/documents/GeneralFinal29.02.08.pdf?.

[59] H Long, S Tait, P Eisen and T Fleming, 'Direction and Purpose of the Mental Health Act 1986'
(Paper presented at the 'The Mental Health Act into the 1990s', Melbourne, Monash University, 29–30
June 1990); J Monahan, 'John Stuart Mill on the Liberty of the Mentally Ill: A Historical Note' (1977)
134 *American Journal of Psychiatry* 1428; J Shapland and T Williams, 'Legalism Revived: New Mental
Health Legislation in England' (1983) 6 *International Journal of Law and Psychiatry* 351.

[60] T Carney, 'Mental Health in Postmodern Society: Time for New Paradigms?' (2003) 10(1)
Psychiatry, Psychology and Law 12.

Communitarian or feminist ethics, with their emphasis on the 'relational' or the 'networked' forms of (often complex and nuanced) human engagements, have been rather neglected to date in mental health law and policy, despite their prominence in areas such as end-of-life decision-making and allocation of scarce health resources (including to groups such as the aged), or concepts of 'competence'.[61] The nearest concrete expression of such philosophies are found in say the 'Ulysses' agreements[62] or supported decision-making available in jurisdictions such as British Columbia, Canada,[63] enabling people to anticipate their future incapacity and write a legally binding instrument that will empower a nominated group of family/friends or others to manage their care while in that future state. Despite the interest in 'capacity-building', or longer standing interest in approaches to distributional fairness (such as the social contract approach of John Rawls's 'veil of ignorance'[64]), there is little to point to by way of concrete examples apart from a few experiments in legal review of access to disability services,[65] and some rare excursions into provision of positive 'socio-economic' rights to health and mental health, or (mainly extra-legal) measures to promote systemic advocacy and self-advocacy.[66]

Contemporary social policy engages ideas such as Amartya Sen's[67] and Martha Nussbaum's[68] very influential work on 'capability' theory—namely concentrating on a person's level of 'functioning' (what they 'are' or 'do') and building and supporting real world abilities to realise those capabilities (what they are 'free' or 'able' to choose to do). Hopper evocatively elaborates for mental health wellness

---

[61] T Carney, 'Judging the Competence of Older People: An Alternative?' (1995) 15 *Ageing and Society* 515; G Mooney, 'Communitarian Claims and Community Capabilities: Furthering Priority Setting?' (2005) 60 *Social Science and Medicine* 247; N Jecker, 'The Role of Intimate Others in Medical Decision Making Aging and Ethics' in N Jecker (ed), *Aging and Ethics: Philosophical Problems in Gerontology* (Clifton, Humana Press, 1991).

[62] On a 'narrative' interpretation, Ulysses contracts set out a holistic statement of a person's values, wishes and preferences, such that current views during a period of illness should neither be accepted or rejected at face value, but 'should be interpreted in the light of the patient's life history, a history informed by narrative work between patient and doctor': G Widdershoven and R Berghmans, 'Advance Directives in Psychiatric Care: A Narrative Perspective' (2001) 27 *Journal of Medical Ethics* 92, 94.

[63] R Gordon, 'The Emergence of Assisted (Supported) Decision-making in the Canadian Law of Adult Guardianship and Substitute Decision-making' (2000) 23 *International Journal of Law and Psychiatry* 61.

[64] J Rawls, *A Theory of Justice* (Oxford, Oxford University Press, 1972).

[65] T Carney and K Akers, 'A Coffee Table Chat or a Formal Hearing' (1991) 2 *Australian Dispute Resolution Journal* 141; T Carney, 'Re-mixing "Access", "Advocacy", "Empowerment" and "Protection"? A Case for a Specialised Division of Labour in Guardianship, Mental Health and Disability Services Adjudication?' (2003) 5 *Newcastle Law Review* 43.

[66] T Carney, F Beaupert, J Perry and D Tait, 'Advocacy and Participation in Mental Health Cases: Realisable Rights or Pipe Dreams?' (2008) 26(2) *Law in Context* 125.

[67] A Sen, 'Capability and Well-Being' in M Nussbaum and A Sen (eds), *The Quality of Life* (Oxford, Clarendon Press, 1993); A Sen, *Commodities and Capabilities* (Amsterdam, North-Holland, 1985).

[68] M Nussbaum, *Women and Human Development: The Capabilities Approach* (Cambridge, Cambridge University Press, 2000).

that, '[a] capabilities-informed "social recovery" will speak to citizenship as well as health. It will worry about what enables people to thrive, not simply survive'.[69] In mental health law this resonates with interest in supported decision-making, mentioned above,[70] and other measures that genuinely empower people with mental illnesses.[71] As mentioned, psychiatric advance directives are one such possible measure for developing the agency strand of this conceptualisation.[72] However, clinical stakeholder views are quite divided about their merit,[73] with up to half of psychiatrists in the United States indicating that they would exercise statutory powers to 'over-ride' objections to treatment.[74]

Consistent with obligations laid down in international human rights instruments, it may be concluded that the liberty interests of patients, understood as their civil rights, dictates retention of some form of historic utilitarian liberal model of mental health laws.[75] The increasingly all-important social and economic rights of the mentally ill, however, cannot be advanced within that framework. Instead, they require grounding in a developmental ('capacity-building') and socially contextualised set of principles, such as the more communitarian, networked, de-centralised approaches for advancing Thomas Humphrey Marshall's agenda of rights of 'social citizenship'.[76]

[69]   K Hopper, 'Rethinking Social Recovery in Schizophrenia: What a Capabilities Approach Might Offer' (2007) 65 *Social Science and Medicine* 868, 875.
[70]   R Gordon, 'The Emergence of Assisted (Supported) Decision-making in the Canadian Law of Adult Guardianship and Substitute Decision-making' (2000) 23 *International Journal of Law and Psychiatry* 61; P Weller, 'Supported Decision-Making and the Achievement of Non-Discrimination: The Promise and Paradox of the Disabilities Convention' (2008) 26(2) *Law in Context* 85.
[71]   BD Kelly, 'The Power Gap: Freedom, Power and Mental Illness' (2006) 63(8) *Social Science and Medicine* 2118.
[72]   A Papageorgiou, M King, A Janmohamed, O Davidson and J Dawson, 'Advance Directives for Patients Compulsorily Admitted to Hospital with Serious Mental Illness' (2002) 181 *British Journal of Psychiatry* 513.
[73]   J Atkinson, H Garner and H Gilmour, 'Models of Advance Directives in Mental Health Care: Stakeholder Views' (2004) 39(8) *Social Psychiatry & Psychiatric Epidemiology* 673; MM Kim, AM Scheyett, EB Elbogen, RA Van Dorn, LA McDaniel, MS Swartz, JW Swanson and J Ferron, 'Front Line Workers' Attitudes Towards Psychiatric Advance Directives' (2008) 44(1) *Community Mental Health Care Journal* 28.
[74]   JW Swanson, V McCrary, MS Swartz, R Van Dorn and EB Elbogen, 'Overriding Psychiatric Advance Directives: Factors Associated with Psychiatrists' Decisions to Preempt Patients' Advance Refusal of Hospitalization and Medication' (2007) 31(1) *Law and Human Behavior* 77.
[75]   Laws authorising the involuntary treatment of people with an addiction, which once mirrored mental health laws, have either been modified to restrict their duration and intensity to 'emergency sobering up', or repealed entirely: T Carney, *Drug Users and the Law in Australia: From Crime Control to Welfare* (Sydney, Law Book Co, 1987); T Carney, 'Complex Needs at the Boundaries of Mental Health, Justice and Welfare: Gatekeeping Issues in Managing Chronic Alcoholism Treatment?' (2006) 17 *Current Issues in Criminal Justice* 347. For example England and Wales excludes addiction from its definition of mental illness (Mental Health Act 1983, s 1(3) [as amended]) and no other provision is made for civil commitment of this group.
[76]   TH Marshall, *Sociology at the Crossroads and Other Essays* (London, Heinemann, 1963).

B.   Is it Possible to Realise Social Citizenship for the Mentally Ill through a 'De-centralised Services Planning' Model?

Consistent with the World Health Organization and professional opinion about the merits of adequately resourced, de-centralised, community-based treatment models, serious thought must be given to building optimal legislative and administrative arrangements to foster sound case planning and to promote client and carer participation.

Patrick Bracken and colleagues frame this challenge as that of adjusting psychiatry to a post-modern world, including finding ways to 'uncouple mental health care from the agenda of social exclusion, coercion, and control to which it became bound in the past two centuries'.[77] They suggest that part of the answer is to 'democratise mental health by linking progressive service development to a debate about contexts, values, and partnerships'.[78] This is conceptually attractive because it offers a way of flexibly engaging with the social networks within which mentally ill people actually live their lives, and in ways more compatible with local values and preferences. Realisation of this vision of a less coercive and more socially inclusive 'partnership' model confronts many barriers. These include the neo-liberal ideas behind the shrinkage of public resourcing of mental health, the service degradation often associated with the 'new public management' approach of outsourcing delivery of services to non-government providers (including under 'contract-for-services' quasi networks of services),[79] and the lower priority given to equity and access issues.[80] This 'crisis of neo-liberalism', does much to account for the limited realisation of the right to 'social participation' (in civil society, employment etc), which lay at the heart of Thomas Humphrey Marshall's conception of 'social citizenship rights'.[81] It is also evident in the United States, as John Petrila outlines in chapter fifteen of this volume. Realisation of social citizenship rights involves the domains of governance, financing, and the organisation and delivery of mental health and cognate services.[82]

---

[77]   P Bracken and P Thomas, 'Postpsychiatry: A New Direction for Mental Health' (2001) 322 *British Medical Journal* 724, 726.

[78]   *ibid*, 727.

[79]   See for instance the loss of 'control' attributed to such trends in Ontario, Canada: R Wilton, 'More Responsibility, Less Control: Psychiatric Survivors and Welfare State Restructuring' (2004) 19(4) *Disability & Society* 371.

[80]   T Carney, 'Mental Health In Postmodern Society: Time for New Paradigms?' (2003) 10 *Psychiatry, Psychology and Law* 12.

[81]   See also T Carney, 'The Mental Health Service Crisis of Neoliberalism—An Antipodean Perspective' (2008) 31 *International Journal of Law and Psychiatry* 101, 108–9; TH Marshall, *Sociology at the Crossroads and Other Essays* (London, Heinemann, 1963).

[82]   S Anfang and PS Appelbaum, 'Civil Commitment—The American Experience' (2006) 4(3) *Israel Journal of Psychiatry and Related Sciences* 209, 214; see also E Grundell, 'Psychiatrist's Perceptions of Administrative Review: A Victorian Empirical Study' (2005) 12 *Psychiatry, Psychology and Law* 68.

Reportedly Germany has made good progress in establishing de-centralised models to advance some of these goals.[83] The Trieste model in Italy also relies on strong local networks to help eliminate reliance on involuntary inpatient treatment.[84] Similarly, Lisa Brophy and colleagues observe the importance of case planning in monitoring and adjusting community treatment order regimes from beginning to end, and the centrality of *social* expertise within the case management team.[85] However, there is much underlying complexity and difference of opinion. For example, there is debate about the viability of 'voucher' models in the United States for empowering people with mental illness to decide and control the way their needs are met.[86] The very construction of people with mental illness as 'consumers' rather than 'citizens' is contested, as is revealed in a New South Wales study of self-support groups.[87] A London study found a serious gap between the rhetoric and the reality of user participation.[88] Moreover the law does not yet have a well-developed portfolio of models and approaches from which to choose, or a strong body of evidence on the basis of which to make a selection of an optimally appropriate approach.

Elsewhere we have argued that systemic and individual advocacy, including lay and self-advocacy in addition to professional representation, should be prioritised.[89] Integration of carers and communities of support are also vital, so great care must be taken to avoid falling into the trap of enacting provisions like Queensland's well-meaning but divisive 'allied person' option, which—unlike the New South Wales 'carer' provisions—failed to recognise their *separate* interests over and above their role in being a spokesperson for the person with mental illness.

Australia's planning statements do aspire to the involvement of carers in planning, such as through 'carers plans'.[90] Despite the Queensland Act going to some lengths to foster such family participation in treatment planning, however,

[83]   A Bramesfeld, M Wismar and K Mosebach, 'Managing Mental Health Service Provision in the Decentralized, Multi-layered Health and Social Care System of Germany' (2004) 7(1) *Journal of Mental Health Policy and Economics* 3.

[84]   J Lesser, *Lessons from Abroad: Australian Mental Health Law and Practice in an International Context* (Melbourne, Mental Health Review Board, 2008) 52–7 available at: www.mhrb.vic.gov.au/documents/GeneralFinal29.02.08.pdf?.

[85]   L Brophy, J Reece and F McDermott, 'A Cluster Analysis of Community Treatment Orders in Victoria, Australia' (2006) 29 *International Journal of Law and Psychiatry* 469.

[86]   For personal care services for the elderly, mental health diagnoses did not alter the level of satisfaction with the voucher model: C Shen, MA Smyer, KJ Mahoney, DM Loughlin, L Simon-Rusinowitz and EK Mahoney, 'Does Mental Illness Affect Consumer Direction of Community-Based Care? Lessons from the Arkansas Cash and Counseling Program' (2008) 48(1) *The Gerontologist* 93.

[87]   N Bolzan, M Smith, J Mears and R Ansiewicz, 'Creating Identities: Mental Health Consumer to Citizen?' (2001) 1(3) *Journal of Social Work* 317.

[88]   D Rutter, C Manley, T Weaver, M Crawford and N Fulop, 'Patients or Partners? Case Studies of User Involvement in the Planning and Delivery of Adult Mental Health Services in London' (2004) 58 *Social Science and Medicine* 1973.

[89]   T Carney, F Beaupert, J Perry and D Tait, 'Advocacy and Participation in Mental Health Cases: Realisable Rights or Pipe Dream?' (2008) 26(2) *Law in Context* 125.

[90]   *ibid.*

families reportedly felt they were still marginalised.[91] The legal option of appointing a family member as an 'allied person' to engage in the planning process for a person with mental illness[92] was rejected as being divisive within the family because only the views of the *patient* (as distinct from the carers) could be conveyed, suggesting to the authors that adult guardianship, as in South Australia, may be a preferable form of planning. As Ian Crombie and colleagues observe, little if any progress has been made toward the *implementation* of these aspirations for carer participation.[93] This is the case even in advanced countries like the United Kingdom, United States of America, Canada and Australasia.

One reason for this is that policy 'dichotomises' carers and the person being cared for, and overlooks the subtle negotiations, emotional dimension, dualities and complex relationships between cared-for and carers. This is shown by Jeanette Henderson's sensitive qualitative research on manic depression (bipolar disorders).[94] Another reason is that too many diverse roles and functions are combined within this single mechanism.[95]

Frankly, however, this is the point where the operationalisation of the communitarian or 'social citizenship' model begins to struggle. While it is quite possible to sketch the philosophical underpinnings,[96] evidence-based examples of successful

[91] L Hallam, 'How Involuntary Commitment Impacts on the Burden of Care of the Family' (2007) 16(4) *International Journal of Mental Health Nursing* 247.

[92] Under the Mental Health Act 2000 (Qld) ss 339–343, the role of the allied person is stated to be to 'help the patient to represent the patient's views, wishes and interests relating to the patient's assessment, detention and treatment under this Act' (s 340). The allied person must be advised of assessment for involuntary detention (s 45(b), the making of involuntary detention orders (s 113(1)(c)), changes to an order (s 120(1)(b)), the ending or revocation of such an order (ss 118(3)(b), 123(b)), tribunal review hearings (ss 189(1)(d), 196(1)(d)), outcomes of review hearings (ss 192(1)(b)), 198(1)(d)). Where the patient lacks capacity, nominations made in advance directives or selections made from other 'statutorily listed' independent persons apply: ss 342, 341. The Mental Health Act 2007 (NSW) also provides for 'carers' (from a statutory list or on nomination: ss 71, 72) to be kept informed (s 68(j)), including being advised of medication (s73(2)(b)), or initial detention for assessment (s 75), MHRT hearings (s 76), and of other significant events such as absconding, discharges or changes of status (s 78), and consultation about discharge planning and follow-up care (s 79).

[93] I Crombie, L Irvine, L Elliott, and H Wallace, 'Carers of People with Mental Health problems: Proposals in Current Policies in Nine Countries' (2007) 28 *Journal of Public Health Policy* 465, 474.

[94] J Henderson, '"He's not my Carer—He's my Husband": Personal and Policy Constructions of Care in Mental Health' (2001) 15(2) *Journal of Social Work Practice* 149, 150: 'Recognising the different individual needs of carers and cared for does not take account of their shared concerns or the experience, complexity and emotional content of care within relationship'.

[95] K Keywood, 'Gatekeepers, Proxies, Advocates? The Evolving Role of Carers under Mental Health and Mental Incapacity Law Reforms' (2003) 25(4) *Journal of Social Welfare and Family Law* 355.

[96] T Carney, 'Culture, Community or Rights: Securing Health in a Post-modern, Privatised World' in D Weisstub and G Pintos (eds), *Autonomy and Human Rights in Health Care: An International Perspective* (Dordrecht, Springer, 2008).

implementation or even plausible approaches for translating those principles into action are much harder to identify.[97] So the final section returns the focus to the roles and processes of MHTs.

IV. Conclusion

The argument ultimately made in this chapter makes a case for broadening the role of mental health tribunals beyond 'hub' responsibilities for monitoring core 'rights protection' provisions through prompt and full interdisciplinary review of involuntary detention, to also include some new 'spokes' which fully engage the medical (treatment) and social (functional implications) aspects of care. Rather than vacating the 'liberty protecting' end of Genevra Richardson and Hazel Genn's[98] spectrum of possible tribunal roles, to move to the opposite pole—that occupied by tribunals or bodies with a 'distributive' function and 'dispute resolution' roles—the argument here is that both roles can be *combined*.

While Nigel Eastman once parodied the lack of legal rigor in mental health tribunals on the basis that they were often 'little more than legalised case conferences',[99] this chapter sees considerable merit in that model, which carries the potential to engage patient concerns about misdiagnosis, inadequacy of treatment (including access to psychosocial support), choice (and side-effects) of medication, and discharge planning. While treatment issues, for instance, can be reviewed in other ways (such as the second opinion system in Britain), tribunals are, as argued by Mary Donnelly in chapter twelve of this volume, the optimal method. Nor is the idea a new one. The British law professor (and tribunal chair) John Wood argued for a broader and more flexible role for tribunals.[100] He has argued that '[a] patient's rights, however that concept is interpreted, are best protected by periodic constructive review, so that needs can be identified and

---

[97] As in the German example: A Bramesfeld, M Wismar and K Mosebach, 'Managing Mental Health Service Provision in the Decentralized, Multi-layered Health and Social Care System of Germany' (2004) 7 *Journal of Mental Health Policy and Economics* 3; A Bramesfeld, U Klippel, G Seidel, F Schwartz and M-L Dierks, 'How do Patients Expect the Mental health Service System to Act? Testing the WHO Responsiveness Concept for its Appropriateness in Mental Health Care' (2007) 65 *Social Science and Medicine* 880.

[98] G Richardson and H Genn, 'Tribunals in Transition: Resolution or Adjudication?' (2007) *Public Law* 116.

[99] N Eastman, 'Mental Health Law: Civil Liberties and the Principle of Reciprocity' (1994) 308 *British Medical Journal* 43, 44.

[100] J Wood, 'Control and Compassion: The Uncertain Role of Mental Health Review Tribunals in the Management of the Mentally Ill' in D Webb and R Harris (eds), *Mentally Disordered Offenders: Managing People Nobody Owns* (London, Routledge, 1999).

pressure exerted to meet them'.[101] Moreover tribunals have exercised such functions in cognate areas such as access to special education services in Britain and
the United States, or support of people with intellectual disadvantage, such as
under Victoria's former Intellectual Disability Services Panel.[102] The Australian
Research Council Linkage study has suggested that tribunals already 'push the
boundaries' into these areas on occasion, but currently it is a very gentle (and
rare) initiative, due to lack of time or a mandate for such action.[103] Greater
involvement is required.

This argument is made mindful of the counter-arguments, including the small
number of tribunals exercising such functions worldwide, their more equivocal
perceived levels of success,[104] doubts about the wisdom of intruding into
resource allocation or clinical decisions in this way, or 'muddying of waters' by
combining too many functions. These are valid areas for further debate and
research. Indeed my current argument is effectively the converse of one I
previously made for a specialised 'division of labour' where *separate* bodies
pursue 'purist' agendas of liberty protection, or facilitation of service access
etc.[105] However, in the contemporary mental health environment—where the
main issue is *obtaining access* to services necessary to promote wellness (rather
than avoidance of excessive retention in treatment or restrictions on liberty)—
the needs of people with serious mental illness now have more in common with
other 'complex needs' groups, where a *broad spectrum* (or 'combination') of
functions is warranted, as under Victoria's (non-coercive), Multiple and Complex
Needs Panel, which places the onus on service providers to meet the assessed
needs of a person.[106]

On its own, an expanded role for tribunals will not realise the social citizenship
entitlements of mentally ill people to more fully participate in the various
domains of access to health care, social supports and community participation
which the Convention on the Rights of Persons with Disabilities enshrines. Such

[101] J Wood, 'The Challenge of Individual Rights: Mental Health Review Tribunals' (1995) 166(4) *British Journal of Psychiatry* 417, 420.

[102] Intellectual Disability Review Panel, *A Right to Be Heard: 20 Years of the Intellectual Disability Review Panel* (Melbourne, Intellectual Disability Review Panel, 2007).

[103] T Carney, D Tait and F Beaupert, 'Pushing the Boundaries: Realising Rights Through Mental Health Tribunal Processes?' (2008) 30 *Sydney Law Review* 329.

[104] Victoria recently replaced its Intellectual Disability Services Panel with newly created roles for three new bodies: a Disability Services Commissioner, a Senior Practitioner, and review rights to the Victorian Civil and Administrative Tribunal: Victoria. Department of Human Services, *About the Disability Act 2006* (2006) available at: www.dhs.vic.gov.au/disability/improving_supports/disability_act_2006.

[105] T Carney, 'Re-mixing "Access", "Advocacy", "Empowerment" and "Protection"? A Case for Specialised Division of Labour in Guardianship, Mental Health and Disability Services' (2003) 5 *Newcastle Law Review* 43.

[106] The Multiple and Complex Needs Panel was established under the Human Services (Complex Needs) Act 2003 (Vic). See also T Carney, 'Complex Needs at the Boundaries of Mental Health, Justice and Welfare: Gatekeeping Issues in Managing Chronic Alcoholism Treatment?' (2006) 17 *Current Issues in Criminal Justice* 347.

reforms will need to be complemented by other provisions (and extra-legal administrative and service arrangements) to facilitate enhanced service quality and co-ordination of mental health, housing, employment and other relevant services, through measures such as *accessible* individual and systemic forms of advocacy or grievance resolution processes. However, if we are to meaningfully engage and promote the participation, socio-economic (citizenship) and civil rights of mentally ill people at all levels of engagement with governmental or civil society, the law needs to play its part by providing greater leverage than is currently the case.

This chapter is predicated on retention of a rights-based, free-standing mental health Act, but broadened to place greater emphasis on recognition of the network of carers, friends and family of a person with mental illness, and on promotion of wellness. Consistent with that wider agenda, it makes a case for renovation of the work of mental health tribunals to reflect a two-strand 'core and penumbra' (or hub and spokes) model: one strand concerned with the core liberty and other civil rights of patients; and a new second strand concerned with realisation of social and economic rights to mental health and related social rights of citizenship.

The elements of a reformed model as sketched in this chapter, it is contended, provide a concrete way of advancing the very worthy, but still unduly vague sentiments favouring 'dignity-based' mental health.[107] Consistent with Jan Brakel's plea to focus on facilitation of treatment, it does so by embracing empowering/educative strategies and *social* rather than medical paradigms, along with maximisation of supported decision-making as endorsed by the CRPD,[108] but in ways which pass the all important 'workability' test.

---

[107] M Donnelly, 'From Autonomy to Dignity: Treatment for Mental Disorders and the Focus for Patient Rights' (2008) 26(2) *Law in Context* 37. Mary Donnelly, 'From Autonomy to Dignity: Treatment for mental disorders and the focus for patient rights' (2008) 26(2) *Law in Context* 37–61.

[108] A Kämpf, 'The Disabilities Convention and its Consequences for Mental Health Laws in Australia' (2008) 26(2) *Law in Context* 10.

12

Reviews of Treatment Decisions: Legalism, Process and the Protection of Rights*

MARY DONNELLY

I. Introduction

Treatment reviews have been described as 'a high water mark of legalism'.[1] It is therefore no surprise that they attract criticism from an 'anti-legalism' perspective. Thus, Nikolas Rose has argued:

> [A]t a practical level, there is no evidence to suggest that hedging the diagnostic process about with procedural safeguards, legally encoding substantive criteria or subjecting psychiatric judgments to judicial review will improve the reliability of diagnoses, their validity or therapeutic utility or transform the relations between expertise and those subject to it.[2]

Commentators more sympathetic to the role of law have also identified the limitations of review. Based on a study in the early 1990s, Philip Fennell found that the second opinion review system then operating in England and Wales was not delivering very much in terms of protecting patients' rights or even in 'inhibiting plans which require megadoses of drugs'.[3] Yet, in respect of treatment decisions, reviews of one form or another remain the most widely adopted legal mechanism for the protection of patient rights.

* I am grateful to my fellow workshop participants at the Prato workshop and to Professor John Mee, Law Faculty, University College Cork for their very helpful insights and suggestions in respect of the arguments made here, although all views expressed and any errors are, of course, my own.
[1] C Unsworth, *The Politics of Mental Health Legislation* (Oxford, Clarendon Press, 1987) 324. Unsworth at 20 was using Shklar's definition of legalism (J Shklar, *Legalism* (Cambridge, Harvard University Press, 1964) 1) as 'the ethical attitude that holds moral conduct to be a matter of rule following and moral relationships to consist of duties and rights determined by rules'.
[2] N Rose, 'Unreasonable Rights: Mental Illness and the Limits of the Law' (1985) 12 *Journal of Law and Society* 199, 206. See also the cost-based critique advanced in K Jones, 'The Limitations of the Legal Approach to Mental Health' (1980) 3 *International Journal of Law and Psychiatry* 1.
[3] P Fennell, *Treatment Without Consent: Law, Psychiatry and the Treatment of Mentally Disordered People since 1845* (London, Routledge, 1996) 217.

This chapter evaluates the success of treatment reviews as a protection for patients' rights. Unlike reviews of admission and detention,[4] there are no internationally agreed standards for reviews of treatment decisions. Accordingly, the chapter draws on the law of three jurisdictions, England and Wales, Victoria (Australia) and Ireland, to study review models in practice. These jurisdictions are interesting, first, because they operate within a similar normative framework. All three jurisdictions permit some degree of compulsory treatment for a mental disorder, including in circumstances where patients have legal capacity,[5] while, at the same time, endorsing a rights-based approach to mental health law.[6] Thus, they present an opportunity to assess the contribution of process rights within a compulsory treatment model. Secondly, between them, these jurisdictions illuminate the main approaches to treatment review. In England and Wales, a new role for judicial review of treatment decisions in certain limited contexts has developed in recent years; Victoria adopts a tribunal review model; and the statutory review schemes in both England and Wales and in Ireland are based on review by fellow professionals (although with significant differences between the jurisdictions in terms of how this is given effect).

The chapter begins by asking what should be expected from treatment reviews when viewed from a human rights perspective. In doing this, the chapter takes the legal context within which review mechanisms operate as a given and investigates how review mechanisms should operate within this context. There are, of course, broader questions about the role of compulsion but these are not the concern of the discussion here. The chapter then considers the different approaches to review and asks how effectively each of them delivers on human rights goals. It shows that, while some forms of review are undoubtedly better

---

[4] Principle 17 of the United Nations Principles for the Protection of Persons with Mental Illness and the Improvement of Mental Health Care, adopted by United Nations GA Res 46/119 of 17 December 1991.

[5] In England and Wales, medication may be compulsorily administered to patients with and without capacity: Mental Health Act 1983 (England and Wales) ss 58, 63. Since 2007, ECT may be compulsorily administered only to patients without capacity except in an emergency situation: Mental Health Act 1983 (England and Wales) ss 58A, 62. In Victoria, medication may be compulsorily administered to patients with and without capacity: Mental Health Act 1986 (Vic) s 12AD, but ECT may be compulsorily administered only to patients without capacity: Mental Health Act 1986 (Vic) s 73 (1). In Ireland, for the first three months following admission, medication may be compulsorily administered only to patients without capacity: Mental Health Act, 2001 (Ireland) s 57, but after three months have passed, medication may be compulsorily administered to patients with and without capacity: Mental Health Act, 2001 (Ireland) s 60. ECT may be compulsorily administered to patients with and without capacity: MHA s 59 (although a Bill amending the MHA in respect of ECT is currently before the Oireachtas: see Mental Health (Involuntary Procedures) (Amendment) Bill 2008. For a comparative summary of the applicable legislative frameworks: see M Donnelly 'From Autonomy to Dignity: Treatment for Mental Disorders and the Focus for Patient Rights' (2008) 26(2) *Law in Context* 37, 38.

[6] Both Australia and the United Kingdom have ratified the Convention on the Rights of Persons with Disabilities (CRPD). Ireland has not yet ratified the CRPD (although it has signed). However, the Mental Health Act, 2001 (Ireland) s 4(3) includes respect for patient rights as an underlying principle in respect of decision-making under the Act.

than others, none delivers full and effective protection for patient rights. It concludes that treatment decisions will always pose particular difficulties for review and that more fundamental changes are needed to the framework within which treatment decisions are made.

II. Treatment Reviews: Establishing a Normative Foundation

As Denis Galligan reminds us, 'each form of process has a normative foundation'.[7] Within the jurisdictions discussed here, the relevant foundation is one which attempts to combine a degree of compulsion with a prioritisation of human rights. In this normative context, three goals are suggested. These are, of course, contestable. However, it will be argued below that the goals identified are grounded in international and domestically applicable human rights instruments. First, treatment reviews must protect individuals against violations of their substantive human rights as protected by the relevant human rights instrument or statute. In England and Wales and in Ireland, this is the European Convention on Human Rights[8] (ECHR) and, additionally, in Ireland, the Constitution of Ireland (*Bunreacht na hÉireann*) 1937. In Victoria, it is the Charter of Human Rights and Responsibilities (the Victorian Charter).[9] The substantive rights in this context are most likely to be negative rights, specifically, the right to be protected from interference. However, this right is limited in application. As noted above, the capable patient's 'right to refuse' treatment has only limited recognition in the jurisdictions discussed here[10] and it is unlikely that any of the applicable human rights instruments will be found to require a major change in this position.[11] However, human rights instruments do require a restriction on the circumstances and the manner in which involuntary treatment may be

---

[7] DJ Galligan, *Due Process and Fair Procedures* (Oxford, Clarendon Press, 1996) 33.

[8] Convention on the Protection of Human Rights and Fundamental Freedoms (European Convention on Human Rights), opened for signature 4 November 1950, CETS No 005 (entered into force 3 September 1953).

[9] The Charter was introduced by the Charter of Human Rights and Responsibilities Act 2006 and became fully operational on 1 January 2008 (the substantive rights provisions having been operational since 1 January 2007).

[10] For detail, see above n 5.

[11] Although s 10(c) of the Victorian Charter of Human Rights and Responsibilities contains an express statement that a person must not be subjected to medical treatment without consent, this is subject to limits: see *Kracke v Mental Health Review Board* [2009] VCAT 646 at [742]–[786].

provided. This restriction derives from the protection which the individual is afforded against inhuman and degrading treatment;[12] and the right to bodily integrity and the right to autonomy.[13]

Secondly, treatment reviews should aim to ensure the delivery of the most appropriate treatment for the person. This goes beyond simply asking whether the treatment violates a person's negative rights and asks additionally whether there are better treatment options and how can these be delivered. This involves a medical or therapeutic aspect but it also involves social and psychological factors. Crucially, it may also require the allocation of resources. It presumes a positive right to appropriate treatment as well as the negative right to avoid unwanted/ unsuitable treatment. Thus, it incorporates the Richardson Committee's 'principle of reciprocity', which recognises that when society requires a person to comply with treatment, it has an obligation to provide appropriate treatment.[14] This focus accords with Article 12(1) of the International Covenant on Economic, Social and Cultural Rights,[15] which requires States Parties to recognise the right of everyone to the enjoyment of

the highest attainable standard of physical and mental health;

with Articles 25 and 26 of the Convention on the Rights of Persons with Disabilities (CRPD);[16] and with Principle 8 of the United Nations Principles for the Protection of Persons with Mental Illness and the Improvement of Mental Health Care (UN Principles), which states that

every patient shall have the right to receive such health and social care as is appropriate to his or her health needs.

Thirdly, the treatment review process itself should be trustworthy not just for the experts but 'for all who may have reason to place or refuse trust' in the process.[17] Thus, the review should be accessible to the people about whom decisions are made and should respect the values of dignity, fairness and participation. A right to fair procedures is recognised in both the ECHR and the Victorian Charter.[18] A requirement for respect for procedural rights is implicit in Articles 12(3) and 13

[12] ECHR Art 3; Charter of Human Rights and Responsibilities (Vic) s 10(b); Irish Constitution Art 40.3.1.
[13] ECHR Art 8; Irish Constitution Art 40.3.1; Charter of Human Rights and Responsibilities (Vic) ss 10(c), 12, 13, 21: see *Kracke v Mental Health Review Board* [2009] VCAT 646 at [775].
[14] Great Britain. Department of Health, *Review of the Mental Health Act 1983: Report of the Expert Committee* (London, Department of Health, 1999) 23.
[15] International Covenant on Economic, Social and Cultural Rights, adopted by United Nations GA Res 2200A (XXI) of 16 December 1966.
[16] CRPD Art 25 recognises the right to health of people with disabilities, while Art 26 requires States Parties to provide habilitation and rehabilitation for people with disabilities.
[17] N Manson and O O'Neill, *Rethinking Informed Consent in Bioethics* (Cambridge, Cambridge University Press, 2007) 167.
[18] ECHR Art 6 and Charter of Human Rights and Responsibilities (Vic) s 24.

of the CRPD[19] and is explicit in the UN Principles (albeit in respect of reviews of admission).[20] The appropriate use of process also has an instrumental value. A process which shows respect for values such as fairness or participation may well have a better chance of delivering the best decision.[21] Additionally, a good process for making treatment decisions may enhance the value of the care provided. Some empirical studies show that patients who have participated in decision-making about treatment and care have higher levels of compliance with treatment and better therapeutic outcomes.[22] This may be the case even in respect of compulsory treatment. A number of studies suggest that the belief that an appropriate and participative process has been observed makes it easier for people to accept the outcome of the process, even if this is not what they hoped for.[23] Bruce Winick argues that inclusion in the decision-making process also enhances individual well-being and self-esteem in a broader sense.[24] For these reasons, a 'good' review process, premised on 'honesty, informed-ness, transparency and patience' is an essential aspect of the protection of patient rights.[25]

III. Rights to Review: Mechanisms in Operation

Viewed in descending order of formality (although not necessarily of effectiveness), reviews of treatment decisions may involve judicial review, review by a specialist tribunal, and reviews by fellow professionals. The first two approaches involve a legal element while the third does not. Because each form of review is especially associated with one of the jurisdictions discussed here, the focus will be on the operation of the review process in that jurisdiction. It is of course possible that judicial review would work differently in, say, the United States, to the way in which it has operated in England and Wales. However, a focus on a particular

---

[19] Art 12(3) requires States Parties to take appropriate measures to provide access by persons with disabilities to the support they may require in exercising their legal capacity. Art 13 requires States to ensure effective access to justice.

[20] UN Principles 17 and 18.

[21] DJ Galligan, *Due Process and Fair Procedures* (Oxford, Clarendon Press, 1996) 131–2.

[22] E Guadagnoli and P Ward, 'Patient Participation in Decision-making' (1998) 47 *Social Science and Medicine* 329.

[23] J Peay, *Tribunals on Trial: A Study of Decision-making under the Mental Health Act 1983* (Oxford, Clarendon Press, 1989) 44–5; D Dennis and J Monahan (eds), *Coercion and Aggressive Community Treatment: A New Frontier in Mental Health Law* (New York, Plenum Press, 1996) 24. See also I Freckelton, 'Mental Health Review Tribunal Decision-making: A Therapeutic Jurisprudence Lens' (2003) 10 *Psychiatry, Psychology and Law* 44, 44.

[24] BJ Winick, 'The Right to Refuse Mental Health Treatment: A Therapeutic Jurisprudence Analysis' (1994) 17 *International Journal of Law and Psychiatry* 99, 100.

[25] I Freckelton, 'Involuntary Detention Decision-Making, Criteria and Hearing Procedures: An Opportunity for Therapeutic Jurisprudence in Action' in K Diesfeld and I Freckelton (eds), *Involuntary Detention and Therapeutic Jurisprudence: International Perspectives on Civil Commitment* (Aldershot, Ashgate, 2003) 337.

jurisdiction provides a detailed picture of the process in operation while at the same time allowing some of the inherent aspects of each process to be identified.

A.   Judicial Reviews of Treatment Decisions

The recognition of a limited right to a judicial review of a treatment decision has been a striking new feature of the law in England and Wales in the decade or so since the incorporation of the ECHR into domestic law. While the statutory framework for review is based on an independent second opinion from a medical professional (typically described as a 'second opinion appointed doctor' or SOAD), in the landmark case of *R (Wilkinson) v Responsible Medical Officer, Broadmoor Hospital*[26] the Court of Appeal found in favour of a patient's right to a judicial review of a treatment decision in certain circumstances. This right derived from the ECHR and, in particular, from the requirement that treatment which may be considered inhuman or degrading under Article 3 must be 'convincingly shown' to be therapeutically necessary.[27] In *Wilkinson* itself, the patient was strongly resistant to the treatment and this put him at serious risk of a heart attack.[28] In these circumstances, Hale LJ stated that 'substantial benefit from [the imposed treatment] would be required for it to be justified'.[29] Significantly, Hale LJ did not focus on the question of the patient's capacity but rather on the question of willingness, noting that 'most people are able to appreciate that they are being forced to do something against their will even if they are not able to make the decision that it should or should not be done'.[30]

(i)   The Extent of the Right to Judicial Review

Wilkinson left open the questions of when exactly a right to a judicial review of treatment decisions will arise and how a review hearing should be conducted. In subsequent cases, the Court of Appeal made several efforts to limit a possible flood of *Wilkinson*-type applications for review.[31] However, in *R (on the application of JB) v RMO, Dr Haddock*,[32] the Court seemed to have become resigned to the fact that patients who requested judicial review of a treatment decision were, in most cases, going to succeed in establishing a right to a hearing.[33] The Court also accepted that the effect of the ruling in *Wilkinson* was that the hearing would

---

[26]   [2001] EWCA Civ 1545.

[27]   As required in *Herczegfalvy v Austria* (1992) 15 EHRR 437 at [82].

[28]   See evidence outlined at *R (Wilkinson) v Responsible Medical Officer, Broadmoor Hospital* [2001] EWCA Civ 1545 at [14].

[29]   *R (Wilkinson) v Responsible Medical Officer, Broadmoor Hospital* [2001] EWCA Civ 1545 at [82].

[30]   *ibid*, at [79].

[31]   *R (on the application of N) v Dr M* [2002] EWCA Civ 1789; *R (on the application of B) v Dr SS and Dr AC* [2006] EWCA Civ 28 at [68].

[32]   *R (on the application of B) v RMO, Dr Haddock* [2006] EWCA Civ 961.

[33]   *ibid*, at [65].

have to be a 'full merits' review as to whether the proposed treatment infringed the patient's human rights and that, accordingly, a patient is entitled to require the attendance of witnesses and to cross-examination of those witnesses.[34] While undoubtedly legally significant, the practical significance of *Haddock* should not be overstated given the structural impediments to access to judicial review. These include patients' lack of knowledge of their rights, unavailability of legal advice and the inevitable stresses and strains of taking a legal action, especially if one is very ill. Thus, for many, perhaps most, patients with mental disorders, judicial review is simply not a realistic option.

(ii) The Contribution of Judicial Reviews of Treatment Decisions

On their own terms, as described in *Wilkinson*, judicial reviews of treatment decisions seek to establish whether 'the decision to impose treatment without consent upon a protesting patient is a potential invasion of [the patient's] rights'.[35] Thus, the focus of judicial review is on preventing violations of substantive ECHR rights. However, it is clear that this takes place against a background of very considerable deference to medical opinion. This deference is evident in Simon Brown LJ's judgment in *Wilkinson* where His Lordship cautioned: '[c]ertainly, however, courts will not be astute to overrule a treatment plan decided upon by the [patient's psychiatrist] and certified by a SOAD'.[36] It is perhaps most effectively summarised by Auld LJ's statement in *R (on the application of JB) v RMO, Dr Haddock* that 'the safeguards provided by the ECHR should not be deployed so as to "cut across the grain of medical good practice"'.[37] At a practical level, this attitude of deference has meant that judicial reviews have not resulted in changes to proposed treatment. Writing in early 2007, Peter Bartlett and Ralph Sandland note that, '[t]o date, High Court judges have felt themselves able to reject *all* medical opinion proffered in support of the patient in *all* cases subsequent to *Wilkinson*, in each case being "convinced" that the treatment should be given'.[38] This has not changed since 2007 and, in fact, on the basis of the volume of reported decisions, the flurry of applications in the wake of *Wilkinson* would seem to be coming to an end.

Notwithstanding judicial deference to the medical profession, judicial reviews have contributed something to the delivery of the most appropriate treatment. This has been achieved through judicial recognition that a broader 'best interests' standard must operate alongside the statutory standard, which, at the relevant

---

[34] *ibid*, at [64].

[35] *R (Wilkinson) v Responsible Medical Officer, Broadmoor Hospital* [2001] EWCA Civ 1545 at [83].

[36] *ibid*, at [31]. See also *R (on the application of N) v Dr M* [2002] EWCA Civ 1789.

[37] *R (on the application of JB) v RMO, Dr Haddock* [2006] EWCA Civ 961 at [33].

[38] P Bartlett and R Sandland, *Mental Health Law: Policy and Practice*, 3rd edn (Oxford, Oxford University Press, 2007) 312.

time, was focused solely on medical efficiency.[39] In *R (on the application of B) v Dr SS and Dr AC*,[40] the Court of Appeal stated that the determination of best interests 'will depend on wider considerations than the simple question of the efficacy of the treatment'.[41] Other relevant factors will be 'whether an alternative and less invasive treatment will achieve the same result' and the 'distress that will be caused to the patient if the treatment has to be imposed by force'.[42] Beyond this, however the judicial review function has not delivered much in terms of developing rights of access to the most appropriate treatment.[43] While Baroness Hale did hint at approval for a principle of reciprocity in *R (B) v Ashworth Hospital*,[44] this was part of a justification for finding that the patient could be treated for a mental disorder different to the one for which he had been admitted, rather than providing any substantive right to treatment.

When considered as a process, the experience of judicial review casts an interesting light on the impact of legal formalities. While judicial review of treatment decisions attracts procedural entitlements to a full hearing with cross-examination and legal representation,[45] the English experience reminds us that this formality is not always facilitative of accessibility, openness and participation. This is evident if the issue of legal representation is considered. A number of commentators have argued that effective legal representation is key to the protection of patient rights.[46] However, legal representation may also serve as a barrier, preventing the person affected by the decision from engaging with the process. If one surveys the judgments in first instance judicial review hearings, there are frequent references to the submissions of the claimants' counsel but much less engagement with what the claimant him or herself has to say. Indeed, in *R (on the application of JB) v RMO, Dr Haddock*[47] Collins J in the High Court rejected the claimant's counsel's application that the claimant himself should be permitted to give oral evidence. The Court already had a written statement from the claimant and, in the view of Collins J, 'it did not seem to me that his evidence would conceivably assist me in reaching my decision'.[48] There is a sense that, in Peter Bartlett's words, the claimant was 'somehow peripheral to the decision at

---

[39] The applicable statutory standard at the time was that 'having regard to the likelihood of its alleviating or preventing a deterioration of [the patient's] condition, the treatment should be given'.

[40] *R (on the application of B) v Dr SS and Dr AC* [2006] EWCA Civ 28.

[41] *ibid.*

[42] *ibid.*

[43] B Hale, 'The Human Rights Act and Mental Health Law: Has it Helped?' (2007) 15 *Journal of Mental Health Law* 7.

[44] *R (on the application of B) v Ashworth Hospital* [2005] UKHL 20 at [31].

[45] *R (on the application of JB) v RMO, Dr Haddock* [2006] EWCA Civ 961 at [64].

[46] M Perlin, 'Fatal Assumption: A Critical Evaluation of the Role of Counsel in Mental Disability Cases' (1992) 16 *Law and Human Behaviour* 39; T Carney, F Beaupert, J Perry and D Tait, 'Advocacy and Participation in Mental Health Cases: Realisable Rights or Pipe-dreams?' (2008) 26(2) *Law in Context* 125.

[47] *R (JB) v Haddock* [2005] EWHC 921 (Admin).

[48] *ibid*, at [14].

issue'.[49] This approach clearly fails to deliver a process which is either fair to, or likely to be trusted by, the person affected by it.

Ultimately, the experience in England and Wales shows the limitations of judicial reviews of treatment decisions. Even leaving aside issues of expense and efficiency, judicial review fails because it is available only to those who have the legal knowledge, the determination and the resources to challenge treatment decisions with which they are unhappy. For most involuntary patients, judicial review is simply not a realistic option. Further, even when judicial review does take place, the chances that a change in treatment will be required are minimal, as is the possibility that more appropriate treatment options will be explored and this treatment provided. Procedurally too, judicial review falls short of providing an open, accessible, inclusive and trustworthy approach to decision-making.

Notwithstanding these criticisms, it should not be concluded that judicial review has had no impact on the protection afforded to human rights in on-the-ground treatment decisions. As Genevra Richardson and Maurice Sunkin note, 'the importance of a piece of litigation in terms of its impact ... may be quite independent of its legal significance'.[50] There is a lack of empirical evidence regarding the impact of the recent use of judicial review in England and Wales on the way in which actual treatment decisions are made. However, judicial statements on ECHR requirements have had a clear influence on the guidance for SOADS (which is discussed further below).[51] Thus, a human rights focus has been, to some degree at least, legitimised and concretised by the possibility of judicial review. Even if one does not think very much of the body of case law from a human rights perspective, at least this body of case law now exists, sending out the clear signal that human rights concerns are not just theoretical aspirations but that they must have immediate practical impact when decisions are being made.

B. Tribunal Reviews

Tribunals provide a less formal, less expensive, faster and more accessible approach to decision-making than traditional courts.[52] In the mental health context, because tribunals will usually include non-legal members, they bring a broader understanding to the task of review, ideally integrating protection for legal rights with an appreciation of the person's medical and social context. The

---

[49] P Bartlett, 'A Matter of Necessity: Enforced Treatment under the Mental Health Act' (2007) 15 *Medical Law Review* 86, 91.

[50] G Richardson and M Sunkin, 'Judicial Review: Questions of Impact' [1996] *Public Law* 79, 91.

[51] See for example, Care Quality Commission, *Guidance for Clinicians and SOADs: The Imposition of Medical Treatment in the Absence of Consent*, revised edn (Nottingham, Care Quality Commission, 2008).

[52] G Richardson and H Genn, 'Tribunals in Transition: Resolution or Adjudication' [2007] *Public Law* 116, 117.

Victorian Mental Health Review Board (MHRB) is typical in this respect, having three members—a legal, a medical and a community member.

Since 2003, the MHRB has been charged with reviewing treatment decisions alongside its review functions in respect of admission and discharge.[53] This review must happen at the same time as the other statutorily required reviews[54] (initial reviews within eight weeks; periodic reviews not more than 12 months apart).[55] Additionally, a patient may appeal at any time against treatment orders or against continuing detention[56] and, if the patient does this, his or her treatment plan must also be reviewed.[57] The treatment review arises in respect of community treatment orders as well as in respect of treatment whilst detained, and the review centres on the patient's treatment plan. Section 19A of the MHA 1986 (Vic) requires that, in drawing up the treatment plan, the authorised psychiatrist must take account of: the wishes of the patient in so far as these may be ascertained; the wishes of the patient's guardian, family member or carer who is involved in providing ongoing care or support to the patient (provided the patient agrees); whether the treatment to be carried out is only to promote the patient's health and well-being; whether there are any beneficial alternative treatments available; and the nature and degree of any significant risks associated with the treatment and any alternative treatment. The review of the treatment plan must consider whether the psychiatrist has complied with these require-ments and whether the plan is capable of being implemented by the approved mental health service.[58] If it does not meet these criteria, the MHRB may require that the plan be revised.[59]

(i)   The Contribution of Tribunal Review

The newness of the Victorian Charter means that there has been little opportu-nity for jurisprudence in respect of Charter-based rights to develop.[60] However, the decision of Bell J, the President of the Victorian Civil and Administrative Tribunal (VCAT) in *Kracke v Mental Health Review Board*[61] lays down an important marker in respect of future applications of the Charter. Bell J found that the MHRB had breached the applicant's right to a fair hearing under section 24 of the Charter because it had failed to conduct treatment reviews within the statutorily mandated time, and he issued a declaration to this effect. Bell J found,

---

[53] Mental Health Act 1986 (Vic) s 22(1)(b), inserted by the Mental Health (Amendment) Act 2003 (Vic).

[54] Mental Health Act 1986 (Vic) s 35A.

[55] Mental Health Act 1986 (Vic) s 30.

[56] Mental Health Act 1986 (Vic) s 29.

[57] Mental Health Act 1986 (Vic) s 35A.

[58] Mental Health Act 1986 (Vic) s 35A(1).

[59] Mental Health Act 1986 (Vic) s 35A(2).

[60] See Mental Health Review Board, *Practice Direction 2007/1: Charter of the Human Rights and Responsibilities Act 2006* available at: www.mhrb.vic.gov.au/publications/practice_directions.htm.

[61] *Kracke v Mental Health Review Board* [2009] VCAT 646.

in respect of the statutory requirement, that '[m]ust means must. The time limits are not guidelines or aspirational'.[62] More generally, Bell J placed compulsory treatment within a human rights framework. While recognising that the Charter did not prohibit compulsory treatment, he recognised compulsion as a limitation on Charter rights and set out in some detail the circumstances in which this limitation may arise, including a requirement for proportionality.[63] In this context, safeguards were crucial. Thus, '[i]f the safeguard is indispensable for the proportionality of the limitation, then the limitation will be incompatible with human rights if the safeguard fails'.[64]

The decision in *Kracke* suggests a requirement for a degree of rigour in the application of the Charter by the MHRB. However, how this requirement will actually impact on everyday tribunal hearings remains to be seen. Mental health tribunals face a number of challenges in building up a rights-based jurisprudence. First, this kind of jurisprudence, in common law jurisdictions at any rate, has developed through adversarial argument and the accretion of precedent. However, as Terry Carney and Fleur Beaupert note, mental health tribunals are 'not *predicated* on the adversarial model, or upon an obligation on the state to "prove" its case as such'.[65] Secondly, quality legal argument is crucial to the development of the law. However, legal representation is not commonplace at tribunal hearings,[66] especially in respect of treatment reviews[67] and, even when lawyers are present, questions may be raised about the quality of the representation provided.[68] Thirdly, the issue of legal knowledge among tribunal members arises. In Victoria, it would seem that treatment reviews are often conducted by one member chosen at random from the three constituencies of the MHRB.[69] In such circumstances, there may be nobody '*capable* of bringing an informed mind to the legal as well as the otherwise largely *medical* case' in respect of the treatment.[70] Even with three-member tribunals, there is a risk that the tribunal make-up may create difficulties in developing a rights-based jurisprudence. Genevra Richardson and David Machin's study of the English Mental Health

---

[62] *ibid*, at [699].

[63] *ibid*, at [742]–[786].

[64] *ibid*, at [767].

[65] T Carney and F Beaupert, 'Mental Health Tribunals: Rights Drowning in un-Chartered Health Waters?' (2008) 13 *Australian Journal of Human Rights* 181, 195.

[66] T Carney, F Beaupert, J Perry and D Tait, 'Advocacy and Participation in Mental Health Cases: Realisable Rights or Pipe-dreams?' (2008) 26(2) *Law in Context* 125, 126. The authors estimate that only 5–10% of MHRB hearings involve legal representation.

[67] *ibid*. The authors note that legal aid tends to be allocated primarily to admission hearings.

[68] See *ibid*, 132–36.

[69] E Grundell 'Psychiatrists' Perceptions of Administrative Review: A Victorian Empirical Study' (2005) 12 *Psychiatry, Psychology and Law* 68, 73.

[70] T Carney and F Beaupert, 'Mental Health Tribunals: Rights Drowning in un-Chartered Health Waters?' (2008) 13 *Australian Journal of Human Rights* 181, 197.

Review Tribunal found that 'the presence of a medical member on the tribunal leads to the danger that the panel will be over-influenced by the medical view in reaching their legal conclusions'.[71]

Because of tribunals' cross-disciplinary make-up, one might expect more from the tribunal model in ensuring the delivery of the most appropriate treatment. As Richardson and Machin note, in a cross-disciplinary context, an examination of the legal issues 'can lead almost inexorably to a wider discussion of the patient's care and future plans'.[72] In addition, the Victorian statutory framework clearly establishes a basis for the MHRB to involve itself in an assessment of the appropriateness of treatment plans.[73] However, before the MHRB can approve a treatment plan, the plan must be 'capable of being implemented by the approved mental health service'.[74] Thus, the Board is restricted to working within the available services and the possibility of using review as a means of demanding access to treatment is limited.

The extent to which the MHRB actually engages with the question of appropriateness is unclear. Most of the respondents to Erica Grundell's study of Victorian psychiatrists were sceptical about the capacity of treatment reviews to bring about positive therapeutic outcomes for patients.[75] This is perhaps unsurprising given Kate Diesfeld and Ian Freckelton's evidence that 'the majority of treatment plans are short and significantly "pro forma", containing little indication of sophisticated and individualised planning to address patients' needs'.[76] However, Grundell also notes that many respondents also identified individual cases in which the review process had resulted in beneficial therapeutic outcomes.[77] Certainly, there are some examples in the case reports of treatment plans being rejected by the MHRB because the psychiatrist failed to comply with section 19A requirements.[78] Terry Carney and colleagues also identify ways in which tribunals have used the review process creatively as a way of negotiating

---

[71]   G Richardson and D Machin, 'Doctors on Tribunals: A Confusion of Roles' (2000) 176 *British Journal of Psychiatry* 110, 115; E Perkins, *Decision-making in Mental Health Review Tribunals* (London, Policy Studies Institute, 2003) reports similar findings.

[72]   G Richardson and D Machin, 'Doctors on Tribunals: A Confusion of Roles' (2000) 176 *British Journal of Psychiatry* 110, 113.

[73]   See Mental Health Act 1986 (Vic) s 35A(1).

[74]   Mental Health Act 1986 (Vic) s 35A.

[75]   E Grundell, 'Psychiatrists' Perceptions of Administrative Review: A Victorian Empirical Study' (2005) 12 *Psychiatry, Psychology and Law* 68, 78.

[76]   K Diesfield and I Freckelton, 'Mental Health Law and Therapeutic Jurisprudence' in I Freckelton and K Petersen (eds), *Disputes and Dilemmas in Health Law* (Annandale, Federation Press, 2006) 104.

[77]   *ibid.*

[78]   See for example, *In the Appeal of P, an Involuntary Patient at Central East Area Mental Health Service* Reference No 07–094, available at: www.austlii.edu.au/au/cases/vic/VMHRB/2007/1.html; *In the Review of P an Involuntary Patient at Mid West Area Mental Health Service* Reference No 07–116, available at: www.austlii.edu.au/au/cases/vic/VMHRB/2007/4.html.

better treatment provision for patients.[79] The cases identified involved 'conciliation and gentle persuasion rather than conflict, with informal contracts being developed between the Tribunal and medical professionals'.[80] The interventions which the tribunals were able to make were 'relatively modest', such as restricting the length of orders so as to permit speedy review by the tribunal or adjourning hearings to allow treatment plans to be developed.[81] As described by Terry Carney and colleagues, insofar as Australian tribunals develop and assert positive rights to services, '[t]hey "nudge" rather than push the boundaries'.[82] However, perhaps the most striking feature, when compared with judicial review, is that they have any impact on the boundaries at all.

In process terms, tribunals adopt a very different approach to that employed by judicial review. On the positive side, the tribunal model provides a chance to escape the confines of legal formality and to craft a more accessible process.[83] However, this can also mean limited procedural protection, especially when the decision relates to treatment rather than to more high-profile matters of admission and discharge. Indeed, Terry Carney and colleagues note that the informality of the tribunal model may be purchased at a cost of failure to test evidence, or an acceptance of hearsay evidence.[84] In such circumstances, medical evidence will be prioritised[85] and the tribunal is likely to tend towards the approval of the treatment plan put forward rather than subjecting this to a critical review.

The fluidity of the tribunal model also means that dynamics can develop quite differently, depending on the people involved and that tribunals can operate in a way which is alienating and demoralising rather than accessible or trustworthy.[86] Important factors in the delivery of 'good' hearings include: whether the person feels confident in the impartiality and fairness of the tribunal;[87] whether he or she is treated with respect or is patronised and made to feel like 'a second class participant' (for example through the selective use of titles);[88] whether or not the

---

[79]   T Carney, D Tait and F Beaupert, 'Pushing Back the Boundaries: Realising Rights Through the Mental Health Tribunal Process' (2008) 30 *Sydney Law Review* 329, 347–53.

[80]   *ibid*, 348.

[81]   *ibid*, 356.

[82]   *ibid*, 356.

[83]   I Freckelton, 'Involuntary Detention Decision-Making, Criteria and Hearing Procedures: An Opportunity for Therapeutic Jurisprudence in Action' in K Diesfeld and I Freckelton (eds), *Involuntary Detention and Therapeutic Jurisprudence: International Perspectives on Civil Commitment* (Aldershot, Ashgate, 2003); T Carney and D Tait, *The Adult Guardianship Experiment: Tribunals and Popular Justice* (Annandale, Federation Press, 1997).

[84]   T Carney, F Beaupert, J Perry and D Tait, 'Advocacy and Participation in Mental Health Cases: Realisable Rights or Pipe-dreams?' (2008) 26(2) *Law in Context* 125, 137.

[85]   *ibid*, 138. Note that the MHRB places particular weight on consultant psychiatrist reports.

[86]   D Tait, 'The Ritual Environment of the Mental Health Tribunal Hearing: Inquiries and Reflections' (2003) 10 *Psychiatry, Psychology and Law* 91.

[87]   I Freckelton, 'Involuntary Detention Decision-Making, Criteria and Hearing Procedures: An Opportunity for Therapeutic Jurisprudence in Action' in K Diesfeld and I Freckelton (eds), *Involuntary Detention and Therapeutic Jurisprudence: International Perspectives on Civil Commitment* (Aldershot, Ashgate, 2003) 313–14.

[88]   *ibid*, 315.

tribunal members behave with arrogance, insensitivity or inattentiveness; and whether the person feels at ease in saying what he or she wishes.[89] In the context of treatment reviews, it is also important that the person feels confident that the tribunal will critically engage with the question of treatment and does not regard treatment reviews as a matter of routine.

It is not clear how effectively the MHRB delivers on these aspects of process in reviews of treatment decisions. A 2002 Report of the Victorian Auditor-General found that 'despite the efforts of the Board to conduct hearings in an informal manner, patients can feel confused, powerless and intimidated by Board processes'.[90] This is confirmed in incidents recounted by Ian Freckelton[91] and by Terry Carney and colleagues.[92] Indeed, a telling narrative quoted by the latter serves as a reminder that informality can sometimes be as off-putting for a person as excessive formality. For the person quoted, 'I guess my biggest problem with the whole thing is that it doesn't feel to me like the real legal system at all'.[93] Experience in other jurisdictions confirms that feelings of confusion, distress, powerlessness, dissatisfaction, and alienation are by no means unusual responses to tribunal hearings.[94] This is not to say that tribunal hearings cannot deliver a 'good' process from the perspective of the person involved.[95] However, it does call into question any presumption that tribunals are inherently able to deliver a better encounter than alternative forms of review.

C. Review by Fellow Professionals

Both of the review models discussed above involve some form of legal review of treatment decisions. However, the core legislative mechanism for treatment review adopted in England and Wales and in Ireland does not involve lawyers at all. Here, the review is undertaken by a fellow professional by means of a second opinion. In both jurisdictions, the second opinion review arises automatically in respect of electro-convulsive therapy (ECT) and where an involuntary patient has been receiving medication for three months. The Mental Health Act 1983

---

[89]   *ibid*, 320.

[90]   Victoria. Auditor-General, *Mental Health Services for People in Crises* (Melbourne, Office of the Auditor-General, 2002) at [5.26] available at: www.download.audit.vic.gov.au/files/mhs_report.pdf.

[91]   I Freckelton, 'Involuntary Detention Decision-Making, Criteria and Hearing Procedures: An Opportunity for Therapeutic Jurisprudence in Action' in K Diesfeld and I Freckelton (eds), *Involuntary Detention and Therapeutic Jurisprudence: International Perspectives on Civil Commitment* (Aldershot, Ashgate, 2003) 322. See also Ian Freckelton, this volume, ch 9.

[92]   T Carney, F Beaupert, J Perry and D Tait, 'Advocacy and Participation in Mental Health Cases: Realisable Rights or Pipe-dreams?' (2008) 26(2) *Law in Context* 125, 137–38.

[93]   *ibid*, 137.

[94]   N Ferencz, 'Patients' Views of the Mental Health Review Tribunal Procedure in England' in K Diesfeld and I Freckelton (eds), *Involuntary Detention and Therapeutic Jurisprudence: International Perspectives on Civil Commitment* (Aldershot, Ashgate, 2003).

[95]   Note the efforts made by the New Zealand Mental Health Review Tribunal, described in K Diesfeld and B McKenna 'The Therapeutic Intent of the New Zealand Mental Health Review Tribunal' (2006) 13 *Psychiatry, Psychology and Law* 100.

(England and Wales), as amended, requires the reviewer or 'second opinion appointed doctor' (SOAD) to assess whether it is 'appropriate for the treatment to be given'.[96] Treatment is deemed 'appropriate' in this context

> taking into account the nature and degree of the mental disorder from which [the patient] is suffering and all the other circumstances of his case.[97]

SOADs must also comply with the Code of Practice to the Mental Health Act 1983[98] and are provided with detailed guidance by the Care Quality Commission, formerly the Mental Health Act Commission. The Irish Mental Health Act 2001 does not provide any express instructions for reviewers and the matter is not addressed in the codes issued under the Act;[99] nor does the Mental Health Commission (the body charged with overview of the MHA 2001) provide detailed guidance on this matter. However, reviewers are bound by section 4 of the MHA 2001, which requires that all decisions under the Act concerning the care and treatment of a person must have the best interests of the person as the principal consideration[100] and that decisions must also give due regard to 'the need to respect the right of the person to dignity, bodily integrity, privacy and autonomy'.[101]

(i)   The Review in Operation

While ostensibly similar, the review mechanisms in England and Wales and in Ireland diverge at a level of detail. In all respects, the English SOAD model is more detailed and careful (whether it is also more effective will be discussed further below). First, under the MHA 1983 (England and Wales), the SOAD is independently appointed by the Care Quality Commission. Under the Irish Act, there is no requirement for external involvement; the second opinion must be given by a second consultant psychiatrist following referral of the matter by the patient's own consultant psychiatrist. Secondly, while both models rely on medical professionals only, the English model requires that the SOAD consult with two other people who have been professionally involved with the patient's treatment (one must be a nurse and the other must be neither a nurse nor a doctor). The Irish model imposes no consultation requirements whatever, including with the patient him or herself.

---

[96]   Mental Health Act 1983 (England and Wales) s 58(3)(b) (as amended by Mental Health Act 2007 (England and Wales) s 6(2)).

[97]   Mental Health Act 1983 (England and Wales) s 64(3) (as inserted by Mental Health Act 2007 (England and Wales) s 6(3)).

[98]   Great Britain Department of Health, *Code of Practice to the Mental Health Act 1983*, revised edn (London, TSO, 2008).

[99]   The Codes of Practice issued under the Mental Health Act 2001 (Ireland), available at: www.mhcirl.ie.

[100]   Mental Health Act 2001 (Ireland) s 4(1).

[101]   Mental Health Act 2001 (Ireland) s 4(3).

Thirdly, there is a difference in the level of detail required and in terms of external audit of how the process is operating. In England and Wales, the involvement of the Care Quality Commission means that all second opinion requests and all SOAD responses are logged. The Care Quality Commission can, at any point, report on how many requests are made, where these come from, how many requests are approved, disapproved or amended and why. Thus, in addition to providing individualised approvals, the English SOAD model allows for a reasonably detailed audit of what is actually going on in practice. The audit aspect of the process is further enhanced by the level of detail required from both the approved clinician and the SOAD.[102] SOADs are legally obliged to provide reasons for their decisions. In its guidance to SOADs in this respect, the Care Quality Commission sets out a detailed list of information which must be included as part of the reasons for the decision.[103] Thus, as well as recognising the patient's right 'to know in useful form and at a relevant time what the SOAD's reasons are for his opinion on the ... proposal to override his will',[104] the requirement to provide reasons constitutes a means of overseeing how SOADs operate in practice.

The scope for audit under the Irish model is more limited. In respect of ECT only, a copy of the relevant form must be sent to the Mental Health Commission, and the Inspectorate of Mental Health Services must report on compliance with the ECT Rules drawn up by the Mental Health Commission (which include the second opinion requirement).[105] Forms in respect of medication remain at local hospital level. The Inspectorate must report on whether the relevant form has been completed and on whether each patient has a treatment plan.[106] Additionally, the Inspectorate inspects a sample of individual prescriptions. For its 2008 inspection, the focus was on the condition of prescriptions, the use of benzodiazepines, polypharmacy in the use of antipsychotics and the use of anti-epileptic medication as a mood stabiliser.[107] While the Inspectorate's work in this regard is

---

[102] Care Quality Commission, *Guidance Note for Commissioners on Consent to Treatment and the Mental Health Act 1983*, revised edn (London, Care Quality Commission, 2008) available at: www.cqc.org.uk. The SOAD must consider the treatment plan as a whole and the relevant form must indicate all drugs prescribed either by name or by the British National Formulary (BNF) guidance on prescription medication. The form must also indicate the maximum amount of drugs allowed in any one category, the route of administration and the dosage, including whether the dosage is in excess of BNF limits.

[103] Care Quality Commission, *Guidance for SOADs: Giving Reasons when Certifying Appropriate Treatment* (London, Care Quality Commission, 2008).

[104] *R (on the application of Wooder) v Feggetter* [2002] EWCA (Civ) 554 at [49].

[105] Mental Health Commission, *Rules Governing the Use of Electro-Convulsive Therapy* (R-S 59(2)2009) (Dublin, Mental Health Commission, 2009). See Mental Health Commission, *Report on the Use of Electroconvulsive Therapy in Approved Centres in 2008* (Dublin, Mental Health Commission, 2009), available at www.mhcirl.ie.

[106] As required by reg 15 of the Mental Health Act 2001 (Approved Centres) Regulations 2006 (SI No 551 of 2006).

[107] For details of the process, see Mental Health Commission, *Annual Report 2008* (Dublin, Mental Health Commission, 2009) 85–88.

undoubtedly valuable, it still falls short of a comprehensive audit of what is going on at treatment level and how the review system is actually working.

(ii) The Contribution of Reviews by Fellow Professionals

Taking the two approaches in turn, it would seem that the Irish approach to review by fellow professionals is clearly inferior to that adopted in England and Wales. It is questionable whether the Irish model can meet any of the goals of review from a human rights perspective. The lack of independent oversight in choice of reviewer means that the review cannot be guaranteed to prevent possible violations of substantive rights. The mechanism provides no meaningful facility for the delivery of appropriate treatment in an individual case (although of course clinicians may choose informally to discuss treatment as part of the second opinion process) and there is limited scope for audit of treatment decisions in general. Finally, from the patient's perspective, it is difficult to see how a review process that is evidently lacking in fairness, openness and opportunity for participation can be trusted as a 'good' process. In a 2006 study (completed before the commencement of the review provisions under the MHA 2001),[108] Elizabeth Dunne found that users of mental health services felt that medication was often the only treatment offered and that it was sometimes over-prescribed.[109] Users also felt that the mode of action of the medication on them was not fully understood by the prescribing personnel and that the medication's side-effects were not always discussed or taken seriously by consultant psychiatrists.[110] Further, many medical personnel were felt to have little or no interest in working with service users to reduce or otherwise modify the dose taken.[111] The treatment review provisions contained in the MHA 2001 does little to require that any of these aspects of care be improved.

It might, of course, be argued that the more general human rights ethos in the MHA 2001 (which established the Mental Health Commission and introduced, for the first time, tribunal reviews of admission and detention) may also impact on treatment decisions and that psychiatrists will use treatment reviews in a way which exceeds the statutory expectations. Because of the limited scope for audit under the Irish model, it is difficult to tell whether this is happening. In its 2008 Report, the Inspectorate described the levels of compliance with and understanding of the purpose and significance of regulations, rules and codes of practice in relation to seclusion, restraint and ECT as 'still disappointing'.[112] However, the Inspectorate also noted 'the beginnings of a cultural shift in terms of increased

---

[108] The review aspects of the MHA 2001 did not commence until November 2006.

[109] E Dunne, *The Views of Adult Users of the Public Sector Mental Health Service* (Dublin, Mental Health Commission, 2006) 30, available at: www.mhcirl.ie.

[110] *ibid*, 31.

[111] *ibid*, 31.

[112] Mental Health Commission, *Annual Report 2008* (Dublin, Mental Health Commission, 2009) 56.

professionalism, accountability and awareness of the importance of governance'.[113] Further, it noted that '[h]uman rights obligations are increasingly
understood'.[114] If this is the case, it suggests that even a very limited and flawed
review mechanism may make some contribution to the climate in which treatment decisions are made.

   While the English SOAD model is undoubtedly better than the Irish model,
this should not distract from the more pertinent question of how effective an
(independent) fellow professional review mechanism is at protecting rights. One
impact of judicial review of treatment decisions in England and Wales has been
greater focus on the role of the SOAD and the affirmation that SOADs are
required to reach an independent conclusion and not simply to approve the
clinician's decision.[115] In this respect, the revised Code of Practice to the MHA
1983 requires SOADs to consider the appropriateness of alternative forms of
treatment, not just that proposed.[116] However, in *R (on the application of JB) v
RMO, Dr Haddock*,[117] Auld LJ took a much more limited view of the SOAD's role.
In his view, 'the SOAD's task is a medical one, to be undertaken on the *Bolam*
principle ... it does not, and could not, properly include a conclusion by him as
to whether his decision is a Convention compliant application of [the statute]'.[118]
Lord Justice Auld's reference to the *Bolam* test for medical negligence is concerning. As Peter Bartlett notes, '[i]t would significantly reduce the value of the SOAD
as a safeguard if his or her role were merely to ensure that a patient was not
treated negligently'.[119]

   Equally concerning is his Lordship's clear rejection of any role for the SOAD in
ensuring the protection of the patient's human rights. While it is certainly true
that SOADs are not courts and cannot be expected to provide a definitive
conclusion on compliance with the ECHR, these remarks suggest that human
rights concerns are entirely irrelevant for the SOAD. If this is the case, then,
unless the person seeks judicial review, English law provides no mechanism to
protect his or her ECHR rights.

   It is difficult to measure how effective the SOAD model is at delivering the
most appropriate treatment. It is clear, however, that reviews have not yielded
large numbers of changes in original treatment decisions. Philip Fennell's study

---

[113]   *ibid*, 57.

[114]   *ibid.*

[115]   *R (Wilkinson) v Responsible Medical Officer Broadmoor Hospital* [2001] EWCA Civ 1545 at
[32]; *R (on the application of B) v Dr SS and Dr AC* [2006] EWCA Civ 28 at [68]; *R (on the application
of JB) v RMO, Dr Haddock* [2006] EWCA Civ 961 at [9].

[116]   Great Britain. Department of Health, *Code of Practice: Mental Health Act 1983*, revised edn
(London, TSO, 2008) at [24.58].

[117]   *R (on the application of JB) v RMO, Dr Haddock* [2006] EWCA Civ 961.

[118]   *ibid*, at [34].

[119]   P Bartlett, 'A Matter of Necessity: Enforced Treatment under the Mental Health Act' (2007) 15
Medical Law Review 86, 92.

from the early 1990s found that agreement between the SOAD and the prescrib-ing doctor was in the region of 96 per cent.[120] Fennell also found that the SOAD's obligation to consult with two other people could often involve consultations with people who had very little knowledge of the patient.[121] He also identified 'surprisingly frequent use of high-dose medication', with almost 13 per cent of approvals involving dosages above the British National Formulary guidelines[122] and extensive use of polypharmacy,[123] which by and large was approved without any expression of concern by the SOAD.[124] The most recent figures show that, in 2008, over 25 per cent of SOAD reviews required some changes in proposed treatment and that over 4 per cent required significant changes.[125]. This repre-sents a substantial increase on the number of changes required in previous years[126] and suggests that SOADs may be becoming more rigorous in the operation of the second opinion review (although it is too soon to draw any definitive conclusions in this respect). Unfortunately, in the absence of an up-to-date equivalent of Fennell's study, it is impossible to ascertain the extent to which practices such as polypharmacy or the prescription of high dosage medication are being prevented through the SOAD review process. However, a range of studies suggests that these practices remain prevalent.[127] If this is the case, then it is questionable whether the SOAD review is delivering the most appropriate treatment for the patient.

Jill Peay's study of clinician responses to a hypothetical case involving the administration of ECT suggests one reason why SOADs have tended not to require significant changes in treatment plans.[128] The study found that SOADs were, in fact, more likely than prescribing clinicians to advocate intervention with ECT, notwithstanding, in this hypothetical case, the patient's strenuous and deep-rooted objections.[129] Further, SOADs were more confident of their conclu-sions.[130] Peay suggests that the SOAD responses may reflect the way in which they frame the decision to be made; SOADs are used to being asked to approve

---

[120] P Fennell, *Treatment Without Consent: Law, Psychiatry and the Treatment of Mentally Disor-dered People since 1845* (London, Routledge, 1996) 208.

[121] *ibid*, 207.

[122] *ibid*, 215.

[123] *ibid*, 202–3.

[124] *ibid*, 203.

[125] Mental Health Act Commission Thirteenth Biennial Report 2007–2009 *Coercion and Consent* (London: TSO, 2009), Figure 50, 154.

[126] Statistics in the Thirteenth Biennial Report *ibid*, show that, in the period 2003–2007, changes were required in approximately 15 % of cases and that significant changes were required in 2% of cases.

[127] See studies cited in Mental Health Act Commission Twelfth Biennial Report 2005–2007 *Risk, Rights, Recovery* (London: TSO, 2008) 203–4.

[128] J Peay, *Decisions and Dilemmas: Working with Mental Health Law* (Oxford, Hart Publishing, 2003) ch 3.

[129] *ibid*, 100.

[130] *ibid*, 100.

treatments so they think in these terms.[131] She also notes that SOADs are more likely to be older and more experienced (a number of her respondents were retired practitioners) and suggests that this may have increased their confidence levels.[132] This may also have impacted on their relative comfort with approving a decision that clearly overrode the patient's deeply-rooted views. After all, the recognition that the patient's views are important, notwithstanding his or her illnesses, is still rather new in mental health care.

As a process, the SOAD review has the advantage of accessibility. It arises automatically where ECT is provided to a patient lacking capacity, and after medication for three months. Further, the review takes place on-site and with minimal disruption. For very ill patients, this may be an important benefit. However, overall, the SOAD process would seem to deliver little in terms of enhancing patients' trust in the system. A 2005 review of the SOAD system found that few patients remembered being given information about the SOAD service in advance of meeting the SOAD, and that most patients did not get a clear indication from the SOAD regarding the purpose of the visit. Lengths of visits varied, with some patients reporting visits of up to an hour and others reporting two to five minutes.[133] While patients reported that SOADs were professional and polite and that they 'looked important' and 'obviously had experience', patients also reported that SOADs did not ask enough questions, were not interested in finding out about the patient, were not spending enough time to get a proper diagnosis or were 'in cahoots' with the doctors at the hospital.[134]

While the contrasting models in England and Wales and in Ireland show that review by a fellow professional can have a different meaning depending on the detail of the surrounding framework, they also show that, regardless of the framework, this review model encounters serious difficulties in protecting human rights. Reviews by judges and tribunals may be criticised for their excessive deference to medical professionals but these mechanisms do at least require the treating professional to justify the decisions which he or she has made in an independent forum, which (one hopes) has an understanding of the significance of rights. These treatment decisions take place in the 'shadow of the law' in a way that decisions approved only by fellow professionals do not. The model also falls short of the goals of delivering the most appropriate treatment for the patient and providing a meaningful and participative process from the patient's perspective. However, the model does have audit potential which could be tapped to enable prescribing patterns to be investigated.

---

[131] *ibid*, 102.

[132] *ibid*, 100.

[133] Mental Health Act Commission, *Review of the Second Opinion Appointed Doctor Service* (London, Mental Health Act Commission, 2006). See the summary of the report findings in Mental Health Act Commission Twelfth Biennial Report 2005–2007, *Risk, Rights, Recovery* (London, TSO, 2008) 196–7.

[134] Mental Health Act Commission Twelfth Biennial Report 2005–2007, *Risk, Rights, Recovery* (London, TSO, 2008) 197.

IV. Conclusion

The preceding examination of treatment review models in three jurisdictions leads to the rather dispiriting conclusion that, although all of the models make some contribution to protecting rights, none of the models delivers a satisfactory level of protection. Of the three models examined, tribunal reviews would seem to have the greatest potential to provide a package which protects substantive rights, ensures the most appropriate treatment and provides an accessible, fair, and participative process. However, the experience of the Victorian MHRB suggests that delivering on this potential encounters significant difficulties.

In the passage quoted in the introduction to this chapter, Rose speaks of transforming 'the relations between expertise and those subject to it'.[135] In order to appreciate the challenges faced by all review models in achieving this, it is helpful to consider the culture within which treatment reviews take place and the legal deference shown to the views of the treating professional in health care decisions generally.[136] There are several reasons for this deference. First, outsiders to the relationship between treating professional and patient inevitably lack the degree of knowledge of the treating professional. Both non-medical professionals, who will feel their lack of medical training, and medical professionals, who will be aware from their own professional experience of the nuances and complexities of individual relationships, will inevitably be inclined to defer to this superior knowledge. Secondly, as Jonathan Montgomery points out, legal deference to the medical profession is based on 'a belief that [medical] practice enshrines moral values and the aspiration to construct a legal relationship between patients and health professionals that enables that morality to flourish'.[137]

Thus, most of the time, there is societal trust in medical professionals, including psychiatrists, to make treatment decisions together with their patients free of external oversight.[138] In circumstances where this is not possible because patients lack capacity, health care decisions are still subject to external review only in a limited set of circumstances.[139] Even within the specific context of mental health law, only a very small proportion of treatment decisions are subject to any form of review. Most reviews arise only in respect of treatment of

---

[135] N Rose, 'Unreasonable Rights: Mental Illness and the Limits of the Law' (1985) 12 *Journal of Law and Society* 199, 206.

[136] Lord Wolff, 'Are the Courts Excessively Deferential to the Medical Profession?' (2001) 9 *Medical Law Review* 1; J Montgomery, 'Law and the Demoralisation of Medicine' (2006) 26 *Legal Studies* 185, 201–2.

[137] J Montgomery, 'Law and the Demoralisation of Medicine' (2006) 26 *Legal Studies* 185, 207.

[138] See General Medical Council, *Consent: Patients and Doctors Making Decisions Together* (London, General Medical Council, 2008).

[139] See for example the limited circumstances in which formal oversight of medical decisions in respect of adults lacking capacity is required in England and Wales as outlined in *Practice Direction E*, issued by the Court of Protection, available at: www.hmcourts-service.gov.uk.

involuntary patients and medication reviews are triggered only at a certain point in the treatment cycle; in England and Wales and Ireland, after three months and in Victoria, towards the end of an eight-week period. In brief, treatment reviews constitute a rare intrusion into the domain of clinical discretion. For many professionals and reviewers, medical and otherwise, this incursion may seem largely unnecessary. Review is a formality necessitated by the law rather than a process to which reviewers are deeply committed.[140] This means that, almost inevitably, treatment reviews will tend towards conservatism.

Placing treatment reviews within a broader health care context also serves as a reminder of the distinguishing feature of the law in respect of treatment for a mental disorder and perhaps the primary reason why treatment reviews are considered necessary in this context. As noted above, in all of the jurisdictions discussed here, treatment decisions are made within a legal framework which accords a lesser degree of protection to the right of autonomy and decision-making freedom of patients with a mental disorder when compared to that accorded to other patients. There is a risk of over-idealising the contribution of the right of autonomy in health care generally.[141] It is a right reserved for patients with capacity, a concept which is both weighted and malleable.[142] Further, it is a right which, in traditional legal discourse at any rate, has yielded relatively little for patients in terms of choice. As Onora O'Neill notes, '[w]hat is rather grandly called "patient autonomy" often amounts to a right to choose or refuse treatments on offer'.[143] However, it must still be recognised that a consequence of the differential approach to the right is that the person with a mental disorder is made less central to the decision-making process; his or her views are less important and easier to override. While differential legal treatment arises only in respect of involuntary patients and is most obviously felt by patients with legal capacity, the impact of this positioning of the patient is broader. For voluntary patients, treatment decisions still take place against a background of the possibility of compulsion in the event of failure to reach agreement.[144] For patients without capacity, the efforts at participative decision-making, which are increasingly recognised outside of the mental health context,[145] are downplayed in a model where even capable patients' views may be overridden. Thus, a different decision-making culture exists in respect of treatment for all patients with a mental disorder.

---

[140] This may explain why professionals interviewed in Victoria were more sceptical about the benefits of treatment reviews, when compared with reviews of admission or discharge.

[141] See M Donnelly, *Healthcare Decision-Making and the Law: Autonomy, Capacity and the Limits of Liberalism* (Cambridge, Cambridge University Press, 2010) ch 1.

[142] See M Donnelly, 'Capacity Assessment under the Mental Capacity Act 2005: Delivering on the Functional Approach?' (2009) 29 *Legal Studies* 464.

[143] O O'Neill, *Autonomy and Trust in Bioethics* (Cambridge, Cambridge University Press, 2002) 37.

[144] A Zigmond and A Holland, 'Unethical Mental Health Law: History Repeats Itself' [2000] *Journal of Mental Health Law* 49, 53; Bernadette McSherry, this volume, ch 16.

[145] See for example the participative aspects of the Mental Capacity Act (England and Wales) 2005 s 4; see also CRPD Art 12.

None of the jurisdictions discussed in this chapter is likely to change their underlying legal position regarding compulsion. Recent reform in England and Wales fell far short of a move to a capacity-based approach to consent to treatment[146] while, on ratifying the CRPD, Australia issued a declaration of its understanding that the Convention allows for compulsory 'assistance or treatment of persons, including measures taken for the treatment of mental disability, where such treatment is necessary, as a last resort and subject to safeguards'.[147] While one might argue that the jurisdictions should change their position, in these political circumstances, it would be a mistake to focus all of one's reform arguments on this issue alone. Therefore, the challenge for treatment reviews is to shift treatment culture in a pro-autonomy direction within a legal model which militates in favour of paternalism rather than the protection of patient rights.

While this chapter has been concerned primarily with evaluating existing review models rather than setting out new ones, it can make a number of suggestions regarding ways in which treatment reviews might be improved. First, issues of deference need to be addressed. Here, it is important to remember that recognition of one's epistemic limitations is an appropriate stance in reaching judgements. A judgement made without awareness of the relevant information may be flawed and certainly would not be trustworthy. However, this does not mean that reviewers cannot engage appropriately with treatment decisions; rather, it shows the need for training, education and commitment on the part of reviewers. It is important that reviewers, as well as the people about whom decisions are made, believe in the process of which they are a part.

Secondly, it is worth considering other options for review besides the individualised top-down model of review currently favoured. A case may be made that audit and accountability should play a greater role in addition to individualised reviews. As noted earlier, the SOAD model affords the possibility of access to information about important matters including prescribing practices and SOADs' reasons for decisions. However, the full accountability potential of the SOAD system is not currently being exploited. While it is not suggested that a generalised accountability measure should or could replace individualised reviews, it could help change prescribing culture and lead to more careful, patient-centred prescribing practices. Done properly, greater accountability and transparency regarding prescribing practices could also improve mental health service users' trust in the system. As Neil Manson and Onora O'Neill note, good systems of accountability 'can improve trustworthiness, and can provide useful evidence for placing trust intelligently'.[148]

---

[146] G Richardson, 'Balancing Autonomy and Risk: A Failure of Nerve in England and Wales' (2007) 30 *International Journal of Law and Psychiatry* 71.

[147] The full text of the Declaration is available at: www.un.org/disabilities; see Annegret Kämpf, this volume, ch 6. For a contrary view of the CRPD see Tina Minkowitz, this volume, ch 7.

[148] N Manson and O O'Neill, *Rethinking Informed Consent in Bioethics* (Cambridge, Cambridge University Press, 2007) 167.

Thirdly, an accessible appeal mechanism, supplemented by a requirement for the provision of information about rights and concrete obligations to facilitate access to the appeal process, should be considered. As noted above, it is unrealistic to expect patients to rely on judicial review to assert their rights in circumstances where a more detailed consideration of legal issues is appropriate. The availability of an effective appeal mechanism could also enhance patient trust in the system as well as protecting human rights.

These are just some preliminary suggestions. A great deal more work is needed perhaps leading ultimately to the development of international standards regarding treatment reviews. Any consideration of alternative approaches to treatment review needs to be grounded in a solid empirical understanding of what is achievable under various kinds of review models. It must also include the input of mental health service users. In both respects, these requirements do not just make good instrumental sense; they are also mandated under the CRPD.[149] However, if, as argued here, current treatment reviews are not providing effective protection for patient rights, it is essential to think about how to improve existing models and whether to create new ones.

---

[149] Art 31 requires that States Parties undertake to collect appropriate information, including statistical and research data to enable them to give effect to the Convention, while Art 33 requires that people with disabilities and their representatives should be involved in monitoring the Convention.

13

Mental Health Law and Its Discontents: A Reappraisal of the Canadian Experience*

JOAQUIN ZUCKERBERG

I. Introduction

This chapter reviews some fundamental questions about the nature of the implementation of mental health legislation dealing with civil committal by looking at the Canadian context. This appraisal is essential in addressing the limitation of rights-based legalism and in re-assessing its role and expectations in relation to persons with mental illnesses. It is hoped that this discussion will assist in the development of policy options for future legal reform initiatives in Canada and other jurisdictions looking to improve their legal systems.

Some of the problems identified are common to the enforcement of law in general. Some reveal inherent contradictions which are perhaps unique to mental health law. This does not necessarily disqualify rights-based legalism as a tool to advance the legal interests of mentally ill persons. It does underscore that mental health laws cannot be created in a social vacuum. Law-makers need to consider the context and culture to which legislation applies.

The chapter first gives an overview of the Canadian legal system and some unique features dealing with consent to treatment. Health in Canada is a provincial matter. Not every province in Canada faces the same challenges, because of differences in the type of legislation and review mechanisms adopted.

The following sections discuss some of the main challenges and dilemmas brought about by the adoption of rights-based legislation in Canada. They are: the application of the 'dangerousness' test; the requirement (or lack thereof) that a person be incapable before being involuntarily committed; the enforcement of

---

* The views expressed in this article are those of the author and do not necessarily reflect the views of any other person or agency.

procedural safeguards established by mental health legislation; and the legal battle over the interpretation of mental health legislation by drawing on criminal law principles. This attempt to import criminal law has also opened up a different though interconnected issue, namely, the role of mental health tribunals (MHTs) in reviewing health practitioners' decisions.

The last part of this chapter explores the questions of legal representation and appeals from MHTs, two essential areas of the review process which may need to be re-addressed in assessing the execution of mental health legislation.

II. Overview of the Canadian Legal System

Constitutionally, Canada has two levels of government, federal and provincial, the jurisdictions of which overlap in many respects. The Canadian Constitution assigns the main responsibility for health to the provinces. Provincial responsibilities include the delivery of medical services and the enactment of laws governing mental health, with each province possessing its own mental health laws. In addition, some provinces have more than one piece of legislation dealing with involuntary patients. For example, the Ontario Mental Health Act 1990[1] is the main legislation dealing with involuntary commitment, but the Ontario Health Care Consent Act 1996[2] sets out procedures and requirements for consent to medical treatment, which includes involuntary patients. These provincial laws were passed as part of a broad movement towards reform across Canada beginning in the late 1970s, which placed a new emphasis on 'legalism', including procedural fairness, improved procedures for assessing capacity, and enhanced protections for the autonomy and self-determination of persons with mental illness.

As with other legal systems of the Western world, Canadian provincial legislation has undergone significant changes which have shifted the legal framework from a paternalistic to a rights-based legal system[3] with a relatively sophisticated model of procedural safeguards—including, for example, the need for a physician's second opinion before committal, the patient's right to be notified of committal and right to review it, access to clinical records, and periodic reviews by a MHT—which in some jurisdictions surpass international legal standards.[4] A review of all of these safeguards is beyond the scope of this chapter.[5]

Perhaps one of the two most noticeable features of Canada's approach towards individuals with mental illnesses is the legal recognition that capable individuals

---

[1] Ontario Mental Health Act, RSO 1990, c M.7.

[2] Health Care Consent Act, 1996, SO 1996, ch 2, Sch A.

[3] A James, 'Psychiatric Power and Informed Consent in Post-World II Canada' (2001) 22(4) *Health Law Canada* 101.

[4] J Zuckerberg, 'International Human Rights for Mentally Ill Persons: The Ontario Experience' (2007) 30(6) *International Journal of Law and Psychiatry* 512.

[5] A comparative review of some of the aspects of these procedural safeguards across Canadian provinces has been conducted by JE Gray, MA Shone and PF Liddle, *Canadian Mental Health Law and Policy*, 2nd edn (Markham, LexisNexis Canada, 2008).

have the right to decide their own treatment regardless of the wisdom of their choice.[6] The best interests of the incapable person are therefore an irrelevant consideration when reviewing someone's capacity.[7] 'Best interest' criteria are therefore conspicuously absent from the provincial legal tests for civil committal. The second feature has been the enactment of the Canadian Charter of Rights and Freedoms[8] ('the Charter of Rights'), which has enabled challenges to a number of mental health laws on the basis of constitutional incompatibility.[9]

The following section reviews one of the main ways in which rights-based legalism has influenced Canadian mental health legislation, namely through the uniform adoption of the 'dangerousness' criteria throughout mental health legislation.

III. Dangerousness

The legal reforms mentioned above led to the abandonment of paternalistic approaches and the adoption of a 'dangerousness' standard for civil committal. This change was promoted on the assumption that 'dangerousness' provided a more objective criterion than other criteria and permitted less reliance on the expertise or discretion of the medical profession. This assumption has been shared by the Canadian courts, which have held that the absence of an 'objective' standard for civil committal, such as dangerousness, constituted a breach of a person's right against arbitrary detainment and imprisonment under the Charter of Rights and Freedoms.[10] However, whether dangerousness provides the intended objective standard or not has been increasingly challenged by the unreliability of assessments about risks of harm, as attested to by the increasing literature on this subject.[11] Some authors have gone even further and argued for the removal of the dangerousness criterion.[12]

---

[6]   *Starson v Swayze* [2003] 1 SCR 722.

[7]   *ibid.*

[8]   Enacted as Sch B to the Canada Act 1982 (UK) c 11.

[9]   Early on, in *Lussa v Health Science Centre* (1983) 9 CRR 350, the Manitoba Court of Queens Bench found that the patient's right under the Charter of Rights had been violated because she had not been properly notified of her rights upon detention.

[10]   *Thwaites v Health Sciences Centre Psychiatric Facility* [1988] 3 WWR 217.

[11]   N Rose, 'Unreasonable Rights: Mental Illness and the Limits of the Law' (1985) 12(2) *Journal of Law and Society* 199; J Cocozza and H Steadman, 'The Failure of Psychiatric Predictions of Dangerousness: Clear and Convincing Evidence' (1976) 29 *Rutgers Law Review* 1084; H Steadman, 'Attempting to Protect Patients Rights Under a Medical Model' (1979) 2 *International Journal of Law and Psychiatry* 185; N Walker, 'Dangerous People' (1978) 1 *International Journal of Law and Psychiatry* 37; H Steadman, 'From Dangerousness to Risk Assessment of Community Violence: Taking the Stock at the Turn of the Century' (2000) 28 *Journal of the American Academy of Psychiatry and the Law* 265.

[12]   MM Large, C Ryan, O Neilssen and R Hayes, 'The Danger of Dangerousness: Why We Must Remove the Dangerousness Criterion From Our Mental Health Acts' (2008) 34 *Journal of Medical Ethics* 877.

The difficulty of the 'dangerousness' test to provide a clear (and 'objective') guideline may also be explained by the law-maker's need to maintain a certain level of abstraction in order to enhance the applicability of the legislation. However, in the mental health context, this vagueness works against the 'objectiveness' upon which the goals of dangerousness criteria are based. Thus, judicial authorities have often found themselves thrown into legal battles over the meaning and scope of the dangerousness test. A discussion of some of the main legal points of contention illustrates the need to re-address those legal terms contained in the test of dangerousness.

A. 'Deterioration'

'Deterioration' is a ground included in many jurisdictions which have adopted the dangerousness test for involuntary admission.[13] A number of Canadian provinces have followed this approach as well.[14] For example, in Ontario the criteria for civil committal were expanded to apply to incapable patients with a recorded history of mental disorder, who may now be committed on the basis of 'substantial mental or physical deterioration'.[15] Although the inclusion of patients who would have not been otherwise committed under the previous existing 'dangerousness' criteria in this province may be been necessary, the ambiguity (or potential unlimited scope) of the 'mental' deterioration standard raises some questions as to whether it can provide a meaningful objective criterion and effective legal safeguard for patients. As an illustration, 'mental deterioration' has been found to include changes in behaviour and mood such as anger and agitation requiring security and seclusion[16] and even 'going from calmness to agitation'.[17] Thus, 'deterioration' may potentially be used to justify 'best interests' considerations. For example, reliance on a 'change in behaviour' which does not lead to 'harm' may conceal a paternalistic consideration. The legality of the criterion of 'substantial physical or mental deterioration', however, appears to have been settled when Manitoba mental health legislation replicating

---

[13] P Appelbaum, 'Almost a Revolution: An International Perspective on the Law of Involuntary Commitment' (1997) 25(2) *Journal of the American Academy of Psychiatry and the Law* 135.

[14] The provinces which include 'mental or physical deterioration' as a ground for involuntary status are British Columbia, Manitoba, Newfoundland & Labrador, Nova Scotia, Ontario and Saskatchewan.

[15] Before December 2000, Ontario's Mental Health Act only allowed involuntary certification on the basis of dangerousness. The Act was amended at that time to introduce a new ground, s 20(1.1), which permits the involuntary detention of members of a select group on the basis of need for treatment. Civil committal in Ontario can now be based on the old dangerousness provisions as well as on the new 'need for treatment' grounds.

[16] *Re SF*, 2007 CanLII 71271 (ON CCB).

[17] *Re SF*, 2007 CanLII 57801 (ON CCB).

these words survived a challenge under the Charter of Rights.[18] The determination of whether evidence advanced to prove 'deterioration' does not include extraneous paternalistic concerns has therefore been left to MHTs.

B. 'Likely'

Provincial legislation in Canada generally requires that the danger or harm that may ensue will be 'likely' to happen.[19] This requirement epitomises some inherent problems of the dangerousness test as shown by the judicial or quasi-judicial reviews of physicians' decisions.

The dangerousness test assumes that physicians have the expertise to foresee the 'likelihood' of the harm. For example, the role of a MHT is to review the adequacy of a physician's opinion and disallow any concern for the patient's best interest as grounds for civil committal. Physicians are therefore left to form their opinions based on their clinical experience in predicting behaviour. At the same time, mental health legislation does not generally require that there be evidence of an overt act that signals danger to the patient or others in order for that danger to be 'likely'.[20] Nor does legislation specify a required time period within which the 'likely' harm must occur.[21] 'Likelihood' may relate to a long-term or short-term probability. In Ontario, there is some limited guidance regarding the 'flexible' nature of the temporal element of the test of dangerousness.[22] The *event* (such as harm, impairment, deterioration and so on) must be anticipated within a reasonable time after discharge. 'Likelihood' includes an element of proximity.[23]

Given the limited legislative guidance and difficulties in foretelling 'likelihood', tribunal members are presumably left to assess the medical opinion regarding 'likelihood' by drawing on their own experience of whether harm or danger is 'likely' to happen in the specific matter before them. However, MHTs may often defer to the physician's opinion, given the view of the physician as an expert and the person most familiar with the patient's case. To borrow from Canadian jurisprudence on standards of review of administrative tribunals,[24] a MHT may end up only reviewing the *reasonableness* (a lower standard) and not the

---

[18] *Bobbie v Health Sciences Centre* [1989] 2 WWR 153 (Man QB).

[19] British Columbia, Quebec, Prince Edward Island and Nova Scotia are the exception. The test under s 17(c)(1) of Nova Scotia's Involuntary Psychiatric Treatment Act, SNS 2005, c 42 is arguably lower than in other provinces because it includes past occurrences as one ground for civil committal without the need to rely on a (future) likelihood of harm.

[20] *Azhar v Anderson* unreported, Ont Dist Ct (28 June 1985).

[21] An earlier version of Ontario's Mental Health Act included a requirement that the serious physical impairment be 'imminent'; however that condition was removed in the current legislation.

[22] *H (Re)*, 2005 CanLII 56630 (ON CCB).

[23] See, eg *Re WS*, 2004 CanLII 46820 (ON CCB); *Re LU* TO-03–0804 (ON CCB), unpublished; *Re HS* 2001 CanLII 8953 (ON CCB) and *Re DS* HA-04–1939 (ON CCB), unpublished.

[24] *New Brunswick (Board of Management) v Dunsmuir* [2008] 1 SCR 190.

correctness (higher standard) of the physician's assessment of 'likelihood'. This results in a degree of deference that may not have been intended by the legislation.

The difficulties involved in determining 'likelihood' become evident in the realm of civil litigation, when courts are asked to assess whether a doctor has failed to follow professional standards. In *Stefaniu v Ahmed*,[25] the patient had been an involuntary patient and his status was confirmed by Ontario's MHT. Two months later, the attending physician made the patient voluntary. A month later (and after being seen by another two physicians) the patient murdered his sister. The Court found that the attending physician had been negligent when she made him a voluntary patient.[26] In contrast, in *Buyze v Malla*[27] the lawsuit arose from the absconding of a voluntary patient from the health facility and his subsequent suicide. The court held that the physician had not breached the standard of care expected from a physician by failing to supervise the patient. The lack of consistency in these decisions attests to the uncertainty surrounding the assessment of likelihood of harm. With limited judicial guidance on this topic, both courts and MHTs continue to rely heavily on medical 'expertise' to determine this question.

C.   'Harm to Others'

The dangerousness test invariably includes harm to a third party as grounds for civil committal. The difficulty in determining whether a specific harm is 'likely' to happen is exacerbated when combined with the ambiguity of the concept of 'harm'. This is an important point that should not be understated. An overbroad interpretation of this concept may cover conduct that may not have been intended to be regulated by the legislation.

Canadian case law has been limited to the consideration of the constitutionality of the term 'serious harm', which is used in a number of provincial statutes. The term has been found not to infringe section 9 (freedom from arbitrary detainment or imprisonment), nor to contravene the principles of fundamental justice protected by section 7 (right to life, liberty, and security of the person) of the Charter of Rights.[28] 'Serious' harm has been found to include harms that relate to the social, family, vocational or financial life of the patient.[29] However, the courts have not dealt with mental harm caused to a third person irrespective

---

[25]   *Ahmed v Stefaniu*, 2004 CanLII 30093 (ON SC); appeal dismissed by the Ontario Court of Appeal 2006 CanLII 34973.

[26]   *ibid.* One of the expert witnesses is quoted by Spiegel J, p 11 at [33] as endorsing the view that 'the best predictor of violence is past violence'. Curiously, the Consent and Capacity Board, Ontario's MHT, has generally rejected past violence as *determinative* of likelihood of harm.

[27]   *Buyze v Malla*, 2008 CanLII 865 (ON SC).

[28]   *Bobbie v Health Sciences Centre* [1989] 2 WWR 153, and *McCorkell v Director of Riverview Hospital*, 1993 CanLII 1200 (BC SC).

[29]   *ibid.*

of any harm to the patient. The term 'mental' (as opposed to 'physical') harm lends itself to different interpretations. As with 'mental' deterioration, there is little guidance as to what 'harm' to someone else may include. Should harm to others include *psychological* harm to a third person, for example, as a result of a previous sexual assault? Or is physical injury necessary?[30] An in-depth review of provincial legislation in Canada is beyond the scope of this chapter. However, it is worth mentioning that provincial statutes vary in their approach to this issue.

In Ontario, harm to others must also be 'bodily'. However, this has not resolved the debate over whether 'mental' harm can be used as grounds for civil committal. Some legal guidance regarding the meaning of 'mental' harm has been sought through reliance on the courts' interpretation of the Criminal Code definition of 'bodily harm', that is, that the latter includes 'psychological' harm.[31] The strength of this interpretation is not clear since, as discussed below, Canadian courts have been reluctant to import principles of criminal law into the mental health context.

A different attempt to define the boundaries of harm to another person distinguishes between harm to the brain and to the mind. Thus, while agreeing that 'the brain (is) an essential physical part of anyone's body and the essence of self', it has been suggested that 'bodily' harm requires harm to the brain rather than to the mind.[32] This dubious distinction between 'brain' and 'mind' provides limited guidance as to whether psychological harm to a third person should be used as a criterion for civil committal. What is certain is that if the psychological harm likely to be caused to another is itself likely to result in serious bodily harm to that other person (all of which must be reasonably foreseeable), then the threat of such consequential bodily harm would satisfy the requirement of 'harm to others'. This reasoning is often enough to dispose of the matter without the need to determine whether the 'harm' envisioned by the legislation is to include 'mental' or 'psychological' harm.[32a] What is evident is that this is an issue which in some jurisdictions needs to be addressed by legislative amendments.

While some jurisdictions require 'bodily' harm to the other person, as in Ontario,[33] others require the 'protection' of others[34] and 'danger' to 'others'.[35] Yet a number of provinces only require 'harm'[36] and New Brunswick has gone as far as to expressly include 'psychological' harm to others in its legislation.

---

[30] *Re HJZ*, 2007 CanLII 23779 (ON CCB).
[31] *Re LI* TO-03-0898 (Ontario Consent and Capacity Board), unpublished. The CCB relied on the Supreme Court of Canada decision of *R v McCraw* [1991] 3 SCR 72.
[32] *Re LA*, 2007 CanLII 19770 (ON CCB).
[32a] For a recent attempt to establish some criteria for 'psychological' harm, see *Re JW*, 2010 CanLII 9881 (ON CCB).
[33] Northwest Territories and Yukon.
[34] British Columbia.
[35] Alberta and Quebec.
[36] Manitoba, Newfoundland & Labrador and Saskatchewan.

Other jurisdictions have addressed this issue by specifically including 'severe mental suffering to others' as a ground for civil committal.[37] In Australia, former New South Wales legislation incorporated 'harassment beyond normal social behaviour that a reasonable person would consider intolerable' in its civil committal provisions.[38] The latter approach represented a very flexible interpretation of harm, which did not require physical *or even mental* harm (the Act was subsequently amended and currently includes a provision that expressly excludes 'anti-social behaviour' as a ground for civil committal[39]). This type of provision may allow physicians to avoid dealing with difficult evidentiary issues involved in determining mental harm to a third person the assessment of which may be beyond their purview, but may also open the door for the detention of individuals whose conduct does not conform to social standards. This underscores a more fundamental problem with the 'dangerousness' test: it may allow the introduction of the decision-maker's subjective view of what is and what is not acceptable social behaviour.

Further research on the application of each jurisdiction's legislation is required to assess whether there is a significant difference in the outcomes of these different approaches. The question as to whether 'harm' to others should be broadly or narrowly defined still remains largely unanswered by the courts.

IV. Capacity and Civil Committal

The previous section discussed various dilemmas posed by the adoption of the dangerousness criteria. This subsection examines a related problem caused by the adoption of mental health legislation with no link established between the need to treat and involuntary committal.

Canadian provinces have adopted different legislative approaches to accommodate the legal need for obtaining the patient's consent to treatment with the dangerousness test. Some jurisdictions require that the person be incapable of consenting to treatment as part of the involuntary status criteria.[40] This ensures that only patients who can be treated will be committed. Therefore, it does not allow for the committal of patients who may not be treated because of a capable refusal but who might cause harm. Other provinces have adopted models that

---

[37]   This is the case in Israel. See J Bazak, 'Rights of the Patient vs. Rights of the Public in the Treatment of the Mentally Ill Law-1991' (1995) 32 *Israel Journal of Psychiatry and Related Sciences* 94.

[38]   Mental Health Act 1983 (NSW) s 5(1)(b).

[39]   Mental Health Act 2007 (NSW) s 16(1)(l).

[40]   Manitoba, Newfoundland & Labrador, Nova Scotia and Saskatchewan.

allow the treatment of capable patients with judicial permission[41] or that simply 'deem' involuntary patients incapable to consent to treatment.[42]

Ontario and the Yukon have adopted an alternative approach by separating capacity and civil committal in the legislation. Thus, an involuntary patient may not be treated if there is a capable refusal. The unintended consequence of leaving some involuntary patients untreated may sometimes result in the latter being confined to psychiatric wards without treatment, or 'warehousing'.[43] Thus, psychiatric facilities may potentially be left to fulfill a custodial, rather than a therapeutic role. This debate has been fuelled in Ontario by the absence of a purpose provision in that province's Mental Health Act.

Courts have addressed this question in a tangential manner. The Ontario Court of Appeal has held that detention without treatment may be a justifiable purpose when dealing with an inmate if it prevents harsher confinement conditions than are necessary to prevent the dangerous effects of a patient's mental illness.[44] In reaching this conclusion, the Court of Appeal held that Ontario's legislative scheme is designed to protect persons who pose a danger to themselves or to others. This was found to be consistent with section 7 under the Charter of Rights.[45] Subsequently, the protection of persons who pose a danger to themselves or to others was used to uphold the civil committal of certain dangerous offenders in Ontario for whom no effective treatment had been shown to exist.[46] Yet, it is not clear whether jurisprudence has evolved to the point where the protection of the patient and other members of society could be argued to be a valid purpose *independent* of the patient's need to be treated.

Whether or not health care facilities are the best equipped institutions to fulfill a custodial role is a question which is beyond the scope of this chapter. There is evidence, however, that decreasing resources in medical care have somehow attenuated warehousing as health practitioners juggle to allocate limited beds to

[41] See, eg Alberta and New Brunswick.

[42] British Columbia Mental Health Act s 31(1) [RSBC 1996] Chapter 288. This provision arguably conflicts with the Charter of Rights and the common law requirement of the need to consent to treatment.

[43] M Gupta, 'All Locked Up with Nowhere to Go: Treatment Refusal in the Involuntarily Hospitalized Psychiatric Population in Canada' in I Freckelton and K Diesfeld (eds), *Involuntary Detention and Civil Commitment: International Perspectives* (Aldershot, Ashgate, 2003).

[44] *Khan v St Thomas Psychiatric Hospital* (1992) 7 OR (3d) 303 (CA). The court indicated that '[t]he point is made more apparent if one considers an inmate who, because of mental illness, presents a high risk of injury to herself or himself. It would be open to a physician to conclude that an inmate who presents a high suicide risk will likely injure himself or herself unless transferred to the custody of a psychiatric facility. This conclusion would remain sound even though extraordinary custodial precautions in jail could alleviate the risk of suicide' (at 296).

[45] The Ontario legislative scheme setting up involuntary admissions has also been found to comply with the Charter of Rights in *Clark v Clark* (1982) 40 OR (2d) 383 (Co Ct) and *CB v Sawadsky* [2005] OJ No 3682. Similarly, the British Columbia civil committal provisions were upheld in *McCorkell v Director of Riverview Hospital Review Panel*, 1993 CanLII 1200 (BC SC).

[46] *Penetanguishene Mental Health Centre v Stock* [1994] OJ No 1545 (Gen Div) at [11].

only the most serious 'treatable' persons with mental illnesses.[47] These findings are compatible with studies which have indicated that the introduction of the dangerousness criteria has not in fact substantially affected the rate of involuntary admissions in a number of North American jurisdictions.[48]

Further, civil committal legislation which requires consent to treatment is predicated upon the need to further individual autonomy and the doctrine of informed consent. This reliance on informed consent has been criticised as failing to reflect the reality of the patient.[49] Presenting the competent patient as the sole decision-maker may ignore the multiple meanings of, and motivations for, a patient's acceptance or refusal of treatment.[50] The dichotomy created by legislation based on principles of autonomy may exclude alternative models of decision-making that may enhance a patient's self-determination in different ways.[51]

It has also been argued that disclosure and consent in physician-patient interactions are in fact generally driven by the need of physicians to convince patients to accept the proposed treatment. Patients may not be informed about the risks and benefits of alternative treatments or the uncertainties intrinsic in most treatment options.[52] Another criticism levelled against the paradigm of informed consent on which this model of civil commitment is built stems from the lack of patient participation in sharing the burden of the decision[53] and the influence of the language employed by the health care worker on the patient's decisions.[54] Additionally, decisions to make a finding of incapacity in a busy

---

[47] M Gupta (above n 43).

[48] RM Bagby and L Atkinson, 'The Effects of Legislative Reform on Civil Commitment Admission Rates: A Critical Analysis' (1988) 6 *Behavioral Sciences and the Law* 45; NC Beck, LR Houge, C Fraps, C Perry and L Fernstemaker, 'Patient Diagnostic, Behavioural and Demographics Variables Associated with Changes in Civil Commitment Procedures' (1984) 40 *Journal of Clinical Psychology* 364.

[49] R Burt, *Taking Care of Strangers: The Rule of Law in Doctor-Patient Relations* (New York, Free Press, 1979) 117–18 and 136. Burt also rejects the converse, a regime of 'doctor [or judge] rule'.

[50] See *ibid*, 1–21, 121–3, recounting the experience of a severely burned patient, who repeatedly asked that treatment for his burns cease so he could die, and exploring the patient's reasons for rejecting treatment. The patient was treated despite his objections, and went on to enrol in and successfully complete law school. Burt concludes that whether the patient's choice was ultimately or solely other-directed, it was very much influenced by his interaction with those around him.

[51] See Israel Doron comparing different models of decision-making guardianship in I Doron, 'Elder Guardianship Kaleidoskope: A Comparative Perspective' (2002) 16 *International Journal of Law Policy and the Family* 368.

[52] BR Rutherford, K Aizaga, J Sneed and SP Roose, 'A Survey of Psychiatric Residents' Informed Consent Practices' (2007) 68(4) *Journal of Clinical Psychiatry* 558.

[53] J Katz, *The Silent World of Doctor and Patient* (New York, Free Press, 1984) 26. See also R Fox, *The Sociology of Medicine: A Participant Observer's View* (Englewood Cliffs NJ, Prentice Hall, 1989) 248–52. For comments to the same effect in the Canadian context, see B Dickens, 'Decision-making in Terminal Care: The Life of One's Days and the Days of One's Life' (1986–1987) 51 *Saskatchewan Law Review* 1.

[54] See BJ McNeil, SG Pauker, HC Sox and A Tversky, 'On Elicitation of Preferences for Alternative Therapies' (1982) 306 *New England Journal of Medicine* 1259. The authors note the discrepancies in

medical practice may sometimes turn on whether the patient consents to the treatment proposed, rather than on the legal test for capacity.[55] Mental health laws may fail to acknowledge the use of coercion on people with mental illnesses.[56] The extent of these medical practices requires further research in order to facilitate a better assessment of the implementation of civil commitment criteria based on a patient's incapacity. It may very well be that the claim of legal models of involuntary committal, which require consent from an involuntary patient in order to provide better protection for a patient's self-determination and autonomy, may be out of touch with medical practice. If that is the case, it raises a critical question concerning the limits of such models in modifying the practices of the medical profession and the need to direct resources towards the education of health practitioners.

V. Procedural Safeguards

Incorporating procedural safeguards into legislation has raised questions about adequate remedies for breaches of such safeguards and the role of MHTs and courts in policing those breaches. This is a highly divisive issue, which finds supporters and objectors on each side of the divide. MHTs are for the most part created by legislation and their jurisdiction is limited to their enabling statute. They therefore have no authority to provide remedies not contained in the legislation, such as monetary compensation. Nor have they generally been given any broad monitoring authority over health care facilities.[57]

Should the failure to follow a legal procedure required for civil committal be grounds for rescinding the involuntary status of a patient? It has been argued that this is necessary if the legislation is intended to have some enforcement mechanism.[58] On the other hand, a failure to follow procedures should not affect the merits of the decision to commit a person. Any remedies arising from a breach of a patient's procedural rights should be pursued through civil litigation (for

patients' treatment choice when the treatment is spoken of in terms of one's percentage chances of living rather than one's chances of dying with that particular therapy. For similar findings relative to the significance of the language used in the context of competent patients' decisions regarding Do Not Resuscitate Orders, see D Murphy, 'Do Not Resuscitate Orders: Time For Re-appraisal in Long-Term-Care Institutions' (1988) 260 *Journal of the American Medical Association* 2098.

[55] See, eg *Re J*, 2008 CanLII 45526 (ON CCB)

[56] See John Petrila, this volume, ch 15.

[57] Newfoundland & Labrador's Mental Health Care and Treatment Act, SNL 2006, c M-9.1 contains a unique provision authorising this province's MHT to make a *non-binding* recommendation to an administrator of a health facility where a violation of a patient's rights has been determined (s 64(c)).

[58] AA Dhir, 'The Maelstrom of Civil Commitment in Ontario: Using Examinations Conducted during Periods of Unlawful Detention to Form the Basis of Subsequent Involuntary Detention under Ontario's Mental Health Act' (2003) 24(2) *Health Law Canada* 9.

example via false imprisonment or battery) or criminal proceedings[59] against the physician or care facility, or by laying a complaint with the professional regulatory body to which the health practitioner belongs.[60]

These two opposing positions are often blurred by the particular procedural safeguard and wording of the provision in question. For instance, should any failure to follow procedural safeguards lead to the termination of a civil committal? If not, what type of circumstances call for termination? Is bad faith or egregious conduct by the health providers required?[61]

The introduction of procedural safeguards also raises questions regarding the legal consequences of the actions of third parties who are also responsible for ensuring the protection of the patient's rights. In Ontario, rights advisors who are independent of the facility where the involuntary patient resides must visit the latter in a timely fashion.[62] Does the failure of these third parties, over whom the physician or facility exercises no or minimal control, invalidate the committal?[62a]

More importantly, declaring a civil committal invalid on the basis of failure to follow a procedural safeguard may not in fact advance the patient's interests. Physicians may restart the certification process leading to civil committal, when the basis for the invalidity was 'procedural' and not 'substantive'. The patient may then be subject to a further committal as soon as the MHT renders a decision based on a failure to follow a procedural safeguard.[63]

The case law dealing with the consequences of failures to follow procedural safeguards reveals complicated and sometimes conflicting decisions by MHTs. This adds uncertainty to the review process and may result in frustration for parties appearing before the MHT, who may sometimes find themselves having

---

[59] In addition to criminal prosecutions under the Criminal Code, a number of mental health statutes create quasi-criminal charges for failure to comply with the legislation. See, eg s 80 of the Ontario Mental Health Act, providing that '[e]very person who contravenes any provision of this Act or the regulations is guilty of an offence and on conviction is liable to a fine of not more than $25,000'.

[60] The effectiveness of these options in Ontario has been questioned. See, eg L Patton, '"These Regulations Aren't Just Here to Annoy You": The Myth of Statutory Safeguards, Patient Rights and Charter Values in Ontario's Mental Health System' (2008) 25 *Windsor Review of Legal and Social Issues* 9. In the European context, see *Storck v Germany* (2006) 43 EHRR 96, where the European Court of Human Rights observed that ex post facto sanctions, in the shape of criminal and civil liability for wrongful detention, do not provide effective protection for the mentally disordered.

[61] The CCB has in a number of decisions held that, if hospital staff were found to have dealt with a patient in an 'egregious' fashion, a panel might for that reason refuse to confirm his or her involuntary status even though the criteria relied on for certification were met at the time of the hearing: see *TS v O'Dea* [2004] OJ No 36; *Re ER* TO 03–0116, unpublished; *Re S* PE-03–0137, unpublished; *Re XX* TO 03–1038, unpublished; *Re ST* TO 03–1221 and 1222, unpublished; *Re SJC* TO 03–1470 and 1503, unpublished; *Re HB* HA-03–0604, unpublished. The Consent and Capacity Board has used this option only once in *Re M*, 2008 CanLII 46900.

[62] Ontario Mental Health Act s 38(3).

[62a] See eg *Re PC*, 2007 (CanLII) 43888 (ON CCB) and *Re JM*, TO 03-1349, unpublished (ON CCB).

[63] In instances when the patient has successfully challenged a committal on procedural grounds, the CCB has encouraged parties to redo the process properly in order to deal with the merits of the application before the tribunal adjourns. See, eg *Re T*, 2008 CanLII 51753 (ON CCB).

to address complicated legal arguments which go beyond the merits of the grounds for involuntary committal, often without the assistance of counsel.

Some jurisdictions, such as Newfoundland and Labrador, have recently amended their mental health legislation to ban challenges to committal on the basis of 'technical' errors.[64] However, whether 'technical' errors equal 'procedural' grounds is not apparent. In any case, the distinction between what is 'procedural' and 'substantive' is not always clear.[65] For example, the requirement that a second medical opinion be sought before a certificate of involuntary status is issued can be considered to be either part of the 'substantive' criteria of involuntary status or a 'procedural' step. Future jurisprudence will be required to define the extent of the application of provisions banning challenges on 'technical' grounds.

In addition, the legislation of Newfoundland and Labrador contains a unique provision authorising the MHT to make a non-binding recommendation to an administrator of a health facility where a violation of a patient's rights has been determined.[66] The power to make recommendations mixes the models of an adjudicative agency with a commission of inquiry (it is worth noting that most Canadian MHTs already give their own members similar powers to the ones given to commissioners appointed under the provincial public inquiries legislation[67]). Given the lack of alternative legal remedies for patients, this may be a promising model for the enforcement of procedural safeguards before MHTs. The combination of an adjudicative model of decision-making with a model predicated on the basis of commissions of inquiry may also provide the basis for a future expansion of the jurisdiction of MHTs. That is, the role of MHTs could also be expanded to *non-binding* recommendations dealing with other matters, such as hospital policies and the provision of non-discriminatory services. This new role should be carefully delineated to avoid the risks of administrative agencies becoming de facto executive agencies or going beyond the original mandate.[68] It remains to be seen whether amendments to mental health legislation such as in Newfoundland and Labrador will remain an isolated attempt or signal a new legislative trend to deal with the uncertainty resulting from the introduction of procedural safeguards in the mental health context.

---

[64] Section 72 of Newfoundland & Labrador's Mental Health Care and Treatment Act, SNL 2006, c M-9.1, allows that province's MHT to confirm a certificate 'notwithstanding a technical defect or error in a certificate of involuntary admission or certificate of renewal'.

[65] For a discussion of this problem in the criminal law context, see GP Fletcher, *Basic Concepts of Criminal Law* (New York, Oxford University Press, 1998).

[66] Newfoundland & Labrador's Mental Health Care and Treatment Act, SNL 2006, c M-9.1, s 64(c).

[67] See, eg Alberta, Manitoba, New Brunswick, Newfoundland & Labrador, Saskatchewan.

[68] Newfoundland & Labrador's MHT has developed a practice by which it recommends *treatment* and changes in hospital policy aimed at the whole system, not for a particular patient, without explicit authority to do so. This has led to complaints from the medical profession about the tribunal exceeding its lack of authority and the impossibility of 'complying' with such recommendations in certain cases.

VI. Importing Criminal Law

A recurrent topic underlying some of the questions raised by the adoption of legalism in Canada is the attempt to use criminal law principles to guide the interpretation of mental health legislation. By and large this attempt favours a patient's case by advancing a stricter interpretation of the law on the basis of the nature and seriousness of the rights affected by the operation of the legislation. In spite of this, Canadian courts have shared the same reluctance as their counterparts in the United States of America to apply criminal law principles when dealing with mental health law, often by distinguishing between the aims of criminal and mental health legislation.[69]

In *Edmonton Journal v Alberta (Attorney-General)*,[70] the Supreme Court of Canada used the 'contextual approach' to recognise 'that a particular right or freedom may have a different value depending on the context'. In *McCorkell v Riverview Hospital*,[71] British Columbia's Supreme Court adopted the contextual approach in rejecting attempts to make the detention of criminals analogous to committal of the mentally disordered.

> [s]tatutes dealing with criminal law are penal in nature; incarceration is a punishment of culpable individuals and serves the objectives of public safety and denunciation of crime. The [British Columbia] Mental Health Act involuntarily detains people only for the purpose of treatment; the punitive element is wholly absent.[72]

Equally, courts have referred to the different objectives of mental health and criminal law in finding that the resort to a committal process at the expiry of a criminal sentence does not amount to a disguised criminal proceeding, since all assessments and determinations are performed by health practitioners who have no connections to the penal system.[73] The courts have also distinguished between criminal and mental health contexts when dealing with mandatory Coroner's inquests into the deaths of prisoners and of involuntary patients.[74]

---

[69] The United States Supreme Court rejected the characterisation of civil commitment as fundamentally punitive in *Addington v Texas*, 441 US 418 (1978), rejecting an argument that the evidentiary standard in commitment hearings should be 'beyond a reasonable doubt'; and in *Kansas v Hendricks*, 521 US 346 (1997), holding that a patient's treatability was not a necessary legal requirement to a constitutionally valid use of civil commitment under Sexually Violent Predator statutes. See discussion in John Petrila, this volume, ch 15.

[70] *Edmonton Journal v Alberta (Attorney-General)* [1989] 2 SCR 1326, 1355–6.

[71] *McCorkell v Director of Riverview Hospital* (1993) 81 BCLR (2d) 273.

[72] *ibid*, at [90].

[73] In *Penetanguishene Mental Health Centre v Stock* [1994] OJ No 1545 (Gen Div) at [9], the Court also referred to the different objectives of the Criminal Code of Canada and Ontario's Mental Health Act: '[t]he former is a penal statute while the latter is a protective statute, designed to protect persons who pose a danger to themselves or to others'.

[74] In *Ontario (Attorney General) v Ontario Human Rights Commission*, 2007 CanLII 56481, the Ontario Divisional Court held that s 10 of Ontario's Coroners Act, RSO 1990, c C.37, did not violate s 1 of Ontario's Human Rights Code, RSO 1990, c H.19, because it did not discriminate on the ground of disability.

A.   The Fruit of the Poisonous Tree

Nowhere is the reluctance of the Canadian judiciary to consider mental health law as being a purely civil matter more patent than in the challenges to the use of 'improperly' obtained evidence by MHTs.

MHTs are usually given broad powers to admit any type of evidence, subject to its relevance.[75] Thus, strict rules of evidence used by the courts do not usually apply to MHTs. Early on, with the introduction of rights-based mental health legislation, the courts established that, in the interest of an expeditious review,[76] a tribunal's admission and reliance on hearsay evidence does not violate section 15 (right to equal protection and benefit of the law without discrimination) or section 7 of the Charter of Rights and Freedoms.[77] This is because mentally disordered persons were found to fall into a special class of persons who require special legislative treatment for their own protection and that of society.[78] Similarly, a MHT can rely on medical opinion which is based largely on previous hospital records, which are hearsay by nature.[79]

The courts' rejection of strict rules of evidence is exemplified by the case of *Re LH*.[80] The patient had been admitted to a psychiatric facility and found incapable with respect to treatment. At some point after the finding was made, it became clear that the written form required to notify the patient of the finding could not be found, nor could the physician prove that rights advice—which is required under Ontario mental health legislation in these circumstances—had been provided. The physician then conducted a further reassessment of the appellant's capacity with respect to the proposed treatment. The MHT confirmed the finding of incapacity by relying on the evidence with respect to the results of the

---

[75]   See, eg Ontario's Statutory Powers Procedure Act, RSO 1990, c S.22, s 15.

[76]   Provincial mental health laws require that hearings before the tribunal be held expeditiously. For example, s 75(2) of the Ontario Health Care Consent Act, SO 1996, ch 2 requires that hearings 'begin within seven days after the day the tribunal receives an application'. These requisites are generally accompanied by stringent time requirements which must be met by the detaining authorities. Thus, certificates of involuntary admission range from the shorter initial period of two weeks (Ontario) to 12 months (Prince Edward Island). The validity of a first and subsequent certificate of detention varies according to each province. In New Brunswick and Alberta it is one month (see, eg Alberta's Mental Health Act s 39), in British Columbia one month, three months and six months thereafter (British Columbia's Mental Health Act s 24), in Manitoba there is an initial period of three weeks and a repeating three-month period for renewals (Manitoba's Mental Health Act s 21(4)) while other provinces have progressive timeframes, such as Ontario's initial period of two weeks, first renewal of one month, second renewal of two months and third and subsequent renewals of three months (Ontario's Mental Health Act s 20(4)).

[77]   *Dayday v MacEwan* (1987) 62 OR (2d) 588, 596. See also *Chandrasena v McDougald* [1989] OJ No 1743.

[78]   *Dayday v MacEwan* (1987) 62 OR 588, 596.

[79]   'The professional opinion of a medical expert which is required by the Mental Health Act necessarily involves an examination of medical charts and a previous history of the patient'. *Rzepski v McCurley* [1990] OJ No 1302 (Ont Dist Ct). See also generally *Starnaman v Penetanguishene Mental Health Centre* (Ont Ct (Gen Div)) [1994] OJ No 1958, at [38]–[40].

[80]   *Re LH*, 2007 CanLII 57084 (ON SC).

treatment of the patient during the period before a new assessment was done and proper notification and rights advice was provided.

On appeal, the patient argued that the Board erred in admitting and considering the evidence obtained during the period when the appellant's legal rights had been breached.[81] The Ontario Superior Court held that where a patient's rights have been interfered with, not all evidence with respect to treatment subsequently provided should be per se inadmissible and not available for consideration by the treating physician and therefore by the tribunal. The tribunal was authorised to admit and consider the evidence concerning the appellant's prior treatment during the 'illegal' period.[82] This decision arguably also applies to the use of evidence obtained from an 'illegal' period in tribunal reviews of civil committal.

The examples above indicate how judicial authorities have shaped the scope of protection of procedural safeguards. The distinction between mental health and criminal law used by the judicial authorities invariably leads to a narrower reading of the patients' rights and remedies. However, while it is true that the purposes of criminal and mental health law are different, what the courts have found to be the purposes of the latter (ie the protection of the public and patient) do not necessarily need to lead to a narrower reading of the patient's rights. In other words, the courts have yet to provide a theory explaining why the lack of a punitive element in mental health legislation inevitably narrows the scope of protection conferred by procedural safeguards.

VII. Role of the Mental Health Tribunal

The introduction of rights-based legalism has not only fuelled the drive to compare mental health law to criminal law but opened a debate about the role of an MHT in overseeing decisions made by health practitioners. Should proceedings before an MHT be 'adversarial', given the seriousness of the rights involved? Or should they be inquisitorial, in light of the 'non-criminal' role that courts have found mental health legislation fulfills and the more flexible rules of evidence which apply to administrative agencies in general?

---

[81] The attempt to use evidentiary principles of criminal law in this case is made obvious (*ibid*, at [30]) where the Court stated that '[t]he question for consideration is whether the violation of the appellant's rights in September, 2006 '*taints*' the evidence of the treatment which followed to the extent that it is inadmissible in respect of the proceeding before the [Consent and Capacity] Board?' (emphasis added).

[82] 'The evidence is clearly relevant to the issue before the Board. One of the fundamental issues which the Board has to consider is the negative and positive benefits of the proposed treatment. Given that the appellant had already received such treatment, the evidence in respect thereto was important. Further, once properly admitted, the question of weight to be given to it was a matter for the Board'. *ibid* at [35].

An adversarial system is premised on the assumption that each dispute involves opposing sides. These adversaries will each present the best evidence and argument in favour of his or her case to an impartial adjudicator. Proceedings are essentially controlled by the parties to the dispute and there is emphasis on the presentation of oral argument by counsel. The role of the decision-maker is more reactive than proactive.

Thus, the adversarial system assumes, because there are two opposing parties, each with an interest in bringing forth the best evidence and in revealing the weaknesses of the opponent's case, that truth and justice will prevail. In the context of an MHT, where the physician, the patient or both may appear unrepresented, this may not be the case.[83] There may often be evidence which neither party produces. Furthermore, where the opposing parties are unequally matched, the system is susceptible to failure. This is especially true at MHTs where the patient is self-represented or only one of the parties has counsel (in Ontario this is generally the patient).

The adversarial approach is also predicated on the basis that its rigidity regarding legal standards better protects the rights of patients. However, several commentators have pointed to the fact that such legal standards have often been relaxed when dealing with mentally ill persons.[84] For example, most MHTs in Canada use a tripartite 'professional-based' panel composed of a physician, a public member and a lawyer member.[85] Other models used by administrative tribunals, such as the 'representational' model, under which two of the three tribunal members act as representatives of the parties (that is, physician and patient), were abandoned in the Canadian context given the bias concerns regarding the positions the 'representative-members' took.[86] Still, is the

---

[83] The various pieces of legislation which establish the jurisdiction of MHTs do not specifically set out which party is responsible to prove that a certificate of involuntary status should be upheld. In Ontario, both the court (see, eg *Azhar v Anderson*, unreported, 28 June 1985 (Ont Dist Ct) 7) and the CCB have consistently held that the burden of proof is on the health practitioner whose decision is being challenged (a finding of incapacity or the issuance of a certificate of involuntary admission). This is not always the case in other jurisdictions, which may place the onus of proof on the applicant (that is, the patient). See, eg s 72 of the Mental Health Act 1983 (England and Wales).

[84] The reasons for this flexibility stem from shifts in judicial philosophy and the biases and prejudices of those charged with protecting the rights of mentally ill persons. This also affects the quality of representation. M Perlin, 'Fatal Assumption: A Critical Evaluation of the Role of Counsel in Mental Disability Cases' (1992) 16(1) *Law and Human Behavior* 39; M Perlin, K Gould and D Dorfman, 'Therapeutic Jurisprudence and the Civil Rights of Institutionalized Mentally Disabled Persons: Hopeless Oxymoron or Path to Redemption?' in D Wexler and B Winick (eds), *Law in a Therapeutic Key: Developments in Therapeutic Jurisprudence* (Durham NC, Carolina Academic Press, 1996); M Perlin, *The Hidden Prejudice: Mental Disability on Trial* (Washington DC, American Psychological Association, 2000).

[85] See, eg British Columbia, Manitoba, Newfoundland & Labrador, Nova Scotia, Ontario and Prince Edward Island. Alberta Mental Health Panels have four members, one of whom is a physician and one a psychiatrist. This model is based on the assumption that the lawyer and medical member bring their professional expertise while the public member provides and represents the view of the public.

[86] The British Columbia Mental Health Review Board was brought into force by amendments to that province's Mental Health Act in April 2005 to replace a longstanding idiosyncratic BC model of

'professional-based' model completely free from bias or the appearance of it?[86a] Tribunal members belonging to the medical profession may tend to agree with health practitioners appearing before an MHT or be given too much deference by the other members, as some data from a number of jurisdictions points out.[87] More research is necessary to assess the extent of the effect that a member's professional background has on the outcome of cases.[88] If that is the case, does the fact that the member is left in a minority properly address this concern?[89] What other alternatives to the 'professional-based' model are available?[90]

More importantly, the assumption that a relaxation of rules of procedure will necessarily lead to a similar relaxation of rules of procedural fairness before MHTs and paternalistic considerations must be questioned.[91] Whether reviews conducted by MHTs are inquisitorial or adversarial in nature may not be as determinative of the outcome of the hearing as the capacity and expertise of

---

party-appointed members for review panel hearings. Under the old Mental Health Act, every review panel hearing was conducted by a three-member panel consisting of a physician appointed by the detaining facility, a person appointed by the detained patient, and a chairperson from a pool of chairpersons appointed for terms of years by the BC Minister of Health under the Mental Health Act. This model raised bias concerns about facilities appointing their own medical staff to panels and patients appointing friends and others with no requirement of impartiality or expertise. The new legislation provides for government-appointed members similar to the rest of Canada. The panel must be composed of a medical, legal and community member who must be neither a physician nor a lawyer.

[86a] See, *DB v Singh*, 2007 CanLII 40204 (ON SC) & *R (PD) v West Midlands and North West Mental Health Review Tribunal* (2004) EWCA Civ 311.

[87] G Richardson and D Machin, 'Doctors on Tribunals: A Confusion of Roles' (2000) 176 *British Journal of Psychiatry* 110, 112.

[88] Since 2005, the CCB has rendered two decisions in which a member dissented with the majority's determination to rescind a certificate of involuntary status. In both of them the dissenter was the physician member. This is of course a very limited number of cases to support a conclusion (CCB database, updated as of January 2009).

[89] A panel of a MHT may be unduly influenced by the medical member's view as revealed by a study of the English Mental Health Review Tribunal. See G Richardson and D Machin, 'Doctors on Tribunals: A Confusion of Roles' (2000) 176 *British Journal of Psychiatry* 110, 115; E Perkins, *Decision-making in Mental Health Review Tribunals* (London, Policy Studies Institute, 2003). In the Australian context, see V Topp, M Thomas and M Ingvarson, *Lacking Insight: Involuntary Patient Experience of the Victorian Mental Health Review Board* (Melbourne, Mental Health Legal Centre 2008) available at: www.communitylaw.org.au/clc_mentalhealth/cb_pages/images/Lacking_Insight.pdf.

[90] Section 34(4) of the United Nations Convention on the Rights of Persons with Disabilities, UN GA Res A/61/611 (2006) provides that the members of the Committee on the Rights of Persons with Disabilities established by the Convention 'shall be elected by States Parties, consideration being given to equitable geographical distribution, representation of the different forms of civilization and of the principal legal systems, balanced gender representation and participation of experts with disabilities'. Consideration of the appointment of expert members of MHTs with mental disabilities is not a legal requirement in any legislation in Canada.

[91] N Rees, 'International Human Rights Obligations and Mental Health Review Tribunals' (2003) 10(1) *Psychiatry, Psychology and Law* 33, 39.

Board members to properly inquire and scrutinise the evidence before them while conducting a fair and impartial process.[92]

Tribunal members in the inquisitorial model are generally active in their questioning of the parties, rather than passively listening to what is brought before them. The members are not restricted to determining a matter on the basis of the case, the issues or the information the parties choose to present.[93] The decision-maker, rather than the parties, directs the process. Discrepancies between the level of representation of the parties, or whether a party is unrepresented (as is often the case before MHTs), become less of an issue. An adversarial model may also harm the therapeutic relationship between physician and patient.[94] Research conducted in the Australian context also suggests that patients before MHTs may sometimes identify the adversarial setting as unfair and as contributing to their powerlessness and lack of equity.[95]

In Canada the role of MHTs is generally defined in their enabling legislation as inquisitorial. Members of MHTs generally have the powers and immunities of commissioners appointed under the specific provincial legislation dealing with public inquiries (Alberta, Manitoba, Nova Scotia, Saskatchewan), or have defined inquisitorial-like powers under the MHT's enabling legislation (Newfoundland and Labrador). Ontario's MHT is one of the few whose role is not defined by the legislation.[96]

Terence Ison argues that

> many, and perhaps most, adjudicative bodies in Canada were established to avoid the problems of the adversary system and operate on some version of an inquisitorial system, though for historical reasons, the use of that phrase has usually been avoided,

---

[92] See, eg I Freckelton, 'Distractors and Distressors in Involuntary Status Decision-Making' (2005) 12(1) *Psychiatry, Psychology and Law* 88, and K Diesfeld, 'Insight: Unpacking the Concept in Mental Health Law' (2003) 10(1) *Psychiatry, Psychology and Law* 63, arguing for the need to deconstruct judgemental clinical descriptors often used before MHTs. See also Ian Freckelton, this volume, ch 9.

[93] RW Macaulay and J Sprague, *Practice and Procedure before Administrative Tribunals* (Toronto, Thomson Carswell, looseleaf) 12–18.

[94] See generally BJ Winick, *Civil Commitment: A Therapeutic Jurisprudence Model* (Durham NC, Carolina Academic Press, 2005).

[95] V Topp, M Thomas and M Ingvarson, *Lacking Insight: Involuntary Patient Experience of the Victorian Mental Health Review Board* (Melbourne, Mental Health Legal Centre, 2008) available at: www.communitylaw.org.au/clc_mentalhealth/cb_pages/images/Lacking_Insight.pdf.

[96] Yukon and British Columbia are the other two jurisdictions. However, Ontario's Mental Health Act s 39(1), which deals with the tribunal's powers to review civil committal, provides that the latter has a 'duty to inquire'. That provision, however, is unique to the tribunal's power to review involuntary status and not to the rest of its jurisdiction. It is highly unlikely that the legislation intended the tribunal to operate in different ways depending on the type of issue it reviews. Ontario's MHT has jurisdiction over approximately 20 different applications, a review of civil committal being only one of them. It is therefore likely that Ontario's MHT is inquisitorial as are the other provincial tribunals. This position has been supported by comments made by the judiciary about the Ontario MHT's duty to inquire in *Tran v Ralyea* [1993] OJ No 1261 and *Kletke v Secker*, Ont Dist Ct 1095/85 (unpublished).

and viewed negatively.[97] The resistance to an inquisitorial model of review has meant that each administrative tribunal in Canada departs from traditional, court-based adversarial hearings to different degrees, perhaps without fully recognising this. Factors influencing the adoption of inquisitorial models have to do with the nature of the issues dealt with by the tribunal, but also with the legal culture of both the members and legal representatives and parties appearing before it. The adoption of and resistance to an inquisitorial approach can be of particular sensitivity in some MHTs, given their hybrid role, which fits neither the adversarial model of a court nor the ill-defined role of other administrative tribunals. MHTs fulfill a dual function. They both adjudicate in disputes between parties (the applicant/patient and the health practitioner) and protect the public interest, namely by balancing a patient's autonomy with public safety.[98] Proceedings before MHTs should therefore be properly regarded as inquisitorial in nature, with elements of an adversarial setting.

Thinking of MHTs reviews as inquisitorial also better suits any potential models of MHTs with jurisdiction to make recommendations regarding hospital policies and/or treatment will be discussed below.

A.   Recommending Treatment

As pointed out above, in common law jurisdictions, administrative tribunals, including MHTs, are creatures of legislation. In Canada, the role of MHTs generally has been limited to listening to the evidence led and placed before it and agreeing or disagreeing with the decision made by the physician, rather than 'questioning' expert evidence given by the presenting physician on the medical diagnosis of the patient. The tribunal's role is to confirm a finding or authorise a course of treatment taken by a health practitioner, not to comment on it.[99]

However, a more 'interventionist' MHT may provide better protection to patients by ensuring that adequate treatment is provided. A potential example of this is the Mental Health Review Board in Victoria, Australia, which since 2004

---

[97]   TG Ison, 'Administrative Law The Operational Realities', paper presented at the Law Society of Upper Canada's CLE Conference, Toronto, 24 February 2009, 3–4.

[98]   Witness to this hybridism were the attempts to define a proper standard of proof for health practitioners before Ontario's MHT. Courts referred to the Board's standard of proof as either proof on an 'enhanced' balance of probabilities or the civil 'balance of probabilities'. The use of the 'enhanced' standard has been subsequently abandoned; J Zuckerberg, 'International Human Rights for Mentally Ill Persons: The Ontario Experience' (2007) 30 *International Journal of Law and Psychiatry* 512, 524. In a similar fashion, the United States Supreme Court rejected the use of the highest standard use in criminal proceedings ('beyond reasonable doubt') in *Addington v Texas* 441 US 418 (1978).

[99]   For example, in *Re A*, 2005 CanLII 12686 (ON CCB) the CCB 'noted that the psychiatric intensive care unit is not a desirable environment for a 15 year-old. However, the Board noted that neither the general psychiatric ward nor the pediatric ward were suitable for Ms. A [the patient]. The Board has no jurisdiction to determine placement of Ms. A but has jurisdiction only to review her involuntary status'.

has had the power to review a patient's treatment plan as part of the conduct of every review of the patient's involuntary status. Although the Victorian Mental Health Review Board has no power to make treatment decisions as such, it does have the power to order the revision of treatment plans which fail to meet the statutory requirements or are not capable of being implemented.[100] Physicians, however, cannot be ordered to follow a specific treatment in a way that is contrary to their ethical obligations and professional judgement.[101] Furthermore, granting an adjudicative body the power to overrule the health practitioner's professional assessment may create a further barrier to the latter's buy-in to the legal system. How should these different considerations be accommodated with an expansive role of an MHT? A possible answer is Nova Scotia's mental health legislation, which gives its MHT the authority

> to make such *recommendations* to the [health facility's] chief executive officer as it sees fit respecting the treatment or care of a patient (emphasis added),

in reviewing involuntary admissions.[102] This is perhaps a compromise position that balances the need to address any concerns arising from the treatment chosen and the proper limits of adjudicative agencies.

B.　Use of Summons and the Right Not to Incriminate Oneself[103]

The confusion generated by the uncertainty of the role of MHTs is highlighted in their power to issue summonses and the approach taken regarding the patients' right not to incriminate themselves.

Administrative tribunals generally have the power to issue summonses[104] and make rules dealing with the disclosure of evidence.[105] It is less clear when an MHT should *compel* parties to testify. The seriousness of the rights adjudicated and the resulting ambivalence as to whether a tribunal's role is adversarial rather than inquisitorial may explain the reluctance of an MHT to issue a summons to a party who has the burden of proof (generally the health practitioner). Should an MHT overturn a health practitioner's decision rather than issue a summons if the practitioner fails to appear at a hearing and the Board does not have enough evidence to make a determination? On the other hand, should an MHT issue

---

[100]　Mental Health Act 1986 (Vic) ss 19A(6) and 35A.

[101]　*British Columbia (Attorney General) v Astaforoff* [1983] 6 WWR 322 (BCSC); *Rotaru v Vancouver General Hospital Intensive Care Unit* 2008 BCSC 318. In the UK context, see *Re R* [1991] 4 All ER 177, 184, 187; *Re J* [1990] 3 All ER 930, 934; on appeal [1992] 4 All ER 614 (CA).

[102]　Nova Scotia's Involuntary Psychiatric Treatment Act s 68(2).

[103]　The discussion under this subsection is based in part on J Zuckerberg, 'Compelling Disclosure of Evidence from Parties before the Consent and Capacity Board' in J Sprague, *Administrative Law Today* (looseleaf), Issue 1–2008.

[104]　For example, s 12 of Ontario's Statutory Powers Procedure Act, RSO 1990, c S.22, provides that a tribunal may require any person, including a party, by summons, to give and produce evidence.

[105]　*ibid*, s 5.4.

summons to the patients? A number of decisions of Ontario's MHT have held that applicants/patients cannot be compelled to testify, borrowing from principles of criminal law against self-incrimination.[106]

The reluctance of an MHT to compel information can also be seen as another aspect of the uncertainty of its role. In fact, the Court of Appeal of Manitoba commented in obiter that it was 'unthinkable' that the provincial Mental Health Review Board, 'enquiring as to whether there are sufficient grounds on which to detain the patient on an involuntary basis, would threaten the patient with a loss of liberty for a failure to answer questions'.[107] Underlying these decisions is the assumption that information in the possession of a patient would operate to the patient's detriment or would fail to contradict the physician's evidence. It is thus not unusual in some jurisdictions for a tribunal to conduct hearings in the absence of the applicant/patient. Administrative tribunals, however,

> are given a broad authority to ask questions precisely to assist the tribunal in having the most information to make the best decision. To what extent should an agency decide not to use that authority and how much can that decision be influenced by a evidentiary provision respecting burden of proof that, after all, is merely a codification of the common law principle that he who avers must prove, and that is, moreover, applicable in most agency proceedings?[108]

Pending judicial guidance, the approach taken by an MHT to the issue of a summons and compellability will depend on the extent to which it sees itself as inquisitorial rather than adversarial and closer to a criminal proceeding.

---

[106] *Re B* OT-06–2899, 2900 and 3015 (ON CCB), unpublished. Whether s 12 of Ontario's Statutory Powers Procedure Act, RSO 1990, c S.22, can validly authorise that province's MHT to compel a patient to testify was litigated in *Hughes v Ontario (Ministry of Health)* [1990] OJ No 724 (Ont Ct (Gen Div)). Unfortunately, the court dismissed the case because it found that the tribunal had not in fact compelled the patient to give evidence using its power under s 12.

[107] *CW v Manitoba (Mental Health Review Board)* [1994] MJ No 401 at [35]. The Court of Appeal set aside a lower court decision on the basis of prematurity. The lower court had quashed a subpoena issued by Manitoba's Mental Health Review Board and had declared that the applicant/patient was not a compellable witness before the Board. Given that it was not clear in the circumstances whether the Mental Health Review Board had intended to elicit evidence from the respondent as distinct from merely interviewing him, the Court of Appeal found the application to the lower court to be premature.

[108] J Zuckerberg, 'Compelling Disclosure of Evidence from Parties before the Consent and Capacity Board' in J Sprague, *Administrative Law Today* (looseleaf), Issue 1–2008.

VIII. Appeals

Rights-based legislation normally includes the right to appeal against the decision made by the MHT to a court.[109] However, as with other areas discussed in this chapter, the implementation of these provisions reveals a mixed picture in terms of effectiveness. This section will focus on the appeal process in the province of Ontario.

Decisions made by Ontario's MHT can be appealed as of right to the court on a question of law or fact or both.[110] The legislation contains special procedures to ensure that appeals are heard promptly.[111] However, on average, it takes approximately eight months from when an appeal is launched until a court renders a decision.[112] The majority of appeals from Ontario's MHT's decisions do not proceed for several reasons, including:

1. The matter became moot before the court was to hear it (for example, the patient is no longer involuntary due to medical improvement);
2. The patient exercised the right to come back to the MHT for a re-determination of the matter before the court was to hear the case;
3. The patient does not pursue the matter due to lack of financial resources (for example, at the appeal stage, legal aid is not given to the patient unless there is an opinion letter from counsel respecting the merits of the appeal);
4. Health practitioners do not pursue the appeal because either they do not want to get involved in legal proceedings and/or the facility where they work is not willing to cover the legal fees (most physicians work on a fee-for-service basis in Ontario).

The limitations of the appeal process are indicated by the significantly low number of appeals from Ontario's MHT which are actually heard.[113] There are also medical implications resulting from the deficiencies of the current appeal process that are particular to Ontario. The legislation in this province provides that a health practitioner who proposes a treatment for a person and finds that the person is incapable with respect to the treatment shall not *begin* the treatment

---

[109] For example, Ontario, Yukon and Manitoba permit appeals from the MHT decision on questions of law and fact. Appeal rights are limited to varying degrees in other provinces. Newfoundland and Labrador and Nova Scotia only permit a right of appeal on questions of law. No further appeal beyond the trial court is allowed in Alberta and Saskatchewan. In British Columbia and Prince Edward Island, a patient only has the right to judicially review the decision (judicial review being a more limited legal recourse than a fully fledged appeal).

[110] Ontario's Health Care Consent Act, SO 1996, ch 2, s 80(1).

[111] The appellant must serve his or her notice of appeal on the other parties and file it with the court, with proof of service, within seven days after he or she receives the Board's decision (Health Care Consent Act, SO 1996, ch 2, s 80(2)).

[112] CCB database.

[113] Only 11% of the appeals received since 2004 by Ontario's MHT were actually heard (CCB database).

(but can continue it if already started before the patient made an application to the MHT) until the appeal against the MHT's decision has finally been disposed of. A health practitioner can only provide interim treatment with the permission of the court.[114] The vast majority of appeals of findings of incapacity regarding treatment are never heard, following the overall pattern of other appeals. The implementation of appeal rights in the mental health context can therefore give rise to significant clinical challenges in the context of untreated patients.

The previous discussion reveals that the implementation of strong procedural safeguards in terms of review of MHTs may be difficult to carry out without further fine-tuning at the appeal level. This requires consideration of fast-track court procedures to be used for appeals from MHTs.[114a]

IX.   Legal Representation

A.   Availability

The need for legal representation before MHT is partly based on the fact that one of the parties belongs to a very vulnerable group whose most fundamental rights are being restricted. The efficacy of a self-represented patient appearing before an MHT is often questionable. International human rights standards provide that a person whose mental capacity is at issue is entitled to be represented by counsel[115] and to choose and appoint counsel to represent him/her.[116] Legal representation should be 'made available without payment by that person to the extent that he or she does not have sufficient means to pay for it'.[117]

Although most Canadian jurisdictions generally meet or exceed international human rights standards, a number of them fail to meet them when it comes to the availability of free legal representation.[118] In some provinces, patients are 'represented' by patient advocates.[119] The limited availability of legal representation stems from a number of factors, including lack of expertise in mental health

---

[114]   Sections 18(3)(d) and 19 of Ontario's Health Care Consent Act, SO 1996, ch 2.

[114a]   The Superior Court of Justice in Toronto has recently implemented a case management system for appeals from Ontario's MHT, namely the CCB.

[115]   Principles for the Protection of Persons with Mental Illness and for the Improvement of Mental Health Care (1992). Adopted by GA res 46/119 of 17 December 1991, available at: www.unhchr.ch/html/menu3/b/68.htm Principle 1(6).

[116]   *ibid*, Principle 18.

[117]   *ibid*, Principle 1(6).

[118]   See J Zuckerberg, 'International Human Rights for Mentally Ill Persons: The Ontario Experience' (2007) 30 *International Journal of Law and Psychiatry* 512.

[119]   New Brunswick. In British Columbia free advocates are employed by the Mental Health Law Program of the Community Legal Assistance Society (CLAS). CLAS is funded by the Legal Services Society, British Columbia's Law Foundation and other sources. Legal aid does not directly cover

law,[120] unavailability of legal aid for patients appearing before the MHT, unwillingness to take legally aided clients in those jurisdictions where legal aid is available, and in certain cases, unwillingness to work with mentally ill clients. In some cases, access to legal representation may also be affected by the short time-frames for scheduling MHT hearings.[121]

This is not a problem that only pertains to MHTs. The Canadian judiciary has undertaken educational initiatives to assist judges to conduct hearings with self-represented parties, given their growing numbers in both civil and criminal matters.[122] This may signal an increasing preparedness to conduct judicial proceedings with unrepresented parties. The systemic availability (or lack thereof) of counsel before MHTs has not yet been litigated in court.[123] However, fiscal restraints and what appears to be the courts' gradual acceptance of unrepresented parties may make it difficult in the future to argue for a right to free legal representation before MHTs. This reality requires revisiting assumptions upon which rights-based mental health legislation is built and the role of MHTs.

Accessibility to legal counsel is also related to the role of the MHT in reviewing the physician's decision. As mentioned before, an inquisitorial model may be better suited to addressing concerns regarding legal representation.

Paradoxically, the acceptance of legalism by the medical profession may be more difficult in those jurisdictions in which patients are provided with a reasonably good level of legal representation, such as Ontario.[124] This is partly due to the lack of legal representation for health practitioners and the adversarial nature of the hearings.[125]

---

representation, but CLAS is funded to hire staff lawyers and paralegals supervised by staff lawyers to represent mentally ill clients at Criminal Code review board hearings and hearings under British Columbia's Mental Health Act.

[120] RM Gordon, 'Legal Services for Mental Health Patients: Some Observations on Canadian and Australian Developments' (1983) 6 *Canadian Community Law Journal* 17.

[121] For example, the Ontario MHT has seven days to schedule hearings (Health Care Consent Act, SO 1996, ch 2, s 75(2)).

[122] Canadian Judicial Council, *Statement of Principles on Self-represented Litigants and Accused Persons* (Ontario, Canadian Judicial Council, 2006) available at: www.cfcj-fcjc.org/research/srl-en.php.

[123] Courts have only addressed the right of patients *to be informed* of the right to counsel in *CB v Sawadsky* [2005] OJ No 3682 and *Chandrasena v McDougald* [1989] OJ No 1743.

[124] Ontario's Mental Health Act also establishes, inter alia, the right of patients to receive rights advice once they are committed. The conduct of rights advisors has also come under some criticism given the perception among some health practitioners that rights advisors may sometimes go beyond their mandate. See in the context of community treatment orders, Dreezer and Dreezer Inc, *Report on the Legislated Review of Community Treatment Orders, Required Under Section 33.9 of the Mental Health Act* (Ontario, Ministry of Health and Long-term Care, 2005) available at: www.health.gov.on.ca/english/public/pub/ministry_reports/dreezer/dreezer.html. This problem appears to repeat itself in other jurisdictions as illustrated by J Vetergaard, 'The Danish Mental Health Act of 1989: Psychiatric Discretion in the New Legalism' (1994) 17(2) *International Journal of Law and Psychiatry* 191, 199.

[125] In this province, while patients had legal representation in approximately 80% of the hearings, the percentage is much lower (approximately 20%) for the doctors (CCB database, updated as of November 2008).

B.   Getting Instructions

The challenges encountered by counsel who represent individuals with mental illnesses before MHTs have been discussed extensively elsewhere.[126] There are some aspects, however, that require further analysis in the Canadian context. One of the most common problems of legal representation before MHTs is the potential ethical and professional conflicts of interest on the part of counsel. Should an MHT allow a lawyer to act for a patient without being concerned about whether or not the client in fact has the capacity to retain and instruct them? Some Canadian jurisdictions have attempted to address this problem by enacting legislation which gives the MHT the authority to order legal representation for a patient and by 'deeming' the patient capable to retain and instruct counsel.[127] This raises further legal difficulties. What is the patient 'deemed' to have capacity for? Should an MHT have to consider the views of a patient regarding legal representation before deciding whether to proceed without counsel? Do provisions that deem a patient capable to instruct counsel apply to the decision not to retain counsel regardless of the person's actual capacity on this issue? If not, should MHTs be making determinations regarding the patient's capacity regarding self-representation? Such determinations may have to be made without any legislative provision for reviewing this type of capacity or relevant evidence (the physician will seldom have expertise on this issue).[128]

Again, a possible answer to these questions may lie with the role (inquisitorial or adversarial) assumed by the MHT and the consequent level of formality and/or intervention during proceedings.[129] An inquisitorial approach may level the inequalities that may exist between parties.

---

[126]   M Perlin, 'The Role and Significance of Counsel' (2005) 42 *San Diego Law Review* 739; PR Tremblay, 'On Persuasion and Paternalism: Lawyer Decision Making and the Questionably Competent Client' (1987) *Utah Law Review* 515; DA Romano, 'The Legal Advocate and the Questionably Competent Client in the Context of a Poverty Law Clinic' (1997) 35 *Osgoode Hall Law Journal* 737.

[127]   See, eg Ontario's Health Care Consent Act, SO 1996, ch 2, s 81(1); Manitoba's Mental Health Act s 58; Newfoundland & Labrador's Mental Health Care and Treatment Act, SNL 2006, c M-9.1, s 70(3).

[128]   To address this issue the Consent and Capacity Board (Ontario) issued guidelines for its members. The guidelines outline the procedure to determine whether the Board should issue an order to arrange for the legal representation of the patient: *Policy Guideline No 2*, 2007 (Ontario, Consent and Capacity Board, 2007) available at: www.ccboard.on.ca.

[129]   Consent and Control Board (Ontario), *Policy Guideline No 2*, 2007 dealing with the Consent and Capacity Board's duty to inquire and elicit evidence when dealing with unrepresented patients.

X. Conclusion

This chapter has pointed to some problems resulting from the adoption of rights-based legalism with limited or no regard to the social and legal environment in which mental health law is implemented. 'Dangerousness' as a criterion for involuntary admission has opened a whole new array of unforeseeable legal dilemmas, which are even more complex in those jurisdictions which permit civil committal without treatment. Similar questions have been raised by the inclusion of procedural safeguards. This at the same time forces a reconsideration of the proper role and procedures of MHTs. The scope and content of rights-based legislation are in a state of development. In some areas, scope and content have been narrowly defined, as with the reluctance to borrow from evidentiary rules used in the context of criminal proceedings and in courts more generally. In others, they remain uncertain and await judicial or legislative clarification.

Another way to measure the introduction of legalism is the effect that rights-based legislation may have on the dignity and sense of justice of people appearing before an MHT (health practitioners, patients, family members and carers). In other words, is the review process established by the legislation fair in the eyes of the parties involved, regardless of the outcome of a legal proceeding? The answer to this question requires further qualitative research.

The problems disclosed by the adoption of rights-based legalism underscore law's inherent limitations as an agent of social change. They also stress the importance of considering the context and culture to which legislation applies. The medical profession generally views itself 'as diagnosticians and providers of treatment rather than custodians'.[130] Education through governing professional bodies, medical schools, training programmes, and so forth appears to be a condition precedent to any successful implementation of mental health legislation.

The current model has also been criticised for its failure to advance the rights of mentally ill persons because it fails to obtain the economic resources needed to improve their status.[131] In Canada, addressing the lack of appropriate funding for mental health services has also been identified as a priority.[132] The failure of rights-based strategies to advance the interests of mentally ill persons is not unique to this area of the law. For example, in the human rights field, similar

---

[130] M Gupta, 'All Locked Up with Nowhere to Go: Treatment Refusal in the Involuntarily Hospitalized Psychiatric Population in Canada' in I Freckelton and K Diesfeld (eds), *Involuntary Detention and Civil Commitment: International Perspectives* (Aldershot, Ashgate, 2003), 174.

[131] See, eg N Rose, 'Unreasonable Rights: Mental Illness and the Limits of the Law' (1985) 12(2) *Journal of Law and Society* 199. For a different view in favour of rights-based legalism, see eg L Gostin, 'Social Historical Perspectives on Mental Health Reform' (1983) 10(1) *Journal of Law and Society* 47.

[132] MJL Kirby and WJ Keon, *Out of the Shadows at Last: Transforming Mental Health, Mental Illness and Addiction Services in Canada*, Report of the Senate Standing Senate Committee on Social Affairs, Science and Technology, (Ontario, Senate of Canada, 2006) available at: www.parl.gc.ca/39/1/parlbus/commbus/senate/Com-e/SOCI-E/rep-e/rep02may06-e.htm.

critiques have been made regarding the excessive focus on 'negative' rights to the neglect of 'positive' rights. Such bias is alleged to have resulted in a failure to deal with what some commentators see as the root causes of injustice and disenpowerment, namely poverty and the unequal distribution of resources. The fundamental debate regarding the application of 'positive' rights to mentally ill persons is outside of the scope of this chapter, although it is worth noting that mental health legislation in Canada is, in tandem with other jurisdictions, highly 'negative' in that it does not provide practical positive entitlements to patients.[133]

The introduction of positive rights in the mental health context is particularly challenging, given the vulnerability and stigma attached to the mentally ill (who often need to rely on the action of rights advocates and consumer organisations). Weak enforcement of positive rights (when they exist) may also be counterproductive by making such rights hollow.

Yet the current model of mental health legislation still represents a profound departure from past medical models based on paternalistic considerations, or the 'best interests' of the patient. Given the limited jurisdiction of MHTs and the limited scope for pursuing civil or criminal actions, thought should be given to the expansion of the jurisdiction of MHTs to make non-binding recommendations regarding treatment and hospital policies and/or the creation of a monitoring body (or the expansion and/or use of the authority of existing organisations such as the Ombudsman) to investigate patient complaints. This will provide procedural 'negative' rights with a more meaningful role as well as strengthening the claim for a 'positive' right to health care.

---

[133] One potential exception is the community treatment order (CTO) provisions provided for in some of the provincial Acts. The latter provide protections against civil liability for some of the people involved in the delivery of the services linked to the CTO (see, eg Ontario Mental Health Act ss 33.1(7) and 33.6). Although the extent of these provisions has not been argued before the courts, they may arguably give rise to a duty to quality of care vis-à-vis the patient.

14

Compulsory Outpatient Treatment and the Calculus of Human Rights

JOHN DAWSON

I. Introduction

This chapter considers whether it is a breach of human rights principles to treat patients involuntarily under a community treatment order (CTO) regime who do not pose an imminent threat of serious harm to themselves or others. This use of CTOs is relatively common in many jurisdictions. A recent review of the research, from the Institute of Psychiatry, found that:

> [t]here is remarkable consistency in the characteristics of patients on CTOs across jurisdictions in very different cultural and geographic settings. [They are] typically males, around 40 years of age, with a long history of mental illness, previous admissions, suffering from a schizophrenia-like or serious affective illness, and likely to be displaying psychotic symptoms, especially delusions at the time. Criminal offences and violence are not dominant features among CTO patients ... [They] are more likely to be severely mentally ill with high hospital admission rate histories, poor medication compliance, and aftercare needs.[1]

The proper legal response to people with this profile is therefore central to debates concerning compulsory outpatient care, particularly in jurisdictions where reasonably comprehensive, publicly-funded, community mental health services are available.

Perhaps the most difficult cases are those in which courts or tribunals must decide whether to continue or renew a person's CTO. The individuals concerned may have a lengthy history of serious mental illness that has had major consequences for their social functioning, but their condition may be stable on the day they appear before the tribunal, following their sustained treatment, first in

---

[1] R Churchill, G Owen, S Singh and M Hotopf, *International Experiences of Using Community Treatment Orders* (London, Institute of Psychiatry, 2007) 109.

hospital, and then under a CTO. When released from compulsory treatment on previous occasions, however, they may not have engaged consistently with outpatient care.

A central question is whether a person in that situation should be released immediately from the CTO. On one view of it, when a person's condition is stable the use of compulsory powers is no longer justified.[2] On another view of it, the tribunal would be entitled, on some occasions, to take a more preventive approach: if there were a strong prospect, for instance, that the person would cease treatment if the order were discharged, and would again require hospital care. On that approach, the tribunal might be entitled to consider the full history of the person's illness, engagement with treatment, and likely prognosis, and might then extend that person's involuntary outpatient care.

The health professionals who treat and maintain contact with the person under the CTO would be acting under the authority of mental health legislation. They would be exercising public functions, or acting as agents of the state, and their intervention could undoubtedly limit that person's human rights. The relevant rights instrument would be engaged, but the threats posed by the person's discharge to voluntary treatment might not be considered particularly serious or imminent. Nor would the person's compulsory community care, at the moment he or she appeared before the tribunal, necessarily be a less restrictive alternative to hospital care. If the person's condition was currently stable, he or she would not be an immediate candidate for inpatient care. The relevant calculus of justification for limiting a person's rights might not be satisfied and that person should be released immediately from the CTO, free to refuse further psychiatric care.

That is not the view that will be advanced here, however. It will be argued, instead, that human rights principles would require the release from a CTO of a person in that situation on *some* occasions, but not others. It would all depend on certain aspects of the human rights calculus, applied to the individual case.

This chapter therefore reviews the central human rights principles that apply to CTOs,[3] and notes certain points of intersection between these principles and empirical research conducted on the operation of CTO regimes. The aim is to consider whether human rights principles permit a preventive approach to be taken to the involuntary outpatient treatment of a person with a serious mental illness who does not currently pose a serious threat of harm.

---

[2]   On this 'dilemma of discharge', see J Dawson, S Romans, A Gibbs and N Ratter, 'Ambivalence about Community Treatment Orders' (2003) 26 *International Journal of Law and Psychiatry* 243; R Mullen, J Dawson and A Gibbs, 'Dilemmas for Clinicians in Use of Community Treatment Orders' (2006) 29 *International Journal of Law and Psychiatry* 535.

[3]   These principles are derived largely from the jurisprudence concerning the Canadian Charter of Rights and Freedoms, enacted by the Canada Act 1982, c 11; proclaimed in force 17 April 1982 ('the Canadian Charter') and the Convention for the Protection of Human Rights and Fundamental Freedoms, opened for signature 4 November 1950, CETS No 005, entered into force 3 September 1953 ('the European Convention').

II. The Calculus of Human Rights

The requirement that states comply with their human rights obligations presents a complex range of legal questions in relation to compulsory outpatient care. The human rights agenda is extensive: it goes to the existence, design, interpretation, and application of a CTO regime. At the very least, it is necessary to consider the impact on human rights of requiring individuals to accept community psychiatric care; whether imposing that requirement can constitute a justified limitation on their rights; and how the legal criteria governing CTOs should be interpreted and applied.

A framework for this discussion can be derived from the structure of a typical human rights analysis of compulsory outpatient care. That analysis is likely to have two main parts. It would focus initially on the impact of community treatment powers on the rights of the individual that are protected by human rights law. The main question posed here would be: *How* are the rights of the individual affected by the operation of a CTO regime? And how *serious* is that impact? The second part of the analysis would focus on matters of justification. What arguments can states make to justify this kind of impact on a person's rights, in order to make a case that the operation of a CTO regime is not a human rights violation overall?

The human rights most directly affected by compulsory outpatient psychiatric care can be described as those protecting a person's 'negative liberty' interests, or their right to be left alone by members of a community mental health team. Section 7 of the Canadian Charter, for example, guarantees the right of an individual not to be deprived of 'liberty and security of person'. The Fifth Amendment to the Constitution of the United States of America declares a citizen is 'not to be deprived of liberty without due process of law'.[4] The European Convention protects the right to 'liberty and security of person' and 'private life'.[5] The New Zealand Bill of Rights Act explicitly guarantees 'the right to refuse medical treatment'.[6]

There is little doubt that these rights can be affected by requiring a person to accept outpatient psychiatric care, particularly continuing medication without

---

[4] This right goes beyond procedural elements to include the notion of 'substantive due process': B Winick, *The Right to Refuse Mental Health Treatment* (Washington DC, American Psychological Association, 1997).

[5] Art 8; P Bartlett, O Lewis and O Thorold, *Mental Disability and the European Convention on Human Rights* (Leiden, Martinus Nijhoff, 2007); K Gledhill, 'Human Rights Instruments and Mental Health Law: The English Experience of the Incorporation of the European Convention on Human Rights' (2006–2007) 34 *Syracuse Journal of International Law and Commerce* 359; R Jones, *Mental Health Act Manual*, 11th edn (London, Sweet and Maxwell, 2008).

[6] New Zealand Bill of Rights Act 1990 (NZ) s 11; P Rishworth, G Huscroft, S Optican and R Mahoney, *The New Zealand Bill of Rights* (Auckland, Oxford University Press, 2003).

consent.[7] In addition, the impact on personal dignity, autonomy, or self-determination, or other values embedded in protected rights, may readily be invoked.[8] Furthermore, some human rights instruments specifically protect the right of individuals to security of their home or property.[9] This would usually include the right of a person to refuse entry into a private residence to members of a mental health team. It is hardly controversial, therefore, to suggest that these 'negative' rights of the individual, to be free of unwanted interference by health professionals acting under the authority of the law, are implicated by the use of compulsory outpatient care.

Nevertheless, a human rights analysis also requires consideration of the *degree* to which such rights are infringed, or the *seriousness* of the impact. These are matters that can be illuminated by empirical research. Involuntary outpatients may be asked to describe, for instance, their experiences of treatment under a well-embedded CTO regime. When recounting their experiences, they may not use the language of human rights instruments, but it is surely relevant to know whether they feel coerced, particularly regarding medication, by health professionals; and whether they feel more or less coerced than during periods of compulsory hospital care, or during other forms of institutionalisation they have known. How do they measure treatment under a CTO against the prior pattern of their life?

The second major aspect of the human rights calculus concerns permissible limitations on rights. Different rights instruments that affirm subtly different rights relevant to the use of CTOs also adopt different approaches to the limitation of those rights. The European Convention, for instance, tends to list the permissible limitations within (or alongside) the statement of each right. Article 8(1) declares:

> Everyone has the right to respect for his private and family life, his [or her] home and his [or her] correspondence.

However, a range of situations is then listed, in Article 8(2), in which such rights may be limited, including their limitation:

> in the interests of . . . public safety, for the protection of public order, health or morals, or for the protection of the rights and freedoms of others.

This permits a broad range of aims to be pursued by the state. The Canadian Charter, in contrast, contains a general 'justified limitations' clause that permits

---

[7] See eg *In re KL* 806 NE 2d 480 (2004) (NYCA). Many human rights instruments also protect the right not to be arbitrarily detained. This right would not apply directly to *outpatient* treatment, except where stringent conditions are imposed on a person's freedom of movement in the community, such as the requirement that they shall not leave a specified address.

[8] The European Court of Human Rights has said of Article 8 of the European Convention, for instance, that 'It covers the physical and psychological integrity of a person', and that 'the notion of personal autonomy is an important principle underlying the interpretation of its guarantees': *Pretty v United Kingdom* (2002) 35 EHRR 1 at [61].

[9] The Fifth Amendment to the Constitution of the United States of America, for example.

limits to be imposed on a range of its protected rights, provided the proper calculus of justification is employed.[10] The Constitution of the United States of America takes a third approach. It appears, on its face, to contemplate very few limits on its declared rights, as many of these are stated in strong, unqualified terms. Nevertheless, through a process of constructive interpretation, the United States courts have identified many implied limits that may be lawfully imposed.[11]

Despite these formal differences, however, there is considerable convergence in the decisions of the courts charged with the enforcement of these different rights instruments as to the general elements of this calculus of justification.[12] The first element concerns the character and importance of the state interests advanced to justify limits on rights. The more important these interests, the more readily may rights be infringed. Ultimately, a fair balance must be struck between legitimate state objectives and specific limits on rights.

The second element concerns the relationship between the means chosen by the state, when limiting rights, and the ends pursued. Here a rational (or reasonable) connection between means and ends will typically be required, to ensure the state's measures are capable of delivering the desired results. The third element concerns the severity and necessity of the means chosen, the central question being: could any less drastic means have achieved the state's legitimate ends?

At all of these points in the analysis, an inquiry is conducted into the means followed to limit rights. The critical principle applied, particularly in European and Canadian human rights law, is that of 'proportionality'.[13] To satisfy this principle, the state must use sufficiently compelling, and effective, and calibrated means to reach its legitimate ends, in order to justify measures that have a particular level of impact on rights.

This structure for the human rights analysis will therefore constitute the framework for the discussion to follow. Three aspects of the empirical research will be discussed that are particularly relevant to this analysis. These concern the manner in which CTOs affect the interests of involuntary outpatients; the efficacy of CTOs in achieving their aims; and the views of health professionals concerning

---

[10] Canadian Charter of Fundamental Rights and Freedoms s 1; *R v Oakes* [1986] 1 SCR 103; P Hogg, *Constitutional Law of Canada*, 5th edn supp (Toronto, Thomson, 2007) ch 38.

[11] See eg *Central Hudson Gas and Electric Corporation v Public Service Commissioner of New York* 447 US 557 (1980).

[12] S Grosz, J Beatson and P Duffy, *Human Rights: The 1998 Act and the European Convention* (London, Sweet and Maxwell, 2000); S Grosz, T Hickman, R Singh and J Beatson, *Human Rights: Judicial Protection in the UK* (London, Sweet and Maxwell, 2008); R Clayton and H Tomlinson, *The Law of Human Rights*, 2nd edn (Oxford, Oxford University Press, 2009). Hogg (above n 10) writes that aspects of the US jurisprudence concerning the calculus of justification bear 'striking similarities' to the approach subsequently adopted by the Supreme Court of Canada in *Oakes* (above n 10), while Clayton and Tomlinson observe that the famous opinion of Dickson CJ, that established the *Oakes* test, draws heavily on the principles of 'proportionality' developed by the European Court of Human Rights.

[13] R Clayton and H Tomlinson, *The Law of Human Rights*, 2nd edn (Oxford, Oxford University Press, 2009) ch 6 D.

the exercise of their community treatment powers. Particular reference will be made to qualitative work conducted by the author's research group on New Zealand's CTO regime.[14]

A.   The Impact of CTOs on Compulsory Patients' Rights

The manner in which the impact of involuntary treatment on individuals with a serious mental illness should be described or conceptualised is perhaps the deepest vein of disagreement in mental health law. Judge Tauro's famous description, for instance, in the Boston state hospital case, of the administration of medication without consent in a psychiatric hospital as 'involuntary mind control', and as 'an unsanctioned intrusion on the integrity of a human being',[15] was strongly criticised by some psychiatrists for resting on 'a basic misconception of the effects of psychotropic drugs'.[16] Paul Appelbaum and Thomas Gutheil have pointed out that Judge Tauro's language reveals no sense that 'it is truly the illness and not the treatment that deserves the label of "involuntary mind control"'.[17] According to Appelbaum and Gutheil, '[p]sychiatrists do not administer neuroleptics in an attempt to "control" minds but to restore them to the patient's control'.[18]

Using the terminology developed by Isaiah Berlin,[19] it might be questioned whether the focus should be on the impact of involuntary treatment on a person's negative liberty, or positive liberty, or both? Does involuntary treatment reduce the freedom of action of individuals, by imposing external constraints on their will, thereby violating their right to be left alone, as Judge Tauro suggests? Or does it advance their liberty, as Appelbaum and Gutheil would have it, by improving their capacity to exercise control over their lives, free of internal

---

[14]   See, particularly, R Mullen, J Dawson and A Gibbs, 'Dilemmas for Clinicians in Use of Community Treatment Orders' (2006) 29 *International Journal of Law and Psychiatry* 535; J Dawson, S Romans, A Gibbs and N Ratter, 'Ambivalence about Community Treatment Orders' (2003) 26 *International Journal of Law and Psychiatry* 243; S Romans, J Dawson, R Mullen and A Gibbs, 'How Mental Health Clinicians View Community Treatment Orders: A National New Zealand Survey' (2004) 38 *Australian and New Zealand Journal of Psychiatry* 836; A Gibbs, J Dawson, C Ansley and R Mullen, 'How Patients in New Zealand View Community Treatment Orders' (2005) 14 *Journal of Mental Health* 357; A Gibbs, J Dawson and R Mullen, 'Community Treatment Orders for People with Serious Mental Illness: A New Zealand Study' (2006) 36 *British Journal of Social Work* 1085; R Mullen, A Gibbs and J Dawson, 'Family Perspective on Community Treatment Orders: A New Zealand Study' (2006) 52 *International Journal of Social Psychiatry* 469; J Dawson and R Mullen, 'Insight and Use of Community Treatment Orders' (2008) 17 *Journal of Mental Health* 269; J Dawson, *Community Treatment Orders: International Comparisons* (Dunedin, University of Otago, 2005); available at: www.otago.ac.nz/law/otagoCTO/index.html.
[15]   *Rogers v Okin* 478 F Supp 1342 (D Mass 1979) 1371.
[16]   PS Appelbaum and TG Gutheil, 'The Boston State Hospital Case: "Involuntary Mind Control", the Constitution and the Right to Rot' (1980) 137 *American Journal of Psychiatry* 720.
[17]   ibid, 721.
[18]   ibid, 721.
[19]   I Berlin, *Two Concepts of Liberty* (Oxford, Oxford University Press, 1958).

constraints within their minds raised by the psychopathology of serious mental illness? Perhaps it is capable of doing both.

Certainly, very significant powers over involuntary outpatients are conferred by a typical CTO regime. Under the New Zealand regime, for instance, a legal duty is imposed on the patient to 'accept treatment' under the direction of their Responsible Clinician, and to accept visits from health professionals, or attend appointments.[20] Designated health professionals are empowered to enter private premises to visit the patient:

at all reasonable times ... for the purpose of treating the patient.[21]

The 'level' of the patient's accommodation, or the degree of support to be available (such as 24-hour nursing cover) may be specified, in practice, as a condition of the patient's community tenure. Swift recall to hospital may proceed if:

the responsible clinician considers that the patient cannot continue to be treated adequately as an outpatient.[22]

Police assistance with that entry and recall process is available, if required.[23] Following recall to hospital, the patient may be treated without consent on the same basis as other compulsory inpatients.[24] These are very significant powers that may undoubtedly limit aspects of a person's freedom.

A CTO in New Zealand does not confer any express power of 'forced medication' in a community setting, nor any express power to restrain a patient in the community for the purpose of administering medication. The main mechanisms for the regime's enforcement are, therefore, the threat of the patient's swift recall to hospital, without going through the complexities of the usual certification process, and the strength of the therapeutic relationships that may be maintained.[25]

Some involuntary outpatients will find their treatment under this kind of regime highly coercive, as was confirmed during a qualitative study of the New Zealand CTO regime.[26] Some patients under CTOs described their experience as being 'restricted', 'ordered', 'pressured', or 'dictated to', or as being under the 'control', 'supervision' or 'surveillance' of the mental health team. One man

---

[20] Mental Health (Compulsory Assessment and Treatment) Act 1992 (NZ) s 29(1).
[21] Mental Health (Compulsory Assessment and Treatment) Act 1992 (NZ) s 29(2).
[22] Mental Health (Compulsory Assessment and Treatment) Act 1992 (NZ) s 29(3).
[23] Mental Health (Compulsory Assessment and Treatment) Act 1992 (NZ) s 41.
[24] Mental Health (Compulsory Assessment and Treatment) Act 1992 (NZ) pt V.
[25] J Dawson, S Romans, A Gibbs and N Ratter, 'Ambivalence about Community Treatment Orders' (2003) 26 *International Journal of Law and Psychiatry* 243; S Romans, J Dawson, R Mullen and A Gibbs 'How Mental Health Clinicians View Community Treatment Orders: A National New Zealand Survey' (2004) 38 *Australian and New Zealand Journal of Psychiatry* 836; R Mullen, J Dawson and A Gibbs, 'Dilemmas for Clinicians in Use of Community Treatment Orders' (2006) 29 *International Journal of Law and Psychiatry* 535.
[26] *ibid.*

described the order as a 'straight-jacket', another as the 'thumb-screws'. Other comments were: 'I have to do what they say'; 'Wham: they can put me straight back in!'; 'It made me a second class citizen'; and 'It was mainly negative, but it saved my life'. One man captured especially the sense of psychological confinement that may be experienced by a person on a CTO, when he said, 'It put me in [a] category hole and a little box'.

Nevertheless, in the New Zealand study, in which a full cohort of patients under CTOs were approached in one region, it was surprising to find that only a small proportion of those interviewed adamantly opposed their involuntary outpatient care.[27] Most indicated that they experienced both positive and negative aspects simultaneously. One man, with a diagnosis of severe bipolar disorder and a history of opiate abuse, who deeply resented his involuntary treatment, said: 'It didn't help me. They forced me to take medication. I hated having my freedom taken away. There was a stigma always in the back of my mind'. Nevertheless, he considered his community nurse 'fantastic'. 'Without her help', he said, 'I would be on the injection right now. She is someone I can really open up to'. Another man who suffered paranoid delusions considered the CTO to be 'like a prison sentence', because he could not go hunting in the forest with his sons. 'My psychiatrist is authoritarian', he declared, 'The injections impair my alertness and energy. They took away my gun licence'. But he also said involuntary outpatient treatment 'brought me back into society as a normal dad. It lifted the burden of monitoring from my wife. It saved my marriage'. His overall conclusion was, 'It's good but there's handcuffs on it'. Many patients' experiences were of this complex, ambivalent kind.[28]

Many individuals disliked the restrictions imposed by the CTO but they still had generally favourable views of the regime.[29] This was mainly because they assessed their experience under the order against their prior patient career, especially in light of their negative experiences of institutions. They considered that community treatment allowed them more freedom and control over their life than hospital care. They appreciated the sense of security the CTO provided, and they often believed they received enhanced access to services in poorly resourced systems. They valued the ongoing support of mental health professionals and supported accommodation providers, and they tended to view the order as a transitional step from a chaotic to a more stable pattern of life. Nevertheless, most still identified negative effects. From the patient's perspective, it seems there can be both significant benefits and drawbacks to treatment under a CTO.

---

[27] A Gibbs, J Dawson, C Ansley and R Mullen, 'How Patients in New Zealand View Community Treatment Orders' (2005) 14 *Journal of Mental Health* 357.

[28] J Dawson, S Romans, A Gibbs and N Ratter, 'Ambivalence about Community Treatment Orders' (2003) 26 *International Journal of Law and Psychiatry* 243.

[29] A Gibbs, J Dawson, C Ansley and R Mullen, 'How Patients in New Zealand View Community Treatment Orders' (2005) 14 *Journal of Mental Health* 357.

B. Parallels with the 'Coercion' Research

The compulsory outpatients interviewed in the New Zealand study therefore exhibited a wide spectrum of views, from complete rejection to total endorsement of their compulsory outpatient care. These results are consistent with many other studies of patients' attitudes to their civil commitment or compulsory hospital care.[30] Numerous studies of patient coercion, conducted since the mid-1990s, for instance, have found wide variation in the perceptions of both compulsory and informal patients concerning the degree of coercion they experience in their mental health care.[31]

The studies typically find that compulsory patients (including outpatients)[32] are more likely to view their experience as coercive than informal patients, as one would expect.[33] But the studies also invariably find that 'objective legal status and subjective feelings of coercion are not equivalent',[34] and that 'formal legal status

---

[30] N Spence, R Goldney and W Costain, 'Attitudes Towards Psychiatric Hospitalisation: A Comparison of Involuntary and Voluntary Patients' (1988) 8 *Australian Clinical Review* 108; G Edelson and V Hiday, 'Civil Commitment: A Range of Patient Attitudes' (1990) 18 *Bulletin of the American Academy of Psychiatry and Law* 65; N Adams and R Hafner, 'Attitudes of Psychiatric Patients and their Relatives to Involuntary Treatment' (1991) 25 *Australian and New Zealand Journal of Psychiatry* 231; T Scheid-Cook, 'Controllers and Controlled: An Analysis of Participant Constructions of Outpatient Commitment' (1993) 15 *Sociology of Health and Illness* 179; R Kaltiala, 'Involuntary Psychiatric Treatment: A Range of Patient Attitudes' (1996) 50 *Nordic Journal of Psychiatry* 27; F Frese, 'The Mental Health Consumer's Perspective on Mandatory Treatment' in M Munetz (ed), *Can Mandatory Treatment Be Therapeutic?* (San Francisco, Jossey-Bass, 1997); S Marriott, B Audini, P Lelliott, Y Webb and R Duffett, 'Research into the Mental Health Act: A Qualitative Study of the Views of Those Using or Affected by it' (2001) 10 *Journal of Mental Health* 33; K Canvin, A Bartlett and V Pinfold, 'A "bittersweet pill to swallow": Learning from Mental Health Service Users' Responses to Compulsory Community Care' (2002) 5 *Health and Social Care in the Community* 361.

[31] L Kjellin and C Westrin, 'Involuntary Admissions and Coercive Measures in Psychiatric Care' (1998) 21 *International Journal of Law and Psychiatry* 31; C Lidz, E Mulvey, S Hoge, B Kirsch, J Monahan, M Eisenberg, W Gardner and L Roth, 'Factual Sources of Psychiatric Patients' Perceptions of Coercion in the Hospital Admission Process' (1998) 155 *American Journal of Psychiatry* 1254; E Elbogen, J Swanson and M Swartz, 'Effects of Legal Mechanisms on Perceived Coercion and Treatment Adherence Among Persons with Severe Mental Illness' (2003) 191 *Journal of Nervous and Mental Disease* 629.

[32] M Swartz, HR Wagner, J Swanson, V Hiday and B Burns, 'The Perceived Coerciveness of Involuntary Outpatient Commitment: Findings from an Experimental Study' (2002) 30 *Journal of the American Academy of Psychiatry and Law* 207; M Swartz, J Swanson and J Monahan, 'Endorsement of Personal Benefit of Outpatient Commitment Among Persons with Severe Mental Illness' (2003) 9 *Psychology Public Policy and Law* 70.

[33] R Nicholson, C Ekenstam and S Norwood, 'Coercion and the Outcome of Psychiatric Hospitalisation' (1996) 19 *International Journal of Law and Psychiatry* 201; B McKenna, A Simpson and T Laidlaw, 'Patient Perception of Coercion on Admission to Psychiatric Services' (1999) 22 *International Journal of Law and Psychiatry* 143; M Swartz, HR Wagner, J Swanson, V Hiday and B Burns, 'Perceived Coerciveness of Involuntary Outpatient Commitment: Findings from an Experimental Study' (2002) 30 *Journal of the American Academy of Psychiatry and Law* 207; E Elbogen, J Swanson and M Swartz, 'Effects of Legal Mechanisms on Perceived Coercion and Treatment Adherence Among Persons with Severe Mental Illness' (2003) 191 *Journal of Nervous and Mental Disease* 629.

[34] V Hiday, M Swartz, J Swanson and HR Wagner, 'Patient Perceptions of Coercion in Mental Hospital Admission' (1997) 20(2) *International Journal of Law and Psychiatry* 227, 237.

should not be considered synonymous with coercion'.[35] Substantial numbers of compulsory patients do not feel coerced, while many informal patients do feel coerced. Patients who feel they have been given a 'voice', or been through a fair process, tend to experience less coercion,[36] and many involuntary patients later revise their opinions and retrospectively endorse their need for compulsory care.[37] Moreover, there is little evidence that involuntary status leads to poorer treatment outcomes.[38]

Nevertheless, these studies consistently identify groups of patients who remain adamantly opposed to their involuntary treatment, and some clinicians interviewed in the New Zealand study observed that patients who remain fully determined not to receive treatment and to avoid contact with a community team are not suitable candidates for involuntary outpatient care. Typical comments were: 'You can't really force someone to rehabilitate'; 'If you haven't got a therapeutic alliance it's pretty useless'; and the patient has 'got to recognise the authority of the order', or its validity, at some level for it to work.[39] Some degree of collaboration between clinician and patient was considered essential to effective use of involuntary outpatient care.[40]

It may still be the case that treatment under a CTO is less restrictive than compulsory inpatient care. This has long been observed[41] and was a consistent theme in our interviews with involuntary outpatients in New Zealand. Many patients under CTOs described the order as a 'stepping stone', 'pathway', or

[35] R Nicholson, C Ekenstam and S Norwood, 'Coercion and the Outcome of Psychiatric Hospitalisation' (1996) 19 *International Journal of Law and Psychiatry* 201, 213. See also Bernadette McSherry, this volume, ch 16.

[36] C Lidz, S Hoge, W Gardner, N Bennett, J Monahan, E Mulvey and L Roth, 'Perceived Coercion in Mental Hospital Admission' (1995) 52 *Archives of General Psychiatry* 1034; V Hiday, M Swartz, J Swanson and HR Wagner, 'Patient Perceptions of Coercion in Mental Hospital Admission' (1997) 20(2) *International Journal of Law and Psychiatry* 227; C Lidz, 'Coercion in Psychiatric Care: What Have We Learned from the Research?' (1998) 26 *Journal of the American Academy of Psychiatry and Law* 631.

[37] N Adams and R Hafner, 'Attitudes of Psychiatric Patients and their Relatives to Involuntary Treatment' (1991) 25 *Australian and New Zealand Journal of Psychiatry* 231; W Gardner, C Lidz, S Hoge, J Monahan, M Eisenberg, N Bennett, E Mulvey and L Roth, 'Patients' Revisions of their Beliefs About the Need for Hospitalization' (1999) 156 *American Journal of Psychiatry* 1385.

[38] R Kaltiala, P Laippala and R Saloknagas, 'Impact of Coercion on Treatment Outcome' (1997) 20 *International Journal of Law and Psychiatry* 311; T Steinert and P Schmid, 'Effect of Voluntariness of Participation in Treatment on Short-Term Outcome in Inpatients with Schizophrenia' (2004) 55 *Psychiatric Services* 786; R Nicholson, C Ekenstam and S Norwood, 'Coercion and the Outcome of Psychiatric Hospitalization' (1996) 19 *International Journal of Law and Psychiatry* 201.

[39] R Mullen, J Dawson and A Gibbs, 'Dilemmas for Clinicians in Use of Community Treatment Orders' (2006) 29 *International Journal of Law and Psychiatry* 535.

[40] *ibid*, 542.

[41] In the empirical literature, see eg T Scheid-Cook, 'Outpatient Commitment as both Social Control and Least Restrictive Alternative' (1991) 32 *Sociological Quarterly* 43.

'bridge' to greater independence from the hospital.[42] CTOs were widely considered to be less restrictive than long-term hospitalisation or imprisonment,[43] and treatment under the CTO was compared particularly favourably to forensic care.

More than 30 per cent of the sample of compulsory outpatients interviewed in the New Zealand study had previously been under the care of the forensic service.[44] Placement on a CTO, under civil mental health legislation, was a well-trodden pathway out of that form of care. Treatment under a CTO was consistently preferred by these patients. It was said: 'The real bad part of my life was in forensics'; 'It's better than the bashings, seclusions and jabs at [hospital X]'; 'I've come straight from the lock-up place'; 'Now I can come and go as I please, go outside, go for walk in the fresh air'. Many patients clearly *believed* their treatment under the CTO had prevented their re-admission to a more restrictive form of care.

There is a limit, however, to the length of time for which a CTO can be viewed as a genuine alternative to hospital care. Patients appearing before courts or tribunals for the renewal or extension of their CTO are frequently described as 'stable'. Their progress may be ascribed to greater compliance with medication and to greater continuity of care provided under the 'structure' of the CTO. In such cases, the order may be used in a largely preventive manner. Thus it is doubtful whether—at the moment the order is renewed—the CTO can legitimately be viewed as an alternative to compulsory hospital care. There is often huge pressure on the remaining hospital beds in heavily de-institutionalised mental health systems, so patients whose condition is considered stable would not usually be immediate candidates for inpatient care.

Although the empirical research indicates that compulsory outpatients have many different views concerning the constraints on their freedom associated with treatment under a CTO, a substantial proportion clearly feel controlled, restricted and under continuing surveillance by the members of a community mental health team. Many outpatients resent the pressure they are under to accept medication, and some are never reconciled to their involuntary treatment.

The coercion studies and the qualitative investigations of patients' views therefore support the common sense notion that the rights of compulsory outpatients to liberty, privacy, and to refuse treatment, that are protected by human rights norms, are significantly limited by compulsory outpatient care, and for some patients the experience of coercion and stigma are central features of the experience. A considerable burden of explanation must therefore lie on the state, under human rights law, to justify using this form of care. To meet that

---

[42] In its report, *Forced into Treatment: The Role of Coercion in Clinical Practice* (Washington DC, American Psychiatric Press, 1994), the Group for the Advancement of Psychiatry wrote: 'As we examined … forced treatment situations, we found repeatedly that initial coercion could lead to greater freedom'.

[43] A Gibbs, J Dawson, C Ansley and R Mullen, 'How Patients in New Zealand View Community Treatment Orders' (2005) 14 *Journal of Mental Health* 357, 362.

[44] *ibid*, 361.

burden, the state must establish that its objectives are sufficiently pressing or important to justify the existence of an involuntary outpatient treatment regime, and to justify its use in particular cases. It must show there is a rational relationship between the measures employed and the outcomes sought. It must show that 'proportionate' measures are used. And it must present convincing arguments that a fair balance is ultimately struck between the interests of the state and the rights of individuals subject to compulsory community care.

III.   The Calculus of Justification

A.   The Interests of the State and Third Parties

Numerous state interests may justify the use of compulsory outpatient treatment, even with patients who pose no serious threat of harm, and these arguments can be expressed in many different terms. The main hope may be that sustained treatment under a CTO will improve the quality of life of people with severe mental conditions whose capacity to make decisions about their psychiatric treatment is significantly impaired. Requiring contact to be maintained with a community service may prevent relapse in their illness, or reduce the severity of its consequences. It may reduce the stress imposed on a person's family or friends, and ensure the person receives sustained attention from the mental health service that they would not otherwise accept.

Many of these potential benefits may not accrue directly to the state, however, although it is the relationship between the state and the individual under compulsory treatment that is the primary focus of the human rights analysis. The benefits may accrue, at least in part, to families, carers and third parties, and there is a risk that their interests will not receive sufficient attention in the analysis if they are not viewed as primary parties to the constitutional relationship between the individual and the state. To count directly in the human rights analysis the interests of families, carers and third parties must be re-cast, therefore, as interests or objectives of the state, which can justify the state's actions during the operation of the CTO regime.

This re-casting, or fixing of the relevant interests on to the state, is not difficult to achieve. The state clearly has strong interests in promoting the health and safety of all its citizens, in fostering the support of families and carers for the mentally ill, and in directing psychiatric services towards those most in need. The interests of third parties to the relationship between the individual and the state must be re-conceptualised in this fashion, however, to count directly in the human rights analysis.

Three possible justifications for the use of CTOs with patients who pose no imminent threat of harm will now be discussed, to illustrate something of the range of arguments available.

(i) Promoting the 'Positive Liberty' of the Mentally Ill

One way to conceptualise the potential benefits of involuntary outpatient treatment for those individuals with a serious mental illness is to consider whether it may promote their 'positive liberty'. This concept of liberty may be less familiar to lawyers than negative liberty—or freedom from interference by others—which is the kind of liberty that is usually considered to be embedded in the notion of human rights.

Positive liberty, in contrast, concerns individuals' capacity for self-governance, or for self-directed activity, or their ability to meet their own goals and maintain important relationships, without their being dominated by internal constraints. Crawford Macpherson calls it 'self-mastery' and says the aim is to remove or minimise impediments to a person's 'developmental power'.[45] Charles Taylor calls it 'the exercise of control over one's own life'.[46] He argues that internal barriers within a person count as obstacles to it. Isaiah Berlin describes it as the capacity for self-direction: 'I wish to be an instrument of my own will', he writes, 'to be moved by reasons, not causes ... conceiving of goals and policies of my own and realising them'.[47]

It is presumably this concept of liberty that Paul Appelbaum and Thomas Gutheil had in mind when they said that the purpose of medication in psychiatry was to restore the patient's control over his or her own mind.[48] Similarly, the New York Court of Appeals declared, in its decision upholding the constitutionality of that State's outpatient commitment statute, that this regime may enable patients 'to live and work freely and productively through compliance with necessary treatment'.[49]

Individuals with a serious mental illness will have goals of their own—to maintain an independent living situation, for example, or an intimate relationship, or contact with their children, or a job. They may be unable to attain those aims, however, when acutely unwell. And yet they may not accept continuing treatment on a voluntary basis. Would compulsory treatment then be justified, to promote their capacity to achieve their own aims, on the basis that the consequences of their illness prevented them from exercising effective control over

---

[45] CB Macpherson, *Democratic Theory: Essays in Retrieval* (Oxford, Clarendon Press, 1973) 113.

[46] C Taylor, 'What's Wrong with Negative Liberty?' in A Ryan (ed), *The Idea of Freedom: Essays in Honour of Isaiah Berlin* (New York, Oxford University Press, 1979).

[47] I Berlin, *Two Concepts of Liberty* (Oxford, Oxford University Press, 1958) 178.

[48] Similar arguments have been made about the meaning of autonomy. Beauchamp and Childress, for instance, describe autonomy as personal rule of self, and say it has two main components: freedom from controlling influences by others, and freedom from personal limitations that prevent meaningful choice: T Beauchamp and J Childress, *Principles of Biomedical Ethics*, 6th edn (New York, Oxford University Press, 2009). Joseph Raz writes: 'It is wrong to identify autonomy with [a] right against coercion ... and to hold that right ... as defeating ... all, or almost all, other considerations': J Raz, *The Morality of Freedom* (Oxford, Clarendon Press, 1986) 207.

[49] *In re KL* 806 NE 2d 480 (2004) 484.

their life? Compulsory treatment might promote a person's positive liberty, in other words, even if it reduces their negative liberty simultaneously.

This kind of issue often surfaces before tribunals, when the patient whose CTO is under review appears to have completely conflicting aims. Patients may express both their desire to maintain an independent living situation, outside hospital, for example, and their desire to cease medication—even though ceasing treatment may have led repeatedly to their hospitalisation in the past.[50] In such cases, the patient's capacity for self-governance may be doubtful, or fluctuating, or may appear to be maintained only by treatment under the CTO. Can the tribunal properly conclude, in those circumstances, that the person so lacks the capacity for self-governance that this would justify continuing his or her compulsory outpatient care?

At the centre of this kind of determination lies the tribunal's assessment of the person's capacity to exercise control over his or her life. But that assessment is not value-free. The way the tribunal interprets and applies the capacity test is bound to be influenced, one way or another, by the relative significance it ascribes to the positive and negative liberty interests of the person under the CTO. If the tribunal attaches considerable importance to the person's ability to govern consistently his or her life, without being dominated by the psychopathology of serious mental illness, it might consider it legitimate to take a longitudinal and predictive view of that person's need for compulsory outpatient care. It might consider all the available evidence concerning the course of that person's illness, and the likely prognosis, and consider capacity for self-governance in that light. And then it might extend the CTO to promote that person's continuing ability to meet his or her chosen ends.

The New Zealand Mental Health Review Tribunal reasoned in this way in a recent case concerning an elderly man with a long history of delusional disorder and seriously disrupted personal relationships, for whom there had been great difficulty finding a placement outside hospital.[51] He informed the tribunal that he had two apparently conflicting desires: his desire to live in the rest home to which he had been admitted solely on the condition that he took medication for his long-standing disorder; and his desire to cease treatment, because, immediately after its administration, it made him feel like he had 'cotton wool' in his head. In deciding to extend his CTO, the tribunal declared:[52]

> It is the applicant's own desire to live in the rest home. However, this conflicts with another desire: to discontinue his medication ... That would prevent him achieving and maintaining a living arrangement that is very much in his interests and desired by him. We consider that this meets the test for seriously diminished capacity for self-care ... It is not the tribunal telling the applicant how and where he must live his own life, it is the

---

[50] These were the facts of *In re EJH*, NZ MHRT, No 07/140, 19 December 2007.
[51] *In re EJH*, NZ MHRT, No 07/140, 19 December 2007.
[52] *In re EJH*, NZ MHRT, No 07/140, 19 December 2007 at [18.2], [19].

applicant himself who desires these things, but if he were free to discontinue his medication he would raise a barrier to his achieving his own goals.

Here the desire to promote the patient's positive liberty interests interacts with the capacity assessment process. It therefore constitutes an important part of the tribunal's justification for limiting this man's rights.

(ii)   Harnessing the Support of Families and Carers

Many further arguments can be made in support of compulsory outpatient treatment that focus on the benefits it may confer on family members, carers or third parties, by modifying the adverse consequences of a person's illness. The interests of these other parties are not necessarily in conflict with those of the person under the CTO. The support of these parties may help promote the social and environmental conditions within which that person's capacities may develop or flourish. As Joseph Raz puts it: '[a]n autonomous personality can only develop and flourish against a background of biological and social constraints which fix some of its human needs'.[53] If a CTO can 'leverage' greater social support for the involuntary patient, or the support of accommodation providers that would not otherwise be available, it may indirectly promote that person's autonomy.

Feminist ethicists have argued that personal autonomy is composed, at least in part, of a cluster, or repertoire, of different skills and capacities that can only be developed in the context of social relationships. They call this 'relational autonomy'.[54] To permit a person with a lengthy history of mental illness to disengage from care and become socially isolated may not promote their autonomy, on that view.

Similarly, Marian Verkerk has argued that placing too much emphasis on the right of a person with a serious mental illness to refuse community mental health care may leave carers in an intolerable bind: 'On the one hand patients are regarded as individuals who have a strong interest in (and a right to) freedom and non-interference; on the other hand many of them have a desperate need for flourishing, viable relationships'.[55] To escape this bind, she suggests, there should be 'a perspective in which "compassionate interference" is not so much a threat to autonomy, but a means of attaining autonomy'.[56] There should be a care perspective on coercion and autonomy, which requires a 'balancing' of the various autonomy interests of the person concerned.

It would be sentimental to suggest that the interests of compulsory outpatients and their families always coincide. Their interests may conflict, or be aligned, or be partly in conflict and partly aligned. CTOs should not be used to reinforce

---

[53]   J Raz, *The Morality of Freedom* (Oxford, Clarendon Press, 1986) 155.

[54]   C Mackenzie and N Soljar (eds), *Relational Autonomy: Feminist Essays on Autonomy, Agency, and the Self* (New York, Oxford University Press, 2000).

[55]   M Verkerk, 'A Care Perspective on Coercion and Autonomy' (1999) 13 *Bioethics* 358, 359.

[56]   *ibid*, 359.

coercive relationships within families, or simply to help families claim resources from the mental health system that should be available regardless of the patient's compulsory status. Nevertheless, families and other informal carers have a major role as stakeholders in involuntary outpatient treatment, and they may only be prepared to provide some forms of support for the patient—continuing accommodation following recent discharge from hospital, for instance—during continuation of a CTO.[57] Supported accommodation providers also have legal and ethical obligations to other residents.

Many people with severe mental disorders live with family members who may experience a considerable burden of care.[58] Family members often have great difficulty accessing resources in the community for their relative,[59] and feel frustrated[60] or poorly consulted[61] in their relations with mental health services. The need to support and consult family members in the treatment of people with severe mental disorders is increasingly recognised as a mainstream aspect of psychiatric practice.[62] Nevertheless, the family members of compulsory outpatients that we interviewed in New Zealand consistently expressed the view that the CTO increased their purchase on the mental health system, that it helped them share the burden of monitoring the patient's condition with members of the community team, and that it promoted greater continuity of care for their relative, greater compliance with treatment, and improved family relationships.[63] Many compulsory outpatients expressed a similar view: that their families had experienced benefits from the CTO.[64]

[57]   R Mullen, A Gibbs and J Dawson, 'Family Perspective on Community Treatment Orders: A New Zealand Study' (2006) 52 *International Journal of Social Psychiatry* 469.

[58]   I Falloon, L Magliano, V Graham Hole and R Woodroffe, 'The Stress of Caring for Disabling Mental Disorders in a Home Based Rehabilitation Service' (1996) 184 *Journal of Nervous and Mental Diseases* 381; P Solomon, 'Research on the Coercion of Persons with Severe Mental Illness' in D Dennis and J Monahan (eds), *Coercion and Aggressive Community Treatment: A New Frontier in Mental Health Law* (New York, Plenum, 1996).

[59]   L Hallam, 'How Involuntary Commitment Impacts on the Burden of Care of the Family (2007) 16 *International Journal of Mental Health Nursing* 247; J Shankar and S Muthuswamy, 'Support Needs of Family Caregivers of People who Experience Mental Illness and the Role of Mental Health Services' (2007) *Families in Society* 302.

[60]   S Hoge, C Lidz, E Mulvey, L Roth, N Bennett, L Siminoff, R Arnold and J Monahan, 'Patient, Family and Staff Perceptions of Coercion in Mental Hospital Admission: An Exploratory Study' (1993) 11 *Behavioral Sciences and the Law* 281.

[61]   L Hallam, 'How Involuntary Commitment Impacts on the Burden of Care of the Family (2007) 16 *International Journal of Mental Health Nursing* 247 R Mullen, A Gibbs and J Dawson, 'Family Perspectives on Community Treatment Orders: A New Zealand Study' (2006) 52 *International Journal of Social Psychiatry* 469.

[62]   Royal Australian and New Zealand College of Psychiatrists, 'Clinical Practice Guidelines for the Treatment of Schizophrenia and Related Disorders' (2005) 39 *Australian and New Zealand Journal of Psychiatry* 1.

[63]   R Mullen, A Gibbs and J Dawson, 'Family Perspectives on Community Treatment Orders: A New Zealand Study' (2006) 52 *International Journal of Social Psychiatry* 469.

[64]   A Gibbs, J Dawson, C Ansley and R Mullen, 'How Patients in New Zealand View Community Treatment Orders' (2005) 14 *Journal of Mental Health* 357.

Although the attention of the law and of clinicians should focus primarily on the rights and needs of the individual patient, the support that families and other carers often experience from a CTO may in fact encourage them to provide assistance to the patient—especially accommodation—that would not otherwise be available. That support may be vital to that person's survival outside hospital. It may promote that person's social inclusion, and it may contribute significantly to the effective exercise of personal autonomy. The support families and other carers appear to receive from CTOs can therefore be fairly viewed, in those circumstances, as an important form of support for the person under involuntary outpatient care.

(iii) The Structural Functions of CTOs

Experienced clinicians often suggest CTOs work in a largely structural manner, through the 'framework' they provide for outpatient care, and through the 'package' of therapeutic measures attached.[65] A CTO may act as a kind of wrap around the therapeutic relationship between clinicians and patient, one that commits health professionals to treatment of the patient as much as it commits the patient to their care. As one clinician commented: 'It is not clear who is under the order, the patient or the nurse'.[66] A CTO may clearly signify to health professionals that certain patients need intensive community supervision, and may in fact enhance their sense of obligation towards the treatment of that patient.

The predominant view amongst psychiatrists surveyed in New Zealand concerning their experience of a well-embedded national CTO regime was that the order may bind into place the necessary community services, encourage compliance with medication, and permit the early identification of relapse.[67] In particular, the CTO regime was seen to clarify the authority of health professionals to maintain contact with the patient, permitting ongoing negotiations about treatment to proceed. CTOs were seen to support the involvement of families and other agencies in care, and to have a significant impact, in some cases, on

---

[65] J Swanson, M Swartz, L George, B Burns, V Hiday, R Borum and HR Wagner, 'Interpreting the Effectiveness of Involuntary Outpatient Commitment: A Conceptual Model' (1997) 25 *Journal of the American Academy of Psychiatry and Law* 5; S Romans, J Dawson, R Mullen and A Gibbs, 'How Mental Health Clinicians View Community Treatment Orders: A National New Zealand Survey' (2004) 38 *Australian and New Zealand Journal of Psychiatry* 836; R Mullen, J Dawson and A Gibbs, 'Dilemmas for Clinicians in Use of Community Treatment Orders' (2006) 29 *International Journal of Law and Psychiatry* 535.

[66] S Romans, J Dawson, R Mullen and A Gibbs, 'How Mental Health Clinicians View Community Treatment Orders: A National New Zealand Survey' (2004) 38 *Australian and New Zealand Journal of Psychiatry* 836, 840.

[67] *ibid.* One Australian study concluded: 'A great advantage of CTOs is their ability to reduce the period of the patient's disturbed behaviour as it is not necessary to wait until the patient is sufficiently ill to justify involuntary admission': K Vaughan, N McConaghy, C Wolf, C Myhr and T Black, 'Community Treatment Orders: Relationship to Clinical Care, Medication Compliance, Behavioural Disturbance and Readmission' (2000) 34 *Australian and New Zealand Journal of Psychiatry* 801, 808.

patients' attitudes to their illness. These complex effects may lead to clinical improvement, enhanced 'insight'[68] and greater stability in the patient's condition. If so, CTOs might be part of the solution to what is widely perceived to be a major failing of de-institutionalisation: the lack of continuity of care.

On the other hand, the New Zealand clinicians also expressed concerns about the adverse impact of coercion on the therapeutic alliance, the potential for long-term use of CTOs to promote dependence on the mental health system, and the difficulties involved in determining the right moment to discharge a person from compulsory outpatient care.[69]

Compulsion was not seen by New Zealand clinicians as a substitute for the provision of an adequate community mental health service. On the contrary, success was seen to depend on the quality and extent of the services provided. There was a perception, however, that placing a patient on a CTO may enhance service provision, and that involuntary outpatients may receive priority for treatment in poorly resourced systems. Perhaps a compulsory treatment order should not be required for this purpose. Compulsion should not be a substitute for good clinical practice, or be simply a vehicle for claiming resources on behalf of a patient. But if a CTO does focus attention on patients who are most in need of treatment, despite their reluctance, it may correct a possible tendency of mental health services to shift their focus to those who are less difficult to engage.

CTOs therefore seem to play a complex structural role that intersects with resource allocation decisions. The Ontario legislature may have had this role in mind when it declared, at the start of its CTO provisions, enacted in 2000, that: '[t]he purpose of a community treatment order is to provide a person with a serious mental disorder with a comprehensive plan of community-based treatment or care'.[70]

(iv) Conclusions on the Calculus of Justification

The above discussion illustrates something of the range of state objectives that may be advanced to justify the limits on rights imposed by a CTO regime, even the rights of patients who present no imminent threat of harm. A court entertaining a human rights challenge to a CTO regime applied to such patients would have to decide whether those objectives were sufficiently pressing, or compelling, or demonstrably justified, to outweigh the serious impact on rights that compulsory outpatient treatment entails—because, as the New York Court

---

[68] On the meaning of this term, see Ian Freckelton, this volume, ch 9.

[69] S Romans, J Dawson, R Mullen and A Gibbs, 'How Mental Health Clinicians View Community Treatment Orders: A National New Zealand Survey' (2004) 38 *Australian and New Zealand Journal of Psychiatry* 836; R Mullen, J Dawson and A Gibbs, 'Dilemmas for Clinicians in Use of Community Treatment Orders' (2006) 29 *International Journal of Law and Psychiatry* 535.

[70] Mental Health Act (Ontario) s 33.1(3) (inserted in 2000, via Bill 68, an Act in memory of Brian Smith, to amend the Mental Health Act and the Health Care Consent Act 1996, known as Brian's Law).

of Appeals has put it, 'the fundamental right of mentally ill persons to refuse treatment may have to yield to compelling state interests'.[71]

There are two major parts to this inquiry: the court must assess both the importance of the state's objectives and the seriousness of the impact on rights. The Canadian jurisprudence suggests the test is whether 'the legislative objective, albeit important, is nevertheless outweighed by the abridgement of rights';[72] or whether there is 'proportionality between the deleterious and salutary effects of the measure';[73] or whether the limit on rights is 'an acceptable price to pay for the benefit of the law'.[74] In making that judgement, the court would have to consider both the potential benefits of CTOs for all parties and the possibility that their use may entail less interference with a person's rights than periodic episodes of compulsory inpatient care.

The court would have to face the fact, however, that many of the positive outcomes claimed for CTOs have not been established by rigorous, quantitative, evaluation research. This leads to the next step in the calculus: whether a rational connection can be established—on the evidence—between the exercise of community treatment powers and their apparent aims.

IV. The Evidence Concerning the Efficacy of CTOs

Many clinicians who work with CTOs *believe* they are a useful tool in the pursuit of core clinical aims for people with a serious mental illness.[75] When Rachel Churchill and colleagues from the Institute of Psychiatry reviewed the evaluation research, however, against the rigorous canons of 'evidence-based medicine',[76] they reached a more sceptical conclusion.[77] They found:

> It is not possible to state whether CTOs are beneficial or harmful to patients ... [R]esearch in this area has been beset by conceptual, practical and methodological problems, and the general quality of the empirical evidence is poor ... The perceptions of CTOs held by different stakeholder groups ... were very mixed, with both positive and negative views expressed ... [T]here is currently no robust evidence about either

---

[71] *In re KL* 806 NE 2d 480 (2004) 485.

[72] *R v Edwards Books and Art* [1986] 2 SCR 713, 768.

[73] *Dagenais v CBC* [1994] 3 SCR 835, 889.

[74] P Hogg, *Constitutional Law of Canada*, 5th edn (supp) (Toronto, Thomson, 2007) para 38–43.

[75] S Romans, J Dawson, R Mullen and A Gibbs, 'How Mental Health Clinicians View Community Treatment Orders: A National New Zealand Survey' (2004) 38 *Australian and New Zealand Journal of Psychiatry* 836.

[76] D Sackett, W Rosenberg, J Gray, R Haynes and W Richardson, 'Evidence-Based Medicine: What it is and What it isn't' (1996) 312 *British Medical Journal* 71; I Chalmers, 'Trying to Do More Harm than Good in Policy and Practice: The Role of Rigorous, Transparent, Up-to-Date Evaluations' (2003) 589 *Annals American Academy of Political and Social Sciences* 22.

[77] R Churchill, G Owen, S Singh and M Hotopf, *International Experiences of Using Community Treatment Orders* (London, Institute of Psychiatry, 2007).

the positive or negative effects of CTOs on key outcomes, including hospital readmission, length of hospital stay, improved medication compliance, or patients' quality of life.[78]

This is an important finding. Nevertheless, it is necessary to distinguish the kinds of evidence that are considered reliable by advocates of evidence-based medicine from the kinds of evidence that would be required to meet the demands of *human rights law*. Somewhat minimal standards of evidence have typically been required by courts inquiring into the connection between a state's objectives and measures taken to limit rights.

The general principle of proportionality requires a state to show that there is 'a reasonable relationship between a particular objective to be achieved and the means used to achieve that objective',[79] or 'a rational connection' between means and ends.[80] Other ways to express this are to say the measures must be 'suitable'[81] or 'necessary'.[82]

There is little consistency evident in the decisions of the courts, however, as to the quality or strength of the evidence that is required to establish this connection on the facts. Justice McLachlin, discussing the position under the Canadian Charter, said a court reviewing the matter 'must determine the actual connection between the objective and what the law will in fact achieve', and that this judgement must be 'based on the facts of the law at issue and the proof offered of its justification, not on abstractions'.[83] Similarly, Richard Clayton and Hugh Tomlinson argue that there should be 'a close and penetrating examination of the factual justification for the restriction' of the right.[84]

Peter Hogg observes, in contrast, that it will often be 'difficult to establish by evidence' that there is 'a causal relationship between the objective of the law and the measures enacted', and that 'the Supreme Court of Canada has not always insisted on direct proof of the causal relationship'.[85] He states that Canadian courts may reach their own conclusions on such matters, based on judicial notice, 'logic', or 'common sense'.[86] Moreover, it seems that expert opinion is sufficient when evidence is required.

---

[78]   *ibid*, 7.
[79]   R Clayton and H Tomlinson, *The Law of Human Rights*, 2nd edn (Oxford, Oxford University Press, 2009) 323.
[80]   *ibid*, 326; *R v Oakes* [1986] 1 SCR 103; *R v Secretary of State for the Home Department, ex p Daly* [2001] 2 AC 532.
[81]   R Clayton and H Tomlinson, *The Law of Human Rights*, 2nd edn (Oxford, Oxford University Press, 2009) 323.
[82]   See *Sunday Times v United Kingdom (No 1)* (A/30) (1979) 2 EHRR 245.
[83]   *RJR-MacDonald v Attorney-General of Canada* [1995] 3 SCR 199, 226.
[84]   R Clayton and H Tomlinson, *The Law of Human Rights*, 2nd edn (Oxford, Oxford University Press, 2009) 354.
[85]   P Hogg, *Constitutional Law of Canada*, 5th edn supp (Toronto, Thomson, 2007) para 38–34.
[86]   *ibid*, para 38–35.

Clayton and Tomlinson may be right that, under European human rights law, 'if there is no evidence to support the justification relied upon then an interference will be disproportionate',[87] and that stronger forms of evidence are required when a measure affects intimate aspects of private life,[88] as is the case with CTOs. But none of the cases suggest the evidence must meet the rigorous standards favoured by the practitioners of evidence-based medicine. Thus evidence of positive professional opinion concerning CTOs would probably suffice. The Royal College of Psychiatrists has long endorsed CTOs in some form.[89] The New Zealand psychiatrists surveyed preferred a mental health system with CTOs by a ratio of eight to one.[90] The Canadian Psychiatric Association has taken the position that CTOs are:

useful in assisting some patients with persistent deficits in insight to follow a treatment regime while living in the community ... [but a] comprehensive package of psychiatric and community support services must be available.[91]

A committee appointed by the American Psychiatric Association to review the evidence concluded that:

mandatory outpatient treatment can be a useful intervention for a small subset of patients with severe mental illness who go in and out of psychiatric hospitals through the so-called 'revolving door' ... [It is] linked to improved patient outcomes when prescribed for extended periods of time and coupled with ... intensive, individualised outpatient services.[92]

Although there is disagreement among commentators about the efficacy of CTOs, that kind of endorsement by professional bodies is probably sufficient to meet the modest demands for evidence of a rational connection between measure and aim set by human rights law. Perhaps this conclusion should be modified, however, by two conditions, based on the caveats entered by the professional bodies that have considered the matter. Those conditions would be: that the use of CTOs should be limited to those who are 'severely mentally ill with high hospital admission rate histories, poor medication compliance, and

---

[87] R Clayton and H Tomlinson, *The Law of Human Rights*, 2nd edn (Oxford, Oxford University Press, 2009) 333.

[88] *Dudgeon v United Kingdom* (A/45) (1982) 4 EHRR 149; *Smith and Grady v United Kingdom* (1999) 29 EHRR 493.

[89] Royal College of Psychiatrists, *Community Supervision Orders* (London, Royal College of Psychiatrists, 1993).

[90] S Romans, J Dawson, R Mullen and A Gibbs, 'How Mental Health Clinicians View Community Treatment Orders: A National New Zealand Survey' (2004) 38 *Australian and New Zealand Journal of Psychiatry* 836.

[91] R O'Reilly, S Brooks, G Chaimowitz, G Neilson, P Carr, E Zikos, P Leichner and P Beck, 'CPA Position Paper: Mandatory Outpatient Treatment' (2003) 48 *Canadian Journal of Psychiatry*, Insert, 1, 5; available at: www.publications.cpa-apc.org/media.php?mid=140.

[92] J Gerbasi, R Bonnie and R Binder, 'Resource Document on Mandatory Outpatient Commitment' (2000) 28 *Journal of the American Academy of Psychiatry and Law* 127, 128.

aftercare needs';[93] and that a comprehensive community mental health service must be available to patients under CTOs.

V. The Least Drastic Means

Finally, to justify the limits placed on patients' rights to liberty, security, or privacy, the state has to show that its CTO regime employs the least drastic, or least restrictive means to achieve its legitimate aims. According to Peter Hogg, in Canada this requirement 'has turned out to be the heart and soul' of the calculus of justification.[94] Canadian courts have 'usually readily accepted'[95] that the State's aims are sufficiently important to justify limits on rights, and that the State's means are rationally connected to those aims. A more searching inquiry has been conducted, however, into the state's use of 'carefully tailored'[96] means.

A full inquiry into the means used to implement involuntary outpatient care would require careful scrutiny of: all powers exercised over involuntary outpatients; all mandatory conditions imposed on their community tenure; and the scope of any discretion exercised by clinicians (or others who manage involuntary outpatients) in the exercise of their powers. A court would have to determine the nature and seriousness of the impact of each of those measures on specific rights, and then judge the necessity for each measure in light of the importance it attributed to the State's aims. Community treatment powers would survive this scrutiny if they impaired the relevant rights 'as little as possible';[97] or impaired them 'no more than is necessary to accomplish' the State's legitimate objectives;[98] or the court considered there was no 'excessive or disproportionate impact' on rights.[99]

Peter Hogg argues that the yardstick employed is a *minimum*, not a *minimal* impact test.[100] This is because the legitimacy of the restrictions on rights has to be measured against the importance of the State's aims, and where those aims are judged to be particularly important very significant limits on rights—that may be much more than minimal—can pass the test. Moreover, a court is likely to grant some deference to the legislature regarding its choice of means.[101] As Richard

---

[93]   R Churchill, G Owen, S Singh and M Hotopf, *International Experiences of Using Community Treatment Orders* (London, Institute of Psychiatry, 2007) 109.

[94]   P Hogg, *Constitutional Law of Canada*, 5th edn (supp) (Toronto, Thomson, 2007) para 38–36.

[95]   *ibid*, para 38–36.

[96]   *RJR-MacDonald v Attorney-General of Canada* [1995] 3 SCR 199, 236 (McLachlin J).

[97]   *R v Oakes* [1986] 1 SCR 103, 138.

[98]   R Clayton and H Tomlinson, *The Law of Human Rights*, 2nd edn (Oxford, Oxford University Press, 2009) 336.

[99]   *ibid*, 342.

[100]   P Hogg, *Constitutional Law of Canada*, 5th edn (supp) (Toronto, Thomson, 2007) para 38–36.

[101]   See *Illinois Election Board v Socialist Workers Party* 440 US 173 (1979) 188, 189 (Blackmun J).

Clayton and Hugh Tomlinson put it, the court must assess the marginal utility of a measure against its marginal impact, while leaving a 'range of reasonable alternatives' to the State.[102]

The critical powers that require scrutiny in this light are those governing: the treatment of an involuntary outpatient in the community; the monitoring of their condition; control over the patient's place of residence, and any other limits on freedom of movement; access to the patient by health professionals, especially powers of entry into private premises; and the power to recall patients swiftly to hospital and re-institute compulsory inpatient care. The question is whether each aspect of those powers is necessary to achieve the State's legitimate aims (in light of the importance of those aims).

A very significant factor for a court to consider in making this final judgement is the prospect that a CTO regime will not achieve its aims if it confers insufficient authority on clinicians, compared with the voluntary approach to treatment, to give them confidence to make active use of the regime.[103]

A.   Treatment Powers

The scope of any powers to treat outpatients without consent will be particularly controversial and open to challenge on human rights grounds, particularly any power to administer medication via injection. The evidence does not suggest that any power to administer medication by force in a community setting needs to be conferred, however, to ensure clinicians make active use of a CTO regime. No such power is expressly conferred by the Australasian CTO regimes, for instance; yet those regimes have attracted the confidence of clinicians, and are widely used.[104] Nor is any power to administer medication by force or through the restraint of an objecting patient likely to be considered a safe or ethical practice by health professionals. A power of that kind would therefore have a disproportionate impact on rights.

No power of forced treatment in the community is conferred by the recently-enacted CTO regime for England and Wales,[105] and the absence of any such power was critical to the New York Court of Appeals's decision in *In re KL*[106] to

---

[102]   R Clayton and H Tomlinson, *The Law of Human Rights*, 2nd edn (Oxford, Oxford University Press, 2009) 329.

[103]   See J Dawson, *Community Treatment Orders: International Comparisons* (Dunedin, University of Otago, 2005), available at: www.otago.ac.nz/law/otagoCTO/index.html. J Dawson, 'Fault-lines in Community Treatment Order Legislation' (2006) 29 *International Journal of Law and Psychiatry* 482, 493, 494; J Dawson, 'Factors Influencing the Rate of Use of Community Treatment Orders' (2006) 6 *Psychiatry* 42.

[104]   J Dawson, 'Fault-lines in Community Treatment Order Legislation' (2006) 29 *International Journal of Law and Psychiatry* 482; S Lawton-Smith, *A Question of Numbers: The Potential Impact of Community Treatment Orders in England and Wales* (London, King's Fund, 2005).

[105]   See Mental Health Act 1983 Pt 4A.

[106]   *In re KL* 806 NE 2d 480 (2004).

uphold the constitutionality of that state's outpatient commitment statute. The court found specifically that Kendra's Law, as it is called, 'does not permit forced medical treatment'.[107] Non-compliance with an outpatient order in New York did not carry any criminal or civil penalty and was not a contempt of court. It 'simply triggers heightened scrutiny on the part of the physician, who must then determine whether the patient may be in need of involuntary hospitalization'.[108] There was therefore no violation of the patient's right to due process. In effect, the threat of reversion to inpatient care, rather than 'forced medication', was the main enforcement mechanism.

B.   Restrictions on Accommodation and Freedom of Movement

Explicit restrictions on the patient's place of residence, or limits imposed on freedom of movement, or on association with other people, will also trigger human rights scrutiny. In particular, if the conditions imposed purport to confine a person to a specific address, under close surveillance, that could constitute a deprivation of liberty that would attract the same substantive and procedural protections as other deprivations of liberty under human rights law.[109]

With regard to patients who pose no serious threat of harm, it is doubtful whether such powers are necessary or required. It is probably sufficient to specify, in certain cases, the kind (or 'level') of accommodation that must be available to a person (the scope of the nursing cover, for instance) and the level of support services required for them to live safely in the community, while leaving them free to move between service providers of the specified kind. That would be a less restrictive approach that might still satisfy the relevant aims.

There are good reasons not to order a vulnerable person to live at a specified community residence. It may prevent effective detention in social circumstances that are not subject to adequate quality control, and it may prevent that person becoming a guaranteed source of income for an unscrupulous entrepreneur.

C.   Powers of Entry

Powers of entry into a private residence are also particularly contentious. They intrude heavily on private life and rights to private property. Yet a major aim of a CTO regime—maintaining contact with the patient—may be thwarted if community health professionals cannot go through the door.

---

[107]   *ibid*, 484.
[108]   *ibid*, 485.
[109]   *Guzzardi v Italy* (A/39) (1981) 3 EHRR 333; *Winterwerp v The Netherlands* (A/33) (1979–80) 2 EHRR 387.

It would only be in rare situations that members of a treatment team might wish to rely on an explicit power of entry conferred by a CTO, to obtain access to a patient. Health professionals can enter private premises with the consent of the occupier. They may enter with the consent of the patient, or, where the patient is living with other family members or carers or resides in supported accommodation managed by others, those other persons may grant lawful entry. In most jurisdictions immediate entry onto private property is also authorised in emergencies to prevent an imminent threat to any person's safety,[110] or generic powers may be available, under mental health or public health legislation, that permit health professionals to enter and investigate the circumstances of vulnerable or unwell people.[111] The conditions of a CTO will usually require patients to attend outpatient appointments where their health can be assessed. It is only where avenues of that kind are inapplicable, or have proved ineffective, that health professionals might need to rely on an explicit power of entry attached to a CTO.

If the members of a community team cannot obtain ready access to the patient, on the other hand, to continue negotiations about treatment and assess the patient's condition, this may substantially undermine their willingness to use the CTO regime—if a cumbersome judicial procedure is required, for instance, that is little different from that required at the 'front end' of a civil commitment regime. There is also a widespread desire to avoid the involvement of the police, if at all possible, in these processes.

It is a considerable challenge, therefore, to design the least drastic powers of entry that can achieve the legitimate aims of a CTO regime. If independent powers of entry are to be conferred by a CTO, they should, at least, be governed by clear legal criteria that indicate their purposes and specify the circumstances in which they can be used, and they should be limited to designated classes of health professional who are currently engaged in the treatment of the patient.

A prior hearing before an independent body should not be required in an emergency, for entry to be lawful. But, in less urgent circumstances, some form of prior hearing, before an independent judicial body, would be required in many jurisdictions, where force, or police assistance, in entry, would be used.

D. Recall to Hospital

While the process of recall to hospital may not be activated frequently in practice, the credible threat of this occurring, should the patient fail to comply with the

---

[110] See, for example, the Police and Criminal Evidence Act 1984 s 17(1)(e), and the discussion of the principles of necessity in the mental health context in *R v Bournewood Community and Mental Health Trust, ex parte L* [1999] AC 458.

[111] A power of this kind is conferred on Approved Mental Health Professionals in England and Wales, for example, by the Mental Health Act 1983 s 115. It does not explicitly authorise entry by force.

conditions of the order, is widely considered by clinicians to be an essential component of an effective CTO regime.[112] If a cumbersome recall process is imposed by law, requiring clinicians to comply with the same kinds of standards and procedures that govern a person's initial certification or commitment, that may substantially reduce clinicians' willingness to use the scheme.

On the other hand, recall to hospital constitutes a form of re-detention of the person, to which comprehensive human rights protections apply.[113] Under European human rights law, this means the *Winterwerp* criteria governing detention for mental health purposes apply.[114] The recall decision must be based on 'objective medical expertise'; the person's condition must be of sufficient severity to warrant his or her involuntary hospitalisation; and the person must be released again if the relevant standards governing involuntary hospitalisation cease to apply. Moreover, the person is entitled to know the reasons for the re-detention, and to have access within a reasonable time to independent review of the need for compulsory hospital care.[115] No prior hearing is required before re-detention proceeds,[116] but the responsible clinicians should consider less restrictive measures first.[117]

Overall, these requirements suggest that an involuntary outpatient should not be recalled to hospital solely due to a failure to comply with the conditions of a CTO. Instead, the outpatient's recall must be 'necessary'. The person's condition must genuinely require involuntary assessment or treatment in hospital, or the admission to hospital must be required to undertake some process—such as a medical examination—that is required to continue the involuntary care. Recall powers or practices that do not meet these parameters, on the other hand, may not constitute the least drastic means of delivering involuntary outpatient care.

VI. Conclusions

This chapter has tried to indicate the likely structure of a comprehensive human rights analysis of a CTO regime. What conclusions can be drawn, therefore, concerning the compatibility of compulsory outpatient treatment with central principles of human rights?

The empirical literature reveals that the impact of a CTO is experienced in many different ways by compulsory outpatients. The order often seems to have both positive and negative effects simultaneously. But community treatment

---

[112] J Dawson, 'Fault-lines in Community Treatment Order Legislation' (2006) 29 *International Journal of Law and Psychiatry* 482.
[113] *X v United Kingdom* (App No 7215/75) (1982) 4 EHRR 188.
[114] *Winterwerp v The Netherlands* (A/33) (1979–80) 2 EHRR 387.
[115] *X v United Kingdom* (App No 7215/75) (1982) 4 EHRR 188.
[116] *ibid*; *In re KL* 806 NE 2d 480 (2004).
[117] *Litwa v Poland* (App No 26629/95) (2001) 33 EHRR 53 at para [78].

powers are clearly capable of intruding on the most intimate aspects of a person's life. The rights of the individual to personal liberty, security, privacy, and property are plainly implicated. The sense of control and surveillance, and the background threat of 'forced medication', may be deeply resented by the person concerned.

The difficulty is, however, that the state also has an important interest in promoting the social inclusion and the personal capacities of people whose ability to govern their lives may be significantly impaired by mental illness, and has a strong interest in preventing their return to compulsory hospital care. The importance of these state objectives make it unlikely that a court would consider a properly-calibrated CTO regime to be an unjustified interference with human rights, provided its standards, powers and procedures are adequately specified by law, and those treated under it have reasonable access to regular, independent review. Moreover, the widespread endorsement of CTOs by members of the psychiatric profession suggests a court would accept that there is a satisfactory connection between the use of community treatment powers and the outcomes sought.

It is likely that the 'least drastic means' test would become, as Peter Hogg suggests, the 'heart and soul' of the human rights inquiry.[118] Its principal focus would be the fine texture of the community treatment powers: the powers provided to treat outpatients, direct their accommodation, enter private premises, and recall them swiftly to hospital care. A court's decisions about the permissible scope of these powers would ultimately be inseparable from its views concerning the importance of the rights at stake, the seriousness of the limits imposed, and the value of the state's aims in operating an effective CTO regime.

The human rights concerns are particularly relevant to decisions made by legislatures concerning the detailed design of a CTO regime. But their relevance does not end there. The human rights concerns go all the way through to the use by courts, tribunals and clinicians—in individual cases—of every power they exercise under the regime.

When deciding to make or continue a CTO in the case of a patient whose condition appears to be stable, and who does not pose an imminent threat of harm, but who has a lengthy history of serious mental illness and many prior admissions after ceasing outpatient care, it is suggested that a tribunal should follow the same principles as bind the legislature in its design of the statutory scheme.

Faced with a decision to extend the CTO of a person in this kind of situation, the tribunal should try to strike a fair balance between protecting that person's rights and recognising important justifications for their limitation. The tribunal should consider carefully whether the CTO seems to be meeting its ostensible aims in the particular case, and whether the powers conferred by the CTO are

---

[118] P Hogg, *Constitutional Law of Canada*, 5th edn (supp) (Toronto, Thomson, 2007) para 38–36.

having a disproportionate impact, in the circumstances, on that person's rights. The whole value of the CTO for this person should be assessed against its impact on rights.

If the person concerned appears highly coerced by the CTO; or involuntary treatment seems to contribute little to the person's capacity to achieve his or her own aims; or it does not pull in the support of others; or it adds little to the overall structure and continuity of the person's treatment programme, then those would all be indicators for the person's discharge from the CTO—because that person's right to be left alone would be significantly compromised, and there would be little offered in return by way of justification.

If the person was less opposed to compulsory outpatient care, on the other hand; or the order appeared to promote his or her 'developmental power'; or it appeared to leverage support from others, or to bind into place a sustained treatment programme in a manner that would not otherwise occur, then those factors would suggest an extension of the CTO—because a different balance would be established between the relevant justifications and limits on rights. That balance could properly influence the tribunal's interpretation of the law and its application in the particular case. The tribunal might then take a more longitudinal and predictive approach to the evidence concerning that person's need for involuntary outpatient care. That approach might commit the tribunal to a greater degree of ethical pluralism in the analysis. But it would constitute a properly contextualised application of the calculus of human rights.

Part 6

Access to Mental Health Services

15

Rights-Based Legalism and the Limits of Mental Health Law: The United States of America's Experience

JOHN PETRILA

I. Introduction

In *Wyatt v Aderholt*,[1] the United States Court of Appeals for the Fifth Circuit provided the following summary of inhumane conditions at Bryce State Mental Hospital, a state institution in Alabama:

> Patients in the hospitals were afforded virtually no privacy: the wards were overcrowded; there was no furniture where patients could keep clothing; there were no partitions between commodes in the bathrooms. There were severe health and safety problems: patients with open wounds and inadequately treated skin diseases were in imminent danger of infection because of the unsanitary conditions existing in the wards, such as permitting urine and feces to remain on the floor; there was evidence of insect infestation in the kitchen and dining areas. Malnutrition was a problem: the United States of America described the food as 'com(ing) closer to "punishment" by starvation' than nutrition …

> Aides frequently put patients in seclusion or under physical restraints, including straitjackets, without physicians' orders. One resident had been regularly confined in a straitjacket for more than nine years. The Evaluation Report on Partlow by the American Association on Mental Deficiency stated that nine working residents would

---

[1]   *Wyatt v Aderholt* 503 F 2d 1305 (1974) 1310. Evidence of inhumane conditions went far beyond those in the appellate court's summary. As a result, the district court entered a lengthy order with very detailed directions to the State on every facet of hospital administration, from the number of staff required to the temperature of hot water. The case stimulated and was emblematic of right to treatment litigation in the United States that resulted in federal judges overseeing the administration of State hospitals, State schools for people with developmental disabilities, juvenile facilities, and jails and prisons. For a discussion of *Wyatt's* impact, see ML Perlin, *Mental Disability Law: Civil and Criminal* (Charlottesville VA, Lexis Law Publishing, 1999) §§ 3A-3, 3A-14.2. The case ultimately ended 33 years after it was initially filed.

feed 54 young boys ground food from one very large bowl with nine plates and nine spoons; 'since there were no accommodations to even sit down to eat,' it was impossible to tell which residents had been fed and which had not been fed with this system. Seclusion rooms were large enough for one bed and a coffee can, which served as a toilet. The patients suffered brutality, both at the hands of the aides and at the hands of their fellow patients; testimony established that four Partlow residents died due to understaffing, lack of supervision, and brutality.

This summary described the environment of a State-operated psychiatric institution in the early 1970s. Conditions in many state psychiatric institutions in the United States at that time were horrific. Many were overcrowded, understaffed, and rife with brutality.[2] Yet State hospitals were the primary venue for psychiatric treatment. In 1955, when the hospital population peaked, there were 558,922 individuals confined in State hospitals.[3] While at least some individuals were classified as 'voluntary' patients, involuntary civil commitment was the usual legal mechanism by which people were confined. Statutory criteria were vague, focused on mental illness rather than behaviour, and allowed indefinite confinement without meaningful access to judicial review.[4]

Mental health law in the United States of America emerged in response to these conditions. Had people with mental illnesses been treated in private, non-governmental facilities, or had conditions been humane, mental health law might not have taken root as part of civil rights law, based on federal constitutional principles. Because the government was the provider of care in State hospitals, lawyers successfully argued that the 14th Amendment to the United States Constitution created governmental duties and procedural and substantive rights requiring enforcement by the federal courts. And because conditions in those institutions often failed to meet even minimum standards of decency, the federal courts required the legalisation of State civil commitment laws in an effort to narrow the universe of people who might become subject to confinement. The legalisation of State commitment laws was not an abstract jurisprudential exercise; rather it marked a specific legal remedy to inhumane institutional conditions. As the West Virginia Supreme Court, in ordering broad revisions of that State's commitment law observed,

> [i]n determining whether there is any justification under the doctrine of Parens patriae for deviation from established due process standards, it is appropriate for this Court to consider that the State of West Virginia offers to those unfortunates who are incarcerated in mental institutions Dickensian squalor of unconscionable magnitudes.[5]

---

[2] D Sobel, 'State Psychiatric Hospitals Forced to Change or Close: Critics Point to Persistent Negligence Across Nation', 10 February 1981, *New York Times* C1.

[3] P Appelbaum, *Almost a Revolution: Mental Health Law and the Limits of Change* (New York, Oxford University Press, 1994) 50.

[4] G Melton, N Poythress, J Petrila and C Slobogin, *Psychological Evaluations for the Courts: A Handbook for Mental Health Professionals and Lawyers*, 3rd edn (New York, Guilford Press, 2007) 326–8.

[5] *State, ex rel Hawks v Lazaro*, 202 SE 2d 109 (1974).

In this context, a rights-based approach to civil commitment particularly, and to mental health law more generally, made sense. By requiring that civil commitment laws provide due process, and by insisting that involuntary commitment based solely on mental illness was not constitutionally valid, the courts reduced the reach of commitment laws. By assuming administrative control of State institutions and mandating State compliance with very detailed operational standards, the courts forced State legislators and governors to improve institutional conditions. And by ruling that the United States Constitution permitted even individuals who had been involuntarily committed to refuse psychotropic medication in at least some circumstances, the courts focused attention on the over-drugging that was a common feature of the forced confinement of many individuals. This era of mental health law also contributed to the de-institutionalisation of State hospitals,[6] though changes in the financing of mental health care, the expansion of social welfare programmes, and advances in treatment philosophy were as important.[7]

Today, the circumstances that gave birth to rights-based mental health law no longer apply to the lives of most people with serious mental illnesses in the United States. State psychiatric hospitals have a greatly diminished role; long-term care for mental illnesses is largely unavailable; and changes in judicial and political philosophies have undercut the constitutional principles at the heart of mental health law. Therefore, it is reasonable to ask what, if anything, a rights-based approach to mental health law can offer, at least in the United States, at this point in time. The rest of this chapter describes the factors that effectively brought the rights-based approach to mental health law to an end, the circumstances in which such an approach has continued utility today, and the ameliorative impact that the adoption of international standards could have on the law in the United States.

II. The Erosion of Rights-Based Mental Health Law in the United States

Judicial application and interpretation of federal constitutional law is a fundamental tenet of the law in the United States, and it is because of this that mental health law in the United States developed in the federal courts based on constitutional principles.[8] The US Supreme Court also spurred reliance on the

---

[6] S Gelman, 'The Law and Psychiatry Wars, 1960–1980' (1997) 34 *California Western Law Review* 153.

[7] D Mechanic and DA Rochefort, 'Deinstitutionalization: An Appraisal of Reform' (1990) 16 *Annual Review of Sociology* 301.

[8] The United States of America of course is not the only country with a written Constitution and Bill of Rights, but not all countries with such documents have a firmly entrenched judicial system

Constitution by advocates for people with mental illnesses, writing in 1972 that involuntary civil commitment was a 'massive curtailment of liberty'.[9] In *Jackson v Indiana*,[10] decided the same year, the Court held that individuals adjudged incompetent to stand trial could be held indefinitely only if they met substantive criteria for civil commitment, and observed: 'it is perhaps remarkable that the substantive constitutional limitations on this power have not been more frequently litigated'.[11]

When challenges to civil commitment laws came, the federal courts were receptive and ruled repeatedly that State civil commitment laws had to be revised to provide substantive and procedural due process.[12] While the courts did not achieve complete consensus on which constitutional provisions gave rise to rights for people with mental illnesses, courts generally relied on the 14th Amendment to the United States Constitution, which prohibits deprivations of liberty without due process of law.[13] Reliance on the 14th Amendment made sense, since the confinement of many people in State hospitals resulted from the involuntary taking of their liberty.

The rapid development and consolidation of this first era of mental health law slowed dramatically in the 1980s for two important reasons. First, the federal judiciary, led by the US Supreme Court grew increasingly conservative about the reach and use of federal judicial power. Secondly, the role of the State psychiatric institution continued to rapidly decline, with most individuals with mental illnesses spending most of their time in non-institutional settings. It soon became apparent that the legal doctrines that served as the foundation of mental health law would be of little utility in this new environment.

The US Supreme Court, with Justice Warren Burger replacing Earl Warren as Chief Justice, made clear its more conservative stance on mental health law issues in *Addington v Texas*,[14] decided in 1978. A unanimous Court rejected an argument that the evidentiary standard in commitment hearings should be 'beyond a reasonable doubt' (the highest standard in law in the United States) because the consequences of civil commitment, and the risk of erroneous decisions at commitment hearings, warranted application of the same standard

---

with broad authority to determine the meaning and effect of constitutional principles. JS Baker, 'How Effective Are Bills of Rights in Protecting Freedom and Civil Liberties?' (1992) 15 *Harvard Journal of Law and Public Policy* 53. For an interesting (and by United States standards somewhat iconoclastic) discussion of the differences between written and unwritten constitutions and the development of the rule of law, see J Pek, 'Things Better Left Unwritten? Constitutional Text and the Rule of Law' (2008) 83 *New York University Law Review* 1979.

[9] *Humphrey v Cady* 405 US 504 (1972) 509.
[10] *Jackson v Indiana* 406 US 715 (1972).
[11] *ibid*, 737.
[12] The seminal case was *Lessard v Schmidt* 349 F Supp 1078 (ED Wis 1972), holding that civil commitment was an even more consequential deprivation of liberty than conviction of a crime.
[13] United States Constitution, amendment XIV.
[14] *Addington v Texas* 441 US 418 (1979).

used in criminal cases. The Court disagreed that civil commitment was fundamentally punitive, writing: 'State power is not used in a punitive sense ... a civil
commitment proceeding can in no sense be equated to a criminal prosecution'.[15]
The Court soon after decided that judicial decision-making was unnecessary in
commitment proceedings involving children.[16]

The Court's decisions effectively ended the further legalisation of civil commitment law, though most States had revised their laws to provide more due process
at commitment hearings and more stringent substantive criteria for commitment. At the same time, through the 1970s and 1980s, the de-institutionalisation
of state psychiatric institutions showed few signs of abating and it became clear
that community services were inadequate to provide care to many of those
needing it.[17] However, litigation designed to force the creation of community
services, based on federal constitutional law, met with little success. In part this
was because the States typically provided little direct service in the community,
and therefore it was not clear that a constitutional challenge based on State action
would lie. More importantly, the US Supreme Court was redefining the relationship between the federal courts and the States and in doing so made it very
difficult to pursue broad judicial remedies against State government.[18] Litigants
in some cases turned to State courts, but with some exceptions, State courts were
reluctant to enter decrees for broad relief.[19]

In 1990, the Congress enacted the Americans with Disabilities Act (the ADA),
the most significant civil rights legislation in the United States since the Civil
Rights Act of 1964. The ADA bars discrimination on the basis of physical and
mental disability in public accommodations, employment, telecommunications
and other areas. The US Supreme Court ruled in 1999 that inappropriate
institutionalisation in a State psychiatric facility constituted discrimination on
the basis of disability.[20] While this suggested that the individuals should be
released to community care, the Court also found that a State could defend itself
by showing that it had a comprehensive, effective plan to place people who were

---

[15]   *ibid*, 428.

[16]   *Parham v JR* 442 US 584 (1979).

[17]   JA Talbott, 'Deinstitutionalization: Avoiding the Disasters of the Past' (2004) 55 *Psychiatric Services* 1112.

[18]   JP Bach, 'Requiring Due Care in the Process of Patient Deinstitutionalization: Toward A Common Law Approach To Mental Health Care Reform' (1989) 98 *Yale Law Journal* 1153.

[19]   State courts have been receptive to cases involving institutional conditions, for example juvenile detention facilities, where evidence of grossly inhumane conditions emerged in a number of jurisdictions. MJ Dale, 'Lawsuits and Public Policy: The Role of Litigation in Correcting Conditions in Juvenile Detention Facilities' (1998) 32 *University of San Francisco Law Review* 675. In at least one case, a State Supreme Court used State law as a basis for ordering improved community services for people with mental illnesses. *Arnold v Arizona Department of Health Services* 160 Ariz 593 (1989). However, for a number of reasons State law provided comparatively little opportunity for group relief, particularly in community settings. See also K Eyer, 'Litigating for Treatment: The Use of State Laws and Constitutions in Obtaining Treatment Rights for Individuals With Mental Illness' (2003) 28 *Review of Law & Social Change* 1.

[20]   *Olmstead v LC, ex rel Zimming* 527 US 581 (1999).

more appropriately treated in community settings. The Court's ruling appeared to advocates to strengthen the rights of individuals with mental illnesses; however, the courts have generally found that the ADA does not require States to create new services, and implementation of community care in most jurisdictions continues to move slowly, despite the spur of *Olmstead*.[21]

As this brief review illustrates, mental health law in the United States emerged as part of civil rights law, using constitutional guarantees as the basis for claims. However, State-operated institutional care was the primary focus. As judicial philosophies shifted, and as the role of State institutions declined, the constitutional approach diminished in utility. The question today is whether a rights-based approach, rooted in constitutional principles, has continuing viability, and if so, in what contexts? The answer to this question is affected by many things, including larger trends in services and political philosophy—factors that are addressed in the next section.

III.   The Current State of the Public Mental Health System in the United States

Each State has its own mental health system and its own laws. Nonetheless, these systems share a number of characteristics. First, resources rarely meet need, and those services that do exist are often disorganised.[22] Adequate housing is particularly scarce. These factors create barriers to access to care for people with serious mental illnesses. Secondly, there is little long-term psychiatric care available in the United States, except for individuals entering care through the courts. Even involuntary civil commitment generally results in a short hospitalisation, and at least one report suggests that hospitalisation beyond the initial involuntary assessment is diminishing.[23] Financial pressures have had an impact on the availability of long-term care as well. Beginning in the 1980s and continuing to the present, public and private providers of mental health care have sought to reduce their costs, often by shortening available periods of both inpatient and outpatient care. There have been reductions in utilisation and cost savings as a result of these measures, though it is not clear that there has been a significant

---

[21]   JDE Smith and SP Calandrillo, 'Forward to Fundamental Alteration: Addressing ADA Title II Integration Lawsuits After Olmstead v LC' (2001) 24 *Harvard Journal of Law and Public Policy* 695.

[22]   President's New Freedom Commission on Mental Health, *Achieving the Promise: Transforming Mental Health Care in America* (Rockville MD, President's New Freedom Commission on Mental Health, 2003) available at: www.mentalhealthcommission.gov/reports/FinalReport/downloads/FinalReport.pdf.

[23]   J Bloom, 'Civil Commitment is Disappearing in Oregon' (2006) 34(4) *Journal of the American Academy of Psychiatry and the Law* 534.

impact on quality.[24] However, the general unavailability of long-term care has implications for the legal principles that might reasonably govern the public mental health system in the United States today.

Thirdly, the traditional 'public mental health system' as it existed through the 1980s no longer exists in many jurisdictions. That system usually had several core elements, including State hospital beds, psychiatric beds in general hospitals, community residences (specialised housing for people with mental illnesses) and outpatient clinics. Individuals with mental illnesses could receive treatment, if available, from within that system. However, several factors have contributed to the fragmentation of that system, including inadequate funding of services, pressures to reduce costs, and the entry of for-profit companies into a service sector that historically had been the province of not-for-profit providers. These trends have resulted in two major shifts in the public mental health system that are relevant here. First, for many people with serious mental illnesses, especially those who live in poverty or are uninsured, access to care is extraordinarily difficult.[25] Secondly, a 'de facto system' of mental health care now exists. However, the 'de facto system' is not really a system of care at all. Rather, it is a descriptive term that recognises that a person with a serious mental illness in the United States today must navigate multiple care providers, with myriad funding sources and rules. It has been described in the following manner:

> Loosely defined, the system collectively refers to the full array of programs for anyone with mental illness. The programs deliver or pay for treatments, services, or any other types of supports, such as disability, housing, or employment. These programs are found at every level of government and in the private sector. They have varying missions, settings, and financing. The mission could be to offer treatment in the form of medication, psychotherapy, substance abuse treatment, or counseling. Or it could be to offer rehabilitation support. The setting could be a hospital, a community clinic, a private office, or in a school or business. The financing of care, which amounts to at least $80 billion annually, could come from at least one of a myriad of sources— Medicaid, Medicare, a state agency, a local agency, a foundation, or private insurance.[26]

As this description suggests, assessment and treatment for mental health and addictive disorders in the United States are provided by many parties, under many auspices; and for many of those entities the provision of such services is a secondary or tertiary responsibility rather than their primary role.

Finally, the conservative political and judicial philosophies that were largely dominant from the mid-1970s through the presidency of George W Bush have had a profound effect on the treatment of people with serious mental illnesses

---

[24] RG Frank and R Brookmeyer, 'Managed Mental Health Care and Patterns of Inpatient Utilization for Treatment of Affective Disorders' (1995) 30 *Social Psychiatry and Psychiatric Epidemiology* 220.

[25] P Cunningham, K McKenzie and EF Taylor, 'The Struggle to Provide Community-Based Care to Low-Income People With Serious Mental Illnesses' (2006) 25 *Health Affairs* 694.

[26] President's New Freedom Commission on Mental Health, *Interim Report to the President*, available at: www.mentalhealthcommission.gov/reports/Interim_Report.htm, p 4.

and addictive disorders. Changes in federal and State sentencing laws that mandated tougher penalties for drug offences brought hundreds of thousands of individuals into jails and prisons. The incarceration rate in the United States per 100,000 population went from 160 in 1972 to 645 in 1997[27] and 775 in 2008, a rate of incarceration five to seven times greater than the rates in other Western countries.[28] In addition, with constitutional scrutiny from the federal courts relaxed, States began to expand their commitment laws. Nearly all States now have outpatient commitment laws, which permit courts to order individuals to adhere to treatment in out-patient settings. All States permit involuntary in-patient commitment when a person is 'gravely disabled', and some States also have begun to create medically-oriented criteria for inpatient commitment, designed to prevent deterioration and relapse.[29] Juvenile law also has been fundamentally altered in many States, with legislation designed to make it far more punitive and much less rehabilitative: The result has been a dramatic increase in the number of children and adolescents in detention facilities and adult correctional facilities.[30] Finally, approximately 20 States have enacted 'sexually violent offender' statutes. These statutes permit the indefinite confinement of individuals convicted of sex-related offences, after their prison terms have expired.[31] The United States is not the only country with such provisions[32] but, as discussed below, the application of these provisions in the United States has resulted in an erosion of due process.

What do these developments mean for people with mental illnesses in the United States? First, access to care is difficult. Secondly, government has increased the reach of its coercive authority in both civil and criminal law; however, because of changes in health care services and payments, long-term care is rare. Thirdly, there has been a tremendous increase in the number (if not the prevalence) of people with mental illnesses and addictive disorders in the criminal justice system. Fourth, long-term mental health care is rare except for individuals who are confined as a result of adjudication of a criminal case or by the extension of a prison sentence through application of sexual offender statutes. As a result, there is a large group of individuals with mental illnesses who

---

[27] JE Kennedy, 'The New Data: Over-representation of Minorities in the Criminal Justice System: Drug Wars In Black and White' (2003) 66(3) *Law & Contemporary Problems* 153.

[28] M Tonry, 'Crime and Human Rights: How Political Paranoia, Protestant Fundamentalism, and Constitutional Obsolescence Combined to Devastate Black America': The American Society of Criminology 2007 Presidential Address (2008) 46 *Criminology* 1, 6.

[29] J Petrila, MS Ridgely and R Borum, 'Debating Outpatient Commitment: Controversy, Trends, and Empirical Data' (2003) 49 *Crime & Delinquency* 157; J Petrila, 'Recent Civil Decisions: Implications for Forensic Mental Health Experts' in A Goldstein (ed), *Forensic Psychology: Emerging Topics and Expanding Roles* (Hoboken NJ, John Wiley & Sons, 2007).

[30] C de la Vega and M Leighton, 'Sentencing Our Children to Die in Prison: Global Law and Practice' (2008) 42 *University of San Francisco Law Review* 983.

[31] JM Fabian, 'To Catch a Predator and Then Commit Him For Life: Analyzing the Adam Walsh's Civil Commitment Scheme Under 18 USC 4248' (2009) 33 *Champion* 44.

[32] M Kelly, 'Lock Them Up—And Throw Away the Key: The Preventive Detention of Sex Offenders in the United States and Germany' (2009) 39 *Georgetown Journal of International Law* 551.

have difficulty in gaining access to care, other than for symptom reduction; and on the other hand, there is a smaller group of individuals confined for long periods of time through judicial action whose prospects for release are dim. State-operated psychiatric institutions today are primarily used for forensic patients; the vast majority of individuals receive mental health treatment, when required, in ambulatory care settings, emergency rooms, and psychiatric beds located in general hospitals.

Given this, legal principles must be responsive to groups of individuals with quite different needs: Finding ways to increase access to services for people in a highly fragmented service system is a different task than assuring that people are not confined indefinitely without due process of law. The relevance of rights-based mental health law therefore may vary, depending on the needs of the individual or group in question. The next section discusses legal issues regarding access and contrasts them with the legal issues regarding long-term, often indefinite, confinement.

IV. What is the role of law when health care is not a right?

The United States is not the only industrialised nation with an inadequate mental health system, nor is it the only country with punitive policies toward a legally designated group of individuals with mental disorders. However, it is unique in not providing universal health coverage. Therefore, any discussion of access to care in the United States must begin with the fact that there is no general right to health care. As a result, individuals have access to care depending on the terms of their insurance plan, rather than as a matter of right, or if uninsured, through emergency rooms and other settings where free care may be provided.

Federal and some State legislatures have attempted to make access to mental health care more generally available by mandating that some levels of coverage must be provided. For example, for people with private insurance, many States and the federal government require 'parity' between coverage for physical health and mental health. As a result the number of insured people with at least some coverage for mental health services has increased.[33] However, for those dependent on public funding for services, the reimbursement rates that providers receive are often below the cost of providing the service, and as noted above, efforts to

---

[33] JM Barrett, 'A State of Disorder: An Analysis of Mental Health Parity in Wisconsin and a Suggestion for Future Legislation' (2008) 1 *Wisconsin Law Review* 1159. However, coverage is not available for all disorders, nor is it necessarily adequate in scope when available. See, eg BA Brunalli, 'Anorexia Killed Her but the System Failed Her: Does the American Insurance System Suffer From Anorexia?' (2006) 12 *Connecticut Insurance Law Journal* 583.

reduce overall costs in these programmes continue. For people without any form of coverage, whether private or public, access to mental health care is extremely difficult, other than in crises, when care may be obtained in an emergency room or through involuntary commitment.

While legislatures have addressed the issue of access in at least a limited fashion, efforts to increase coverage and access through litigation have fared poorly. Most people who are privately insured obtain insurance as part of employment, with employees and employers each paying a part of the insurance premium. Insurance companies are legally obliged to provide coverage consistent with the insurance contract that specifies the health benefits that will be provided. There has been extensive litigation in both federal and State courts in the last two decades regarding the administration of insurance benefits, particularly in response to cost-cutting efforts. While the legal landscape is confused, it is fair to say that such litigation has been unsuccessful in forcing new benefits to be added to an insurance contract.[34] In publicly funded plans, available benefits are specified legislatively. Because the costs of such programmes have risen dramatically over the years, and constitute mandatory spending for the governments that finance them, governments have moved aggressively to control inflation in costs. As with privately financed insurance plans, litigation can force the provision of existing benefits, but cannot be used to enlarge coverage beyond that mandated legislatively.

Given this legal landscape, contract law has more utility than constitutional law in assuring that individuals obtain services legally due them through publicly or privately financed insurance plans.[35] However, available remedies are limited and in the absence of universal health care, individuals are left with the benefits provided in whatever insurance plan they are fortunate enough to obtain. There are simply no good legal theories available to expand coverage beyond that provided in the plan, nor are there legal theories that can force an insurer to provide coverage for an individual who is uninsured.

V. The Situation of People with Serious Mental Illnesses Facing Long-Term Confinement

While many people with serious mental illness have difficulty obtaining access to long-term care, there are comparatively small groups of individuals who face indefinite confinement in psychiatric facilities. One group is forensic clients,

---

[34] RF Rich, CT Erb and LJ Gale, 'Judicial Interpretation of Managed Care Policy' (2005) 13 *Elder Law Journal* 85.

[35] J Petrila, 'From Constitution to Contracts: Mental Disability Law At the Turn of the Century' in L Frost and R Bonnie (eds), *The Evolution of Mental Health Law* (Washington DC, American Psychological Association, 2001).

defined here as those individuals, charged with a criminal offence, who enter care after being found either incompetent to stand trial or not guilty by reason of insanity. As noted earlier, the number of State psychiatric hospital beds in the United States has declined dramatically and, increasingly, access to those beds is available primarily through the criminal courts.[36] While there are problems associated with the care of these individuals—for example, long waiting lists that cause unnecessary delays in access to treatment for competency restoration[37]— legal rules governing the disposition of these issues are long established and generally clear.

Another group, however, faces a more problematic legal situation. These are individuals committed indefinitely as 'sexually violent predators', almost always after expiration of their prison sentences. Historically, a number of States had statutes that permitted the civil commitment of individuals who had committed sexual offences. These statutes, usually called 'sexual psychopathy' laws, were rehabilitative in nature, though confinement could be indefinite. Such statutes had begun to fall into disrepute by the 1970s, in part because treatment was considered ineffectual.[38] However, in response to brutal and highly publicised sexual offences, State legislatures began adopting a new type of sexual offender statute in the 1990s. These Sexually Violent Predator (SVP) statutes have been adopted in approximately 20 States and a number of other countries.[39] SVP statutes in the United States are not rehabilitative in any sense, even though individuals are confined in psychiatric facilities. In fact, legislatures have explicitly acknowledged this fact. For example, the Kansas legislature, in a preamble to its legislation, stated the statute authorised the commitment of individuals

> who do not have a mental disease or defect that renders them appropriate for involuntary treatment ... [but who] have antisocial personality features which are unamenable to existing mental illness treatment modalities.[40]

---

[36] An excellent analysis of this issue can be found in J Bloom, 'The Majority of Inpatient Psychiatric Beds Should Not Be Incorporated by the Forensic System' (2008) 36 *Journal of the American Academy of Psychiatry and the Law* 438.

[37] In Florida, a State law requires a State forensic hospital to admit someone found incompetent to stand trial within 15 days of receipt of the order. However, because of an inadequate number of beds, individuals waited in jail for months and a waiting list of nearly 300 people developed. After State judges began finding the director of the responsible State agency in contempt of court in individual cases where access within the statutory time was not available, the State moved to eliminate the waiting list through new resources. Associated Press, 'Mentally Ill Inmates Get State Boost', *St Petersburg Times*, 4 May 2007.

[38] Group for the Advancement of Psychiatry, Committee on Psychiatry and Law, *Psychiatry and Sex Psychopath Legislation: The 30s to the 80s* (Washington DC, American Psychiatric Association 1977).

[39] See P Keyzer, 'The "Preventive Detention" of Serious Sex Offenders: Further Consideration of the International Human Rights Dimensions' (2009) 16(1) *Psychiatry, Psychology and Law* 262; WL Fitch, 'Sexual Offender Commitment in the United States: Legislative and Policy Concerns' (2003) 989 *Annals of the New York Academy of Science* 489.

[40] Kansas Sexually Violent Predator Act (1994), Preamble.

One of the unanswered questions from the constitutional era of mental health law was whether the States could use civil commitment laws for what effectively is preventive detainment. In other words, did a State have to provide treatment to people who were civilly committed, or could individuals be confined in the absence of treatment? The Kansas legislature made clear (as did other legislatures) that it believed the class of people it was subjecting to indefinite, involuntary confinement, and who had already been punished for a criminal act, were untreatable. It is difficult in this light to read an SVP statute as anything other than a form of preventive confinement. Given this, a challenge to the constitutional validity of SVP statutes was inevitable. When that challenge came, the US Supreme Court in 1997, by a 5–4 vote, ruled the statutes constitutional.[41] In its opinion, the Court rejected a number of assertions of unconstitutionality, including a claim that the statutory definition of mental illness was unduly broad. On the question of whether the person's treatability was a necessary legal predicate to a constitutionally-valid use of civil commitment, Justice Thomas was explicit for the majority:

> While we have upheld state civil commitment statutes that aim both to incapacitate and to treat, we have never held that the Constitution prevents a State from civilly detaining those for whom no treatment is available, but who nonetheless pose a danger to others … *It would be of little value to require treatment as a precondition for civil confinement of the dangerously insane when no acceptable treatment existed* (emphasis added).[42]

This is a sweeping grant of State authority, particularly when exercised through civil rather than criminal law. In a later case, the Court concluded that remedies available to criminal defendants (such as the prohibition against double jeopardy) were not available to individuals committed under SVP laws, because in the Court's view, SVP statutes were not punitive.[43]

These decisions together provide grant States great discretion in the commitment and confinement of individuals adjudged sexually violent predators. While States enjoyed broad authority to civilly commit individuals at the beginning of the mental health law era, the courts eventually circumscribed that authority through the imposition of procedural safeguards in the commitment process, through requirements that State institutions meet minimal safety and treatment standards, and through creation of a 'right to refuse treatment' in some circumstances. However, these limitations have far more limited effect in today's legal environment.

The US Supreme Court has expressed little interest in whether States exercise a real rather than rhetorical commitment to providing treatment to individuals held under SVP statutes; a legislative promise of treatment has satisfied at least

---

[41] *Kansas v Hendricks* 521 US 346 (1997).
[42] *ibid*, 366.
[43] *Seling v Young* 531 US 250 (2001).

some of the Justices.[44] At the same time, the Court has recognised that challenges to institutional conditions might be brought under federal or State law, and in at least one case a federal grand jury investigation resulted in imposition of a federal court decree requiring changes in one State's SVP facility.[45] However, it is worth remembering that many State SVP statutes state explicitly that individuals who commit sexual offences are not amenable to treatment. The primary purpose of such statutes is community protection through confinement, not the rehabilitation of the offender.

Many individuals committed under SVP statutes have committed horrific offences, and so it is not difficult to understand a lack of legislative or public interest in the conditions of confinement. The erosion of due process rights in SVP hearings, often abetted by expert testimony, is more troubling.[46] Three issues are relevant here. These include a lack of proper gate-keeping by courts in deciding on the admissibility of evidence, problems in the provision of expert testimony on the question of future risk, and an insistence that a class of people is inherently untreatable.

Courts in the United States have broad authority over the admissibility of expert testimony. The US Supreme Court has broadened that authority through its decisions in *Daubert v Merrell Dow Pharmaceuticals*[47] and *Kumho Tire Company v Carmichael*.[48] Those decisions create a template for courts in considering admissibility, and the court is to consider whether such testimony is based on scientific method, among other criteria. However, in SVP hearings, courts have been reluctant to reject testimony based on risk assessment tools with at least questionable validity and reliability. Rather, testimony is readily admitted, with courts generally being of the view that any challenges go to the weight of the evidence rather than admissibility.[49]

Judicial reluctance to play an aggressive gate-keeping role would be less significant if expert testimony on risk were rigorous and precise. However, a review of reported cases reveals testimony that often overstates the scientific merits of risk assessment tools, confuses risk assessment methods, and ascribes to the individual defendant risk probabilities that are more appropriately ascribed to a *group* of individuals. For example, in the case of *In re Wilson*[50] the court stated that the assessment tool entitled the 'Rapid Risk Assessment for Sex

---

[44] In *Kansas v Hendricks*, Justice Thomas, writing for the majority, noted that while it might appear that Kansas provided only 'meager' treatment, State officials had told the Court they were committed to providing adequate treatment and had for the purposes of *Hendricks* satisfied any constitutional obligation: *Kansas v Hendricks* 521 US 346 (1997) 369.

[45] *Turay v Seling* 108 F Supp 2d 1148 (WD Wash 2000).

[46] For a full review of these issues in the United States, see RA Prentky, E Janus, H Barbaree, BK Schwartz and MP Kafka, 'Sexually Violent Predators in the Courtroom: Science on Trial' (2006) 12 *Psychology, Public Policy and Law* 357.

[47] *Daubert v Merrell Dow Pharmaceuticals* 509 US 570 (1993).

[48] *Kumho Tire Company v Carmichael* 526 US 137 (1999).

[49] *Washington v Strauss* 20 P 3d 1022 (2001).

[50] *In re Wilson*, WL 1182807 (2000).

Offender Recidivism' was 'highly predictive of sexual offenses'. In a case involving the Sex Offender Risk Appraisal Guide, an expert testified that based on his score, there was a 59 per cent chance the defendant would re-offend within 10 years and a 45 per cent chance the defendant would re-offend within seven years. Eric Janus and Robert Prentky, who have been sharply critical of the conduct of SVP hearings, wrote about this testimony:

> By ascribing a risk directly to the defendant, this testimony obscured the critical steps that must be taken to link the [actuarial risk assessment] results to the legally relevant measures: the 'fit' of the instruments to the legal categories, the process of generalizing from the development or validation samples to the defendant, and the band of potential error defining the score and its associated probability.[51]

In other cases, an expert 'mixes' risk assessment based on an actuarial tool with clinical judgement, as a result overstating and diluting the scientific merits of the former method. In *State v Keinitz*[52] the prosecution's expert witness testified that he had added 10 points to the defendant's score on the Violence Risk Appraisal Guide (VRAG) based on his own clinical judgement. As a result, the probability of the defendant's future risk was presented as being more than 50 per cent. However, while the creators of the VRAG originally proposed the use of clinical judgement to complement the score achieved on the VRAG, they no longer believe that is appropriate. Instead they write:

> What we are advising is not the addition of actuarial methods to existing practice, but rather the replacement of existing practice with actuarial methods. This is a different view than we expressed a decade ago, when we advised the practice of adjusting actuarial estimates of risk by up to 10% when there were compelling circumstances to do so … We no longer think this practice is justifiable: Actuarial methods are too good and clinical judgement is too poor to risk contaminating the former with the latter.[53]

The defendant faces indefinite confinement as a result of testimony on his or her future risk but the lack of rigour in some expert testimony creates the impression that prediction of the *individual's* future risk has a degree of scientific certainty that, to date, is unwarranted.

These issues are compounded by testimony that people labelled as psychopaths (which includes many people committed under SVP laws) are inherently untreatable. As noted earlier, legislatures have described the class of people that SVP laws are supposed to reach as not amenable to treatment. Some researchers lend support to this view. For example, a recent review concluded that 'psychopaths are fundamentally different from other offenders and that there is nothing "wrong" with them in the manner of a deficit or impairment that therapy can

---

[51] ES Janus and RA Prentky, 'Forensic Use of Actuarial Risk Assessment With Sex Offenders: Accuracy, Admissibility, and Accountability' (2003) 40 *American Criminal Law Review* 1443, 1496.

[52] *State of Wisconsin v Keinitz* 585 NW 2d 609 (Wis App 1999).

[53] VL Quinsey, GT Harris, ME Rice and CA Cornier, *Violent Offenders: Appraising and Managing Risk*, 2nd edn (Washington DC, American Psychological Association, 2006) 197.

"fix".[54] However, this ascribes difficulties in treating a class of people to the individuals themselves, rather than to inadequacies in current treatment modalities. In addition, there is modest evidence that treatment can ameliorate risk with some individuals who meet the criteria for psychopathy.[55] Therefore, testimony that a person who is a 'psychopath' is inherently untreatable is not only scientifically dubious, but provides a court further rationale for simply warehousing the person.

In short, SVP hearings may feature inadequate judicial oversight of admissibility, scientifically questionable testimony on future risk, and therapeutic nihilism on the issue of the person's amenability to treatment. One can argue that many individuals committed as SVPs warrant indefinite confinement. However, this does not excuse the erosion of due process rights, nor does it warrant reliance on testimony that is often far less scientifically grounded than presented.

VI. Rights-Based Mental Health Law in the United States of America in the 21st Century

The public mental health system in the United States has changed dramatically since the emergence of mental health law. The constitutional principles at the heart of mental health law developed to address issues that are far less common today. Nor are those principles responsive to the problem of access to care, the dominant problem faced by the majority of people with serious mental illnesses. At the same time, there are groups of individuals, such as those committed as sexually violent predators, who face long-term confinement with little legal protection. What role might rights-based mental health law play in this environment?

A. A Rights-Based Approach is Essential for People Facing Long-Term Confinement

First, it is clear that a rights-based approach is essential for people who face indefinite and/or preventive confinement. The application of unbridled state authority readily leads to abuses, as Abu Ghraib and Guantanamo vividly illustrate. While legal oversight of SVP proceedings is often lacking, the application of constitutional principles assures at least some scrutiny of the confinement of a much despised population.

---

[54] GT Harris and ME Rice, 'Treatment of Psychopathy: A Review of Empirical Findings' in C Patrick (ed), *Handbook of Psychopathy* (New York, Guilford, 2006) 568.

[55] See for example, J Skeem, J Monahan and E Mulvey, 'Psychopathy, Treatment Involvement, and Subsequent Violence Among Civil Psychiatric Patients' (2002) 26 *Law and Human Behavior* 577.

While a constitutional, rights-based approach is necessary in the case of involuntary confinement, it is not necessarily adequate. The courts created mental health law through the extension of constitutional principles, absent specific textual language requiring such results. The history of mental health law since its creation illustrates the weakness of such an approach. While the 14th Amendment's requirement that the State may not deny liberty without due process of law may be immutable, its interpretation certainly is not. Rather, judicial interpretations of constitutional rights and their reach have changed with the advent of a more conservative, punitive approach in both criminal and civil law in the United States. The US Supreme Court first encouraged challenges to civil commitment laws, eventually circumscribed such challenges, and ultimately has given States very broad authority to confine people who have a mental illness. In each case, the same constitutional provisions were applied. What had changed was the judicial philosophy of the majority of Justices on the Court.

This may reflect broader weaknesses in the United States' constitutional system. Michael Tonry, for example, argues that criminal justice policies in the United States are almost always more punitive than those of other democracies in part because of an 'obsolete constitutional system'.[56] He describes the Constitution of the United States as 'designed to address eighteenth-century not twentieth-century or twenty-first century problems', which he believes makes the United States 'almost uniquely vulnerable to the policy excesses associated with the paranoid style and religious fundamentalism'.[57]

Reliance on constitutional law as the lynchpin of mental health law assuredly has not led to a fixed body of law that looks first to protect the rights of the most vulnerable. There is also considerable support for the proposition that this approach had less impact than might have been imagined given the sweeping challenges to the exercise of State authority. For example, Paul Appelbaum, in a comprehensive review, characterised what occurred as 'almost a revolution'.[58] In his view, decision-makers (whether judges, lawyers, family, or health care professionals) make decisions based on a sense of equity and the best interests of the individual. Strict adherence to legal principles gives way when it conflicts with such interests. Michael Perlin attributes this to 'sanism', which he describes as a fundamental, but often unacknowledged prejudice against those with mental illnesses, and argues that it leads to paternalistic decision-making at the expense of individual autonomy.[59] Regardless of *why* paternalism often prevails (and

---

[56] M Tonry, 'Crime and Human Rights—How Political Paranoia, Protestant Fundamentalism, and Constitutional Obsolescence Combined to Devastate Black America': The American Society of Criminology 2007 Presidential Address (2008) 46 *Criminology* 1, 4.

[57] *ibid*, 18.

[58] P Appelbaum, *Almost a Revolution: Mental Health Law and the Limits of Change* (New York, Oxford University Press, 1994).

[59] M Perlin, *The Hidden Prejudice: Mental Disability on Trial* (Washington DC, American Psychological Association, 1999).

whether it is a good or bad thing in a given case), it seems clear that even at the height of the constitutional movement, legal standards were often relaxed in the presence of mental illness.

There are also prominent legal scholars in the United States who counsel flexibility in situations in which a rights-based approach would suggest a more rigid approach. Bruce Winick and David Wexler in particular have argued that 'therapeutic jurisprudence' is the most appropriate legal response to resolving the problems of individuals with mental illnesses: They define therapeutic jurisprudence as an approach that

> simply seeks to focus attention on an often neglected ingredient in the calculus necessary for performing a sensible policy analysis of mental health law and practice— the therapeutic dimension—and to call for a systematic empirical examination of this dimension.[60]

They have applied this framework to issues such as civil commitment, where Winick argues that a legal model represents a significant improvement over a medical model, but also concludes that a legal model gives power to 'judges and lawyers who often fail to understand the clinical needs of the patient. By placing primary emphasis upon legal rights, the legal model often neglects the therapeutic needs of the patient'.[61] Therapeutic jurisprudence has been criticised on the ground that it may substitute one form of paternalism for another, but there is no mistaking the influence it is having on practice, for example, in the development of therapeutic courts such as mental health courts.[62] Therapeutic courts, by definition, operate differently than traditional criminal court, forgoing the adversarial process. The underlying philosophy of such courts is that a strict adherence to the legalistic model of the criminal court undermines the ability of a court to address the individual's needs.

While a rights-based approach is essential in bounding State authority when indefinite confinement is at issue, it is vulnerable to political changes, shifts in judicial philosophy, and the biases and prejudices of those charged with protecting individual rights. In sum, it addresses some, but not all issues faced by people with mental illnesses.

---

[60] DB Wexler and BJ Winick (eds), *Essays in Therapeutic Jurisprudence* (Durham NC, Carolina Academic Press, 1992) xi.

[61] BJ Winick, *Civil Commitment: Toward a Therapeutic Jurisprudence Model* (Durham NC, Carolina Academic Press, 2005) 5.

[62] J Petrila, 'Book Review: Paternalism and the Unrealized Promise of "Essays in Therapeutic Jurisprudence"' (1993) 10 *New York Law School Journal of Human Rights* 877; J Petrila, 'An Introduction to Special Jurisdiction Courts' (2003) 26 *International Journal of Law and Psychiatry* 3.

B.   International Law Principles would be an Important Addition to Mental Health Law in the United States

The United States does not have universal health coverage and access to health care is not a legal right. Adoption of universal health coverage with a decent mental health benefit would improve access to care for many individuals who at present have no coverage. President Obama appears committed to incrementally increasing access to health care for uninsured Americans. Whether this ultimately leads to universal coverage, or an improvement of mental health coverage, is an open and politically complex question.

In the absence of universal coverage and given changing constitutional interpretations, mental health law in the United States also would benefit by adopting the human rights approach embedded in various international conventions, particularly since the use of coercion is an international issue.[63] The European Convention of Human Rights (the European Convention) provides an excellent starting point for this approach. While the European Convention does not address mental health issues in great or explicit detail, Gostin has identified three issues where mental health and human rights intersect, namely: coercive mental health policies infringe on human rights; intrusions into human rights can be harmful to mental health; and there is a synergistic relationship between respect for human rights and individual mental health.[64] The European Convention does not address universal access to care, but Larry Gostin believes it is particularly important in three other substantive legal areas, including the compulsory detention of individuals with mental illnesses; conditions of confinement and intrusive treatments; and protection of the rights of citizenship.[65]

The United Nations Convention on the Rights of Persons with Disabilities (the CRPD)[66] and its optional protocol goes much further than the European Convention. While the United States was not one of the 139 signatories at the time it was adopted by the United Nations General Assembly, President Obama has signalled his intention for the United States to be a signatory.[67] The CRPD commits nations ratifying it to prohibit discrimination on the basis of disability in a wide variety of areas. It also explicitly provides for access to care as a fundamental guarantee. It adopts the principle of reasonable accommodation as a cornerstone, much as the Americans with Disabilities Act (the ADA) does.

---

[63]   J Dawson, 'Factors Influencing the Use of Community Treatment Orders' (2007) 6 *Psychiatry, Psychology and Law* 42.

[64]   L Gostin, 'Human Rights of Persons with Mental Disabilities: The European Convention of Human Rights' (2000) 23 *International Journal of Law and Psychiatry* 125.

[65]   *ibid.*

[66]   United Nations Convention on the Rights of Persons with Disabilities (CRPD) (adopted by GA Res A/Res/61/106 24 January 2007).

[67]   Available at: www.whitehouse.gov/the_press_office/Remarks-by-the-President-on-Rights-of-Persons-with-Disabilities-Proclamation-Signing/ 24 July 2009.

However, the CRPD goes beyond the ADA, in framing equal rights and access for people with disabilities as basic human rights.

There is significant political and judicial hostility toward using international law in interpreting law in the United States.[68] When the Supreme Court outlawed the death penalty for offences committed when the defendant was a juvenile, Justice Kennedy wrote extensively in his majority opinion about the status of the death penalty internationally, concluding that the United States stood virtually alone in permitting its use with juveniles.[69] Justice Scalia, dissenting, wrote that the notion that the United States should conform its laws to international law should be 'rejected out of hand'. In addition, the administration of George W Bush refused to sign many international agreements as a matter of policy. However, placing the United States' law in an international context, specifically in the context of an international commitment to human rights, might provide more predictable footing for mental health law than that provided by constitutional standards. It is probable that under the Obama administration, the United States will eventually ratify the CRPD. At the same time, the uneasy relationship between international law and US constitutional law is likely to continue given American judicial and political realities.

C.   A More Complete Understanding of the Relationship between Coercion and the Exercise of Choice is Essential to the Evolution of Mental Health Law

A rights-based approach to mental health law emerged in part in response to the systematic use of coercion in public mental health systems, through involuntary civil commitment, physical restraint and forced drugging. However, recent research into the use of coercion with people with mental illnesses being treated in community settings suggests that 'coercion' is a more complex and nuanced topic than debates over rights might suggest. It is clear that community treatment orders are not the only occasion in which treatment staff, judges and others use strategies designed to induce an individual to adhere to treatment. These include pre-conditioning access to money and housing on treatment adherence, and judicial orders to receive treatment in lieu of longer jail terms.[70] In a five-site

---

[68]   United States' courts are not alone in considering international standards in decisions applying a nation's fundamental laws. See eg Y Shany, 'How Supreme Is the Supreme Law of the Land? Comparative Analysis of the Influence of Human Rights Treaties Upon the Interpretation of Constitutional Law Texts by Domestic Courts' (2006) 31 *Brooklyn Journal of International Law* 341. Shany examines court decisions from the United States, Canada, Israel, South Africa, Australia and the United Kingdom in which the courts did (or more frequently did not) consider international human rights treaties in their decisions.

[69]   *Roper v Simmons* 543 US 551 (2005).

[70]   J Monahan, A Redlich, J Swanson, P Robbins, P Appelbaum, J Petrila, H Steadman, M Swartz, B Angell and D McNiel, 'Use of Leverage to Improve Adherence to Psychiatric Treatment in the Community' (2005) 56 *Psychiatric Services* 37.

study in the United States, nearly one-half of 1,000 individuals in community mental health care reported that they had experienced one or more of these forms of leverage (or coercion, depending on one's perspective) in their lives, suggesting that this is a ubiquitous issue in care.[71]

One critique of a purely rights-based approach to mental health law is that it can reduce arguments over core issues such as civil commitment to an ideological debate without recognising the various issues subsumed within the topic of 'coercion'. Bonnie and Monahan, in an effort to reframe the debate, suggest that the threshold question in considering whether something is coercive should be whether it improves or detracts from the person's legal 'base-line' at that point in time. They consider outpatient commitment to be coercive, because it detracts from the person's current 'base-line', that is, living in the community without court order. However, enrolment in a mental health court, in lieu of serving time in jail or prison, might be non-coercive.[72] If the 'offer' to the person improves his or her legal base-line, then they argue that it is possible to apply contract principles by creating incentives for the person to accept the offer. Others disagree with the use of 'contract' in this context. In the view of these critics, the power differential between the representative of the State and the individual with mental illness is too significant to permit the give and take associated with contract negotiation, particularly in the context of the criminal justice system.[73] Regardless, Bonnie and Monahan shift the debate from a generalised, ideological debate about coercion to a discussion that incorporates the emerging knowledge regarding the various ways in which legal officials and treatment providers use coercion and leverage to influence behaviour.

Research into coercion also has begun to illustrate that criminal justice decision-makers sometimes explicitly adopt strategies that mimic those used by caregivers in creating a therapeutic alliance. One study of a mental health court, using standardised instruments, found that defendants experienced the court as both fair and non-coercive, which reflected the judge's belief that giving voice to defendants was important in their willingness to accept treatment.[74] Another study of specialised probation (in this context, probation designed for individuals with mental illnesses) found that probation officers with specialised caseloads adopted different and more flexible strategies for addressing violations of proba- tion conditions than those with 'as usual' caseloads. The use of such strategies

---

[71] *ibid.* Use of money as leverage ranged from 7 to 19% of patients; outpatient commitment, 12 to 20%; the use of criminal sanctions, 15 to 30%; and housing, 23 to 40%.

[72] R Bonnie and J Monahan, 'From Coercion to Contract: Reframing the Debate on Mandated Community Treatment for People with Mental Disorders' (2005) 29 *Law and Human Behavior* 485.

[73] J Skeem and JE Louden, 'Mandated Treatment as a Condition of Probation: Coercion or Contract?' (Paper presented at the Annual Meeting of the American Psychology—Law Society, Hyatt Regency Jacksonville Riverfront, Jacksonville FL, March 2008).

[74] NG Poythress, J Petrila, A McGaha and R Boothroyd, 'Perceived Coercion and Procedural Justice in the Broward Mental Health Court' (2002) 25 *International Journal of Law and Psychiatry* 517.

was viewed favourably both by the officers and those on probation, and was thought to contribute to positive outcomes.[75] Further research undoubtedly would reveal much more about the factors that make adherence to treatment more likely. Such research could shed light on whether and to what degree treatment adherence depends on the actions of the party exercising leverage, the impact on the individual of threats or use of coercion, and the relative degree of choice and autonomy exercised by the individual.

VII. Conclusion

Rights-based mental health law emerged in the United States to respond to serious human rights violations in a public mental health system that no longer exists. People with mental illnesses had few legal rights and were subject to indefinite involuntary confinement in State-operated psychiatric institutions where conditions were often fundamentally inhumane. Mental health law, anchored in the United States Constitution, provided legal rights that expanded autonomy, created due process standards for civil commitment, and forced States to improve institutional conditions. However, barely more than a decade after mental health law emerged, several factors, including broader changes in judicial and social attitudes, brought the constitutional era to an end.

Today, the public mental health system in the United States is dramatically different for most people with serious mental illnesses. Access to care rather than protection from care is the dominant issue for most individuals. On the question of access, constitutional law has little to offer. Universal health care, with guaranteed access, will require an act of Congress. In the interim, only contract law provides a reasonable legal basis for enforcing an individual's right to health care benefits contained in privately- and publicly-financed health plans, and such litigation is rarely pursued.

At the same time, when indefinite confinement is permitted, as in the case of sex offenders, a rights-based approach is essential. Yet changing constitutional standards have provided States with great authority to confine people regardless of whether they can be treated, and expert witnesses contaminate judicial hearings that lead to such confinement through assertions that their testimony is far more scientific than it is.

Given these developments, what are the critical elements of an ideal 'mental health law' in the United States today? First, access to a guaranteed level of coverage is essential. Secondly, constitutional law would be vigorously applied when the stakes for an individual are at their highest: In the civil context, these

---

[75] J Skeem, J Encandela and JE Louden, 'Perspectives on Probation and Mandated Mental Health Treatment in Specialized and Traditional Probation Departments' (2003) 21 *Behavioral Sciences & the Law* 429.

are situations where a person faces indefinite confinement. Thirdly, law would reflect a preference for autonomy, but would be also recognise that not all efforts to constrain the exercise of autonomy are coercive. This could mean a more flexible application of legal standards in some situations. For example, as Winick has suggested, the standard for competency to decide might be relaxed if the decision in question was clearly in the person's interests.[76] Fourthly, rehabilitation and treatment would be clearly articulated legal duties when the State takes away liberty, in contrast to the current posture of the courts that diminishes the importance of treatment in some situations. Fifthly, international law would be drawn on where appropriate, to reinforce the notion that there are fundamental human rights involved in the care of people with mental illnesses, that cannot be modified by changing judicial interpretations of constitutional principles.

Adoption of these principles would not be a panacea. Law, alone, will not provide more service capacity, better housing, or case management. But given the impact of mental illnesses on individuals, families, and communities, the foundation of mental health law should not shift as judicial philosophies and societal attitudes shift. While a rights-based approach is essential in establishing this foundation, in the United States at least it is insufficient standing alone.

---

[76] BJ Winick, *Civil Commitment: A Therapeutic Jurisprudence Model* (Durham NC, Carolina Academic Press, 2005).

16

The Right of Access to Mental Health Care: Voluntary Treatment and the Role of the Law

BERNADETTE MCSHERRY

I. Introduction

What is now generally termed the 'right to health' was first set out in 1948 in Article 25(1) of the Universal Declaration of Human Rights:[1]

> Everyone has the right to a standard of living adequate for the health and well-being of himself [or herself] and of his [or her] family, including food, clothing, housing and medical care and necessary social services.

The past two decades have seen a developing exploration of what is meant by the right to health and the issue of access to health care services. Article 12(1) of the International Covenant on Economic, Social and Cultural Rights[2] requires governments to recognise

> the right of everyone to the enjoyment of the highest attainable standard of physical and mental health.

In 2000, the United Nations Committee on Economic, Social and Cultural Rights published General Comment No 14,[3] which provides a detailed interpretation of the right to the highest attainable standard of health. Paragraph 9 states that 'the right to health must be understood as a right to the enjoyment of a variety of facilities, goods, services and conditions necessary for the realization of the

---

[1] Universal Declaration of Human Rights, GA Res 217A(III), UN Doc A/Res/3314 (10 December 1948).

[2] International Covenant on Economic, Social and Cultural Rights, opened for signature 16 December 1966, 993 UNTS 3 (entered into force 3 January 1976).

[3] UN Committee on Economic, Social and Cultural Rights, General Comment No 14: The Right to the Highest Attainable Standard of Health (Art 12 of the Covenant) UN Doc E/C12/2000/4 (11 August 2000).

highest attainable standard of health'. Paragraph 43(a) sets out a core obligation on States Parties to ensure 'the right of access to health facilities, goods and services on a non-discriminatory basis, especially for vulnerable or marginalized groups'.

What the right to health may mean in relation to those with disabilities is now very much on the agenda.[4] Article 25 of the Convention on the Rights of Persons with Disabilities[5] recognises that persons with disabilities have

> the right to the enjoyment of the highest attainable standard of physical and mental health without discrimination on the basis of disability

and, under paragraph (b), requires States Parties to

> [p]rovide those health services needed by persons with disabilities specifically because of their disabilities, including early identification and intervention as appropriate, and services designed to minimize and prevent further disabilities.

The scope of the right to the enjoyment of services in relation to the realisation of the highest attainable standard of *mental* health remains to be explored more fully. In particular, it is timely to raise the question as to whether there is a role for the law in supporting the right to enjoyment of specific services for individuals with mental illnesses.

This chapter outlines the current laws in relation to 'voluntary' patients and considers the arguments for and against such provisions. It examines whether legal provisions can assist in providing a framework for enabling individuals with mental illnesses to gain access to services that aid their enjoyment of the highest attainable standard of mental health.

II. Access to Services and the Right to the Highest Attainable Standard of Mental Health

As outlined above, Article 25(b) of the Convention on the Rights of Persons with Disabilities requires States Parties to

> [p]rovide those health services needed by persons with disabilities specifically because of their disabilities.

While it would seem that this immediately requires States Parties to ensure that all health services including mental health services are properly resourced and accessible in the form of hospitals and community services, the right to the

---

[4] See, eg LO Gostin and L Gable, 'The Human Rights of Persons with Mental Disabilities: A Global Perspective on the Application of Human Rights Principles to Mental Health' (2004) 63 *Maryland Law Review* 20.

[5] Convention on the Rights of Persons with Disabilities, GA Res 61/106, opened for signature 30 March 2007, UN Doc A/Res/61/611 (entered into force 3 May 2008).

enjoyment of the highest attainable standard of physical and mental health is subject to 'progressive realization' and resource constraints.[6] This means that what is required of a developed state is of a higher standard than developing countries, but 'all states are expected to be doing better in five years time than what they are doing today'.[7]

Peter Bartlett rightly points out in chapter seventeen that most of the chapters in this collection are concerned with mental health systems in countries with developed economic and legal cultures, where moves towards 'rights-based legalism' for the treatment of individuals with mental illnesses have been on the political agenda for decades. Mental health systems in such developed countries obviously vary in scope and practice, but there is growing evidence that accessibility (or the lack thereof) is a key issue for those wanting treatment, particularly in the community.[8] Taking the Australian mental health system as an example, the findings of many enquiries suggest that access to proper treatment, particularly for those with high-incidence mental disorders such as depression and anxiety, is wanting. In 2003, the Mental Health Council of Australia released a report which found that 'current community-based systems fail to provide adequate services'.[9] It pointed out that Australia spends approximately seven per cent of its health budget on mental health, whereas other 'first world' countries spend 10 to 14 per cent.[10]

Two years later, the *Not for Service* report, which was prepared by the Mental Health Council of Australia and the Brain and Mind Research Institute in association with the Human Rights and Equal Opportunity Commission,[11] echoed the findings of the 2003 Report. It stated:

> It seems that, even where there has been good policy or law, the policy has not been translated into reliable, high quality health care ... while stand-out programs can be identified, there is no clear evidence of a systemic commitment to improved access to quality care.[12]

---

[6] International Covenant on Economic, Social and Cultural Rights, opened for signature 19 December 1966, 993 UNTS 3, art 2(1) (entered into force 3 January 1976).

[7] P Hunt and J Mesquita, 'Mental Disabilities and the Human Right to the Highest Attainable Standard of Health' (2006) 28 *Human Rights Quarterly* 332, 342.

[8] This is also discussed by Joaquin Zuckerberg and John Petrila, this volume, chs 13 and 15.

[9] G Groom, I Hickie and T Davenport, 'Out of Hospital, Out of Mind!' *A Report Detailing Mental Health Services in Australia in 2002 and Community Priorities for National Mental Health Policy for 2003–2008* (Canberra, Mental Health Council of Australia, 2003) 1, available at: www.mhca.org.au/Publications/documents/OutofHospitalOutofMind.pdf.

[10] *ibid*, 3.

[11] Mental Health Council of Australia, Brain and Mind Research Institute and Human Rights and Equal Opportunity Commission, *Not for Service: Experiences of Injustice and Despair in Mental Health Care in Australia* (Canberra, Mental Health Council of Australia, 2005) available at: www.hreoc.gov.au/disability_rights/notforservice/documents/NFS_Finaldoc.pdf.

[12] *ibid*, 38.

The *Not for Service* report measured the data collected against the National Standards for Mental Health Services, which the National Mental Health Working Group endorsed in December 1996.[13] Standard 11.1 sets out that the relevant mental health service should be accessible to the defined community. The report found that Standard 11.1.4, which requires that the mental health service should be available on a 24-hour basis, and Standard 11.1.2, which requires that '[t]he community to be served is defined, its needs regularly identified and services are planned and delivered to meet those needs', are not being met in many Australian States.[14] Instead, because of 'the inability of consumers and carers to access mental health services during times of crisis, police are increasingly being called to assist, as they are available 24 hours a day 7 days a week'.[15]

In March 2006, the Senate Select Committee on Mental Health's First Report reiterated these findings and stated that the

> high levels of stigma, high rates of death, low levels of access to services, and poor employment outcomes for people with mental illness are amongst the indicators that show that there must be reforms in mental health if these tragic statistics are to be improved.[16]

Recommendation 2.4 of the Senate Select Committee's Final Report recommends that the Australian Health Ministers agree to

> Reform the National Mental Health Strategy to guarantee the right of people with mental illness to access services in the least restrictive environment, to be actively engaged in determining their treatment and to be assisted in social reintegration and underpin those rights with legislation.[17]

Since the Senate Select Committee's Final Report in April 2006, the then Commonwealth Government pledged AUS$1.8 billion in new funds for a five-year action plan for better mental health services.[18] In July 2006, the Council of Australian Governments (COAG) reached agreement on a National Action Plan

---

[13] *National Standards for Mental Health Services*, endorsed by the Australian Health Ministers' Advisory Council's National Mental Health Working Group (December 1996) available at: www.health.gov.au/internet/main/publishing.nsf/Content/mental-pubs-n-servstds.

[14] Mental Health Council of Australia, Brain and Mind Research Institute and Human Rights and Equal Opportunity Commission, *Not for Service: Experiences of Injustice and Despair in Mental Health Care in Australia* (Canberra: Mental Health Council of Australia, 2005) 498, dealing with Queensland, available at: www.hreoc.gov.au/disability_rights/notforservice/documents/NFS_Finaldoc.pdf.

[15] *ibid*, 499, dealing with Queensland. See also *ibid*, 833 for a national overview.

[16] Australia. Parliament. Senate Select Committee on Mental Health, *A National Approach to Mental Health—From Crisis to Community*, First Report (Canberra, Select Committee on Mental Health, 2006) 4, available at: www.aph.gov.au/Senate/committee/mentalhealth_ctte/report/report.pdf.

[17] *ibid*, 6.

[18] Prime Minister of Australia, John Howard, 'Better Mental Health Services for Australia' (Press Release, 5 April 2006).

on Mental Health aimed at improving the co-ordination and collaboration between governments, private mental health service providers and non-government organisations.[19]

While these are steps in the right direction, a National Survey of Mental Health and Wellbeing conducted by the Australian Bureau of Statistics in 2007 indicated that only 35 per cent of individuals with a mental disorder of 12 months in duration received any care.[20] In 2008, it was admitted by the Victorian Government Department of Human Services that 'current arrangements and service cultures mean that individuals with mental health problems receive inadequate services compared to those with physical health conditions'[21] and the situation is much the same across Australia.

The Victorian Government Department of Human Services has stated that 'services are too focused on the most severely mentally ill'.[22] The same can be said of mental health laws. Genevra Richardson has referred to domestic mental health legislation as being designed to promote the protection of the patient, the protection of others and the provision of access to health care.[23] Rights-based criticisms of involuntary commitment laws have generally concentrated on interference with personal autonomy and patients' rights to refuse treatment. However, the developments outlined at the international level suggest that there may now be a shift emerging, from a focus on laws dealing with the involuntary treatment of those with serious mental illnesses and protecting the rights to liberty and autonomy, to developing laws that encourage a right to mental health for *all* individuals with mental illnesses, supported by a right to access appropriate mental health services.[24] This may also reflect a shift away from a focus on the civil/political right to refuse treatment under an autonomy model of mental health laws to a focus on the social/economic right to treatment.

The one aspect of mental health laws that may assist in developing the right to the enjoyment of the highest attainable standard of physical and mental health concerns 'voluntary' admissions to mental health services. The next section outlines existing laws in this regard.

---

[19]　Council of Australian Governments, *National Action Plan on Mental Health 2006–2011* (14 July 2006) available at: www.coag.gov.au/coag_meeting_outcomes/2006–07–14/docs/nap_mental_health.pdf.

[20]　Australian Bureau of Statistics, *4326.0—National Survey of Mental Health and Wellbeing: Summary of Results, 2007* (Canberra, Australian Bureau of Statistics, 2008) 23 available at: www.ausstats.abs.gov.au/ausstats/subscriber.nsf/0/6AE6DA447F985FC2CA2574EA00122BD6/$File/43260_2007.pdf.

[21]　Victorian Government Department of Human Services, *Because Mental Health Matters: A New Focus for Mental Health and Wellbeing in Victoria: Consultation Paper* (Melbourne, Department of Human Services, 2008) 13 available at: www.health.vic.gov.au/mentalhealth/reformstrategy/documents/mhmatters-rep08.pdf.

[22]　*ibid.*

[23]　G Richardson, 'Balancing Autonomy and Risk: A Failure of Nerve in England and Wales?' (2007) 30 *International Journal of Law and Psychiatry* 71.

[24]　S Bell, 'What Does the 'Right to Health' Have to Offer Mental Health Patients?' (2005) 28(2) *International Journal of Law and Psychiatry* 141.

III. The 'Truly' Voluntary: Access to Services

A number of jurisdictions have legislative provisions dealing with voluntary admissions. For example, in Australia, the Tasmanian legislation contains a provision which states that hospital admission with the patient's consent is preferable to involuntary admission,[25] while the Northern Territory legislation sets out the general principle that a person should only be admitted as an involuntary patient

> after every effort to avoid the person being admitted as an involuntary patient has been taken.[26]

New South Wales, South Australia, Tasmania and the Northern Territory all have provisions dealing with the admission of voluntary patients.[27] There are differing levels of complexity relating to these provisions. South Australia takes a 'minimalist' approach in stating that a person may be admitted on his or her own request and may leave the treatment centre at any time.[28] The other three jurisdictions include provisions dealing with the refusal of a request for admission as a voluntary patient. In Tasmania, a medical practitioner must explain why the admission is refused and provide information about other available medical services.[29] If the refusal is on the basis that the applicant does not have a mental illness, the applicant has a right to a second opinion from another medical practitioner.[30] In New South Wales, the applicant can apply to the medical superintendent for a review of a decision not to admit the applicant,[31] and in the Northern Territory, the applicant can appeal to the Mental Health Review Tribunal against a refusal to admit him or her.[32]

The New South Wales and Northern Territory Acts also have provisions dealing with the review of voluntary patients. In New South Wales, at least once every 12 months, the Mental Health Review Tribunal must review voluntary patients who have been in a mental health facility for a period of more than 12 months.[33] In the Northern Territory, at least once every six months, the Mental Health Review Tribunal must review the admission of a voluntary patient who remains in the relevant treatment facility for longer than six months.[34]

---

[25] Mental Health Act 1996 (Tas) s 18.
[26] Mental Health and Related Services Act (NT) s 10(a).
[27] Mental Health Act 2007 (NSW) ch 2; Mental Health Act 2009 (SA) pt 3; Mental Health Act 1996 (Tas) pt 4, div 2; Mental Health and Related Services Act 1998 (NT) Pt 5.
[28] Mental Health Act 2009 (SA) s 8.
[29] Mental Health Act 1996 (Tas) s 20.
[30] Mental Health Act 1996 (Tas) s 21.
[31] Mental Health Act 2007 (NSW) s 11.
[32] Mental Health and Related Services Act (NT) s 25(9).
[33] Mental Health Act 2007 (NSW) s 9.
[34] Mental Health and Related Services Act (NT) s 122.

The Northern Territory has separate provisions for treatment after voluntary admission. It enables treatment only where the individual concerned has given 'informed consent' or a guardian gives his or her consent to the treatment.[35] The Northern Territory Mental Health Review Tribunal held, in *In the Matter of 'A'*[36] that reviews of voluntary patients encompassed those under guardianship orders and that such a review encompassed examining whether the person will benefit from continuing to be admitted as a voluntary patient. The problem for the Tribunal in this case was that 'A' had an intellectual disability and he was being kept as a voluntary patient at the Royal Darwin Hospital because there was no other appropriate facility to care for him. The Tribunal found that 'A' could be said to be benefiting from being a voluntary patient in a very 'loose sense' because the alternative would be to discharge him and not have him receive any care at all. The Tribunal called for the Northern Territory Government to establish 'tailor-made' treatment facilities for individuals such as 'A' so that it did not have to make similar decisions in the future.

All of these legislative provisions deal with individuals who have been admitted as inpatients. This indicates that the law may serve a role in providing access to hospital services, but not necessarily to outpatient community services. A further limitation in relation to putting such legislative provisions into action is the issue of identifying the 'truly' voluntary. This involves a consideration of whether the individual concerned has given his or her 'informed consent' to admission and treatment.[37] The debates concerning what is meant by 'informed consent' and 'capacity to consent' will not be canvassed here; suffice it to say that the issue of consent is particularly relevant in relation to what have been termed the 'incapacitated but compliant'[38]—a group of individuals that needs special attention as outlined in the next section of this chapter.

IV. The 'Incapacitated but Compliant'

The relationship between voluntary and involuntary admissions is complex and the description 'incapacitated but compliant' may in fact refer to those with milder forms of mental illness rather than those with severe forms of mental illnesses such as schizophrenia or bipolar disorder. Involuntary admission usually

---

[35] Mental Health and Related Services Act (NT) s 54(1).

[36] *In the Matter of 'A'* (Unreported, Mental Health Review Tribunal (NT), 25 August 2000) available at: www.nt.gov.au/justice/docs/courts/mentalhealth/decision_a.pdf.

[37] See, for example Mental Health and Related Services Act (NT) s 25(3): 'A medical practitioner ... must examine the person and may admit the person as a voluntary patient if satisfied, following the examination, that the person has given informed consent to his or her admission'. And s 54(1): 'A person who is admitted to an approved facility as a voluntary patient may only be treated under this Act where— (a) the person gives his or her informed consent to the treatment; or (b) a guardian of the person gives his or consent to the treatment'.

[38] *HL v United Kingdom* (2005) 40 EHRR 32 at [52].

takes place after what has been termed 'informal coercion' has proven inadequate.[39] Bernice Pescosolido, Carol Boyer and Keri Lubell have pointed out that 'voluntary' mental health admissions often occur after the individuals concerned have been 'pushed' into care by family, clinicians and friends, a process they refer to as 'extralegal coercion'.[40] Coercion may also exist in the sense that the individual is informed that unless he or she continues to comply with the 'voluntary' treatment regime, he or she will be treated as an involuntary patient.[41]

There thus exists a group of patients who can be classified as not truly voluntary, but are 'compliant' either because of cognitive impairments, because of a lack of understanding of their rights, because of the fear of being given involuntary status, or because of the pressure of others.

The lack of legislative procedures for those in this group was considered by the European Court of Human Rights in the case of *HL v United Kingdom*.[42] HL was born in 1949 and had suffered autism since birth. He had a long history of behavioural problems and special care needs. He was unable to speak and his cognitive abilities were such that he lacked the capacity to consent or object to medical treatment. For over 30 years he was cared for in the Bournewood Hospital, being an inpatient in the Intensive Behavioural Unit since the late 1980s.

In March 1994, HL lived with two paid carers, Mr and Mrs E, while the Hospital remained responsible for his care and treatment. From 1995 onwards, HL attended a day-care centre on a weekly basis.

On 22 July 1997, while HL was at the day care centre, he became agitated and started banging his head against the wall. He was taken to the accident and emergency unit at the hospital and was admitted as an inpatient. A doctor considered making him an involuntary patient, but decided not to because he was compliant and did not resist being admitted. It was not until 12 December 1997 that HL was released back into Mr and Mrs E's care.

In the meantime, around September 1997, HL, represented by his cousin and 'next friend', made an application for judicial review of the hospital's decision to admit him, for a writ of habeas corpus and for damages for false imprisonment. The High Court refused the application on the grounds that HL had been properly admitted under the common-law principle of necessity.

---

[39] T Carney, D Tait, A Wakefield, M Ingvarson and S Touyz, 'Coercion in the Treatment of Anorexia Nervosa: Clinical, Demographic and Legal Implications' (2005) 24(1) *Medicine and Law* 21.

[40] B Pescosolido, C Boyer and K Lubell, 'The Social Dynamics of Responding to Mental Health Problems' in C Aneshensel and J Phelan (eds), *Handbook of the Sociology of Mental Health* (New York, Kluwer Academic/Plenum, 1999) 449.

[41] V Hiday, M Swartz, J Swanson, R Borum and H Wagner, 'Coercion in Mental Health Care' in P Backlar and D Cutler (eds), *Ethics in Community Mental Health Care: Commonplace Concerns* (New York, Kluwer/Plenum, 2002).

[42] *HL v United Kingdom* (2005) 40 EHRR 32.

On appeal, the Court of Appeal found that HL's detention had been unlawful.[43] This was on the basis that the right to detain a patient for treatment for mental disorder could only be exercised under the Mental Health Act 1983 (England and Wales). The Mental Health Act Commission estimated that if this judgment were to be put into practice and applied to others in similar circumstances to HL, 'there would be an additional 22,000 detained patients resident on any one day and an additional 48,000 compulsory admissions per year under the 1983 Act'.[44]

The Hospital Trust appealed to the House of Lords, which upheld the appeal.[45] Lord Goff (with whom Lord Lloyd and Lord Hope agreed) delivered the principal judgment and held that patients who were compliant, but lacked capacity to consent, could be treated on the basis of the common-law doctrine of necessity and did not have to be detained as involuntary patients under the Mental Health Act 1983 (England and Wales). The drawback to this approach, as Lord Steyn observed, was that individuals like HL would not have their detention subject to an extensive scheme of statutory safeguards.[46]

An application was then made to the European Court of Human Rights. It found that HL's detention had breached Article 5(1) of the European Convention on Human Rights, which states that

everyone has the right to liberty and security of person.

One of the exceptions is the 'lawful detention' of 'persons of unsound mind'.[47] Whether or not a person is of unsound mind must be determined by objective medical evidence.[48]

The European Court of Human Rights found that HL had been deprived of his liberty because he had been under continuous supervision and had not been free to leave.[49] Further, he was of unsound mind in that he was 'suffering from a mental disorder of a kind or degree warranting compulsory confinement which persisted during his detention between 22 July and 5 December 1997'.[50] Ultimately, the main issue was whether or not HL's detention could be considered 'lawful' in the sense of avoiding 'arbitrariness'.[51] The Court found that the detention was not lawful in this sense because of the lack of any fixed procedural rules governing HL's detention, particularly the lack of any requirement for the

---

[43] *R v Bournewood Community and Mental Health NHS Trust, ex parte L* [1998] 2 WLR 764 (EWCA Civ).

[44] *HL v United Kingdom* (2005) 40 EHRR 32 at [36].

[45] *R v Bournewood Community and Mental Health NHS Trust, ex parte L* [1999] AC 458 (HL).

[46] *ibid*, 492–3.

[47] Convention for the Protection of Human Rights and Fundamental Freedoms (European Convention on Human Rights), opened for signature 4 November 1950, 213 UNTS 221, art 5(1)(e) (entered into force 3 September 1953).

[48] *Winterwerp v Netherlands* (1979) 2 EHRR 387.

[49] *ibid*, at [91].

[50] *ibid*, at [101].

[51] *ibid*, at [119].

clinical assessment of the continuation of the disorder warranting detention.[52] The Court did not order monetary compensation for the detention, but did order that HL's costs be paid by the state.

The effect of this decision was to reinforce that 'informal' admission procedures are not appropriate for those individuals who lack the capacity to consent to treatment, but who are compliant with it. This mirrors the approach taken by the majority of the Supreme Court of the United States in *Zinermon v Burch*,[53] in which procedural safeguards were deemed necessary for voluntarily admitting an individual who lacked the capacity of give informed consent. The Court in that case, however, did not specify what those procedural safeguards should be.

In March 2005, the British Government released a 'consultation document' setting out its proposed response to the European Court's decision.[54] This set out a new approach of 'protective care' which would require legislation governing admission procedures, as well as processes for review and appeals. A summary of responses was then circulated by the Department of Health.[55]

Subsequently, Schedule A1 was added to the Mental Capacity Act 2005 (England and Wales) by Schedule 7 of the Mental Health Act 2007 (England and Wales). This schedule sets out a new system relating to certain individuals detained in hospitals and care homes for treatment purposes. This new system came into force on 1 April 2009. If an individual lacks the capacity to consent to treatment because of conditions falling within the ambit of the term 'mental disorder',[56] the Primary Care Trust (for hospitals) or the local authority (for care homes) must carry out an assessment to ensure, amongst other matters, that detention for care or treatment is in the person's best interests.[57] It is estimated that around 21,000 assessments will be carried out across England and Wales between 2009 and 2010.[58] In making a 'best interests' assessment, the assessor

[52] *ibid*, at [120].
[53] *Zinermon v Burch* 494 US 113 (1990).
[54] Department of Health, '*Bournewood' Consultation: The Approach to be Taken in Response to the Judgment of the European Court of Human Rights in the 'Bournewood' Case Consultation Document* (March 2005) available at: www.dh.gov.uk/en/Consultations/Closedconsultations/DH_4113613.
[55] Department of Health, *Protecting the Vulnerable: The 'Bournewood' Consultation: Report of the Public Consultation on the Government's Proposed Response to the 'Bournewood' Case* (The Judgment of the European Court of Human Rights in the Case of *HL v the United Kingdom*): Summary of Responses (London, Department of Health, 2006), available at: www.dh.gov.uk/prod_consum_dh/ groups/dh_digitalassets/@dh/@en/documents/digitalasset/dh_4137959.pdf.
[56] Mental Capacity Act 2005, para 14(1) of sch A1 refers to a mental disorder as that defined under the Mental Health Act 2007 (England and Wales), but also includes learning disabilities within the term's ambit. Section 1(2) of the Mental Health Act 2007 defines mental disorder as 'any disorder or disability of the mind' while s 3 excludes any dependence on alcohol or drugs from the term's ambit.
[57] Mental Capacity Act 2005 sch A1, para 33(1).
[58] *Mental Capacity Act Deprivation of Liberty Safeguards Implementation/Commissioning Q&A, February 2009* available at: www.dh.gov.uk/prod_consum_dh/groups/dh_digitalassets/documents/ digitalasset/dh_094793.pdf.

must take into account any relevant care plan or needs assessment.[59] Once detention is authorised, a representative is appointed to support and look after the interests of the person.[60]

The need for legislative provisions governing the detention of those who are not 'truly' voluntary but 'compliant' would seem to be of utmost importance following the European Court of Human Rights decision, but many mental health acts still focus solely on involuntary admission and treatment. In Australia, only the Mental Health and Related Services Act (NT) contemplates the voluntary admission and treatment of those who are unable to give their informed consent, and the provisions in this Act assume that a guardian has been appointed under the Adult Guardianship Act (NT) to make a decision on behalf of such an individual.[61]

The reasons for the omission of provisions dealing with 'voluntary' admission and treatment are explored below. The next section, however, deals with some of the benefits of having such provisions.

V. The Arguments In Favour Of the Legal Regulation of Voluntary Admissions and Treatment

In 1974, David Wexler wrote that 'the law will probably move increasingly away from coercive procedures and toward a model of voluntary hospitalization and treatment'.[62] This shift has taken some time to occur, but the development of international human rights frameworks has provided an impetus for such a shift.

The majority of individuals receiving mental health care are treated on a voluntary basis[63] and there are many benefits of having legislative provisions dealing with voluntary admissions. Such provisions signify a preference for voluntary over involuntary detention and treatment, which can lead to a lessening of the fear associated with accessing mental health services. Karna Halverson points out that '[v]oluntary admission avoids the stigma associated with a court

---

[59] Mental Capacity Act 2005 sch A1, para 39(3).

[60] Mental Capacity Act 2005 sch A1, para 137.

[61] Adult Guardianship Act 1988 (NT) s 54(3).

[62] DB Wexler, 'Mental Health Law and the Movement Toward Voluntary Treatment' (1974) 62(3) *California Law Review* 671, 675–6.

[63] In the United States of America, for example, it is estimated that just over 70% of admissions are voluntary: K Halverson, 'Voluntary Admission and Treatment of Incompetent Persons with a Mental Illness' (2005) 32(1) *William Mitchell Law Review* 161, 163 and references therein.

determination of incompetency'.[64] Related to this is the idea that voluntary admission and treatment avoid the adversarial process that often attaches to involuntary civil commitment laws.[65]

Voluntary admissions also aid in ensuring that individuals with mental illnesses maintain autonomy, which can lead to more co-operation with treatment and a 'stronger alliance with treatment personnel'.[66] If the aim of hospitalisation is not only to provide treatment, but also to provide some form of structure and protection from the pressures of external responsibility,[67] then being in hospital on a voluntary basis can only enhance such an experience.

In relation to international human rights frameworks, having laws that focus on voluntary admissions can also help recognise not only the right to autonomy, but also the rights to dignity, privacy and physical and mental integrity under the Convention on the Rights of Persons with Disabilities.[68] These rights have become the focus of the recent jurisprudence of the European Court of Human Rights and are part of a developing framework 'which addresses the needs of all patients with mental disorders'.[69]

More specifically, a right to appeal against a refusal to admit an individual for treatment may help place pressure on governments to ensure more people are being treated by and gaining access to mental health services than is currently the case in a crisis-driven treatment culture. Finally, some form of review process can help ensure that certain individuals are not detained for longer than necessary and are able to exercise their right to be discharged. This need not be a cumbersome process, as currently, voluntary commitment 'vastly reduces the administrative burden on the treating facility'.[70]

[64] K Halverson, 'Voluntary Admission and Treatment of Incompetent Persons with a Mental Illness' (2005) 32(1) *William Mitchell Law Review* 161, 164.

[65] DH Stone, 'The Benefits of Voluntary Inpatient Psychiatric Hospitalization: Myth or Reality?' (1999) 9 *Boston University Public Interest Law Journal* 25, 29.

[66] PS Appelbaum, 'Voluntary Hospitalization and Due Process: The Dilemma of *Zinermon v Burch*' (1990) 41 *Hospital and Community Psychiatry* 1059, 1060.

[67] PS Appelbaum and TG Gutheil, *Clinical Handbook of Psychiatry and the Law*, 4th edn (Philadelphia PA, Lippincott, Williams & Wilkins, 2007) 61.

[68] Convention on the Rights of Persons with Disabilities, GA Res 61/106, opened for signature 30 March 2007, UN Doc A/Res/61/611 (entered into force 3 May 2008).

[69] M Donnelly, 'From Autonomy to Dignity: Treatment for Mental Disorders and the Focus for Patient Rights' in B McSherry (ed), *International Trends in Mental Health Laws* (Anandale, Federation Press, 2008) 37, 57.

[70] SC Kellogg, 'The Due Process Right to a Safe and Humane Environment for Patients in State Custody: The Voluntary/Involuntary Distinction' (1997) 23 *American Journal of Law and Medicine* 339, 344.

VI.   The Arguments Against The Legal Regulation of Voluntary Admissions and Treatment

The jurisdictions that do not have provisions dealing with voluntary admission and treatment sometimes justify this on the basis that:

(a) voluntary patients should be regarded the same as any patient in mainstream medical facilities in order to reduce discrimination or 'stigma' attached to those with mental illnesses;

(b) if both voluntary and involuntary patients are detained in the same or similar facilities, the former could be subject to the overt or covert threat of being made an involuntary patient;[71] or

(c) legal regulation leads to inflexible and cumbersome processes for review.

These three justifications for omitting voluntary admission and treatment procedures in mental health acts will be discussed in turn.

A.   Discrimination

A major justification for *not* having specific legislation governing the voluntary admission of those with mental illnesses is that to do so differentiates them from all other voluntary health care patients, thus discriminating against or stigmatising those with mental illnesses. This argument came to the fore in Victoria in 1995 when provisions relating to the admission of voluntary patients were repealed.[72] During the second reading of the Mental Health (Amendment) Bill 1995 (Vic), the then government Minister for Malvern, Robert Doyle, stated that removing regulation of voluntary inpatient admissions was less stigmatising and did not mean removing access to treatment:

> You would not attach a voluntary-patient label to someone coming in for a hip replacement or for any general service in our hospitals. Why, then, would we attach

---

[71] H Watchirs, *Application of Rights Analysis Instrument to Mental Health Legislation: Report to Australian Health Ministers' Advisory Council Mental Health Working Group* (Canberra, Commonwealth Department of Health and Aged Care, 2000) 4, available at: www.health.gov.au/internet/main/publishing.nsf/Content/360B8042750B3170CA2571F100079B16/$File/rights.pdf.

[72] Mental Health (Amendment) Act 1995 (Vic) ss 4(a) and 10. This Act was passed on 5 December 1995. When the Mental Health Act 1986 (Vic) was first being drafted, the members of the Consultative Council on Review of Mental Health Legislation (Dr David Milton Myers, Professor Richard Ball and Deirdre Fitzgerald) used this same argument in recommending that the new Act omit any mention of voluntary patients: Victoria. Consultative Council on Review of Mental Health Legislation, *Report of the Consultative Council on Review of Mental Health Legislation* (Melbourne, Health Commission of Victoria, 1981) 24. This recommendation was ignored: JRB Ball, 'The Mental Health Act of Victoria' (1995) 27(1) *Australian Journal of Forensic Sciences* 35. Section 7(4) of the Mental Health Act 1995 (Vic) originally enabled a right of appeal to the Chief Psychiatrist against a refusal to admit a person as a voluntary patient.

such a stigmatising label to someone seeking voluntary help for a mental illness? . . .
People who are mentally ill and admitted voluntarily will have the same informal status
in a hospital as any other patient. That in no way prevents people able to consent to
treatment from seeking and receiving treatment in an in-patient mental health service
and it does not restrict the range of services available.[73]

The problem with this argument is that those with mental illnesses do not have
access to services on an equal basis with those with physical illnesses. In Australia,
the Senate Select Committee on Mental Health pointed out in 2006 that

many people currently do not seek treatment for their [mental] illness, and there is little
point striving for reduction in the stigma and increased awareness, if people find there
is no support available when they take the first step toward getting help.[74]

Discrimination thus already exists in relation to access to treatment. There is
some reason to believe that regulating voluntary admissions may have the
opposite effect to that set out by Robert Doyle, in the sense that if mental health
laws place more emphasis on voluntary admissions and treatments, involuntary
treatment will be seen as a last resort, thus leading to an increased willingness to
be treated.

Of course this issue is very much linked to proper resourcing for mental health
services, which will enable more voluntary admissions and treatment. During the
second reading of the Mental Health (Amendment) Bill 1995 (Vic), the then
Member for Albert Park, John Thwaites, in opposing the repeal of the legislative
provision dealing with voluntary admissions, stated that

[the] real reason for the removal of that provision is resources. The government wants
to reduce the number of people being admitted for psychiatric treatment, and the way
to do so is simply to prevent voluntary patients having the right to appeal against
refusals to admit them.[75]

While this may not have been the overt intention of the government of the time,
it can be argued that denying a right to appeal against a refusal to be treated
means that involuntary admission and treatment becomes the default setting for
those with serious mental illnesses. That is, the emphasis is placed on crisis-
driven mental health services rather than on prevention, care and treatment for
those who have not yet reached crisis point.

---

[73] Victoria, *Parliamentary Debates*, Legislative Assembly, 25 October 1995, 815 (Robert Doyle).

[74] Australia. Parliament. Senate Select Committee on Mental Health, *A National Approach to Mental Health—From Crisis to Community: First Report* (Canberra, Select Committee on Mental Health, 2006) 17, [2.26] available at: www.aph.gov.au/Senate/committee/mentalhealth_ctte/report/report.pdf.

[75] Victoria, *Parliamentary Debates*, Legislative Assembly, 25 October 1995, 811 (The Hon John Thwaites).

If the focus of mental health laws is shifted towards the regulation of voluntary treatment, including a right to appeal against a refusal to provide treatment, then the discrimination that attaches to involuntary detention and treatment may well be lessened.

B. Coercion

Helen Watchirs has outlined the argument that legislative provisions relating to voluntary admission and treatment of necessity lead to both voluntary and involuntary patients being detained in the same or similar facilities, thus leading the former to be subject to the overt or covert threat of being made an involuntary patient.[76] This argument concerning coercion, however, does not seem to be a consequence of legislative provisions in themselves, but is related to the way in which mental health care is delivered. In many countries governments have moved towards 'mainstreaming' by incorporating mental health care into health care in general, rather than having specialised psychiatric institutions.[77] The argument is therefore that involuntary patients are in a class of their own and should be treated separately from 'voluntary' patients.

However, as stated above, those with mental illnesses do not access or receive treatment on an equal basis with those with physical illnesses. This may partly be because of a fear of being treated involuntarily, but it would also appear that the availability of services, particularly in the community, is wanting.

There is little doubt that coercive practices currently exist, but this does not seem to be directly related to the argument that coercion follows from voluntary and involuntary patients being treated in the same or similar facilities. The situation is much more complex. There are some reports that individuals may contrive to arrange to be involuntarily committed to ensure they obtain treatment, with some mental health professionals also employing involuntary mechanisms to admit willing patients.[78] Perceived coercion is strongly related to factors other than legal status alone.[79] Virginia Aldigé Hiday, Marvin Swartz, Jeffrey Swanson and H Ryan Wagner, in providing an overview of studies into coercion, have concluded that

---

[76] H Watchirs, *Application of Rights Analysis Instrument to Mental Health Legislation, Report to Australian Health Ministers' Advisory Council Mental Health Working Group* (Canberra, Commonwealth Department of Health and Aged Care, 2000) 4, available at: www.health.gov.au/internet/main/publishing.nsf/Content/360B8042750B3170CA2571F100079B16/$File/rights.pdf.

[77] Concerning the link between lack of regulation for voluntary patients and mainstreaming, see, for example, Victoria, *Parliamentary Debates*, Legislative Council, 31 October 1995, 479 (The Hon Rob Knowles).

[78] SK Hoge, CW Lidz, M Eisenberg, W Gardner, J Monahan, E Mulvey, L Roth and N Bennett, 'Perceptions of Coercion in the Admission of Voluntary and Involuntary Psychiatric Patients' (1997) 20 *International Journal of Law and Psychiatry* 167, 168.

[79] HD Poulsen, 'The Prevalence of Extralegal Deprivation of Liberty in a Psychiatry Hospital Population' (2002) 25(1) *International Journal of Law and Psychiatry* 29.

from one-fifth to one-third of involuntarily hospitalized patients report having wanted to be hospitalized at the time of their legally coerced admission [whereas] approximately half of legally voluntary patients report having felt a large element of coercion in the decision leading to their hospitalization.[80]

It would seem, then, that the argument that provisions dealing with voluntary admission and treatment will inevitably *lead* to coercive practices is too simplistic an argument to bear much weight.

C.   Cumbersome Processes

One of the arguments put forward by the UK government in *HL v United Kingdom* was that for 'voluntary' patients, it wished 'to avoid the formal statutory procedures of compulsory psychiatric committal for incapacitated patients unless absolutely necessary, the informality, proportionality and flexibility of the common-law doctrines being considered distinctly preferable'.[81]

There is certainly a perception that statutory regulation of clinical practice leads to costly and unnecessary legal protections.[82] It may also be argued that having a right to appeal against a decision to refuse treatment opens the floodgates to the judicial review of clinical decisions, which pleases neither clinicians nor judges.

The new scheme for 'deprivation of liberty safeguards' under the Mental Capacity Act 2005 (England and Wales) does appear complex, with its regime of assessors, representatives, managing authorities and supervisory bodies.[83] However, regulation does not need to be overly complex. Review processes can be streamlined, with the need for the review of voluntary admissions and treatment being perhaps less onerous than for those involuntarily detained. A well-structured and clearly defined legal framework would go some way towards combating this particular argument. Otherwise, as signalled by the decision in *HL*, the absence of any legal criteria governing the 'compliant, but incapacitated' can lead to unjustifiable breaches of the fundamental right to liberty.

---

[80]   VA Hiday, MS Swartz, J Swanson and HR Wagner, 'Patient Perceptions of Coercion in Mental Hospital Admission' (1997) 20(2) *International Journal of Law and Psychiatry* 227, 228.

[81]   *HL v United Kingdom* (2005) 40 EHRR 32 at [80].

[82]   See, eg SK Hoge, CW Lidz, M Eisenberg, W Gardner, J Monahan, E Mulvey, L Toth and N Bennett, 'Perceptions of Coercion in the Admission of Voluntary and Involuntary Psychiatric Patients' (1997) 20 *International Journal of Law and Psychiatry* 167, 169.

[83]   D Bruckard and B McSherry, 'Mental Health Laws for those "Compliant" with Treatment' (2009) 17(1) *Journal of Law and Medicine* 16.

VII. Conclusion

As pointed out in the Introduction, Article 25(b) of the Convention on the Rights of Persons with Disabilities[84] requires States Parties to

> [p]rovide those health services needed by persons with disabilities specifically because of their disabilities.

The majority of individuals accessing mental health services do so on a voluntary basis, but mental health laws generally ignore this fact by focusing solely on involuntary detention and treatment.

Is there a role for the law in supporting the right to the enjoyment of certain services? Having legislative provisions relating to voluntary admission and treatment, particularly in relation to appealing against a decision to refuse treatment, must be a step in the right direction in ensuring the delivery of the highest attainable standard of mental health care. Of course this approach raises questions concerning the scope of judicial review, options for remedies and potential conflicts caused by judges 'forcing' doctors to treat certain individuals or demanding that the government spend more money resourcing mental health services. This needs further exploration and it may be that more emphasis on 'optimal administrative arrangements', as explored by Terry Carney in chapter eleven of this volume, including ensuring a right to a second opinion or enabling judges to order a case conference, would be preferable to just having the judicial power to order that treatment be given to certain individuals.

Nevertheless, the argument can be made that failing to have a legislative framework for voluntary admissions breaches 'the right of access to health facilities, goods and services on a non-discriminatory basis, especially for vulnerable or marginalised groups'.[85] The emphasis on finding ways to ensure equality under the Convention on the Rights of Persons with Disabilities requires that marginalised persons should be supported to reach equal participation in society. This requires the provision of adequate and appropriate services. If mental health laws shift the focus more towards voluntary admission and treatment rather than focusing solely on involuntary admission and treatment, then there is at least a possibility that adequate resourcing of services and a reduction in counter-therapeutic coercive practices may follow.

---

[84] Convention on the Rights of Persons with Disabilities, GA Res 61/106, opened for signature 30 March 2007, UN Doc A/Res/61/611 (entered into force 3 May 2008).

[85] UN Committee on Economic, Social and Cultural Rights, *The Right to the Highest Attainable Standard of Health* (Art 12 of the International Covenant on Economic, Social and Cultural Rights), General Comment No 14 (22nd Sess), UN Doc E/C12/2000/4, 11 August 2000, para 43(a).

17

Thinking About the Rest of the World: Mental Health and Rights Outside the 'First World'*

PETER BARTLETT

I. Introduction

The considerable preponderance of literature relating to mental health law is framed in the context of economically advantaged countries, primarily in North America, Western Europe and Australia and New Zealand. These origins are reflected in a specific set of assumptions regarding mental health law. These assumptions in part relate to the nature of the legal subject. These are countries where modern legal forms flow from a broadly post-enlightenment mentality, where individual rights and liberties are the stuff of national identity. Rights to control civil confinement, or to control mandatory psychiatric treatment, have developed in these jurisdictions in the context of this broader legal culture.

The economic and cultural context also shapes the context of litigation in other ways. Extensive, politically developed and largely benevolent (if often paternalistic) psychiatric professions, coupled with increasingly active user groups, have made a significant impression on the form and organisation of services. Relative to other parts of the world, people with mental disorders in economically advantaged countries benefit from access to inpatient and outpatient specialist care of a comparatively high standard, availability of modern psychiatric treatments, and programmes of care, support, accommodation and

* While much of my understanding in this area has benefited from my work with the Mental Disability Advocacy Center (MDAC) in Budapest, including as a board member for that organisation, the views expressed are my own and do not necessarily reflect the views of that organisation (nor, of course, the University of Nottingham nor the Nottinghamshire Healthcare NHS Trust). I have further benefitted from involvement in a project to reform the mental health law in Lesotho, a project graciously funded by the Nuffield Foundation. My thanks to Rachel Jenkins of the Institute of Psychiatry, King's College London, for providing generous comments on a draft of this chapter, and to the participants at the Prato workshop for their insights.

financial assistance within the community. The form and standards of all of these programmes are quite appropriately the subject of ongoing research, debate, complaint, and litigation. Nonetheless, the existence of these standards of care fundamentally affects the approach to and the context of litigation in these nations.

This developed economic and legal culture is in the background of many of the papers in this volume. Insofar as the authors in this volume question the appropriateness of 'rights-based legalism', it is in the context of societies where moves towards such legalism have been on the political agenda for decades. At least some of the mores of that legalism are already integrated at least to some degree into the practices of compulsion in psychiatry: anyone who was going to be amenable to a legalistic or human rights approach is already talking that talk, although not necessarily always walking that walk as much as we would like. The question in these developed countries is less likely to be 'was all that ever a good idea', than 'have we achieved as much through this route as we can hope for'.

Outside this rather narrow band of developed countries, the situation is markedly different. Human rights as understood in developed countries, and in particular the human rights of persons with mental disabilities, are not as high on the political, justice, social or professional agendas. Social Services are grossly underfunded by the standards of developed countries, and have to operate in a context of far lower government expenditure on the health, educational and social sectors as a whole. Institutional standards may often be distressingly poor. In countries where large mental hospitals and other related institutions have been long established, such as those in central and eastern Europe, there is often little or no local experience of de-institutionalisation and transition from central institutions to local comprehensive care. Mental health legislation and regulation often ranges from the minimal to the non-existent. Frequently, such legislation as there is has become significantly out-dated. Certainly, there is often no history or tradition of legalism of the sort that developed 'western' nations now largely take for granted.

The questions to be addressed by this chapter are thus rather different to the others in this volume. It is not whether we have achieved as much as we could hope for, but rather is the rights-based endeavour worth promoting at all in such a markedly different resource, professional and cultural context? Or would people with mental disabilities in these countries be better served by some other form of reform agenda?

It will be clear from what follows that rights-based legalism is not enough on its own. At a minimum, provision of an appropriate infrastructure of services (however we wish to define 'appropriate'), more direct involvement of users throughout the mental health system, and widespread challenges to stigma throughout these societies are also required. This will not be news to the readers of this volume from economically advantaged countries, as it reflects experience in the developed world over the last roughly 40 years. The question is not whether rights-based legalism is enough; it is instead whether it should be a part of the way forward.

II. Rights as a Model

If we are to discuss the desirability of 'rights-based legalism', it is of course necessary to define the field. At the beginning of the twenty-first century, rights may mean a wide variety of things. Within classic human rights, there are a variety of 'fundamental' rights, essentially to be free from state intervention: the right to liberty, the right to security of the person (sometimes taken to include a right to make decisions regarding medical treatment), the right to judicial processes and equality before the law, and the right to privacy, for example. Variations on these rights are contained in most post-enlightenment human rights instruments—the European Convention on Human Rights,[1] the African Charter of Human and Peoples' Rights,[2] the Canadian Charter,[3] the American Bill of Rights,[4] and so forth. Most of these instruments currently offer some form of legal redress for individuals who consider that their rights under these instruments has been infringed. The issues of access to justice that have long been the stuff of socio-legal analysis are of course important limitations for potential litigants, but in most of the world, these rights are at least in theory enforceable.

Over the twentieth and early twenty-first centuries, human rights law has moved increasingly into rights of social participation, however. Some of these rights are also part of the traditional corpus—the right to vote, for example—but in recent decades the number and scope of these rights have been expanding. Rights to standards of services and standards of institutional care, and rights to health care are obvious examples. The recent United Nations Convention on the Rights of Persons with Disabilities, discussed elsewhere in this volume, provides a particularly broad array of these rights to participation.[5] These rights can be interesting in the context of mental health law, as they change the way those involved in the system are grouped. For the classic legal rights, persons with mental health problems are often pressing their right against their treatment provider: civilly detained patients litigating for their freedom against their

---

[1] Convention for the Protection of Human Rights and Fundamental Freedoms (European Convention on Human Rights), opened for signature 4 November 1950, CETS No 005 (entered into force 3 September 1953).

[2] African Charter on Human and Peoples' Rights, opened for signature 27 June 1981, 1520 UNTS 217 (entered into force 21 October 1986).

[3] Canadian Charter of Rights and Freedoms, Constitution Act, 1982. Enacted as Schedule B to the Canada Act 1982 (UK) c 11 (entered into force 17 April 1982).

[4] The Bill of Rights is the name by which the first 10 amendments to the Constitution of the United States of America are known. They entered into force on 15 December 1791.

[5] United Nations Convention on the Rights of Persons with Disabilities, adopted 13 December 2006, GA Res 61/106. UN Doc A/Res/61/106 (entered into force 3 May 2008). See in particular rights to accessibility (art 9), freedom from exploitation (art 16); community living (19), education (art 24), health (art 25), habilitation and rehabilitation (art 26), work and employment (art 27), adequate standards of living and social protection (art 28); participation in public and political life (art 29), participation in cultural life, leisure activities and sport (art 30). See also Oliver Lewis, this volume, ch 5; Annegret Kämpf, this volume, ch 6 and Tina Minkowitz, this volume, ch 7.

treating psychiatrist, for example. Second generation rights, however, may instead be about systemic provision, and thus service providers and service users may be united on the same side. A service user litigating for better mental health services may well be supported by his or her treatment team, not litigating against them. The real target of such litigation may be those in government in charge of resource allocation.

Enforceability of these second generation rights by aggrieved individuals will depend on the instrument in which they are contained. Often, the most relevant rights (such as the right to health, and the right to community living) are circumscribed with language that limits the effect of the right, or are not directly enforceable by individuals. One way of engaging with the desirability of 'rights-based legalism', therefore, would be to ask whether substantive buttressing and more direct enforcement of these rights would be an appropriate way forward, since 'rights-based legalism' will be beneficial only if relevant rights are available for enforcement.

The trend in recent years has been to require that these rights are provided in a non-discriminatory fashion. Of particular relevance for current purposes, non-discrimination on the basis of disability has increasingly become a matter of legal and public policy. In developed countries, this has placed the law relating to people with mental disabilities in a new context. Justifications for legal interventions are no longer as clear as they once were—a topic for a different time, but an important topic nonetheless. For current purposes, the point is that in human rights law, the mere existence of a mental disability is no longer an obvious justification in itself for differential legal treatment, nor for the deprivation of rights. This is not of course to say that human rights law need be blind to different circumstances. Requirements to make 'reasonable accommodation' to accommodate the needs of persons with disabilities are an obvious example where consideration of difference is in itself a human rights requirement. Such concepts are generally intended to buttress the rights of affected individuals however, not to restrict them.

That may be taken as the broad structure of human rights. Any departure from these rights raises particular theoretical problems. By definition, these rights are meant to be universal: they are to apply to everybody, in all countries signing the relevant instrument. Allowing a 'pick and mix' approach to people who warrant human rights protection raises dangerous precedents within countries: if some groups do not warrant protection, why not others?

A considerable amount of debate regarding mental health law and service provision in developed nations has in recent years moved away from rights-based analysis. Even a number of papers in this volume seem to consider that the key rights issue is now optimising service provision and good outcomes, as defined by medical indicators. Questions of coercion become re-phrased to make them appear human rights neutral.[6] Expressly or by implication, the classic rights questions about whether people with mental disabilities should be permitted to refuse compulsion, or the development of firm and objective criteria for compulsion, are viewed as somehow old-fashioned, quaint, 'SO 10 years ago'. Yet moves away from strong affirmations of human rights in our own countries undercut the credibility of human rights arguments abroad. In an international context, departures from universality also raise problems of credibility for the human rights project overall: how are we to pressure a nation known for human rights violations to comply with human rights instruments, if our own countries nation are themselves choosing to depart from those 'universal' norms when convenient to do so? Whether this is an appropriate approach for developed countries is outside the scope of this chapter, but for the sake of persons in other countries, both within the mental disability field and outside it, for whom fundamental rights have not been achieved and may have real import, this is not a position we should sleep-walk into.

The pursuit of these rights however implies a level of legalism. As noted above, access to courts for the determination of civil rights is itself a part of the human rights framework, and a move from it may itself imply a human rights violation.

'Rights-based legalism' may perhaps be taken to extend beyond the territory of traditional human rights, defined in international treaties and post-enlightenment national constitutions. In many countries, legal regulation of matters relating to mental disability extends into areas that are not necessarily pivotal to human rights as defined above, and these areas may at least in theory be subject to litigation. English law, for example, allows judicial challenge of a broad array of decisions made by a public authority, including the National Health Service, and occasionally litigation has arisen in a psychiatric context that does not raise obvious human rights issues. We have in recent years seen an application challenging an individual's categorisation as 'psychopathic' rather than 'mentally ill', for example.[7] These cases are very much the exception, however. English litigation in the mental health field is overwhelmingly about the scope of basic freedoms, in particular rights to liberty and freedom from involuntary treatment.

The arguments for rights-based legalism outside the classic human rights context are quite different than for fundamental human rights issues. Here, the arguments are likely to reflect skirmishes over power at a relatively specific level, the micro-theatres of power that make Foucauldeans salivate. A defence of rights-based legalism in this context might be based on the protection of some form of power to the individual, which might in turn be taken to protect some vestige of personal dignity. It might also be defended as a punitive/threatened

---

[6] See, eg R Bonnie and J Monahan, 'From Coercion to Contract: Reframing the Debate on Mandated Community Treatment for People with Mental Disorders' (2005) 29(4) *Law and Human Behavior* 485.

[7] *R (on the application of B) v Ashworth Hospital Authority* [2005] UKHL 20.

procedural 'stick' in the background, which practitioners will avoid by better engagement and communication with their patients/clients, an outcome that seems highly desirable. The fact that such disagreements do not engage with fundamental human rights thus does not necessarily mean a rights-based approach is inappropriate.

Indeed, the use of law as a structure to these debates opens a somewhat different view of human rights in mental health. Human rights, clearly in one sense, is a set of principles and standards to which everyone in society is entitled—a top-down vision defining how state action is restricted. But human rights can also be viewed from the bottom up—a way in which a framework is created for marginalised peoples to engage with (and to insist on engagement with) the decisions that affect them, either as groups or as individuals. Without that engagement, human rights law rather misses the point, since that engagement is fundamental to the dignity of individuals and peoples that human rights law presupposes. The right to refuse treatment is perhaps a helpful example. Certainly, the right to refuse treatment is important because of classic political doctrines concerning limitation of state power; but it is a reasonable speculation that this is not the key concern of many people with mental disabilities who want the right to refuse. Anecdotal evidence would suggest that few people with psychiatric disabilities want to refuse all medication or treatment. For them, the right to say 'no' is not about refusal of everything; it is about creating a long-stop that requires the treatment provider to engage with them about the decisions that will affect them. It is thus about articulation of the self, and about the individual claiming his or her own dignity. It is about the determination not simply to become a passive clinical object. This makes it about a very different vision of human rights, and perhaps the most important vision. Without this legal protection, the risk is that overworked clinicians use power as convenience, to reach the 'right' clinical decision.

In practice, litigation that is clearly outside the scope of human rights discourse is relatively rare. Much more frequent is litigation that, although taken by the domestic courts to be outside the scope of human rights law, nonetheless arguably engages human rights issues. In England in the last few years, for example, we have seen courts fail to find that the European Convention on Human Rights is engaged, let alone violated, in the cases, respectively, of an individual lacking capacity being institutionalised over the objection of competent family carers,[8] and of a competent and objecting individual being given psychotropic medication.[9] Human rights lawyers might see things rather differently from the courts in these cases, and, at least occasionally, Strasbourg has

---

[8]　*Re S (Inherent Jurisdiction: Family Life)* [2002] EWHC 2278 (Fam), esp at [39].
[9]　*R (on the application of PS) v Responsible Medical Officer* [2003] EWHC 2335 (Admin).

shared this different view.[10] For these issues, the distinction between human rights and other rights-based legalism appears tenuous.

For purposes of the discussion that follows, the focus will be on decisions within this somewhat broader ambit of human rights, focusing on compulsory treatment, provision of services, institutional standards, detention, guardianship and other civil rights. From the discussion that follows, it will be clear that these issues appear to be relevant in central Europe and Africa, and they are included in international instruments of which the relevant countries are parties—most notably the European Convention on Human Rights and the African Charter on Human and Peoples' Rights. Both of these treaties have courts to interpret their provisions, so in strategic terms, we can understand that we are talking not merely about rights as a discursive mechanism, but also a mechanism with some enforcement attached. For purposes of the distinctions drawn above, it will be taken that these generally engage with human rights issues. 'Purely' non-human rights related decisions, such as the categorisation question noted above, will not form a part of this discussion.

III. What it's Like In the Rest of the World

Basic demographic information regarding care in southern Africa and central Europe is contained in table 1. The first point that becomes obvious from that table is that 'the rest of the world' is not a homogenous place, and southern Africa is in many ways as different from central Europe as both are from economically privileged countries. Indeed, there is considerable variation between countries in each of these regions, and no doubt within countries themselves. Nonetheless, a few generalisations may be made.

A. Southern Africa

Much of Africa is, of course, chronically poor. It is not uncommon that average annual Gross Domestic Product (GDP) is less than US$1000 per person. It is an environment where often there have never been psychiatric services as would be recognisable to a western European. Overall health budgets are miniscule,

---

[10] Compare, for example, *R v Bournewood Community and Mental Health NHS Trust, ex parte L* [1999] 1 AC 458 to *HL v United Kingdom* [2005] 40 EHRR 761.

Table 1: Comparative Demographic Data

	Area (K km²)	Population (M)	Average GDP $US	MH Budget as % of Health Budget	Per 10,000 Population				Per 100,000 Population				Area per psychiatrist (x 1000 Km²)
					MH Beds (Total)	MH Beds in MH Hospitals	MH Beds in General Hospitals	MH Beds in other settings	Number Psychiatrists	Number of MH Nurses	Number Psychologists	Number of social workers	
S Africa													
Angola	1,247	16.4	2,235	0	0.13	0.70	0.60	0.00	0.00	0.00	0.00	0.00	
Botswana	582	1.8	7,183	1%	1.10	0.70	0.40	0.00	0.40	9.00	0.30	3.00	80.00
Congo	342	4.0	1,400	N/A	0.06	–	0.06	–	0.03	0.10	0.26	N/A	342.00
DR Congo	2,345	58.8	154	N/A	0.17	0.15	0.009	0.009	0.04	0.03	0.01	0.40	100.00
Gabon	268	1.4	4,928	.3%	0.70	0.60	0.06	0.00	0.30	1.00	0.50	2.00	67.00
Lesotho	30	2.1	714	7%	0.80	0.30	0.50	0.00	0.05	0.20	0.09	1.20	30.00
Malawi	118	13.6	263	2%	0.37	N/A	N/A	N/A	0.00	2.50	0.00	0.00	
Mozambique	799	21.2	333	N/A	0.23	0.20	0.04	0.01	0.04	0.01	0.05	0.01	21.00
Namibia	824	2.1	3,193	N/A	1.50	1.50	0.0	0.00	0.20	0.00	6.00	6.00	206.00
South Africa	1,228	48.3	5,683	N/A	4.50	4.00	0.38	0.12	1.20	7.50	4.00	20.00	2.00
Swaziland	17	1.1	2,455	.3%	2.00	2.00	0.0	0.00	0.10	10.00	0.10	0.10	17.00
Zambia	753	12.0	925	0	0.50	0.17	0.18	0.07	0.02	5.00	0.04	0.04	150.00
C Europe													
Bosnia iH	51	4.0	2,568	N/A	3.60	2.40	1.0	0.20	1.80	10.00	0.50	0.03	0.70
Bulgaria	111	7.6	4,839	2.5%	8.30	4.10	1.90	2.30	9.00	15.00	0.90	0.30	0.16
Croatia	57	4.5	14,495	N/A	10.06	8.02	0.98	1.06	8.70	N/A	N/A	N/A	0.14

Czech Rep.	79	10.4	21,187	3%	11.40	9.80	1.50	0.20	12.10	33.00	4.90	N/A	0.06
Estonia	45	1.3	10,046	N/A	10.20	8.00	2.10	0.00	13.00	0.00	N/A	N/A	2.60
Hungary	93	10.1	14,094	8%	9.60	2.30	7.20	0.10	9.00	19.00	2.00	1.00	1.00
Latvia	64	2.3	9958	6.3%	13.80	13.50	0.30	0.00	10.00	40.00	2.00	0.50	0.27
Lithuania	65	3.4	15,300	7%	10.00	8.60	1.10	0.30	15.00	36.00	5.00	N/A	0.13
Poland	313	38.1	11,483	N/A	7.80	5.20	1.20	0.60	6.00	18.40	3.40	0.60	0.14
Romania	238	22.6	2618	3%	7.60	5.50	2.00	0.20	4.10	8.90	4.50	N/A	0.26
Slovakia	49	5.4	20,075	5%	9.00	6.00	3.00	0.00	10.00	32.00	3.00	1.00	0.91
Comparitors												
Australia	7,682	20.7	39,300	9.6%	3.90	1.20	2.70	1.00	14.00	53.00	5.00	5.00	2.60
France	547	63.4	36,417	8%	12.00	7.00	3.0	2.00	22.00	98.00	5.00	N/A	0.04
UK	244	60.9	37,400	10%	5.80	N/A	N/A	N/A	11.00	104.00	9.00	58.00	0.04
USA	9,800	306.0	47,025	6%	7.70	3.10	1.30	3.30	13.70	6.50	31.10	35.30	0.23

Sources
Sources for data columns 1–3: UK and Australia GDP: Central Intelligence Agency, *World Fact Book* (Washington DC, CIA, 2009). All other figures UK Foreign Office website (available at: www.fco.gov.uk), accessed 23 February 2009. Some figures predate the recent economic difficulties. Source for data columns 4–11: World Health Organization, *Mental Health Atlas 2005* (Geneva, WHO, 2005).

sometimes as low as a few dollars per capita per year.[11] Mental health budgets are in turn a small proportion of that, and are largely devoted to staff salaries and a small number of inpatient beds. In a number of southern African countries, there appears to be virtually no state investment in mental health services at all. In others, where figures were available, in most cases the mental health budget was less than two per cent of the health budget. Mental health tends to be under-funded in most countries of the world, relative to the impact of mental health on quality-adjusted life years (QuALYs);[12] but these figures are extreme, particularly when placed in the context of tiny overall health budgets.

The result is minimal specialist service provision. According to the World Health Organization in 2005, there were no psychiatrists in either Angola or Malawi.[13] Elsewhere, psychiatrists are exceptionally rare. Only in the Republic of South Africa (RSA) does the number exceed 0.5 per 100,000 population. Zambia, for example, has one psychiatrist in government practice for roughly 12 million people. Psychiatric nurses, social workers and psychologists are in similarly short supply. Kenya has 250 psychiatric nurses in the country, but the rate of produc-tion is far less than the rate of loss to retirement, mortality and brain drain (both overseas and internal). Indeed, in 2009, Kenya only produced one psychiatric nurse for the country.[14]

This situation is further complicated by the physical size and geography of these countries. Outside the RSA, the average area per psychiatrist ranges from roughly 17,000 km² in Swaziland, to 342,000 km² in the Congo. To put that in context, the comparable number for Australia is 2600 km², for the United States of America, 230 km², and for France and the United Kingdom, 40 km² per psychiatrist. Averages in this context must of course be approached with care. In practice, mental health professionals, and psychiatrists in particular, are likely to be concentrated in urban areas. For these urban populations, specialist services will be considerably more accessible than for people outside these urban areas. For people in rural areas, the concentration of services in cities and the sparse coverage of primary care means that the nearest medical facilities may be a very long way away indeed, a difficulty exacerbated by limited public transport infrastructure.

Available treatments are limited. New generation antipsychotic drugs are unlikely to be available in the public sector, because of price. Training in new

---

[11] Statistics from the WHO in 2002 show for example that the per capita expenditure on health in Burundi was US$3 per year; in the Democratic Republic of the Congo US$4 per year; in the Central African Republic US$ 11 per year; and in Chad and Malawi, US$14 per year: World Health Organization, *Global Health Atlas*, available at: www.apps.who.int/globalatlas/.

[12] World Health Organization, *The World Health Report 2001: Mental Health: New Understanding, New Hope* (Geneva, WHO, 2001) ch 3.

[13] World Health Organization, *Mental Health Atlas* (Geneva, WHO, 2005) also available online at: www.apps.who.int/globalatlas/default.asp. Since the WHO report, Malawi has successfully recruited a psychiatrist.

[14] My thanks to Rachel Jenkins of the Institute of Psychiatry, King's College London, for this example.

psychological therapies is limited and a shortage of specialists means that in any event, even where training is available, continuing supervision is difficult. Bed provision is similarly minimal, and such facilities as there are may be under-staffed. The result is that facilities may be of poor quality. One African psychiatrist writes:

> Most mental hospitals in Africa are located in the 'economic ghettos' of cities, and the forensic units are in turn located in the 'ghettos' of these hospitals, in locations often termed maximum security units. Though located in hospitals, these units are practically extensions of prisons, only worse because they exist as 'orphan' units that do not belong to either the medical or prison systems. In addition to the lack of adequate facilities, most countries have an average of one psychiatrist to a million. Those patients with the added need for forensic care have even less, and therefore for many people commitment to one of these units means a life sentence on a daily dose of chlorpromazine, carbamazepine and malnutrition.

> A visit to many of these institutions leads to despair about the state of human rights and dignity in our continent. Those who are considered lucky are seen by a demoralized, poorly trained, and inadequately paid doctor who passes by the ward once every few weeks, to see only those patients who are most disturbed. For those who are of no trouble, there is no review.[15]

Formalised community support programmes are extremely rare, and indeed are logistically impractical on a national basis, when numbers of potential clients are compared with numbers of available specialist staff. Therefore there has long been recognition that in low-resource settings especially, but also in richer countries, involvement of primary care is crucial and integration of mental health into primary care is essential for population access to mental health care.[16] While there can be little doubt that this is a desirable way forward, it is not an unproblematic strategy. Its drivers are at least partly a lack of professional and financial resources. While getting better use out of minimal resources is of course desirable, it should not detract attention from the other problem, that mental health is often significantly under-resourced in the region, with reference to overall health budgets.

While some family structures apparently continue to be strong, factors such as poverty, the journeying of breadwinners to seek employment and the death of potential carers (for example, from HIV) has made sustained family care increasingly problematic. Certainly, the anecdotal reports are that stigma against people with mental disabilities who return from institutional care is often entrenched, and sometimes violent.

The treatment picture is complicated by the existence of traditional healers, who are often the first port of call for the vast bulk of people who suffer from

---

[15] FG Njenga, 'Forensic Psychiatry: The African Experience' (2006) 5(2) *World Psychiatry* 97.
[16] For a recent discussion, see A Alem, L Jacobsson and C Hanlon, 'Community-based Mental Health Care in Africa: Mental Health Workers' Views' (2008) 7(1) *World Psychiatry* 54.

mental health problems. There has been little research on the effectiveness of these treatments in terms of health and social outcomes. Harmful practices have been documented by some practitioners. Nonetheless, traditional healers are often well embedded in the community. They are seen to understand the cultural and community context, and as noted, are a reality in the care system. They do not necessarily work in opposition to the western-style psychiatrists. In Lesotho, for example, hospital workers have told me that traditional healers may often house a person released from hospital, and aid in their re-integration into the local community.[17] Nonetheless, the framework of traditional healers can create complexities. It would seem that little if any research has been done as to how the remedies of these healers interact with the medications prescribed by physicians prescribing western medicines. Further, the cultural structure of the traditional approach can intersect awkwardly with western medicine. When a patient identifies his or her condition as flowing from demonic possession, for example, it may be difficult for a psychiatrist to determine how far this flows from psychosis, and how far from the fact that this is how the culture articulates some forms of mental condition.

The legislative framework in these countries is sometimes left over from colonial days. While some countries have produced new Acts,[18] others have no legislative framework, leading to a lack of meaningful criteria for compulsory admission or compulsory treatment. Similarly, guardianship legislation is rudimentary, and rarely allows partial guardianship, for example. In practice, in much of the Southern African region, the overwhelming sense is of the absence of meaningful legal regulation in the mental health context.

Consistent with this, there appears to be no tradition of engagement of people with mental health problems with the legal system. Legal representation or formal advocacy is not a fixture of the mental health system. Again, this should be placed in perspective: in Lesotho, the state provides defence lawyers to criminally accused persons only in capital cases. It is thus perhaps unsurprising that they are not routinely provided to psychiatric patients.

---

[17]   Regarding traditional healers and integration with other medicine, see for example O Ayon-rinde, O Gureje and R Lawal, 'Psychiatric Research in Nigeria: Bridging Tradition and Modernisation' (2004) 184 *British Journal of Psychiatry* 536; SC Moukouta and E Pewzner-Apeloig, 'Thérapies traditionnelles-thérapies moderns en milieu psychiatrique au Congo. Syncrétisme ou interference?' (2002) 160 *Annales Médico-psychologiques, Revue Psychiatrique* 353.

[18]   In southern Africa, the Republic of South Africa has particularly good legislation: see Mental Health Care Act, 2002 (RSA Act no 17, 2002) s 32. While not really in southern Africa, other African countries have also passed new legislation in recent years. See Tanzania, Mental Health Act, 2008 (Act no 21/08); Kenya, Mental Health Act c 248 (1991); and Egypt, which passed new legislation (Law for the Care of mental Patients) in 2009.

B. Central Europe

Central Europe raises very different questions. Certainly, these countries are relatively poor by western European standards, but they are considerably wealthier than the African countries discussed above. As table 1 shows, the average annual GDP per head is roughly US$10,000 to 20,000—significantly below western European comparitors, but significantly higher than the African examples. Similarly, from a simple demographic point of view, there are a much wider range and stronger concentration of services. Where figures are available, mental health appears to account for something in the range of three to seven per cent of health budgets. Once again, this is an under-fund relative to impact of mental disorders on QuALYs, but these are in general much higher proportions than the African numbers, and are further based on significantly higher health budgets.

This follows through into service provision. In the southern African countries outside the RSA, there are 0.13 to 1.5 mental health beds per 10,000 population; in central Europe, these numbers are generally between 7.5 and 14—notably higher than in the comparitors in developed nations, reflecting in part the ongoing focus on institutional rather than community services in the region. Psychiatrists and other mental health professionals are similarly much more readily available, with up to 15 psychiatrists per 100,000 population. And while organised community care provision is extremely limited in central Europe, there are generally state financial benefits available to people with mental disabilities. While certainly not generous, these benefits do allow a financial cushioning of the transition between institution and community.

Central Europe is thus not a culture where mental health care does not exist. Instead, the issues are about its nature. There may be no shortage of institutions, but the institutions are often sadly inadequate. The reports of the European Committee for the Prevention of Torture (CPT) and other investigative bodies have chronicled serious deficiencies in institutional care in the region. In a 2002 visit to Karlukovo State Psychiatric Hospital in Bulgaria, for example, the CPT found that meat, fresh vegetables and fruit were only rarely available, and the daily per capita allowance for food was less than half a Euro. In practice, the institution relied on donations of food from relatives of the inmates. The CPT noted a connection between the limited food and the mortality rate in the institution.[19] While this is certainly a particularly clear example of institutional deprivation, institutions do seem to be generally large and depressing. The common use of 'cage beds' and 'net beds' in significant parts of the region—beds covered by bars or netting to preclude the occupant from leaving the bed or, often, from standing up—is one indication of the intensity of control and general

---

[19] European Committee for the Prevention of Torture CPT/Inf (2004) 21 (visit of April 2002) at paras [132]–[134]. For a more detailed discussion of CPT reports in the context of psychiatric facilities, see P Bartlett, O Lewis and O Thorold, *Mental Disability and the European Convention on Human Rights* (Leiden, Martinus Nijhoff, 2007).

oppressiveness that is still not uncommon.[20] An absence of community-based care means that people may remain in these institutions for long periods of time, particularly if they have chronic disabilities such as learning disabilities.

These are countries that remain influenced by their Soviet past. In a legal context, this means that there are almost always legal structures surrounding confinement,[21] often buttressed with procedural protections. Thus in much of central Europe, civil psychiatric detention may only occur upon the order of a court, for which a lawyer is provided. The problem with these procedural protections is that they are often in form only. The report of the Mental Disability Advocacy Center (MDAC) relating to Hungary provides a particularly clear example of how these rights lack real meaning. Lawyers often meet clients only at the court on the day of the hearing, and hearings last only a few minutes.[22] Indeed, it would seem that in some countries lawyers do not view it as part of their role in these hearings to challenge the confinement, raising the question as to what purpose the hearings are actually meant to achieve.[23] The parallels with the empirical literature on the United States of America 30 years ago are striking.

Once the individual is admitted, plenary guardianship often follows almost as a matter of routine, often with the director of the hospital or social care home being appointed as the guardian. Here, the unreformed nature of the legal systems does create real problems in rights protection. Consistent with classic Roman law, a person under guardianship loses legal personality. He or she ceases to be a legal agent who may enforce his or her rights, and this is regardless of the de facto functional capacity of the individual to make the specific decisions in question.

Southern Africa and central Europe are thus fundamentally different conceptually. Southern Africa is poor, in a world where law is, and has always been, largely absent in the field of mental health. Central Europe is a world still in the shadow of its Soviet past, with large psychiatric facilities, battalions of psychiatric professionals, and a tradition of legal process (although not meaningful legal involvement). These contexts follow through into the questions of service provision, and the question of the place of rights in these regions. For southern Africa, the question is how to build an appropriate system essentially from scratch; in central Europe, the question is how to 'turn the super-tanker'.

What they share is a history of political and social indifference to mental health issues. In neither region has there been the political support for the development of adequate mental health programmes, nor of the user involvement movement,

---

[20] Regarding cage beds in particular, see Mental Disability Advocacy Center (MDAC), *Cage Beds: Inhuman or Degrading Treatment in Four EU Accession Countries* (Budapest, MDAC, 2003) available at: www.mdac.info/documents/118_MDAC_Cage_Bed_Report.pdf.
[21] The obvious exception is Latvia, which appears to have no functioning mental health legislation.
[22] Mental Disability Advocacy Center (MDAC), *Liberty Denied* (Budapest, MDAC, 2004).
[23] P Bartlett, T Simmins, M Derić and M Zadro, *An Analysis of the Mental Health Regulations in Bosnia and Herzegovina with Recommendations* (Sarajevo, Council of Europe, 2008).

that has occurred in economically advantaged countries over the last roughly 40 years. In both regions, the question is how to kick-start change.

IV. Rights over the Self

Unless we are to abandon the rule of law completely regarding mental disability in these jurisdictions, the legal starting point must be the assurance of an appropriate legal structure in domestic law. That, along with relevant domestic policy and the financial resources, provides the legal groundwork for the provision of a system of care and support for people with mental disabilities. The specific content of such law and policy is a much wider subject than can be addressed in this chapter. Suffice it to say that, as noted in the first section of this chapter, the legal and cultural traditions are not in place for what people in economically privileged countries would view as appropriate standards of care, and appropriate standards and provision of community-based care in particular.

It is appropriate to remember where the real arguments for this sort of rights lie. Perhaps most significant is the application of power to the individual. Sometimes the authorities are wrong, or at least not so clearly right that they should be allowed to do what they want. Sometimes these errors are manifest— the ambulance attendants bring the wrong person to hospital, for example, or there are clear and material errors in the medical record upon which compulsion is based. One hopes that such egregious errors are uncommon, but experience indicates that they certainly occur. Much more frequently, issues of compulsion will be in a grey area of: how does a legal standard apply to the situation of this individual? This does not alter the fact that the effects on the individual are likely to be substantial—deprivation of liberty, enforced treatment, loss of control over property, for example—and he or she must have a right to ensure that the decision meets the appropriate standards.

The arguments for such rights also concern the governance of those who care for people with mental disabilities, be they professionals or family members. These individuals exercise power. It may be a platitude, but it is nonetheless a valuable platitude that power unchecked is a recipe for power abused. Certainly, the provision of individual rights to challenge these carers is not on its own a sufficient check for such power, but it enforces a particular relationship between the carer and the individual. The experience in economically advantaged countries is that the move towards engagement with users, the rise of the user involvement movement, and the consequent reshaping of mental health policy occurred in parallel with the development of and increased exercise of individual rights of service users. While it is difficult to see that such correlations can be researched with rigour—there are too many confounding variables—it is intuitively arguable that the new, engaged and active role accorded to service users flows, to a relevant degree, from the fact that this active role could be enforced: a culture has developed in these countries where service users can, in a judicial or quasi-judicial forum, have their voices heard and require carers to justify their actions. Engagement without such enforcement becomes a crumb dropping from the master's table, at the master's behest; and in this day and age, that is no way to build a mental health system.

As noted above, these rights often do not currently exist in a meaningful way outside economically advantaged countries. In Latvia and in much of southern Africa, there appears to be no functioning mental health law, let alone a law which creates the opportunity for service users to challenge or engage with the decisions regarding compulsion that are made about them. In much of central Europe, as noted above, persons found incapable under a judicial process, sometimes without notifying them of the hearing,[24] lose their legal personhood, and no longer have standing in court. Furthermore, even in those parts of central Europe where court hearings occur as a matter of routine, they appear often to be mere formalities, with little meaningful engagement with users and their rights.

On some of these points, the situation in central Europe in particular bears some relationship to the American situation in the 1960s: law and institutions exist; the question is how to make the law relevant at the local level. That would suggest that the development of a legal culture for service users might be an appropriate way forward, to take better and meaningful advantage of the existing frameworks. In southern Africa, by comparison, little relevant law exists, let alone a legal culture prepared for litigation in this area. In both cases, we are a long way from a world where it can be taken for granted that users of psychiatric services and people with learning disabilities can in practice contest their rights, and where they will be taken seriously by the legal system.

The difficulties of developing litigation in this area are not merely formal, however. It is not merely that there is no culture of litigation, it is also that the user may well be in an institution where order is maintained by the effect of long-standing institutionalisation, by coercion, or occasionally by violence. Certainly, in a total institution, life for an individual challenging the institution is unlikely to be made pleasant by the institutional staff. It is fair to ask how their safety is to be assured in the roughly six years it now takes between an application to the European Court of Human Rights and its final determination, plus of course the time required for the prerequisite exhaustion of domestic remedies.

Perhaps as problematic is the question of what can rights look like in these cultural contexts? The issues for central Europe and southern Africa appear different here, as central Europe is markedly more culturally similar to western Europe: society within individual countries is not generally based on ethnic or

---

[24] See, eg *Shtukaturov v Russia* (App No 44009/05) judgment 27 March 2008. For more detailed discussion of guardianship in central Europe, see the reports of MDAC, available at www.mdac.info.

cultural tribes; court systems, legal systems and psychiatric systems exist in a broadly similar way to the rest of Europe; and there is not generally the grinding poverty of much of southern Africa.

How relevant are the cultural differences between the economically privileged countries in which human rights have developed and southern Africa? Obviously, such differences exist and cannot be ignored, but they must be approached with come care, since 'cultural difference' can frequently become a mask for stigma and oppression. The African Charter on Human and Peoples' Rights, for example, specifically protects the role of the family as 'the natural unit and basis of society'.[25] This has led to some debate as to whether families should have a particularly strong role in African mental health law.[26] While the role of families in African society, both in practice and in their human rights charter, may be significant, it is not obvious how it should be translated into mental health law. The reality is that mental disability still carries considerable stigma in much of Africa, and the risk is that families will choose not to offer care within the family, but instead to leave an individual in an institutional setting as long as possible. As such, the risk is that this becomes a right to exclude the person from the family rather than to include them.

That said, it is difficult to see that a system of law and rights can work without engagement with local culture. Quite how we should expect that to work in southern Africa is an open question. Certainly, unless patterns of service provision change dramatically, it is difficult to see that the western model of tribunals, with a psychiatrist, a lay person and a lawyer, can function: there are simply not enough psychiatrists. It does not of course follow that rights cannot be pursued. The RSA, which like the rest of southern Africa has a shortage of psychiatrists in some parts of the country, has expanded the psychiatric role on the review board to include other mental health professionals.[27] That might provide a different model. Alternatively, in some parts of southern Africa, indigenous courts still exist, and have an active role in the community. One might imagine that they might appropriately be used for determination of matters of dispute in this area. How successful that approach would be no doubt depends on a variety of external factors: Do the courts function effectively and with the respect of all who would be party to disputes about psychiatric coercion? Can they readily be trained with the necessary legal knowledge to apply the statute? And are there issues of stigma among the court officers that would preclude application of a rights-based law in the way the law intends? Whatever is decided, the court or

[25] African Charter on Human and Peoples' Rights (ACHPR), opened for signature 27 June 1981, 1520 UNTS 217 (entered into force 21 October 1986) art 18.
[26] See, eg the article by Dr Ahmed Okasha in the newspaper *Al-Masry al-Youm*, 4 March 2009.
[27] See Mental Health Care Act 2002 (RSA) s 1(xvii), 20(2)(a).

court-like body must have the confidence of service users, mental health professionals, and the local community. We still know very little of how these practicalities will play out in domestic contexts in southern Africa: we are still too near the beginning of the process of legislative development.

For any of this to work, of course, local policy-makers must come to understand the relevance of the issues. It does seem that a critical mass of those charged with care of people with mental disabilities is aware of the problems and the issues of stigma surrounding service users, but it is far from obvious in either central Europe or southern Africa that this constitutes a majority of psychiatric professionals, let alone a national consensus. If we are to see meaningful entrenchment of human rights values in psychiatric and learning disability services in these countries, significant changes of attitude will be required among the bulk of practitioners, policy-makers, governments and the public.

That reminds us that the provision of individual rights is only one part of a much bigger project, involving changed attitudes to users of psychiatric and learning disability services and to the provision of mental health services. If individual rights are merely a part of that larger picture, they are nonetheless an integral part. Appropriate provision of services in the twenty-first century requires safe environments for users, an end to unregulated coercion, an atmosphere of trust between users and service providers, enhanced dignity for service users and a move towards engagement of service users in their care. For these to become more than policy 'tick boxes', they must be buttressed by mechanisms of enforcement, and those must include mechanisms for the individual service users to ensure that standards are applied in their cases. Nonetheless, individual rights are clearly part of a bigger picture.

V. Issues of Systemic Litigation and Enforcement

As is well-known in economically privileged countries, individual rights have their limits, and this is nowhere more evident than in the psychiatric and learning disability realms. It has been acknowledged since the ground-breaking paper of Janet Gilboy and John Schmidt over 30 years ago[28] that coercion frequently occurs outside law, in situations where 'voluntary' patients do not perceive themselves as having real choices in their psychiatric admission or treatment. Further, a significant proportion of users of psychiatric and learning disability services will be in a position of sufficient vulnerability that they will not be able to instigate legal proceedings. This vulnerability may, as noted above, flow from conditions in the individual's place of care: he or she may not feel that it is safe to 'rock the boat'. It may also of course flow from the individual's disability. While

---

[28] J Gilboy and J Schmidt, '"Voluntary" Hospitalization of the Mentally Ill' (1971) 66 *Northwestern University Law Review* 429. See also Bernadette McSherry, this volume, ch 16.

certainly many people with mental health problems or learning disability are able to stand up for their own rights, the reality is that some are not. Further, and perhaps more significantly, successful litigation of individual rights may provide a remedy to the individual litigant, but may fail to address over-arching and systemic problems in the mental health care system.

Some of the mechanisms to address these problems will not necessarily involve litigation. Boards of inspection, for example, may be an important way to police and enhance standards of care provision, even if they have no right to go to court to enforce their concerns. Their efficacy will however be determined by the appropriateness of appointments made to the boards, and how effective the extra-legal mechanisms are to ensure that their recommendations or findings are acted upon. Even in developed democracies, there are numerous examples of reports and notices of violation issued by these inspection panels left gathering dust, making no meaningful difference. In these circumstances, access to courts by these boards (combined with sufficient budgets to make such access practicable) may be important.

Of greater relevance to the theme of this volume is systemic litigation, either by way of test-case, class action, or other mechanism. The efficacy of this approach in the economically developed world has been patchy. In England, there has been little litigation to enforce standards of service provision, and such litigation as has occurred has by and large been unsuccessful.[29] In the United States of America, by comparison, some early cases relating to standards of care and justifications for confinement were instrumental in establishing the human rights culture in a psychiatric context.[30] To what degree does systemic litigation represent a way forward for southern Africa and central Europe?

Any optimism must be limited. At best, litigation will only be as strong as the right protected in the formal legal instrument, and key rights in this area are often, to use the prevailing euphemism, 'aspirational'. As an obvious example, the right to health appears in a wide variety of international legal instruments, but is generally qualified by reference to the 'best *available*' standard of health, or with an express reference to affordability.[31] This rather woolly language severely limits the potential success of litigation, providing courts with an invitation to avoid the difficult economic decisions that health care choices involve. Further, many of

---

[29] See, eg *R v Gloucestershire County Council, ex parte Barry* [1997] 2 All ER 1 (HL); *R (on the application of K) v Camden and Islington Health Authority* [2001] EWCA 240; *R (on the application of Stennett) v Manchester City Council* [2002] UKHL 34 is something of an exception, as it requires the state to pay community aftercare services that are mandatory under the Act, although it does not define what services are mandatory under the Act.

[30] *Addington v Texas*, 441 US 418 (1979); *O'Connor v Donaldson*, 422 US 563 (1975); *Schmidt v Lessard*, 414 US 473 (1974); *Romeo v Youngberg*, 644 F 2d 147 (3rd Cir 1980).

[31] See, eg ACHPR art 16; International Covenant on Economic, Social and Cultural Rights, UN GA res 2200A (XXI), 21 UNGAOR Supp (No 16) at 49, UN Doc A/6316 (1966), 993 UNTS 3 (entered into force 3 January 1976) art 12; European Social Charter (Revised), ETS 163, arts 1(11), 11.

these rights are contained in international instruments that have no enforcement mechanisms for individuals, and may not be incorporated into domestic law.

Nonetheless, there are some indications that systemic litigation may sometimes be a useful way forward. In Bulgaria, for example, recent cases brought jointly by the Mental Disability Advocacy Center (MDAC) and the Bulgarian Helsinki Committee have resulted in findings that Bulgaria's failure properly to educate children with intellectual disabilities constituted a violation of the European Social Charter,[32] and that differential payments to people receiving community benefits based respectively on age, learning disability, and mental health problems was discriminatory under Bulgarian domestic law. In Russia, an MDAC test-case relating to procedures of guardianship has resulted in findings both at the European Court of Human Rights and the Russian Constitutional Court that the procedures for assessing incapacity and awarding guardianship must be fundamentally altered, to allow significant involvement of the person allegedly lacking capacity.[33] In the event that these cases result in significant systemic reforms, real and tangible results may follow for large numbers of people. At the international level, European Court of Human Rights jurisprudence has established broad framework requirements for civil detention,[34] although it has been less helpful in establishing minimal standards of care in facilities.[35]

A caveat is appropriate, however, in that the existing structures of human rights import an agenda as to what sorts of right are important. There is little doubt that it is easier under the European Convention on Human Rights for example, to ensure standards of care in facilities than it is to require the provision of care services in the community. The result of litigation in this area, therefore, might well be that funds are spent to improve facilities, at least to the point that they are no longer violating human rights. This presents advocates with a dilemma. If expenditure is made in this way, people will still be in the institutions; merely in marginally less bad institutions (or, conceivably, good institutions?). It is difficult to see that governments that are required to spend money on these institutions will quickly abandon them for community models of care: the focus on institutional models of care is thus buttressed, not challenged. At the same time, is it really acceptable not to litigate the standards of care in these places, and thus to leave people in manifestly sub-standard conditions, in the hope that community services may come?

It is not obvious that the human rights priorities necessarily match the priorities of the service users. To take a concrete example, I have in central

---

[32] *Mental Disability Advocacy Center (MDAC) v Bulgaria*, European Committee of Social Rights, complaint 41/2007, decision of 10 June 2008.

[33] See *Shtukaturov v Russia* (App No 44009/05) judgment 27 March 2008; see also decision of Russian Constitutional Court, 27 February 2009.

[34] See *Winterwerp v The Netherlands* (1979) 2 EHRR 387.

[35] See, eg *Herczegfalvy v Austria* (1992) 15 EHRR 437, where prolonged handcuffing of an individual did not violate the prohibition of inhuman or degrading treatment.

Europe visited a ward where everyone was dressed only in nappies. There was no obvious reason for this—the residents did not appear to be incontinent. Unsurprisingly, I found this situation distressing, and I suspect if the situation found its way to litigation, there would be a good chance that a court would make a finding of degrading treatment. It is much less obvious that the people on the ward viewed the situation as intolerable. The visit did not allow me to speak with the residents, but it is further fair to wonder whether the matters that were of concern to them are matters that human rights law would rate as important.

VI. Conclusion

In the background of much of this discussion has been the discursive power of rights. In the period after the fall of the Berlin Wall, there was tremendous enthusiasm in central Europe for engagement with the western European conceptions of rights, in part as a way of drawing a line under the events of the previous half century. While the subsequent 20 years have taken some of the bloom off the rose in this regard, rights continue to have discursive power in these countries.

Africa, once again, is different: with the exception of the RSA, human rights do not appear to be articulated as the marker for distinction from an old and oppressive régime. Instead, the risk is that human rights are perceived as merely the latest form of colonialism, creating a much more ambiguous climate for reform. That said, African nations are signing up to the key United Nations human rights instruments, and Africa does have its own charter of human rights,[36] buttressed by its own African Court of Human and Peoples' Rights.[37]

Insofar as the discursive power of rights and law can be harnessed to the advantage of people with mental disabilities, it may well be a helpful tool in bringing about systemic reform to mental health services. It allows service users to be re-created as persons with a role and a stake in the care system—a development largely taken for granted in economically privileged countries, but which is still largely absent in central Europe and southern Africa.

So where does this leave us? Rights do matter. They matter because sometimes they matter in individual cases; they matter because sometimes the political culture of rights and also their discursive impact can influence governments into useful action. Certainly, both those objectives are important. We have also known, since the earliest days of the law and society movement, that rights only

---

[36] African Charter on Human and Peoples' Rights, opened for signature 27 June 1981, 1520 UNTS 217 (entered into force 21 October 1986).

[37] Protocol to the African Charter on Human and People's Rights on the Establishment of an African Court on Human and Peoples' Rights, 9 June 1998, OAU Doc OAU/LEG/EXP/AFCHPR/ PROT (III).

matter if accompanied by political and social advocacy, before, in parallel with, and after litigation. There can be little doubt that this is a lesson that must also be applied in central Europe and southern Africa. Rights do not happen in a vacuum. They happen as part of social and political movements. They are, however, a necessary part of those movements.

Index